THE LIFE OF
James Cardinal Gibbons

HIS EMINENCE

JAMES CARDINAL GIBBONS

From a portrait by Marie de Ford Keller,
presented by the Cardinal to Miss Mary
O. Shriver, December 16, 1920.

THE LIFE OF
James Cardinal Gibbons
Archbishop of Baltimore
1834-1921

By

JOHN TRACY ELLIS
PROFESSOR OF AMERICAN CHURCH HISTORY
IN THE
CATHOLIC UNIVERSITY OF AMERICA

With a Prefatory
Note to the Replica Edition
By the Author

VOLUME I

CHRISTIAN CLASSICS, INC.
WESTMINSTER, MARYLAND
1987

Nihil obstat:
  John K. Cartwright
  Censor deputatus
Imprimatur:
  ✠ Patrick A. O'Boyle
  Archbishop of Washington
  September 16, 1951

First Published, 1952
Replica Edition, 1987

ISBN: 0 87061 144 5

Prefatory Note

THIRTY-FIVE years have passed since this biography of Cardinal Gibbons appeared. It has been out of print for a long time and the repeated requests for it have had to go unfilled. The initiative for the present reprint was taken by Monsignor George G. Higgins, a friend to whom I am beholden for this and many other favors. I am equally indebted to Mr. John J. McHale, Director of Christian Classics, Inc., for his willingness to issue a reprint of this work.

In the generation since the publication of the original edition there have been new currents and moods of thought in historiography, such as the increased emphasis on people's history, or 'history from below,' as it has been termed. This trend, as far as ecclesiastical history is concerned, may legitimately be considered in part as a reflection of Vatican Council II's concept of the 'people of God.' Were I writing the Gibbons story today this contemporary emphasis would probably find a stronger expression. It would not, however, represent a radical departure from the original approach, for I have always been convinced that the biography of a churchman can and should embrace a treatment of the people he served, and this, I believe, was done substantially in the chapters on Gibbons as Archbishop of Baltimore and as American citizen. At a time when many have questioned the character and current relevance of the Church, it is to be hoped that the life story of James Gibbons which involved practically all significant aspects of American Catholicism from the Civil War to beyond World War I will help to shed light on the Church of the United States. In that regard Gibbons would have shared in the view of Cardinal Newman when the latter declared:

> A number of answers can be given to the question, What is the Church? We are far from saying that in so complicated a question *only* one, or perhaps that any *one*, is right and true; but whatever is right, whatever wrong, surely we must go to history for the information.[1]

John Tracy Ellis

The Catholic University of America
May 25, 1987

---

[1] John Henry Newman, *Essays Critical and Historical*. New York: Longmans, Green and Company. 1897. II, 253.

v

Preface

THERE were many times during the more than six years in which the life of Cardinal Gibbons was in preparation, that the writer felt the truth of an observation made some weeks after the cardinal died, when it was said, "He will have no biographer probably to do him justice."[1] His career was so long and eventful, the problems with which he dealt so varied and delicate, and the impression he left on the American mind so extraordinary and enduring that it seemed an impossible task, a generation after his death, to recapture the spirit of the man and to recount and weigh with the significance and balance which they deserved the great events in which he had played so leading a role. And yet if a full knowledge of the splendid accomplishments and the unique contribution of the Cardinal of Baltimore to both Church and State were not to be lost to future generations, if the striking lessons and the wonderful heritage which he bequeathed to those who came after him were not to be forever dimmed in the memory of Americans of every class and creed, it was necessary that the work should be undertaken, and that before all those who had known the cardinal in life had passed away.

From the time that the writer first acquired a close knowledge of the history of American Catholicism, he had no doubts concerning the prime position which James Gibbons had occupied in that history, but it was quite another matter to tell his story in a manner that would pay fitting tribute to his greatness. In a desire that the career of Gibbons should be set forth with all the amplitude which its significance seemed to merit, the work assumed proportions which went quite beyond the original intention, but it is to be hoped that the importance of his life for the history of both Church and State in the United States will have justified its length.

It was from one of the writer's dearest friends that there

---

[1] William J. Kerby, "James Cardinal Gibbons. An Interpretation," *Catholic World*, CXIII (May, 1921), 147.

came the original suggestion to write the cardinal's life, and it was that friend's sustained interest that encouraged him to approach the authorities of the Archdiocese of Baltimore about the matter. To the Right Reverend John K. Cartwright, rector of St. Matthew's Cathedral, Washington, is owed, therefore, the initial stimulus which set the work in motion in July, 1945, and through every step of the way he remained vitally concerned about its progress. Monsignor Cartwright not only bore patiently the seemingly interminable discussions over points that arose as the biography advanced, but he gave a close reading to the manuscript and offered numerous criticisms of a constructive and judicious character that added immeasurably to whatever merit of style and balanced judgment the work may have. Two other dear friends and colleagues of the Catholic University of America performed a similar service by their conscientious reading of the manuscript chapter by chapter as it was written. To the Very Reverend Louis A. Arand, S.S., president of Divinity College, the writer will always be grateful for his many sound criticisms and enlightening observations. The Reverend Henry J. Browne, archivist of the University, was also most helpful with criticisms and suggestions made during his reading of the manuscript and, too, with numerous references to archival and published sources which, as he encountered them in his own research, he passed on to the writer with an unfailing generosity that was in the best tradition of co-operative endeavor. To these three men, then, above all others, an immense obligation was incurred during the past six years. While their ideas added greatly to whatever merits the work may possess, needless to say, the ultimate responsibility for any errors of judgment, fact, or omission rests solely with the writer and not with his friends.

Insofar as the spirit which informed this work from the outset is concerned, the writer tried to keep before his mind the admonition which Pope Leo XIII addressed on August 18, 1883, to three cardinals of the Roman Curia in his famous letter, *Saepenumero considerantes,* on historical studies. In that document, which has rightly been regarded ever since as a charter for Catholic historians, the Pontiff urged that they always bear in mind the rule which he quoted from Cicero, namely, "that the first law of history is, not to dare to utter falsehood; the second, not to fear to speak the truth; and, moreover, no room must be left for suspicion of partiality or prejudice."[2] It was a rule of which Cardinal Gibbons heartily approved. When Edmund S. Purcell's *Life of Cardinal Manning* appeared in 1896 the author's use of so much private correspondence of a character uncomplimentary to Manning shocked some ecclesiastics, and at least one, Thomas W. Croke, Archbishop of Cashel, grew so alarmed that he destroyed most of his private letters as a consequence.[3] On the contrary, Gibbons after reading the two volumes of Purcell made the comment that to his mind the candor of the work had made the portrait of Manning more convincing since it had not represented him as superhuman.[4]

Just a year after Purcell's work appeared the Cardinal of Baltimore published his book called *The Ambassador of Christ.* In that volume he outlined his ideas on what should constitute a good biography. In the main he drew the illustrations for his standards of objectivity from the New Testament where, as he stated, the denial of Peter, the early persecution of the Church by Paul, the worldly ambition of James and John, and the incredulity of Thomas were fearlessly recorded without any attempt at extenuation or palliation. Gibbons quoted with approval the remark that Leo XIII had made some years before to Cardinal Manning, to the effect that it had been too much the fashion in writing history to omit what was unpleasant, and that if the historians of the previous century had written the Gospels, for example, one might never have heard of the fall of St. Peter or of the treachery of Judas. Gibbons was pleased at the improvement he had noted in the more recent biographies, and it was his conviction, as he expressed it, that:

> The public man, whether churchman or layman, who has never committed an error of judgment, or who was never betrayed into any moral delinquency, will hardly ever be credited with any great words or deeds worthy of being transmitted to posterity.[5]

It was in this fashion, therefore, that the writer endeavored

---

[2] *Ave Maria,* XIX (September 29, 1883), 761.

[3] Patrick J. Walsh, *William J. Walsh, Archbishop of Dublin* (Dublin, 1928), pp. 159–160.

[4] Allen Sinclair Will, *Life of James Cardinal Gibbons, Archbishop of Baltimore* (New York, 1922), II, 934.

[5] *The Ambassador of Christ* (Baltimore, 1896), p. 253.

as far as possible to allow the documents to speak for themselves so that the reader might have all the evidence before him, and thus in the final analysis make up his own mind where to place the blame for actions and words which he might regard as unworthy of their authors. Wherever the full understanding of a situation demanded the relating of incidents of a controversial nature, these were given in the conviction that in the long run candor could only serve the cause of truth, and in so doing it would reflect credit upon the Church and upon Catholic historical scholarship. Such was the spirit in which Ludwig von Pastor wrote his monumental *History of the Popes,* and it was scholarship informed by that ideal that won for Pastor the high commendation of Pope Leo XIII in the latter's letter of January 20, 1887, to the church historian in which he complimented him upon the completion of his first volume and urged him to speed his efforts to finish the history of the Papacy of modern times.[6] In attempting to write the biography of Cardinal Gibbons the writer can say sincerely that he tried to remain true to the principles enunciated by the Pontiff in his letter of 1883, and thus to leave no room for suspicion of partiality or prejudice. How far he has succeeded, however, in attaining his objective is not for him but for the reader to judge.

When one reflects upon the number of obligations that are incurred during the course of a work of this kind he becomes conscious of two things: first, of how much he owes to the help of others, and, second, of the duty he has to give public expression to that obligation. In the first instance the writer would wish to express his appreciation to his ordinary, the Most Reverend Patrick A. O'Boyle, Archbishop of Washington, for the interest which he manifested in the biography of Gibbons and, too, for the consideration which he showed of the absorbing and time-consuming nature of the work. The writer is likewise not unmindful of the deep debt of gratitude which he owes to the memory of the late Archbishop of Baltimore and Washington, Michael J. Curley, who not only readily gave permission for the use of the rich archival treasures of his premier see, but who extended to the writer through weeks at a time the warmest hospitality of his household. Only slightly less is owed to Arch-

---

[6] Ludwig von Pastor, *History of the Popes* (St. Louis, 1923), I, vi.

bishop Curley's chancellor, the Right Reverend Joseph M. Nelligan, present pastor of Immaculate Conception Church, Towson, Maryland, who, both in his official capacity and in his role as a friend, was untiring in his efforts to put every possible facility at the writer's command. And at the hands of the priests and the sisters of 408 N. Charles Street, the old residence of Cardinal Gibbons, he found the kindliest treatment during his many weeks of research in the archives. He is indebted, too, for a critical reading of certain chapters of the work to the Reverend Joseph McSorley, C.S.P., of the Church of St. Paul the Apostle, New York, and to his colleagues, Professors Martin R. P. McGuire and John T. Farrell of the Catholic University of America. The Very Reverend Timothy Canon Gunnigan, pastor of St. Mary's Church, Ballinrobe, County Mayo, Ireland, not only read the chapter on Gibbons' boyhood in Ireland and offered a number of corrections and suggestions, but he proved a most gracious host on the three-day visit which the writer paid to Ballinrobe in June, 1950. He remembers with equal gratitude the Most Reverend James Fergus, Bishop of Achonry, who during the time of his pastorate in Ballinrobe gathered data on Gibbons' Irish connections from relatives and old friends of the cardinal, and who received the writer at his present home in Ballaghadereen where he extended to him the warmest and most generous welcome. The Reverend W. Kailer Dunn, assistant secretary of the Catholic Near East Welfare Association, not only helped in the gathering of data about Gibbons, but he sacrificed hours of his time in driving the writer about Baltimore and its environs for interviews with various persons who had known the cardinal.

If a biography of an important personage is to be truly definitive, it is inevitable that the biographer must impose himself upon the staffs of many archives, libraries, and research centers. In this category the writer's obligations again have been very numerous. During his survey of the various archival centers which yielded correspondence of Cardinal Gibbons or of his contemporaries he experienced more than a spirit of mere politeness; in many cases professional service was accompanied by a personal hospitality which made his two- or three-day stops much more enjoyable. For kindnesses of this character he is genuinely grateful to the Most Reverend Peter L. Ireton,

Bishop of Richmond; the Most Reverend Thomas J. Toolen,
Bishop of Mobile; the Most Reverend John J. Boylan, Bishop
of Rockford; and to their chancery officials. He wishes likewise
to express thanks for similar courtesies and assistance to the
Right Reverend Howard J. Carroll, general secretary of the
National Catholic Welfare Conference; the Very Reverend
Pierre Boisard, S.S., superior general of the Society of St.
Sulpice in Paris; the Right Reverend Giuseppe Monticone,
general archivist of the Congregation of the Propaganda Fide
at Rome; the Reverend Thomas T. McAvoy, C.S.C., archivist
of the University of Notre Dame; the Reverend Bartholomew
F. Fair, custodian of the collections of the American Catholic
Historical Society of Philadelphia at St. Charles Borromeo
Seminary; the Reverend Jeremiah J. Brennan of St. Joseph's
Seminary, Yonkers, New York; the Right Reverend Charles
J. Plauché, chancellor of the Archdiocese of New Orleans and
the Marist Fathers of Notre Dame Seminary in that city; the
Right Reverend William J. Gauche, rector of St. Gregory
Seminary, Cincinnati; the Reverend Robert F. McNamara of
St. Bernard's Seminary, Rochester; the Reverend Hugh J.
Phillips of Mount Saint Mary's College, Emmitsburg; the Very
Reverend Harry C. Koenig of St. Mary of the Lake Seminary,
Mundelein; the Right Reverend Walter J. Leach, vice-chancellor
of the Archdiocese of Boston; the Right Reverend Edward J.
Hickey, former chancellor of the Archdiocese of Detroit; the
Reverend William J. O'Shea, S.S., of St. Mary's Seminary,
Roland Park, Baltimore; the Reverend Edward A. Ryan, S.J.,
of Woodstock College; the Reverend Joseph I. Malloy, C.S.P.,
archivist of the Paulist Fathers; the Abbé Alphonse Chapeau of
the Catholic Institute of Angers for assistance in the Manning
Papers in London; the Right Reverend John L. Manning,
chancellor of the Diocese of Charleston; the Right Reverend John
Krol, chancellor of the Diocese of Cleveland; the Reverend
Thomas B. Finn of the Diocese of Covington; the Right
Reverend Dorance V. Foley, former chancellor of the Archdiocese of Dubuque; the Reverend Paul L. Love, archivist of
the Archdiocese of Baltimore; Dr. Leo F. Stock of the Carnegie
Institution of Washington; and Miss Elizabeth Bradley of the
Baltimore chancery office. The writer would wish to include
as well all those who assisted him in any way on his visits to

these archives and, too, those who furnished him with copies of letters from archives which he did not have an opportunity to visit in person.

Among the many other obligations incurred was that to the Committee on Grants-in-Aid of Research of the Catholic University of America which generously assigned to the writer from the funds at their disposal $950 to cover the cost of typing the manuscript and for traveling expenses to distant archives. Moreover, he is conscious of the debt he owes to the staffs of a number of libraries for the courteous and efficient service which they rendered to him. Mr. Eugene P. Willging, director of the Mullen Library of the Catholic University of America, and his staff deserve a special word of thanks, and the personnel of the Library of Congress, especially those of the Division of Manuscripts and the Newspaper Reference and Thomas Jefferson Rooms, were also of great assistance. Mention should likewise be made of the staff of the Enoch Pratt Free Library of Baltimore for their help in running down many items about Gibbons' Baltimore career, as well as the library of the Theological College at the Catholic University of America for the loan of books.

To the writer's graduate students an expression of thanks is also due for providing him with references to aspects of the life of Cardinal Gibbons which they discovered in pursuing their own research projects. To those who knew the cardinal in life and who gave their time in interviews, which were extremely enlightening in information which could not be found elsewhere, the writer is likewise under obligation. Mrs. Adelaide Y. Cahill performed her exacting task as typist in a most efficient manner and the writer's secretary, Mrs. James S. Boss, was always most willing and helpful in checking numerous items of reference. The Misses Rosabelle A. and Josephine M. Kelp should likewise be thanked for their efficient work in preparing the index. To the Reverend Aloysius K. Ziegler, head of the Department of History in the Catholic University of America, and to his colleagues in the department, the writer is appreciative of the interest and consideration shown to him during the preparation of the biography. If there should be any others who have rendered a service to this work in any way and whose names have been omitted through inadvertence, the writer can only beg them in their generosity to forgive the oversight and to accept herewith his sincere thanks for their help.

Finally, in grateful memory mention should be made of the Right Reverend Peter Guilday, late professor of American church history in the Catholic University of America, whose splendid pioneer efforts created a special field of historical investigation for the writer and many others who came after him. Monsignor Guilday showed a lively interest in the life of Cardinal Gibbons during the two years it was in progress before his death in July, 1947. As the one who was chosen to replace him, it is a pleasant duty to record this fact to the memory of the writer's professor and friend, who directed his graduate training and who gave him the stimulation to pursue historical research. A similar memory remains of the late Thomas F. O'Connor of St. Louis University, whose rich fund of knowledge of the American Church was always at the writer's disposal, and who before his untimely death in September, 1950, had manifested a deep interest in everything that pertained to the biography of Cardinal Gibbons.

JOHN TRACY ELLIS

Washington, D. C.
October 10, 1951

Acknowledgments

THE author wishes to thank the respective publishers for permission to quote from the following books bearing their imprint: Harvard University Press (Elting Morison's edition of *The Letters of Theodore Roosevelt*); Charles Scribner's Sons (Nicholas Murray Butler, *Across the Busy Years*); Yale University Press (Wilbur L. Cross, *Connecticut Yankee: An Autobiography*); Harper & Brothers (Anson Phelps Stokes, *Church and State in the United States;* Francis C. Kelley, *The Bishop Jots It Down*); Appleton-Century-Crofts, Inc. (Thomas A. Bailey, *A Diplomatic History of the American People*); Macmillan Company (Arthur M. Schlesinger, *The Rise of the City, 1878–1898;* Homer C. Hockett, *Political and Social Growth of the American People, 1492–1865*); J. P. Lippincott Company (Joseph Fort Newton, *River of Years*); University of Minnesota Press (George M. Stephenson, *John Lind of Minnesota*); Alfred A. Knopf, Inc. (Thomas Beer, *The Mauve Decade*); Dodd, Mead & Company (G. K. Chesterton, *What I Saw in America*); E. P. Dutton & Company, Inc. (Allen Sinclair Will, *Life of Cardinal Gibbons*).

KEY TO FOOTNOTE ABBREVIATIONS

AAB	Archives of the Archdiocese of Baltimore
AABo	Archives of the Archdiocese of Boston
AAC	Archives of the Archdiocese of Cincinnati
AANO	Archives of the Archdiocese of New Orleans
AANY	Archives of the Archdiocese of New York
AASP	Archives of the Archdiocese of St. Paul
ACHSP	American Catholic Historical Society of Philadelphia Collections
ACUA	Archives of the Catholic University of America
ADC	Archives of the Diocese of Cleveland
ADR	Archives of the Diocese of Richmond
ADRo	Archives of the Diocese of Rochester
AMSMC	Archives of Mount Saint Mary's College
ANCWC	Archives of the National Catholic Welfare Conference
APF	Archives of the Paulist Fathers
AUND	Archives of the University of Notre Dame
AWC	Archives of Woodstock College
LC	Division of Manuscripts, Library of Congress
MP	Manning Papers, Church of St. Mary of the Angels, Bayswater, London

Contents

Illustrations

Frontispiece. Portrait of Cardinal Gibbons painted by Marie de Ford Keller and presented by him to Miss Mary O. Shriver, December 16, 1920.

Scenes from Gibbons' boyhood in Ballinrobe, County Mayo, Ireland (*facing p. 14*).

Gibbons in 1866, five years after his ordination as a priest (*facing p. 60*).

Gibbons as the youngest bishop in the American Church, 1868 (*facing p. 73*).

St. Peter's Cathedral in Richmond, 1876 (*facing p. 120*).

The cardinal's Charles Street residence in Baltimore (*facing p. 165*).

The Third Plenary Council of Baltimore, 1884 (*facing p. 203*).

Gibbons' titular Church of Santa Maria in Trastevere (*facing p. 307*).

Gibbons at the age of fifty-seven in 1891 (*facing p. 376*).

The cardinal's silver episcopal jubilee at Washington, October 26, 1893 (*facing p. 422*).

John Ireland, Archbishop of St. Paul (*facing p. 653*).

THE LIFE OF
James Cardinal Gibbons

CHAPTER I

Childhood in Baltimore and Ballinrobe

IT WAS on July 23, 1834, that James Gibbons was born in a simple dwelling on the west side of Gay Street, just north of Fayette Street, in the city of Baltimore. Twelve days later, on August 4, this fourth child of Thomas and Bridget Gibbons was baptized by Father Charles I. White, an assistant priest at the Cathedral of the Assumption.[1] Thus was inaugurated an association on the part of the future cardinal with this venerable building that would deepen as time went on and finally be brought to a close nearly eighty-seven years later when his mortal remains would lie in state in the central aisle of the cathedral preparatory to his solemn funeral and burial in the crypt beneath the sanctuary. It would be almost forty-four years after the baptism that its subject, by now Archbishop of Baltimore, would make the following entry in his diary:

> This morning the Rev. Dr. C. I. White Pastor of St. Matthew's Church, Washington, was buried in Mt. Olivet cemetery, having died on the 1st. About twenty five of the clergy of the diocess [*sic*] were present at the obsequies in St. Matthew's Church which was filled to repletion, many distinguished Protestants & some of the foreign ministers being present. I preached on the occasion. It was this ven. priest that baptized me. . . .[2]

James was the first boy in the Gibbons family. His two oldest sisters, Mary and Bridget, had been born in Ireland

---

[1] Baptismal Register G, 1838–1854, p. 456. The entry under August 4, 1834, records that John and Anna Hanaher acted as sponsors at the baptism. There is a discrepancy in dates on this particular volume of the register. All unpublished sources in Baltimore cited throughout this work are in the archives of the Archdiocese of Baltimore unless otherwise noted.

[2] Diary of Cardinal Gibbons, April 4, 1878, p. 103. In his early years Gibbons spelled "diocese" as "diocess" rather consistently.

in the mid-1820's before the family emigrated to the United States, and Catherine, the youngest girl, was born in the first house occupied by the Gibbons' on Patterson Street in Baltimore on July 23, 1831, exactly three years before the birth of James.[3] Nearly three years after James' birth the second son, John, arrived on May 4, 1837, in a house on Frederick Street, Baltimore, and was baptized in St. Patrick's Church.[4] The youngest child, Thomas, was born about 1842 after the family had returned to the old country.[5]

The Ireland out of which Thomas Gibbons and his wife, the former Bridget Walsh, emigrated with their two small daughters about 1829 was, indeed, an unhappy land.[6] True, that year marked the attainment of one of the chief aims of Daniel O'Connell in the passage of the act of Catholic Emancipation by the British Parliament. But while this measure threw open public and municipal offices to the Catholics, it conferred no benefit upon the numerous class of small farmers to which both Thomas Gibbons and the family of his wife belonged. In one respect the bill made the position of this class even worse since it restricted the vote to those whose land valuation was £10 or over. Completely disfranchised, with no fixity of tenure or redress against rack rents and eviction, the

---

[3] Shahan Papers. John T. Gibbons to Thomas J. Shahan, New Orleans, November 24, 1923. Information on the early years of the Gibbons family was supplied for Bishop Shahan by the brother of the cardinal after the latter's death. The Shahan Papers were used by the writer at Holy Angels Rectory, Philadelphia, where they are presently in the custody of the Right Reverend Bernard A. McKenna.

[4] *Ibid.*

[5] In the records of the Louisiana Historical Library, Cabildo, New Orleans, there is the entry under St. Patrick's Cemetery #1 of Thomas Gibbons who died on June 19, 1865, at the age of twenty-three. The information contained in this record would tend to confirm that given to the writer by Mrs. Albert H. Start [Margaret Gibbons] of New Orleans, niece of Cardinal Gibbons, in an interview of January 25, 1948. Thomas, the cardinal's youngest brother, fought in the Confederate Army during the Civil War and died unmarried.

[6] It is impossible to determine with certainty what year the Gibbons family emigrated from Ireland. John Gibbons, in the letter to Thomas Shahan cited in footnote 3, said 1829, while information gathered in Ireland for the writer and related in a letter of January 21, 1946, stated that "it was most probably 1831." The birth of Catherine Gibbons in Baltimore on July 23, 1831, would, however, incline one to believe it was the earlier date. The writer wishes to express his thanks to the Most Reverend James Fergus, Bishop of Achonry, who took the pains to gather a good deal of important data from Thomas Canon O'Malley, J. Canon Cunnane, and others and send it to the writer.

small farmers of Ireland were entirely at the mercy of the powerful landlords.

Thomas Gibbons had been born in 1800 at Gortnacullin, Tourmakeady, County Mayo, a small village situated high up on the slope of the Tourmakeady Mountain and commanding a fine view of the beautiful expanse of Lough Mask. His wife, who was three years younger than himself, was a native of Tooreen, a village in the Partry district located on the opposite side of Lough Mask. The two villages lay within the parish of Ballyovey in the Archdiocese of Tuam.[7] While both families belonged to the class of small farmers, James Walsh, the cardinal's maternal grandfather, was also the village school-master. Unfortunately, the disappearance of both parish and school records for many settlements in Ireland in the early nineteenth century does not permit the historian to speak with more exactitude on the early lives of the father and mother of James Gibbons. Precisely when and why the Gibbons family emigrated to the new world it is impossible to say, but in all likelihood poverty was the compelling reason. That general conditions in Ireland did not improve during the early years of their married life is certain. As one historian of Ireland has said:

> The country had in fact since 1796 been under a terrorism which survived both the Rebellion, the Union, and Emancipation, a terror-ism in which the normal ascendancy was reinforced by an Orange bigotry which meant to keep the power in Protestant hands in spite of emancipation and to make rebels and 'Croppies' (for so they called the discontented) 'lie down,' as their song ran.[8]

Whether it was discouragement with the state of his business in Westport, the largest town in the region, or eviction from his landholding that prompted Thomas Gibbons to seek a better life beyond the seas cannot be determined. At any rate, it was just at a time when thousands of his fellow countrymen were abandoning their homeland that Gibbons and his family set out. "After a slight setback in 1828 emigration increased annually to the record years of 1831 and 1832, during each of which

---

[7] For details on the Irish background of the family the writer is indebted here to the three clergymen named in footnote 6.

[8] Edmund Curtis, *A History of Ireland* (New York, 1937), p. 364.

over 65,000 passengers left Ireland for America."[9] The family settled first in Canada, but after a brief stay they found the northern climate too severe so they started south and ultimately came to Baltimore where they took up permanent residence around 1830.[10]

In Baltimore the Gibbons fortunes picked up considerably. The father found employment as a clerk with the firm of William Howell and Son, described as "commercial merchants," which had a prosperous importing business in its establishment located on south Gay Street not far from the house where his first son was born in 1834. He had the responsibility of guarding the money brought by some of the clipper ships which traded in and out of the port of Baltimore at that time and, too, of delivering to the captains of these vessels sums of money needed when they sailed on new voyages.[11]

The Gibbons family arrived in Baltimore at a time when the city was in the flush of prosperity. Its population of 80,625 in 1830 made it second only to New York among the cities of the United States and ahead of Philadelphia by several hundred.[12] Among the total population were 18,911 colored persons of whom 4,123 were slaves.[13] Since Baltimore was the first southern city of any size which a traveler coming south from Boston and New York would meet, the presence of the Negroes in such numbers attracted the comment of foreign visitors especially.

[9] William Forbes Adams, *Ireland and Irish Emigration to the New World from 1815 to the Famine* (New Haven, 1932), pp. 159–160.

[10] It is impossible to say exactly the year of their arrival in Baltimore. It is likely that they came by ship from Canada, but there were no regularly kept records of the port of Baltimore until 1834.

[11] Allen Sinclair Will, *Life of Cardinal Gibbons, Archbishop of Baltimore* (New York, 1922), I, 2–3. Will had the advantage of going over his manuscript in an earlier edition of 1911 with the cardinal himself or with his secretaries, so presumably the information given here on the early history of the family is accurately stated. Richard J. Matchett (Ed.), *Baltimore Director, Corrected up to September, 1835* (Baltimore, 1835), listed householders by name and frequently, too, by occupation. Thomas Gibbons is listed as living at 49 north Gay Street but no occupation is given (p. 97). The Matchett *Director* for 1833 gives the location of the Howell firm as 48 Gay Street (p. 96).

[12] Hamilton Owens, *Baltimore on the Chesapeake* (Garden City, 1941), p. 244.

[13] William Travis Howard, Jr., *Public Health Administration and the Natural History of Disease in Baltimore, Maryland, 1797–1920* (Washington, 1924), p. 173. That Baltimore was growing rapidly can be seen in the fact that four years later — the year Gibbons was born — the city's population had reached 98,901. *Ibid.*, pp. 178–179.

An Englishman by the name of Abdy was in Baltimore in 1834 and his observations led him to remark:

> There are a good many free blacks in Baltimore, the merchants of which prefer them to the whites as porters and carmen. So well known are they for their superior honesty and civility, that the storekeepers and tradesmen are used, as I have been informed by more than one reputable person, to tell their customers that they will not be answerable for any goods they may send out, when entrusted to white people.[14]

Six years after Abdy another English visitor to the city wrote:

> We just staid long enough at Baltimore to admire its commanding site, neat streets, and handsome dwelling houses; examine the columns, two in number, a hundred times described, which give it the sounding title of "The Monumental City," buy a ticket in the lottery (which, of course, turned up a blank), and make some passing observations on slavery, this being our first experience of a State cursed with that foul blot.[15]

Baltimore's fine harbor facing down Chesapeake Bay gave it an easy claim on much of the increasing international trade into which the young American Republic was then entering. Just two years before James Gibbons was born the *John Gilpin*, a Baltimore clipper, had set out in 1832 and covered 34,920 miles in 189 days and seventeen hours, an average of over 183 miles a day, a record which, according to Baltimoreans, set the world agog.[16] This brisk and growing world commerce naturally encouraged industry and by 1833 Baltimore boasted three sail factories, seven carpet factories, three engine works, three glassware factories, a copper mill, two shot towers, five chemical works, four breweries, two distilleries, a snuff factory, and a sawmill. Moreover, the increasing business of the city found a channel for its funds through ten chartered banks and two private banking companies, and the population was served for news by five daily and six weekly newspapers.

---

[14] E. S. Abdy, *Journal of a Residence and Tour in the United States of North America* (London, 1835), II, 55.

[15] Thomas Colley Grattan, *Civilized America* (London, 1859), I, 163.

[16] J. Thomas Scharf, *The Chronicles of Baltimore* (Baltimore, 1874), p. 473. Another Baltimore clipper, the *Ann McKim*, went around the Horn and back in 167 days, arriving in Baltimore on June 16, 1834, about a month before Gibbons was born. Owens, *op. cit.*, pp. 253–254.

Baltimore was proud, too, of its hotels. As one visitor put it, "The establishments for entertaining strangers and travellers are numerous. *Barnum's* or *The City Hotel,* is the most distinguished."[17] That Barnum's did enjoy a good reputation we know, for the highly critical Charles Dickens stopped there on his tour in 1842 and he wrote of it:

> The most comfortable of all the hotels of which I had any experience in the United States, and they were not a few, is Barnum's in that city: where the English traveller will find curtains to his bed, for the first and probably the last time, in America; and where he will be likely to have enough water for washing himself, which is not at all a common case.[18]

The "genteel private residences" of those years were to be found in the neighborhood of Exchange Place, Monument Square, and along Charles and Calvert Streets. The Baltimore Library Company and the Mercantile Library Association afforded the more studious Baltimoreans with materials for reading while the bookstores of Cushing & Brother and John Murphy near St. Paul Street handled the sale of new books for eager readers. A common practice throughout the United States in the early nineteenth century was present in full force in Baltimore in the form of a lively traffic in lottery tickets which were sold in aid of a wide variety of causes. The lottery was thrust upon the attention of all by every scheme "that ingenuity or greed could devise."[19]

But the family of Thomas Gibbons in the early 1830's would have little time or money for the entertainments at Barnum's Hotel, the fine dinners in the mansions near Monument Square, or the purchase of new books at Murphy's. Nor would they find much in common with the city's "literary" set which numbered at the time Francis Scott Key, John Pendleton Kennedy, Jared Sparks, Rembrandt Peale, the painter, and William Gwynn, editor of the *Federal Gazette.* The Gibbons'

---

[17] Charles Varle, *A Complete View of Baltimore With a Statistical Sketch* (Baltimore, 1833), pp. 55–59, 79–80.

[18] Charles Dickens, *American Notes for General Circulation* (London, 1842), II, 25.

[19] Henry Stockbridge, Sr., "Baltimore in 1846," *Maryland Historical Magazine,* VI (March, 1911), 25.

lived far from the world of this group of Baltimoreans who had organized themselves into the Delphian Club and met in the "quaint porticoed house, shaded by five stately elms, in Bank lane, in the rear of Barnum's Hotel, which they dignified by the name of 'Tusculum.' "[20] Rather the main interests of this immigrant Irish family of modest means lay in the practice of the deep Catholic faith which they had brought with them from Ireland, in the simple pleasures of their own home and that of their neighbors, and in making the most of their frugal living.

At the time of their arrival in Baltimore James Whitfield, English-born fourth Archbishop of Baltimore, was ruling the premier see of the United States. There were five regular parishes in the city along with the chapels of St. Mary's Seminary and the Carmelite convent; and sixty-eight priests, including the Sulpician and Jesuit Fathers, ministered to the growing Catholic settlements in the city, the State of Maryland, and the District of Columbia which comprised the archdiocese. The number of Catholic people in the Archdiocese of Baltimore was then approaching 80,000. The Gibbons family belonged to the cathedral parish where Archbishop Whitfield was assisted by Fathers Edward Damphoux, S.S., Peter Schreiber, and Charles I. White.[21] The imposing cathedral which had been dedicated in 1821 was already well established as one of the principal objects of attraction in Baltimore. In May, 1829, James Stuart, an English visitor, had attended services in the cathedral on his trip to Baltimore and he thought, as he said, that he "never saw an assemblage of handsomer women than in the cathedral on a Sunday. The interior of that church is well fitted up, and

---

[20] Clayton Colman Hall (Ed.), *Baltimore. Its History and Its People* (New York, 1912), I, 134.

[21] *United States Catholic Almanac for 1834* (Baltimore, n.d.), pp. 48–51. The estimate of the numbers of the Catholic population was given by Samuel Eccleston, fifth Archbishop of Baltimore, in a letter of January 31, 1838, to the Society for the Propagation of the Faith. In this letter he spoke of the unpleasantness then rampant from Protestant bigotry in Baltimore. He likewise lamented the great scarcity of priests for carrying on the work of the Church, and he mentioned that if he had more priests he felt great good could be done among the Negro population, both slave and free. He said, "Je ne crois pas qu'il y ait dans ce pays, sans excepter les Sauvages, aucune classe d'hommes au milieu de laquelle il fût possible d'opérer plus de fruit." *Annales de la propagation de la foi* (Lyon, 1834), X, 497–499.

there are a few good pictures. The organ is very fine."[22] In March, 1830, another Englishman, by the name of James Boardman, attended Mass in the Cathedral of the Assumption and this non-Catholic guest set down his impressions of what he had seen and heard on that Sunday morning. He wrote:

> The service was conducted with considerable splendor, aided by most delicious music; and the sermon, like almost all I have had the pleasure of hearing from the pulpits of the Church of Rome, inculcated good works, and contained no uncharitable allusions to those who professed a different creed. The crowded congregation consisted chiefly of Irish, of which nation there are great numbers in Baltimore. Among the assembled throng in this holy place, one individual in particular arrested our attention from the moment of his entrance. It was the venerable Charles Carroll, the last survivor of that patriot band, who pledged "their lives, their fortunes, and their sacred honour," to establish the liberties of their country. This highly respected gentlemen [sic] who is the grandfather of the present Marchioness of Wellesley and Carmarthen . . . was then in his ninety-second year, yet walked down the aisle with a vigorous step.[23]

The year of the birth of James Gibbons was a memorable one for Baltimore. Although the city had experienced some years of high prosperity, the wave of speculation and reckless expansion which overtook the United States generally in the early 1830's showed its evil consequences in Baltimore at an earlier date than in other parts of the country. On March 24, 1834, the Bank of Maryland announced that it was unable to prosecute business any longer and the news "fell with a heavy shock on this community."[24] Baltimore had seen the beginning of the first public railroad in the Baltimore and Ohio in 1828, and the same year marked the opening of two lines of steamboats plying between the city on the Chesapeake and south Atlantic ports.

This was but a part of the expansion which the Monumental City was undergoing in these years. President Andrew Jackson,

---

[22] James Stuart, *Three Years in North America* (Edinburgh, 1833), I, 392.

[23] A Citizen of the World [James Boardman], *America and the Americans* (London, 1833), pp. 259–260. For the Baltimore Irish of these years, cf. Martin S. Rushford, "A Social Study of the Irish in Baltimore, 1815–1858," an unpublished master's dissertation, The Catholic University of America (1933).

[24] Scharf, *op. cit.*, p. 467.

who had experienced the ire of thousands by his veto of the Second Bank of the United States and his proclamation against the South Carolina nullifiers of the tariff of 1832, now felt the organized anger of his enemies as hard times spread. A public protest meeting was held in Monument Square in Baltimore on April 23 where resolutions were framed against the Jackson administration and in favor of the formation of a state branch of the Whig Society. A week later the United States Insurance Company suspended payment and the depression deepened.[25] Hundreds of Baltimoreans felt cheated and aggrieved and as the months passed and the pinch of poverty became more acute their indignation at the Bank of Maryland directors mounted.

> When nearly a year and a half elapsed and no satisfactory statement had been made to the creditors the poor people who had lost largely refused to tolerate longer the "law's delay," or the mutual recrimination of the bank directors. Other institutions had become bankrupt in consequence of this failure, and the people divested of between two and three millions declined to be pacified by further statements.[26]

The result of this public temper was a minor riot on August 6, 1835, which led to further disturbances of the peace and destruction of property until Mayor Jesse Hunt recognized the seriousness of the situation and called upon General Samuel Smith to assume control with armed defensive parties. Only then was order restored, "and the bank directors who had fled the city were requested to return, as they were assured their property rights would be enforced and protected."[27]

It was in this atmosphere that James Gibbons was born on July 23, 1834, in the house on north Gay Street which stood until 1892 when it was razed to make way for a plaza to accommodate parades and public meetings near the present city hall. All during the three years which the Gibbons family spent in Baltimore after the birth of their first son the general economic conditions of the country showed a steady decline and finally, a few weeks after the inauguration of Martin Van Buren

---

[25] *Ibid.*, p. 469.
[26] Hall, *op. cit.*, I, 140–141.
[27] *Ibid.*, I, 141.

as President on March 4, 1837, the aggravated situation became a real financial panic with the banks of New York City suspending payment on May 10. "Bankruptcies multiplied in every direction. . . . Twenty thousand wage-earners were thrown out of work, wages were cut, and the cities were crowded with the unemployed."[28] It is probable, indeed, that the effects of the panic of 1837 were felt by Thomas Gibbons and his family. He belonged to the class of merchant clerks whose fortunes would be directly touched by the general stoppage of business. However, there is no evidence to show that it was adverse economic circumstances that prompted the elder Gibbons to leave Baltimore in this year 1837 and to return to Ireland. On the contrary, it would appear that if he had sufficient funds to transport himself, his wife, and his five children across the Atlantic in this critical time, he had made good during his residence in Baltimore and that he had not been too seriously damaged by the untoward events that were carrying many of his fellow workers and their families to ruin. In fact, Thomas Gibbons' health had shown a deterioration for some time, and his physician had advised a sea voyage in the hope that it might improve.[29] The family intended at the time of their departure to return to Baltimore and with that in mind they left their furnishings and effects in the care of some cousins by the name of Geary.[30]

The three-year-old lad who left the United States with his family in 1837 could naturally not have known much about the land of his birth at so early an age. And yet one of the few recollections he did retain of the period was associated with the presence of President Jackson at a celebration in Baltimore. Over eighty years later he wrote to a correspondent:

---

[28] Homer Carey Hockett, *Political and Social Growth of the American People,* 3 ed. (New York, 1941), p. 578.

[29] Will, *op. cit.,* I, 10. An effort to learn the name of the ship and date for the return of the family to Ireland was not successful. In a letter of June 3, 1948, to the writer from J. N. Weathertum of the Statistics Division of the Board of Trade in London it was stated, " . . . it is regretted that the information which you require is not available, as no passenger lists relative to voyages prior to 1890 are in the possession of this Department."

[30] Interview of the writer with the niece of Cardinal Gibbons, Mrs. Thomas J. Stanton [Mary Swarbrick], New Orleans, January 25, 1948. The *Baltimore Director, Corrected up to May, 1837* (Baltimore, 1837), p. 140, gives Thomas Gibbons, laborer, living on Frederick Street south of Water Street.

I was always interested in Andrew Jackson for personal reasons. When I was an infant in the year 1837, General Jackson received an ovation in Baltimore. The procession escorting him through the city happened to pass our residence and my mother held me up in her arms to contemplate the hero of New Orleans, the President of the United States.[31]

It was an odd circumstance that this memory of the seventh President of the United States should be the sole recorded impression of the earliest years of one who was destined to know personally more American presidents than any churchman of his time.

When the Gibbons family returned to Ireland in 1837 it was naturally to the neighborhood of their former residence in County Mayo. What had begun as an extended holiday lengthened itself into a stay of sixteen years after Thomas Gibbons determined upon remaining in the land of his birth. It was in the vicinity of Ballinrobe, a small town which as late as 1940 had only 1,350 inhabitants, in the southern part of Mayo and to the east of Lough Mask, that the father bought land and began anew the task of providing for his family. Since Ballinrobe was only about ten miles from his native Gortnacullin it was a region with which Mr. Gibbons was quite familiar. In Bridge Street, on a site presently occupied by John B. Staunton, Gibbons carried on a grocery business and also had a publican's licence for the sale of liquor.[32] The family lived in a dwelling which stood on a hill and years later the house was occupied by a boyhood friend of the cardinal who retained a clear memory of their earlier associations.[33]

---

[31] Letter of Gibbons to Samuel G. Heiskell quoted in Will, *op. cit.,* I, 10. In a letter of July 19, 1920, to Gibbons from Heiskell of Knoxville, Tennessee, author of *Andrew Jackson and Early Tennessee History,* 2 ed. (Knoxville, 1920), Heiskell thanked him for his letter of July 14 and stated he was particularly glad to learn, as he said, "First that you saw Andrew Jackson. You are the second person I know of, now living, who saw Andrew Jackson" (128-F). The correspondence from the archives of the Archdiocese of Baltimore will be cited hereafter only by the index number.

[32] James Fergus, at the time pastor of St. Mary's Church, Ballinrobe, to the writer, January 21, 1946. Will, *op. cit.,* I, 11, speaks of Gibbons senior buying land near Ballinrobe and that he "settled down again to the life of a farmer." It is possible, of course, that Gibbons had his business in Ballinrobe and at the same time ran a small farm. Mention of "his father's customers" in the information sent by Bishop Fergus would indicate that Mr. Gibbons was in business. Cf. also Edward A. D'Alton, *A Short History of Ballinrobe Parish* (Dublin, 1931).

[33] Will, *op. cit.,* I, 11.

At about the age of seven years James Gibbons started to school. His first lessons were learned from a Mr. Jennings in the company of Francis J. MacCormack, a future Bishop of Galway, who recalled nearly a half century later in writing to congratulate Gibbons on the honor of the red hat, "It is now over forty years since we began our Latin studies under Mr. Jennings in Abbey St."[34] The scene of his earliest schooling held a fond memory for Gibbons, for it is told of him that on one of his later trips to Ballinrobe as an American bishop he visited Abbey Street to see if the tree, under the branches of which he used to sit as a boy studying his lessons, still stood in one of the gardens.[35] Following his earliest instruction with Jennings he was sent to a private classical school conducted by a Mr. John J. Rooney in the Cornmarket at Ballinrobe. Among his schoolmates here in the group of about fifty boys were Thomas and Robert Tighe of the Heath, Claremorris, whose father was then one of the prominent businessmen in Ballinrobe. Thomas afterward became a member of the British Parliament and held a number of important offices while Robert became a major in the British Army.[36] There was also Charles Sillery, a Protestant lad, who ultimately attained to the rank of major general by following the career of his father, Captain Sillery, who was stationed for a considerable time with his company of British troops in Ballinrobe.[37]

The boy who seemed to be the closest friend of young Gibbons during his school days in Ireland, however, was Charles Clark. Clark was the son of one of the Gibbons' neighbors, a

---

[34] 80-0-16, MacCormack to Gibbons, Ballaghadereen, March 10, 1886. Mac-Cormack was at the time Bishop of Achonry; in 1887 he was promoted to Galway.

[35] James Fergus to the writer, Ballinrobe, January 21, 1946.

[36] Years later Robert Tighe solicited the aid of Gibbons for a nephew who was seeking a job in Baltimore. At that time he said, "I dined about two years ago with his Lordship, Dr. MacCormack, Bishop of Galway, and we talked over old times and the pleasant school boyhood days we all spent together in old Ballinrobe. I was very pleased to hear from my brother at the Heath, that you looked so well when staying with him" (90-D-3, Tighe to Gibbons, Kingston-on-Thames, Surrey, August 28, 1892).

[37] Shahan Papers, John T. Gibbons to Shahan, New Orleans, February 18, 1924. Over fifty years later Gibbons was in correspondence with General Sillery who wrote him that he was gratified by the cardinal's remembering him and writing to him after so many years since, as he expressed it, "I know that in your exalted position, your time is very valuable" (91-Q-10, Sillery to Gibbons, Jersey Island, July 29, 1893).

The ruins of old St. Mary's Church on the edge of town where Gibbons served Mass as a boy.

Abbey Street. The site of the first school attended by Gibbons is the fourth building from the right.

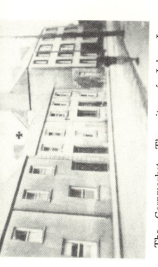

The Cornmarket. The site of John J. Rooney's school which Gibbons attended is the third house from the left.

Looking down Bridge Street. The house occupied by the Gibbons family is the third from the right with the name of J. B. Staunton over the door.

Scenes from Gibbons' Boyhood in Ballinrobe, County Mayo, Ireland
(Courtesy of Very Reverend Timothy Canon Gunnigan)

Protestant, and a few years older than James. Speaking of Clark's religion, James' younger brother, John, wrote later that he [Clark] "was the only young man in town of that persuasion although there were a few Protestant families living there."[38] That there was a close tie between James Gibbons and Charles Clark we know from a letter the former wrote to his old schoolmate a quarter century later. After expressing joy at hearing from his friend and learning that he had been following his career, he made reference to what was probably the occasion of their parting years before in speaking of "that memorable morning to which you so feelingly allude." Gibbons then continued:

> How gratifying it will be to both of us to retrace our steps and revisit once more together those familiar spots where we unbosomed ourselves and where our hearts were knit like those of Jonathan and David. Our friendship has proved lasting, resisting time and all counter affections, because it was based on virtue. When I look back on that early period of my life, like you I attribute much of my subsequent strength against temptations to our pure and healthy conversations, serious and mature beyond our age. Surely our guardian angels must have been with us.[39]

It was in these early years in Ireland that James Gibbons first showed the love of study that characterized his entire life. He was so eager to learn that he disliked missing a single day at school. As his brother wrote of him years later in speaking of this period of James' life, "Mother on a few occasions would desire him for some purpose to absent himself but he would plead and plead until she gave him permission to go."[40] And yet Gibbons was, nonetheless, a real boy for all his love of books. Visits to some of his father's customers in Brownstown held a special attraction for him with the prospect of swimming in Lough Carra. He liked especially to swim, run, and hike and to play cricket, handball, and marbles. In fact, a mark on one of his fingers that he bore through life was the scar from an injury experienced in a game of cricket.[41] He was the envy of the

---

[38] *Ibid.*, November 24, 1923.

[39] Gibbons to Clark, Charleston, South Carolina, September 5, 1869. A copy of this letter was enclosed in the material sent to the writer by Bishop Fergus.

[40] Shahan Papers, John T. Gibbons to Shahan, New Orleans, November 24, 1823.

[41] Will, *op. cit.*, I, 13.

neighborhood in playing marbles and his brother related that on one occasion, "I saw him sell as many as a shilling's worth and still his pockets were full."[42] On the long walks around the countryside — a recreation which delighted him even in old age — he had as a companion his friend Charles Clark. Reared as he was in the home of deeply religious people it is small wonder that young Gibbons early manifested a love for the Church and its ceremonies which showed itself in his serving Mass at St. Mary's Church in Ballinrobe from his earliest years until the time that he returned to the United States.

It is unfortunate that no records of Rooney's school remain, if any were ever kept. The early 1840's when James Gibbons started to school were a period of great tension in Irish education. In 1831 the British government had devised a system of national schools for Ireland with government support. But the provision for religious instruction in these schools satisfied no one, and the Catholics, Presbyterians, and Church of Ireland people all objected to it from various angles. It was in 1834 that the doughty and colorful John MacHale had become Archbishop of Tuam whose ecclesiastical jurisdiction embraced Ballinrobe. Although the Irish hierarchy was divided on the question of the national schools, with Archbishop Daniel Murray of Dublin siding with the government, MacHale would have nothing to do with the national schools in his archdiocese. He forbade attendance at these schools on the part of the children of his people and he redoubled his efforts to secure the Franciscans, Christian Brothers, and the Sisters of Mercy in towns like Westport, Ballinrobe, and his see city to obviate the difficulty.[43]

Schools like those of John Rooney which young Gibbons attended were, therefore, private in character and helped to supplement the scarcity of Catholic schools properly so-called. Fortunately for James' later career the instruction given by Rooney seems to have been strong in the classical tradition. As his brother later stated, "The school in town which he attended could not be much improved on for the acquiring of correct English, Greek and Latin but nothing else. . . ."[44] With his quick

---

[42] Shahan Papers, John T. Gibbons to Shahan, New Orleans, November 24, 1923.
[43] Bernard O'Reilly, *John MacHale, Archbishop of Tuam* (New York, 1890), I, 473.
[44] Shahan Papers, John T. Gibbons to Shahan, New Orleans, November 24, 1923.

mind he took in the rudiments of these languages and laid the foundations so well that when he later began his training for the priesthood in Maryland, after an absence of some years from school, he encountered no serious difficulties. Moreover, it was in Ballinrobe that Gibbons received his introduction to the classics of English literature and of history, two subjects which, as we shall have reason to see, absorbed much of his reading time in after years. No one disputed Rooney's ability to instruct, but there was a tradition to the effect that because the fellow was somewhat slovenly and uncouth in manner some of the townspeople of Ballinrobe decided that they would employ another teacher for their boys. The story that Gibbons refused to transfer his allegiance from the man who had served him so well in his lessons was entirely in keeping with his fidelity to old friends which he displayed throughout his life. When he was challenged to give the reason for his refusal to follow the crowd, he replied that he would learn as much in one week from Rooney as he would in a month from the new teacher.[45] Both in school and at play young Gibbons showed characteristics of this kind which were to mark him later as a student in Maryland, and the comment written of him by one of his companions in Ballinrobe in after years was the sort of thing said of him by both professors and classmates at St. Charles and St. Mary's. Thomas Tighe recalled him as "a most gentle, amiable boy, very studious and clever, and a great favorite."[46]

When James Gibbons was only eight years old the spring and summer of 1842 brought severe distress to many in County Mayo in the form of famine. While it proved in no way as devastating as the frightful visitations that began in 1845, it was sufficient to arouse the indignation of Archbishop MacHale at the failure of the British government to bestir itself in behalf of his suffering people. MacHale wrote Sir Robert Peel, the Tory prime minister, in June, 1842, begging for government aid, a request he made repeatedly in later years but with no marked success.[47] The presence of famine and the failure of the government to give relief emphasized the wrongs under which the Irish

---

[45] Information contained in communication of James Fergus to the writer, January 21, 1946.

[46] Will, *op. cit.*, I, 13, citing a letter from Tighe of May 27, 1909.

[47] O'Reilly, *op. cit.*, I, 597–601.

people were then laboring, and it gave point to the arguments of the Young Ireland Party which they voiced through their newspaper, the *Nation,* founded in this same year of 1842.[48] Daniel O'Connell was still stirring Irish hearts with his speeches for repeal of the Union of 1801, a campaign in which he found no more sincere and constant supporter than Archbishop MacHale of Tuam. In fact, in the elections of December, 1840, the archbishop had campaigned actively throughout County Mayo for repeal.[49]

The difficult conditions that overtook Ireland in 1842 were mild, however, compared to the scourge which set in with the failure of the potato crop in 1845. Through the succeeding two years famine stalked the countryside and, "it was in the part of the country so especially dear to the Archbishop of Tuam, in Galway and Mayo, that the distress was most extreme, that starvation and fever were mowing down the populations, and that Landlordism was busy with its hellish work of exterminating."[50] The very region in which the Gibbons family lived was one of the hardest hit, and although there is no record of their experiencing actual hunger the cholera, or "famine fever" as it was called, did strike the family and on April 20, 1847, Thomas Gibbons died of this disease. James was not yet thirteen years of age at the time of his father's death, and it is not unlikely that this eldest boy in a family of six children felt the altered circumstances in their home more keenly than his younger brothers. The elder Gibbons, removed by death at the early age of forty-seven, was laid away in the Kilkieran Cemetery at Partry and just two years later his youngest daughter, Catherine, was buried beside him.[51] Catherine, James' youngest sister, who had been born in Baltimore exactly three years before him, died on April 27, 1849, at the age of seventeen. The death of Catherine caused so much grief to James that for a time he lost his appetite.[52]

---

[48] Curtis, *op. cit.,* p. 366.

[49] O'Reilly, *op. cit.,* I, 483–520.

[50] *Ibid.,* I, 652.

[51] James Fergus to the writer, Ballinrobe, January 21, 1946. On June 14–15, 1950, the writer visited the scenes of Gibbons' boyhood in Ballinrobe and went to the cemetery at Partry where the graves of Mr. Gibbons and his daughter are enclosed by a fine iron fence bearing a small plaque which reads: "Affectionately erected by Right Revd. James Gibbons, D.D., Vicar Apostolic of North Carolina, U. S."

[52] *Ibid.* The story of Gibbons' grief over his sister's death was related to the writer by Mrs. Mark Shriver of 607 St. Paul Street, Baltimore, in an interview

Up to the time of the father's death the meager records of these years would indicate that the circumstances of the family had been relatively good. True, the Gibbons' were never a wealthy family, but the father seems to have been fortunate in his business enterprises and while their means were always modest there was no trace of dire poverty. However, with the passing of the head of the house the affairs of the widow and her six children naturally did not prosper as before. What disposition Mrs. Gibbons made of her husband's business and land it is impossible to say but, at any rate, for the next six years she continued to live at Ballinrobe and to care as best she could for her growing children.

At a time when Ireland was so profoundly disturbed as it was in these very years no family of the lower classes, such as that of Bridget Gibbons, could entirely escape being affected adversely. The great famine which had originally struck in September, 1845, had continued for two and a half years with almost incredible losses of life, health, and spirit on the part of the population of Ireland. In the summer of the year in which Mr. Gibbons died it was estimated that three millions of the island's total population of about eight millions were being kept alive either by public works or charity. However, the potato crop of that year 1847 showed a fairly good yield and by March, 1848, the worst suffering of the people was at an end. Politically, however, conditions were far from happy. Daniel O'Connell continued his agitation for home rule to the end of his life.

> "Monster meetings" were attended by thousands marching in military array though without weapons to some point where their beloved "Dan" swayed them with an extraordinary blend of eloquence over Ireland and vitriolic or humorous, though often coarse, attacks on her enemies. On the sacred Hill of Tara it is said a quarter million of people listened to him.[53]

And when O'Connell died at Genoa in May, 1847, on his way to Rome there were left at home the more radical Young Irelanders who directed Irish political ambitions into more danger-

---

of March 7, 1947. She told it in connection with relating the cardinal's sympathy to her in the death of her little daughter. Gibbons cited his own reaction to his sister's death years before to show Mrs. Shriver how he understood her sorrow.

[53] Curtis, *op. cit.*, p. 365.

ous paths. Hopes rose again when an Irish franchise act passed Parliament in 1850 and raised the total electorate to about 160,000 voters, and the same year witnessed the formation of the Tenant Right League which had as its main objective the winning of fair rents for the tenant farmers and security from eviction. Although in the general elections of 1852 the league was able to return fifty members to Parliament, its over-all success was hardly more than trivial.[54] An alert youngster like James Gibbons could hardly have been a witness to these events without an impression having been made upon him. On at least one occasion when two local men by the name of Moore and Higgins were running for Parliament against Isaac Butt, young Gibbons and some of his schoolmates acted as clerks in the election at Ballinrobe in order to save the popular candidates the expense of hiring men.[55] But beyond this one episode there is no record of any activity or reaction on James' part to the political ferment taking place around him.

So seriously had the differences over political questions aroused the Irish people just at this time that they had even brought about a divided hierarchy in the Catholic Church of Ireland. Archbishop Paul Cullen of Dublin, who in general followed the sympathetic attitude toward the British government of his predecessor, Daniel Murray, found a powerful adversary in Archbishop MacHale. An acute crisis ensued in the relations between the two archbishops and their respective followers in the hierarchy over the exposure of corruption on the part of three Irish politicians by the names of John Sadleir, William Keogh, and Edmund O'Flaherty, all of whom held minor posts in the coalition ministry of the Earl of Aberdeen and Lord John Russell. Ultimately all three left the government more or less in disgrace, but what angered MacHale was the silence of the Archbishop of Dublin in the face of what the former regarded as the patent corruption practiced by the three men in their public trusts. Enemies of the Archbishop of Tuam reported MacHale to Rome as having been guilty of engaging in politics and slighting his episcopal duties, and they stated as well that Protestantism was making ominous advances in his archdiocese by reason of his neglect of duty. The complaints to Rome occasioned a letter of rebuke

54 *Ibid.*, p. 372.
55 Shahan Papers, John T. Gibbons to Shahan, New Orleans, November 24, 1923.

from Pope Pius IX in October, 1852, to which MacHale sent a strong defense of himself on January 23, 1853.[56] The inside story of this trouble among the Irish bishops was doubtless not known to their people in all its details, although their differences of opinion on political questions were a matter of common knowledge. It was the same John MacHale who as the bishop of the Gibbons family conferred the sacrament of confirmation on the future American cardinal.

All in all conditions in both Church and State were anything but promising in the early 1850's in Ireland, and it is not surprising that Mrs. Gibbons should have begun to turn her eyes back across the Atlantic and to entertain the wistful hope that there in the United States where they had experienced a relatively good fortune and where there were so many greater opportunities she might find a place for herself and her children. Emigration to the new world had by now become an old practice among the Irish. While the numbers leaving Ireland for America had shown a fairly steady increase since 1815, the famine of the 1840's had, of course, accelerated the pace. The year 1846 created a new record with 109,000 emigrants departing for North America and the succeeding year saw the number doubled.[57] With so many of their friends and neighbors seeking a fresh start in the United States it might well have offered confirmation of the wisdom of her decision to Mrs. Gibbons, and the latter part of 1852 found her and the children making preparations to leave the sad land of Ireland forever.

In circumstances such as this second coming to the United States one would normally expect Bridget Gibbons to return to Baltimore. That she had a love for the place there is no doubt. Years later her second son, John, related that in Ireland his mother and his sister, Catherine, had talked much about Baltimore and "its numerous attractions in comparison to those elsewhere,"[58] and what he called "the relating of pleasant reminiscences about the attractions of the Monumental City," was a favorite pastime in the home at Ballinrobe. But it was precisely because of those fond memories that Mrs. Gibbons did not wish now to return to the city on the Chesapeake. They had been the hap-

[56] O'Reilly, *op. cit.*, II, 433–453.
[57] Adams, *op. cit.*, p. 239.
[58] Shahan Papers, John T. Gibbons to Shahan, New Orleans, November 24, 1923.

piest days of her life and to go back to Baltimore without the
partner with whom she had shared her joy in the 1830's was
more than the widow could bear. It was this sentiment that decided Bridget Gibbons to choose New Orleans rather than Baltimore as the site of the family's future home.[59]

It was not at all uncommon at the time for large families to
split up on the trip to America and this was the way the Gibbons
family determined to make the voyage. Accounts of their trip
differ, but it seems fairly clear that James, John, and their sister,
Bridget, came first, sailing from Liverpool in January, 1853, on
a ship bound for New Orleans, and that they were followed later
by the mother with Mary and Thomas.[60] At any rate, after
having been about two months at sea the ship on which James
and John were traveling struck a sand bar off the Bahamas near
midnight of March 17. Fortunately, there was not a high wind
and at daybreak the passengers were taken in small boats to
the island and eventually made their way to Nassau. The Gibbons' were befriended by a Protestant gentleman by the name
of Johnston who offered them the hospitality of his home while

---

[59] Interview of the writer with Mrs. Thomas J. Stanton, New Orleans, January
25, 1948. Mrs. Stanton related that the cardinal's mother, her grandmother, lived
with the family of her daughter and son-in-law, Mr. and Mrs. George Swarbrick,
in her late years and that as a young girl the granddaughter, Mrs. Stanton [Mary
Swarbrick], heard the old lady several times give this as the reason why she
chose New Orleans rather than Baltimore as a future home in 1853.

[60] Will, *op. cit.,* I, 16–17, has Mrs. Gibbons embarking with all her children at
Liverpool in January, 1853. The information gathered by Bishop Fergus, however,
states that, "James, John and Brigid went first. . . . The Cardinal's mother and
Mary joined the family later." John Gibbons told Bishop Shahan in his letter
of February 18, 1924, about the shipwreck in the Bahamas and he spoke of the
time "when he and I" (meaning James and himself) met the mishap, making no
mention of their sister, Bridget, or any of the rest of the family being with
them. In his previous letter to Shahan of November 24, 1923, he had stated that
after his father's death "a portion of the family accompanied Uncle Martin
Gibbons to America and the latter's descendants now live in Dayton, Ohio. A little
later our whole family were once more reunited in this City of the South." It
seems clear, therefore, that the Gibbons family came to the United States in
1853 in two groups, but the exact identity of the two parties is impossible to
establish from the evidence at hand. A check of the WPA Survey of Federal
Archives in Louisiana at the National Archives, Washington, entitled "Passenger
Lists taken from Manifests of the Customs Service, Port of New Orleans, 1850–
1861" (1941), failed to reveal the names of any of the family entering the
port in 1853. However, the foreword to the typed copy of the passenger lists
states that "this compilation does not pretend to be a complete list of all passengers
entering this port between January 15, 1850, and May 18, 1861. . . ."

they were waiting for a ship to continue their journey.[61] After a delay of some days they sailed again and landed at New Orleans in the spring of 1853. In a short time the rest of the family followed and with them all now reunited in the metropolis of the South they could make definite plans for beginning what would be a new chapter in the life of each of them.

[61] Nearly forty years later Gibbons received a letter from a D. C. Johnston in Dayton, Ohio, who said he was the only son of William P. Johnston who befriended Gibbons with his brother and sister when they came out from Ireland. But Johnston said it was in his father's house on Louisiana Avenue in New Orleans, not in the islands, and that the sister was Mary, not Bridget. If Johnston's account was correct it would alter several of the minor details concerning the events of the journey. (AAB, unclassified, Johnston to Gibbons, Dayton, May 18, 1892).

CHAPTER II

Priesthood and Episcopacy

THE city where Bridget Gibbons and her five children cast their lot in the spring of 1853 had long since become the leading port of the South. Three years before the family arrived there New Orleans had a total population of 119,523, of whom 91,431 were whites and 28,092 were free and slave Negroes.[1] There was still a good deal of the old world atmosphere about New Orleans with its narrow streets and the quaint shops and dwellings that projected their interesting balconies over the sidewalks. The architecture that greeted a visitor was quite different from that which he saw in other large American towns. Not only was there a difference in architecture, but enough of the inhabitants of the city had retained the Latin features of their forebears who had built New Orleans to draw the comment of strangers. Six years before the Gibbons' came to the city Alexander Mackay, an English traveler, was there for some time, and he remarked, "As you walk the streets, the Anglo-American countenance is the exception in the stream of faces which you meet, whilst French is the language chiefly spoken around you." Mackay thought that "there are few towns on the surface of the globe possessing such a medley of population as New Orleans."[2]

More than once in the first months of their residence in New Orleans the older Gibbons children must have questioned the wisdom of their mother's choice in selecting this city for their future home, for the year 1853 proved to be one of the worst in the long and turbulent history of the metropolis of the South. In May a virulent form of yellow fever, brought in by boats

---

[1] John S. Kendall, "New Orleans' 'Peculiar Institution,' " *Louisiana Historical Quarterly*, XXIII (July, 1940), 869.

[2] Alex. Mackay, *The Western World; or Travels in the United States in 1846-47*, 4 ed. (London, 1850), II, 294, 302.

from Jamaica or Brazil, broke out and swept through the city with devastating effects. The death toll mounted until the climax was reached during the week of August 14 when 1,288 casualties were reported. In all from June 1 to October 1 New Orleans recorded over 11,000 deaths from all causes among its people, and it is generally agreed that due to unregistered deaths the total number exceeded that figure.[3] Added to the general havoc caused by the epidemic of yellow fever was the spirit of political violence. It was in 1853, too, that a group of Whigs introduced the Know-Nothing Party into Louisiana. The familiar pattern that marked the advent of the Know-Nothings elsewhere in the country showed itself as well in New Orleans, and when the threatening campaign for mayor finally came to an end in March, 1854, election day did not pass without leaving several killed and a considerable number of residents seriously wounded. These disorders continued for the next four years and with Charles M. Waterman winning the mayoralty in 1856 New Orleans saw the inauguration of an administration during which "the city was kept in turmoil by the animosities of the two opposing political parties."[4] So bad had it become that in his message to the legislature in 1857 Governor Robert C. Wickliffe informed that body that "organized ruffians" were keeping nearly one third of the New Orleans electorate from the polls.[5]

If the family of Bridget Gibbons in those first months had to bear with the anxiety caused by the yellow fever and the unpleasantness of finding themselves in a city torn by political strife, they had at least the consolation of knowing that New Orleans was a friendly milieu for the practice of their religion. At the time of their arrival Archbishop Anthony Blanc had been ruling the See of New Orleans for over seventeen years. The percentage of Catholics among the total population was high, and within the city itself there were seventeen parishes to care for the spiritual needs of the people.[6] Catholicism was strong in Louisiana; in fact, so strong was it that the Know-Nothings

---

[3] Roger Baudier, *The Catholic Church in Louisiana* (New Orleans, 1939), pp. 374–375.

[4] John S. Kendall, "The Municipal Elections of 1858," *Louisiana Historical Quarterly*, V (July, 1922), 361.

[5] *Ibid.*, pp. 361–362.

[6] *Metropolitan Catholic Almanac and Laity's Directory for the Year of Our Lord 1853* (Baltimore, 1853), pp. 97–98.

were at pains to disguise their anti-Catholic bias there. When the Louisiana branch of the party sent off six delegates to the national convention in Philadelphia in 1855 one Catholic was deliberately included in the delegation, and upon the convention refusing to seat the Catholic member the other five non-Catholic Louisiana delegates withdrew.[7] New Orleans had been founded by Catholics and in the intervening years it had not lost its Catholic tone and character. When Mackay was there in 1847 he observed this fact and he commented:

> The creole population being almost entirely Catholic, much of the manners of continental Europe is visible in New Orleans. These were established before the cession, and the soberer character and severer tenents of the American and Protestant population have not yet been able to make much headway against them.[8]

When the family came to New Orleans James Gibbons was nearing his nineteenth birthday. While his mother had ordered her furnishings and effects in Baltimore to be sold and the money sent to her,[9] the amount of capital which this Irish widow had at her disposal was limited. For that reason it is not strange that James, the oldest son, should feel it necessary to find work and thus help support his mother, sisters, and younger brothers. Fortunately, he secured employment as a clerk in the store of William C. Raymond located at 71 Camp Street where the proprietor maintained "a complete assortment of the most choice family groceries."[10] The association between young Gibbons and his Presbyterian employer proved happy from the outset and years later the cardinal's brother, speaking of this relationship, said he could hardly give adequate expression "to the feelings of the young employee towards his lovable and conscientious employer. . . ."[11] Not long after entering Raymond's employ James Gibbons fell a victim to the yellow fever then rampant in New Orleans. His oldest sister, Mary, nursed him at a great

---

[7] John S. Kendall, "The Municipal Elections of 1858," *Louisiana Historical Quarterly*, V (July, 1922), 360. Cf. W. Darrell Overdyke, *The Know-Nothing Party in the South* (Baton Rouge, 1950), pp. 218–223, which stresses the point that in that region the Know-Nothings were often more anti-foreign than anti-Catholic.

[8] Mackay, *op. cit.*, II, 306.

[9] Interview with Mrs. Thomas J. Stanton, New Orleans, January 25, 1948.

[10] *Cohen's New Orleans Directory for 1855* (New Orleans, 1855), p. 195.

[11] Shahan Papers, John T. Gibbons to Shahan, New Orleans, February 18, 1924.

risk to herself. Following the current practice he was kept in bed under heavy coverings to induce perspiration, hot baths were prescribed, and the amount of food allowed him was reduced to almost nothing. Through the sweltering heat of August this trial continued and for a time his weakness became so extreme that his life was despaired of.[12] James' brother wrote of this episode years later:

> During his sickness Mr. Raymond visited him every morning for about a month which must have been a great inconvenience to him as we lived a distance from his residence and on leaving he would say, take the best care of him no matter what it costs. On one occasion he had quite a dispute with the doctor, fearing that he was giving him too much medicine.[13]

At length he made a slow but certain recovery and was able to return to work. So satisfied was Raymond with the services of his young clerk that he raised his salary each year and — an unusual practice, to be sure — advances in salary were made for the previous year as well as for the coming year.[14]

While James Gibbons found both pleasure and profit in serving the wealthy sugar and cotton planters who patronized Raymond's to purchase stock that would last them and their slaves for months ahead, the hardy river men seeking provisions for their trips up the Mississippi, and the families in the neighborhood, it was not long before it became apparent that he had other plans for his future, regardless of how promising a career might beckon to him from the business world. From the time he was a little lad serving Mass in the chapel back in Ballinrobe his religion had meant more to him than it did to most boys.

James' interest in religion was deep enough that he thought nothing of going a distance from his family parish church in New Orleans to hear a band of famous missionaries who came to St. Joseph's Church, opposite Charity Hospital, the second week in February, 1854, to open a ten-day mission. The priests who preached the mission were Alexander Czvitovicz, Francis X.

---

[12] Allen Sinclair Will, *Life of Cardinal Gibbons,* I, 18–19.

[13] Shahan Papers, John T. Gibbons to Shahan, New Orleans, November 24, 1923. Some years later George Swarbrick, brother-in-law of James Gibbons, became manager of Raymond's store and ultimately held a partnership in the business. *Ibid.*

[14] *Ibid.*

Masson, Isaac T. Hecker, Clarence Walworth, and Augustine Hewit, all members of the Congregation of the Most Holy Redeemer and the last three converts to the Church.[15] Young Gibbons attended faithfully the exercises of the mission, and although he did not have the good fortune to hear Father Hecker, who had been taken ill with pneumonia on the voyage from New York,[16] he did find enlightenment and inspiration in the sermons of the other distinguished preachers. For some time previous to the mission the young man had been considering the priesthood as a vocation. But like every serious-minded youth contemplating a step of this kind he recalled years later "that for some time I hesitated and did not know whether I should serve God in the Church as a priest, or as a layman in the world."[17] Among the factors which influenced his mind at this time was his close reading of Orestes Brownson whose apologetic essays in his famous *Review* quickened young Gibbons' interest and helped to stimulate him to thoughts of how much he might accomplish for the Church in the priesthood.[18] It happened that during the mission at St. Joseph's Father Walworth delivered a spirited talk on the priesthood. It was Walworth's sermon that settled James Gibbons' doubts and solidified his decision to devote his talents and effort to this high calling.[19]

At this particular time there was stationed at St. Alphonsus Church in New Orleans another Redemptorist priest by the name of John B. Duffy. He had distinguished himself in a special way during the yellow fever epidemic of 1853 by his constancy and

---

[15] John F. Byrne, C.Ss.R., *The Redemptorist Centenaries* (Philadelphia, 1932), pp. 264–265. Hecker, Walworth, and Hewit left the Redemptorists in 1858 and founded the Paulist Fathers. St. Joseph's Church in New Orleans where the mission was preached, bears a striking similarity in its exterior to St. Thomas Church, Wilmington, North Carolina, where Gibbons was installed as vicar apostolic in 1868.

[16] Will, *op. cit.,* I, 19.

[17] *Catholic University Bulletin,* XXIV (December, 1918), 150. This entire issue of the *Bulletin* is devoted to the golden jubilee of Cardinal Gibbons as a priest, celebrated in Baltimore on October 20, 1918.

[18] Albert E. Smith and Vincent de P. Fitzpatrick, *Cardinal Gibbons, Churchman and Citizen* (Baltimore, 1921), p. 30.

[19] Ellen H. Walworth, *Life Sketches of Father Walworth* (Albany, 1907), pp. 130–131. Miss Walworth related that she met Gibbons in a bookstore in Baltimore where in conversation he confirmed the influence of Father Walworth's sermon upon him in New Orleans.

zeal in behalf of the sick, and this attention to the stricken, added to his generally high moral character, made Father Duffy, in the words of a Redemptorist historian, "the most popular Redemptorist ever assigned to New Orleans. . . ."[20] Duffy not only visited the numerous victims of the fever while taking care of his regular parish duties, but he was able as well to complete the construction of a new school in St. Alphonsus Parish during the same difficult year of 1853. Moreover, "In the midst of his ministry and work for the school, Father Duffy found time, in leisure moments to give Latin lessons to a number of boys who had manifested a desire to become priests."[21]

Once his decision had been made, then, it was to John Duffy that young Gibbons turned for instruction in Latin in the hours after his work at Raymond's grocery store. Under the guidance of this splendid priest the earlier lessons of Jennings and Rooney, learned some years before in Ireland, again came alive in the mind of the young man. It was from his priest mentor, too, that there came the inspiration to pursue his priestly studies in the city of his birth. Father Duffy had begun his novitiate as a Redemptorist in Baltimore in 1847 and after his ordination in 1849 he was there a second time as *socius* to the novice master.[22] His residence in Baltimore had brought Duffy into contact with the Sulpician Fathers and his observations of them as trainers of future priests in their three schools in and near Baltimore had made him a warm admirer of these men. He, therefore, suggested to James Gibbons that it was to the Sulpicians in Baltimore that he should go to study for the priesthood. It was a suggestion which the churchman never regretted, for as he stated publicly on the occasion of his golden jubilee as a bishop, "I followed the Redemptorist's advice, and never shall I regret that I placed myself under the care of the Sulpicians, who are eminent in learning, but more eminent in piety."[23] Another priest who, it was said, aided Gibbons in his preparations for entrance to the preparatory seminary was Father James J. Duffo, S.J., who

[20] T. L. Skinner, C.Ss.R., *The Redemptorists in the West* (St. Louis, 1933), p. 104.

[21] *Ibid.*, p. 101.

[22] *Ibid.*, p. 100.

[23] *Catholic University Bulletin*, XXIV (December, 1918), 150.

taught the humanities at the College of the Immaculate Conception in New Orleans in the early 1850's.[24]

While the determination of her eldest son to become a priest and to leave home to study in far-off Baltimore created a certain tinge of sorrow in the heart of Mrs. Gibbons, the devout widow was so happy at the thought of James becoming a priest that it outweighed her sense of loneliness at his impending departure. Years before when the family was living in Baltimore Bridget Gibbons had attended the funeral of the mother of Father Charles I. White, the priest who had baptized James. There she saw the body of Mrs. White borne from the church by priests as her pallbearers, and she later related that she prayed that the child she was then carrying in her womb might be a boy and a priest.[25] The advice of Father Duffy to her son that he should pursue his studies in Baltimore could hardly have been displeasing to the mother. All through the years since she had left the city on the Chesapeake she had spoken to her children about it. Long after this time the cardinal's brother, recalling these reminiscences of his mother and James' decision to study in Baltimore, wrote, "Do you wonder then that all of us including the Cardinal, in particular, had great love for Baltimore and wished to be there. . . ."[26] Certainly the selection was not made because

---

[24] Will, *op. cit.*, I, 20. Roger Baudier in a letter to the writer of June 17, 1948, stated that he had spoken of this priest to James J. O'Brien, S.J., of Loyola University, New Orleans, who told him that he [O'Brien] once asked the cardinal about Duffo and that "His Eminence stated that Father Duffo had no hand in shaping his vocation." There is no mention of Duffo in any of the contemporary sources on this period of Gibbons' life. The few biographical details known about him were furnished to this writer in a letter of June 17, 1948, from Edmond F. X. Ivers, S.J., from the records of the Society of Jesus at Woodstock College. Many years later when Bishop William Henry Elder of Natchez was being talked of as coadjutor to Archbishop Alemany of San Francisco, Elder wrote to Gibbons from Vicksburg on October 29, 1878, to say how he did not wish to go to San Francisco and he intended to inform Rome of his attitude. He added, "Your old friend Fr. Duffo experienced & prudent encourages me to make these representations to the Holy See" (74-B-7). Since the Woodstock records show Duffo as working in Vicksburg at this time there is no doubt but that this man was the same Jesuit who was supposed to have known Gibbons in New Orleans years before, but it is not possible to prove that he helped him with his preparations for the priesthood.

[25] Interview with Mrs. Thomas J. Stanton, New Orleans, January 25, 1948. The story that Mrs. Gibbons was opposed to her son becoming a priest as related by Covelle Newcomb in her fictionalized account of Gibbons entitled *Larger Than the Sky* (New York, 1945), pp. 40–43, is quite without foundation.

[26] Shahan Papers, John T. Gibbons to Shahan, New Orleans, November 24, 1923.

of the lack of Catholic schools in Louisiana, since at the time the Vincentians were in charge of St. Vincent de Paul Seminary at Assumption and the Jesuits had three schools where young Gibbons could have made his preparatory studies, namely, St. Charles College at Grand Coteau, the College of SS. Peter and Paul in Baton Rouge, and the College of the Immaculate Conception in New Orleans.[27]

Father Duffy not only made the original suggestion of the place for study, but he prepared the way by writing to Archbishop Francis P. Kenrick of Baltimore asking him if he would accept Gibbons as a student at St. Charles College. The archbishop replied on June 9, 1855, as he noted in his letter register, "consentiens ut juvenis Gibbons in Marylandia natus, in sem. S. Caroli acciperetur."[28] From the outset young Gibbons was enrolled as a student for the Archdiocese of Baltimore,[29] so that it was not a question of his merely going to Baltimore to study but of his electing to lead his life permanently in that part of the country. Precisely why he chose to affiliate himself with Baltimore rather than with the Archdiocese of New Orleans where his family had established their residence, it is impossible to say. The extant records suggest only that his determination to spend his priestly life in Baltimore rather than in New Orleans was prompted by the love which he had come to have for the city of his birth from hearing his mother and sisters speak about it.

At the time that James Gibbons set out from New Orleans for Baltimore in the late summer of 1855 he was twenty-one years of age. The long journey of over a thousand miles could

---

[27] *Metropolitan Catholic Almanac and Laity's Directory for the Year of Our Lord 1855* (Baltimore, 1855), pp. 109–110.

[28] AAB, Literarum Registrum, 1851–1862, p. 82. The writer is indebted to Michael J. Curley, C.Ss.R., for calling this entry to his attention in a letter of March 12, 1948. The failure to find Duffy's letter to Kenrick giving young Gibbons' qualifications was rendered all the more regrettable when the writer discovered a letter of November 15, 1872, to Gibbons himself in which Duffy described through four pages the characteristics of a student by the name of John E. Reilly of New Orleans whom he was recommending to Bishop Gibbons for his Diocese of Richmond (72-M-4).

[29] ASMS, Ordinations, St. Mary's Seminary, Volume I. After each of the ordinations of James Gibbons recorded in this book — without pagination — are the words "ex diocesi Baltimorensi." The Register, St. Mary's Seminary, I, 90, likewise states in regard to his entrance to St. Charles: ". . . his application was received by the Abp. of Baltimore for this diocese." In the Register his birthday is incorrectly given as July 18, 1834.

not be made by rail all the way since the through route from
Baltimore to Cincinnati and St. Louis was completed only in the
summer of 1857.[30] Gibbons, therefore, took the easier and cheaper
transportation afforded by the steamboat up the Mississippi and
then over the Ohio River to Cincinnati. Not long before his death
he described this first journey to Baltimore in the following
words:

> As for transportation, in 1855 I set out from New Orleans to
> Baltimore. Arriving by boat at Cincinnati, I there took the
> Baltimore and Ohio to a point west of the Allegheny Mountains.
> Here I detrained and continued the journey over the mountains by
> stage. I was exactly 16 days en route from New Orleans to
> Baltimore.[31]

In the eighteen years that had elapsed since he left Baltimore
for Ireland the city had grown to a metropolis of 188,251 persons,
of whom nearly twenty-five per cent were foreign-born. The heavy
immigration of the preceding years had added hundreds of
Germans and Irish to the native population, and with both groups
highly organized, "either or both could swing a close election."[32]
The presence of so many foreign-born Catholics, of course,
fanned the flames of hatred among the Know-Nothings who had
appeared in Baltimore politics three years before. In fact, at the
very time that young Gibbons reached the city it was in the
midst of a noisy election campaign. In Ellicott City, not far
from Baltimore where Gibbons was to begin his studies at St.
Charles College, the bitterness was so intense in the autumn of
1855 that the Know-Nothings followed the adjournment of one
of their own mass meetings by an invasion of a meeting of the
Union Party, "and set up such a shouting that it was impossible
for the meeting to proceed."[33] Election day in November was

[30] Clayton Colman Hall (Ed.), *Baltimore, Its History and Its People,* I, 480.

[31] Baltimore *Catholic Review,* February 19, 1921, which published at this time
the last article written by Gibbons before his death.

[32] Hamilton Owens, *Baltimore on the Chesapeake,* p. 261.

[33] Lawrence F. Schmeckebier, *History of the Know Nothing Party in Maryland*
(Baltimore, 1899), p. 28. While Gibbons was still at St. Charles the Sulpician
community in the city of Baltimore suffered occasionally from rough treatment
in the streets. The diary of François Lhomme for January 7, 1857, for example,
recorded: "Three rowdies attacked the seminarians during a walk; they threw
stones and even fired a pistol. Rev. Flamnant was struck with a stone; Rev.
Fredet had his nose smashed" (ASMS, p. 20). Whether or not these attackers were
Know-Nothings Lhomme did not say.

marked by rioting and disorders, but "the success of the Know-Nothings was complete. Baltimore City and thirteen out of twenty-one counties were ranged in the Know-Nothing column."[34] This phenomenon, of course, was nothing new to James Gibbons, for he had witnessed the rowdiness of the nativist bigots in his home city. Through most of his student days in Baltimore the Know-Nothings would reign supreme, being dislodged from the city government only in October, 1860, after a period which a Maryland historian has stated, "will always be looked back to as one of violence and disorder."[35]

The tactics of the Know-Nothings led to many unpleasant incidents for the Catholic people of Baltimore at this time, but here as elsewhere the movement against the Church failed to check its growth. Archbishop Kenrick and his suffragan bishops had, indeed, the hardihood to hold the Eighth Provincial Council in that May of 1855 in the face of the opposition, and the Archdiocese of Baltimore with its nearly 120,000 Catholics and 127 priests[36] continued its advance in a quiet way which gave little real provocation to these critics. Out in the countryside near the village of Ellicott City the institution to which James Gibbons directed his steps was still in a somewhat embryonic stage. St. Charles College had opened its doors on October 31, 1848, with Father Oliver L. Jenkins, S.S., as president and the entire personnel under his care in those first months consisted of Father Edward Caton, a deacon, a housekeeper, and four boys as students.[37] But it was not long before other students were attracted to this preparatory seminary conducted by the Sulpician Fathers, and by 1855, the year of Gibbons' matriculation, the forty-two students were sufficiently crowding the accommodations to warrant making a dormitory on the third floor of the building and thus creating room "for about seventy." Likewise in September, 1855, "a large room on the east end of the second floor was

[34] Schmeckebier, *op. cit.*, p. 29.

[35] *Ibid.*, p. 115. Cf. also Sister Mary St. Patrick McConville, *Political Nativism in the State of Maryland* (Washington, 1928).

[36] *Metropolitan Catholic Almanac and Laity's Directory . . . 1855* (Baltimore, 1855), p. 77.

[37] [George E. Viger, S.S.], *Golden Jubilee of St. Charles' College, Near Ellicott City, Maryland, 1848–1898* (Baltimore, 1898), p. 12. Cf. also John J. Tierney, S.S., "St. Charles College: Foundation and Early Years," *Maryland Historical Magazine,* XLIII (December, 1948), 294–311. The figures given for student enrollment by Tierney on page 306 differ from those of Viger in some particulars.

fitted up as a community chapel, where services could be carried on with more splendor."[38] The charges were $100 for board and tuition for a school year, payable half yearly in advance.[39]

At the time of Gibbons' entrance to St. Charles its faculty consisted of Father Jenkins as president; J. B. Randanne, who taught Latin at the college for eleven years; Pierre Frédet, the author of several textbooks in history; Hugh F. Griffin; and Jean-Baptiste Menu. Menu was later described as "one who was to play a part second only to that of Father Jenkins in the history of the College."[40] Living conditions were rather primitive in the single building which served the community for all purposes, and the young man from New Orleans suffered from the cold that first winter with the dormitory heated by only one central stove, and this during a season which was the coldest winter on record in Maryland since 1817.[41]

One of the first acquaintances which Gibbons made was Ridgley Dorsey whose home was in Woodstock, Maryland. Upon Gibbons paying his respects to Father Jenkins when he arrived the latter called Dorsey and said, "Dorsey, this is young Gibbons. Take him downstairs to supper."[42] With that abrupt introduction there began a friendship which lasted throughout their school days both at St. Charles and St. Mary's Seminary. James Gibbons was, of course, quite unfamiliar with the discipline which obtained in an institution for the training of future priests, and one of the first rules which he observed with some misgiving was the silence of the boys as they passed to their meals and again in the morning when they filed into the hall for prayers. The warm and friendly spirit of the new arrival from New Orleans overflowed with questions and greetings, but when he experienced nothing but silent gestures and an icy stare from the superior in answer to his salutation Gibbons subsided with some reluctance and resigned himself to keeping the rule.

If the disciplinary regulations of the college were at first a trial for the young man there were two phases of the life at St. Charles which James Gibbons found thoroughly to his liking,

---

38 *Ibid.*, p. 32.
39 *Metropolitan Catholic Almanac . . . 1855*, pp. 66–67.
40 Viger, *op. cit.*, p. 36.
41 Will, *op. cit.*, I, 27–28.
42 *Ibid.*, I, 26.

namely, study and recreation. Father Randanne was a hard task-master in his Latin classes, but Gibbons, drawing on the good foundation he had laid in Ballinrobe, experienced no difficulty. The professor was accustomed to call for the reading of certain passages by the students and then to request their translation of the lines. When he was not satisfied with the rendition he would ask that it be read and translated again. On one occasion he made that request of Gibbons; whereupon the latter repeated exactly the translation he had given the first time. A third effort did not move the student from his sense of the particular passage of Tacitus, and since he felt he was right not even the darkening countenance of Randanne could budge him.[43] This characteristic of holding to a position when he was convinced of the correctness of his view was one which he carried through life, although Gibbons was ready enough to change his mind when the reason-ableness of an opposite opinion had been presented to him. The same Father Randanne who taught Latin also exercised some supervision over the students' recreation. On his arrival at St. Charles Gibbons had brought two suits of clothes cut in the style of the day. But in playing prisoners' baseball and football the breeches soon gave way and Randanne had a suit of his own design made for him. Gibbons later stated that the vest came up to the chin and the coat went down to his heels so that "John L. Sullivan could have gotten into the legs of the trousers." But fit or no fit, Randanne's sole reaction to the ridiculous garment was, "I will cure you of your vanities."[44]

In the college at Ellicott City, just as at Rooney's school back in Ballinrobe, Gibbons enjoyed athletics. He played with vigor at the outdoor sports and once more engaged in the long hikes through the countryside on free days with his friends, especially Dorsey. Across the Frederick turnpike from the college campus was Doughoregan Manor, the ancestral estate of Charles Carroll of Carrollton, of which the property of St. Charles had once formed a part. The vast stretches of the estate with its large orchard were a special attraction for the students on their out-ings. Among the associates of James Gibbons in his recreations at St. Charles were several men who later attained prominence

---

[43] *Ibid.,* I, 29–30.
[44] Smith-Fitzpatrick, *op. cit.,* p. 33.

in the American Church. There was Thomas M. A. Burke who in 1894 became the fourth Bishop of Albany and who in later years stated of the cardinal that at the college he "endeared himself to everybody by his amiability and obliging disposition."[45] At St. Charles, too, Gibbons first met John S. Foley, the son of a well-known Baltimore Catholic family, who in 1888 had the pleasure of having his old friend, by then a cardinal, consecrate him as fourth Bishop of Detroit. Foley recalled their time at St. Charles in after years, and he said of the young Gibbons of those days:

> Whatever he did was done with all his might and that is the philosophy of his story. He engaged in his studies in the same earnest, indefatigable fashion that he exhibited at football or in the racquet court, and his mind was as active as his body, full of spring and resiliency. He was a youth, too, of noble and generous impulses and his unaffected modesty was the most charming trait of his character.[46]

One of the dearest and most enduring of all the friendships formed by Gibbons by reason of his association with St. Charles College, however, was that of T. Herbert Shriver.[47] It was on a visit to the college as a priest that Gibbons met Shriver and the friendship ripened into a deep and abiding affection, not only for Herbert himself but for the whole Shriver family, and to the very end of his long life this family was probably his closest association among the laity. The fact that Herbert left St. Charles and did not complete his studies for the priesthood affected in no way the love that Gibbons had for him and his family.

At the end of the first year young Gibbons received a first premium in Greek and in second year French and a second premium in church history, Latin, English, and elocution. These honors were awarded to him at the commencement held on July 13, 1856.[48] It was a performance which he repeated a year later when he was one of a graduating class of five and again carried off a first premium in Greek, French, rhetoric, and elo-

---

[45] Will, *op. cit.*, I, 34.

[46] Quoted in *ibid.*, I, 33.

[47] Interview with Miss M. Madeline Shriver, Union Mills, Maryland, July 9, 1945.

[48] *Catholic Mirror,* July 19, 1856.

cution and a second premium in church history and Latin.[49] Moreover, it was at the commencement on July 12, 1857, that Gibbons was selected to make the students' address. He had been told at first that Archbishop Kenrick would preside and with that in mind he had written his speech; circumstances prevented the archbishop from attending and another prelate was announced as the ranking dignitary. Young Gibbons rewrote part of his oration to fit the new circumstance. Finally he was informed that the second prelate had likewise dropped out of the picture and that the neighbor and friend of the college, Colonel Charles Carroll, would preside. Once more the oration was revised, and now Gibbons devoted most of his speech to a summary of the attainments of Carroll's distinguished ancestor, Charles Carroll of Carrollton, and the part the latter had played in winning American independence and in giving the property on which St. Charles College stood. In closing he spoke for his classmates in thanking the colonel for allowing them the freedom of his vast estates since, as he said, "we enjoyed the same privileges in passing through them as if they had been a portion of St. Charles." In its final form Gibbons' speech was sufficiently good that Father Jenkins "showed his appreciation of the oration by making a copy of it to be preserved."[50]

It must have been with a happy heart that James Gibbons looked forward to the end of his second year at St. Charles and the prospect of a return to his family in New Orleans. True, he felt regret at leaving the college, but many of his friends would be with him again in the fall when he planned to enter the major seminary in Baltimore, and whatever regret he experienced was lightened by the thought of seeing once more the dear ones from whom he had been so long separated. A short time after reaching New Orleans he wrote a letter to his friend, Ridgley Dorsey, which so well described his trip home and his summer occupations that it is worth reading in full:

> What shall I say that thou art doing in the region of Woodstock. Are you meditating on Brownson or Locke, pouring over Goldsmith's

---

[49] *Ibid.*, July 18, 1857.

[50] Viger, *op. cit.*, pp. 28–29, quoting Oliver L. Jenkins' journal. A typed copy of the speech was furnished to the writer through the kindness of the Reverend William J. Fletcher of St. Mary's Church, Newington, Connecticut.

'Deserted Village,' or locked in the embraces of your beloved Johnson? I hope at least, my dear friend, that you are enjoying yourself. I am scarcely yet settled at home, having arrived on last Saturday, after a journey of nearly three weeks. I have seen many strange things in my travels; after studying the theory of things for two years I have taken a practical view of the world. By a trip down the Ohio and Mississippi you can see the world in miniature. You are sure to encounter in the boat Yankees and Southerners, French, Dutch, English, with a good supply of the ubiquitous race — the Irish. There is no better school for politics, for here the merits of all parties are diligently discussed. You may judge from the length of time I was coming down that I had enough of time to make observations. I cannot attempt to give you the least idea of the beauty of scenery to be met with in these rivers. It is, I suppose, the longest and most majestic scene to be met with after a confinement of fourteen days on a boat.

I was telling you that I feared a disappointment in a boat at Cincinnati and my fears were realized. After arriving in that city on Wednesday p.m., I was obliged to remain until the following Saturday, when I took passage on the David Gibson. I spent the first Sunday in Louisville, where I attended vespers at Bishop Spalding's magnificent new Cathedral, and the following Sunday I spent in Memphis, Tenn., where we were discharging freight. The third Sunday found me once more in the bosom of my family. I need not tell you what happiness we mutually felt in meeting once more after so long an absence.

I have done very little in the way of study since I came home. My leisure hours are principally spent in paying visits and writing letters to our St. Charles friends. I try to read some English works, but I am crowded by so many of them that I cannot lay my mind down to get through one at a time. I read a chapter in "Blackwood's Magazine" and then pick up "Macauley's [sic] England," "Chateaubriand," or some other religious book. I had intended to ride out on the cars to see Venissat,[51] but I was informed yesterday by the Archbishop that he had arrived safely.

The weather at present is very hot, but the city is remarkably healthy. This, in fact, would be one of the most agreeable cities in the Union were it not for these modern locusts — the mosquitoes. They have a particular attachment for me, as you could judge from

---

[51] Ferdinand Venissat, a French student at St. Charles College, 1854–1857. Cf. *A Complete List of the Students Entered at Saint Charles College, Ellicott City, Maryland, Since the Opening, October 31, 1848* (Staten Island, New York, 1897), No. 97.

my physiognomy. I am spending my time very agreeably, and I hope the same for you. Please to give my respects to the Reverend Gents at St. Charles, if you see them. I hope you will favor me with a letter. I intend to leave the 1st of September, so in order to receive yours it must be sent before the 20th. I remain, your sincere friend in Christ, James Gibbons.

P.S. Pray for me.[52]

The letter to Dorsey reveals among other things the taste for serious reading of Gibbons as a student, a characteristic which he was destined to show all through life. It was on this trip down the Ohio in late July, 1857, that he met for the first time Martin John Spalding, at that time Bishop of Louisville, and later destined as Archbishop of Baltimore to be the man who would urge upon the Holy See the promotion of the young Father Gibbons to the episcopacy. The occasion of the meeting came about through Archbishop Kenrick's request that Gibbons deliver some pamphlets for him to the Bishop of Louisville. Aside from this single letter we have little further knowledge of how he spent the month's holiday with his family. His health was not good during his visit and when he returned to Baltimore in the autumn he still showed the effects of the "fever and ague which he brought from New Orleans. . . ."[53] By that summer John, his oldest brother, was twenty and Thomas, the youngest member of the family, was about fifteen. The Gibbons children were, therefore, now fairly well advanced toward maturity and the earnings of John and the girls supplemented their mother's modest income in a way that maintained them in a frugal but decent comfort.

The four weeks of happy, carefree vacation were swift in passing and September 1 found James again upon his long journey to Baltimore. This time it would be to the mother seminary of the United States, old St. Mary's on North Paca Street, that he would go as a student for philosophy and theology. So eager had he been to get the utmost from his training that

---

[52] New York *Freeman's Journal*, October 21, 1893. This letter, written from New Orleans and dated August 7, 1857, was published in connection with Gibbons' silver jubilee as a bishop.

[53] W. S. R. [Wendell S. Reilly, S.S.], "Cardinal Gibbons as an Alumnus," *The Voice*, VIII (May, 1931), 14, quoting notes on Gibbons made by François P. Dissez, S.S. Reilly also used the diary of Lhomme, a typed copy of which is kept in the archives at St. Mary's Seminary, Roland Park.

he had actually requested Father Jenkins to permit him to return to St. Charles for an extra year in the classics. But Jenkins had long since come to have a high respect for the mental abilities of the young man from New Orleans and he saw nothing to be gained by delaying in this way his advance toward the priesthood. It was out of obedience, then, to his superior's judgment that James Gibbons entered St. Mary's in 1857 instead of the following year, and Jenkins characterized the new student at St. Mary's for the benefit of Father François Lhomme, the superior, as one who possessed, *"Bon esprit; talent."*[54]

The student body into which Gibbons entered on September 10, 1857, at St. Mary's Seminary consisted of thirty-two young men.[55] It was a considerably smaller number than he had left behind at St. Charles where in that year of 1857 seventy-seven boys were enrolled.[56] Lhomme presided over the house as superior; Joseph P. Dubruel was the treasurer; Stanislaus Ferté taught moral theology; Alphonse J. Flammant, dogma; J. M. Gervais, moral philosophy; and Alexis J. Elder acted as pastor. In the following year François P. Dissez joined the faculty. Among these professors it was to Dissez that Gibbons became especially attached and the friendship which was formed in 1858 endured through half a century until the night in 1908 when the Cardinal Archbishop of Baltimore stood sadly at the bedside of his old professor of philosophy and watched as he breathed his last.[57]

The same fidelity to friends was noted of Gibbons at St. Mary's as had been true of him at Ballinrobe and St. Charles. Old friends were with him from the college in the seminary on Paca Street as, for example, his favorite Ridgley Dorsey, but Dorsey encountered difficulties with his Latin and that, together with ill-health, ultimately prompted the faculty to advise him "to reenter the world."[58] There was another friend from St. Charles days by the name of Joseph Onthank who showed promising talents, but Onthank contracted tuberculosis and

---

[54] *Ibid.*

[55] *Metropolitan Catholic Almanac and Laity's Directory for the Year of Our Lord 1857* (Baltimore, 1857), p. 65.

[56] Viger, *op. cit.,* p. 31.

[57] Reilly, *op. cit.,* p. 14.

[58] ASMS, Student Record Book, n.p.

died prematurely. During his friend's illness Gibbons demonstrated his rare gifts for kindness and human sympathy, and Father Dissez later commented that "his tenderness [was] exercised in a special way towards his excellent and severely tried friend. . . ."[59] There were classmates like John Gaitley who later served as a fellow priest with Gibbons in the archdiocese and of whom the faculty commented that he was "fatigued by the end,"[60] and John P. Hagan, ordained with Gibbons, of whom the faculty wrote that, "He was found often in bed."[61] After a year at St. Mary's Gibbons and five of his classmates made their official entrance into the clerical state with tonsure conferred on them in the seminary chapel on September 15, 1858, by Archbishop Kenrick.

During the previous year Father Dissez taught Gibbons philosophy and he gave him a grade of eight and a half out of a possible ten for the first semester. While he was second in rank in the class at first he ultimately came out in first place and was appointed on April 29, 1858, the "master of conference." It was the function of the master of conference to preside at the review of the subject matter already seen in class and to prepare "by this review the public weekly examination called the *dominicale*."[62] That James Gibbons had made an outstanding record during his four years in the seminary is certain from the evidence left in the records of the institution. It was the custom at that time to give grades on the basis of ten. The over-all comments of the faculty in this case testified to the high esteem they entertained for him. Gibbons' report read as follows:

1. Talents & capacity more than ordinary, especially facility.
2. Success 9.
3. Disposition & temper: amiable, equanimity; cheerfulness; zeal for duty, great ardor for study, & almost too great eagerness for knowledge; for some time inspired some fears lest he might not take the right direction.
4. Regularity 9; virtue 9.

---

[59] Reilly, *op. cit.*, p. 14.

[60] ASMS, Student Record Book, n.p.

[61] *Ibid.*

[62] Reilly, *op. cit.*, p. 14. Dubruel's diary for October 30, 1860, recorded the funeral of Father Lhomme and added, "Two seminarians prayed by his remains, during the day that lapsed from death to burial. Mr. Gibbons kept watch during night" (p. 22), ASMS.

5. Preaching very successful; judgment, exposed to be carried by his imagination.
6. Manners.
7. Observations: gained the esteem & affection of all.[63]

These grades and comments by his instructors quite thoroughly refute the opinion which has been expressed now and then over the years that James Gibbons did not possess a fine mind and that his seminary record had not been an impressive one.

His spiritual director during his early seminary days was Father Stanislaus Ferté, the first in a long line of Sulpician confessors who guided Gibbons' conscience to the very end of his life.[64] Father Dissez, who knew Gibbons intimately as a student, gave this summary of his career at St. Mary's Seminary:

> James Gibbons manifested the *bon esprit* at St. Mary's as at St. Charles' by his affability, politeness and kindness towards all, superiors and fellow-students. He was a regular and edifying seminarian. He profited by all opportunities to increase his knowledge. Even in recreation he liked to ask his Professors about the subject-matter of his studies or readings. He had a special zeal for the study of Holy Scripture; in his private rule he set apart one hour to read it every day.[65]

Through all these four years at St. Mary's the Sulpicians themselves bore the expenses of this candidate for the Archdiocese of Baltimore. In the ledger of the financial accounts of those years there appears under the name of James Gibbons the item, "Entered 10th 7th 1857 — Supported by the house, not for clothes," and the account runs to a final entry for May 6, 1861, and closes with the comment, "Borne by the house $615.00."[66] It is small wonder, then, that Gibbons should have felt a lifelong gratitude to the Sulpicians, but in the years to come he more than repaid these good priests for their expenditures in his behalf by establishing three burses at St. Charles College, giving $15,000 for the chapel fund of St. Mary's, and bestowing on the two institutions combined a gift of $50,000 "to help them extend the grounds of St. Charles."[67]

---

[63] ASMS, Student Record Book, n.p.

[64] Reilly, *op. cit.*, p. 14.

[65] *Ibid.*

[66] ASMS, Seminarians, 1854–1864, p. 111.

[67] Reilly, *op. cit.*, p. 15.

As his training advanced Gibbons received minor orders on June 16, 1859, and by the summer of 1861 he was ready to receive the subdiaconate on June 28, and the diaconate on June 29. Finally, with five of his classmates, he was raised to the priesthood on Sunday, June 30, 1861.[68] He had received all his orders from tonsure through priesthood from Archbishop Kenrick, and the ceremonies on each occasion had been conducted in the chapel of St. Mary's Seminary. Over a half century later he spoke of the ordaining prelate as "the first really great man whom I can remember to have known intimately. . . ."[69]

At the time of James Gibbons' ordination to the priesthood the entire country was in a state of intense excitement and fear. The long and bitter controversy over the slave issue had culminated on April 12 in the attack on Fort Sumter, and the actions of the Union and Confederate governments made it clear during the succeeding weeks that the last chance to avert civil war had been lost. Nowhere did the force and bitterness of the conflict divide the population more than in Baltimore. The state had in 1860 a population of 515,918 white persons, but the presence of 171,131 Negroes, of whom 87,189 were slaves, added, of course, to public anxiety.[70] Maryland was generally speaking southern in sympathy, and it had been linked for long years by close commercial, social, and historical ties to the South. On the other hand, Baltimore was the only city south of the Mason and Dixon Line that had large manufacturing interests which bound it to the North. The result was fatal to a peaceful community and it could be said in truth that, "There never was a house divided against itself in sharper contrast than Maryland in 1861."[71]

In answer to President Lincoln's call on April 15 for 75,000 volunteers the Sixth Massachusetts Regiment approached Baltimore four days later on its way to the fighting front. The

---

[68] ASMS, Ordinations, St. Mary's Seminary, I, n.p.

[69] James Cardinal Gibbons, "My Memories," *Dublin Review,* CLX (April, 1917), 164.

[70] Charles Branch Clark, "Slavery and Emancipation in Maryland, 1861–1865," *Maryland Historical Magazine,* XL (December, 1945), 295.

[71] Matthew Page Andrews, "Passage of the Sixth Massachusetts Regiment through Baltimore, April 19, 1861," *Maryland Historical Magazine,* XIV (March, 1919), 60.

troops were set upon by the angry Baltimoreans of southern views and the result of the encounter left four soldiers killed and thirty-six wounded with twelve citizens of the city killed and a considerable number seriously injured.[72] The outbreak of violence within the city naturally heightened the uneasiness of everyone and Charles Howard, president of the Board of Police, wrote General Isaac R. Trimble two days after the fight with the Massachusetts soldiers to the effect that "a large number of our fellow Citizens have apprized this Board that they are organizing themselves into Associations for the defense of the City; various rumours having led them to believe that its safety is seriously endangered."[73]

In circumstances of this kind it is not strange that there was strong sentiment for the secession of Maryland from the Union. William Howard Russell was in Baltimore during the week of the episode with the troops from Massachusetts, and he stated that he was visited at the Eutaw House "by some gentlemen of Baltimore, who were highly delighted with the news and I learned from them there was a probability of their State joining those which had seceded. The whole feeling of the landed and respectable classes is with the South. . . ."[74] No chances were taken by the government at Washington, however, and on the night of May 13 Federal Hill near Baltimore was occupied by Union troops under General Benjamin F. Butler and the city was overawed by the military. Governor Thomas H. Hicks, who had been elected on a Know-Nothing platform in 1857, called an election for representatives to Congress. Election day, June 13, just about two weeks before Gibbons' ordination, passed off quietly and Baltimore bore the appearance of loyalty. While there was no interference by the troops in the election they were present in numbers and were "ever ready to preserve order."[75]

But the relative quiet of the voting in June set no precedent, for the general election in November was attended by wild excitement and disturbance, although it decided once and for all

---

[72] *Ibid.*, pp. 70–71.
[73] "Baltimore and the Crisis of 1861," *Maryland Historical Magazine*, XLI (December, 1946), 259.
[74] William Howard Russell, *My Diary North and South* (New York, 1863), p. 36.
[75] Charles Branch Clark, "Maryland in the Special Session of Congress, July, 1861," *Maryland Historical Magazine*, XXXVI (December, 1941), 387.

the status of Maryland within the Union. The Union victory at the polls was accomplished by the arrest of twenty-nine secessionists in the state legislature, and the passage of measures aimed to weed out men of these views from public life. By this means only about 10,000 out of Baltimore's 40,000 voters were allowed to vote.[76] After the balloting in November all practical hopes of the secessionists were dashed, many sympathizers with the South fled, and "Maryland became in fact as well as in name a loyal state."[77] Anthony Trollope, in Baltimore at the time of the election, stated that one resident had told him, "When this is over every man in Baltimore will have a quarrel to the death on his hands with some friends whom he used to love."[78]

While the political fate of Maryland was sealed by the election of November, 1861, the die-hards continued all through the war to cause incidents which "clinched any argument in favor of severity as against leniency towards the South."[79] A severe censorship of the press was enforced by the federal authorities in the city and during the war nine Baltimore newspapers were suppressed either temporarily or permanently, and two of the nine were forced to suspend publication because of the arrest of their editors. The Catholic press was no exception and on September 29, 1863, Michael J. Kelly, P. J. Hedian, and John B. Piet, publishers of the *Catholic Mirror,* were arrested on orders of General Robert O. Tyler because their printing press had published an inflammatory pamphlet by Frank Key Howard called *Fourteen Months in American Bastilles.* While they were released on October 3, Kelly and Piet were arrested a second time on May 23, 1864, at the orders of General Lew Wallace and sent to Fort McHenry on the charge that their bookstore and printing press were printing and circulating Confederate books and articles.[80] The *Catholic Mirror* was suspended during the week of May 23–30

---

[76] William A. Russ, Jr., "Disfranchisement in Maryland (1861–67)," *Maryland Historical Magazine,* XXVIII (December, 1933), 319.

[77] Charles Branch Clark, "The State Elections of 1861," *Maryland Historical Magazine,* XXXVII (December, 1942), 399.

[78] Anthony Trollope, *North America* (London, 1862), II, 464.

[79] Russ, *op. cit.,* p. 328.

[80] Sidney T. Matthews, "Control of the Baltimore Press During the Civil War," *Maryland Historical Magazine,* XXXVI (June, 1941), 162–164.

and resumed publication only after the release of its editors some days later. In October, 1864, J. and C. Kreuzer, proprietors of the *Katholische Volkzeitung* of Baltimore, were warned by General Wallace against publishing any anti-government tracts, threatened with suspension of their newspaper should the order be disobeyed, and commanded to submit each issue to the provost marshal for examination.[81]

Such were the general conditions in which Father James Gibbons inaugurated his priesthood in Baltimore. While the young priest, who was twenty-seven that summer, had lived all his life in the United States south of the Mason and Dixon Line with a consequent coloring of his views by southern associations, he did not favor the South during the Civil War. Years later he recorded his views of the conflict of the 1860's when he wrote:

> It was from His Grace [Archbishop Kenrick] that I imbibed a strong attachment to the Union. I had been born a Southerner and brought up a Southerner, and my heart was, of course, with the Southern States. Indeed, my brother was actually fighting in the Army of the Confederacy; but I could never believe that secession would succeed, and even if it should succeed I could not help but see that it would be the destruction of what was already a growing, and what might become a very great nation. Therefore my head was always with the Union.[82]

It was not easy, therefore, for a priest with opinions of this kind to practice his religious ministrations in the Baltimore of these years. So intensely did many of the Baltimore Catholic clergy feel about the righteousness of the Confederate cause that in the first year of the war the priests of the cathedral parish actually refused to read Archbishop Carroll's prayer for the civil authorities because it contained a petition for the preservation of the union of the American people. The reading of this prayer at Mass was a custom that had been followed for years in the cathedral. Archbishop Kenrick finally decided that he would read it himself, and as Gibbons related:

> I suppose during the reading of that prayer he suffered more than one could well imagine; for when he mentioned the Union of

---

81 *Ibid.*, p. 167.
82 *Dublin Review*, CLX (April, 1917), 165–166.

the States, many people got up and publicly left the Cathedral, and those who remained expressed their dissent from the Archbishop's petition by a great rustling of papers and silks.[83]

Archbishop Kenrick was deeply affected by the strain under which his clergy and people were compelled to live, and it was the belief of Gibbons that there was "no doubt that what seemed to be the breaking up of the Union in 1861 very much hastened his death."[84] The archbishop died suddenly in the night of July 6–7, 1863, just three days after the great battle was fought at Gettysburg.

Gibbons' first parochial experience came when he was assigned by Archbishop Kenrick as an assistant to Father James Dolan, pastor of St. Patrick's Church, in the neighborhood of the city called Fell's Point. It was a rough section of the town stretching along the water front where the Patapsco River reaches out to meet Chesapeake Bay. The inevitable elements of society found in large port cities were present in numbers at Fell's Point, but back a few blocks from the water front there were rows of modest but respectable dwellings which housed many fine families of both native and immigrant stock. The pastor of St. Patrick's was himself a hardy character, although beneath his brusk manner was a warm Irish heart which responded quickly to the spiritual needs of his people. Father Dolan had been a man of great independence of action and view all his life and he had not particularly welcomed the young assistants sent by the archbishop to help him. In fact, they had come in a fairly steady procession of recent years and they had left just as regularly. Therefore, when the parishioners saw the slender young priest of medium height and attractive smile appear in their pulpit one Sunday morning in July, 1861, they wondered how long this preacher, whose first sermon they enjoyed so much, would last among them.[85] As a matter of fact

[83] *Ibid.*, p. 165.

[84] *Ibid.*, p. 164.

[85] Will, *op. cit.*, I, 45, quoting John Malloy, one of the parishioners at the time. Thirty-seven years later when Gibbons presided and preached at the dedication of the new St. Patrick's Church on November 20, 1898, he said in part: "This sacred spot is especially dear to me. After leaving the seminary it was here that I celebrated my first Mass; it was here I preached my first sermon, it was here I began to break the bread of life for the faithful and to exercise the functions of the ministry." John T Reilly, *Collections in the Life and Times of Cardinal Gibbons* (McSherrystown, 1898–1899), V, 371.

he lasted only about six weeks, although that should not lead one to the conclusion that the pastor was solely responsible for his assistant's quick move since the practice of appointing newly ordained priests to country pastorates was fairly common then and for years thereafter.

If James Dolan was not a priest of the most elegant manners, he was one who watched with a sharp eye for the best interests of the Church and the Catholic people of his neighborhood. St. Patrick's was already nearly seventy years old as a parish when James Gibbons came there, its foundation having been laid by Father Antoine Garnier, S.S., in 1792. In the intervening time Baltimore had grown, and particularly of late years the expanding sections of the parish farther out made it plain that another church should be constructed for the convenience of the people living at what were then the extreme eastern boundaries of the city. For that reason Dolan had purchased ground in a section known as Canton, and there built a small church which he called St. Bridget's. For the first few years St. Bridget's had served as a mission from St. Patrick's, but it ultimately got its own pastor in the person of Michael O'Reilly. With the transference of Father O'Reilly in mid-summer, 1861, to Mount Savage, Maryland, the *Catholic Mirror* announced that he would be succeeded by Father Gibbons. After paying tribute to O'Reilly the editor concluded, "The congregation of St. Bridget's will, no doubt, find in Father Gibbons, a worthy successor to their late esteemed pastor."[86] In this way did Father Dolan see that provision was made for his mission parish and at the same time rid himself at St. Patrick's of another assistant whose services he did not feel he needed.

Finding himself a pastor only six weeks after ordination, the young priest went promptly to work and his first officially recorded act was the baptism of Barsine Elizabeth Young, a convert, on August 15, 1861.[87] It was not a pleasant situation

---

[86] *Catholic Mirror,* August 17, 1861. For the parish to which Gibbons was first assigned, cf. *Souvenir Book. Sesquicentennial of Saint Patrick's Parish, 1792–1942* (Baltimore, 1942). The impression that Dolan did not want an assistant is strongly conveyed in Will, *op. cit.,* I, 45–47, who quotes the pastor of St. Patrick's as having said in his blunt way at the time of Gibbons' appointment to St. Bridget's, "Canton is a good school for a young priest." *Ibid.,* I, 47.

[87] Baptism Register, August 29, 1858 to December 10, 1865, p. 42. This volume is kept at St. Brigid's Rectory, Baltimore. The spelling of the name was later

into which James Gibbons found himself so suddenly projected. While the simple church was adequate for the religious services of his small congregation, there was no rectory and he had to make his home in a few small rooms which had been built against the wall of the church with no provision for light or ventilation and with the boards of the floor resting on the ground. The neighborhood had not yet been built up and the only house close at hand was that of Mrs. Bridget Smyth, one of his parishioners, who was exceedingly kind to the young pastor. This good woman acted as a housekeeper for the priest's rooms and she sent one of her sons to sleep there each night because the lonely location was thought to be dangerous in that neighborhood filled with rough characters.[88]

While the number of people in the parish was not great they were widely scattered and this necessitated long and sometimes exhausting trips for Father Gibbons in all kinds of weather. Most of his parishioners were quite poor with the heads of families employed in the copper works and rolling mills of Canton or as agricultural workers who tilled their small farms and market gardens. Naturally these people could not contribute much to the support of their pastor, and it, therefore, taxed the ingenuity of Gibbons to find ways to meet expenses and to improve the parish. At length he decided upon renting Carroll Hall in the city with a view to holding a fair. Upon inquiry he discovered that the manager was not at all inclined to rent the building to him and only after a great amount of pleading did he finally persuade the fellow. The explanation for the man's conduct was given after he felt more reassured about his prospective tenant. He told Gibbons, "I thought you were a Yankee."[89] The fair was a real success and from the revenues of this and succeeding entertainments of a similar kind enough money was raised to enable the young pastor to erect a neat brick rectory alongside the church with no additional burden upon his people.

---

changed from "Bridget" to "Brigid." The last baptism record in this book signed by Gibbons on December 3, 1865, was over the name of J. P. Gibbons (p. 95). It is one of only two times that the writer found him using a middle initial; precisely what his middle name was the extant records do not reveal.

[88] Will, *op. cit.*, I, 47–48. Will got his account of the assistance of Mrs. Smyth from members of her family.

[89] *Ibid.*, I, 50.

During these years of the Civil War the Catholic Church like all institutions of the nation felt the strain. The number of priests available for parish work in the Archdiocese of Baltimore was far below the requirements, and so early in 1862 Archbishop Kenrick asked Father Gibbons if he would assume charge of St. Lawrence O'Toole Church at Locust Point. This small church, the cornerstone of which had been laid on July 22, 1855, by the archbishop,[90] was situated a mile away from St. Bridget's across the Patapsco River. The task of serving in this dual capacity proved to be a severe one on the frail constitution of Gibbons. He found that each Sunday morning he had to leave Canton at six o'clock and row in a skiff across to Locust Point where he would hear confessions, say Mass, preach, baptize, and attend sick calls at St. Lawrence's. He would then row back across the river to Canton in time for the high Mass at St. Bridget's at ten-thirty where he would likewise deliver a sermon. All this early morning travel was done, of course, fasting and while he came through the ordeal without too serious consequences it did leave him with a lifelong ailment in the form of bad digestion. At Locust Point in these war years his congregation consisted, among others, of many ship and dock workers. It was one blessing that the war had brought to Baltimore in the form of a greatly increased amount of employment on the steamboats engaged in the fighting at sea. It was within the confines of St. Lawrence's that this activity was at its height in the very years Gibbons had charge of the parish.

> At Locust Point the Union developed a great depot for the con-
> centration and distribution of war supplies — an area so congested
> at times that vessels had to remain at anchor awaiting their turns
> at the piers. Steamboats crowded the numerous and active shipyards,
> either building for the Union or being overhauled after rough usage
> in the Potomac and Hampton Roads and in the campaign along the
> coasts of the States lying to the southward, for which these erstwhile
> media of commerce and good will were converted into transports,
> blockaders and gunboats.[91]

In this second water-front church Gibbons recorded, on March

---

90 32B-Z-1, Acta Episcopalia of F. P. Kenrick, p. 130.
91 William J. Kelley, "Baltimore's Steamboats in the Civil War," *Maryland Historical Magazine*, XXXVII (March, 1942), 42.

6, 1862, his first baptism of a child by the name of Edward Gallagher, and the registers of the parish show his constancy in serving the community up to his transfer to the cathedral in November, 1865.[92]

Beyond the exacting duties entailed in caring for his two parishes the young pastor found time to act in the capacity of a volunteer chaplain at the two principal military posts in Maryland. Fort Marshall was located not far from St. Bridget's and Fort McHenry, of *Star Spangled Banner* fame, was within the boundaries of the parish of St. Lawrence at Locust Point. On one occasion at Fort McHenry in July, 1864, Gibbons heard the confession of a Confederate prisoner and then sought to get some nourishment for the man who had not been properly provided for by the hospital doctor. For this act of kindness, performed, as he wrote later, "merely to help a suffering fellow-creature, irrespective of his politics, I was told my services would no longer be acceptable at the fortress, and that I need not return."[93] The doctor in question, James H. Curry, sent a communication on July 18 recommending that Gibbons' pass be revoked, "he having conversed with a prisoner of War in the Hospital, and without any permission."[94] The priest wrote out a full explanation of his action at the hospital and he ended by saying, "The undersigned far from knowing that he was doing wrong in giving the ministrations of his religion to the Prisoner, made known the fact to Dr. Curry and intimated to him the request of the Prisoner that a little wine be furnished to him."[95] But Curry was not to be appeased by the explanation forwarded to him by General William H. Morris, and he returned it to the general with the recommendation:

> I do not think the necessity exists for a general pass to enable the Reverend Gentleman to give the "ministrations of his religion" to the patients. If in any particular instance a patient desires to see a Priest of the Roman Catholic Faith certainly no objection would be offered to the request. But in as much as the Rev. Jas. Gibbons has

---

[92] Baptismal Register, Our Lady of Good Counsel Church, Baltimore. The name of the parish was later changed from St. Lawrence O'Toole to its present name.

[93] *Dublin Review*, CLX (April, 1917), 166.

[94] 71-H-1, Curry to J. Gales Ramsay, Fort McHenry, July 18, 1864, copy.

[95] 71-H-2, signed statement of Gibbons as pastor of St. Bridget's Church, Canton, July, 1864.

stepped beyond the bounds of propriety in the one case, I most hastily recommend that no General pass be furnished him.

But if a patient desires to see him or he desires to see a Union soldier in the hospital I have no objection to a special pass being given for each visit.[96]

Exactly what type of pass was ultimately issued to Gibbons we do not know, but he explained the sequel himself. "However, I did return, since I threatened to make known to the higher authorities what had taken place; and men who exercise martial law with little regard for the feelings of those below them are often very sensitive as to the feelings of those above them."[97] It was another example of Gibbons' persistence when he felt he was in the right.

The young chaplain had a variety of experiences during those days of war. In the same summer of 1864 a Confederate soldier by the name of John R. H. Embert had obtained leave to visit his family in eastern Maryland but during his stay he was arrested as a spy and condemned to death. Embert was a Catholic and the case reached the attention of Father Gibbons, his confessor, who interceded in his behalf. At first he had no success. Two other soldiers were condemned to die for the same offense at midnight of August 29. On the previous evening a number of prominent Baltimoreans begged John S. Gittings, president of the Northern Central Railroad, to appeal to President Lincoln to pardon the prisoners. Lincoln was under an obligation to Gittings by reason of the latter's kindness to Mrs. Lincoln and her sons in 1861 when an attempt on the President's life forced him to leave his wife and children in Harrisburg and proceed to Washington alone. Mr. and Mrs. Gittings befriended the President's family and for that reason Lincoln naturally felt grateful. However, stanch Democrat that he was, Gittings did not fancy going to Washington now to ask the favor of Lincoln, but at length Mrs. Gittings was prevailed on to make the trip and the President readily agreed to intercede and save the condemned soldiers.

Word did not reach Father Gibbons of the presidential reprieve and he appeared that evening to prepare Embert for

---

[96] *Ibid.*, a copy of the communication of Curry, July 30, 1864, to General Morris, was written on the opposite side of the above statement of Gibbons.

[97] *Dublin Review*, CLX (April, 1917), 166.

death, only to learn the joyful news that his sentence had been commuted to imprisonment for the duration of the war. Not long after the war when Gibbons was stationed at the Baltimore cathedral Embert came to see him. He recalled how the priest had exerted himself to save his life and had been pleased to lose the chance of seeing a knot tied around his neck; he informed Father Gibbons that he was now asking him "to tie a more pleasing knot," since he wanted him to officiate at his marriage, which he did.[98] At another time he was called to attend a soldier at Fort Marshall whom he found to be in a delirium from fever. In an effort to bring him back to his senses Gibbons began to ask him questions. To the query as to where he was born, the soldier answered, "Ireland." To the question of what part of Ireland, the sick man replied the western section, and finally the priest learned it was Ballinrobe. He then inquired if he knew the pastor of Ballinrobe and the soldier replied yes, he was his brother. At once Gibbons exclaimed, "You are Hal Conway!" In such strange circumstances did the chaplain discover an old schoolmate from Ballinrobe.[99]

Despite the hazards of war Father Gibbons undertook a visit to his family in New Orleans while the conflict was still on. Times were even harder there than they were in Baltimore and once the city fell in May, 1862, to the Union forces of General Benjamin Butler and Captain David G. Farragut the severity imposed by the federal commanders must have made living hard for the Gibbons family and their friends.[100] The young priest had doubtless been greatly weakened by his strenuous work in the two parishes and military forts, for his obvious illness alarmed his family lest he might be lapsing into tuberculosis. For this reason his sister Bridget, Mrs. George Swarbrick, persuaded him to go over to Lewisburg, Louisiana, for a prolonged rest and there the resilient spirit and basically healthy constitution of Father Gibbons revived and he recovered his strength.[101] It was most likely in 1864 that this trip was

---

[98] Will, *op. cit.*, I, 55–57.

[99] *Ibid.*, I, 58. The pastor of Ballinrobe at the time was actually Thomas Hardiman but he had as a curate Peter Conway. Cf. D'Alton, *A Short History of Ballinrobe Parish*, pp. 59–60.

[100] Cf. Howard Palmer Johnson, "New Orleans under General Butler," *Louisiana Historical Quarterly*, XXIV (April, 1941), 434–536, for conditions in the city during these years.

[101] Interview with Mrs. Thomas J. Stanton, New Orleans, January 25, 1948.

made, and it would be interesting to know if he was the James Gibbons who arrived at New Orleans on the *Champion* from New York on November 3, 1864.[102] While it is probable he made the trip by boat it cannot, of course, be established with certainty that the passenger of that name was the James Gibbons we know.

After his recovery from the threat of tuberculosis and a long visit with his mother, brothers, and sisters Father Gibbons returned to his post of duty in Baltimore. One of the priestly tasks which he fulfilled with special profit to his people and pleasure to himself was preaching. There is every evidence for the belief that Gibbons was from the outset what one might truthfully call an effective preacher. There was nothing of the fiery orator about him, nor was there anything distinguished in his style of composition. But he did have to a marked degree the gift of putting religious truths in a simple and attractive dress that held the attention and won the conviction of his audiences. From the very beginning of his priesthood he spoke to the people on simple yet basic subjects. Among his extant sermons which bear a date the very first one carried the title "Good Use of Time," in which he drove home the point that we can gain eternity by a good use of our time. Another early sermon was on "Peace," preached at St. Joseph's Church in Baltimore just three weeks after his ordination, a subject which was particularly appropriate to be heard by a congregation distracted by war. Subjects like pride, the love of God, mortal sin, the resurrection of the body, and how the word of God was to be heard are found among the sermons for this period of Gibbons' life, and they all bear the same unadorned recitation of dogmatic truths illustrated by homely illustrations calculated to clarify the meaning of the preacher.[103]

The accidental appropriateness of one of Father Gibbons' sermons probably struck his listeners with a peculiar poignancy. The long and painful ordeal of the Civil War had just come to an end five days before with the surrender of General Lee

---

[102] National Archives, Survey of Federal Archives in Louisiana, WPA of Louisiana, Passenger Lists, Port of New Orleans, 1864–1866, p. 65.

[103] 71-D through W, contains handwritten copies of these early sermons of Gibbons with dates running from January 1, 1861, up to March, 1899. He kept copies of many of his sermons and preached them on repeated occasions.

at Appomattox Courthouse. It was Good Friday night, April 14, 1865, and Gibbons was preaching at St. Joseph's Church in Baltimore. Strangely enough he dwelt with special emphasis upon the deep ingratitude of the Jews and the peculiarly base treachery of Judas toward our Lord. In the course of his remarks he said:

> Imagine a great and good ruler, who had done everything to deserve the confidence and affection of his subjects, and who had lived only for his country and had no desire but for his country's good, imagine such a ruler struck down by the hand of an assassin! Would you not feel, my brethern, a deep indignation at his murder?[104]

In the light of the fact that it was only an hour or two after Gibbons' sermon that same evening that President Lincoln fell at Ford's Theater from the bullet of Wilkes Booth, the coincidence must have given the priest's words a meaning for his audience far beyond what he himself intended. On the following day Archbishop Spalding of Baltimore promptly issued a public letter to the priests and people of his archdiocese in which he deplored the assassination and said he felt confident that his Catholic subjects would willingly unite, "with their fellow-citizens in whatever may be deemed most suitable for indicating their horror of the crime, and their feeling of sympathy for the bereaved."[105] On April 21 the body of the murdered President was brought into Baltimore on the way to its last resting place at Springfield, and when a stop was made to permit the remains to lie in state for two hours in the rotunda of the Exchange, a military and civic procession was formed to escort the casket in a manner that would be expressive of the respect and esteem of the citizens for the dead President.[106] It was characteristic of James Gibbons that he should be among the clergy who marched in procession to the Exchange on that April morning.

The war years had brought a major change to the Archdiocese of Baltimore. When Archbishop Kenrick died in July, 1863,

---

[104] *Dublin Review,* CLX (April, 1917), 167.

[105] *Catholic Mirror,* April 23, 1865.

[106] J. Thomas Scharf, *Chronicles of Baltimore,* p. 634. ASMS, Diary of Joseph P. Dubruel has the following entry for April 21, 1865: "Lincoln's remains passed through the city. Students went with the clergy, Dr. Coskery leading the procession" (p. 25).

the normal interval before the appointment of a new archbishop was lengthened by the exigencies of war and by the delicate task which faced the Holy See in filling the premier see of the United States — a city southern in sympathy although lying within the Union lines — with a candidate who would offer satisfaction to the varied groups involved. There were rumors afloat that the government at Washington was actively interesting itself in the appointment to Baltimore, and Martin John Spalding, Bishop of Louisville, wrote in his journal under date of February 7, 1864, "There appears to be no doubt that the Government has interfered at Rome in regard to the appointments to the sees of Baltimore and New York."[107] In any case, the selection finally fell upon Spalding himself, and it proved to be a very happy one. Spalding, who was fifty-four years of age at the time and had been a bishop for sixteen years, was the son of parents who had been born in Maryland and emigrated to Kentucky in the 1780's. He was, therefore, of old Maryland stock and this factor helped to make his appointment a highly popular one. The long vacancy of over a year in Baltimore was finally filled when its seventh archbishop took possession of his see on July 31, 1864. Little did the pastor of St. Bridget's at Canton realize how much lay in store for him at the hands of this man whom he had first met as a seminarian on his trip down the Ohio River in 1857.

The war had come to an end in the spring of 1865 and there was a slow return everywhere to normal times with the welcome healing of the old wounds. Maryland finally worked its way out of the harsh military rule of General Lew Wallace, and by the end of that year the more congenial civil government was again in sight. As one Maryland historian expressed it:

The end of the year 1865 saw the passing away of what might be called the typical conditions of Civil War times. Almost coincident with the new year began the self-reconstruction of Maryland. In the ensuing period the registration act was finally repealed and the de-

---

[107] Quoted in J. L. Spalding, *The Life of the Most Rev. M. J. Spalding, Archbishop of Baltimore* (New York, 1873), p. 258. Spalding says of this rumor, "This brief sentence is the only reference which I have been able to find among his papers to a subject to which he seems not have given more than a passing thought." No mention of any such interference appeared in Leo F. Stock, *United States Ministers to the Papal States. Instructions and Despatches, 1848–1868* (Washington, 1933).

feated Union party split up into two factions. The radical wing became the Republican party in the State, and the conservatives joined the triumphant Democrats, in whose hands lay the destinies of Maryland for many years.[108]

This return to peace likewise relieved the burdens of Father Gibbons as volunteer chaplain at Forts Marshall and McHenry. It was his belief that he could now devote himself with all his energies to his two parishes of St. Bridget and St. Lawrence. He seemed perfectly content in his humble post, and his mind was filled with plans for the improvement and expansion of his parochial duties. But the young pastor had not reckoned with the new archbishop.

As the months passed Archbishop Spalding managed to get about a good deal in his new field of labor, acquainting himself with his priests and people, seeking sites for new buildings, and surveying generally the task that lay ahead of him. Naturally he met Father Gibbons shortly after his arrival in Baltimore as he did the other city pastors, and he took a very strong liking to this wiry little priest whose pleasing and gracious manner complemented so well his piety and administrative ability. It was not long before the personal attraction of Gibbons gave to the archbishop the idea that he could best serve the archdiocese by employing his talents as secretary to himself and as a member of the busy cathedral household.

According to the cardinal's first biographer it was in June, 1865, that Archbishop Spalding first mentioned to Gibbons the proposal he had in mind.[109] The immediate reaction was a

---

[108] William Starr Myers, *The Self-Reconstruction of Maryland, 1864–1867* (Baltimore, 1909), p. 39.

[109] Will, *op. cit.*, I, 63. That Archbishop Spalding was considering the incardination of his priest nephew, John Lancaster Spalding of the Diocese of Louisville, into the Archdiocese of Baltimore is evident from their correspondence. Writing from Venice on September 19, 1864, to his uncle the young priest said he would leave it "entirely to you as to whether I am to go to Baltimore or to Louisville" (37-A-5). Only a few days after his arrival in Baltimore the archbishop wrote his nephew and remarked he knew he had not yet been assigned to any particular duty, and he added that, "a little touch of self-interest — enlightened I trust — makes me less sad at the contingency as it may possibly induce the new Bishop to give you to me. I could soon employ you and both constantly and usefully. However, we must leave this to the march of events, which God alone can dispose for the best" (37-E-40, Spalding to Spalding, Baltimore, July 26, 1864, copy). One wonders if the elder Spalding had succeeded in inducing Bishop Peter J. Lavialle of Louisville to release his nephew if he would have made him his

favorable one, flattered as he was by the compliment of the archbishop seeking his close and intimate association. But then doubts began to trouble him. He was happy in Canton, his people were fond of him, and they were of the poorer and less favored classes among the Catholics of Baltimore. Did he not have a clear duty to remain with them? In his perplexity the young priest turned for advice to Father Henry B. Coskery, Vicar-General of the Archdiocese of Baltimore. He begged Coskery to intercede with Archbishop Spalding to change his mind and leave him where he was. On his return to St. Bridget's from his visit to Coskery conflicting emotions arose once more and he began asking himself if he was stubbornly adhering to his own wishes rather than yielding obedience to his superior. Was it a case, in other words, of persisting in his own will against that of his archbishop? Questions of this kind tormented him all during that Saturday evening and far into the night; but Sunday morning settled his doubts. Before preparing to say his Masses he sat down and wrote a letter to Father Coskery, revoking the appeal of the day before, stating he stood ready to obey the archbishop's wish in his behalf whatever it might be. With that done, and the letter delivered to the vicar-general by a student who was at the time in the rectory, he experienced a new calm and began his customary Sunday morning duties in his usual serene manner.[110]

Although the original proposal of the change of Gibbons from Canton to the cathedral had been made in the summer, it was not until nearly Christmas that he took his departure from St. Bridget's. In the meantime the news spread and a committee of the parishioners waited on the archbishop and pleaded with him to leave their pastor with them. Spalding, in turn, stated his own pressing needs for the services of a priest secretary, and although he appreciated their wishes, he said that he felt he could not satisfy them in this particular regard. Gibbons was still at St. Bridget's in late November, as we know from his letter to Thomas A. Becker, a former member of the cathedral household, concerning the archiepiscopal library there. He wrote Becker to say that he appreciated his instruction

---

secretary and then not have found need to call Gibbons to this position at the cathedral.

[110] *Ibid.*, I, 64–65.

concerning the care of the books which would be one of his new duties but, he said, "as I am a perfect novice in my new function, I shall be obliged to trouble you again for a few additional explanations." He added that he was "yet in Canton" and had not so far seen the library of the cathedral. Gibbons sympathized with Becker's regret at leaving Baltimore a short time before. "I can indeed appreciate your feelings, for if I am so distressed at abandoning my home Parish, I can well imagine your grief at parting with a place and with gentlemen so congenial to your good taste." He closed by asking Becker to address his next letter to the cathedral.[111] Finally the transfer of Father Gibbons became official and the *Catholic Mirror* for December 16, 1865, carried the following notice:

> Our Most Rev. Archbishop, who had returned in good health from his arduous visitation of the Eastern Shore counties of his diocese, announced on Sunday last [December 10] that the Rev. Father Gibbons, of Saint Bridget's church, Canton, has been transferred to the Cathedral to act there as an assistant pastor; with the installation of this Rev. pastor, his Grace further announced a very desirable change in the arrangements of the parochial Mass. At the close of the half past eight o'clock Mass on Sundays, there is to be an instruction by Father Gibbons, and after the 1st of January a Sunday School is to be opened at the Cathedral, under the direction of the same Rev. gentleman. We congratulate the Cathedral congregation on the acquisition of so excellent, exemplary and intelligent a priest as Father Gibbons, and welcome him with all our heart to his new domicil [*sic*]. Father Gibbons' place at St. Bridget's has been filled by the appointment of Rev. John F. Gately [*sic*] of Bryantown, as his successor. . . .

Thus the first and only pastorate of James Gibbons was brought to a close after four and a half years, and there came to St. Bridget's in his place one of the five classmates with whom he had been ordained in 1861 in the person of John T. Gaitley. Father Peter McCoy succeeded him as pastor of St. Lawrence's at Locust Point.[112]

It was a matter of no surprise that Archbishop Spalding was not long in Baltimore before he felt the need of a capable

---

111 71-J-1, Gibbons to Becker, Baltimore, November 24, 1865.

112 *Sadlier's Catholic Directory, Almanac and Ordo for the Year of Our Lord 1867* (New York, 1867), p. 55.

priest to act as his secretary. There confronted him now duties and obligations far beyond the range of those he had experienced during his years as a bishop in Louisville. Baltimore was, in a sense, the Catholic capital of the United States. Here were held the councils of the American Church and here, too, was directed much of the important business of the Holy See with the American bishops. Before the establishment of the Apostolic Delegation in 1893 the Archbishop of Baltimore served as the channel through whose hands passed most of the correspondence affecting transactions of general importance to Rome and to the Church of the United States. Obviously, Spalding, whose health was already seriously impaired by a severe bronchial and gastric disorder, was not in a position to carry the burden alone. He thus found a great amount of relief in being able to give over to the alert and competent young Father Gibbons much of the business at hand.

One of his duties as secretary was to accompany Spalding on his visitation tours throughout the archdiocese, an experience which stood Gibbons in good stead when he himself was called on to govern the see some years later.[113] While the major part of his work during the next two and a half years would be devoted to secretarial services for the archbishop, he found time, too, for the priestly ministrations which he loved so well and performed with so much profit to souls. He assisted Fathers Henry B. Coskery and Thomas Foley, the other members of the archbishop's household, in hearing confessions regularly in the cathedral, taking his turn at the parish Masses, and in preaching and giving instructions in the truths of the Catholic faith in the successful Sunday school which he began conducting soon after his arrival. In this way the knowledge as a parish priest which he had learned at Canton and Locust Point was kept fresh in his mind and the enrichment which it gave to his own priestly life was not lost.

Archbishop Spalding was in Baltimore only a few months when he began laying the plans for the holding of a plenary

---

[113] Gibbons likewise accompanied the archbishop occasionally on his holidays. For example, Richard L. Burtsell, the New York canon lawyer, recorded in his diary under date of August 14, 1866: "We met Abp. Spalding at Saratoga; he is quite dignified. He had with him as Secretary F. Gibbons, I understand, quite a smart priest" (AANY, Burtsell Diary, January-November, 1866).

Gibbons in 1866, five years after his ordination as a
priest. Seated is the Very Reverend Henry B. Coskery,
Vicar General of the Archdiocese of Baltimore.

council of the American Church. As early as March, 1865, his nephew, Father John Lancaster Spalding, was writing him from Rome in regard to the copies of European conciliar legislation which the archbishop had requested.[114] The archbishop pursued this interest through the coming months and by August he was outlining for Bishop John Timon of Buffalo his reasons for convening a council.[115] The plans materialized slowly, and by February, 1866, Pope Pius IX gave the council his approval and designated Spalding as apostolic delegate. The archbishop, in turn, sent out on March 19 the letter of convocation to the American hierarchy. This activity, of course, increased greatly the amount of correspondence which had to be handled by the archbishop's office, and through the spring and summer Gibbons was kept very busy with the arrangements for the council. Not only did it entail a fairly constant correspondence with the forty-some bishops at the time in the United States, but accommodations had to be found for them during their stay in Baltimore, details of ceremonies in the cathedral had to be worked out, and in addition the general superiors of the religious orders and the theologians to the bishops had to be cared for.

The first preliminary meeting of the Second Plenary Council was convened at Archbishop Spalding's residence on October 4 and the solemn opening of the council took place three days later in the cathedral. Among the officers appointed for the discharge of the conciliar business was the archbishop's secretary, who was named to the post of assistant chancellor of the council. It would be his task to help Father Thomas Foley who acted as chancellor of the gathering. It was Gibbons' first experience of a council of the Church, for although he was in Baltimore in May, 1858, when the Ninth Provincial Council was held, he was then only a student in St. Mary's Seminary and he knew no more of the proceedings than what he could gather from watching the processions to the cathedral, being present at one or more of the solemn Masses, and from hearing snatches of gossip about the bishops who visited the seminary. Now as a minor official of the council he came into direct contact with the six archbishops besides Spalding, the thirty-

---

[114] 37-A-8, Spalding to Spalding, Rome, March 13, 1865.
[115] Letterbook of Archbishop Spalding, p. 150.

seven bishops, and the large number of distinguished priests who were in attendance as theologians and superiors of religious orders. It was James Gibbons' first formal introduction to the leaders of the American Church, and it was at this gathering that he met the men with whom he was so soon to be associated in the hierarchy of the United States. It was in October, 1866, that men like Peter Richard Kenrick, Archbishop of St. Louis, John McCloskey, Archbishop of New York, James Roosevelt Bayley, Bishop of Newark, John J. Williams, Bishop of Boston, and William Henry Elder, Bishop of Natchez, had an opportunity to observe the spirit and work of the young priest who in a few years would be of their number and with whom they would have occasion to deal in an intimate way on the problems confronting American Catholicism.

Needless to say, Father Gibbons played a very minor role in the council. And yet this agreeable young priest was to be the subject of the bishops' judgment before they left Baltimore. One of the main items of business of the hierarchy was the outlining of new dioceses to be suggested to the Holy See in order that the Church might keep pace with the expanding nation. In a session which was held on October 13 there arose the subject of choosing fitting names to be submitted to the Holy See for filling the vacant Diocese of Erie. Bishop Josue M. Young had died on September 18, just three weeks before the council opened, and it was necessary, therefore, to make provisions for the see. In the original *terna* drawn up on October 13 for Erie the name of Gibbons was put in second place, but later in the same session his name was placed first on the *terna* chosen to fill the projected Vicariate Apostolic of North Carolina which the bishops were proposing to the Holy See. When the prelates met for their session on October 17 a number of these *ternae* were made final and the minutes reveal that the list for Erie omitted Gibbons while the *terna* for North Carolina carried his name as first with that of Matthew O'Keefe, pastor of St. Mary's Church, Norfolk, Virginia, second, and Jeremiah J. O'Connell, O.S.B., pastor of St. Peter's Church, Columbia, South Carolina, third.[116]

---

[116] 39A-D-4, Minutes of the Second Plenary Council. Aside from his duties as assistant chancellor the printed minutes of the council reveal nothing more of Gibbons' activities than the fact that he served on three occasions as deacon of

The opinion of Gibbons' qualifications for the episcopal office as submitted by the council to the Congregation of the Propaganda was a very high one. It recounted his academic training, his parish experience, and his secretarial services, all of which were said to have been performed with the greatest honor to him. In conclusion it was remarked, "The Delegate believes him the most worthy of all for the Episcopacy." That such was, indeed, the opinion of Spalding was evident from his letter to Alessandro Cardinal Barnabò, Prefect of the Propaganda, written on November 8, in which he spoke in the most glowing terms of his secretary. Besides repeating his attainments as a student, pastor, and secretary the archbishop noted that Gibbons was pious, prudent, full of zeal, in good health although not robust, and firm in his ideas. Furthermore, he preached well, especially to youth, enjoyed the best reputation among those who knew him, and was beloved by all. In fact, said Spalding, "He is a priest in every respect perfect."[117] It was obvious that the Archbishop of Baltimore was the principal promoter of his young secretary for the episcopacy, and during the succeeding months his determination that Gibbons should wear a miter never flagged.

In the spring of 1867 Archbishop Spalding decided upon a trip to Europe to attend the celebration in Rome marking the centennial of the martyrdom of St. Peter. His health had been very poor of late and it was hoped that the voyage would prove beneficial to him. During his absence the archbishop kept in touch by mail with Baltimore, and in answer to two letters recently received from him Gibbons wrote Spalding on July 21 to give him news of his archdiocese. He told the archbishop that the construction work on the west gallery in the cathedral was progressing slowly, although a few days before a large iron beam weighing 7,000 pounds had come down with a frightful crash. Little real damage was done, but Gibbons

pontifical Masses celebrated by Archbishops Kenrick, Alemany, and Odin. Cf. *Concilii plenarii Baltimorensis II. . . . Acta et decreta* (Baltimore 1868), pp. lxxii, lxxviii, lxxxvii.

[117] For a copy of Spalding's letter of November 8, 1866, to Barnabò and a summary of the materials on Gibbons submitted to the cardinals of Propaganda at their meetings on September 15, 23, and 27, 1867, the writer is indebted to Monsignor Giuseppe Monticone, general archivist of the Congregation of the Propaganda Fide, who presented them to him in Rome on May 10, 1950. They were copied from the Acta, anno 1867, vol. 232, ff. 342, 364 rv, 402v–403, 413v–414v.

stated, "Not having an abiding faith in the strength of the ropes, I vacated my confessional before the beam fell and escaped a shock." Collections for St. Mary's Training School, a favorite project of the archbishop, were showing a gratifying return, and Father Edward McColgan had purchased land at Mount Washington on the Northern Central Railroad for a future parish. That the bishopric was still in the mind of Spalding for his secretary we know from Gibbons' reply:

> As your Grace seems determined to inflict a mitre on me, I think it would be a good idea to send me on from France some of the Episcopal paraphernalia. I have the blues since I read your letter. To leave Baltimore is hard enough, but to lose the genial company of the archiepiscopal house costs me a good deal, — more than I can say in words. You see I take it seriously, because your letter appears serious. But if your Grace remains the other side of the Atlantic for five years, I won't mind. The longer you stay the better because the longer my exile is deferred.[118]

While his letter to his superior revealed a note of resignation, there surely was no enthusiasm, and among other things it showed how reluctant he was to leave Baltimore. The city of Baltimore was throughout his long life the place above all where James Gibbons loved to be and the thought of leaving it brought readily to his mind a sense of exile.

Since Father Coskery, the vicar-general, had accompanied the archbishop to Europe, the burden of parochial work was increased during their absence for Father Thomas Foley, the chancellor of the archdiocese, and Father Gibbons. The arch-

---

[118] 36A-J-2, Gibbons to Spalding, Baltimore, July 21, 1867. On July 3, 1867, Spalding had written a letter from Rome to "Rev. Dear Friend," which was marked *"Private."* At the close of this letter he said, "Tell Joseph that I am able to confirm all that I wrote him a few days ago about executive business, except Delaware, of which I am not altogether certain, but still think in my opinion probable" (71-N-1). This statement would mean that Spalding had won confirmation of Gibbons as Vicar Apostolic of North Carolina. The letter may have been sent to Thomas Foley, the chancellor, who told Spalding a few weeks later that the news he had relayed about the new bishops had appeared in the New York papers and that Gibbons "couldn't sleep" when he heard it. Foley said that whenever Gibbons heard anyone speak of North Carolina, "he pours a torrent of inquiries from his mouth, equal to the deluge" (34-A-3, Foley to Spalding, Baltimore, August 16, 1867). The Joseph referred to in Spalding's letter of July 21 was probably Joseph Dubruel, S.S., who was at the time superior of St. Mary's Seminary in Baltimore and a member of the archbishop's council.

bishop returned to Baltimore in the middle of October and upon his arrival home the customary round of business, official visitations, and reception of callers was resumed in the residence on Charles Street. One of the interesting features of residence in the archbishop's house was the opportunity it offered for meeting distinguished guests. In December Jefferson Davis and his wife called to see Archbishop Spalding, and Gibbons wrote to his friend, Herbert Shriver:

> Last week, Ex President Davis, for whom you fought so bravely, called with his lady, on the Archbishop, and spent over two hours in our house. I had the honor of an introduction to him, and found him just what I expected, a quiet, grand, thinking man, with care and intelligence blended on his forehead.[119]

Added to the responsibilities of the clergy in Baltimore in these days was the collection of funds for relief of the many sufferers in the South. Conditions in the southern states after the war were very bad, indeed, and Baltimoreans showed their southern sympathies again by the generous manner in which they responded to the many appeals for help which reached them from the South. The *Catholic Mirror* of Baltimore was filled at this time with such appeals and notices of benefit entertainments being held to gather money for relief. A foreign visitor to Baltimore in the winter of 1867 stated, "Balls and bazaars were being got up, while I was there, for the openly avowed purpose of collecting funds to support those families in the South which had been reduced to poverty by the late war." Moreover, the same visitor learned that a considerable emigration had taken place from the South to the friendly environment of Baltimore on the part of those who "would not live under negro domination as long as they had the means of living elsewhere."[120] Another traveler from abroad who had recently come to Baltimore by way of the West Indies, New Orleans, up the Mississippi, and then to Cincinnati and Pittsburgh thought

---

[119] ASMS, Gibbons to Shriver, Baltimore, December 22, 1867. A series of thirteen letters here from Gibbons to Shriver running from August 25, 1867, to March 19, 1869 — with one of December 4, 1886 — reveal, *inter alia,* the affection of the priest for this student and his efforts to keep him in St. Charles College to continue his studies for the priesthood.

[120] F. Barham Zincke, *Last Winter in the United States* (London, 1868), pp. 32–33.

Baltimore "the first even tolerably clean city I had seen since I entered the States." He liked the dome of the Cathedral of the Assumption but, he added, "the interior is choked with hideous rented pews." He concluded, "If, which heaven forbid! I were compelled to fix my residence in an American city, I think I should fix on Baltimore."[121]

In January, 1868, there was introduced into the Maryland legislature a bill for strengthening the public school system throughout the state, and before the adjournment of the session this measure became a law. In the new law a state tax of ten cents was levied on each $100 of taxable property to support the public schools, but no provision was made for any aid to schools under denominational control, nor was any account taken of the need for religious instruction of children attending the public schools. Naturally the Archbishop of Baltimore was anxious about the increasing burden of support for his parochial schools and he felt that the state should be willing to give some form of financial assistance to the private schools conducted under Catholic auspices. With this in mind he asked Gibbons to prepare a report to be submitted to the Maryland state senate which would demonstrate the saving to the State of Maryland from the Catholic schools. Gibbons took pains to give a detailed account of the matter as it affected the city of Baltimore. He reported that the average attendance at the cathedral Sunday school for the year 1867 had been 500 while the Catholic parochial schools of the city had numbered 7,089 children. Allowing, as he stated, a minimum annual cost per child of $5 it would amount to a saving of $37,945 to the state on the part of the Catholics of Baltimore alone, to say nothing of other parts of the state. Although the report seemed to offer a cogent argument to the mind of the archbishop and his secretary, the terse entry for February 1, 1868, in the official proceedings of the Maryland senate indicated the fate that awaited it. It read, "The President presented the petition of the Parochial Free Schools under the control of the Catholic Church in the city of Baltimore, from the Archbishop of Baltimore. Which was read and referred to the Committee on Education."[122]

[121] Greville John Chester, *Transatlantic Sketches* (London, 1869), pp. 258–259.
[122] Cornelius F. Thomas (Ed.), *The Life Story of His Eminence James Cardinal*

While tasks of this kind were occupying his time the threat of the miter of North Carolina finally became a reality. In the middle of February Father Gibbons wrote to his friend, Herbert Shriver, and he said:

> The long threatened documents from Rome have come at last, or at least official letters from Cardinal Barnabo confirming most of the nominations made at the late Plenary Council. Among the batch was one for your devoted friend myself. It was stated in the letter that the Bulls would be sent forthwith. Already the archbishop in his kindness is preparing for me some of the Episcopal paraphernalia. In contemplating those shining but oppressive insignia I compare myself to a Bull decked out for the sacrifice. "Ego enim jam delibor." Do pray for me dear Herbert, that if I accept this appalling burden, the very thought of which makes me gloomy, although I try to keep up a cheerful appearance, — God may give me light and strength necessary for the tremendous office. Should I finally determine to go to N. Carolina, and unless I change my mind, I am destined to go, I intend to make a retreat at St. Charles; when I will spend a few days with my old Preceptors, and will have the pleasure of seeing you and my young friends.[123]

Although Gibbons was still showing some reluctance at accepting the office of Vicar Apostolic of North Carolina and hinting that he might yet refuse it, in the end Archbishop Spalding had his way and the young priest gave his consent to undertake the work. The news soon became public, and on February 22 Bishop James F. Wood of Philadelphia wrote to congratulate him and to hope for, "Many consolations and a continual increase in the flock committed to yr. care of which you will be the vigilant, zealous and loving Pastor."[124] On March 14 St. Mary's Seminary conferred on Gibbons the doctor of divinity degree in view of his being named a bishop.[125]

Once the decision had been made plans could mature for the consecration of the young priest as a bishop of the Church. The date was set for Sunday, August 16, and the invitations went out

---

Gibbons (Baltimore, 1917), p. 9. *Journal of the Proceedings of the Senate of Maryland* (Annapolis, 1868), p. 142. For the 1868 school bill in Maryland, cf. Leo J. McCormick, *Church-State Relationships in Education in Maryland* (Washington, 1942), pp. 197–199.

[123] ASMS, Gibbons to Shriver, Baltimore, February 19, 1868.

[124] 71-O-2, Wood to Gibbons, Philadelphia, February 22, 1868.

[125] ASMS, Dubruel's Diary, p. 25.

some weeks in advance. John McGill, Bishop of Richmond, wrote
to thank Gibbons for his invitation which he hoped to be able
to accept. McGill said:

> You have the prospect of a field of labour where the need is great
> and the resources are very limited, but you will have the consolation
> to feel, that only love of God and zeal for souls, could be an in-
> ducement to acquiesce in the demands of the Holy Father. I hope
> God will give you success, and, amid your works, numerous con-
> solations to lighten the burden that you are to carry.[126]

Richard V. Whelan, Bishop of Wheeling, asked to be excused
from the consecration due to the pressure of other engagements
and he added, "But you will have my fervent prayers for the
occasion. A life of labor is before you and I trust that God will
strengthen you for the work."[127] Gibbons, the first alumnus of
St. Charles to become a bishop, must have beeen especially
pleased by the reply of an old friend of his college days, Thomas
M. A. Burke. Burke, himself a future Bishop of Albany, congratulated the bishop-elect and he then said, "I feel that the
hand of God has been in your appointment and that in it, neither
ambition nor human influence had any share." He went on to
tell his friend that he knew the work in North Carolina would
be hard, but he consoled him with a series of questions which
offered a program of labor which, read in the light of the future
cardinal's career, might seem almost prophetic:

> How many churches will there not spring up under your fostering
> care? How many young levites by your encouragement will con-
> secrate themselves to God in the sacred priesthood? How many
> converts will be added to the fold of Christ? With what tender care
> will the poor despised children of Africa be instructed in the saving
> truths of our holy religion. In a word what charitable and religious
> institutions will spring up as monuments to your zeal?[128]

Father James McDermott of Glens Falls, New York, who was
with Gibbons at St. Mary's, wrote that he would have to miss
the consecration on account of the diocesan retreat and he continued, "but as our good professor poor Mr. Flamant [*sic*] used
to say, 'we must bear all afflictions patiently, even that of being

---

[126] 71-Q-1, McGill to Gibbons, Richmond, July 7, 1868.
[127] 71-O-2, Whelan to Gibbons, Arlington, July 8, 1867.
[128] 71-Q-4, Burke to Gibbons, Albany, July 23, 1868.

a bishop.' " All Gibbons' old fellow students in northern New York were happy over the appointment, said McDermott, "and none more so, I sincerely assure you, than your friend of room number 50 in old St. Mary's."[129] Bishop Jeremiah F. Shanahan, consecrated only a month before as the first Bishop of Harrisburg, assured Gibbons he would be in Baltimore for the festivities on August 16, and he added that he would send his congratulations unless, as he expressed it, "you feel as I have felt, the circumstances do not require any such well meant extravagances."[130]

Two days before the consecration of Gibbons he received a request from D. & J. Sadlier Company, publishers of the *Catholic Directory,* for a report on the Church in North Carolina in order that it might be inserted in its proper place in the directory for 1869.[131] It was a request which he was in no position at the time to satisfy, for he as yet knew precious little himself about the state of Catholicism in the area to which he was being sent. The same day brought a letter which must have touched him deeply, a brief note from Father Dolan at St. Patrick's in Baltimore under whom he had first served as a priest. Dolan enclosed a check for $100 which he said was to assist him in his new mission, with the promise as well of a missal and two chasubles.[132]

At length the great day arrived when James Gibbons was to be made a bishop. Thomas A. Becker, a priest of the Diocese of Richmond, was consecrated first Bishop of Wilmington, Delaware, at the same ceremony. The Baltimore *Sun* reported that, "Long before the hour named for the beginning of the services, Charles, Mulberry and Cathedral streets were filled with people, anxious to see the procession of priests and prelates announced to proceed from the archiepiscopal mansion to the sacred edifice."[133] Archbishop Spalding was the consecrator of these two

---

[129] 71-Q-6, McDermott to Gibbons, Glens Falls, August 9, 1868.

[130] 71-Q-7, Shanahan to Gibbons, Glen Riddle, Pennsylvania, August 11, 1868.

[131] 71-Q-9, Sadlier to Gibbons, New York, August 15, 1868. Sadlier told the bishop that the late appearance of the directory the previous year had entailed "a direct and severe pecuniary loss" and was the subject of general complaint and they were, therefore, trying to avoid a repetition this year.

[132] 71-Q-8, Dolan to Gibbons, Baltimore, August 15, 1868. The pastor at Fell's Point died on January 12, 1870, and Scharf recorded that he was one who "was respected and admired by all for his virtues, charities, and usefulness . . . " (*op. cit.,* p. 682).

[133] August 17, 1868.

priests who had been members of the cathedral household and the co-consecrators for Gibbons were Patrick N. Lynch, Bishop of Charleston, and Michael Domenec, C.M., Bishop of Pittsburgh. Besides the consecrators five other bishops were reported by the press in attendance at the ceremony: William O'Hara of Scranton, Jeremiah F. Shanahan of Harrisburg, James Roosevelt Bayley of Newark, John McGill of Richmond, and Richard V. Whelan of Wheeling. The preacher for the occasion was Thomas Foley who knew the two new bishops intimately from his association with them at the cathedral. Addressing Gibbons he said:

> And you, Right Reverend Sir, are to go to the large State of North Carolina. It appalls one to think of that State of nearly a million of inhabitants, with but few altars, and one or two priests to minister to them. This is the work, which the Holy Ghost, which the Supreme Pontiff, which the united body of our Bishops in Council assembled, have cut out for you, a work which plainly speaks the character which you hold with them.
>
> It would not do for me to speak from personal observation, and with the feelings which I bear towards you. You have been associated with us, like your Right Reverend Companion, at this altar. You were of our household and home. We have had the opportunity of observing in both, not only those great characteristics, which ought to be found in every Christian priest, but also those interior traits of virtue which embellish and complete the man of God. . . . Again I say to you that I cannot congratulate you on going to North Carolina, but I do rejoice for the honor which the Church of God has conferred on you, and I do congratulate your flock, few and scattered, upon the advantage they are to derive from the Apostolic mission you are to establish in that State, which in a religious sense may be called a desert. It will not be long, I predict, before that desert will be made to bloom and produce much fruit, and your vicariate, now so poor and uninviting, will be able to compare with other dioceses of longer existence in religious prosperity.[134]

The *Catholic Mirror,* in speaking of Gibbons' career at the cathedral, wrote: "No incumbent of the Cathedral ever won more rapidly or deservedly on the affections of its congregation. As a

---

[134] *Catholic Mirror,* August 22, 1868. The editors of the *Mirror* curiously enough seemed to know very little about Gibbons' personal background. They said, "Bishop Gibbons we believe is a native of Baltimore, although his family now reside in New Orleans. If not born in Baltimore, he was reared from early boyhood in Maryland, etc."

confessor and preacher, as a laborious servant of the sick, the dying and the disconsolate, he showed himself to be always a ready and willing priest."[135]

At the time of his consecration James Gibbons had just passed his thirty-fourth birthday. He was at the time the youngest among the more than 1,000 bishops scattered throughout the Catholic world and, of course, the youngest in the hierarchy of the United States. The ecclesiastical jurisdiction which he had inherited in North Carolina being only a vicariate apostolic and not a diocese, he was given the title of Bishop of Adramyttum, one of the many dioceses which had long ago passed out of existence but whose titles were reserved for titular bishops of missionary territories. Any priest ordained only seven years and having only slight knowledge of the exacting duties of episcopal administration might well entertain misgivings at the prospect which confronted him. Gibbons was never what one might call an adventuresome man, nor was he particularly endowed with the gifts of initiative and originality; but, on the other hand, once he felt that his course was right and good he pursued it with courage and determination. If the thought of his impending departure from the Baltimore he loved so well to the North Carolina of which he knew little or nothing might have caused him to grow faint, his deep trust in the designs of Providence buoyed him up and the receipt of a letter from Wilmington, North Carolina, a few days after his consecration brought a ray of hope. Mr. Alfred L. Price of the Wilmington *Journal* wrote to the new bishop on a matter of business and he closed his letter by saying, "You will be warmly received by all Catholics and many who are not."[136]

---

[135] *Ibid.*

[136] 71-Q-10, Price to Gibbons, Wilmington, North Carolina, August 17, 1868.

CHAPTER III

On the Missions in North Carolina

ALTHOUGH Bishop Gibbons was consecrated on August 16 it was not until November 1 that he was installed in his little pro-cathedral at Wilmington, North Carolina. His health was not too good that summer and he was advised that it would be safer for him to wait for cooler weather before undertaking his work in the South. Meanwhile he was not idle. Since his appointment to the vicariate dated from March 3, 1868, when the Holy See erected the new jurisdiction and named Gibbons to the post, he had had ample time to make some preliminary plans for the task ahead. Baltimore friends were generous to the young bishop-elect, and he was able to send off to Wilmington a few days before his consecration a check for $6,000 to purchase a lot adjoining St. Thomas Church. Alfred L. Price, publisher of the Wilmington *Journal,* and father of Thomas F. Price, the first priest of North Carolina, carried through the transaction for Gibbons and told him he thought it a good buy. "Two years before the war," said Price, "it was sold for $500 and about $2,700 expended on it, in good money."[1]

During the late summer and autumn Bishop Gibbons was kept busy performing various episcopal functions in and around Baltimore. A week after his consecration he returned to his old parish of St. Bridget's at Canton where he confirmed ninety-four persons on August 23. "The parishioners . . . flocked around the pastoral residence to pay their respects to their old and beloved pastor, and congratulate him on his promotion to the Episcopacy."[2] The new bishop preached in different city

---

[1] 71-Q-10, Price to Gibbons, Wilmington, August 17, 1868.
[2] John T. Reily, *Passing Events in the Life of Cardinal Gibbons* (Martinsburg, 1890), p. 274. Reily published ten volumes of miscellaneous materials in the life of Gibbons between this volume and the last which came out in 1905.

Gibbons as the youngest bishop in the American Church after his consecration as Vicar Apostolic of North Carolina on August 16, 1868.

churches on succeeding Sundays, and on September 13 he paid a visit to his former parish of St. Lawrence at Locust Point and the same day dedicated the Passionist Monastery of St. Joseph on Frederick Road. Two weeks later found him at St. Patrick's in Cumberland where some of the congregation through their pastor presented the bishop with the sum of $200.[3] On September 18 at Frederick, Maryland, Gibbons performed the first priestly ordinations of his episcopal career when he ordained two Jesuits, Charles Bahan and James Pinasco, the first in a long line of 2,471 priests who received holy orders at his hands.[4]

In early September the bishop received his first authentic report on the state of Catholicism in North Carolina from Father Henry P. Northrop. The latter told him that only three towns in the vast area which he covered had churches, namely, Raleigh, Edenton, and New Bern, although fifteen other towns and villages were named as stations where the priest visited occasionally. "Besides these," said Northrop, "there are other small points where one or two Catholics reside. Some I have visited, others I have not. In fact, on every trip, I 'start' a few, which being out of my appointed tract, I have to put off until the next time." The priest enumerated a total of about 250 Catholics for all these settlements, and he named six other small towns and suggested that the bishop look them up on a map and he would then have, as he said, "almost all the spots where there are any representatives of the faith, as far as *I know,* tho' I am sure we will discover still others in our trip next month."[5]

While the number of priests at the disposal of Bishop Gibbons to serve the Catholics was pitifully small considering the size of

---

They have different titles, betray careless arrangement and very loose editing; yet there are items in these volumes which cannot be found elsewhere.

[3] *Ibid.,* p. 275.

[4] John T. Reily, *Collections and Recollections in the Life and Times of Cardinal Gibbons* (Martinsburg, 1892–1893), p. 104. The final figure of 2,442 priestly ordinations was given by Gibbons in his own hand under date of May 25, 1920 (Diary, p. 308), although he ordained twenty-nine Jesuits the next month which raised the total to 2,471.

[5] 71-R-1, Northrop to Gibbons, New Bern, September 9, 1868. Northrop actually belonged to the Diocese of Charleston. Gibbons made an early plea to Bishop Lynch for his services when he said, "I trust that you will leave Father Northrop with me as long as you can" (Archives of the Diocese of Charleston, Gibbons to Lynch, Baltimore, February 28, 1868, copy). The writer is indebted to the Reverend Richard C. Madden, pastor of St. Andrew's Church, Myrtle Beach, South Carolina, for copies of a number of letters from the Charleston archives.

his jurisdiction, he was encouraged to learn that he had several students then in school on whom he might count to help in the years ahead. The bishop visited St. Charles College before leaving for North Carolina and solicited candidates for the vicariate among the student body of his old school. Among the students was one by the name of Denis J. O'Connell to whom the bishop apparently took an immediate liking. Young O'Connell wrote him to say he was grieved to learn of his illness and he hoped it would improve, for, as he said, "there is a heap of work to be done there [North Carolina] to make it a flourishing diocese." Herbert Shriver had taken an interest in O'Connell at Gibbons' suggestion, and as a consequence life had been made very pleasant for the lad at St. Charles.[6] In the light of the exceedingly close friendship that developed between Gibbons and O'Connell in after years this first evidence of their relationship is of more than ordinary interest.

By the autumn the new bishop's health had improved and immediate plans could be made for his installation which had been set for the feast of All Saints, Sunday, November 1. The little party, consisting of Archbishop Spalding, Gibbons, and Bernard J. McManus, pastor of St. John's Church in Baltimore, left the city on October 29. In speaking of the young bishop's departure the *Catholic Mirror* stated that Gibbons left with the prayers and best wishes of all the priests and people of the Archdiocese of Baltimore. It remarked, "No one reared and educated among us probably has been more generally esteemed and beloved; and for no one will more devout prayers be offered up to Almighty God."[7] The churchmen arrived in Wilmington on Friday evening, October 30, where they were the guests of Colonel Francis W. Kerchner, a former Baltimorean.

On Sunday morning St. Thomas Church was crowded to capacity despite the fact that a heavy rain "descended in copious torrents." After Archbishop Spalding had led Bishop Gibbons to his throne and formally installed him, the latter celebrated the pontifical high Mass with McManus as assistant priest, Northrop as deacon, and Mark S. Gross as subdeacon. Present in the sanctuary were three other priests: Jeremiah J. O'Connell,

---

[6] 71-R-8, O'Connell to Gibbons, St. Charles College, October 29, 1868.

[7] November 7, 1868.

O.S.B., of Columbia, South Carolina; Lawrence P. O'Connell of Charlotte, North Carolina; and Timothy Bermingham, Vicar-General of the Diocese of Charleston. Following the gospel, Spalding preached the sermon during which "for more than an hour [he] riveted the marked attention of the congregation by a solid, logical, and impressive discourse." He traced the derivation of the Church from Christ through the establishment of St. Peter's see in Rome, and then told his audience that their new bishop had received the unanimous vote of the bishops of the United States in council at Baltimore two years before and that he had come to them bearing his commission from the Bishop of Rome. He went on, "I know him well. He is beloved by all that knew him in Baltimore. . . . I know you will like him. He improves upon acquaintance. Though he will be found uncompromising in his principles of faith, he will be charitable to all, assist all, irrespective of sect or creed."[8] In the afternoon Bishop Gibbons presided at pontifical vespers and preached, and as he confided to his diary, "Many Protestants attended both services."[9]

The advent of James Gibbons to North Carolina occurred at a time when the state was still in a sad condition of disruption following the Civil War. The carpetbaggers had taken over the government there as elsewhere in the South and the rule imposed by them and the emancipated Negroes, whom they used for their own selfish purposes, made life anything but pleasant for the native white population of the state. Gibbons' first experience was such as to arouse grave misgivings in his mind about the future. Years later he recalled:

> The night I arrived in Wilmington, there was a torch-light procession of the emancipated slaves, many of them now holding office and domineering over their former masters. If one can imagine an enormous crowd of negroes, most of whom were intoxicated, all of whom were waving torches in the blackness of the night, one can very easily imagine the first impressions of a new and very young Bishop.[10]

He had, of course, known of the general conditions before he arrived, and two months before one of his priests had written him from New Bern offering a somewhat detailed picture. He said:

---

[8] *Ibid.,* November 14, 1868.
[9] Diary, p. 1.
[10] "My Memories," *Dublin Review,* CLX (April, 1917), 167.

The political sky down here looks very dark. The excitement is intense & growing under the influence of processions & flag presentation-processions, public speaking & whiskey. We have had one or two petty disturbances, which people look on as the precursors to more serious ones. The election of Grant will result, if we must believe the professions of our friends here, in a general stampede & desertion of the town to carpet baggers & scallawags. I am afraid our little church will suffer from the secession which is threatened & which in some instances will be carried out.[11]

A constitutional convention had met in Raleigh in January, 1868, and during the course of the following weeks that body — controlled by the Republicans with a smattering of carpetbaggers and Negroes — adopted a new constitution for North Carolina. The document contained, to be sure, most of the features necessary to admit the state again into the Union. In the campaign preceding the vote on adoption of the constitution and the election of new officials there was widespread corruption accompanied by deep bitterness on both sides. "Personal encounters were of frequent occurrence among the candidates, and the most violent personal abuse was common."[12] The Republicans, however, carried the election and the Conservatives, or old Democrats, elected only one member of Congress, one judge, and one solicitor. The new legislature met on July 2 and ratified the fourteenth amendment and nine days later President Andrew Johnson announced that North Carolina had fulfilled the congressional requirements for statehood.

Meanwhile the Freedmen's Bureau and the Union League were pursuing their course throughout the state and the activities of these agencies of reconstruction, together with the scandalous frauds over the railroads perpetrated by the legislature, gave abundant cause, in the minds of many North Carolinians, for the organization of the Ku Klux Klan as a defense measure. These conditions in the public life of the community naturally led to a decline in morals generally. Crime increased and theft became a common occurrence. "Live stock was stolen until in some communities the raising of sheep and hogs was aban-

---

[11] 71-R-1, Northrop to Gibbons, New Bern, September 9, 1868.

[12] J. G. de Roulhac Hamilton, *Reconstruction in North Carolina* (New York, 1914), p. 285. This work is of a definitive character for the political and economic history of North Carolina during the years when Gibbons was resident there.

doned."[13] Wages were low and money extremely scarce with only six banks in the state with a combined capital of less than one million dollars. As a leading historian for this period of North Carolina has summarized it:

> In the daily life and in business alike, uncertainty was the chief characteristic of the attitude of the people. No one knew what to expect of the future and it became increasingly difficult to plan for it. . . . It was a gloomy population that inhabited North Carolina, and, viewed from any standpoint, the economic outlook for the future was dark.[14]

Such were the general conditions of the Vicariate Apostolic of North Carolina when its young bishop arrived. Since the ecclesiastical jurisdiction covered the entire state it meant that Bishop Gibbons' responsibility extended over 49,412 square miles. According to the census of 1870 there was a total of 1,071,361 inhabitants of whom over ninety-six per cent were living in rural areas. The overwhelmingly rural character of North Carolina was emphasized by the fact that Wilmington, the largest town in the state, had only 13,446 people, while Raleigh, the capital, numbered but 7,790, and New Bern was next with 5,849.[15] The bishop could find no large concentrations of population here such as he had been accustomed to in New Orleans and Baltimore. Moreover, his problem was aggravated by the widespread illiteracy since the school system all over the state had largely broken down during the war. True, the new constitution of 1868 had made provision for schools, but the narrow interpretation of the courts given to Article VII forbidding counties or towns from going into debt for schools only added to the "tragically persistent and continuing indifference of the majority of the people to the blighting effects of illiteracy."[16] Added to these handicaps was the immense Negro population recently emancipated. Before the erection of the vicariate the state had been included within the Diocese of Charleston, and only the summer before Gibbons' consecration Bishop Patrick N. Lynch had reported the uni-

---

[13] *Ibid.,* p. 420.

[14] *Ibid.,* pp. 425–426.

[15] *Sixteenth Census of the United States: 1940* (Washington, 1942), pp. 771–772. The over-all figures of previous census returns in this volume give an excellent basis of comparison for population growth.

[16] Charles L. Coon, "School Support and Our North Carolina Courts, 1868–1926," *North Carolina Historical Review,* III (July, 1926), 399.

versal disaster that had befallen his diocese to the Society for the Propagation of the Faith. Speaking of the emancipated slaves he said, "I have for my portion 750,000, of whom 20,000 at most are Catholics." Lynch told the society of the havoc in his see city, and that outside of it, as he put it, "there is everywhere only ruins and suffering."[17]

At the outset Bishop Gibbons had the assistance of only three priests to help him bear his burden — Mark S. Gross who was with him in Wilmington, Henry P. Northrop, who covered the many stations in the northeastern part of the state, and Lawrence P. O'Connell, who had charge of the missions in the southwestern area with his residence at St. Peter's Church in Charlotte.[18] Gross was ordained for Baltimore but volunteered for the North Carolina missions, and Northrop belonged to the Diocese of Charleston but was loaned to Gibbons by Bishop Lynch. Lawrence O'Connell was named vicar-general by the young bishop. A fourth priest, James A. Corcoran, who had recently served at Wilmington and belonged to the Diocese of Charleston, had been called to Rome as one of the theologians to make preparations for the Vatican Council. Needless to say, there were no Catholic schools, hospitals, or any other kind of diocesan institution. The modest little Church of St. Thomas the Apostle in Wilmington, which was constructed of brick with stucco finish, had been dedicated in July, 1847.[19] Since there was no residence for the clergy, the bishop and Mark Gross had to accommodate themselves as best they could in the four small rooms attached to the rear of the little church until they could get money enough to enlarge the building and in this way provide more commodious living quarters. With the few Catholics of North Carolina scattered in small groups throughout the length and breadth of the state there was no knowing exactly how many souls fell within Gibbons' spiritual jurisdiction and when it came time to make the first report the closest approximation was "about 700,"[20] or less than one

---

[17] Patrick N. Lynch to the Society for the Propagation of the Faith, Charleston, June 17, 1867, *Annales de la propagation de la foi* (Lyon, 1868), XL, 80–90.

[18] *Sadlier's Catholic Directory, Almanac, and Ordo for the Year of Our Lord 1869* (New York, 1869), pp. 302–303.

[19] Cf. *St. Thomas the Apostle Catholic Church* (Wilmington, 1947), a souvenir booklet published to commemorate the centennial of the church.

[20] *Sadlier's Catholic Directory . . . 1869*, p. 303. For the general conditions of

per thousand in relation to the total population of the state. From every human viewpoint it was a discouraging prospect that faced Bishop Gibbons in November, 1868. Archbishop Spalding sensed his loneliness when he departed after the installation and upon his return to Baltimore he wrote him, "I was truly affected when I left you on Monday morning; I thought you looked like an orphan & desolate." He assured the bishop that he would pray that God would give him a brave apostolic heart which would suffer the privations for His honor and glory. "I have not a doubt of your ultimate success. You will reap in joy after sowing in tears. Courage!" Spalding went on to say that he had sent a report to the Prefect of the Congregation of the Propaganda in Rome about Gibbons which, as he remarked, "your modesty could scarcely recognize, but which I look to you to make true in the future as I believe it has been in the past."[21] It was evident that Spalding was leaving no stone unturned to bring the qualities of the young bishop to the attention of the Holy See. After his return to Baltimore with the archbishop, Father McManus, too, wrote an encouraging letter to his friend. He was going down that evening to St. Patrick's for a visit with Father James Dolan and, as he said, "won't I miss somebody. Those nice walks and social chats we used to have together are now things of the past, and the Peanut State owns half of my poor self." Regardless of how much he missed his friend, McManus felt he had a "glorious future" before him, and he concluded by saying he felt certain that Gibbons would be "agreeably disappointed when you go through the diocese and the consciousness that you are planting *'good seed corn,'* for the Lord, will be too much consolation for even little privations you may have to endure."[22]

---

the Church in the South in the post-war years, cf. the unpublished master's thesis of Vincent de Paul McMurry, S.S., "The Catholic Church and Reconstruction, 1865–1877," The Catholic University of America (1950).

[21] 71-S-2, Spalding to Gibbons, Baltimore, November 5, 1868. That week saw the election of Ulysses S. Grant to the presidency which accounts for Spalding's closing remark: "F. Foley laughed at our making a 'Bee-line' for home on Monday, not taking into account the election on Tuesday."

[22] 71-S-1, McManus to Gibbons, Baltimore, November 3, 1868. How deeply attached Gibbons was to McManus was revealed twenty years later when on February 28, 1888, he confided to his diary the following entry: "Mgr. B. J. McManus, the dearest friend I have had among the clergy, died this morning. Deus det tibi pacem suam, amice cordis mei!" (p. 222).

To be sure, these letters from old friends in Baltimore brought their joy to the lonely young bishop in North Carolina, but there was much work to be done and no good could come of spending time lamenting Baltimore. Five days after his installation Gibbons entered his first item in the parish register when he wrote, "I baptized conditionally Abraham Franklin, aged 53 years, after having received his profession of faith. Bernard Gorman, spr."[23] Thus was the first in a lengthy series of adult converts received into the Church at James Gibbons' hands in North Carolina. That same day he wrote to his old classmate of Ballinrobe days, Francis MacCormack, who was then a priest in Westport, asking him if he would intercede to get him a community of Sisters of Mercy from Ireland for his vicariate.[24] On November 10 the bishop left Wilmington with Father Gross on the first visitation tour of his jurisdiction during which he traveled 925 miles by rail, stage, and steamboat, visited sixteen towns and stations, confirmed sixty-four persons of whom sixteen were converts, and baptized sixteen of whom ten were converts.

This tour which lasted four weeks carried Gibbons through the principal towns of central and eastern North Carolina. On his second night in Fayetteville he preached to a packed church with the Presbyterian and Methodist ministers in attendance; at Goldsboro he preached in the town hall. At New Bern he found the largest Catholic congregation so far, about 110 souls. Here, too, Gibbons confirmed twelve of whom half were converts, and before leaving New Bern he preached at the Sunday high Mass to a large congregation, "the great majority of whom were Protestants." After leaving New Bern he made a stop at Swift Creek to visit a family by the name of Nelson, and he recorded in his diary, "I confirmed Mr. & Mrs. Nelson in the garret, the only unoccupied place at our disposal." At Plymouth he baptized and confirmed Isaac Swift who was once a rich planter, but Gibbons remarked, "he is now his own wood-cutter." A visit to Raleigh, the state capital, brought the bishop in contact with some of the prominent men in the state government. One, Colonel Robert M. Douglas, son of the late Senator Stephen A. Douglas of Illinois, was a Catholic and associated at the time with the regime of Governor William W. Holden, then in disrepute with

---

[23] Register of St. Thomas Church, Wilmington, November 6, 1868, No. 628.
[24] Diary, November 6, 1868, p. 1.

conservative North Carolinians. The attorney general of the state, William M. Coleman, expressed his interest in the Catholic religion and the bishop was asked to send him some books to read, "with a view of becoming a Catholic." December 17 found him once more in Wilmington with his first visitation tour completed.[25] Through the next eight years he continued to make these periodic visits to various sections of the state, seeking out stray Catholics, administering confirmation in the small parishes and stations, and generally stimulating the Catholic people to a renewal of their religious fervor by his public sermons and private conferences.

If the visitation tour was the occasion for fresh anxieties in the mind of the young bishop, it likewise brought its consolations. When Edward Conigland, one of the most outstanding lawyers in North Carolina at the time, learned Gibbons was coming to Halifax he wrote to offer the hospitality of his home. "I have only to say that my house and all that I have are at your disposal," he said, "and I shall consider myself and children very highly honored if you & Father Northrop will stop with us during your sojourn in Halifax all, or a portion of the time." Conigland confessed that he had led a quite irregular religious life as Northrop knew, but, as he added, "God in His goodness, has never taken away from me the light of the Faith, although it would seem that the Catholic who neglects his religious duties is practically an infidel." The lawyer had just lost his wife and he wondered if her influence in eternity had not turned him back to religion.[26] Conigland was to be the instrument through which the bishop was able to accomplish much good for the Church in the succeeding years. Attorney General Coleman wrote soon after Gibbons' visit with him in Raleigh to make further inquiries regarding the Mass and to apologize for the write-up of the bishop's talk which had appeared in the *Standard,* "the bad taste of which is only to be pardoned by the well meaning of the writer."[27]

---

[25] *Ibid.,* November 10–December 17, 1868, pp. 2–11.

[26] 71-S-6, Conigland to Gibbons, Glen-ivy near Halifax, November 21, 1868.

[27] 71-S-8, Coleman to Gibbons, Raleigh, December 19, 1868. Why Coleman should take exception to the lengthy editorial in the North Carolina *Standard* of Raleigh on December 15, 1868, it is difficult to see. Three days before the same paper had announced Gibbons' coming and since, as they said, it was his first visit to Raleigh they suggested that he be greeted by "a large and attentive

Gibbons himself attested to the cordial reception he had received everywhere on his tour when he told Archbishop Spalding that he had been welcomed "both by Protestants & Catholics." He said he found the people in four or five places clamoring for churches and "the public generally, irrespective of religion, expressing a willingness to contribute liberally." Everywhere he went he found large and enthusiastic audiences for his sermons, "whether in churches or court houses." He went on, "I hope curiosity was not the only motive. Even intelligent people are strangely ignorant of our faith." He pictured for the archbishop some of the hardships, too. "Sometimes we have to share the same room & the same *bed,* to see the day-light through many a crevice, to live on corn bread. But more frequently we enjoy all the luxury of the season." In Raleigh he received every mark of respect. "Yesterday I preached twice in the Catholic Church to crowded houses. The Legislature now in session, turned out en masse. It is here particularly that the Church gains in public estimation by the conservative cause she pursued during the war."[28]

Near the end of the year 1868 Bishop Gibbons received his first benefaction from the Society for the Propagation of the Faith in France. He was sent the sum of 8,000 francs, or about $420.[29] These donations from the society continued all during the nine years he exercised jurisdiction over the vicariate and amounted in all during Gibbons' time in North Carolina to the sum of 57,280 francs, or a little over $3,000. Needless to say, this financial help from abroad was a wonderful assistance to the struggling Church in that area. Gibbons later said of the help sent to him by the society, "I can scarcely see how the work could have gone without such aid. The certainty of the annuity

audience of our citizens." In the *Standard's* editorial comment on the bishop's sermon he was praised for his delivery, subject matter, and polish, and the writer ended by saying he hoped the bishop would "often favor our city with his presence." The only expression used which Coleman could possibly have objected to was that the sermon was so good that "an angelic auditory might have listened to it with pleasure and profit." Knowing Gibbons as we do, it is more than likely that instead of being offended by the *Standard's* write-up he was probably highly pleased.

[28] 34-B-9, Gibbons to Spalding, Raleigh, December 15, 1868.

[29] 71-S-4, President de l'oeuvre de la propagation de la foi to Gibbons, Paris, November 10, 1868.

was a relief to my mind, whilst it gave a stimulus to fresh undertakings. . . ."[30]

Meanwhile the talk which the bishop had delivered the previous September at St. Charles College, where he had invited any student who was unattached to a diocese to interest himself in North Carolina, bore fruit. Young John Doyle wrote from the college to say he had obtained permission from Bishop William McCloskey of Louisville to leave that diocese, and he would now like to affiliate with the vicariate.[31] This was welcome news, of course, but as badly in need of priests as he was Gibbons was compelled to exercise great circumspection in permitting seminarians and priests to join his little band. Those who had experienced trouble elsewhere did not make good prospects for the Church of North Carolina, and the bishop was grateful to Archbishop Spalding for warning him about a seminarian recently dismissed from Baltimore.[32] Several years later he received the applications of two priests, one of whom confessed intemperance at an earlier period and the other said he had been in ill-health some years before but was now restored. Across the top of both letters Gibbons wrote in the words, "offer declined," showing that he realized the danger in taking chances with men who might prove a liability rather than an asset to the vicariate.[33] Gibbons' caution in this matter saved him future heart-

---

[30] James Cardinal Gibbons, "Reminiscences of North Carolina," *United States Catholic Historical Magazine,* III (1889–1890), 338. This paper dated February 18, 1891, was prepared for a meeting of the United States Catholic Historical Society on May 25 of that year. In the absence of Gibbons it was read by Father James J. Dougherty, director of the Home of the Immaculate Virgin in New York. The sums assigned to the Vicariate of North Carolina for the years 1868–1876 can be found in the annual and semi-annual reports in the *Annales de la propagation de la foi,* Volumes XLI–XLIX.

[31] 71-S-5, Doyle to Gibbons, St. Charles College, November 19, 1868.

[32] 71-S-10, Spalding to Gibbons, Baltimore, December 22, 1868. Even before his consecration Gibbons showed this caution. When Bishop Lynch of Charleston wrote him concerning a certain Canadian priest who was looking for incardination, he offered as an excuse for declining to take him the failure of his own bulls to arrive up to that time, and the bishop-elect then added, "Besides it occurred to me that the same peculiarity of temper which led to his removal from the diocese of Kingston, would also militate against him in this new field" (Archives of the Diocese of Charleston, Gibbons to Lynch, Baltimore, June 14, 1868, copy).

[33] 72-D-3, Peter Cody to Gibbons, Cleveland, February 2, 1871; 71-D-4, J. Molloy to Gibbons, Knoxville, Tennessee, February 21, 1871.

aches, and after two years time he was cheered by the report that his five students at St. Charles College all gave promise of making the type of priests who would serve the North Carolina missions with credit.[34]

In the matter of recruiting religious women Bishop Gibbons at first encountered disappointment. His appeal to Ireland for Sisters of Mercy, sent a few days after his arrival at Wilmington, met with a refusal. Francis MacCormack answered in Christmas week that the sisters at Westport were unable to send out a colony to North Carolina due to a scarcity of numbers. He suggested that he try Ballinrobe, his old home, and MacCormack closed his letter by saying he hoped to see Gibbons soon, "when you will recognize — in your old school-fellow — a fat little priest."[35] Although the bishop followed up the suggestion and opened negotiations for the sisters at Ballinrobe,[36] nothing came of it. At length by August, 1869, he decided to seek the assistance of sisters nearer home. He first wrote to the Sisters of Our Lady of Mercy in Charleston who had been founded by Bishop John England and offered to furnish a residence for them in Wilmington at his own expense, as well as to help them recruit novices in Baltimore and Wilmington. Having received a favorable reply and secured the permission of Bishop Lynch and Father Timothy Bermingham, the sisters' ecclesiastical superior, he made a trip to Charleston to conclude the transaction.[37] Gibbons secured the services of three sisters who arrived in Wilmington on September 20 and took up their temporary residence in the home of a Mr. Rose. They spent the first few weeks getting their permanent residence in order, and, on October 11, 1869, these sisters opened the Academy of the Incarnation for girls, and by January 3, 1871, they began a parochial school under the title of

---

[34] 72-D-2, S[tanislaus] Ferté, S.S., to Gibbons, St. Charles College, February 15, 1871.

[35] 71-S-9, MacCormack to Gibbons, Westport, December 22, 1868. MacCormack looked forward to the time when Gibbons would visit Ireland and they could go over again the ground they used to cover together which was "endeared to us by many recollections — John J. Rooney, etc."

[36] 71-T-3, Thomas Hardiman to Gibbons, Ballinrobe, January 25, 1869.

[37] Archives of the Diocese of Charleston, Gibbons to "Respected Dear Mother," Ashville, August 10, 1869, copy; 71-W-5, Sister Mary Agatha to Gibbons, Charleston, August 26, 1869; 71-W-6, Lynch to Gibbons, Philadelphia, August 30, 1869; Diary, September 2, 1869, p. 18.

St. Peter.[38] In this way did North Carolina obtain its first Catholic teaching sisters and the help which they were able to give the young bishop and his few priests in the task of instructing the children in their faith was, indeed, very great.

Christmas week of 1868 had brought a gossipy letter from James Dolan, Gibbons' old pastor in Baltimore. Dolan did not think much of the collection recently taken up in Baltimore for the American College in Rome and he felt the money might better be spent on St. Mary's Seminary at home. He said there was a rumor that Spalding was looking for a coadjutor. "I have heard," he wrote, "that the A.B. in consequence of the great weight of the affairs of the American Church is looking for a *'Helper.'* If the old man gets me, he will *regret* it *only once* & [in] me may find a Master. Such things have happened & can happen again. . . ."[39] The prospect of Dolan as Coadjutor Archbishop of Baltimore must have brought a smile to Gibbons!

About this time Bishop Gibbons began to get the first in a long series of requests for books of instruction in the Catholic faith. He told Archbishop Spalding that he had just received such a request from "a very high functionary whom I met in Raleigh," and he intended to send him Spalding's own *General Evidences of Catholicity.*[40] A few weeks later his friend, Edward Conigland, sought books for an interested Episcopalian friend and Gibbons recommended John Milner's *End of Controversy* and Richard Challoner's *The Catholic Christian Instructed.* He took occasion in replying to Conigland to recommend to him the fair he was holding that spring in Wilmington for the benefit of a sisters' residence and also the cause of a church at Halifax. He said:

38 Diary, p. 24.

39 71-S-11, Dolan to Gibbons, Baltimore, December 22, 1868.

40 34-B-10, Gibbons to Spalding, Wilmington, December 22, 1868. Spalding's book had been published in Louisville in 1847. This letter reveals Gibbons' sympathy for worthy seminarians. He mentioned a boy whose health seemed to be hopelessly gone, and he then said, "But I have great sympathy for the poor young man, whose widowed mother I know is indigent. If he has any strength left, he could teach catechism & S. school, act as sacristan & general factotum, & I would be very glad even to ordain him, if there were any sure prospects of his recovery." The same letter told of his being puzzled in finding it the custom in North Carolina to publish the banns between a Catholic and Protestant who wished to marry. He said he found no law against it in the legislation of the Second Plenary Council, "& yet the practice is unknown in Baltimore in whose footsteps I wish to walk."

I wish you & Mr. McMahon could secure a little Church in or near Halifax. The sooner you have a church, the more frequent you may find the visits of a priest. I have already six students in college, candidates for the Ministry in N. C. I am obliged to pay for all of them. You may imagine the difficulty I have to contend with in trying to make all ends meet. When some of these young men are ordained, you may expect to see a priest more frequently.[41]

The bishop spent a few days early in 1869 in New Orleans with his family and by this time his brother John's grain business was doing so well that John was able to give him "a handsome present in money & horse" for the work in North Carolina. Gibbons continued to lament the lack of books of instruction, and he told Spalding after his return from New Orleans that while the danger of losing the faith was not great for the Catholics of Wilmington, he did fear for those living in the rural areas. "My one remedy," he said, "is the circulation of books. I have exhausted my supply. . . . I wish I had about a dozen copies of the 'Evidences.' "[42] It was from his experiences with prospective converts and his strong feeling of the need of books on instruction that there gradually took shape in Gibbons' mind — urged on by Father Mark Gross — the idea of writing a book which would give the essentials of Catholic doctrine in a simple way. Thus was there slowly adumbrated *The Faith of Our Fathers,* born of Gibbons' experiences in the missions of North Carolina and Virginia, and destined to have such remarkable success as a work of apologetic literature.

His friend, the Archbishop of Baltimore, was a churchman whose wide experience in church councils had brought a deep conviction as to their usefulness. Spalding decided to convoke the Tenth Provincial Council of the Province of Baltimore in April, 1869, and he turned to his youngest suffragan to prepare the pastoral letter which would be issued to the priests and faithful at the close of the council. The archbishop outlined for Gibbons the subjects he believed should be emphasized in the pastoral, and since he wanted the document to be fresh, terse, and practical, he said, "I therefore commit it to a fresh hand guided by a fresh heart." He told the bishop to write it out in

[41] University of North Carolina Library, Conigland Papers, Gibbons to Conigland, Wilmington, February 17, 1869.
[42] 36A-J-3, Gibbons to Spalding, Wilmington, February 25, 1869.

Wilmington and when he arrived in Baltimore, as he said, "you can see a great number of pastorals which I have, & fill up."[43] Gibbons stated that while writing pastoral letters was "sacred and untrodden ground" for him he would do the best he could and the suggestions of the archbishop would, of course, be his guide.[44]

Thomas Foley, chancellor of Baltimore, had the task of making the arrangements for the council, and it must have amused Gibbons to be requested to send the chancellor "the names of your Theologians & also the names of superiors of Seminaries and Heads of Religious Orders in your Vicariate, who will accompany you." Apparently Father Foley had only the vaguest idea of the condition of the Church in North Carolina. Foley told him the kind of copes he would need together with his crozier and miter, and he ended by saying the archbishop had appointed Gibbons to preach the closing sermon of the council.[45] The vicar apostolic replied that he had no seminary and no religious orders of either men or women in the entire state. "You will," replied Gibbons, "consequently enroll me as a single passenger." That he was glad of an opportunity of returning to his native city was evident, for he remarked to Foley, "I feel in going back to Baltimore, like a boy returning home to spend the holidays. 'Nature will out.' "[46] Meanwhile he was encouraged in receiving word that Edward Conigland was seriously thinking of building a church at Halifax and he wrote Conigland to say he would stop there overnight on his way to the council. The visit would afford the bishop an opportunity to transact another item of business which had been on his mind for some time. "I desire in conformity with the ordinances of the Church," he said, "to make my will. And as you are conversant with the laws of N.C. you are the most fitting person to consult."[47]

The council in Baltimore opened on Sunday, April 25, with Archbishop Spalding, his twelve suffragan bishops, and Abbot

---

[43] 71-U-1, Spalding to Gibbons, Baltimore, March 4, 1869.

[44] 36A-J-4, Gibbons to Spalding, Wilmington, March 6, 1869.

[45] 71-U-2, Foley to Gibbons, Baltimore, March 30, 1869.

[46] Gibbons to Foley, Wilmington, April 1, 1869, a letter furnished to the writer through the kindness of Monsignor Edward P. McAdams, pastor of St. Joseph's Church, Washington, D. C.

[47] University of North Carolina Library, Conigland Papers, Gibbons to Conigland, Wilmington, April 3, 1869.

Boniface Wimmer, O.S.B., of St. Vincent's Abbey at Latrobe, in attendance. The main business of the council was to decide upon the best means to carry into execution the decrees of the Second Plenary Council of 1866, and to advise with one another concerning the coming general council of the Church which would convene at Rome in December. The bishops were in session one week and on the closing day, Sunday, May 2, Gibbons preached the sermon in the cathedral. His subject was "The Divine Mission and Unerring Authority of the Catholic Church." The preacher emphasized the unchangeableness of Catholic doctrine and the unerring authority of the Church in pronouncing upon matters of faith and morals, but in the light of the great controversy that marked the Vatican Council soon to open, it is interesting to note that he said nothing directly on the subject of papal infallibility.[48] The conciliar meeting at Baltimore in the spring of 1869 was the young bishop's second experience of this kind, and while the two gatherings of 1866 and 1869 were slight, indeed, in comparison with the Vatican Council, they afforded Gibbons some knowledge of how the Church transacted her business through the medium of councils. The pastoral letter, written by Gibbons and published at the end of the meeting, urged the cause of Catholic education upon parents for their children and pointed out the dangers of a purely secular education. While the number of converts to the Catholic Church in the United States had been gratifying, the pastoral did not fail to mention that Catholics were obliged "to confess with sorrow, that a great number are lost to the Church." The bishops' approval of the Catholic Publication Society of New York was renewed and protectories and orphan asylums were warmly recommended to the generosity of the people. Among the abuses condemned were birth control and the dangerous amusements of obscene theatrical performances, indecent literature, and the "modern fashionable dances, commonly called German or Round dances. . . ." The care and concern of the Church for the Negroes was expressed, and on the subject of their welfare the pastoral said:

> We therefore desire that separate schools and churches be established for the blacks, wherever, in the judgment of the Ordinary,

[48] *Catholic Mirror*, May 8, 1869. On this council cf. *Concilii Baltimorensis II . . . acta et decreta* (Baltimore, 1870).

they may be deemed practicable and expedient. Where special schools and churches are not erected for them, every facility should be afforded for their religious and moral training, as far as circumstances will permit.[49]

Some weeks after the close of the council Spalding received a letter from Archbishop John B. Purcell of Cincinnati inquiring about the pastoral which the latter had read in a Catholic paper. Spalding told Purcell, "Bishop Gibbons of N. Carolina, a most promising young Prelate, wrote the Pastoral, I only making some suggestions as to the matters to be treated & the order of the same."[50] The day after the council closed Gibbons had the joy of celebrating Mass in the cathedral and giving his first communion to old William Shriver for whose conversion Mrs. Shriver and their children had been praying for many years.[51]

Upon Bishop Gibbons' return to Wilmington in the spring of 1869 he made ready for his second major visitation tour, this time through the missions served by Father Lawrence P. O'Connell in and around Charlotte. He left home in July and by the first week in August he had reached Morgantown where they could find only three Catholics. One of these was a Mr. McGraw who had ten children, all Protestants, a fact which prompted Gibbons to say in his diary, "a sad instance of the result of mixed marriages."[52] He and Lawrence O'Connell continued traveling through the small towns and settlements for some weeks and finally, on August 16, he arrived home again after having gone 985 miles by rail and stage, visited eleven towns, counted 376 Catholics in O'Connell's missions, confirmed 106 of whom thirty-three were converts, and baptized six of whom four were converts.[53] Gibbons' friend, the Archbishop of Baltimore, wrote to say that he had heard he had returned to Wilmington "like a conquering hero," and he wanted to greet and congratulate him. "When will you honor us with the light of yr. countenance? We are in darkness." Spalding reminded Gibbons of

---

[49] *Ibid.*, May 15, 1869.
[50] AUND, Cincinnati Papers, Spalding to Purcell, Baltimore, May 19, 1869.
[51] *Catholic Mirror*, May 8, 1869.
[52] Diary, August 5, 1869, p. 16.
[53] *Ibid.*, p. 18.

his engagements for confirmation in Baltimore that autumn, and he asked him to add another for the chapel of St. Mary Star of the Sea at Federal Hill.[54]

These engagements in Baltimore were, of course, welcome to the bishop from North Carolina, for they enabled him to visit his friends as well as to make collections for his missions. The particular confirmations referred to by Spalding were to be performed prior to their departure for the Vatican Council. Late in August Gibbons received a letter from James A. Corcoran written from Rome. As noted previously, he had gone to Rome as the representative of the American hierarchy at the meeting of the theologians, called to draw up the schema for the coming council. Corcoran, who had previously been the pastor of St. Thomas Church in Wilmington before his departure for the Holy See, told Bishop Gibbons that the newspapers had falsely reported the theologians as having finished their work. Such was not the case. While it was his intention to return to Wilmington when he had finished his business in Rome, he told the bishop, "there is no telling when the Council will end. Some of the most sanguine look to its completion by Easter next; but there are many others high in station and of far-sighted penetration, who indulge no such hope." Corcoran rightly predicted, "Here are matters which will create animated and prolonged discussion. Theologians here may [have] considered them all settled, cut and dry and simply ready for acceptance. But the Bishops, many of them at least, will think otherwise." He commented on the recent changes in the government of Napoleon III and their relation to Pius IX's regime, and he said Garibaldi's son had been in Rome about a month before. The papal government knew it but did not molest him, content merely to let him know they were aware of his presence. "This may be diplomacy," said Corcoran, "but it is not to my taste."[55]

Just about this time Gibbons' friend, Thomas Foley, got an unofficial word of his appointment as coadjutor bishop and administrator of the Diocese of Chicago. He had recently been to

---

[54] 71-W-7, Spalding to Gibbons, Baltimore, August 30, 1869.

[55] 71-V-10, Corcoran to Gibbons, Rome, July 24, 1869. Corcoran approved getting sisters from Charleston rather than Baltimore. "The Charleston Sisters are better adapted and are personally popular with the Protestants of Wilmington. They will do an immensity of good. . . ."

Chicago where his reception was not very cordial, although in St. Louis Archbishop Kenrick treated him with great kindness. The thought of inheriting the troubled situation in Chicago disturbed Foley, and he told his old friend in North Carolina:

> I consider myself free to decline, because I told our own Abp. as well as this other I was unwilling to accept. . . . If our dear Lord will only pass me over and let me stay where I am I shall be grateful to Him. If I can do nothing else, I think I may perhaps ship over to Rome in September, and put a stop to troubles by a personal appearance.[56]

Some months after this Foley was appointed to Chicago and was consecrated while Gibbons was out of the country in Rome. While the situation of the Church in Chicago was quite different from that in North Carolina, the troubled administration there of late years made Gibbons realize that his former Baltimore housemate merited his sympathy.

The early autumn found the Vicar Apostolic of North Carolina in Charleston where he completed arrangements for getting the Sisters of Our Lady of Mercy for Wilmington. While there he wrote to his old friend, Charles Clark, whom he had known in Ballinrobe and he remarked to him that his brother, John, and his brother-in-law, George Swarbrick, had lately visited him in North Carolina since he could not himself get down to New Orleans before the Vatican Council. He told Clark that since he had come to North Carolina, "I have been mentally and physically occupied with little or no respite. . . . My position is no sinecure. You must pray for me that I may [have] strength to hold out." He closed by saying that he hoped to visit Ireland on his way home from the council in Rome.[57] Not long before leaving Wilmington he wrote to suggest to his lawyer, Edward Conigland, that the latter write an article for the Wilmington *Journal* explaining the advantages which would accrue to the community from having the sisters who were soon to arrive from Charleston.[58] Conigland did as he was requested and the result pleased Gibbons very much:

---

[56] 71-W-2, Foley to Gibbons, Baltimore, August 6, 1869.

[57] Gibbons to Clark, Charleston, September 5, 1869, copy sent to the writer in a letter from Canon Fergus of Ballinrobe, January 21, 1946.

[58] University of North Carolina Library, Conigland Papers, Gibbons to Conigland, Sumter, South Carolina, September 7, 1869.

I read with interest & pleasure your timely and happily constructed article on the Sisters of Mercy. You are the right man
in the right place. Allow me to say that you are a little Jesuitical —
no mean compliment. No reader can tell whether you are a Jew,
Turk or Papist. The sisters will arrive this evening, as I am informed
by telegraph. I leave Wilmington on Monday next, but regret that
I cannot make any stay in Halifax.[59]

The time had now arrived for the bishop to leave his vicariate
to be gone for over a year. The final entry in his diary was that
of September 20 noting the arrival of the sisters and it would
be October 4, 1870, before he would again take up his pen to
record his activities in North Carolina. Previous to sailing he
had a number of engagements to fulfill in Baltimore, such as the
confirmations already referred to and various other functions
like the rededication of St. Joseph's Church at Texas, Maryland,
recently renovated by the pastor, Lawrence S. Malloy, who
asked Bishop Gibbons to perform the ceremony on one of the
Sundays he would be in Baltimore.[60] There were many activities
of this kind to occupy his time during the weeks before he left
the United States and on October 20, the day the archbishop
and his party sailed on the *Baltimore,* there was a gala farewell
in their honor. The *Catholic Mirror* said:

> The 20th of October will be a day long remembered by the Catho-
> lics of Baltimore, as having witnessed public demonstration of the
> warm regard and sincere respect in which the highest dignitary of
> the Church in the United States is held by the people of his Diocese,
> irrespective of creed. The departure of Most Rev. Archbishop Spald-
> ing and his brother Bishops and priests for Rome was naturally the
> occasion of a manifestation by the Catholic community of their
> regret at a separation which will probably last many months. . . .
> During the last eight days, the archiepiscopal residence had been
> thronged with visitors, who came to take their leave of their vener-
> able and beloved prelate, and many were the offerings brought to
> him, either for his personal use or for that of the Holy Father.[61]

---

[59] *Ibid.,* Gibbons to Conigland, Wilmington, September 20, 1869.
[60] 71-Y-2, Malloy to Gibbons, Texas, Maryland, September 9, 1869.
[61] October 23, 1869. Sailing with Spalding and Gibbons were Bishops Wood
of Philadelphia, McGill of Richmond, Domenec of Pittsburgh, Mullen of Erie,
and O'Gorman of Nebraska. Also in the party were Bernard J. McManus, pastor
of St. John's Church, Baltimore; Placide L. Chapelle, pastor of St. Mary's Church,
Rockville, Maryland; and Charles O'Connor, vice-rector of the American College,
Rome. The *Baltimore* sailed from Locust Point pier to Bremen via Southampton.

It would be difficult to imagine any event in history that would be better calculated to give a young missionary bishop a true concept of the majesty and universality of the Catholic Church than the Vatican Council. It was now over 300 years since the last ecumenical council had concluded its sessions at Trent in 1563. The number and complexity of problems facing the Church in the mid-nineteenth century seemed ample reason for calling the bishops of the world to Rome to confer and advise regarding the doctrinal and moral aspects of these questions. It was on December 6, 1864, that Pope Pius IX had made known to the cardinals his intention of convoking a general council, and from that time on for the next five years the time and effort of many of the officials of the Holy See were given over to its preparation. The leading bishops of the world were consulted for their views on holding a council and after a majority had responded favorably five commissions of consulting theologians were named. These theologians numbered just an even hundred and were at work by the early days of 1869.[62] Among them the sole representative of the American hierarchy was James A. Corcoran. By the late autumn of 1869 all was in readiness and the Eternal City was filling up with bishops from every corner of the globe.

The departure of Archbishop Spalding and his party on October 20 left them time to visit in France for some weeks prior to the opening of the council in Rome. While in Paris they were the guests of the general motherhouse of the Sulpician Fathers. Gibbons later informed one of his Sulpician friends in Baltimore, "We both had a very pleasant time with your brethren in Paris from whom we received every kindness."[63] The visit to the French capital gave to the Vicar Apostolic of North Carolina an opportunity likewise to visit the headquarters of the Society for the Propagation of the Faith to thank them in person for their financial aid to him and to explain in more detail the pressing needs under which his vicariate still labored. After the visit to Paris the prelates made their way southward through France and at Marseilles they took a boat for Civita Vecchia and

---

For a description of the farewell celebration, cf. the Baltimore *Sun,* October 21, 1869.

[62] Cuthbert Butler, *The Vatican Council* (New York, 1930), I, 90. This two-volume work, based on the letters of Bishop William Ullathorne of Birmingham written during the council, is an excellent over-all account.

[63] ASMS, Gibbons to Dubruel, Rome, March 13, 1870.

crossed the Mediterranean by that route. On board ship Gibbons met a Chinese bishop on his way to the council who told him that by the time he reached Rome he would have traveled 23,000 miles.[64] Of the sixty-some bishops in the United States at the time forty-five attended the council with eighteen of them, including Gibbons, resident at the American College and others scattered in various religious houses throughout Rome. During all his time away from home Bishop Gibbons remained close to his episcopal patron, Archbishop Spalding. He later wrote of their association:

> I was his inseparable companion in our voyage across the Atlantic, during our sojourn in England, in France, in Italy and in Rome. For ten months we sat at the same table and slept under the same roof.[65]

The solemn opening of the Vatican Council took place with Pius IX presiding in person over the first public session on December 8, 1869, the feast of the Immaculate Conception. There were over 650 bishops present, and the ceremonies which began at eight-thirty were not concluded until three-thirty in the afternoon; but as one of the bishops who was present wrote in a letter of the same day, "it was magnificent beyond description, and well worth a little fatigue."[66] The Basilica of St. Peter was filled with nearly 50,000 people who had crowded in to watch the unusual pageantry and when the session finally ended and the throng began to move toward the doors Bishop Gibbons became separated from Archbishop Spalding in whose carriage he was accustomed to ride. Soon he was hopelessly lost and, as he said, "as much bewildered as a stranger would be in a London fog." The rain was coming down in torrents and a carriage was not to be had for any price. With the American College a mile or more away and Gibbons still wearing the cope and miter, the thought of walking home was,

---

[64] James Cardinal Gibbons, *A Retrospect of Fifty Years* (Baltimore, 1916), I, 11–12. During the course of the council Gibbons and Bishop Lynch of Charleston wrote jointly a number of articles describing the events in Rome which were published in the *Catholic World* in eight unsigned installments between February and September, 1870 (Volumes X–XI). In 1916 the cardinal reprinted these articles with a preface in the volume cited above.

[65] *Catholic Mirror,* March 30, 1872, which prints the full text of Gibbons' sermon at the month's mind Mass for Spalding in the Baltimore cathedral.

[66] Butler, *op. cit.,* I, 164. Bishop Kerril Amherst of Northampton was the writer of the letter.

of course, out of the question. Finally after a long wait and when it was already growing dark he spied a solitary bishop left on the portico awaiting a carriage. He said he felt it was his last chance, so he marshaled his best French and begged a ride. The bishop looked at him, smiled good-naturedly, and replied in English that his carriage was already engaged to carry five but he would crowd him in somehow. "Rarely did our English tongue sound so sweet in my ears," said Gibbons, "and seldom was an act of kindness more gratefully accepted."[67] He later learned that his benefactor was a bishop from Australia.

When it is remembered that there were 1,025 bishops in the Catholic world who were privileged to attend the Vatican Council and that James Gibbons was number 930 in point of rank, it can easily be understood how insignificant a part he played in the proceedings.[68] He was conscious of his humble station as the youngest prelate in the vast assembly and he, therefore, had nothing to say in the public sessions. But his obscurity among so many distinguished figures of the Church did not lessen his interest in the council's activities. As he later wrote:

> Although my youth imposed upon me a discreet silence among my elders, so keen was my appreciation of my good fortune at being present among these venerable men that I cannot remember to have missed a single session, and I was a most attentive listener at all the debates.[69]

Here for the first time Gibbons had a chance to see the leading bishops of Christendom in action. It was in the Vatican Council that he first saw and heard Henry Edward Manning, Archbishop of Westminster, whom he pronounced "unquestionably, the most attractive figure among the Episcopate of England." That Manning held a special place in Gibbons' impressions of the council personalities is evident from his published reminiscences. Manning delivered the longest oration of the council, a speech lasting an hour and a half, but Gibbons liked it and thought it "a most logical and persuasive argument, and, like all his utterances . . . entirely free from rhetorical ornament and from any effort to arouse the feelings or emotions." The young bishop from North

---

[67] Gibbons, *op. cit.*, I, 2–3.
[68] Joannes Dominicus Mansi, *Sacrorum conciliorum nova et amplissima collectio* (Arnhem & Leipzig, 1927), V (53), 1087.
[69] Gibbons, *op. cit.*, I, 1.

Carolina studied Manning carefully, commenting on his sunken eyes, high and well-developed forehead, fleshless face, and splendid voice. "When he wishes to gain a strong point, he rallies his choicest battalion of words, to each of which he assigns the most effective position; while his voice, swelling with the occasion, imparts to them an energy and a power difficult to resist."[70] Little did James Gibbons realize as he listened to Manning in Rome in the spring of 1870 how much this English churchman would mean to him in the years ahead when, as Archbishop of Baltimore, he faced grave problems, a partial solution to which he always seemed to find in the counsel of the Cardinal of Westminster.

It was at the council, too, that Bishop Gibbons met Archbishop Patrick Leahy of Cashel, "who was perhaps, the most graceful orator among the English-speaking Prelates." The primate of Hungary, John Cardinal Simor, Archbishop of Esztergom, astounded Gibbons by telling him he used four different languages in administering his archdiocese of a million souls, a feat which sounded even more remarkable than that of the vicar apostolic from China who sat next to him in the council chamber and told him he was obliged among his people to employ six different dialects of Chinese.[71] To the Vicar Apostolic of North Carolina, whose proficiency in speaking foreign languages was never exceptional, these recitations must, indeed, have appeared wonderful. Others who drew the attention of Gibbons in the council were Bishops Félix Dupanloup of Orléans, the most

---

[70] *Ibid.,* I, 21–22; 155–156. Almost a half century later Shane Leslie, biographer of Cardinal Manning, asked Gibbons to give his impressions of Manning as he knew him in the Vatican Council. Gibbons replied: "I recall as if it was but yesterday, his memorable speech, which though in a foreign tongue, and the longest one made at the Council, held us spellbound by its beautiful diction and sound logic. It was most incisive, each word, every sentence, the charming, forceful expression of his masterful mind. He not only spoke for himself, on the doctrine of Infallibility, but played the part of the Council's whip, going about among the other members, and by irresistible argument bringing them into line, in support of the Doctrine.

"Again in Rome, on the occasion of one of his sermons, I went somewhat prejudiced to hear him speak, but came away charmed and with the utmost admiration.

"These memories of Cardinal Manning are so dear to me, so impressive, that it seems only yesterday that I saw him, listened to him, and admired him" (MP, Gibbons to Leslie, Baltimore, March 26, 1914).

[71] *Ibid.,* I, 9.

pronounced opponent among the French of the definition of papal infallibility; William von Ketteler of Mainz, also a strong inopportunist; Joseph Strossmayer of Bosnia, the greatest Latin orator in the assembly; and Joachim Cardinal Pecci, Bishop of Perugia. Pecci took no part in the public debates of the council, but Gibbons described the future Leo XIII, with whom he was destined to have such close relations, as "one of its most influential members, and the weight of his learning and administrative experience was felt in the committee to which he was appointed."[72]

The spirit in which the discussions were conducted impressed Gibbons. He remarked he could safely say that in none of the leading parliaments of the world "would a wider liberty of debate be tolerated than was granted in the Vatican Council."[73] He maintained that he listened in the council chamber to the debates on the issue of papal infallibility and he heard "far more subtle, more plausible, and more searching objections against this prerogative of the Pope than I have ever read or heard from the pen or tongue of the most learned and formidable Protestant assailant."[74] The young American bishop listened with close attention as the theological arguments flowed from the opposing sides with a wealth of erudition unfolding finely delineated theories. He thought he detected in all this argumentation three main systems of thought, namely, the English, German, and French. It was a demonstration not at all familiar to American ears. Commenting on the lack of speculative thought in the United States, he remarked:

> We owe it, probably, to the fact that with us all men are so busy trying to amass fortunes that they have little time and less taste for such abstruse speculations.[75]

As the great issue of defining the Pope's infallibility arose in the council it became evident that there would be prolonged discussion and heated controversy. Gibbons realized at an early date that the end was not going to come nearly so soon as some had anticipated. In mid-March he wrote to Joseph P. Dubruel, S.S., on business concerning his students in Baltimore and he said at that time:

---

[72] *Ibid.*, I, 27–28.   [74] *Ibid.*, I, 20.
[73] *Ibid.*, I, 13.   [75] *Ibid.*, I, 87.

There is not the slightest prospect of the Council coming to a close in June next, nor probably short of two years. It is my intention, D. V. to leave Rome in July, if I am allowed. I can afford neither the time nor money to remain longer from home.[76]

On March 6, just a week before he wrote this letter, the draft of the papal infallibility decree as drawn up by the theologians had been put into the hands of the bishops and it was clear that it would invite opposition. The succeeding weeks were filled with argument and counter-argument in private discussions while the public sessions debated other questions. During that spring the report of the commission *De fide catholica* was also the subject of controversy and when the whole of the schema on this subject was voted on April 12 eighty bishops returned a *placet juxta modum*. Those voting this qualified approval were obliged to hand in a statement in writing of their objections to the constitution *De fide* as it stood. Among them were seventeen American prelates including Gibbons. The objections of the Americans were confined for the most part to the phrase "Sancta Romana Catholica Ecclesia" as contained in the constitution. They objected likewise to a number of cases where the term "anathema sit" was employed. The point in the first instance was the objection to placing "Roman" before "Catholic" in the official title of the Church. Gibbons' objection read that the word "Romana" ought to be omitted, but if it was included then the other marks of the Church should likewise appear, "una, sancta, catholica, apostolica atque Romana."[77] The question was thoroughly debated and in the final voting on April 24 the 667 bishops present gave a unanimous *placet* to the constitution *De fide catholica* with the official wording for the Church amended as the objectors had asked, that is, to read "Sancta Catholica Apostolica Romana Ecclesia."

The American hierarchy were divided on the subject of the definition of papal infallibility. When on January 1, 1870, a petition was issued asking that the doctrine be defined it was

---

[76] ASMS, Gibbons to Dubruel, Rome, March 13, 1870. The mention of Gibbons lacking money to remain longer in Rome recalls the amusing remark attributed to Pius IX on the expenses of the council: "Non so se il Papa uscirà di questo Concilio fallibile od infallibile; ma questo è *certo* che sara fallito." Butler, *op. cit.*, I, 170 n. 1.

[77] Mansi, *op. cit.*, III (51), 398. For a full discussion of this question cf. Butler, *op. cit.*, I, 277–283.

circulated among the bishops, and 380, including nine Americans, signed it. But contrary petitions arose at once against the definition, and one, suggesting that the question not be brought before the council at all, carried the names of twenty American bishops. Archbishop Spalding, the nominal leader of the Americans, had originally believed that a definition was unnecessary, that the Catholic people already believed the doctrine, and that what was needed was to condemn all errors opposed to it. However, after being in Rome for some months and observing the pressure brought by certain outside elements to prevent the definition, the Archbishop of Baltimore changed his mind and drew up his own *postulatum* calling for the definition in council. Meanwhile, however, Spalding was himself named to the committee *De postulatis* and he, therefore, felt that propriety demanded that he should drop out from advocating any special matters before the council. His senior suffragan, James F. Wood of Philadelphia, then took up Spalding's *postulatum,* secured the signatures of four American bishops, and forwarded it to the presiding cardinal. In the debates that ensued between May 14 and June 30 at one time or another seven American bishops mounted the rostrum to make speeches for or against the definition, and finally on June 30 the last American to speak in the Vatican Council, Augustin Vérot, S.S., Bishop of St. Augustine, referred to as "l'enfant terrible" of the gathering, made his supreme effort against the definition. When a request that the debates on papal infallibility be closed was put to a vote and passed on June 3 the action gave rise to a protest at this closure to which nine Americans affixed their signatures. Most bitterly opposed of all was Archbishop Peter R. Kenrick of St. Louis who on June 9 published his famous *Concio* at Naples, regarded by many as the strongest written protest made during the entire council to the definition of papal infallibility.[78]

To all this theological discussion and controversy James Gibbons was an interested listener, but he took no active part. When it came time for the final public session on July 18 to pass on the question of papal infallibility he voted with the majority as did most of the Americans, although a number of bishops from the United States had absented themselves and gone home

---

[78] Raymond J. Clancy, C.S.C., "American Prelates in the Vatican Council," *Historical Records and Studies,* XXVIII (1937), 39–55.

rather than vote in favor of the decree, and one, Edward Fitzgerald of Little Rock, at the last moment decided to attend and vote against it. Fitzgerald and Bishop Luigi Riccio of Cajazzo in the Kingdom of Naples were the only two among 535 bishops voting who returned a *non placet*. During the final voting a violent electrical storm broke over Rome so that the historic occasion was marked by a dramatic and quite unexpected impressiveness. Gibbons sat through the final session which had convened at nine o'clock, and when the vote was made known a burst of applause and congratulations to the "Papa infallibile" broke out and swelled through St. Peter's until the sound of the Sistine Choir was drowned in the din. This sort of thing happening in a church was strange to most of the Americans present, but, as Gibbons said, "there are times when feeling is so powerful as to break through all ideas of conventionality."[79]

During the nearly eight months that Bishop Gibbons spent in Rome he had many an unforgettable experience. The vicar apostolic from North Carolina, who was within five days of his thirty-sixth birthday on the occasion of the formal definition of papal infallibility, had met personally many of the greatest men in the Church through his close association with Archbishop Spalding. He was present, too, on January 29, 1870, when Pius IX paid a special compliment to the Americans by coming to the chapel of the American College to pronounce the decree declaring Giovanni Ancina as venerable. He was proud to meet the Pope personally, and he was proud, too, to hear his friend, Spalding, greet the Pontiff in Latin in the name of the American hierarchy.[80] Even though he had taken little or no active part in the deliberations of the council the gathering had afforded him a golden opportunity to exercise his very pronounced faculty of learning from others. To sit week after week and listen to the finest minds in the Church debate doctrinal and moral problems not only refreshed Gibbons' own knowledge but gave to it an enrichment which he never lost. He had shown from the time he was a small boy in Ireland an avidity for learning that continued into his mature years, and during the months of the council he lost no chance to add to his store of knowledge on every score.

One lesson Gibbons learned on his trip pertained to the rela-

---

[79] Gibbons, *op. cit.,* I, 184.
[80] *Ibid.,* I, 60–63.

tions of Church and State. He had been from his early years a warm admirer of the manner in which those relations were conducted in the United States. The European sojourn in 1869–1870, where he observed the practical working of union of Church and State in some of the countries he visited, only solidified Gibbons in his preference for the American system. When he and Archbishop Spalding left Rome in July they traveled across western Europe on their way to the British Isles. At Annecy in Savoy they were the guests of Bishop Claude M. Magnin who received them in his splendid palace "before which guards marched up and down." The vicar apostolic from North Carolina, surveying the magnificence of the building with its fine appointments, and thinking, perhaps, of his four small rooms back in Wilmington, congratulated his host, to which the latter replied, "Monsignor Gibbons! all is not gold that glitters. I cannot even build a sacristy without government approval."[81] The incident made a profound impression on James Gibbons' mind, and it served to reconcile him more than ever to the independent poverty in which he administered his vicariate in the United States. It was but the first of many such impressions gathered by Gibbons on the operation of union of Church and State as he observed it during his numerous trips to Europe. With each new view of the old world system he became a stronger defender of the mutually free and amicable relationships governing Church and State in his own country.

The long debates in the Roman heat left Bishop Gibbons in a weakened condition which the holiday in the British Isles would do much to overcome. In fact, just before the breaking up of the council Father Corcoran went to his room to discuss a matter of personal business where, he said, "I found you so feeble & prostrate, that I would say nothing of it."[82] But the visit to London helped to revive him, and his weeks in Ireland, where he called on many old friends in and around Ballinrobe, gave him the relaxation that he needed. Late in September Gibbons sailed from Queenstown on the *City of Brussels* which had on board a considerable number of American churchmen.

---

[81] *Catholic University Bulletin,* **XXIV** (December, 1918), 151. In his *Faith of Our Fathers,* 83 ed. (Baltimore, 1917), p. 246, Gibbons stated that it was at Annecy in Savoy that this incident occurred.

[82] 82-B-2, Corcoran to Gibbons, Charleston, October 5, 1870.

On the way across the Atlantic the ship encountered a frightful storm which caused it to pitch in a way that terrified most of the passengers. Gibbons proved himself a source of real courage and strength in the emergency. Years later one of his fellow passengers on the voyage recalled the incident to him when he said:

> No picture stands out more clearly in my life than yours on the morning of the great storm, when with barometer in hand and the word of cheer on your lips you sustained the failing courage of many. To you all looked for the word of hope, and I recall it as you announced the upward tendency of the Mercury and the abatement of the storm.[83]

By October 4 the bishop was again in Wilmington after an absence of over a year. While he was away the church had been enlarged and its equipment improved. The enlargement of 24 by 40 feet was in the main intended as living quarters for the clergy, and Gibbons was pleased with the improvement which, as he wrote, "forms my present commodious dwelling."[84]

Conditions in North Carolina had not greatly improved during Gibbons' absence. In January, 1870, the carpetbagger legislature had passed a bill giving Governor Holden power to declare a county in a state of insurrection. This effort to awe the inhabitants by military force led to the recruiting of armed bands of men who in several places engaged the state troops, with the result that in some counties a situation approximating civil war ensued through the spring and summer. The Conservatives were determined to be rid of the Republican regime once and for all and by dint of extraordinary effort and the general disgust of the people for the Holden administration, the election on August 4 resulted in a sweeping victory for the

---

[83] 121-W, D[aniel] J. Riordan to Gibbons, Chicago, June 10, 1919. Monsignor Riordan, pastor of St. Elizabeth's Church in Chicago, was the brother of Archbishop Patrick W. Riordan of San Francisco.

[84] Diary, October 4, 1870, p. 19. The total cost of the improvements, including the lot and the purchase of a marble altar and some paintings, was $7,000. That even a modest expenditure of this kind took a serious toll on his slender resources we know from a letter Gibbons wrote to Bishop Lynch about two months later. He remarked at that time, "I deeply sympathize with your Lordship in your heavy financial crosses & am already beginning to feel the weight of my own burden" (Archives of the Diocese of Charleston, Gibbons to Lynch, Norfolk, Virginia, December 11, 1870, copy).

Conservatives. The new legislature met on November 21, less than two months after Bishop Gibbons' return to Wilmington from Europe, and within a few weeks the governor had been impeached. The trial was set for January 30, 1871, and through the course of the next two months North Carolinians watched with interest as the abuses of the administration they so much detested were exposed to public view. One of the counsel for Holden was Edward Conigland, the lawyer of James Gibbons. Hamilton described him as "an orator of great power, full of fire and energy, and thoroughly Celtic in temperament. He had long been regarded as one of the ablest members of the bar of the State and his opening speech was awaited with great interest."[85] Bishop Gibbons followed the impeachment trial with close attention, and when Conigland sent him a copy of his major speech the bishop said he liked its clearness of argument and earnestness of tone. "Your eloquent rebuke of certain newspapers prejudicing the case, meets with my hearty approval."[86] A few days later in a second letter Gibbons again mentioned his pleasure at Conigland's speech and he told the lawyer that it was not often he could praise public speeches. "I think whatever may be the result of the trial," he remarked, "that Gen. Holden ought to feel under lasting obligations to you."[87] But despite all Conigland's efforts Governor Holden was convicted on March 22 and removed from office, and North Carolina moved another step closer to overthrowing the Reconstruction regime.

Although conditions were not so bad at the time in North Carolina as they were in other states of the South the recovery was yet far from complete. All the staple crops such as cotton, corn, and wheat showed a marked decline for the years since 1860 and whereas that year had produced a yield of 33,000,000 pounds of tobacco by 1870 it was only a little over 11,000,000 pounds. With the state dependent for the most part on the prosperity of its predominantly rural areas the fortunes of the towns were adversely affected also. Industry had as yet made little impression upon North Carolina and out of a population

---

[85] Hamilton, *op. cit.*, p. 551.
[86] University of North Carolina Library, Conigland Papers, Gibbons to Conigland, Wilmington, March 5, 1871.
[87] *Ibid.*, Gibbons to Conigland, Wilmington, March 10, 1871.

of over a million people only 13,622 were employed in manufacturing establishments. Not until 1869 did Brodie Duke open his two-room tobacco factory at Durham, so the tremendous wealth and expansion of that industry was as yet far in the distance.[88] The school system of the state was sadly enmeshed in politics and showed little progress. While there were twenty-two institutions calling themselves colleges, "probably none . . . deserved a rating above a secondary school." The students at the University of North Carolina numbered only thirty-five in 1869 and finally on February 1, 1871, the university was compelled to close from lack of patronage and did not reopen until September, 1875.[89]

These conditions compelled an uphill fight for the Catholic Church throughout the state, to say nothing of the handicap of the overwhelming Protestant population and the prejudice which operated against Catholics in North Carolina. Yet by 1870 the efforts of the bishop and his four priests on the missions had succeeded in increasing the number of Catholics, either through searching out lapsed ones or by conversions, to a total of 1,200 which was about 500 above the number when Gibbons came there in 1868.[90] But the resources were so meager that the bishop had to depend on outside aid. It was with that thought in mind that he wrote to the Bishop of Albany and some of his friends in that diocese asking if he might go there to beg. He received a hearty welcome from Bishop John Conroy who told him, "Be kind enough to make my house your home when you can come & I am sure that any of our priests will be honored by your visit."[91] His friend, James McDermott, responded encouragingly and said he thought there was scarcely a priest in the Diocese of Albany, "who will not give you a passibly [sic] decent Collection."[92] Just at this time Archbishop Spalding reached Baltimore from Europe and he told Gibbons that he had been given "a grand Reception —

[88] Archibald Henderson, *North Carolina. The Old North State and the New* (Chicago, 1941), II, 344–348, 359.

[89] *Ibid.*, II, 366–367.

[90] *Sadlier's Catholic Directory . . . 1870* (New York, 1870), pp. 311–312. The immigration from abroad in these years which brought great increases of population to the dioceses of the North and West touched the South hardly at all.

[91] 72-C-2, Conroy to Gibbons, Albany, November 2, 1870.

[92] 72-C-4, McDermott to Gibbons, Glens Falls, November 17, 1870.

twice as grand as that of *our* departure . . . yr. presence alone
was wanting. My children of Balto. turned out in mass, & I
love them more than ever."[93] He urged him to visit Baltimore,
a plan which Gibbons had in mind to follow on his way north
to Albany. But before setting off for the North the bishop
completed the work on his first pastoral letter to his people
on the temporal power of the Pope, a document which pleased
John Murphy, the publisher in Baltimore, so much that he
volunteered to make Gibbons no charge for the printing job.[94]
Likewise, before his departure for New York he delivered a
public lecture on temperance in the theater at Wilmington on
the invitation of the local temperance society, "the members
of which," said Gibbons, "with one exception, are non-
Catholics."[95] The lecture was a sufficient success to prompt the
president of the state council of the Friends of Temperance
at Raleigh to write him two days later asking that he repeat
it there,[96] and the Wilmington society sent him a formal
resolution of thanks for his effort in their behalf.[97] He was
not able to go to Raleigh at this particular time, but he did
fill the engagement later that year.[98]

On his way to Albany in late March, Gibbons stopped off
at Baltimore to visit his friends. On March 19 he delivered a
lecture on the Papacy and the temporal power in the hall of
the Maryland Institute. Gibbons gave the lecture, so he thought,
for the benefit of a parochial school fund of one of the Baltimore
parishes, but the pastor decided to give over the receipts to
the bishop himself, "and the change in the programme giving
the benefit to his own diocese was made without his knowledge. . . ."[99] Apparently he showed signs of poor health, for
the archbishop wrote him a warning note and told him he
was really uneasy about him. Spalding continued, "you looked

---

[93] 72-C-3, Spalding to Gibbons, Baltimore, November 16, 1870.

[94] 72-D-1, Murphy to Gibbons, Baltimore, February 2, 1871. The pastoral of
fifteen pages was dated January 27, 1871, and entitled *A Circular Letter on the
Temporal Power of the Popes Addressed to the Clergy and Laity of the Vicariate
Apostolic of North Carolina* (Baltimore, 1871).

[95] Diary, February 21, 1871, p. 24.

[96] 72-D-5, Theo. N. Ramsay to Gibbons, Raleigh, February 23, 1871.

[97] 72-D-6, Jas. W. King to Gibbons, Wilmington, February 25, 1871.

[98] Diary, August 17, 1871, p. 25.

[99] *Catholic Mirror,* March 18 and April 1, 1871.

so thin & so fatigued. Do not kill yourself, for Providence has yet great designs on you for His glory & the good of the Church."[100] A few days later the bishop answered his friend from Albany and thanked him for his interest in his health which, he said, "thank God, has improved, since I came to Albany. My work though considerable, will allow me intervals of repose."[101] He would be in New York State until mid-June and then the archbishop could count on his being in Baltimore for the confirmation tour he had outlined for him.

His reception by the clergy of the Diocese of Albany was very cordial and Gibbons was able to collect a considerable sum of money from the priests and people to take back to his vicariate. The first week of June found him stopping with Bishop Conroy in Albany with his tour of the diocese about ended. He confessed to his friend, Father Joseph Dubruel, that his labors had been "very arduous," but they were now nearly finished and by June 14 he hoped to be in Baltimore. Just at this time the full details of the horrors of the Paris Commune were coming through. Among the victims of the communards during the "Bloody Week" from May 21–28 was Archbishop Georges Darboy of Paris who was executed as a hostage. Gibbons had seen and heard Darboy in the Vatican Council the year before. He told Dubruel, "The recent events in Paris are too shocking to be dwelt upon. I learned a few days ago, through an Irish channel, that Rev. Mr. Hogan of St. Sulpice, Paris, one of your confreres, had escaped, or was released from prison & had gone for security to Ireland. You could ill spare so good a man."[102]

During June and part of July Bishop Gibbons filled engagements to confirm in a number of parishes in the Archdiocese of Baltimore. The archbishop had gone off to Warm Springs, Virginia, for his health, and from there he told the young bishop he saw no objection to his lecturing to the temperance people in Raleigh, "provided you take care not to endorse that Temperance organization. . . ."[103] While on his tour he

---

[100] 72-E-1, Spalding to Gibbons, Baltimore, April 8, 1871.

[101] 36A-J-5, Gibbons to Spalding, Albany, April 10, 1871.

[102] ASMS, Gibbons to Dubruel, Albany, June 3, 1871. John B. Hogan, S.S., was a prominent Sulpician who later served as the first president of Divinity College at the Catholic University of America.

[103] 72-E-3, Spalding to Gibbons, Warm Springs, July 13, 1871.

confirmed and preached at Barnesville, a little village in Montgomery County. Not long afterward a woman wrote him that she was present on that occasion and she was now seeking further information. "Believe me I shall never forget your sermon nor you. I am a Protestant and have been an earnest searcher after truth. Whether I have found it or not remains yet to be tested."[104] The inquiry of Mary Louise Wood was one of the first among dozens which were sent to Gibbons by Protestants after hearing him preach or reading one of his books.

With his confirmation tour completed in Maryland the bishop returned to North Carolina where he complied with the request of the Raleigh temperance society to deliver his lecture in Metropolitan Hall on August 17.[105] While the reception given to his spoken and written words had been on the whole highly favorable up to this time, he did not altogether escape the sting of criticism. Spalding forwarded a letter he had received from England, as he said, "written probably by some apostate Irish Catholic, from which you will perceive that your fame has overstepped the boundaries of America. Some of the criticism may be of service to you — while I attach very little importance to the missive."[106] Precisely what the critic was talking about we have no way of knowing as the letter was apparently destroyed or lost. The health of Archbishop Spalding was beginning to show serious signs of deterioration just at this time and he wrote Gibbons on September 29, "I was nearer death for two days than I ever was probably before." But his people prayed for him and he was then feeling better. "In fact," he said, "I don't see how I am going to die; they will not let me."[107]

It was in the fall of 1871 that there occurred one of the most remarkable incidents of James Gibbons' North Carolina career. A country doctor by the name of John C. Monk was living with his family at a small rural settlement called Newton Grove in Samson County between Raleigh and Wilmington. The doctor had for some time been giving serious thought to the subject of religion. He chanced on an old issue of the New

---

[104] 72-E-5, Wood to Gibbons, Petersville, Maryland, July 22, 1871.
[105] Diary, p. 25.
[106] 72-F-3, Spalding to Gibbons, Baltimore, August 25, 1871.
[107] 72-F-7, Spalding to Gibbons, Baltimore, September 29, 1871.

York *Herald* which contained a copy of a sermon by Archbishop John McCloskey on the subject of the true Church.
He was so impressed by what he had read that he sent off a letter
addressed to "Any Catholic Priest in Wilmington, N. C." in
which he asked for further enlightenment. Mark Gross answered
the call by a visit to Newton Grove where he began a series
of instructions for the doctor and preached in the open to the
people from the neighboring countryside. Dr. Monk's position
of influence in the community proved to be a powerful attraction
for a number of others and soon there sprang up a very
lively interest in Catholicism in a region where before it had
only been the subject of ridicule and reprobation. At length
the doctor finished his instructions and came to Wilmington
where, on October 27, 1871, Bishop Gibbons baptized him
after receiving his profession of faith.[108] He proved to be so
ardent a Catholic and set so splendid an example that soon
his wife and children, his brother and his family, and a number
of their neighbors followed him into the Church.

In March, 1872, Gibbons fulfilled his promise to Dr. Monk
to visit Newton Grove. It was a trip he never forgot. He had
to rise at four o'clock in the morning to catch a very early
train out of Wilmington and, there being no carriages about,
he was compelled — with the aid of a small boy — to carry
his heavy traveling bag filled with mission articles a distance
of a mile to the station. Upon arrival at Newton Grove in a
very severe storm he was met by Monk's brother on horseback,

---

[108] St. Thomas Church Baptismal Register, October 27, 1871, No. 566. A search
of the New York *Herald* for the first six months of 1871 revealed the text of only
one sermon of Archbishop McCloskey. That was in the issue of January 2 with
the story of the dedication of St. Ann's Church in East 12th Street, New York,
where McCloskey had presided and preached the previous day. The theme of the
sermon was the unity of God's Church as the most conspicuous of its marks.
McCloskey spoke of the unity that exists in God Himself, of how He gave His
Son in His visible body to be the Saviour of mankind, how all men were united
to Christ, but how a body had to be united to a head. He pointed out the
chaos that would have ensued had Peter preached what he pleased in Rome while
James was preaching something different in Jerusalem. From this McCloskey
pressed his point on the necessity of unity of belief in essential dogmas, the harm
that had been done by quarreling sects with their contradictions and discord,
and he ended with the statement that in the Catholic Church alone could one
find the unity of belief which must mark the true church of Christ. While it is
impossible at this late date to say for sure that this is the sermon Dr. Monk read,
its general plan of development would make it seem very likely that it was.

accompanied by a neighbor with his carriage. He later wrote that Monk carried an ax "to cut our way through the forests, for the sleet and snow had covered the country, and bowed to the earth, and in many places across our course, the pine saplings that grew in dense bodies up to the margin of the road." For twenty-one miles they had to cross the country through the teeth of wind, rain, sleet, and snow. "After a short exposure I was all but frozen by the violence of the storm and intense cold."[109] Gibbons recovered quickly, however, after reaching his destination and the next day he celebrated Mass in Dr. Monk's home and preached to a large gathering of people. In a short time others entered the Church and ultimately a crude little wooden church was constructed to accommodate them when the priest came on his occasional visits. Naturally this movement drew criticism and before long some of the Protestant ministers in the neighborhood had begun a crusade of petty persecution, but the more they inveighed the more did the people flock to the little church to hear the priest's instructions. Dr. Monk died on September 10, 1877, at the early age of fifty-one, but not before he had the joy of seeing his own family and that of a number of his neighbors embrace the Catholic faith. Forty years later the last of the original band of converts at Newton Grove died when Anna Monk [Mrs. Underwood], the daughter of the doctor, suffered a stroke like her father. At that time her son, a Benedictine at Belmont Abbey, wrote to James Gibbons and reminded him of the circumstance of his mother's conversion at his hands, and he said she had seen the little parish at Newton Grove "grow from it's infancy to the present large Congregation, and was the last of the three that formed the foundation of that Mission."[110] Experiences such as these — and he had several others which were not so striking — gave heart and courage to Gibbons to continue his efforts in spite of all difficulties.

---

[109] "Reminiscenses of North Carolina," *United States Catholic Historical Magazine,* III (1889–1890), 346.

[110] 115-H, Francis Underwood, O.S.B., to Gibbons, Belmont, North Carolina, April 23, 1917. The writer visited Newton Grove on May 10, 1947, where the pastor, Alphonsus Schonhart, C.Ss.R., told him that there were then 340 white and ninety-five colored members of this rural parish. Virtually the whole countryside is of the Catholic faith, the most solidly Catholic rural community in North Carolina.

The same month that had witnessed Dr. Monk's baptism in Wilmington also saw the opening of St. Thomas' School in the basement of the church with twenty boys under the care of Fathers Gross and James B. White.[111] During that month, too, Wilmington had its first reception of a young woman as a candidate for the Sisters of Our Lady of Mercy and the bishop preached at the ceremony on October 15.[112] Just at this time disaster and ruin befell the diocese of his friend, Thomas Foley, when on October 9–10 a large portion of the city of Chicago was destroyed by fire. The quick sympathy of the Vicar Apostolic of North Carolina was aroused for his stricken friend to whom he sent off a gift in money from his own slender resources. John Foley, brother of the bishop in Chicago, wrote to thank Gibbons and he said, "I am sure no amount received by him will be more highly appreciated. Who would have thought that Chicago would need aid from N. Carolina?"[113]

The new year of 1872 brought alarming reports from Baltimore concerning the condition of Archbishop Spalding. John Murphy, the publisher, informed Gibbons on January 2 that his recovery was very doubtful,[114] and two days later Father Dubruel told him the archbishop had been anointed. "He may recover yet," said Dubruel, "but is continually in danger of being strangled. . . . His sufferings are great. We are all praying for him."[115] But before the ordeal of the archbishop was ended death struck in another part of the Province of Baltimore when John McGill, Bishop of Richmond, died on January 14. On his return from the funeral in Richmond two days later Gibbons found awaiting him a telegram appointing him administrator of the vacant diocese, this by the will of Archbishop Spalding, seconded by Bishops Wood, Lynch, and Becker.[116] The telegram was followed by a letter from Becker written from Richmond. He and Lynch of Charleston had examined the papers of the late Bishop of Richmond and set all in order as far as they

---

[111] Diary, October 2, 1871, p. 28.
[112] 72-F-8, Sermon on "Reception of a Sister," first delivered at Wilmington, North Carolina, October 15, 1871.
[113] 72-G-2, Foley to Gibbons, Baltimore, November 13, 1871.
[114] 72-H-1, Murphy to Gibbons, Baltimore, January 2, 1872.
[115] 72-H-3, Dubruel to Gibbons, Baltimore, January 4, 1872.
[116] Diary, January 14–16, 1872, p. 29.

were able. They were then setting out for Baltimore to confer with Spalding. Becker wrote:

> I shall explain to the Abp. my views, & give my decided voice in your favor, without drawback or fear, praying that God's will may be done, on earth as in heaven. Do not be "effrayed." Our Lord will aid & assist you. The future is bright for you, for you have an old diocese to rule, with young, and as I think, good priests, all well disposed toward yourself. Pax tibi, & I will write from Balto.[117]

Regardless of how reluctant Gibbons might be to take on the added burden there seemed no way out. Wood of Philadelphia wrote from Baltimore to say that the archbishop wished him to repeat what he had already communicated by wire and, he added, "to say also that he wishes you to take up your abode, at least for the present, in Richmond."[118]

James Gibbons was a person who by nature disliked radical changes in his customary way of living. When he was appointed to the cathedral in Baltimore he was reluctant to leave St. Bridget's Parish; now that he had become used to his home in Wilmington after over three years there he was again loath to leave it. However, he did not feel he could refuse the appointment of the archbishop so he wrote him his assent.

> I must first bless God for your escape the 3rd time, from the jaws of death. Father McManus kept me informed almost daily, by telegram or letter, about yr. condition.
>
> The Bishops at the funeral insisted on my accepting the administration of Richmond, sede vacante. Your Grace's Confirmation was before me last night on returning to Wilmington.
>
> I start on Monday to commence operations, & judging from what I saw, I have a mare magnum to explore.

---

[117] 72-H-7, Becker to Gibbons, Richmond, January 17, 1872.

[118] 72-H-8, Wood to Gibbons, Baltimore, January 18, 1872. Over two years later Bishop Becker discovered among his papers a note written by Archbishop Spalding on January 31, 1872, just a week before his death. Becker told Gibbons both he and Thomas Foley were present when it was written and could vouch for its authenticity, and he added, "It shows at once what the Mt. Rev. Abp. thought of you, and is the last piece of writing done by that active hand." The Spalding note read as follows: "I hereby appoint the Rt. Rev. Bishop Gibbons, administrator, with full powers, for the Diocese of Richmond, and I strongly recommend him to the Holy See as Bishop, his present position continuing V. Ap. of North Carolina. This is my vote & opinion. Addressed to all the Suffragans of the Province. M. J. Spalding, Archbp. Balt." (72-H-9, Becker to Gibbons, Wilmington, Delaware, March 28, 1874).

I will spend some days in Richmond, & if I get into the mud, somebody will be responsible. I hope not to be obliged to bore you with difficulties.

The papers have published the news of the funeral obsequies. Every thing passed off well.

Possibly I may have the pleasure of seeing you next week. Our congregation prayed earnestly for you.

I suppose your Grace is too feeble yet to write. May your full recovery be speedy.[119]

Five days later he wrote from Richmond what proved to be his last letter to Archbishop Spalding. He had then been in the Virginia capital for some days and he said everything was going on satisfactorily and he was "overhauling the late Bishop's accounts & papers." He would come to Baltimore soon and get Bishop McGill's will. Fortunately, he had the assistance of the Mayor of Richmond, Anthony M. Keiley, a prominent Catholic lawyer, "who has furnished me," said Gibbons, "with all necessary information, as to the course I am to pursue." Gibbons told Spalding in closing that he rejoiced to hear that the archbishop seemed to be improving in health.[120]

Just two weeks later Martin John Spalding died on February 7. Gibbons confided to his diary: "Archbishop Spalding died. A great light is extinguished in Israel. I attended his funeral, having before his death, given him the H. Viaticum & read for him the Profession of Faith."[121] In the death of Spalding, Gibbons lost a powerful friend who had exerted every effort during the previous seven years to advance the young churchman whom he had taken into his official family in December, 1865. It was fitting, therefore, that Gibbons should have been present at the end to assist at the death and funeral of one who had meant so much to him. On March 20 the month's mind Mass was celebrated for the late archbishop in the cathedral of Baltimore, and Gibbons was selected to preach the sermon. He traced his relationship to Archbishop Spalding from 1865 to his death and he said that their friendship was of a most intimate and affectionate nature. "I reverenced him as a father, and he deigned to honor me as a son." He spoke,

---

[119] 36A-J-6, Gibbons to Spalding, Wilmington, January 18, 1872.

[120] 34-B-12, Gibbons to Spalding, Richmond, January 23, 1872.

[121] Diary, February 7, 1872, p. 29.

too, of their repeated trips together when, as he remarked, he was selected to accompany the archbishop, "because I could be better spared to the Cathedral than either of my two cherished companions, one of whom is now the honored bishop of Chicago, and the other has just followed his master to his eternal reward" [Coskery]. He then recalled his association with Spalding during their trip to the Vatican Council when for ten months he was daily in his company. "During all this time I had an excellent opportunity of studying his character, and of observing those hidden springs which gave motive power to his public acts."[122] He did not forget his friend in the way that means most to a priest when he sent Father Dubruel at St. Mary's Seminary a request for twenty-five Masses to be offered by the Sulpician Fathers for the repose of Spalding's soul.[123]

Bishop Gibbons appreciated the fact that the life of Archbishop Spalding had been one of more than ordinary importance to the history of the Catholic Church in the United States. He was glad, therefore, to find among a list of private instructions left to him by the dead prelate that the archbishop directed Gibbons to give over all the necessary documents for the writing of his biography to Father Isaac Hecker of the Paulist Fathers. He told Hecker this news and further informed him that on his next trip to Baltimore he would secure the documents from the archives and send them to him.[124] A Baltimore layman by the name of J. Fairfax McLaughlin who had admired Spalding, expressed his intention of writing the biography of the archbishop, but Gibbons informed him of Spalding's request for Hecker to do the work. McLaughlin readily enough agreed to drop his projected work on which he had already gathered some material, although he regretted, as he said, that "I did not speak to you on the subject when you were here."[125] Gibbons suggested to Hecker that as soon as he could get around to forwarding the Spalding papers he would do so, and he would send him, too, a copy of Spalding's instructions to Hecker in regard to the biography which, he added, "*I would suggest to*

---

[122] *Catholic Mirror,* March 30, 1872.
[123] ASMS, Gibbons to Dubruel, Wilmington, Holy Saturday, 1872.
[124] 72-H-15, Gibbons to Hecker, Wilmington, April 2, 1872.
[125] AAB, unclassified, McLaughlin to Gibbons, Baltimore, May 9, 1872.

you to publish in the papers."[126] In this way further disappointments such as that suffered by McLaughlin might be averted. Actually Hecker did not undertake the biography but instead he and Augustine Hewit, C.S.P., suggested that it be done by Father John Lancaster Spalding, the late archbishop's nephew, who was then resident in New York. Gibbons approved of their choice and he told young Spalding, "You may rest assured that I will furnish you all the aid in my power, both in materials & suggestions." He would facilitate his access to documents in Baltimore that could not be removed from the archives and he consented as well to note down all the personal traits, anecdotes, and reminiscences he could recall about the archbishop and would keep the paper for him.[127] Spalding was grateful for the proffered assistance of Gibbons in the work and he asked if he might enjoy perfect freedom in consulting him as to difficulties which might present themselves. He disliked bothering him in the matter but, as he said, "your great kindness gives me confidence."[128] The biography eventually came out in the next year and for so early a date after the death of its subject it proved to be a good piece of work.

The responsibility of Bishop Gibbons for administering the vacant See of Richmond along with his own vicariate was, of course, a heavy one. It necessitated repeated trips between Richmond and Wilmington with a good deal of added travel in visiting the scattered missions of the Church in Virginia and North Carolina. In early June Bishop Whelan of Wheeling wrote him to say he had heard a rumor that Ignatius Persico, Bishop of Savannah, was seriously ill. He added, "I trust we are not exposed to lose another of the Prelates of our already suffering Province." Whelan took occasion to warn Gibbons against exerting himself too much. His friends knew that he was not strong and some of them feared that the double burden might prove too much for him. The Bishop of Wheeling told him:

> I trust your own health is good. You must allow me as an old hunter to advise you to look for game during the coming months in the mountain regions of Virginia & N. Carolina. Richmond is

[126] 72-I-1, Gibbons to Hecker, Wilmington, May 1, 1872.
[127] 34-B-13, Gibbons to Spalding, Richmond, July 12, 1872.
[128] 72-I-8, Spalding to Gibbons, New York, July 22, 1872.

not healthy at this season, and the first year it is likely to be still more dangerous for you. You may find in healthier portions of the field confided to you quite enough for the exercise of your zeal. As we cannot yet spare you from the ranks I hope you will turn my advice to account.[129]

But any hope that Gibbons might have entertained of being relieved of one of the two jurisdictions which he had been administering since January was dashed when on August 29, 1872, he received a letter from Cardinal Barnabò, Prefect of the Congregation of the Propaganda, announcing that he had been named by Pius IX as Bishop of Richmond and enclosing the bulls, but stating that he was to retain the administration of the Vicariate of North Carolina until the Holy See would appoint a new vicar apostolic.[130] The bulls for his promotion to Richmond bore the date of July 30, and it soon became known that on the same day James Roosevelt Bayley, Bishop of Newark, had been named eighth Archbishop of Baltimore to succeed Spalding. The appointment to Baltimore brought joy to Gibbons. He quickly sent off a letter to Bayley in which he said he had just learned the news through a private dispatch. "I am permitted at last, to give vent to my feelings, by expressing my heartfelt gratitude to God & congratulations to you. The wishes of my heart are now fulfilled. You will be glad to learn, that you have been the desired of Balto, as I have reason to know, for many opened their hearts freely to me on the subject."[131] Bayley himself was not nearly so enthusiastic about the move from Newark to Baltimore, and while he thanked Gibbons for his congratulations he made it clear that he was in

---

[129] 72-I-3, Whelan to Gibbons, Wheeling, June 4, 1872.

[130] 72-J-2, Barnabò to Gibbons, Rome, August 5, 1872; on August 11 Barnabò transmitted to Gibbons his faculties as Bishop of Richmond (72-J-3,4,5,6).

[131] 41-S-1, Gibbons to Bayley, Wilmington, August 12, 1872. Just at this time a report appeared in the press that William H. Elder, Bishop of Natchez, had been named to Baltimore. The report met the strong approval of Bishop Thomas Foley in Chicago who wrote to Gibbons to say he was glad it was Elder and not Bayley.

Foley remarked: "It would have been an error to place a convert from the Episcopal ministry in the first see of the country, and a catastrophe to have placed some other people in the same" (72-J-7, Foley to Gibbons, Chicago, August 16, 1872). Bayley, of course, was a convert to Catholicism. On Bayley, cf. the definite biography of Sister M. Hildegarde Yeager, C.S.C., *The Life of James Roosevelt Bayley, First Bishop of Newark and Eighth Archbishop of Baltimore, 1814–1877* (Washington, 1947).

no way elated over his promotion. If he did have to go to Baltimore, "one of the consolations it will bring with it," he wrote, "will be that I will be nearer to you, and that we will often see one another, take counsel together. I count upon you as my right hand man."[132]

Congratulations began to reach Gibbons from his friends as the news of his appointment spread through the country. Thomas Foley told him he was happy to testify to his profound sense of joy at his removal from Adramyttum to Richmond. "The journey," said Foley, "has no doubt been very fatiguing on account of the immense distance between the two sees."[133] The Bishop of Wilmington got the news in Rome. He said he had written the Holy See from Bremen in favor of Gibbons as the only suitable appointment. He told his friend that Bishop Lynch of Charleston would have gotten Baltimore instead of Bayley, "had he not had himself embroiled with the U.S. Gov. This is the only reason why he was not put there." He went on to describe how critical conditions were in Rome for the Church with the anti-clericalism of the Italian government making life uncomfortable for churchmen. "We go out none at all except in a carriage, and then are insulted." Becker had become aware of the strange position of Miss Ella Edes, a convert newspaperwoman, who was acting as a correspondent for the New York *Herald* and the *Freeman's Journal* from the Eternal City. He said, "The female writer (from Rome) in the 'Freeman's Journal' seems to have been appointed a sort of minutante or minatrice. She has tried to interview yrs truly but without success as yet. . . ."[134] James Gibbons himself was destined to have some annoying experiences at the hands of this woman in the years ahead.

As late as the first week of September Bayley confided that he was still hesitating about Baltimore and did not know what to do. "I would go to Rome immediately," he wrote, "if I thought that I would be successful, but Archbishop McCloskey

---

[132] 72-J-8, Bayley to Gibbons, Newark, August 18, 1872.

[133] 72-J-7, Foley to Gibbons, Chicago, August 16, 1872.

[134] 72-J-9, Becker to Gibbons, Rome, August 20, 1872. Lynch's trouble with the government referred to by Becker arose from his acting as an unofficial agent for the Confederacy during the Civil War. Cf. Leo F. Stock, "Catholic Participation in the Diplomacy of the Southern Confederacy," *Catholic Historical Review*, XVI (April, 1930), 1-18.

tells me it would do no good." Bayley doubted if he could preside at Gibbons' installation in Richmond but he made it known that he would make an effort to do so. Before he was even out of Newark the archbishop-elect hinted at what soon became a cherished plan for his successor in Baltimore when he told Gibbons, "When I can find time, I wish to write you a confidential letter in regard to Baltimore, in order to get your advice — but if I have to go there, there may be some opportunity of seeing you before I do so."[135] Three weeks later Bayley felt safe in telling Bishop Gibbons that he would install him in Richmond. As for the sermon on the occasion, he favored Gibbons himself as the preacher but that detail they could settle between them later. "I would offer to pontificate on the occasion," he said, "but I am such a poor singer, that it would not give much eclat to the ceremony."[136]

Meanwhile Gibbons made his preparations for leaving North Carolina. On September 5, a week after receiving the bulls, he wrote to Pius IX and Cardinal Barnabò accepting the appointment as Bishop of Richmond.[137] On October 6 he preached his farewell sermon in St. Thomas Church wherein he reviewed the history of the Church in North Carolina and in Wilmington, paying tribute to Judge William Gaston, Father Thomas Murphy, founder of the Wilmington parish, Dr. James A. Corcoran, and others. He remarked that he believed he could conscientiously say he had devoted all his poor energies to the advancement of Catholicism in the North Carolina missions. He would not detain them with an account of the anxious days and nights he had spent in thinking how he could improve the Church in the vicariate, but whether at home or abroad, he said, "my heart was in N.C. & in Wilmington." About $30,000 had been spent in Wilmington alone since he came, on the church, sisters' residence, and school, and he left it with a debt of "about $7,000 which Providence will enable us to meet in due time." Whereas thirty-one years before there had been only seven Catholics in Wilmington there were now 400 and that was a notable increase. The bishop then paid his final tribute to the people themselves:

---

[135] 72-K-3, Bayley to Gibbons, Newark, September 6, 1872.
[136] 72-K-6, Bayley to Gibbons, Newark, September 27, 1872.
[137] Diary, September 5, 1872, p. 30.

You can bear me witness that I never indulged in flattery which would be unbecoming the House of God, nor shall I do so now. Yet I cannot forbear saying a few words of commendation. I would be doing violence to my own feelings, if now on the eve of leaving you, I did not bear testimony to yr. unfeigned piety which always edified me; to your spirit of obedience which consoled me, & to your unbounded liberality which encouraged me in my difficulties. In future times, the best tribute of praise I can pay to other congregations, is to tell them they are as pious, as docile & as generous as the people of Wilmington.[138]

In the interval since Gibbons' arrival in 1868 the number of priests in the vicariate had increased to eight, there were two parochial schools, a number of new churches and mission stations, and the total Catholics in North Carolina, 1,400, was double the number reported for the state four years before.[139] Speaking of Gibbons' departure from North Carolina, one of the missionary priests wrote some years later, "The transfer of Bishop Gibbons was universally regretted." O'Connell felt that it was especially the bishop's ability to speak and to write attractively, as well as his personal amiability and unaffected manners that had won him friends and admirers. He remarked that the amount of labor which Gibbons was capable of accomplishing seemed incredible; his travels over the state employed all modes of conveyance, "new and obsolete," and his visitation tours brought an acquaintance with his people so that, according to this writer, "He knew all the adult Catholics in North Carolina personally and called them by name." Gibbons' method of apologetics for the Church likewise drew admiration, for he could always refute error, "without wounding charity or interrupting the amenities of social intercourse."[140]

While Bishop Gibbons continued as the administrator of the Vicariate of North Carolina when he was promoted to the See of Richmond, his permanent residence would now be in Virginia's capital and only for brief periods during the next five years would he be in North Carolina on the business of the Church.

---

[138] 72-L-4, sermon preached by Gibbons on his farewell to North Carolina, October 6, 1872.

[139] *Sadlier's Catholic Directory . . . 1872* (New York, 1872), p. 327.

[140] J[eremiah] J. O'Connell, O.S.B., *Catholicity in the Carolinas and Georgia* (New York, 1879), pp. 397–398.

He told his Wilmington Catholics when he preached his farewell sermon, however, that he would always take a lively interest in their happiness. "Like an absent father who reads with nervous hands the letters of his devoted children far away, I will watch you my spiritual children, for such you still remain."[141] He never lost his high regard for these North Carolinians, and in after years he stated that he found the audiences which he had addressed in that state more receptive to the teachings of the Church than he had those in Virginia.[142]

At thirty-eight years of age, then, with four years of experience as a bishop James Gibbons set out from Wilmington for Richmond in the middle of October, 1872, where the Catholics of the Old Dominion were prepared to welcome in his person the fourth bishop of their episcopal see.

---

[141] 72-L-4, sermon of Gibbons at Wilmington, October 6, 1872.

[142] Interview of the writer with Louis O'Donovan, July 9, 1945. Monsignor O'Donovan served Cardinal Gibbons as secretary from 1909 to 1919. In the summer of 1950 an historical marker was erected at Third and Dock Streets in Wilmington, just a half block west of St. Thomas Church, to commemorate Gibbons' installation there in 1868 (*North Carolina Catholic,* July 28, 1950).

CHAPTER IV

Bishop of Richmond

THE installation of James Gibbons as fourth Bishop of Richmond took place in St. Peter's Cathedral on October 20, 1872. The prediction of the Richmond *Daily Dispatch* on the day before the ceremony that, "the cathedral will doubtless be thronged to its utmost capacity by an interested congregation,"[1] was more than fulfilled. In fact, so great a crowd desired to gain entrance to the cathedral that they lined the sidewalks for nearly a block before the doors were opened, and when they were given the signal for entering the building "there was a rush so great that the utmost efforts of a squad of police . . . were necessary to prevent accidents."[2] James Roosevelt Bayley, eighth Archbishop of Baltimore, installed Gibbons and the pontifical Mass was celebrated by Thomas A. Becker, Bishop of Wilmington. There were about thirty-five priests present for the occasion, including practically all of the clergy of the Diocese of Richmond, with a number from Baltimore, Philadelphia, and North Carolina. During the Mass Archbishop Bayley preached a brief sermon, but at the end of the ceremony the principal address was given by Bishop Gibbons himself. He paid tribute to his three predecessors in the See of Richmond and to the priests of the diocese, but a major portion of the sermon was directed to the laity. Gibbons had words of special commendation for the faithful, and he linked their loyalty to the Church with their loyalty to the nation when he said:

> And we have unbounded confidence in your enlightened obedience, beloved children of the laity. It has been tauntingly said by the enemies of the Church that the submission of the Catholic laity

---

[1] October 19, 1872.

[2] *Ibid.*, October 22, 1872.

Old St. Peter's Cathedral and bishop's residence, Richmond, Virginia, in 1876, the center of Gibbons' labors from October, 1872, to October, 1877.

to their pastors was forced and servile, and that their loyalty to their Church would melt away amid the free air of America. The Catholics of the United States have triumphantly repelled, by their acts, the insulting insinuation. As there are none more loyal than they to their country, so there are none more devoted to their Church.[3]

The installation passed off very happily and the Richmond *Daily Enquirer* could truly say that it "was one of the most splendid religious ceremonials ever witnessed here."[4]

The Diocese of Richmond comprised eight counties in the State of West Virginia together with all of the State of Virginia except twenty counties which were under the jurisdiction of the Dioceses of Wilmington and Wheeling. The combined area which now became the spiritual responsibility of Bishop Gibbons covered 34,808 square miles. It was not a new ecclesiastical jurisdiction as had been the case with North Carolina when he went there in 1868. The Diocese of Richmond had been established originally by the Holy See on July 11, 1820, and although there was a period of nearly twenty years during which the see had been administered by the Archbishop of Baltimore, it had had a resident bishop for over thirty years preceding the advent of James Gibbons. In the year of Gibbons' arrival in Richmond the diocese had fifteen churches, an equal number of chapels and stations, five schools for girls with about 800 students, eight schools for boys that served 600 students, one hospital, two orphan asylums caring for 119 orphans, and a total estimated Catholic population of around 17,000. To care for the spiritual needs of the people and institutions over Virginia and the counties of West Virginia in the diocese there were at the time seventeen priests with nine students preparing for the ministry in various seminaries.[5]

While the situation of the Catholic Church in Virginia was, indeed, an improvement over that which Gibbons had found in North Carolina four years before, the overwhelmingly non-Catholic character of the population made it missionary territory insofar as Catholicism was concerned. In 1870 the total popula-

---

[3] *Catholic Mirror,* October 26, 1872.

[4] October 22, 1872.

[5] *Sadlier's Catholic Directory, Almanac and Ordo for the Year of Our Lord 1872* (New York, 1872), pp. 335–337.

tion of Virginia was 1,225,163 which meant that only a fraction over one in seventy-two were Catholics. Moreover, like North Carolina the population was largely rural and scattered with more than eighty-eight per cent of the inhabitants living in rural areas. There was only one fairly large city in Virginia at this time, namely, Richmond which had a population of 51,038, while Norfolk's 19,229 and Alexandria's 13,570 placed them as the only two other communities in the state with a population of over 10,000.[6] Richmond's population was almost equally divided at the time between the two races with 27,928 whites and 23,110 Negroes. But the Virginia capital was showing signs of development as an industrial center with iron works, flour mills, and a large cotton mill doing a fairly thriving business by the time Gibbons reached the city and there was every indication of future growth. Moreover, railroad communication was opened between Richmond and the West in February, 1873, and this contributed to the city's prosperity.[7]

Yet the Civil War had ended only seven years before and few states of the Confederacy had suffered more from the marauding armies than the Old Dominion. Vast stretches of the battle area of eastern Virginia had been devastated and toward the west the Shenandoah Valley had been laid waste by military order. While many towns suffered severe damage at the hands of the troops, the countryside was even more systematically destroyed.[8] Recovery was relatively rapid in some areas and yet it took years for the disruption to wear off and a fully normal life to return. Virginia had been readmitted to the Union in January, 1870, and had fortunately escaped the worst features of carpetbag rule which afflicted some of her neighbors. Nevertheless, the presence of heavy debts plagued the state and the Republican Party rule was strong enough to prevent real reform until the election of November, 1873, when General James L. Kemper, a Conservative, defeated the Radical candidate for governor, Robert W. Hughes. The Conservatives gained further ground in succeeding years and by 1877, the

---

[6] *Sixteenth Census of the United States: 1940. Population* (Washington, 1942), I, 1099–1100.

[7] W. Asbury Christian, *Richmond. Her Past and Present* (Richmond, 1912), p. 336.

[8] Matthew Page Andrews, *Virginia. The Old Dominion* (New York, 1937), p. 527.

year Gibbons left Virginia, there were only nine Republicans and one Negro left in the Virginia legislature.[9] The state's first formal effort to establish a public school system came only with the passage of the bill of July, 1870, but the system did not get under way seriously much before 1872, and all during Gibbons' residence in Virginia the facilities for public instruction left much to be desired.[10]

Shortly after coming to Richmond, Bishop Gibbons was faced with the problem of providing teachers for a school for boys in the cathedral parish. Up to this time the practice of having religious sisterhoods teach boys had not been very widespread through the American Church. This would account for the separate schools for boys and girls mentioned above in connection with the Diocese of Richmond. Gibbons did not feel he could obtain the Christian Brothers to teach the boys so he decided to ask Archbishop Purcell of Cincinnati, who had sisters in some of his parochial schools for boys, if they had proved successful. He said, "I write to the oldest & consequently the most experienced Prelate in the U. States, that he might give the benefit of his advice to the Benjamin of the Episcopate family, on a certain point." The bishop then outlined his problem, said he believed sisters would do as well as brothers as teachers for boys, and ended by confessing, "But I distrust my own unripe judgment in this matter."[11] This request made of Purcell provides a good illustration of how strongly inclined Gibbons was to turn to others for advice on serious problems. He showed this characteristic all through life, but it was especially marked in his younger years.

The new year of 1873 brought a letter from the Paris headquarters of the Society for the Propagation of the Faith with a donation of 2,800 francs or about $150 for the Diocese of Richmond, the first benefaction of a series while Gibbons was bishop there which would ultimately total over 34,000 francs or $1,700 for his years in the diocese.[12] Needless to say, these sums were speedily put to work in advancing the work of the

---

[9] Richard L. Morton, *Virginia Since 1861* (Chicago, 1924), pp. 165–177.
[10] *Ibid.*, p. 244.
[11] AUND, Cincinnati Papers, Gibbons to Purcell, Richmond, November 30, 1872.
[12] 72-N-1, President de l'oeuvre de la propagation de la foi to Gibbons, Paris, January 4, 1873.

missions throughout the state. It was not easy to find the money to help support priests on the mission and to pay for the expenses of students who had become candidates for the diocesan priesthood. While the number of priests available was not great, at the time they were apparently all that Gibbons felt he could support, for he asked the rector of All Hallows College in Ireland to cancel any adoption of students for Richmond since, as he said, "I am now, and will be for some time, amply supplied with priests."[13]

However, he was not so plentifully supplied that he did not object to the loss of one of the best men in the diocese when Father Francis Janssens was proposed for the rectorship of the American College in Louvain. Bishop Becker had advanced Janssens' name, and he had added, "I suppose Bp. Gibbons may object; but 'in conflictu praeceptorum praevalet fortius'; his needs are as nothing compared with the good you can accomplish yonder."[14] Gibbons did object and the intervention of Archbishop Bayley at Rome helped to save Janssens for the Diocese of Richmond since, as the archbishop said, a good rector could be found in Belgium but "it would be very difficult for Bishop Gibbons to replace you."[15] If there were priests to spare Father Lawrence O'Connell, Gibbons' vicar-general for North Carolina, said he needed one; he had written the bishop that he had heard of two new priests and he would like to have one of them to help him on the missions near Charlotte. "I love to get a young zealous, ardent & working priest," he said.[16]

One of the most interesting candidates for the priesthood then preparing for Richmond was John B. Tabb, who later attained considerable fame as a poet and as a close friend of Sidney Lanier. Tabb was a convert from the Protestant Episcopal Church who had been baptized by Gibbons in September, 1872, at the age of twenty-seven. When he decided to study for the priesthood the bishop sent him to St. Charles College and at the end of the first school year he wrote for

---

[13] 72-O-5, Gibbons to W[illiam] Fortune, Richmond, June 21, 1873, copy.

[14] AANO, Becker to Janssens, Wilmington, Delaware, January 9, 1873.

[15] *Ibid.*, Bayley to Janssens, Baltimore, July 5, 1873.

[16] 72-O-15, O'Connell to Gibbons, Charlotte, October 26, 1873. O'Connell told Gibbons that he could guarantee $200 on the Concord mission for another priest if he could get him, and since the board cost only $6 or $7 a month in that county he believed a priest could "live comfortably there on $100.00 a year."

instructions as to how he was to spend his summer holiday, adding that he wished to return to the college in the fall for at least twelve months more. He said a recent letter from Alfred A. Curtis, himself a convert, had expressed the wish that Gibbons would promptly send him on to St. Mary's Seminary but, he added, "I prefer to 'make haste slowly' in so serious a matter."[17] It was a case where both the student and the professors were agreed, for Father Stanislaus Ferté wrote Tabb's bishop just at this time that Father Menu, his Latin professor, "is of opinion that he truly needs another year; whilst his disciplinary training would also be materially benefited by another year's stay at the College."[18] William P. Price was at St. Charles at this time, studying for the Vicariate of North Carolina. He, too, wrote of plans for his summer to Bishop Gibbons and he said he could not close without saying something about Tabb. He wrote:

> I do not believe I have met a funnier man. In some respects, he is like a child. That is, he is so innocent. When we wish to have a good laugh, and that is pretty often, as you know from experience that college boys like to have a good laugh, we get Mr. Tabb in a crowd, and start him off on Jokes. I often laugh at him so much I am exhausted. Indeed you will have a good priest when he is ordained. He puts his soul and body into everything he does.[19]

There is a curious note in the correspondence of the early years of Gibbons' episcopacy from a number of students studying under his auspices. For example, young Price in the letter cited above expressed his wonderment at a message sent by Gibbons to his students at St. Charles College through Ferté, the president. He wrote, "I have been conjecturing, at least trying, to find out the meaning. If I have not met your expectations let me [know], Dear Bishop, and I will try to do better hereafter." A year or two before this Patrick Moore, a student for North Carolina enrolled at St. Charles, told Gibbons that he had received his recent letter, "and am very much grieved that mine of the 17th inst. has caused you so much displeasure." Moore expressed his regret for the previous letter that had

---

[17] 72-N-14, Tabb to Gibbons, Ellicott City, May 20, 1873.

[18] ADR, Ferté to Gibbons, St. Charles College, May 21, 1873.

[19] *Ibid.*, Price to Gibbons, Ellicott City, May 22, 1873.

given offense.[20] Even the favorite, Denis O'Connell, apparently did not escape, for he wrote from the American College in Rome in early 1875 offering profuse apologies after learning that Gibbons had sent a message through another that O'Connell had been guilty, as he expressed it, "of treating you with disrespect."[21] Since it proved impossible to find the supposedly offending letters it is difficult for the historian to determine just what was the true situation in regard to Gibbons and his students. But that he demanded in his dealings with them in these early years a rather exacting standard of conduct and, perhaps, showed a hypersensitive reaction to their manner of acting and dealing with him in correspondence there seems to be no doubt. Whatever the root of the difficulty might have been it was a peculiar phenomenon in the earlier years of Bishop Gibbons which seemed to disappear almost entirely in his later life.

A few weeks after the arrival of James Gibbons in Richmond there was organized in the cathedral parish a Catholic temperance society with Father Janssens as president and Mr. James Sherry as vice-president.[22] The charter members numbered fifty and their activities received the approval and co-operation of the bishop who gave his hearty blessing to the temperance movement now and all through his life, although at no time was he a teetotaler. In the fall of 1873 the cathedral school for boys at Ninth and Marshall Streets was dedicated. With this accomplished through an expenditure of $37,000 facilities were provided for the 187 boys who entered a few days after the opening, and the see city of the diocese now had a school for Catholic boys which met its needs.[23] A few weeks after the dedication of St. Peter's School, the bishop was visited by the assistant mother of the Little Sisters of the Poor who came to inspect a building on Brooke Avenue which Gibbons had proposed as a home for the aged poor of his diocese.[24] This became a favorite project of the bishop's and through the generosity of William Shakespeare Caldwell, a wealthy layman of New

---

[20] 72-E-4, Moore to Gibbons, Norwalk, Connecticut, July 17, 1871.
[21] 72-T-2, O'Connell to Gibbons, Rome, January 27, 1875.
[22] Diary, December 1, 1872, p. 36.
[23] *Ibid.,* September 28, 1873, p. 47.
[24] *Ibid.,* October 14, 1873, p. 48.

York, he was later able to make his dream a reality. Caldwell had begun his benefactions to the Diocese of Richmond when his Christmas letter of 1873 enclosed a check for $350 to be distributed among the boys' school, the orphanage, and the St. Vincent de Paul Society.[25] Every financial aid was welcome to the Bishop of Richmond, for his expenses were high and he had just received word that the cost of sending a student, not on a burse, to the American College in Rome would be $350 in currency.[26]

The affection which Gibbons had for Baltimore and all that it represented must have caused him some uneasiness of mind as he began to hear rumors that they were not taking very well to their new archbishop. Bishop Thomas Foley in Chicago kept in close touch with Baltimore through his family, and in one of his letters to Gibbons he said, "I am very much afraid things are going in a poor way at home. It is said his Grace is to spend the winter in Florida. If Dr. Tyndall, the atheist, were to apply his prayer-gauge to the appointment of Bishops, he would find sometimes the Holy Spirit had but an infinitesmal part in the choice."[27] Foley's opinion of Archbishop Bayley was shared by his priest-brother, John, who was a pastor in Baltimore. Six months after Thomas' letter the brother wrote from Baltimore to Gibbons to describe the serious fire and the grave danger in which the cathedral was placed by the conflagration. He said he met Father John Dougherty, chancellor of the archdiocese at the time, on the street after the fire, who told him that a number of dispatches had come in from friends of the cathedral, even distant bishops, "but not even a single word from our own venerable Metropolitan. Indeed, my dear Bishop, you can form no idea of ecclesiastical affairs here."[28] Archbishop Bayley had not wanted to come to Baltimore in the first place, and although he performed his duties in a conscientous way insofar as his enfeebled health permitted, his frank nature let it be known that he was not altogether happy there, a fact which sensitive Baltimoreans felt keenly.

A factor that played an important part in the absences of

25 72-P-9, Caldwell to Gibbons, New York, December 23, 1873.
26 72-P-6, John J. Williams to Gibbons, Boston, December 7, 1873.
27 72-N-2, Foley to Gibbons, Chicago, January 6, 1873.
28 72-O-10, Foley to Gibbons, Baltimore, July 28, 1873.

Bayley from Baltimore and his seeming lack of interest there was his impaired health. For most of the five years he was Archbishop of Baltimore he suffered from poor health and the last year or two it was grave enough to hinder seriously his administrative work. Gibbons must have intimated to Bayley that he had heard he was going to Florida for the winter, for the archbishop wrote to assure him he was only joking with Bishop Vérot and that he had no more idea of going there, as he said, "than I have of going to the celestial empire — tho' I would like to go there, if it was the *real* celestial empire." He confided to the Bishop of Richmond, "It seems to be getting worse instead of better here — so many letters — so many matters of business that I can hardly find time to say my prayers. . . ." He likewise remarked that he did not like the new life of Archbishop Spalding by his nephew. It was not a lifelike portrait, the book was too philosophical and sententious, and the style was poor, giving Bayley a feeling that when reading it he was "riding over a 'corduroy' road."[29] For one who loved the Church of Baltimore as Gibbons did the consciousness of the archbishop's discontent there and the fact that the priests and people were aware of this was, of course, painful. In the years immediately ahead he would exert himself as best he could to overcome the difficult situation, but this favorite suffragan of the Archbishop of Baltimore could do little to make his native city congenial to Bayley.

The end of Gibbons' first year in Richmond witnessed a severe shock to the community as a consequence of the financial panic which had broken in New York in September. The last weeks in September found the banks of Richmond closing with the people rushing madly to try to save their money. The inevitable paralyzing effects on business followed with a number of factories shutting down and others cutting their force so that a great number of people were thrown out of employment. The winter of 1873–1874 brought a depression which was almost as bad as that suffered immediately after the Civil War. Mayor Anthony M. Keiley solicited the aid of the ministers of the city in helping to organize relief drives to assist those who were in dire need and it was not until the late spring that conditions

---

[29] 72-P-2, Bayley to Gibbons, Baltimore, November 8, 1873.

began to right themselves. As one historian has expressed it, "The panic of 1873 was not soon to be forgotten in Richmond."[30] Bishop Gibbons and his clergy gave all the help they could to the sufferers during the emergency. In the last days of the year the bishop solemnly dedicated the Diocese of Richmond and the Vicariate of North Carolina to the Sacred Heart in an impressive ceremony at which Bishop William H. Gross of Savannah "preached an admirable discourse on the Sacred Heart. The church was packed with people, a large proportion being Protestants. . . ."[31]

During the course of his repeated missionary journeys through the States of Virginia and North Carolina Gibbons encountered some strange experiences. Early in 1874 he had gone south to Halifax, Virginia, on such a tour and there on a dark, rainy night he had preached to about twenty persons who assembled in the courthouse to hear him. About four-thirty the next morning he was awakened by the barking of dogs and soon discovered that there was a thief in his room. The bishop called out several times but received no answer; whereupon he jumped out of bed and the robber ran, leaving behind Gibbons' vest which contained about $150. He later wrote, "It was fortunate that I did not seize him, as he probably would have overpowered me."[32] From southern Virginia the bishop traveled on to New Bern, North Carolina, where he confirmed. It had been his intention to continue a tour of the North Carolina missions in the region of New Bern, but he was suddenly called home by the serious situation which had arisen in one of the Virginia parishes over the conduct of the pastor. Gibbons confided to his diary, "I think his mind is impaired & that he is hardly responsible for his acts."[33]

Trouble with unruly priests was, of course, one of the most disagreeable things with which the bishop had to contend. Fortunately, he did not have to suffer too much from this source, but one of the severest trials of his life as a bishop was just ahead of him with the pastor at Raleigh, North Carolina. Father J. V. McNamara had a serious difference with Bishop Gibbons when the former forbade his people to hold a ball on St. Patrick's

---

[30] Christian, *op. cit.*, pp. 341–342.
[31] Diary, December 28, 1873, p. 49.
[32] *Ibid.*, January 4, 1874, p. 51.
[33] *Ibid.*, January 12, 1874, p. 52.

night because he felt scandal would arise from it. The bishop disagreed with him and the incident brought on a crisis in their relations which had been strained since the priest first began to serve the Raleigh congregation in 1869. As Mark Gross explained to James A. McMaster, editor of the New York *Freeman's Journal,* to whom McNamara had appealed, the latter had been gravely disobedient for years, had given scandal, and abused his people through his ungovernable temper.[34] Finally Gibbons' patience was worn out and he suspended him. When the bishop went to Raleigh in the spring of 1874 to try to bring order to the parish, McNamara, as the bishop described it, "had the hardihood to sit in the sanctuary on last Sunday during late Mass, & attempted to speak after I had preached, but I forbade him. . . ." Gibbons went on to say that the priest "had been a source of almost constant affliction to me since I gave him Faculties in 1869. . . ."[35] McNamara appealed to the Holy See and the bishop was compelled to defend his own course of action by writing to Alessandro Cardinal Franchi, the Prefect of the Congregation of the Propaganda. Ultimately McNamara was replaced as pastor at Raleigh and the incident was liquidated, but it had been a sore trial of anxiety and embarrassment to the young bishop which he did not soon forget.

North Carolina gave rise to another disturbing incident just at this time which was of a different character. Thomas Atkinson, Protestant Episcopal Bishop of North Carolina, had in May, 1874, delivered an attack in Wilmington on the Catholic teaching on the sacrament of penance and the moral influence of the confessional. Gibbons regarded the attack as serious enough to warrant an answer. He, therefore, prepared a fairly elaborate reply to Bishop Atkinson and had it printed in the form of a brochure with the title of *The Sacrament of Penance and the Moral Influence of Sacramental Confession.* In it the Bishop of Richmond endeavored to answer the two main charges of Atkinson, namely, the alleged human origin and immoral tendency of confession, and the religious superiority of Protestant over Catholic countries. In regard to the first point Gibbons traced from Scrip-

---

[34] AUND, McMaster Papers, McNamara to McMaster, Raleigh, Easter, 1874; Gross to McMaster, Raleigh, April, 1874. McNamara had been installed as pastor by Gibbons on July 11, 1869, Diary, p. 13.
[35] Diary, April 10, 1874, p. 55.

ture the divine origin of the sacrament and outlined in some detail the spiritual and psychological advantages derived from a sincere confession of one's sins. The second part of the brochure sought through history to disprove Atkinson's contention in relation to such points as the relative number of murders, percentage of illegitimacy, etc., as between Protestant and Catholic nations.[36] The controversy stirred the curiosity of a number of people in North Carolina and the Episcopalian rector of St. Thomas Church in Windsor wrote for a copy of Gibbons' reply to Atkinson and added a further request that he tell him the second, third, and fourth bishops in the See of Rome after St. Peter. "I wish," he said, "to trace the Apostolic Succession to my own satisfaction."[37] Wootten told Gibbons in a second letter that it was his belief that St. Paul, and not St. Peter, was the first Bishop of Rome, although he confessed that "this is but an opinion & detracts nothing from the Succession. . . ." He closed his letter by saying he was greatly obliged to Bishop Gibbons for the response to his request, and he added, "I should be pleased to know you, & should an opportunity offer I will with your permission make myself known to you."[38]

James Gibbons was again in North Carolina in June, 1875, when he spent most of the month on a tour of the missions. It was on this trip that he was first made the offer of a large tract of 500 acres of good land west of Charlotte by Father Jeremiah O'Connell. O'Connell had in mind that the farm would afford an opportunity for the bishop to engage the services of a group of religious who might, in the main, live off its produce and at the same time take care of the Catholics in the surrounding settlements. Gibbons acted promptly and first tried to secure the Redemptorists, but in that effort he failed. He was willing to turn over the farm, valued by O'Connell at $65,000 "including the gold mine existing in it,"[39] to any religious order who would take it on the terms of caring for the missions in the region. After about six months of effort and negotiation the bishop finally succeeded when Abbot Boniface Wimmer, O.S.B., of St.

---

[36] 72-R-1, copy of Gibbons' pamphlet published at Richmond in 1874.
[37] ADR, Edward Wootten to Gibbons, Windsor, North Carolina, September 23, 1874.
[38] *Ibid.*, Wootten to Gibbons, Windsor, September 29, 1874.
[39] Diary, June 26, 1875, p. 72.

Vincent's Abbey, Latrobe, Pennsylvania, agreed to send a colony of Benedictine monks to cultivate the farm in Gaston County. Herman Wolfe, O.S.B., a former Lutheran minister, was appointed the first prior, and on March 25, 1876, Gibbons transferred the deed to the Benedictines. A private agreement was entered into between Bishop Gibbons and Abbot Wimmer "to surrender the property to the Bishop of N. Carolina," as it read, "should it be ever diverted from its legitimate purposes, viz. the establishment of an agricultural farm & a Catholic college. The Fathers are also bound to evangelize the neighboring county, & do the work of missionary priests."[40] The conclusion of this transaction cheered Gibbons a great deal as he foresaw immense good to come from a community of monks in western North Carolina. Writing of this Benedictine foundation some years later, he gave first credit for it to Abbot Wimmer. Gibbons said of it, "I regarded this Abbey with unbounded satisfaction. . . . My intimate knowledge of the poverty of the past made me keenly relish the richness of this spiritual Foundation. In my judgment it is most intimately related to the best interests of Catholicity in the Southland."[41]

This Benedictine foundation at Belmont, North Carolina, served to compensate Bishop Gibbons for some of the disappointments he had to undergo in relation to the Church in that state while he continued as vicar apostolic. In response to an inquiry of John O'Kane Murray, the author of a popular history of the American Church, concerning the number of converts to Catholicism made during his episcopacy, Gibbons stated that about thirty-five per cent of those he had confirmed in North Carolina had been converts while the figure for the State of Virginia was fourteen per cent of those confirmed. In both states, he maintained, the more frequent conversions came from the enlightened classes, "especially when they have met with adversities," and it was the Protestant Episcopal Church which furnished the largest number of converts to Catholicism of all the Protestant

---

[40] *Ibid.*, March 25, 1876, p. 79.

[41] "Reminiscences of North Carolina," *United States Catholic Historical Magazine*, III (1889–1890), 351. Abbot Vincent Taylor, O.S.B., of Belmont Abbey in a letter of December 2, 1947, to Anselm Biggs, O.S.B., stated that the archives of the abbey contained no letters or documents from Gibbons.

denominations.[42] One of the last recorded visits to North Carolina which Gibbons made before his promotion to Baltimore was in the late winter of 1876. He traveled to Greensboro by boat on the Tar River and preached that night in the Methodist church. As he wrote, "The Methodist bell summoned the people to church, & some Protestant ladies sang & played on the occasion. The attendance was large."[43] A few weeks later he reached Raleigh on Easter Tuesday where he confirmed and preached, for as he told Archbishop Bayley, "preaching is almost the alpha & omega of Episcopal life in N. Carolina."[44] It was now over seven years since Gibbons had assumed charge of the Church in North Carolina and while its progress still left much to be desired it could truthfully be said that his repeated visitation tours and his sermons and ministrations had done much to give spirit and courage to the few priests and scattered laity who were spread over the vast stretches of the Old North State.

One of the most appealing forms of charity which could recommend itself to any bishop is the care of the aged poor. The Bishop of Richmond was conscious of his responsibility for these unfortunate ones, but it was only through the generosity of William Shakespeare Caldwell that he was enabled to do anything practical about it. In the early spring of 1874 Caldwell wrote Gibbons to say that he was deeding the house and furniture which he owned at the corner of Ninth and Marshall Streets in Richmond to the bishop for the purpose of an old people's home under the care of the Little Sisters of the Poor. He added that he had provided in his will for an endowment of $20,000 to help support the home, and he urged Gibbons to seek incorporation of it by the Virginia legislature and to provide for the legal security of the property through the bishop's own will.[45] Gibbons acted promptly and a bill for the incorporation of the home for Richmond's aged Catholic poor was unanimously passed by the legislature and signed by the governor.[46] Mr. Caldwell, unfortunately, did not live to see the fulfillment of his project. Bishop Gibbons was warned on May 23 by a letter

[42] AUND, New York Papers, Gibbons to Murray, Richmond, January 28, 1876.
[43] Diary, February 16, 1876, p. 78.
[44] 40-G-3, Gibbons to Bayley, Richmond, March 23, 1876.
[45] 72-Q-5, Caldwell to Gibbons, New York, March 29, 1874.
[46] Diary, April 21, 1874, p. 55.

from Caldwell's daughter that his condition was critical, and as a matter of fact he died that day.[47] It took some time for the preparations to be made to receive the sisters but on October 13 six Little Sisters of the Poor headed by Sister Virginia arrived in Richmond where they took possession of their home. Henceforth worthy cases of the poor and infirm aged of the diocese would receive the care and attention they deserved.

While Bishop Gibbons busied himself with this and other projects for the improvement of his diocese he kept in frequent touch with his metropolitan in Baltimore, and it was evident from their correspondence that the ties of friendship between Gibbons and Bayley were growing closer as time passed. In early March, 1874, he told the archbishop that the Bishop of Wheeling, Richard V. Whelan, had recently spent a week with him in Richmond during which the latter's health seemed to improve. Alluding to Whelan's previous service as Bishop of Richmond, Gibbons said, "I was deeply moved when I saw him yesterday preaching in the church of which he was appointed Bishop 33 years ago. It was the first time he saw our congregation since 1848."[48] Some days later he expressed his disappointment on learning that Archbishop Bayley was not coming to Richmond for a visit. "I saw a bright spot looming up towards the Ides of March, & I looked & behold it was not."[49] When the trouble with Father McNamara in Raleigh reached a crisis Gibbons related the whole story to Bayley, and he confessed that the incident of the priest threatening to make a speech at Mass on Sunday, "was the most trying moment of my life."[50]

On July 7 Bishop Whelan of Wheeling died and Bayley wrote a week later to express his regret to Gibbons that he was not able to attend the funeral. The death at Wheeling necessitated, of

---

[47] 72-Q-9, Minnie Caldwell to Gibbons, New York, May 23, 1874; Diary, May 23, 1874, p. 60.

[48] 41-S-2, Gibbons to Bayley, Richmond, March 2, 1874.

[49] 41-S-3, Gibbons to Bayley, Richmond, March 12, 1874

[50] 41-S-4, Gibbons to Bayley, Richmond, April 23, 1874. Three years later Cardinal McCloskey of New York made inquiry of Gibbons about McNamara. In reply Gibbons related the facts in the case and told the cardinal that McNamara had sent him a long telegram to the effect that he was appealing his case to Rome. Gibbons told McCloskey, "To forestall his action, I sent his Eminence Cardinal Franchi (through Dr. Chatard) a detailed account of the transaction, & that ended the matter" (AANY, Gibbons to McCloskey, Baltimore, December 18, 1877).

course, action on the part of the archbishop to fill the vacancy. Bayley consulted the Bishop of Richmond as to the best way of securing the votes of the suffragan bishops of the Province of Baltimore in this matter, and then he raised the question of his own succession in Baltimore.

> There is one point connected with this affair which it is necessary for you to know, and that is, that at the same time that I write to the Suffragans in regard to Wheeling I intend to ask their consent to my requesting the Holy See to name you Coadjutor of Baltimore cum jure successionis so that you will have to keep in mind, in choosing three names for Wheeling, the probability of having soon to name a successor to the Bishop of Richmond.[51]

From intimations previously given by Bayley it is fairly sure that this was not the first time that Gibbons learned what the Archbishop of Baltimore had in mind for him. The bishop was away from Richmond when the archbishop's letter arrived, but a week later he answered to give his recommendations for the vacant See of Wheeling. He listed the names of Matthew O'Keefe of Norfolk, John J. Kain of Harpers Ferry, and Frederick Wayrich, C.Ss.R., as his choice for the Wheeling *terna*. Then on the subject of the archbishop's letter which touched himself Gibbons said:

> I would rather be silent than speak about the coadjutorship. It has started various conflicting thoughts in my mind. I have a grounded fear that I would not satisfy Your Grace's expectations, & that I would not improve on closer acquaintance.
> One thing would reconcile me to the marriage, the reasonable prospect of your long life. I shall say no more but silently pray that God's will may be done. Things are now thank God, in such splendid order in this diocese, that I have little trouble in directing affairs.[52]

It would seem apparent from the bishop's reply to Bayley that he was not altogether unwilling to make the change suggested. But whatever might have been Gibbons' "conflicting

---

[51] 72-Q-13, Bayley to Gibbons, Madison, New Jersey, July 14, 1874.

[52] 41-S-5, Gibbons to Bayley, Richmond, July 22, 1874. Gibbons told Bayley that at Bishop Whelan's funeral, "The Patriarch from Cincinnati was there, & was very naturally selected as the speaker. He very kindly invited me to speak, but although primed & loaded, I would not go off. On the following Sunday I discharged my gun in Martinsburg, one of Bp. W's first missions."

thoughts" at the proposal that he should be promoted to the coadjutorship of Baltimore, they were soon set temporarily at rest. Bayley told him he had reflected on the matter and decided to defer it until Wheeling was filled and Philadelphia was made a metropolitan see. *"Then* it *must* come, for reasons which I will tell when I see you." In closing the archbishop urged the Bishop of Richmond to come to Baltimore later and spend a week with him, "& get yourself gradually accustomed to the peculiar atmosphere of Baltimore & the delightful odors of the basin, which is [*sic*] particularly fragrant and diffusive this summer."[53] Although the subject of the coadjutorship was thus postponed, it was not forgotten and through the next three years the steps taken by the archbishop made it a virtual certainty that James Gibbons' residence in Richmond would be terminated before very long.

Toward the end of 1874 the interest of the English-speaking world was enlivened on both sides of the Atlantic by the public controversy between Cardinal Manning and William Ewart Gladstone over the issue of papal infallibility. The American press gave the controversy considerable space and the New York *Herald* solicited the opinions of a number of American Catholic bishops for publication. A reporter of the *Herald* called on Gibbons in Richmond to ask his views. The bishop told him that while the Archbishop of Baltimore had given a full discussion to the question in his interview, he would be willing to express his opinion. He recalled that the Vatican Council had created no new doctrine, "but confirmed an old one." He likened the decree of papal infallibility to decisions of the Supreme Court when it decided constitutional questions. The decision of the justices embodied no new doctrine but rather a new form of words, since the judgment was based on the letter and spirit of the Constitution. So when the Catholic Church defined a new dogma of faith the definition was nothing more than a new form of expression given to an old doctrine, "because the decision must be drawn from the revealed word of God, and based upon the constant tradition of the Church." Gibbons stated he found it rather singular that Gladstone should be frightened by the tyranny of the Pope whereas he was completely silent on the

[53] 72-Q-14, Bayley to Gibbons, Madison, New Jersey, July 24, 1874.

tyranny being practiced just then by Bismarck against the Church in Germany. He said he attended all the sessions of the Vatican Council during which this question was debated and "not one of the Bishops resisted the definition on the ground that it would in the slightest degree alter the relations existing between the temporal and spiritual power." The New York *Herald* of November 29, 1874, carried the Gibbons interview, along with a sympathetic editorial note which closed with a reference to the bishop's surprise at Gladstone's silence regarding Bismarck's policies, "and this surprise," added the *Herald,* "most persons are obliged to share."

The opening of the new year brought a severe illness to Gibbons which was caused by a cold and a kidney infection. He was compelled to confine himself to the house for nearly a week, "an unusual imprisonment for me," as he told Archbishop Bayley, and the illness prompted him to run up to Baltimore to consult Dr. McSherry.[54] But the bishop overcame the difficulty and was able to resume his activities. The spring of 1875 brought a batch of new appointments from the Holy See to the American Church and among them was that of the pastor of St. Peter's Church, Harpers Ferry, West Virginia, John J. Kain, who was named Bishop of Wheeling. Kain dreaded the prospect and he wrote Gibbons to say he had a preaching engagement in Richmond on St. Patrick's Day and he hoped he would be in town, "so that I may be able," he said, "to consult with you, first of all."[55] James F. Wood had at the same time been accorded the honor of becoming the first Archbishop of Philadelphia, and Gibbons wondered if he would not expect his former brother-suffragans to be present for the conferring of the pallium. He told Bayley he did not know whether his engagements would permit the trip to Philadelphia, although, as he remarked, "I should like to do him every honor in my power."[56]

But even more important than the Philadelphia ceremony would be the conferring of the biretta on the first cardinal of the United States, John McCloskey of New York, which was scheduled for April 27. Once more Gibbons inquired of his friend Bayley if he thought bishops outside of the Province of

[54] 41-S-7, Gibbons to Bayley, Richmond, January 16, 1875.
[55] 72-T-3, Kain to Gibbons, Harpers Ferry, February 16, 1875.
[56] 41-S-8, Gibbons to Bayley, Richmond, March 2, 1875.

New York would be expected to attend. "If duty, or even courtesy requires it, I shall make it my business to be present. In that case I shall reach Baltimore on Tuesday morning, the 20th, & hope to be there in time to accompany Your Grace to New York."[57] The solicitude shown in these requests for the feelings of his fellow bishops on the occasions of their celebrations was one which Gibbons demonstrated all through his life. Whenever he could free himself from diocesan business he always made a point of being present at functions of the Church in various parts of the country. Only toward the end of his career when old age made traveling a more trying experience for him did he curtail this activity which seemed to give him relaxation and pleasure and, of course, an opportunity to show consideration for the churchman in whose honor the function was held.

In the spring of 1875 the bishop made a trip to Emmitsburg where he succeeded in winning the promise of Sister Euphemia Blekinsop, the superior, for a group of her sisters to teach in a school he hoped to open in the parish at Petersburg, Virginia. Eventually in January, 1876, the Daughters of Charity of St. Vincent de Paul were sent and the school was opened on February 1 of that year with ninety children, including thirty-five boys who, as Gibbons wrote, "at my request of Mother Euphemia, they are permitted to teach."[58] The bishop accompanied the sisters to Petersburg and on Sunday, January 30, in his sermon at the high Mass he formally introduced them to the parishioners.

Shortly before President Grant had caused a considerable stir by his message to Congress in the early days of December, 1875, when he had recommended a constitutional amendment forbidding the teaching of "sectarian" matters in any school supported wholly or in part by public funds, and the exclusion from school funds and taxes of any school which was conducted by a religious denomination. Grant likewise recommended a tax on church

[57] 41-S-9, Gibbons to Bayley, Richmond, April 12, 1875.
[58] Diary, April 11, 1875, p. 70; February 1, 1876, p. 77. On his visit to Emmitsburg in April, 1875, Gibbons noted: "My niece Mary Swarbrick is there at school." This was the future Mrs. Thomas J. Stanton with whom the writer had an interview in January, 1948, at New Orleans. The bishop also noted that he went on from Emmitsburg to Baltimore, where, he said, "I paid my respects to the Ablegate Mgr. Roncetti who was staying at the Archbishop's house." Cesare Roncetti had come to the United States to bring the red biretta for Cardinal McCloskey of New York who received it on April 27, 1875, at a ceremony which Gibbons had attended.

properties. Gibbons was again interviewed by a reporter from the New York *Herald.* He said that if the constitutional amendment proposed by Grant were carried out it "would reduce our American Republic to the condition of things existing in pagan Rome." The bishop further commented on the dangers of a more centralized government and the effects it would have on individual liberty and education. He championed the rights of the family and the states in matters of education against the federal government, and he expressed himself as believing that if education were handed over to the latter, "it will give the administration an overwhelming patronage, which would destroy all balance of power and reduce minorities to a mere cipher." Gibbons said he could not see how both religion and paganism could be excluded from the schools, "for if an education excludes all religion it is necessarily pagan, there being no medium between the two terms." He was equally vigorous in opposing Grant's suggestion concerning the taxing of church property, and to him such action would be putting a premium on infidelity and avarice while making "religion and philanthropy odious by imposing a penalty on those who maintain Christianity and support charitable houses." The bishop closed the interview by saying that he did not believe the American people would ever be found advocating "or even indorsing such novel legislation."[59]

Gibbons had made a second trip to Emmitsburg in September, 1875, in the interests of getting further sisters for parish schools in his diocese. While he was there, as he told Archbishop Bayley, Sister Euphemia, the superior, had shown him the archbishop's future mausoleum. "May it long remain empty of its guest," said Gibbons. He confessed to Bayley that he wished he could contemplate death with the complacency of the archbishop. "I declaim tolerably well on death in *general;* but when the question is narrowed down to *myself,* ah! there's the difficulty." He further told the Archbishop of Baltimore how happy he was at the recent election of John Lee Carroll as Governor of Maryland. "It appeared to me that his defeat would have deterred Catholics from presenting themselves as candidates, & would tempt politi-

---

[59] *Ibid.,* December 10, 1875, p. 76. The printed interview is inserted here in the diary and was written under a Richmond date line of December 10, 1875. The Grant proposals can be found in James D. Richardson's edition of *Messages and Papers of the Presidents* (New York, 1897), X, 4228–4289.

cal parties virtually to exclude them from aspiring to places of honor, as used to be the law in Great Britain. All honor to my native state." Gibbons said he had been urged to attend the dedication of the Cathedral of the Holy Name in Chicago, and he added, "as I had no vacation in the summer, I am inclined to go for a few days." The Jesuits had just concluded a mission at the cathedral and the bishop's reactions to their efforts revealed the high value which he always placed upon maintaining friendly relations with those outside the Church. He told Bayley, "They carried out my wishes to the letter, by avoiding controversy in their sermons. My little experience in this region, has convinced me that polemical discussions don't effect as much good as moral discussions interlarded with some points of doctrine."[60] With the same idea in mind Gibbons associated himself closely with the civic life of Richmond and when the unveiling of the statue of Stonewall Jackson took place on October 26, 1875, in Capitol Square he was on the speakers' stand with the general's widow and the other distinguished guests. Nearly 40,000 people turned out for the event and "it proved to be the greatest day of the kind since the unveiling of the Washington Monument."[61]

Early in the year 1876 Bishop Gibbons received a communication from Rome which disturbed him greatly. He was informed by the Prefect of the Congregation of the Propaganda that Bishop Kain of Wheeling had petitioned the Holy See for a redistribution of the territories of the Dioceses of Richmond and Wheeling so that the state lines might be observed. As the boundaries then stood, seventeen counties and a part of Craig County in Virginia were in the Diocese of Wheeling while eight counties of West Virginia were in the Diocese of Richmond. Kain's proposal was to make the diocesan lines identical with the state boundaries. While the proposed change would enlarge Gibbons' territory it would diminish the number of Catholics living in his diocese. He quickly informed Archbishop Bayley of Kain's move and he protested vigorously the loss of what he

---

[60] 41-S-10, Gibbons to Bayley, Richmond, November 5, 1875. In reporting the success of the mission one of the Jesuits stated there were over 2,400 confessions and 2,109 communions. Reflecting Gibbons' pleasure he said, "After my closing exhortation on Sunday evening, the Bishop arose and addressed the congregation in one continued strain of happiness." P.M. to "Rev. dear Father," November 23, 1875, *Woodstock Letters*, V (1876), 50–51.

[61] Christian, *op. cit.*, p. 349.

regarded as the "most populous Catholic territory," of the Diocese of Richmond. He outlined in detail his reasons: the present division was made by the Archbishop of Baltimore with the concurrence of his suffragan bishops; no regard was paid heretofore in the United States to state lines in mapping out dioceses; Martinsburg, the center of the Catholic population of the counties in question, was ninety-six miles nearer to Richmond than to Wheeling; the former Bishop of Wheeling had never, to Gibbons' knowledge, challenged the boundaries while Bishop Kain, "being scarcely warm in his seat," and only eight months in the see, had now questioned them to Rome. Gibbons said he already had responsibility for 92,000 square miles — an area the size of all Italy! He could not, therefore, assume charge of this further territory. He was writing to Rome to lodge his protest at Kain's action and he thought Bayley ought to know the facts since, as he remarked, "you are the proper arbiter in such cases, though I am sorry to trouble you, burdened as you are with your immediate charges."[62]

Bayley heartily agreed with the Bishop of Richmond and said he had no previous knowledge of the matter except a vague allusion to it some time before when Kain mentioned the strange division of the two dioceses. "Before he wrote to Rome," said Bayley, "he was bound in courtesy at least, to have conferred with you about the matter." Bayley asked for further information and he said he felt Gibbons' protest to the Holy See would prevent action at least until it had been fully examined into.[63] Some days later the Archbishop of Baltimore was in possession of a map sent for his examination and he wrote to say that he would suggest that Gibbons inform Cardinal Franchi and quote him [Bayley] as agreeing with the judgment of Gibbons. "It might seem disrespectful if I were to write directly, when my opinion has not been asked. . . ."[64] At length the Holy See refused to consider the proposed change of diocesan boundaries and Franchi so informed Bishop Gibbons.[65] Although the inci-

---

[62] 40-G-1, Gibbons to Bayley, Richmond, January 19, 1876, *Private.*

[63] ADR, Bayley to Gibbons, Baltimore, January 21, 1876.

[64] *Ibid.,* Bayley to Gibbons, Baltimore, January 31, 1876.

[65] 72-V-3, Franchi to Gibbons, Rome, March 2, 1876. Twelve years later when the See of Richmond was vacant and Gibbons had been for some time Archbishop of Baltimore he presided over a meeting of the bishops of the Province of Baltimore, of which all were present except Northrop of Charleston. At this

dent doubtless put something of a strain on Gibbons' relations with his episcopal neighbor, Kain himself did not lose hope and in the spring he wrote that he could not be present for a church function in Savannah and he all the more regretted it, "for I should like to renew the proposition which I once made to you, to petition the Holy See to transfer to Richmd. that part of Va. which is now in this diocese." Kain said he knew Gibbons was well aware of all the conditions involved but the next incumbent of the See of Richmond might not be so, and he explained that he was not referring, as he said, to Gibbons' "early demise, but to the probability of other changes to which none will give a heartier acquiescence than myself."[66] Whatever annoyance Gibbons experienced at the rather untactful way in which Kain had sought a change in their diocesan boundaries, it was not the cause of a break in their friendship. Gibbons had recommended Kain as one of the candidates for the See of Wheeling and when the latter was consecrated there on May 23, 1875, the Bishop of Richmond had acted as one of the co-consecrators and preached the sermon. In the years ahead the two men were even closer friends and when Gibbons became Archbishop of Baltimore he found no more prompt co-operator in all the business of the Church than he did in John J. Kain.

As time passed the health of Archbishop Bayley showed further deterioration and this prompted him to re-open the question of the coadjutorship for Bishop Gibbons. Bayley wrote to Cardinal McCloskey in New York early in 1876 and he told the cardinal that his doctor said he must either resign the See of Baltimore or get a coadjutor. He said he believed that it would be better to ask Rome for a coadjutor, but it did not seem necessary to him that three names should be submitted to the Holy See. "Bp. Gibbons of Richmond would be 'the right man in the right place.' " Of Gibbons the archbishop remarked, "He is clear headed — sensible — a good administrator — is very popular in Baltimore, and would be most acceptable to Clergy & people." Bayley informed McCloskey that he would appreciate

---

meeting the prelates agreed to ask the Holy See to regulate the boundaries of the Dioceses of Richmond and Wheeling in accordance with the state lines of Virginia and West Virginia (Diary, July 1, 1888, p. 225). However, no change was made by Rome.

[66] 72-V-8, Kain to Gibbons, Wheeling, April 7, 1876.

it if the latter would second his efforts in Rome by writing to the Prefect of Propaganda "that it is all right."[67] Some weeks later Bayley similarly solicited the help of Archbishop Purcell of Cincinnati. He outlined the case for Purcell much as he had done for McCloskey, and he then added:

> I would fight on usque ad finem, but it would do no good, and Religion would suffer. The Doctors say that the trouble comes from gouty secretion — and of course will grow no better. Since I began this letter, I had to stop and do nothing for over an hour, not being able to see enough to go on with it. It is now thirty years since I became Secretary to Bishop Hughes, and I have worked myself out. It is not every one who has your power of endurance.[68]

That Bayley was in earnest there was no doubt, for he dispatched letters to Archbishops Kenrick, Wood, and Williams with the same request, and on April 3 he addressed letters to all his suffragan bishops and to Cardinal Franchi on the same subject.[69] Meanwhile James Gibbons maintained silence and allowed the matter to be advanced by Bayley before both the Holy See and the American hierarchy.

With the very large number of Negroes in both Virginia and North Carolina the task of their evangelization presented itself as a serious one to the bishop and his few priests in the two states. Hampered as he was by lack of men and money, Gibbons had been able to do hardly more than to scratch the surface by way of making a start in this important work. For that reason the chance of enlisting the aid of the Mill Hill Fathers of England, a group especially dedicated to missionary work among the Negroes, presented a strong attraction to the Bishop of Richmond. Gibbons had known of their work in Baltimore where late in the year 1871 four of these men had been established by Herbert Vaughan, their superior, with the hearty approval and assistance of Archbishop Spalding. When Vaughan had completed an extensive tour of the United States in 1872 in behalf of this work he noted in his diary shortly before sailing that Gibbons, who had recently been in Baltimore, told him that his men were "highly esteemed by the Vicar-General and the clergy."[70] Two

---

[67] AANY, Bayley to McCloskey, Baltimore, January 22, 1876.

[68] AUND, Cincinnati Papers, Bayley to Purcell, Baltimore, March 16, 1876.

[69] 43-N-1, Archbishop Bayley's Diary, March 24, 1876; April 3, 1876.

[70] J. G. Snead-Cox, *The Life of Cardinal Vaughan* (London, 1910), I, 179–180.

years later Vaughan and Canon Peter Benoit brought out a new group of missionaries to the United States and on this occasion the question of Mill Hill Fathers for the Diocese of Richmond was discussed with Gibbons. At that time the bishop had inquired also about the possibilities of getting the Mill Hill Sisters to come to Richmond.

Many months later, after Benoit had returned to London, he wrote Gibbons to say that he had discussed the matter with the sisters' superior and they had agreed that, "As their community is young & composed almost exclusively of converts we both think that it is in all respects better not as yet to undertake such a distant & for them unknown work." However, since Gibbons had told him on his visit to Richmond that after a time he did want to do something for the very large number of Negroes he had in his episcopal city, Benoit now asked if he was interested in having two priests come out to inaugurate the project. Canon Benoit also inquired if two or three Daughters of Charity could not be set apart "for the negro children in order that you may not have to embark at once into too heavy expenses."[71] Bishop Gibbons replied and accepted his proposal for sending out two priests to Richmond for work among the Negroes. As he wrote, "I promise to pay traveling expenses & one thousand dollars a year for 3 years. I guarantee them $1000 a year, supplying whatever may fall short of that amount in the contributions of their congregation."[72] Due to a scarcity of priests, however, the English society did not actually begin their work in Richmond until 1885, about eight years after Gibbons had left the diocese.

In the midst of his diocesan duties James Gibbons found time to do a considerable amount of preaching outside of his own spiritual jurisdiction. It was evident that he had begun to acquire a reputation as a preacher, for the calls for his services increased as time went on. As we have seen, he was the preacher at the consecration of John J. Kain in Wheeling in May, 1875. In September of the same year he gave the students' retreat at St. Charles College in Ellicott City.[73] On May 25, 1876, he preached the sermon at the consecration of the cathedral of Baltimore,

---

[71] 72-V-6, Benoit to Gibbons, Mill Hill, London, March 30, 1876.
[72] Diary, June 7, 1876, p. 80.
[73] 41-S-10, Gibbons to Bayley, Richmond, November 5, 1875.

and three days later Gibbons was the preacher at the dedication of St. Peter's Church at Newcastle, Delaware, where Father Benjamin J. Keiley, a future Bishop of Savannah, was then pastor. Again, on May 13, 1877, he was in Charleston where he preached at the consecration of John Moore as second Bishop of St. Augustine.[74] He had plenty of practice for this work, of course, on the numerous occasions where his presence called for sermons in the missions of Virginia, and at times the talks were delivered in strange places and under unusual circumstances. For example, late July of 1876 found Gibbons in southern Virginia where at Danville he delivered a sermon in the evening at the Odd Fellows' Hall and found fourteen Catholics to attend his Mass in a private home the next morning, while at Covington ten days later he preached and confirmed in the Methodist church.[75] Although the circumstances were at times strange, nonetheless the bishop gleaned a wealth of experience and knowledge of the non-Catholic mentality from these visits through rural Virginia and North Carolina and it was this enrichment of mind that gave to his first and most famous book, *The Faith of Our Fathers,* an approach and a tone which rapidly made it the *vade mecum* of so many non-Catholic Americans whose interest had been aroused in the doctrines of the Catholic Church.

For a long time Bishop Gibbons had been turning over in his mind the possibility of writing a book in which, by a clear exposition of Catholic truths, he would serve both uninstructed Catholics and those outside the Church who were seeking further information on its teachings and practices. Gibbons had felt keenly the need of books of instruction from his earliest days on the missions in North Carolina and we have already seen him asking Archbishop Spalding in Baltimore to send him copies of the latter's apologetic works for distribution. Books were an especially desirable avenue of knowledge in areas like North Carolina and Virginia where there were so few Catholic schools and such a pitifully small number of priests and sisters to help with instructions. Years later, when lecturing on his career in the South, Gibbons emphasized the importance of books of reli-

[74] Diary, May 28, 1876, p. 80; May 13, 1877, p. 87. The text of the sermon at Baltimore can be read in Gibbons' *A Retrospect of Fifty Years,* II, 1–16.
[75] *Ibid.,* July 20, 1876; July 30, 1876, p. 81.

gious instruction for the southern missions. He recalled that
Bishop John England of Charleston, the first Catholic bishop in
the Carolinas, had followed the practice of building up a little
library at the mission centers wherever he could, and Gibbons
added, "This medium of conversion I fully recognized. A good
book is a powerful ally."[76] He stated that it was at the urgent
insistence of Father Mark S. Gross that he started to give the
matter of writing a book serious consideration. Pursuing this task
with the same measured pace which marked most of his undertakings, it took a long time for the project to reach a practical
plane.

However, by the early months of 1876 the greater part of the
manuscript had been completed by the bishop. John B. Tabb
who, as has been mentioned, had been received into the Church
in 1872 and then sent to St. Charles College by Gibbons, was at
the time in Richmond teaching in St. Peter's School.[77] Tabb, who
was a rare student of the English language and who had a splendid background, of course, for appreciating the non-Catholic
American mind, was asked by the bishop to go over his manuscript. This Tabb did and when he had finished with his stylistic
corrections Gibbons sensibly submitted the manuscript to the

---

[76] "Reminiscences of North Carolina," *United States Catholic Historical Magazine*, III (1889–1890), 344.

[77] Francis E. Litz, "Father Tabb," *Catholic University Bulletin*, XII (July,
1944), 8–9. Litz mentioned the statement of William McDevitt in the latter's
article, "Father Tabb at St. Charles College" (*Catholic World*, CLVI [January,
1943], 412–419), that Gibbons had Tabb "to copyread (and largely to rewrite),"
the book (p. 412); but he confesses that the assertion of McDevitt was uncor-
roborated. William McDevitt was a close friend and associate of John Tabb. The
fact that McDevitt had Gibbons meeting Tabb for the first time in Richmond
"about 1875" (*ibid.*) would indicate that he was not too accurate as to details
since the bishop had received Tabb into the Church in 1872. In 1945 McDevitt
published from the Recorder-Sunset Press a little book entitled, *My Father,
Father Tabb. At Home and at College.* In this unpaginated brochure he mentioned
the criticism which arose in Baltimore over his remark concerning the authorship
made in the *Catholic World.* He maintained that Tabb told him ten years later
that he "very largely rewrote some chapters of the work, so far as style is
concerned." But aside from this statement the only evidence submitted to sub-
stantiate it is that the wealth of literary allusions and quotations in *The Faith
of Our Fathers* would seem to indicate that a person of greater literary cultivation
than Gibbons had a hand in the work. But McDevitt does not say that Gibbons
was all his life a constant reader of the Scriptures and the classics of Roman and
English literature and that his other published works, such as *The Ambassador
of Christ*, bear a similar characteristic.

trained eye of a theologian in sending it to Father Camillo Mazzella, S.J., professor of theology at Woodstock College. Mazzella read the work and then sent on the copy to John Murphy, the publisher, in Baltimore by whom the book was going to be brought out. When Murphy received the copy from Mazzella he wrote Gibbons as follows:

> In reply to your esteemed favor of the 4th Father Mazella [sic] sent a Bundle of your Copy to me yesterday, without any message. I subsequently met him accidentally in the Cars, and he told me that he would send the remainder in a few days. As we had no time to enlarge on the subject, he simply stated that it was very good, or something to that effect. He will no doubt write to you when he has examined all. I have read the Introduction and was very much pleased with it. It is plain and practical. Before commencing this work, in order to guard against any misunderstanding please give me your ideas as to the style of Book you would like, the price you desire it to be sold at. . . .[78]

Apparently the bishop left most of the details in Murphy's hands and in good measure relied on the publisher's judgment, for some days later Murphy told him he appreciated the confidence he placed in him, "but business calls for exact understanding." Therefore, he would issue the volume in two different styles, one cloth to sell for $1 and the other paper to sell for 50 cents, and Murphy would allow him 5 cents on each cloth copy and 2½ cents on each paper copy sold until 10,000 copies had been disposed of. "After which," said the publisher, "the percentage is to cease. By both the above you will observe that I assume all risks as to change in prices, etc."[79] In another few days Murphy made acknowledgment of the receipt of a letter from Gibbons, and he said, "You will see from the spirit manifest in connection with your Book that I predict and anticipate a large sale for it." He assured the author that no expense or effort would be spared to put out a pleasing volume and to co-operate with Gibbons' desire to enlighten the American public on Catholicism, "a matter," said Murphy, "that I feel you have the faculty of doing in a more practical way than most of our good clergy and Bishops."[80]

Late in 1876 the proofs of the forthcoming book were ready

---

[78] ADR, Murphy to Gibbons, Baltimore, September 15, 1876.
[79] *Ibid.*, September 18, 1876.
[80] *Ibid.*, September 23, 1876. An effort to locate Gibbons' correspondence with

for correction, and Bishop Gibbons came to Baltimore where he and young J. Henry Furst, of the printing firm of J. H. Furst Company, went over the proofs and put them in form for the final printing. Before the end of the year *The Faith of Our Fathers* had been published and the first complimentary and review copies had been distributed. One of the first letters of commendation on the work came from Father Jean B. Menu, S.S., at St. Charles College. He compared the book to Bossuet's *Exposition of the Doctrine of the Catholic Church* which had been responsible for the conversion of many Protestants in France. Menu thought Gibbons' work, "more readable than that of Bossuet. . . . Evidently your object was not to make money, for I understand that the price is as low as it can be." The Sulpician had heard about Tabb's part in reading the work, but he thought he had been the proofreader. He said he had gone over the pages looking for errors in the hope of catching Tabb. "It would be so sweet to find fault with Mr. Tabb for his negligence. I thought I had found two, at least one, but upon consultation I saw that I was myself in error."[81]

This first literary effort of James Gibbons proved to be an immediate success. Letters poured in upon him from all directions with many of the American hierarchy sending their congratulations. Bishop Louis de Goesbriand of Burlington, Vermont, for example, said he found it much more readable than other books of its kind and, he added, "with remarkable flavour of that charity which the Enfants of Mr. Olier know how to communicate to their pupils."[82] By the early spring of 1877 a copy of *The Faith of Our Fathers* had reached Panama where a certain Herrigue Lewis inquired of James A. McMaster of the New York *Freeman's Journal* if he might translate it into Spanish.[83] Murphy, the publisher, was naturally elated at the sales and he wrote Gibbons to say that in consideration of

---

Murphy proved unsuccessful. Thomas B. Kenedy of P. J. Kenedy and Sons, the firm that took over the Murphy business, told the writer in a letter of July 8, 1948, "We have no correspondence of his [Murphy's] other than that which treats in the known course of business." James P. Walsh of the Baltimore law firm which handled the Murphy estate wrote on July 12, 1948, " . . . I received only the business correspondence of recent years. . . ."

[81] 73-A-2, Menu to Gibbons, St. Charles College, January 3, 1877.

[82] 73-A-7, De Goesbriand to Gibbons, Burlington, January 17, 1877.

[83] 73-A-16, Lewis to McMaster, Panama, April 16, 1877; 73-C-9, Lewis to Gibbons, Panama, June 15, 1877.

the unexpected demand and the prospects of a larger sale than was at first anticipated, he would voluntarily agree to extend the copyright on the book "until the Sales & Payments amount to Twenty Thousand (20,000) Copies of One Thousand Dollars."[84] A few days later Father Charles J. Croghan, pastor of St. Joseph's Church in Charleston, told the bishop that he was delighted with the book and had distributed fifty copies of it among his Sunday school children. "You hit upon the right matter; the style is admirable. Your vocabulary contains no *'maxillafrangent'* words. Everything in the book is as clear as a sunbeam."[85] Since it was especially for groups such as Croghan's in Charleston that the bishop had intended his volume, this letter doubtless brought him more than ordinary satisfaction. Father Daniel E. Hudson, C.S.C., editor of *Ave Maria* at the University of Notre Dame, was quick to sense the book's value and he suggested a translation into German which could be done, if Gibbons consented, by a professor of German at Notre Dame who was a convert from the Lutheran ministry.[86] Gibbons readily assented to the German translation and Hudson told him that he had put a copy of the fourth revised edition into Professor Otto Schnurrer's hands and told him to go to work.[87]

The fact that the book had not as yet been on the market six months and had already gone through a fourth revised edition gives an idea of the popularity with which it was received. The mail that came in on the subject of Gibbons' *The Faith of Our Fathers* in the first months was almost entirely sympathetic and favorable. However, Adolphe Pinsoneault, former Bishop of Sandwich, wrote him from Montreal, stating his disagreement with Gibbons in shifting the blame for the Spanish inquisitors to the King of Spain rather than to the Pope. Pinsoneault felt Gibbons had de-emphasized too strongly the Church's part in the Inquisition in Spain. He suggested, therefore, that he revise his remarks in this particular since Gibbons' judgment on the question "will pass for absolute truth in America just as the strangely erroneous statements of Mgr. Hefele and other liberal Catholic writers did in Europe."[88]

---

[84] 73-A-19, Murphy to Gibbons, Baltimore, April 27, 1877.
[85] 73-A-20, Croghan to Gibbons, Charleston, April 30, 1877.
[86] 73-B-13, Hudson to Gibbons, Notre Dame, May 25, 1877.
[87] 73-C-2, Hudson to Gibbons, Notre Dame, June 5, 1877.
[88] ADR, Pinsoneault to Gibbons, Montreal, June 10, 1877.

Aside from this single exception the first reactions to the volume received by the author were universally favorable. Three years after the publication of the book, it is true, an answer appeared in a volume entitled *The Faith of Our Forefathers* by Edward J. Stearns, examining chaplain of the Protestant Episcopal Diocese of Easton. Stearns' efforts at refutation, however, were not at all successful, and at the time that his work came out Gibbons' volume had already gone through thirteen reprints and had sold about 65,000 copies.[89]

The phenomenal success which *The Faith of Our Fathers* was destined to have in convincing many Protestants of the truth of the Catholic position began to show itself at an early date. In June, 1877, Gibbons received a letter from a woman in Baltimore who told him she had been reared a Protestant but had a respect and reverence for many Catholic practices. But other Catholic doctrines, as she said, "of which I was ignorant, I accepted as the empty, meaningless ceremonies I had been taught to consider them." Recently while on a visit to St. Mary's County she had come on the bishop's book. "I was charmed with it, and discovered that my predilection for the Church was because I was a Catholic at heart." She was now under instructions to become a Catholic and she wanted the author to know of her gratitude for *The Faith of Our Fathers*.[90] Edgar P. Wadhams, first Bishop of Ogdensburg and himself a convert, told Bishop Gibbons that he had distributed many copies of the work, and he found "no better book for the instruction of Catholics & to give information to Protestants."[91]

Gibbons had sent a copy to Pope Pius IX to be presented by Louis E. Hostlot, vice-rector of the American College in Rome. Hostlot told him that in the audience when he presented the volume the Pope had expressed his pleasure at learning of its success and his special joy that "the bishops were taking up their pens in the defence of Mother Church, and for this 'tell the bishop of Richmond that I send him a special blessing with

---

[89] For an analysis of Stearns' answer to Gibbons, cf. "Archbishop Gibbons and his Episcopalian Critic, Dr. Stearns," by A. de G., *American Catholic Quarterly Review,* V (January, 1880), 84–104. Stearns' book was published by Thomas Whitaker in New York.

[90] 73-C-10, Virginia Walter to Gibbons, Baltimore, June 18, 1877.

[91] 73-D-8, Wadhams to Gibbons, Ogdensburg, July 21, 1877.

the hope that he will continue the good fight.' "[92] A Mr. George B. P. Taylor, who had for years been seeking the truth in religion, wrote at this time to say that a reading of the book had brought him peace of mind at last and, he added, *"all of my doubts have been removed. . . ."* He wanted the bishop to know that his wish expressed in the preface, that should the perusal of the volume bring one soul to the knowledge of the true Church his efforts would have been well repaid, was fulfilled in his case. He thanked Gibbons, therefore, for what he called, "the Heavenly information that you have been pleased to make known to poor deluded creatures like myself."[93] Another convert from Episcopalianism told the author that he had been converted some years before, but he wanted Gibbons to know the part which a reading of *The Faith of Our Fathers* had recently played in the conversion of his mother. The book had settled the doubts under which the old lady had labored for many months. "I cannot refrain from adding that this old lady, now in her seventy-fifth year, was more than once obliged to close the book because of her conviction of its force and truth, and with tears to ask the Good God for grace and strength to sacrifice her pride and face the bitter and vindictive persecution of her own children."[94] All these testimonies of the value of his book reached the bishop before it was in circulation hardly more than six months. The years ahead would bring him a constant flow of letters of a similar kind as *The Faith of Our Fathers* passed through edition after edition and rose to the top of the list among the most widely read books on religion in the English language.[95]

---

[92] 73-D-9, Hostlot to Gibbons, Rome, July 24, 1877. It must have been agreeable news to Gibbons to learn from the rector of the Roman college of the unusual record made by his student, Denis O'Connell. Hostlot said, "Mr. O'Connell has given the greatest satisfaction during his course. His talent is remarkable. At his examination for the degree of D.D., his success has been so marked, that the degree was conferred on him by the Cardinal & professors with acclamation, they refusing to vote by ballot as is usual on such occasions. The cardinal prefect moreover came out of the room expressly to congratulate him. H. E. Card. Franchi, as well as several of the professors have come to the college to inform me of the same. His character, I am glad to state, is in accordance with his talent. He has always been obedient, & remarkably humble, having no pretensions. In all, if Mr. O'Connell continues to be what he has shown himself to be here in the College, he will be a most useful member to the Church."

[93] 73-D-11, Taylor to Gibbons, Ridge, Maryland, July 27, 1877.

[94] 73-D-12, E. Ashfield to Gibbons, Washington, D. C., July 28, 1877.

[95] One of the most recent evidences of the influence of *The Faith of Our Fathers*

At the time that the details of Gibbons' book were being worked out the rumor of the Baltimore coadjutorship arose again and the bishop heard of it rather constantly thereafter in one form or another. In the spring of 1876 the Coadjutor Archbishop of St. Louis, Patrick J. Ryan, told him that he would do his best to get a group of the Sisters of St. Joseph of Carondelet for Gibbons' missions, although he thought the latter should not be planning so far as a year in advance. "Suppose," said Ryan, "you should be *translated* in the interim? Suppose you should be found in the quiet, respectable rank of the Coadjutors of the Country. . . . But I must not joke or hint even." Ryan said on his next trip to the East he would certainly visit Richmond if Gibbons were still there, and if he had meanwhile been promoted he stated, "I will do myself the honor & pleasure of calling to congratulate you in your new home in — well the place to which you will be translated!"[96] That summer the Bishop of Savannah, William H. Gross, C.Ss.R., and his priest-brother, Mark, were in Rome. While there the latter wrote to Gibbons to say that his brother had visited Cardinal Franchi, Prefect of the Propaganda, and he found the cardinal "much exercised in mind" about the Archdiocese of Baltimore in relation to the appointment of a coadjutor. Bishop Gross had spoken frankly of the poor health of Archbishop Bayley to Franchi, and Mark Gross added, "You were not forgotten," although it was the impression of the Bishop of Savannah from his talk with Franchi "that Rome will not at present appoint a coadjutor."[97] Meanwhile Bayley's health did not improve and he wrote Gibbons from Seton Hall College in New Jersey in August asking if he would come to Baltimore several weeks hence so they could consult on the names to be forwarded to the Holy See to fill the Dioceses of St. Augustine and Richmond. Bayley confessed, "I am completely hors du combat."[98]

---

in bringing converts into the Church was that of the distinguished historian, Carlton J. H. Hayes, who said in his address on November 12, 1949, in accepting the Cardinal Gibbons Medal of the Alumni Association of the Catholic University of America, "Personally I like to recall that some fifty years ago I read and re-read his *Faith of Our Fathers* — I was then a Baptist — and answered the call" (*The Catholic University of America Bulletin*, XVII [January, 1950], 2).

[96] 72-V-9, Ryan to Gibbons, St. Louis, April 7, 1876.
[97] 72-W-2/1, Gross to Gibbons, Rome, July 22, 1876.
[98] 72-W-4, Bayley to Gibbons, South Orange, New Jersey, August 4, 1876.

John Lancaster Spalding had recently been named as first Bishop of Peoria and he acknowledged Gibbons' letter of congratulation with thanks, to which he added, "though I am sure you are too wise to think that I am really to be congratulated upon my appointment to the See of Peoria. It seems to me that the last thing a sensible man ought to desire is to be a bishop, at least in the United States. I hope there may be some right way of escaping this responsibility and that some one more fit to build up a new diocese may be appointed." Spalding told him he had heard the news about his possible promotion to Baltimore and he sincerely hoped it was true. He had not yet seen a copy of *The Faith of Our Fathers,* but he had heard good reports of it, and he said, "If someone does not get ahead of me I shall notice it in the Cath. World."[99] That winter Michael A. Corrigan, Bishop of Newark, had gone to Rome and he wrote Archbishop Bayley from the Eternal City to say that in an audience the previous evening he had given Pius IX a report on Bayley's health, which he said, "in the hurry of the moment I fear I depicted in too black colors." The Pope showed his concern and Corrigan felt there would not be "the slightest difficulty" about a coadjutor as soon as the necessary documents were forwarded to the Holy See. He closed by saying, "It is surprising though how much 'red tape' there is here, and how exact they are in requiring compliance with what strikes us as unnecessary formalities."[100]

As much as James Roosevelt Bayley might have wished to expedite the matter of Gibbons' transfer to Baltimore he found he must comply with Propaganda's demand that a *terna* of three names be sent for the coadjutorship. He informed Archbishop Williams of Boston that besides the *terna* of himself and his suffragans Rome wanted letters from the other American metropolitans. Would Williams, therefore, please write to Rome and, as he remarked, "if you can, urge the appointment of Dr. Gibbons who is the right man." Bayley told the Archbishop of Boston that the three names he had forwarded to the Holy See had been, in order of preference, Bishops Gibbons, Thomas Foley of Chicago, and Thomas A. Becker of Wilmington.[101] Meanwhile Gibbons

[99] 72-W-7, Spalding to Gibbons, New York, December 30, 1876.
[100] 40-T-3, Corrigan to Bayley, Rome, February 9, 1877.
[101] AABo, Bayley to Williams, Richmond, February 15, 1877.

accepted Spalding's invitation to act as a co-consecrator at his elevation to the episcopacy by Cardinal McCloskey in New York on May 1, and the cardinal, in turn, sent word that he would favor him by becoming his guest during his stay in the city.[102] Just at this time Denis O'Connell, who was approaching his ordination to the priesthood in Rome, wrote to say that he had delayed writing to his bishop because, as he phrased it, of "the daily expectation of your elevation to the Metropolitan See of Baltimore." He told Gibbons that either from the United States or from the Propaganda rumors had continually been coming of late that the matter would be announced the following week, "and with them a reason for another week's delay." Young O'Connell rejoiced at the prospect of the bishop's advancement, but it saddened him to think it would separate them since he felt grateful for all Gibbons' kindnesses and, as he expressed it, "[I] frequently consoled myself with the promise of passing my life under the government of the unassuming and gentle Bishop that took me to fish with him in Mr. Cox's pond and dealt with me so familiarly in his apostolic journeys through No. Carolina's forests." He had gone so far as to ask the rector of the college if he might not bind himself personally to Gibbons, rather than to the diocese, but the rector had disapproved and said he could "do much good for the cause of God in Virginia." O'Connell was to be ordained on May 26, and he would then await Gibbons' instructions as to what he was to do.[103]

At length the appointment of James Gibbons as Bishop of Jonopolis and Coadjutor Archbishop of Baltimore with the right of succession was made. His first news of the action of Rome reached him on May 15, 1877, in the form of a telegram from James A. McMaster, editor of the New York *Freeman's Journal,* which read: "You are preconized coadjutor of Baltimore cum jure successionis. Accept my congratulations."[104] Within twenty-four hours the news was flashed over the country and the congratulations of his friends began to come in. Thomas Foley in Chicago rejoiced for both the bishop and his own native city of Baltimore in a prompt wire of congratulation.[105] The thought of

---

[102] 73-A-14, Spalding to Gibbons, New York, March 28, 1877; 73-A-17, McCloskey to Gibbons, New York, April 18, 1877.

[103] 73-B-2, O'Connell to Gibbons, Rome, May 3, 1877.

[104] 73-B-4, McMaster to Gibbons, New York, May 15, 1877, telegram.

[105] 73-B-7, Foley to Gibbons, Chicago, May 16, 1877, telegram.

Gibbons in the premier See of Baltimore, with its rich memories for Catholicism in the United States, filled Bernard F. Ferris, pastor of Sacred Heart Church in Pittsburgh, with joy. He concluded a long and enthusiastic letter by saying, "I am sorry for Richmond but glad for Baltimore & the United States."[106] Father Pierre P. Denis, president of St. Charles College, sent the congratulations of the bishop's alma mater and asked if he would preside at the commencement on June 28, and Denis' Sulpician confrère, Joseph Dubruel, vicar-general of Baltimore, asked Gibbons to verify the report when he said, "Will you be kind enough to let me know the real state of things; if true I will congratulate you, the archdiocese, and even my poor self."[107] Bishop Corrigan of Newark, with whom Gibbons was destined to have many interesting, if not always tranquil, relations in the years ahead, wrote, "May God be praised for his appointment which has been so earnestly prayed for, and may His Holy Spirit be always with you to guide and direct you for our common good!"[108] Gross of Savannah said he knew that both the clergy and laity of Baltimore would receive the news with the greatest pleasure. "I know of only one," said Gross, "who will regret the appointment and that is, your own dear diocese of Richmond."[109]

On May 26, 1877, Denis J. O'Connell was ordained a priest in Rome by Raffaele Cardinal Monaco. On the day following his ordination he wrote a lengthy letter to his superior, the Bishop of Richmond, in which he described for him the ceremony of his first Mass in the Church of Santa Croce in Gerusalemme. He said that while he knew Gibbons rejoiced with him in his priesthood he did not know if he should accept congratulations on the latter's promotion to Baltimore. The young priest told his bishop, ". . . God has great designs upon you, and his finger is most strangely apparent in the course of your life. Whatever else awaits you here, the government of many cities certainly awaits you hereafter." O'Connell said that following dinner that day the new priests were received by Cardinal Franchi. He remarked that he told Franchi he had taken away his bishop. "How so?"

[106] 73-B-6, Ferris to Gibbons, Pittsburgh, May 16, 1877.
[107] 73-B-9, Denis to Gibbons, Ellicott City, May 18, 1877; 73-B-5, Dubruel to Gibbons, Baltimore, May 16, 1877.
[108] 73-B-11, Corrigan to Gibbons, Newark, May 20, 1877.
[109] 73-B-12, Gross to Gibbons, Columbus, Georgia, May 21, 1877.

he asked. "You have given him to Baltimore." "Oh, si, si," he exclaimed laughing, "Monsig. Gibbons, for they all wanted him." Dr. Edward McGlynn of New York was present on the occasion and at this point he entered the conversation:

> "And cum jure successionis too, Eminenza," interposed Dr. McGlynn who stood near. "Yes," replied the cardinal, "all the Bishops were in favor of him, and the people of Baltimore were most eager to obtain him." "And he is young," added the Dr., "not much above thirty." "Thirty four" his Eminence responded. Then Dr. McGlynn continued: "He is most amiable and learned and has written some very valuable works, especially one on the Faith." "Si, si," said the cardinal, "io so," [I know it] "e molto bravo."[110]

Doubtless Gibbons found this description of the reactions in Rome to his interest, even if it did reveal that the Prefect of Propaganda and McGlynn had missed his age by almost ten years. Gibbons' episcopal neighbor to the south, Patrick N. Lynch of Charleston, sent his belated congratulations some weeks later. He hoped Gibbons would be as happy in Baltimore as Baltimore would be to have him. "Of course the mitre will be heavier and the thorns sharper. But so it is with Bishops and Archbishops." Lynch revealed his own mood by saying that he had lately been ill "and also in the dumps." Bishop Moore was getting on splendidly in his new Diocese of St. Augustine, but Lynch thought that "one year hence he may feel the burden and the contradictions." The Bishop of Charleston told Gibbons that the latter's sermon at Moore's consecration the previous month had proved "a hit." In fact, Lynch remarked, "It delighted the protestants who still speak of it with admiration. Was it to escape a temptation to vanity, that you ran away from us so quickly?" He asked Gibbons if he might come to Richmond soon to take up a collection for his diocese. "I have just now a little under forty dollars to my name and I must do my best to pay eight hundred within four weeks. The two or three hundred I might get in Richmond would be of invaluable aid to me."[111]

All during June the messages of congratulation continued to reach Gibbons. Bishop Jeremiah F. Shanahan of Harrisburg rejoiced to know that they would now be near neighbors and he

---

[110] 73-B-8, O'Connell to Gibbons, Rome, May 27, 1877.
[111] 73-C-1, Lynch to Gibbons, Charleston, June 4, 1877.

hoped Gibbons would come to see him often.[112] When the news became official Ryan of St. Louis wrote "as the senior coadjutor" in the country to welcome him into their ranks and to indulge his fondness for a play on words when he said that though "you have not here a lasting city," he hoped he would "be preserved many years to explain & to vindicate the 'Faith of Our Fathers.' "[113] Bishop Kain of Wheeling stated that he had long been convinced of the need for a change in Baltimore. He paid tribute to the many excellent traits of character of Archbishop Bayley, but he felt the latter was "a failure at the helm of that noble old ship which so many illustrious hands have steered before him." Therefore, regardless of his feelings in the matter, Gibbons should accept. Kain had written his opinion to Rome of the Baltimore situation six months before, and it was his interest in the welfare of the metropolitan see which, he said, "caused me to place your name first on the list which I sent to Rome."[114]

Early in July, 1877, Bishop Gibbons left Richmond for a three-week holiday trip to Niagara Falls, Montreal, Portland, and Boston. He was accompanied by Father John T. Gaitley, pastor of St. Bridget's Church in Baltimore, a classmate of the bishop's from St. Mary's days.[115] In April of that year Archbishop Bayley had undertaken a trip to Europe in the hope that the waters of Vichy might restore his health.[116] Late in June he was joined at Vichy by Archbishop Wood of Philadelphia who had just come from Rome bearing to Bayley a letter from the Holy See with the bulls of appointment for Gibbons as coadjutor of Baltimore. Wood informed the Bishop of Richmond that the official documents of his appointment were dated May 29 and that Bayley had asked him to reconvey them to him with the request that he enter on the administration of the Archdiocese of Baltimore as soon as he could. Bayley had written to Rome asking that every faculty be given Gibbons so that he could assume the administration *"with the least possible delay,"* and Wood added that it was the express wish of the Archbishop of Baltimore that he tell Gibbons that every faculty he could personally impart to him was his. Wood mentioned

[112] 73-C-5, Shanahan to Gibbons, Harrisburg, June 10, 1877.
[113] 73-C-7, Ryan to Gibbons, St. Louis, June 12, 1877.
[114] 73-C-8, Kain to Gibbons, Newburg, West Virginia, June 15, 1877.
[115] Diary, July 26, 1877, p. 88.
[116] Yeager, *op. cit.,* p. 456 ff.

that while Bayley's health was somewhat improved, he was "by
no means *well.*" He said the archbishop hoped to make his *ad
limina* visit to Rome before leaving Europe, and Wood added
confidentially that he feared Joseph Dubruel, the Sulpician vicar-
general of Baltimore, did not enjoy, as he expressed it, "to the
extent which might be desired the affection and confidence of
the Revd. Clergy! Quis sit culpandus nescio."[117] A week later
Bayley himself wrote to Gibbons and renewed the grant of all
the faculties he could give him for the administration in Baltimore, instructed him as to where he would find the keys to his
desk, the important papers and documents he might need, and,
should it prove necessary, how he might secure money from the
cathedraticum fund in the Savings Bank. He said he intended
to leave Vichy as soon as Archbishop Wood was able to travel
and he would go to Hamburg in Hesse for a month, on to an
English watering place for another month, "and then home, if I
determine to come home." If he decided to remain in Europe
he would go to Rome for the visit *ad limina.*[118]

Congratulatory messages continued to reach Bishop Gibbons
in the days of this summer and he must have been kept busy
acknowledging the good wishes of his many friends. His old
professor and confessor in the seminary, Paulinus F. Dissez, S.S.,
told him his promotion to Baltimore was "for us indeed a family
blessing." Dissez felt the appointment was a reason for congratulating himself "for having a little part in the direction of
your ecclesiastical studies."[119] The Prefect of Propaganda meanwhile forwarded Gibbons' faculties to him so that when he
entered on his new work in Baltimore he would have official
warrant for doing so.[120] The faculties sent by Franchi arrived in
Richmond on August 1 and the next day Gibbons had a letter
from Dubruel saying the bulls had been forwarded to him by
Archbishop Wood. Gibbons noted in his diary, "May God give
me light to know my duty & strength to fulfill it."[121] A week later
Father Dubruel traveled to Richmond and placed the documents
in the hands of the new coadjutor.[122] One of Gibbons' favorite

---

[117] 73-C-13, Wood to Gibbons, Vichy, France, June 27, 1877.
[118] 73-D-2, Bayley to Gibbons, Vichy, July 3, 1877.
[119] 73-D-3, Dissez to Gibbons, St. Charles College, July 3, 1877.
[120] 73-D-4, Franchi to Gibbons, Rome, July 5, 1877.
[121] Diary, August 2, 1877, p. 89.
[122] ASMS, Diary of Joseph P. Dubruel, S.S., August 10, 1877, p. 29.

Richmond priests, Francis Janssens, was then on a holiday in the Netherlands with his family. He wrote the bishop to say that while he congratulated him on his promotion, the thought of their separation was a hard one and he would ever retain a fond remembrance of the five years they had spent together. Janssens had been informed that he was designated by Archbishop Bayley to be administrator of the See of Richmond on Gibbons' departure. He said he heard it whispered here and there that he might be the next bishop, and he pleaded with Gibbons, "if you will add one more act of kindness to the many you have shown me, pray use yr. influence to counteract it; the very idea of being a Bishop now frightens me, and I feel entirely incompetent for such a responsibility, — my youth, inability, foreign blood, lack of piety and many other things make me unfit for such a position."[123]

In August the Archbishop of Baltimore returned from Europe but his condition grew so critical that late in the month Gibbons hurried to Newark and on August 29 anointed him.[124] These were trying days for the bishop who was expected to wind up his affairs in Virginia and North Carolina while at the same time attempt to keep the administration of the Archdiocese of Baltimore in some kind of order. On September 5 he wrote his acceptance of the Baltimore assignment to Pius IX and Cardinal Franchi, and he then seconded Bayley's appointment of Janssens as administrator of Richmond during the vacancy.[125] When Janssens arrived home from Europe late that month the administration of the diocese was turned over to him by the bishop. One of the last important public appearances of James Gibbons in Richmond came on September 19 when he preached the sermon in St. Peter's Cathedral at the Mass celebrated during the convention of the Irish Catholic Benevolent Union. He told the delegates that his nearly ten years of residence in Virginia and North Carolina had taught him that religious animosity was not nearly so bad as it was sometimes painted. He said he had daily commingled and conversed with peoples of all religious creeds,

> and unless I have very much mistaken the character and disposition
> of those people, I can say to you with confidence, that you will here

---

[123] 73-E-5, Janssens to Gibbons, Tilburg, Holland, August 27, 1877.
[124] Diary, August 27, 1877, p. 89.
[125] *Ibid.*, September 5, 1877, p. 89.

seek in vain for social ostracism or religious animosity. Prejudices indeed there may be & are among us, but they are relegated to the private family & to the churches. You will find in the public walks of life, a broad religious toleration & a social fraternal spirit. And the friendly smile you will see before you on Richmond's face, will reflect the warm & generous feelings of Richmond's heart. . . .

Gibbons made a strong plea for the co-operation of the Catholic laity with the clergy. "Without you we can do little or nothing. We clergy & you people have the same interests. We stand or fall together." He paid high tribute to their organization and was at pains to picture the benefits which derived from societies such as theirs, providing they lived up strictly to their constitution.[126]

Ten days after this sermon Bishop Gibbons received a telegram telling him that Archbishop Bayley was reported to be dying. He made another hurried trip to Newark and remained with the archbishop until death closed his useful career on the morning of October 3.[127] The ceremonies of the funeral in Baltimore, at which Cardinal McCloskey of New York headed a group of nineteen bishops, the burial beside the grave of the late archbishop's aunt, Mother Elizabeth Seton, at Emmitsburg, and the many details attendant on these events took all of Gibbons' time during early October. Three days before the funeral the new archbishop began to exercise one of his functions as metropolitan when he sent telegrams to the suffragan bishops of the Province of Baltimore announcing the approaching nominations to the vacant See of Richmond and the Vicariate of North Carolina. The funeral of the archbishop afforded the bishops a good opportunity to discharge this duty, and on October 10 Archbishop Gibbons had informed Bishop Moore of St. Augustine, who could not be present, that their selections for Richmond, in order of preference, had been Silas M. Chatard, rector of the American College in Rome; John J. Keane, assistant pastor of St. Patrick's Church in Washington; and Henry P. Northrop, pastor of St. Patrick's Church at Charleston.[128] Within a few days Gibbons was asked by Archbishop Joseph S. Alemany

---

[126] 73-E-11, Handwritten copy of sermon to the delegates of the ninth convention of the Irish Catholic Benevolent Union, Richmond, September 19, 1877.

[127] Diary, September 28–October 3, 1877, p. 90.

[128] 73-F-12, Moore to Gibbons, St. Augustine, October 16, 1877.

of San Francisco to fulfill another duty of the metropolitans of the country, namely, to write Rome and express his views on the proposed *terna* of names for the coadjutorship of San Francisco. Alemany gave Gibbons the three names with Bishop William Henry Elder of Natchez at the head of the list and asked him if he would please second the request in a letter to Cardinal Franchi.[129]

Following the funeral of Archbishop Bayley and the transaction of the most pressing business in Baltimore, the new archbishop returned to Richmond to complete his packing and to take final leave of his people. On Sunday, October 14, he preached his farewell sermon in the cathedral to, as he wrote, "a very large congregation among whom I am told, there were many Protestants."[130] The clergy of the diocese gave a farewell dinner in his honor on October 16 and presented to Gibbons a beautiful chalice as a token of their esteem and gratitude for his services to them and their people in the Diocese of Richmond.[131] While Gibbons naturally felt regret at departing from Virginia where he had spent five happy years, he did so with the satisfaction that he had been able to do a great deal to advance the cause of religion in the state. In the five years since 1872 the number of churches had been increased by seven to a total of twenty-two, nine more chapels and stations had been added to the fifteen of 1872, and there were eight more priests in the diocese now to make a total of twenty-five scattered over the towns and country stations of Virginia and West Virginia.

While the number of orphan asylums remained the same and the general Catholic population had increased by only about 1,000 in the intervening years, there had been a marked development in the matter of parochial schools. In 1872 there had been five so-called "female academies" and eight parochial schools for boys, whereas by the time Gibbons left the diocese there were

---

[129] 73-F-10, Alemany to Gibbons, San Francisco, October 12, 1877. At this time a vacant diocese was usually filled by the Holy See from a *terna*, or list of three names, submitted by the metropolitan and his suffragan bishops; a vacant archdiocese followed the same procedure except that in addition the opinions of all the metropolitans of the country were likewise solicited by Rome.

[130] Diary, October 14, 1877, p. 90. The pulpit of old St. Peter's Cathedral in Richmond from which this final sermon was delivered has inscribed on it the names of the bishops of the see, a list which indicates the notable ecclesiastics who served in this relatively small diocese.

[131] *Ibid.*, October 16, 1877, pp. 90–91.

fourteen parochial schools each for boys and girls with six academies for the latter.[132] This increase in the facilities for Catholic education in the diocese, with the attendant number of religious women at hand for the work, must have given a special satisfaction to the bishop as he surveyed in retrospect his years in Richmond. Even the Vicariate of North Carolina was able to boast of four parochial schools in the year Gibbons went to Baltimore, whereas nine years before there had been none.[133] Moreover, as their departing bishop informed them in his farewell sermon, the people of the Diocese of Richmond were left with no large debt for all the activities of the previous years, there being only a small amount due on the property of the Daughters of Charity on Fourth Street in Richmond.[134]

At length on October 19 James Gibbons took his farewell of Richmond. The Richmond *Daily Dispatch* of the following day noted that "there was a number of leading Catholics at the depot to see him off." The *Dispatch* further stated that it had been the intention of the Catholics of the city to present the archbishop with a set of vestments, but they did not arrive before he left the city. The vestments would be put on exhibition at the cathedral hall so all could see them and then they would be forwarded with a letter from the Honorable Anthony M. Keiley who had acted as chairman of the presentation committee. A few days later the vestments were forwarded to Baltimore and with them the letter of Mayor Keiley in which he said:

> Its value, were it a hundred fold greater, would feebly image the reverent respect and affectionate gratefulness with which the name of Bishop Gibbons will ever be borne in the hearts of the faithful of this city and see.
>
> You have filled your diocese with monuments of your enlightened zeal and fervent piety; you leave it tarnished by the memory of no scandal, and weighted by the burden of no debt; and you bear to your new home the palm of successful labors and a faithful duty, and the crown of a good will, genuine and universal.[135]

One of the most touching final tributes from Richmond came to Gibbons in a letter of E. Courtney Jenkins. He told him he had

---

[132] *Sadlier's Catholic Directory, Almanac and Ordo for the Year of Our Lord 1878* (New York, 1878), pp. 357–360.

[133] *Ibid.*, pp. 416–417.

[134] *Catholic Mirror*, October 20, 1877.

[135] 73-G-9, Keiley to Gibbons, Richmond, October 31, 1877.

been in the cathedral on the previous Sunday for the bishop's farewell sermon and he then realized what they had all lost by his departure. He recalled that through the wanderings and demoralization of war he had once strayed from his Catholic faith, but in later years it had been restored to him through, as he said, "*your* blessed instrumentality." It was for that reason especially that Jenkins felt so keenly the departure of one who had meant so much to him.[136] In the years ahead there would be many priestly consolations of this kind to give fresh courage and a new spirit to the heart and effort of Gibbons when the grave problems of the American Church at times weighed heavily upon him.

Thus three months beyond his forty-third birthday this man who had now completed nine years in the episcopacy found himself the archbishop of the premier See of Baltimore, his native city. At so early an age was he placed in the seat of a Carroll, a Kenrick, and a Spalding, a position which, although not so by official act of Rome, carried with it the practical primacy of the Catholic Church of the United States. From all the indications given of his wisdom, virtue, and ability through the years up to 1877 there seemed every reason to believe that the choice for this high post had been a happy one. The day of his arrival in Baltimore he noted in his diary that he had immediately entered on his new duties. He listed the clergy of the household as Thomas S. Lee, rector of the cathedral; William E. Starr, chancellor of the archdiocese; and Alfred A. Curtis, secretary of the archbishop; and he added, "all pious zealous & accomplished gentlemen as far as my observation & information enables me to judge."[137]

---

[136] 73-F-14, Jenkins to Gibbons, Richmond, October 20, 1877.
[137] Diary, October 19, 1877, p. 94.

CHAPTER V

First Years as Archbishop of Baltimore

THE Baltimore to which Archbishop Gibbons returned in the autumn of 1877 was a larger and more important city than he had left nine years before. The population had increased to a total of 332,313 by the census of 1880, of which 53,729 or a fraction over sixteen per cent were colored. The state in general had by that year 934,943 persons of whom almost sixty per cent were residents of rural areas.[1] While the processes of industrialization were at work in Maryland as elsewhere along the Atlantic coast in these years, the scales had not as yet been tipped strongly in favor of urban against country life. Besides Baltimore the state had but one other city of more than 10,000 population in 1880, namely, Cumberland with 10,693, and the state capital at Annapolis was still a quiet little town with only 6,642 people. Forty miles from Baltimore, and embraced within the limits of the Archdiocese of Baltimore, was the national capital which counted in 1880 a population of 177,624.[2] Outside of Baltimore and Washington, therefore, the responsibility of the new archbishop would be confined in a considerable degree to small towns and rural settlements.

Politically speaking the State of Maryland had recently undergone a reform movement. Both the Republican and Democratic Parties had been largely boss-ridden since the Civil War until the election of 1875 brought a reform administration headed by John Lee Carroll of Howard County as governor. Carroll had been backed by Arthur P. Gorman, the most powerful figure in Democratic politics in Maryland at the time and a man who as United States senator was to wield great influence in Maryland

---

[1] *Sixteenth Census of the United States: 1940. Population* (Washington, 1942), I, 463–464.

[2] *Ibid.*, I, 201.

The cardinal's Charles Street residence in Baltimore with the Cathedral of the Assumption in the background. He first moved to this house in December, 1865, as secretary to Archbishop Spalding where he resided until October, 1868, when he left it as a bishop for North Carolina. He returned to the residence in October, 1877, as archbishop and died in the room to the rear of the second floor on the left on March 24, 1921.

politics for years to come.[3] Governor Carroll, the great-grandson of the signer of the Declaration of Independence, was a Catholic and the relations between the governor and the archbishop were marked by mutual respect and esteem. After his inauguration as governor Gibbons had written to congratulate him, and Carroll had said in reply, "I have but one purpose in mind and that is to try & elevate the party and to act in all things for the dignity & honor of our grand old state."[4] The bitter opposition to him as a Catholic in the campaign of 1875 had, of course, aroused the keen sympathy of his coreligionists, as well as that of fair-minded non-Catholics.

But despite Governor Carroll's hope to conduct his administration in a way that would redound to the "dignity" of the state, a situation arose in the second year of his term which necessitated a resort to force. The financial panic which visited the United States in the fall of 1873 was so severe that the recovery from its evil effects was long delayed. Large industrial and commercial firms finding their profits drastically curtailed sought means of retrenchment, and the discharge of employees and reduction of wages offered themselves as remedies to the managers. There ensued a very serious and widespread wave of unemployment which brought acute hardships to thousands of American wage earners and their families.

Among the business enterprises which had suffered from the panic was the Baltimore and Ohio Railroad. In the summer of 1877 the management of the road had endeavored through a discharge of employees and a ten per cent cut in wages to reduce a part of their losses. With a great number of Baltimore laborers already in dire straits the railroad's latest action appeared in the eyes of their workers to be just cause for a strike. When the strike came the B. and O. management sought to break it by introducing substitutes for the strikers at the company plants; whereupon in July the strikers retaliated by violence and began to destroy property in Cumberland. Governor Carroll made public an announcement that he would send state troops to Cumberland, and when the threat of violence arose a few days later in Baltimore he telegraphed President Hayes and asked for

---

[3] Clayton Colman Hall, *Baltimore. Its History and Its People*, I, 245–246. On Arthur P. Gorman, cf. *Dictionary of American Biography*, VII, 434–435.
[4] 72-V-5, Carroll to Gibbons, Annapolis, March 29, 1876.

federal troops. The government at Washington responded and soldiers were sent into the city from Fort McHenry while warships sailed up the bay, landed marines, and General Winfield S. Hancock took command. The action of the military restored order by July 23 and on August 1 the strike of the B. and O. workers was broken.[5] Carroll's action, of course, made him unpopular in labor circles, and the resentful mood of many of the city's populace was still felt when James Gibbons arrived nearly three months later to take over his new position.

Although the Archdiocese of Baltimore embraced at that time the District of Columbia and the entire State of Maryland with the exception of the eastern shore, the combined area was less than 10,000 square miles, which was an immensely reduced jurisdiction to that which Gibbons had under his care in either North Carolina or Virginia. The visitation tours throughout the archdiocese, with its relatively good transportation system, would be simple in comparison to those he had experienced in the South. Moreover, the fact that Baltimore was the oldest see in the country and had known for many years a numerous and devoted Catholic population, accounted in good measure for the highly developed state of the religious institutions at the time that Gibbons assumed control. There were then in the city of Baltimore twenty-one parishes of which five were designated as German and Bohemian, while Washington had eleven parishes of which two were for the Germans and one for the colored Catholics. The archdiocese numbered likewise sixty-six elementary schools, some of which were free and others at which a tuition fee was charged. The large number of parochial schools was in part due to the fact that there were at the time in some instances separate schools for boys and girls in the same parish. The academies for boys and novitiates for religious numbered nine and the academies for girls totaled thirteen. Higher education was well served by St. Mary's Seminary, Mount Saint Mary's College in Emmitsburg, St. Charles College, and the two Jesuit institutions of Georgetown and Woodstock Colleges. Organized Catholic charity took care of the less fortunate in a house of the Good Shepherd, a home for the aged poor conducted by the Little

Sisters of the Poor, and six hospitals. The archdiocese had a total of 126 churches and thirty-five chapels and stations to serve the religious needs of both city and rural residents with a total of 234 diocesan and religious priests to minister to the 200,000 Catholics.[6]

The decorum with which Baltimore observed Sunday in these years was a subject for comment among foreign visitors. One traveler in the fall of 1878 said, "I passed a Sunday here. This is a great church-going place." The same man observed that, "The religious position of the blacks is also very good; they are excellent Christians."[7] But a year later another visitor found Baltimore's manner of keeping Sunday a bit too austere for his taste. He related that the ringing of church bells on Sunday morning was a frightful nuisance, and when he was "wicked enough" to try to get shaved he failed, nor could he buy an appetizer before dinner on a Baltimore Sunday. "Beyond church-going there was nothing to do; and one could scarcely go to church morning, afternoon and evening. . . . I could not help being struck with astonishment by the perfection to which Sabbath-keeping had been brought in Baltimore." The stranger was delighted, however, on Monday when Baltimore again came to life and proved to be a "very vivacious and cheerful city, full not only of commercial bustle and activity, but of social amenity and refinement."[8] The sort of Sunday regime to which these foreign visitors adverted was much to the liking of Archbishop Gibbons and later in his life, when Sunday laws began to be seriously relaxed, he joined with other ministers of religion in protesting the lowering of the moral tone of the Lord's day.

Before an archbishop can exercise the full powers of a metropolitan or perform certain episcopal functions which require its liturgical use such as ordinations, he must have requested of the Holy See and received the symbol of his jurisdiction, namely, the pallium. For that reason the new Archbishop of Baltimore lost no time in asking Rome for this insignia of his full powers, but he was informed by Louis E. Hostlot, vice-rector of the

---

[6] *Sadlier's Catholic Directory . . . 1878* (New York, 1878), pp. 60–73. The total number of Catholics is not given in this issue of the *Directory*, but the issue for 1880 gives the figures as 200,000 for the Archdiocese of Baltimore, *op. cit.*, p. 60.

[7] Sir George Campbell, *White and Black. The Outcome of a Visit to the United States* (London, 1879), pp. 257, 263.

[8] George Augustus Sala, *America Revisited* (London, 1882), I, 120–140.

American College, that the pallia were conferred only in a consistory and he could not tell Gibbons when one would be held, although he said there would be one soon. Hostlot had followed instructions in asking for *ad interim* powers for the archbishop which he would send on as soon as he had received the rescript. Meanwhile he said he would carry out the formalities concerning the pallium, and though the business would entail "a little 'feeding' of pontifical masters of ceremony, who are indispensable on such occasions," he would attend to all details. "I will have satisfaction," he said, "in occasionally growling at their procrastination so that matters will come out all right in the end."[9]

In order to expedite the reception of the pallium Gibbons had requested his friend, the young Father Denis J. O'Connell, to act as procurator for him in Rome. O'Connell arrived in Rome on November 1 and all through November and December, 1877, he kept writing to the archbishop with detailed explanations of his progress and his disappointments in the matter of the pallium. On November 5 he informed Gibbons that he had secured for him from the Congregation of the Propaganda ordinary power of confirming and extraordinary power for ordaining, but the pallium itself would have to await the consistory. Pius IX's health was not good and, therefore, no date had been set for the ceremony.[10] Bishop Corrigan of Newark wrote Gibbons just at this time to say he would be glad to be present in Baltimore for the conferring of the pallium and to give the archbishop some information he had recently learned about how the archiepiscopal cross was to be used in the solemn conferring of confirmation. Corrigan thanked Gibbons for sending on a $5,000 draft to carry out the provisions for charity in the will of the late Archbishop Bayley. Speaking of Bayley, he wrote, "I miss our dear friend very much. Hitherto in all my troubles I was accustomed to lean on him, and seek his advice. Now there is a feeling of loneliness."[11]

While Archbishop Gibbons awaited definite action by the Holy See in regard to the pallium there were a number of tasks of his new office which he could perform without further delay. The day after Archbishop Bayley's funeral he held the meeting of

---

[9] 73-G-8, Hostlot to Gibbons, Rome, October 31, 1877.

[10] 73-H-7, O'Connell to Gibbons, Rome, November 5, 1877. Propaganda's grant of faculties to Gibbons was contained in four documents signed on November 4, 1877 (73-H-3-4-5-6).

[11] 73-H-11, Corrigan to Gibbons, Seton Hall College, November 7, 1877.

the suffragans of his province for the filling of the See of Richmond. At that time the three names chosen, as mentioned previously,[12] had been Chatard, Keane, and Northrop. Although Chatard's name was first on the *terna,* the archbishop confided to his diary that he believed the removal of the rector of the American College in Rome just at that time would prove injurious to the institution and for that reason he wrote a letter to Cardinal Franchi, "strongly recommending Rev. Fr. Keane...."[13] Some days later he preached the first sermon in the cathedral since his appointment to Baltimore when on the third Sunday of Advent he spoke on the "Presence of God." The practice of Sunday preaching in the cathedral was one which Gibbons followed all through the forty-four years of his life as Archbishop of Baltimore. Although business often called him away from the city he usually managed to preach at least once a month at the Sunday high Mass and these sermons ultimately became occasions which the Catholics of the city greeted with considerable anticipation.

Another project to which Gibbons gave his attention during his first weeks in Baltimore was the support of St. Mary's Industrial School for homeless boys. This institution had been a favorite one with Archbishop Spalding who founded it in September, 1866, with the Xaverian Brothers in charge. In the intervening years it had accomplished great good for the city's orphan boys by teaching them trade skills and inculcating a moral tone in their lives. Since it had a strong claim to the support of the community, Gibbons did not hesitate to invite the Baltimore members of the state legislature to a meeting where he "exposed to them the services wh. the institution was rendering to the cause of religion & morality & the claims it has on a continuance of city & state patronage." He noted in his diary that several of the state legislators present "spoke warmly of the institution."[14] Gradually, then, the administration of the archdiocese became more familiar to the new ordinary, and in his first months he was served by Joseph P. Dubruel, S.S., as his vicar-general with William E. Starr the chancellor, Thomas S. Lee the rector of the cathedral, and the convert priest, Alfred A. Curtis,

---

12 Cf. *supra,* Chap. IV, p. 160.
13 Diary, December 7, 1877, p. 96.
14 *Ibid.,* December 16, 20, 1877.

as his secretary. These priests had been on the scene in Baltimore for some time and they were able, therefore, to acquaint Gibbons with the details of many of the problems which confronted him.

In the many letters which Denis O'Connell wrote to Archbishop Gibbons from Rome in the last weeks of 1877 while he was waiting for the consistory, he managed to give him many interesting items of Roman news and gossip. On November 13 he said there was some talk among unauthoritative persons of "creating a resident American dignitary in Rome — Monsig. Chatard." New cardinals were also rumored for the coming consistory, and O'Connell had been going about trying to learn if an American would be among them. He confessed that he had "caught nothing reliable yet, but Card. McCloskey was appointed without any previous noise," and he quoted Dr. Ubaldo Ubaldi as saying openly that Baltimoreans had felt the antiquity of their see slighted "by Papal preference for New York." Rome at this time, said O'Connell, was filled with apprehension concerning the possible designs of the secular governments on the next conclave. An item of more immediate interest to an American was contained in O'Connell's brief sentences, "Father Hecker's October article caused some talk. Miss Edes will read some parts of it to his Eminence."[15] Ella Edes, a convert news-

---

[15] 73-I-1, O'Connell to Gibbons, Rome, November 13, 1877. The unsigned article was entitled "The Outlook in Italy," *Catholic World*, XXVI (October, 1877), 1–21. The author was critical of Italian Catholics for permitting the Church to be maneuvered into an embarrassing position vis-à-vis the State. He asked, "What has beguiled so large a number of people of Italy, once so profoundly Catholic, that now they should take up the false principles of revolution, should accept a pseudo-science, and unite with secret atheistical societies?" He drew a comparison between the favorable position of the Church in the United States and that in Latin countries, and insofar as remedies for Italian Catholicism were concerned Hecker declared, "The balm that will cure the present wound in Italy is not likely to be found in a closer alliance of the church with the acutual state" (p. 19).

Regarding Miss Edes, a little insight into her favorable position in Rome can be gleamed from an entry in the diary of Archbishop Robert Seton at the New York Historical Society under date of June 20, 1905. Seton had recently visited Edes and he wrote of her that she was "long a correspondent of some newspaper. A great friend of Card. Barnabò. Says he was her confessor. Grew blind as he grew old and she used to go up to Propaganda every evening and talk to him and tell him the news." Although Barnabò had died some years previous to the Hecker article, Edes, who was a resident in Rome into the twentieth century, continued to exercise influence on American Church matters there long after his death.

paperwoman in Rome, was not friendly to Gibbons' interests as we shall have reason to see. The cardinal to whom the Hecker article would presumably be read was most likely Franchi, the Prefect of Propaganda.

Two days later O'Connell wrote again to say that he had that day had an audience of Pius IX whose "great frame," as he expressed it, "is nearly worn." He had asked the Pope's blessing for the new Archbishop of Baltimore which the Pontiff had given, and then,

> . . . shaking his closed hand as if threatening an enemy [he] said with great vehemence, "e gli dia la forza ed il coraggio." His earnestness made a profound impression on all present. This happened in the chamber of the Tapestries. They are the words to you of Christ's Vicar-maybe of Christ, and seem to indicate that you are raised up for a struggle.[16]

Ten days later O'Connell was writing in a less solemn tone to say that the date of the consistory was still uncertain due to Pius IX's health, but it was now virtually settled that there would be no American cardinals. He commented, "Italy has certainly its share and England, with its few Catholics, has two."[17] It is difficult to escape the impression that by these repeated references to an American cardinal O'Connell was teasing Gibbons with the prospect of the red hat coming to Baltimore. That O'Connell himself was making a good impression in Rome that winter we know from Hostlot's testimony to Archbishop Gibbons. The Roman vice-rector commented on the industry, tact, and knowledge of the young American priest. He said that several of the officials of Propaganda had expressed their surprise to him at O'Connell's knowledge in philosophy, theology, and "even in the higher ecclesiastical administration." This prompted Hostlot to say that he had often thought of what an advantage it would be to the diocese if O'Connell, as he put it, "could stop here some time longer to continue & perfect himself in canon law and other studies pertaining thereunto. . . ."[18] In the light of O'Connell's succession to the Roman rectorship in 1885 and his long and valuable service to Gibbons as an unofficial agent at the Holy

---

[16] 73-I-4, O'Connell to Gibbons, Rome, November 15, 1877.

[17] 73-I-13, O'Connell to Gibbons, Rome, November 26, 1877.

[18] 73-I-15, Hostlot to Gibbons, Rome, November 27, 1877.

See these early evidences of his success in Rome are of more than ordinary interest.

During the course of the next month seven long letters reached Baltimore from O'Connell in which he chronicled the ups and downs to which he was subject in the matter of the pallium. The date was once set but the Pope took sick and again the consistory had to be postponed; but at length on December 28 Pius IX assembled the College of Cardinals in his library when the pallia for the new archbishops were postulated for and given out. Cardinal Manning of Westminster was present and Dr. O'Connell told Gibbons that following the consistory, "I declared to Card. Manning your esteem for his person, and presented the compliments of the season. The old cardinal was pleased to hear it and salutes you most respectfully." A final letter told the Archbishop of Baltimore that his agent would sail on the *Germanic* on January 10. The ailing Pontiff was growing more feeble as time went on, and, as O'Connell said, "If he closed his eyes and stretched himself, he would be taken for a corpse." O'Connell told Gibbons that Miss Edes was grateful for the picture of Archbishop Bayley which he had sent her, and he added, "she says she made you coadjutor, at least hastened your nomination. Bishop Corrigan wrote her to do so."[19]

With the troublesome problem of the pallium finally settled Archbishop Gibbons could now make definite plans for the ceremony of its formal bestowal in his cathedral. The date was set for February 10, 1878, and his invitations were soon dispatched to the American hierarchy. Bishop Thomas Foley wrote from Chicago that he would be there, and he added, "You are promoted because you merited it, and you have won your place without ambitioning it."[20] Archbishop Wood was first invited to confer the pallium on Gibbons, but he regretted that his health made it impossible for him to accept.[21] The archbishop then turned to his senior suffragan, Patrick N. Lynch of Charleston, who consented to perform the ceremony. The prospect of the trip to Baltimore may have cheered Lynch a little, for he told Gibbons that because of the crushing load of debt he was then carrying he

---

[19] 73-K-9, O'Connell to Gibbons, Rome, December 30, 1877. The other O'Connell letters from Rome at this time were written on November 27, December 4, 5, 12, 19, and 28 (73-I-16; J-2-J-3; J-10; K-1; and K-8).

[20] 73-L-11, Foley to Gibbons, Chicago, January 15, 1878.

[21] 73-M-4, Wood to Gibbons, Philadelphia, January 18, 1878.

did not believe, as he expressed it, that a man, "under sentence of death, feels more gloomy and sad than I do — and have done ever since Christmas."[22] A pressing invitation to Bishop Corrigan in Newark told him that Gibbons would be "more than disappointed by any excuse."[23] Corrigan replied that he would be present and he suggested to the archbishop that he invite George Conroy, Bishop of Ardagh and Apostolic Delegate to Canada, who was in the United States at the time.[24] Gibbons had met Conroy at Westport in Ireland on his visit in the fall of 1870 and he was glad to get word that the delegate was coming to Baltimore for the ceremony.[25]

On January 22 Denis O'Connell arrived in Baltimore with the long sought pallium.[26] With everything in readiness for the ceremony the plans were temporarily halted when news reached the United States that Pius IX had died on February 7. Gibbons felt a certain hesitation in proceeding with the arrangements for the pallium, but on February 8 he received a telegram from Cardinal McCloskey of New York which read, "Don't postpone ceremony."[27] The decision was made, therefore, to go ahead, even if the external pomp of the procession from the rectory to the cathedral and the use of an orchestra were to be omitted. Besides Archbishop Gibbons and Archbishop Williams of Boston, there were eleven American bishops in attendance along with Bishop Conroy of Ireland. Lynch celebrated the pontifical Mass and preached, after which Gibbons himself responded. In his remarks the latter explained the significance of the pallium and the advantage Catholics in large centers enjoyed in having an opportunity to witness the grandeur of solemn church ceremonies. Gibbons mentioned his experience in the South in receiving converts into the Church who had never seen a celebration of this kind since "their worship was in a place no better than a log cabin."[28] Following the Mass a dinner was served to the guests and in the evening John Lancaster Spalding, Bishop of Peoria, delivered a lengthy eulogy at pontifical vespers on Pope Pius IX. At the end of the day the vicar-general of the archdiocese, Joseph

---

[22] 73-M-10, Lynch to Gibbons, Charleston, January 22, 1878.

[23] AANY, Gibbons to Corrigan, Baltimore, January 21, 1878.

[24] *Ibid.*, Gibbons to Corrigan, Baltimore, February 1, 1878.

[25] 73-N-11, Conroy to Gibbons, Brooklyn, February 2, 1878.

[26] Diary, January 22, 1877, p. 98.

[27] 73-N-16, McCloskey to Gibbons, New York, February 3, 1878, telegram.

[28] Baltimore *Sun,* February 11, 1878. The *Catholic Mirror* of February 16, 1878, gave the story of the conferring of the pallium in great detail.

Dubruel, confided to his diary a brief comment on the events in which he said, "Bishop Lynch's address was very good, but still better was the answer of Arch. Gibbons."[29]

On the following day the archbishop dedicated the new building at St. Mary's Seminary, an event attended by most of the prelates who had come to Baltimore for the pallium. Bishop Conroy delivered the sermon on the subject of the renewal of clerical promises at the dedication. The apostolic delegate remained as Gibbons' guest for a week, and they made a round of visits to religious institutions in and near Baltimore. On February 18 the guest, whom Gibbons characterized as "a gifted & accomplished Prelate," was present at the pontifical requiem in the cathedral celebrated by the archbishop for Pius IX. On this occasion Father John J. Keane, assistant at St. Patrick's Church in Washington, preached what Gibbons called "a magnificent discourse" on the late Pope. Two days later the archbishop received a cable from the Associated Press announcing that Joachim Cardinal Pecci, Bishop of Perugia, had been elected Pope and had taken the name of Leo XIII. The misgivings concerning the possible interference of the Italian government in the conclave had not been in any way borne out and the election came on the third ballot only forty-eight hours after the opening of the conclave. Gibbons stated in his diary that the leading candidates for the papal throne had been reported to be Cardinals Franchi, Bilio, DeLuca, and Panebiancho. He closed his diary entry by saying, "Card. McCloskey did not arrive in time for the conclave, having arrived in Tusculum [*sic*] from New York on the 18th."[30] A week after the election the Archbishop of Baltimore dispatched a letter of congratulations and good wishes from himself, the priests, and the people to the new Pontiff.[31]

James Gibbons was not many months in Baltimore before the archdiocese suffered the loss by death of two of its most prominent priests. Charles I. White, pastor of St. Matthew's Church in Washington, who had baptized him, died the first week in April and three weeks later, Joseph P. Dubruel, S.S., the archbishop's vicar-general, died on Easter Saturday, April 20.[32] The Bishop of Newark wrote his sympathy on the death of the vicar-

---

[29] ASMS, Diary of Joseph P. Dubruel, S.S., February 10, 1878, p. 29.

[30] Diary, February 11–20, 1878, pp. 100–102.

[31] 73-P-1, Gibbons to Leo XIII, Baltimore, March 1, 1878, copy.

[32] Diary, April 4, 23, 1878, pp. 103–104.

general, and in replying Gibbons confessed that the loss of one "whose counsel was very precious to me," was a real sorrow. "But as you well say," he continued, "death to a Sulpitian is precious in the sight of God."[33] On May 10 the archbishop appointed Father Edward McColgan, pastor of St. Peter's Church, as vicar-general,[34] a post in which he was to serve for twenty years. The death of Dubruel had deprived the Sulpicians of the United States of their superior and the superior-general in Paris asked the archbishop for his advice as to a successor, and at the same time requested that a Sulpician be not again appointed vicar-general of the archdiocese as the duties entailed in the two positions were too much for one man to fulfill properly. Father Henri Joseph Icard assured Gibbons, however, that the Sulpicians would be happy to assist him in any other way they could.[35] In reply the archbishop agreed with Icard that it was very difficult for the same man to fill simultaneously the offices of vicar-general and superior of the seminary, and for that reason he would comply with the request made of him. As to the successor of Dubruel, Gibbons was persuaded that Alphonse L. Magnien was the most worthy to succeed as Sulpician superior. He would be very acceptable to the clergy and the archbishop thought he had the qualities necessary to govern the seminary and to give satisfaction to those outside of the community.[36] Shortly thereafter Magnien was appointed as superior.

The prestige of his office as Archbishop of Baltimore soon brought to Gibbons requests for various writing assignments which he often did not have the time to undertake. The corresponding editor of the *American Catholic Quarterly Review* was hopeful of an article from him since, as he said, he felt that the widening influence of the journal would be furthered, "if we can secure contributions from such pens as yours."[37] The archbishop begged off, however, and suggested the name of Dr. Ganns in his place.[38] A few weeks after the death of

---

[33] AANY, Gibbons to Corrigan, Baltimore, April 23, 1878.

[34] Diary, May 10, 1878, p. 105.

[35] 73-S-10, Icard to Gibbons, Paris, May 19, 1878.

[36] Archives of the Society of St. Sulpice, Paris, Gibbons to Icard, Baltimore, June 4, 1878.

[37] 73-N-7, George Wolff to Gibbons, Philadelphia, January 30, 1878.

[38] 73-N-10, Wolff to Gibbons, Philadelphia, February 1, 1878. The only priest of this name in the *Catholic Directory* of that year was Henry G. Ganns,

Father White, John Gilmary Shea, historian of the Church in the United States, asked the archbishop's permission to examine White's collection of historical materials which, he said, he understood were being transferred to the archives in Baltimore;[39] and about the same time Benjamin J. Webb of Louisville requested Gibbons to write a sketch of the life of Bishop John McGill for the history of the Church in Kentucky which he was preparing.[40]

The early summer of 1878 found the archbishop on a visitation tour in southern Maryland. In driving between two small missions the party came to a wide creek and when the carriage reached the center of the creek one of the horses stopped and refused to move. Gibbons and his priest companion sat for nearly an hour until finally they saw a man at a distance whom they hailed and he procured a boat for them in which they were rowed ashore. As the archbishop wrote, "the refractory horse was unharnessed in the water, & the carriage drawn ashore, & a kind neighbor supplied us with another horse. Our young driver was very exultant because he did not even swear during the long ordeal."[41] Two weeks later he was scheduled to give confirmation at Doughoregan Manor, the estate of Governor Carroll. The governor invited him to be his week-end guest, and he told the archbishop that if he would inform him what train he was taking, "my carriage shall be in waiting to bring you up with any assistant you may select."[42] Gibbons spent the week end with the governor and his family and on Monday he presided at the commencement at St. Charles College. In the fall of that year the archbishop was present again at Ellicott City on November 4 for the patronal feast of St. Charles Borromeo. At that time William H. O'Connell, later Archbishop of Boston, was a student there and he wrote his impressions of Gibbons. He said the Archbishop of Baltimore struck him as "a very holy man, and withal very keen, too. He is almost emaciated,

assistant at St. Mary's Church, Lykens, Pennsylvania. Gibbons did write an article for the *Review* five years later entitled "The Law of Prayer," VIII (October, 1883), 577–596, and thereafter he was an occasional contributor to its pages. Cf. X (October, 1885), 696 ff; XIII (January, 1888), 1 ff; XIII (October, 1888), 577 ff.

[39] 73-R-6, Shea to Gibbons, Elizabeth, New Jersey, April 26, 1878.
[40] 73-R-7, Webb to Gibbons, Louisville, April 27, 1878.
[41] Diary, June 12, 1878, p. 108.
[42] 73-T-8, Carroll to Gibbons, Doughoregan Manor, June 26, 1878.

and the Southern boys adore him." O'Connell related that Gibbons addressed the students, and afterward he asked him to bless a rosary for him. In the course of his remarks on Gibbons the writer gave a description of his physical features which is of interest. He wrote:

> His face is thin — his features, large and bony. His eyes are lanterns; they transform his whole face — very bright and keen if rather small. He bears himself with simple dignity, and one sees at once the genuine priest and gentleman. . . . His voice is very pleasant and he speaks in a clear-cut manner. I should think he was a very careful, orderly painstaking man in everything; and then his face, not handsome, but very pure and noble, as if he had known great difficulties and had patiently worked them out.[43]

Although Archbishop Gibbons naturally felt closer to the Sulpicians by reason of his schooling than to other religious communities in his archdiocese, he was on friendly terms with all. When Father James Perron, S.J., of Woodstock College wrote him to say he was having a copy of Father Emilio M. de Augustinis' new book sent to him, Gibbons thanked him and said the new work would be a complement to that of Mazzella whose departure from Woodstock, he added, "I so much regret."[44] The distinguished Jesuit theologian, who had been in the United States since 1867, had recently been recalled to Rome. During his time in this country Gibbons had contact with Mazzella, not only as a critical reader of his manuscript of *The Faith of Our Fathers,* but also in his capacity as moderator of the theological conferences for the clergy of the Archdiocese of Baltimore.[45]

His efforts to remain on friendly terms with the various institutions in his jurisdiction, however, did not extend to the point of surrendering his convictions. For example, when the

---

[43] William Cardinal O'Connell, *The Letters of His Eminence William Cardinal O'Connell Archbishop of Boston* (Cambridge, 1915), I, 29–30. This volume of letters was edited by O'Connell years after their supposed dates of origin, but the full names of the persons to whom they were addressed were not given. For example, the letter quoted above bore the date of November 23, 1878, and was addressed merely to "Dear James." The writer had no opportunity to examine the original correspondence.

[44] AWC, Gibbons to Perron, Baltimore, October 9, 1878.

[45] On Mazzella, cf. Brendan A. Finn, *Twenty-Four American Cardinals* (Boston, 1947), pp. 381–391, a work which generally speaking, however, has to be used with caution.

president emeritus of Mount Saint Mary's College in Emmitsburg, John McCaffrey, objected to the rumored reintroduction in the churches of the archdiocese of the prayer of Archbishop Carroll for civil authorities, on the grounds that the people did not like it and that it might give occasion to the civil power for an opening wedge to dictate religious practices,[46] the archbishop assured McCaffrey that "any suggestion coming to me from so venerated & learned a source" would command his respectful attention. Nonetheless, he said he could see nothing to condemn and much to admire in the prayer, and he added, "Nor do I see how the recitation of this prayer can be construed with any sense of justice, into a badge of ultra submission to the civil powers." Gibbons would give the matter serious consideration before recommending it throughout the archdiocese, but as far as he knew it had never been interrupted in the cathedral since it had been inaugurated by Archbishop Kenrick.[47] Gibbons always showed a strong inclination to demonstrate his regard for the civil authorities and the nation's customs. For example, three years after this incident with McCaffrey he told Bishop Gilmour of Cleveland that he was going to issue an order for public prayers on Thanksgiving Day. "We should not let Protestants surpass us," he wrote, "in our expression of loyalty & devotion to our country."[48]

The pressure of diocesan business was, of course, constant and of a great variety. In January, 1879, the archbishop was informed that the superior of the Mill Hill Fathers did not wish his men in Baltimore to be engaged for ministrations to the whites. It had been reported to the superior that Gibbons had recently asked one of these priests to say Mass at the penitentiary on a Sunday when over 200 whites and only twenty colored were in attendance. The last general chapter of the society had legislated to the effect that the members should devote themselves exclusively to the Negroes and the request was made, therefore, that the archbishop please not ask the Mill Hill men in the future to undertake work for the whites.[49] The need of more nursing sisters in Baltimore had been felt for some time and Gibbons availed himself of his trip to Europe

[46] 74-A-4, McCaffrey to Gibbons, Emmitsburg, October 11, 1878.

[47] AMSMC, Gibbons to McCaffrey, October 16, 1878.

[48] ADC, Gibbons to Gilmour, Baltimore, November 14, 1881.

[49] 74-G-4, P[eter] Benoit to Gibbons, London, January 7, 1879.

in the spring of 1880 to seek the services of the Bon Secours Sisters in Paris. In October of that year he informed the superior that a residence was ready to receive them and in July, 1882, a larger and better house was blessed by Gibbons for these women whose services to the sick proved so beneficial to the city's unfortunate.[50] Further facilities for the care of Baltimore's orphans were likewise provided when on December 28, 1881, Gibbons installed four Sisters of St. Francis from England, all of whom were converts, in their new home on St. Paul Street where they assumed charge of a foundling asylum and school for colored children.[51] The growing foreign-born population of the city prompted the archbishop in July, 1882, to request the provincial of the Redemptorists in Vienna to send him several Bohemian priests who could help to care for the increasing number of Bohemians who were at this time crowding into St. Wenceslaus Parish.[52]

When the time neared for the celebration of Baltimore's sesquicentennial the archbishop sent out a circular to his clergy instructing them to have the various parish societies prepared to march in the parade on October 14. Moreover, the *Te Deum* was ordered to be sung in all the churches after vespers on Sunday, October 17, and the priests were urged to preach on the event and to give thanks to God who in His mercy, said Gibbons, "has cast our lot in a city founded on the land of the Catholic Carrolls . . . a city whose inhabitants in the past have witnessed the most interesting events of Catholic history in this country." The Catholic people should be told to enter into the spirit of the occasion with their fellow citizens, but to avoid "all sinful excess" during the days of the celebration.[53] When the sesquicentennial was held on October 11–19, 1880, "the city gave itself over to gaiety and enjoyment with an abandon never before known. The city fathers appropriated $10,000 and private citizens added $20,000 to the Sesqui-Centennial fund."[54] Some months later when President James

---

[50] Diary, April, October 19, 1880; July 8, 1882, pp. 139, 144, 162. For the early history of these sisters in Baltimore, cf. James M. Hayes, *The Bon Secours Sisters in the United States* (Washington, 1931), pp. 50–91.

[51] Diary, December 28, 1881, pp. 155–156.

[52] *Ibid.*, July 22, 1882, p. 161.

[53] *Ibid.*, September 24, 1880, p. 145.

[54] Hall, *op. cit.*, I, 253.

A. Garfield was shot on July 2, 1881, by an assassin Gibbons at once wrote a circular letter to the clergy in which he urged prayers for the stricken chief executive. He said:

> You will, therefore, with all the power at your command, urge your people to pray during Mass and at other times for the recovery of His Excellency, and on Sunday next, should he then still survive you will say in his behalf before or after Mass, and together with all your people the Litany of the Saints; as at once entreating God to spare his life and also as making an act of expiation for a crime which appertains to us as a nation and not only concerns but tarnishes us all.[55]

A copy of the circular letter was forwarded by the archbishop's secretary to Mrs. Garfield with an expression of sympathy. The quick response of Gibbons to these city and national events was a further exemplification of the keen interest he showed in associating himself with the joys and sorrows of the community of which he was a part. He never lost an opportunity to express this interest and pride, and one could see it in so simple a thing as the archbishop's letter of thanks to the president of the Baltimore and Ohio Railroad for the renewal of his annual pass when he congratulated him on the success that the road had experienced under his administration, a fact, as he said, "which is a subject of just pride to every citizen of Maryland."[56]

In the early days of 1879 Archbishop Gibbons lost one of his dearest personal friends when Bishop Thomas Foley, Coadjutor and Administrator of Chicago, died on February 19. Bishop Becker offered the pontifical requiem and Gibbons preached the eulogy. After recounting some of the salient facts of Foley's life the preacher revealed his personal sorrow. He said:

> And now bear with me one moment, for the grief of my own heart is great. I have spoken of the loss that you, Chicago and his family have sustained, and yet his death has inflicted on my heart an anguish and a wound which only time and the mercy of God can heal, and which can only be appreciated by those who know what true friendship is.[57]

---

[55] Diary, July 2, 5, 1881, pp. 151–152.
[56] LC, Robert Garrett Papers, Gibbons to L. M. Cole, Baltimore, January 1, 1880.
[57] Baltimore Sun, February 25, 1873.

When four years later the archbishop suffered the loss of his own mother the fact of the speedy burial of the dead in New Orleans and the great distance between the two cities did not permit him to attend the funeral. In his diary for May 8, 1883, he wrote, "My dear Mother died last night at the age of 80 years. May she rest in peace."[58] A week later he extended his thanks to Archbishop Francis X. Leray of New Orleans for, as he put it, "your great kindness and charity in presiding at the funeral service of my dear Mother. I beg you also to thank for me your devoted clergy who were present on the same occasion."[59]

Amid the varied duties which engaged Gibbons' attention as archbishop he managed to find time for some writing. One of his first publications after his return to Baltimore was a pastoral letter on the subject of "Christian Education." In it the archbishop gave a fairly lengthy description of the evil effects of a purely secular education. He estimated that at the time there were 17,500 children enrolled in the parochial schools, academies, and colleges of the Archdiocese of Baltimore, besides, as he added, "1,600 children who are clothed, supported and educated in our industrial schools and asylums." He said that from the evidence submitted "the conclusion is forced upon us, that Catholic Parochial Schools must be established and fostered, if we would preserve the faith of our children." After an appeal to Scripture and to history to illustrate his argument, he ended with a strong exhortation to parents to heed the duty which they had to see to it that their children were given the benefits of a religious education.[60] Bishop Tobias Mullen of Erie wrote Gibbons about the pastoral, "It is excellent reading on a most important subject, in fact the most important that can engage the solicitude of prelates, priests or people. . . ."[61] From England Bishop Herbert Vaughan of Salford likewise stated that he had read the letter with much interest, and he recommended the *Tablet* as a source wherein Gibbons would find a "continuous stream of information and comment on this the question of

---

[58] Diary, May 8, 1883, p. 168.

[59] AUND, New Orleans Papers, Gibbons to Leray, Baltimore, May 14, 1883.

[60] *Catholic Mirror*, January 27, 1883. The pastoral letter called forth an approving editorial in the *Freeman's Journal* of January 27, 1883.

[61] 77-B-4, Mullen to Gibbons, Erie, January 25, 1883.

the day."[62] Some months after the appearance of the pastoral letter Gibbons and the Abbé Alphonse Magnien made a visit to St. Joseph's Academy in Emmitsburg where he spoke to the sisters and complimented them on the work they were doing for the education of young girls. On this occasion he took the opportunity to urge them to work for the canonization of Mother Elizabeth Seton, their American foundress, and he said, "I would myself very gladly take the initiative, if I had any encouragement from here; the first movement must naturally begin here. . . . You remember too that American canonized Saints are very rare birds, and Mother Seton's name would add another to the very short list."[63]

The relations of Archbishop Gibbons in these years to the other major Catholic school in Emmitsburg illustrate his sense of responsibility to the institutions in his archdiocese and at the same time his generosity to charitable causes. Mount Saint Mary's College had been founded in 1808 and had given splendid service through the years to the American Church. Gibbons had no connection with the college other than that as ordinary of the diocese in which it was situated, since he was never there as a student. When John McCaffrey, the former president, reported that all was going well at Mount Saint Mary's in the early autumn of 1880 Gibbons replied that he rejoiced to hear it, and he added, "I am warmly interested in its welfare."[64] However, matters were not as good as McCaffrey thought and a few months later the college found itself in one of the most severe financial crises of its history. In the emergency the archbishop wrote a circular letter "appealing to the alumni for aid in behalf of the College."[65] But the efforts to avert catastrophe seemed at first to have failed and Gibbons told Father Patrick H. Hennessy that from what he read in the papers it would seem that "it is all over now. . . ." He continued that the archbishops of Baltimore had never had any control over the finances of the college, "nor even any knowledge" of such except of an official character.[66]

[62] 77-C-1/1, Vaughan to Gibbons, Salford, February 8, 1883.
[63] Archives of St. Joseph's Central House, Emmitsburg, Annals, August 3, 1882.
[64] AMSMC, Gibbons to McCaffrey, Baltimore, October 2, 1880.
[65] *Ibid.*, Gibbons to "My dear Doctor," Baltimore, January 8, 1881.
[66] *Ibid.*, Gibbons to Hennessy, Baltimore, February 28, 1881.

In the emergency at Emmitsburg it seemed wise that Father William J. Hill should retire from the presidency and with that in mind Gibbons suggested the names of three priests whom, as he said, "you might sound."[67] He told Silas Chatard that he regarded Byrne as "facile princeps," and to prove his interest in Mount Saint Mary's he added, "As an earnest of my good will I propose to go to New York on the day after Palm Sunday & confer with the Cardinal on the subject of the College."[68] At length William Byrne, Vicar-General of the Archdiocese of Boston, was the man selected. In order to save the old college from closing, an advisory board was appointed to assist in its finances and Gibbons agreed to take the chairmanship and treasurer's post on this board.[69] In his capacity as treasurer he had received in donations $15,625 by the following October, and he reported the sum to Byrne and added, "My own donation is available at any time."[70] Through the efforts of the advisory board and the loyalty of the alumni Byrne could report by March, 1882, that the court had released the college from the custody of the receiver. The president revealed himself as sensible of the assistance that Archbishop Gibbons had given when he said:

I must avail myself of this opportunity to thank Your Grace for your kind co-operation, generous support and wise counsel in this whole struggle. I hope that neither your patience, charity or indulgence has been exhausted by our proceedings so that I may venture to ask to be allowed to make heavy drafts on them soon.

Byrne then proposed that Gibbons become a member of the college council.[71] Although he had given both time and money to Mount Saint Mary's in the crisis, the Archbishop of Baltimore was not willing to become an official member of what was variously termed in the correspondence the "council," "board," and "corporation." By the early spring of 1882 the worst of the crisis was over and Gibbons told Byrne that it was to him as president that there was due "the chief credit for the resuscitation of the College. You had a dark road before you

---

67 *Ibid.*, Gibbons to "My dear Doctor," Baltimore, March 23, 1881.
68 AANY, Gibbons to Chatard, Baltimore, April 2, 1881.
69 ADC, Corrigan to Gilmour, New York, April 12, 1881.
70 AMSMC, Gibbons to Byrne, Baltimore, October 28, 1881.
71 76-O-2, Byrne to Gibbons, Emmitsburg, March 7, 1882.

& you faced it."[72] Three years later the archbishop again
expressed his concern for Mount Saint Mary's when he said
he had taken, "& will continue to take an active interest in
the College. . . ." Nonetheless, he still declined to permit his
name to appear officially in what he called "the list of [the]
active Board. My name would be a mere figure-head."[73]

The manner in which Gibbons responded to the dire straits
of the Emmitsburg college was typical of the way he met
demands upon his purse from worthy causes. When the yellow
fever epidemic broke with such devastating effects in the
South in the fall of 1878, the archbishop within three weeks
sent off checks varying in size from $100 to $500 to a total
of $3,000 acknowledged by the grateful recipients. He directed
his charities mainly to New Orleans, Tennessee, and Mississippi
with requests that they be given to the particular missions or
orphanages most in need.[74] Among many others Bishop Elder
of Natchez told Gibbons, "The liberal contributions that you
and others have sent, have been a great service already."
During the epidemic word reached Baltimore that Elder had
died of the yellow fever; whereupon there had been celebrated
a requiem Mass and a sermon preached on Elder's sacrifice.
The Bishop of Natchez wrote of this false report, "And what
shall I say in acknowledgment of the Requiem Mass & the
funeral sermon! Well — if the Mass did not get me out of
Purgatory, it helped to get me out of my sick bed. And for
the sermon, — I cannot say much about that, until I see it or
hear it."[75] Gibbons continued his help to the yellow fever victims
well into the autumn, and as late as November 4 Elder was
acknowledging an additional check of $500 from him.[76]

Among the charities which the Archbishop of Baltimore
patronized in these years was an annual donation of $100 to
the support of Dr. Levi Silliman Ives, the convert Protestant
Episcopal Bishop of North Carolina.[77] He likewise used the
collections taken up throughout his archdiocese by the Society

[72] AMSMC, Gibbons to Byrne, Baltimore, March 9, 1882.

[73] *Ibid.*, Gibbons to "Rev. Dear Father," Baltimore, June 30, 1885.

[74] The latter part of Box 73 and the first part of Box 74 of the Gibbons
Papers, AAB, contain several dozen letters of thanks from recipients of checks for
the yellow fever victims in the South.

[75] 74-A-8, Elder to Gibbons, Vicksburg, October 14, 1878.

[76] 74-C-3, Elder to Gibbons, Vicksburg, November 4, 1878.

[77] 73-T-11, John M. Farley to Gibbons, New York, July 3, 1878.

for the Propagation of the Faith to assist less favored missionary areas of the Church in the United States. For example, Archbishop Joseph S. Alemany of San Francisco received nearly $600 from this source in 1878 for his difficult missions in Utah.[78] And when in the next year bankruptcy overtook Archbishop Purcell in Cincinnati, Gibbons contributed $4,460[79] to the fund being raised by the American bishops, in addition to writing Purcell several letters of encouragement and sympathy. The old Archbishop of Cincinnati was grateful for what he termed, "the most kind letters you were pleased to write to me and of me."[80] Shortly after the Purcell failure in Cincinnati word reached the United States of the great suffering in Ireland as a consequence of the war over the Land League. In the crisis which had come to the Irish peasants Archbishop Gibbons in February, 1880, directed that there be sent nearly £3,000 for relief purposes with £400 earmarked for Archbishop MacHale of Tuam and a like sum for his old schoolmate, Bishop McCormack of Achonry.[81] These various sums dispensed by Gibbons during these years were but a small amount of the benefactions which he gave to a wide variety of charities all through the time that he was Archbishop of Baltimore.

One of the principal duties of a metropolitan is to serve as a guide and counselor to the suffragan bishops of the province over which he presides. In the early years of Gibbons as Archbishop of Baltimore there arose a number of problems in the suffragan sees of the province which demanded his direction and advice. We have already seen his efforts in behalf of the vacant See of Richmond and his recommendation to Rome that Father Keane should be named to the diocese. After a long delay, occasioned in part by the bulls being misdirected and sent to the dead letter office in New York,[82] they arrived in

---

[78] 74-F-8, Annual Report of the Propagation of the Faith for the Archdiocese of Baltimore for the Year Ending November 30, 1878.

[79] 74-U-7, John J. Williams to Gibbons, Boston, December 16, 1879. The trouble in Cincinnati arose from the failure of the archbishop's brother, Father Edward Purcell, who had for nearly forty years been conducting a private banking business for small depositors. Cf. John H. Lamott, *History of the Archdiocese of Cincinnati, 1821–1921* (New York, 1921), pp. 171–207.

[80] 74-L-4, Purcell to Gibbons, Cincinnati, March 18, 1879.

[81] Diary, February 17, 26, 1880, p. 137. On the subject of American reaction to this Irish crisis, cf. James J. Green, "American Catholics and the Irish Land League, 1879–1882," *Catholic Historical Review*, XXXV (April, 1949), 19–42.

[82] *Ibid.*, August 1, 1878, p. 111.

Baltimore on August 1, 1878, with the name of John J. Keane as the new bishop. The fact that the diocese had been vacant for nearly a year probably prompted them to hasten the ceremony of consecration and the date was fixed for August 25 at St. Peter's Cathedral in Richmond. Keane chose Gibbons to consecrate him, the first of twenty-three such ceremonies which the archbishop was to perform in the years ahead. Gibbons reached the Virginia capital three days in advance of the event which gave him an opportunity to visit his friends there. The consecration of Keane brought together the bishops of the province, and they used the opportunity to draw up for the Holy See a *terna* for the vacant Vicariate of North Carolina. Their choices were Mark Gross, Henry Northrop, and Francis Janssens in that order.[83] Gibbons found real satisfaction in consecrating and installing Keane as fifth Bishop of Richmond and his own successor in that see, for he had taken a liking to the thirty-nine-year-old prelate and had been impressed by the fine work he had done at St. Patrick's in Washington. He had a special admiration for the exceptional ability which Keane had shown as a preacher.[84]

Another of Gibbons' suffragan bishops, John Kain of Wheeling, warned him against accepting lectures for charitable causes since he was already burdened with too many duties. Kain said that

---

[83] *Ibid.,* September 2, 1878, p. 113 ff. Someone had written a letter to Rome complaining against Gross' lack of knowledge of theology to be a bishop. Gibbons defended Gross against the charge made to Giovanni Cardinal Simeoni, Prefect of Propaganda (*ibid.,* January 24, 1880, pp. 135–136). At length news of the appointment of Gross to North Carolina came through on March 17, 1880, but he declined the honor and Rome accepted his resignation, notice of which reached Gibbons on October 25, 1880 (*ibid.,* p. 145). A new *terna* was drawn up on November 24 and Gibbons informed Simeoni of this action on December 5, 1880, but fault was found with the list and on May 7, 1881, a new *terna* was forwarded to the Holy See (*ibid.,* p. 149). It was from this list that the third name, Henry Northrop, was finally selected and word reached Gibbons on October 15, 1881. Gibbons consecrated Northrop in the cathedral of Baltimore on January 8, 1882 (*ibid.,* p. 158).

[84] Securing a bishop for Richmond lessened the archbishop's burden since the administrator was timid about making decisions and referred questions of a serious nature to the metropolitan. For example, Janssens told Gibbons in January, 1878, that the Richmond Italians wanted to have a requiem for the recently deceased Victor Emmanuel II, but he said, "I do not like to take the responsibility of such an act upon myself." Therefore, he turned to Gibbons for advice and said he would confer a favor on him by *"telegraphing* at once," what he should do (73-L-9, Janssens to Gibbons, Richmond, January 14, 1878). The answer of the archbishop was not available.

on his recent visit to Baltimore he thought Gibbons looked "worn & overtaxed," and it occurred to him to remind the archbishop "of Tom Jenkin's complaint about the expense of burying Archbishops."[85] Some months later the same bishop complained to Gibbons of how the Society for the Propagation of the Faith in Paris had overlooked the Diocese of Wheeling and he said, "Perhaps a few lines from you to the Directors would induce them to change their minds. . . . I shall be very grateful for your good offices in this important matter."[86] A similar appeal for the archbishop's moral support with the Paris society soon reached him from Bishop Keane in Richmond. Keane told him he found the finances of the diocese in a bad way and was able to get only from $20 to $30 a month to live on from the cathedral parish.[87] Gibbons advised his friend to write a strong letter to Paris; this Keane did and sent it to the archbishop with the request that he add an endorsement to his appeal.[88] When the latest disbursement of funds by the Paris society became known Keane felt aggrieved at getting only $233 for North Carolina, "and Richmond passed by without a word." He was hopeful, however, as he said, "that after reading your letter & my statement they will deal with us more kindly." During the time that Gibbons had been Bishop of Richmond he had tried, as we have seen, to improve the facilities for the colored Catholics there. Keane now told the Archbishop of Baltimore:

> Our work among the colored people, which I have proclaimed as only an attempt to carry out a project which you had long matured, & had bequeathed to me, meets with much success. They crowd the Cathedral, & behave in a way that would reflect credit on any white congregation. Their spirit towards us is already greatly changed — and soon I will commence catechism classes on week evenings, to gather any harvest the Lord may give us.[89]

As early as 1879 Thomas A. Becker, Bishop of Wilmington, who was likewise a suffragan of Baltimore, had grown discouraged and depressed there and had submitted his resignation

---

[85] 73-Q-12, Kain to Gibbons, Wheeling, April 15, 1878.
[86] 74-E-4, Kain to Gibbons, Wheeling, December 14, 1878.
[87] 74-F-6, Keane to Gibbons, Richmond, December 23, 1878.
[88] 74-G-1, Keane to Gibbons, Richmond, January 1, 1879.
[89] 74-I-5, Keane to Gibbons, Richmond, February 5, 1879.

to the Holy See. Giovanni Cardinal Simeoni, the new Prefect of Propaganda, asked Gibbons for his judgment in the case, and the archbishop replied with high praise for Becker's zeal and industry and said he believed he might be happier if he were transferred to a diocese where there was more episcopal work, especially one where there was a large number of German Catholics "whose idiom he uses."[90] Actually it was seven years before Becker was freed of Wilmington when in 1886 he became the sixth Bishop of Savannah. On February 26, 1882, Gibbons lost one of his suffragan bishops in the death of Patrick N. Lynch of Charleston. Lynch had attained a great deal of notice during the Civil War when he acted as an agent for the Confederate government in Europe. The archbishop attended the funeral and celebrated the requiem Mass on March 1. Three weeks later at a meeting of the bishops of the province in Baltimore a *terna* for Charleston was drawn up with William Wayrich, C.Ss.R., Patrick W. Riordan of Chicago, and Daniel J. Quigley, vicar-general of Charleston, as the names submitted and in that order.[91] Once more a long delay ensued, and when no appointment had been made by September, Gibbons wrote to Simeoni urging action, "& recommending the selection of Rev. Father Riordan in preference to the others."[92]

While awaiting a bishop for Charleston the Archbishop of Baltimore tried to be of as much help as he could to Quigley, the administrator, who in the spring of 1883 thanked him for what he termed, "your many acts of kindness which seemed to me to go beyond my official position."[93] About the same time the vicar-general of Richmond, Augustine Van de Vyver, acknowledged the metropolitan's check of $100 in offerings for Masses to be distributed among the poor priests of the diocese, and he said, "This token of your affection permits me to express again my sincere sentiments of love and gratitude towards you."[94] When he was in Paris in the fall of 1883 Archbishop Gibbons made a strong plea in behalf of the hard-pressed Henry Northrop who had meanwhile become Bishop of Charleston,

---

[90] Diary, September 12, 1879, p. 127, copy of Latin letter to Simeoni.
[91] *Ibid.*, February 26, 1882, p. 160.
[92] *Ibid.*, September 9, 1882, p. 163.
[93] 77-F-5, Quigley to Gibbons, Charleston, April 4, 1883.
[94] 77-F-6, Van de Vyver to Gibbons, Richmond, April 5, 1883.

while continuing as administrator of North Carolina. He told Northrop:

I have just returned from the Bureau of the Prop. of the Faith where I made a strong speech in your favor to Mr. Certes. I represented to him as powerfully as words came to me, the extreme poverty of the missions of N. & South Carolina, the trials you endured, & the absolute need of funds for the subsistence of yourself & clergy. . . .

On reaching Rome, I intend to embody in a letter to him the substance of my remarks today, which will be submitted to the council.

I shall also employ in your behalf the good offices of the Super. Curé of S. Sulpice who holds a leading place in the councils of the Prop. of the Faith. You have sown, I have watered, may God give the increase.[95]

Gibbons had not been in Baltimore a month as archbishop when he was appealed to by John Moore, Bishop of St. Augustine, who said he had two bright boys whom he would like to send to the American College in Rome and he inquired if the two burses maintained by the Archdiocese of Baltimore might not be assigned to the Florida youths.[96] The archbishop did give one of the Baltimore burses to Bishop Moore's student and the suffragan wrote his thanks, telling him at the same time about the yellow fever then raging in Florida and saying that the injury done to the business prospects of the region around St. Augustine, for that winter at least, was incalculable.[97] In ways such as these did James Gibbons endeavor to fulfill the responsibilities which were his as metropolitan of the Province of Baltimore, and these early activities were, of course, to continue through the nearly forty years ahead during which he presided as the principal dignitary of the province.

Both as ordinary of Baltimore and as an American metropolitan Archbishop Gibbons was called on constantly to give his judgment to the Holy See on the qualifications of men for the episcopacy. Often his choice for a vacant diocese was taken by Rome, as in the case of Keane for Richmond. Yet that was

[95] Archives of the Diocese of Charleston, Gibbons to Northrop, Paris, October 23, 1883.

[96] 73-H-12, Moore to Gibbons, St. Augustine, November 8, 1877.

[97] 73-I-7, Moore to Gibbons, St. Augustine, November 20, 1877.

not always true, for although, as we have seen, he wrote a special letter to the Holy See in September, 1882, recommending Riordan for Charleston, actually Northrop was named bishop. When it came time to fulfill the instruction of the Second Plenary Council of Baltimore that names be submitted to Rome every three years for the episcopacy, Gibbons sent those of Placide L. Chapelle, Jeremiah O'Sullivan, and George W. Devine of his own archdiocese and Denis J. O'Connell of Richmond.[98] Eventually all these men became bishops except Devine.

While it was a simple matter for the Archbishop of Baltimore to select names which he regarded as suitable for the episcopal office from among his priest acquaintances, it was at times anything but simple for him to give an informed judgment on the filling of vacancies in distant dioceses. When in 1878 the question of a coadjutor for Archbishop Alemany in San Francisco was raised and Bishop Elder of Natchez was prominently mentioned, Gibbons wrote to Rome, "exposing reasons why Bp. Elder should be permitted to remain in Natchez or that his departure for S. Francisco should be delayed." He said he did this at the request of the vicar-general and clergy of Natchez.[99] Meanwhile, however, the financial disaster in Cincinnati prompted the proposal that old Archbishop Purcell should have a coadjutor. After the original *terna* of April, 1879, proved a failure, since Edward Fitzgerald of Little Rock and Bernard McQuaid of Rochester both refused to be considered, the suffragans of Cincinnati in September of that year drew up a new list on which Elder was placed first.[100] Gibbons was heartily in favor of Elder for the Cincinnati position, and he warmly recommended the choice to Rome.[101] As he told Gilmour in a letter from Annapolis:

> On my return to Baltimore I shall forward a letter to Rome strongly urging the appointment of Dr. Elder. The only circumstance that may defeat your desire is his previous appointment to San Francisco. But I trust the desperate state of affairs in Cincinnati — which I shall not fail to represent — will determine the Holy See to reconsider its previous action.[102]

---

[98] Diary, February 4, 1881, p. 147.
[99] *Ibid.*, November 16, 1878, p. 119.
[100] 74-R-9, Gilmour to Gibbons, Cleveland, September 29, 1879.
[101] Diary, October 11, 1879, pp. 128–129.
[102] ADC, Gibbons to Gilmour, Annapolis, October 6, 1879.

When the news reached San Francisco of Elder's possible change
Alemany protested to Gibbons at the loss of a prospective co-
adjutor, but if it could not be averted then he asked that the
Archbishop of Baltimore suggest one of the young and energetic
bishops of the East to help him in San Francisco.[103] Ultimately
Elder was appointed to Cincinnati in 1880, and Archbishop
Alemany had to wait three more years before he obtained
assistance in the person of Patrick W. Riordan as coadjutor.

During the summer of 1880 Cardinal McCloskey of New
York likewise appealed to Gibbons for his assistance in getting
a coadjutor of his choice. He wrote him while the archbishop
was still in Europe, giving him the *terna* of the Province of
New York, and he said, "Will your Grace be kind enough
to write to Card. Simeoni giving your opinion — which I hope
will be a favorable one."[104] The New York case moved more
rapidly and within two and a half months McCloskey got as
his coadjutor with the right of succession Bishop Corrigan of
Newark, the third name on his list. Corrigan told Gibbons
that the one favor he wanted to ask of him before he left for
Rome, "was to try and avert this fearful load." Now that it had
happened he could, as he said, "only humbly commend myself
to your prayers — amazed at the thought that I am bidden to
carry a cross which your Predecessor told me, years ago in
your room, that even he would not dare to carry."[105]

In his effort to do something for Alemany in San Francisco
Gibbons had recommended John Kain of Wheeling as coadjutor
there. He added in his diary, "The Bishop of Richmond would
be an admirable choice also, but he would dread the responsibility."[106] A year elapsed without any action being taken and
then Gibbons noted that Alemany, "after consulting with me,"
had recommended Keane, Spalding, and Gross of Savannah to

---

[103] 75-B-7, Alemany to Gibbons, San Francisco, February 24, 1880.

[104] 75-H-2, McCloskey to Gibbons, New York, July 14, 1880. There is no way
of knowing what Gibbons did about the Lynch candidacy for the New York
coadjutorship when he was in Rome, but three months later when the news broke
that Corrigan had been appointed Gibbons told Lynch, "I was expecting to congratulate you soon on your transfer to a more responsible field. I wrote to Rome
on the subject as late as Sept. 4th. But I am sure that none will bow to
the decision of the Holy See more willingly than yourself" (Archives of the
Diocese of Charleston, Gibbons to Lynch, Baltimore, October 16, 1880, copy).

[105] 75-K-1, Corrigan to Gibbons, Newark, October 1, 1880.

[106] Diary, March 11–13, 1880, p. 139.

Rome in that order, and he added, "I have written today to Card. Simeoni strongly advising the confirmation of Dr. Keane or of Dr. Spalding."[107] Apparently Gibbons had changed his mind about Keane for San Francisco during the ensuing year. Spalding, however, refused to leave Peoria. He told Gibbons, "There is an impression in Rome that I may be induced to accept the coadjutorship of San Francisco. This is a mistake. My present responsibility is greater than my ability and my conscience will not permit me to go to San Francisco."[108] Spalding at the same time strongly recommended Father Patrick Riordan of Chicago and at length in 1883 he was named.

Besides helping to provide for vacant sees Archbishop Gibbons was expected to interest himself in grave situations that arose from time to time in various American dioceses. For example, by the spring of 1879 an acute financial crisis had arisen in the Archdiocese of New Orleans under the administration of Archbishop Napoleon J. Perché. The vicar-general in a letter to Gibbons painted a frightful picture of conditions and begged him to intervene at Rome for a coadjutor as necessary to avert ruin.[109] This grave opinion was seconded by Elder of Natchez who told him the same week that he had heard of the appeal that had been made to Baltimore. While Elder said he understood "why you would not like to interfere directly," yet conditions were truly critical with Perché then in Europe asking for new loans on bonds that would mortgage the whole of the properties of the Church.[110] When Simeoni informed Gibbons that Perché had asked for a coadjutor and had proposed Bishop Francis X. Leray of Natchitoches, Archbishop Gibbons concurred in the appointment of Leray, but stated that if it were to be made, a successor should be named to Natchitoches as soon as possible.[111]

Much of this type of business, to be sure, fell to the lot of all the archbishops of the United States, but the amount of it that reached the Archbishop of Baltimore was especially great since he exercised, in the absence of an apostolic delegate, many of the functions that would normally have been performed by

---

[107] *Ibid.,* February 3, 1881, p. 147.

[108] 76-C-9, Spalding to Gibbons, Peoria, August 30, 1882.

[109] 74-N-2, G. Raymond to Gibbons, New Orleans, May 17, 1879.

[110] 74-N-3, Elder to Gibbons, Natchez, May 23, 1879.

[111] Diary, June 2, 1879, pp. 124–125.

such an official. The years up to 1893 were crowded for James Gibbons with tasks of this kind, and even after the appointment of the delegate in that year it continued for a considerable period due to the unfamiliarity of the first delegate with American customs and, too, to the fact that by 1893 Gibbons' stature had clearly placed him as the first Catholic churchman of the United States.

The archbishop had not been long in Baltimore before he began to receive invitations to social functions in Washington. In March, 1878, for example, he was the dinner guest of Senator Francis Kernan of New York where the two senators from Virginia with several others were also present.[112] These contacts with public men were regarded by Gibbons all during his life in a serious way. Nor did he fail to inform the Holy See when he believed they had made a contribution to the cordial relations between Church and State. For example, in early July, 1879, he wrote Cardinal Simeoni telling him "of the good feeling which now subsists between the civil authorities and the Church," and he instanced the attendance of President Rutherford B. Hayes at the commencement of Georgetown College, and the recent action of the Governor of Maryland in signing a law which remitted "to a great extent" the tax on church property.[113] But the knowledge that the archbishop was acquainted with and esteemed by public men brought its annoyance, too, in the form of increasingly heavy demands for his intervention in behalf of office seekers or their friends. One of the earliest examples of this reached him in this same summer of 1879 when Ellen Ewing Sherman appealed to Gibbons for her brother, General Charles Ewing, who, she said, would like to be Governor of Utah. "I would be most happy if your Grace would write a few lines to the President in regard to this."[114] Whenever the archbishop felt that he could recommend a person in good conscience for an appointment of this kind he did so.

In the fall of the same year Archbishop Gibbons was asked and gave his support to a project of national scope when he subscribed for five shares of stock at $100 each in the recently

---

[112] *Ibid.*, March 25, 1878, p. 102.
[113] Diary, July 6, 1879, p. 126.
[114] 74-Q-2, Sherman to Gibbons, Oakland, Maryland, August 5, 1879.

organized Irish Catholic Colonization Association. The association had come into being for the purpose of colonizing the western states with Catholic settlers who would till the soil and strengthen the Church in rural areas. Bishops Ireland and Spalding were prominent in its founding and Mr. William J. Onahan of Chicago acted as secretary. It was Onahan who informed Gibbons that his payment for the capital stock he had subscribed was now due and payable.[115] John Ireland wrote him enthusiastically of the plans of the association for settling Irish Catholic farmers in Nebraska and Minnesota, and he said their success was due in very great measure to the endorsement given the movement by the leading bishops of the United States. He closed with a typical flourish, "The one name of the Archbishop of Baltimore on our list did more than fifty discourses from little bishops of the West."[116]

Although most of the time of Archbishop Gibbons was given over to the transaction of purely diocesan business or to problems, such as the above, which arose within the Church of the nation, considerable demands were made upon him, too, for the proper handling of relations between the Holy See and the American Church. When Bishop George Conroy, Apostolic Delegate to Canada, came to the United States in the winter of 1878 it was Gibbons who provided the delegate with a secretary and traveling companion in the person of Denis O'Connell. There seemed to be some difficulty at first about O'Connell's being released from his duties in Richmond and the delegate wrote Gibbons from Cincinnati that it might be better not to press matters further, adding, "I will manage to do without any one."[117] However, the difficulty was soon adjusted and O'Connell joined Bishop Conroy for the trip to the Far West, writing to Gibbons that the delegate spoke of Baltimore as " 'the best equippaged diocese in the world' and he has a high appreciation and a sincere regard for your Grace." One can infer that the twenty-nine-year-old priest was getting valuable experience with Conroy for his later services to Gibbons since he closed his letter by saying, "He gives me many useful hints on conduct towards others";[118] and a month later O'Connell

[115] 75-A-11, Onahan to Gibbons, Chicago, January 17, 1880.
[116] 75-C-1, Ireland to Gibbons, St. Paul, March 2, 1880.
[117] 73-P-4, Conroy to Gibbons, Cincinnati, March 8, 1878.
[118] 73-Q-1, O'Connell to Gibbons, San Francisco, March 25, 1878.

confessed that on the trip he had "learned much of human nature; much that will serve me all my life." He told Gibbons that the delegate feared the archbishop worked too hard and would break down if he continued. O'Connell explained to Conroy that Gibbons had worked for the past ten years and had not broken down, and that it was his intention to "economize power" when he had learned the details of his archdiocese, to which he added, "But he did not change his opinion."[119] At the end of his tour across the United States the apostolic delegate returned to Canada and from Quebec he wrote to the Archbishop of Baltimore:

> Now that I have reached Canada I feel it a duty to thank Your Grace for your kindness in sending Dr. O'Connell with me. I am well pleased with him.
> I hope you will carry out your intention of taking him to your diocese. I believe you will do well to make him useful in your own personal service.[120]

Although the suggestion of transferring Father O'Connell from the Diocese of Richmond was not followed immediately, the special talents of the young priest were not forgotten by Gibbons and five years later, when the time came for preparations to be made for the Third Plenary Council, he summoned O'Connell from his parochial work in Virginia to assist him in Baltimore and Rome.

In his capacity as Archbishop of Baltimore Gibbons was made a member of the executive board of the American College in Rome, and it was to him that there was sent the correspondence about the college since he was secretary of the board. When in 1878 Pope Leo XIII requested that the student body of twenty-one at the college be doubled, Gibbons was asked by the board at its meeting in New York on July 17 to communicate this wish to the metropolitans of the United States."[121] Four years

---

[119] 73-R-3, O'Connell to Gibbons, Marysville, California, April 21, 1878.
[120] 73-S-9, Conroy to Gibbons, Quebec, May 18, 1878. An effort to obtain the report of Conroy on American Catholicism was not successful. Monsignor Giuseppe Monticone, general archivist of the Congregation of the Propaganda, informed the writer in a letter of May 14, 1950, that "the most diligent search has been made in the different *fonds* of the archives, but the above-mentioned report of Monsignor Conroy has not been found."
[121] 73-U-3, Hostlot to Gibbons, Rome, July 17, 1878; 73-V-1, Gibbons to the Archbishops of the United States, Baltimore, August 6, 1878, copy.

later when certain unspecified rumors began to circulate about the rector of the college which were harmful to his good name, Gibbons told Archbishop Elder he believed the charges should be thoroughly investigated in justice to Monsignor Hostlot and to the college itself.[122] While he was anxious to see the question of the rectorship fairly settled, he told Elder in another letter, "I do not wish to take any action without the concurrence of his Eminence of New York, & am willing to act with him."[123] It was through Hostlot that the archbishop sent his letter of congratulation to Leo XIII on his recent encyclical, *Aeterni patris,* which encouraged the study of scholastic thought. Therein he thanked the Pope in the name of the suffragan bishops and priests of the Province of Baltimore and said he would urge both seminarians and lay students to study the works of St. Thomas Aquinas. The Roman rector informed him that he had presented the letter and the Pontiff had expressed his thanks, to which Hostlot added, "Yours is the first from our episcopate."[124]

About the same time Archbishop Gibbons was asked to interest himself in the rectorship of the American College of Louvain, an institution of which he knew even less than that of Rome. Monsignor John de Nève had served as rector since 1860 but in October, 1871, he was compelled to relinquish the position through illness. He later recovered his health and in 1880 he came to the United States in an effort to interest the hierarchy and the alumni in the college. Some of de Nève's friends were supporting him for another term in the rectorship and Gibbons was appealed to in the matter. Knowing little of the circumstances of the Louvain institution, the Archbishop of Baltimore sensibly did not commit himself. De Nève visited Louisville where Bishop McCloskey was likewise a bit reluctant to support him for the rectorship. As he wrote to Elder, "All things considered, it may after all be a risk to put him back, & for my part, as Archbishop Gibbons doesn't seem to care to take up the question, I shall, so far as I am concerned, leave the solution of the difficulty to the wisdom of Rome; & from

---

122 AAC, Gibbons to Elder, Baltimore, June 28, 1882.
123 *Ibid.,* n.d.
124 74-A-10, Hostlot to Gibbons, Rome, January 17, 1880. A copy of Gibbons' Latin letter to Leo XIII can be found in his diary under date of December 15, 1879, pp. 130–131.

what I can see, Rome is quite as unwilling to touch it as Dr. Gibbons."[125] Bishop Caspar H. Borgess of Detroit told Gibbons that on de Nève's initiative he had written him while he was in Rome concerning the Louvain matter, although he was not enthusiastic about the college and said its utility "seems to be of the past." However, he was so persistently pressed about the question that Gibbons would oblige him, as he said, "by giving your opinion on the subject for my final action in the affair."[126] This was only one of the many questions affecting the welfare of the American Church in its European connections which Gibbons was called on to help solve, and although de Nève did resume the Louvain rectorship in 1881 it was not through the intervention of the archbishop since his knowledge of the case was never sufficient for him to assume leadership in the matter.

In February, 1880, the Archbishop of Baltimore had printed a circular letter to his clergy informing them that shortly after Easter he was going to Rome where he would inform the Pope of the fidelity of his priests and people. He asked them to be generous to the collection for Peter's Pence on Easter Sunday, and he stated that Father McColgan would be the administrator of the archdiocese in his absence.[127] Less than two weeks before sailing Gibbons wrote Simeoni discrediting the rumors that the German Catholics in the United States were unjustly treated by the Irish bishops, and protesting against the removal of women from church choirs which, he said, in his judgment would be "impracticable & inexpedient."[128] Gibbons sailed for Rome on the *City of Chester* on April 22, accompanied by Fathers Alfred Curtis, Bernard McManus, John Foley, and Augustine Van de Vyver.[129] Before reaching Rome the party visited Liverpool, London, and Paris. It happened that Cardinal Manning was in Rome when he reached there, and Gibbons invited him to dinner at the American College, an invitation which Manning would be pleased to accept if, he said, "I am able to leave the

---

[125] AAC, McCloskey to Elder, Louisville, July 15, 1880.

[126] Archives of the Archdiocese of Detroit, Letterbook, November 14, 1879–December 31, 1880. Borgess to Gibbons, Detroit, August 24, 1880. On the Louvain college, cf. J. Van der Heyden, *The Louvain American College, 1857–1907* (Louvain, 1909).

[127] Diary, February, 1880, p. 140. A copy of the printed circular is pasted in here.

[128] *Ibid.*, April 10, 1880, p. 141.

[129] *Ibid.*, April 14, 1880, p. 142.

Vatican in time. On that day I have to be at a Congregation."[130] The meeting with Manning would give Gibbons an opportunity to discuss problems which the American and English Churches had in common with the Holy See. During his three weeks' stay in the Eternal City the Archbishop of Baltimore had two private audiences of Leo XIII and several conferences with Cardinal Simeoni and Lorenzo Cardinal Nina, the Secretary of State.[131]

That Gibbons did not neglect during his Roman visit the various questions affecting the American Church we know from his correspondence with Archbishop Elder. He told him that when he arrived in Rome there was a plan underway for increasing the Peter's Pence from the United States. It involved designating two bishops who would go from one diocese to another, or as an alternative, setting up confraternities, "presided over by distinguished ladies," under the supervision of the pastors. He concluded, "I gave the Card. a lengthened opinion in writing condemning in strong terms the two plans proposed, & adding that the plan already in vogue among us was the only feasible one. The H.F. not only approved of my suggestions, but incorporated them in a letter to the Abps. of the U.S. of which I am the bearer."[132]

After a return journey through northern Italy, Austria, and Germany where he witnessed the Passion Play at Oberammergau, the archbishop stopped at Amsterdam, Brussels, and Paris and then crossed to England. He visited Lulworth Castle where Archbishop John Carroll had been consecrated in 1790 and then went on to Birmingham where with Father Curtis he called on Cardinal Newman at Edgbaston and took breakfast with him. They spent the morning conversing with the great English cardinal and Gibbons later remarked, "I need not say with what keen pleasure I listened to the wealth of anecdote and narrative that flowed so abundantly from his well-stored mind."[133] After a month in Ireland he sailed from Queenstown

---

[130] 75-G-5, Manning to Gibbons, English College, Rome, May 17, 1880.

[131] Diary, September 3, 1880, p. 142.

[132] AAC, Gibbons to Elder, Verona, June 8, 1880.

[133] 99-P-1/4, text of Gibbons' sermon preached in the cathedral of Baltimore on April 6, 1902, commemorating Leo XIII's silver papal jubilee. The cardinal mentioned his visit to Newman in the summer of 1880 in connection with his audience of the Pope some weeks before. Referring to the audience, he said "I well remember with what eagerness and delight I determined to thank the Holy Father for having invested John Henry Newman with the sacred purple. Few official

on the *City of Chester* on August 25. The archbishop arrived in Baltimore on the evening of September 3 after an absence of four and a half months and noted in his diary, "Our entire trip, thank God, was devoid of mishaps."[134] Ten days later he spoke in the cathedral on his voyage to Europe, describing the Passion Play, the Cologne cathedral which, he said, he liked even better than St. Peter's, and his audiences of Leo XIII. He told the congregation that he might speak at great length on his observations of the governments of Europe and their relations to the Church, but he would content himself with saying, as he put it, that he was "proud to own that whatever be the faults and drawbacks of our own system & they are not a few, still I would infinitely prefer to live under our own flag than any Gov. of contin. Europe, for with us liberty is not a name, but a living reality."[135]

In these years before the *Code of Canon Law* had yet appeared to regulate definitely the relations of bishops and priests and the legislation of the councils of Baltimore had not adequately defined their mutual rights, there was considerable uneasiness on the part of many American prelates over the lack of precise legislation on the matter. When Bishop McQuaid was in Europe in 1878 he discovered that the English bishops avoided difficulty on this score by naming their priests as administrators of parishes rather than as rectors or pastors. The English system recommended itself to McQuaid and he told Bishop Corrigan, "We must come to some such arrangement in America."[136] The question of the removal of a pastor also bothered Corrigan and he remarked to Gibbons that the chief point of one of McQuaid's Roman memorials to Simeoni had been, *"Must a Prelate consult the Commission before making any transfer of a Pastor from Church to Church, against the will of the latter?"* The commission spoken of was a body of priests appointed to help the bishop judge in controverted cases, and Corrigan stated that Rome had already drawn up an affirmative reply and was

---

acts of the Sovereign Pontiff were received with more genuine satisfaction by the English-speaking world than this practical and graceful recognition of the eminent services rendered to religion by England's illustrious scholar and divine."

[134] Diary, September 3, 1880, p. 142.

[135] 75-I-5, text of the sermon given by Gibbons on September 12, 1880, in the Cathedral of the Assumption, Baltimore, in his own handwriting.

[136] 74-D-6, Corrigan to Gibbons, Newark, November 26, 1878, quoting McQuaid's letter of November 11 to him from Tours.

prevented from sending it only by the strong objections of Bishop McQuaid.[137] Gibbons, who was no specialist in canon law and who had, like the other bishops, only the Baltimore conciliar legislation as a guide, doubtless consulted the professors in his seminary for help in such matters. A month before the opening of the Fourth Provincial Council of Cincinnati he advised Elder on the question of the relations between bishops and priests. He said:

> Under the heading "disciplina Ecclesiastica," the relations of Bishops & priests, I would advise you to assert the broad principle that priests, even Rectors may be removed without trial by the Bishops from one place to another whenever in his judgment the interests of religion call for such a removal (the Bishop of course in all cases acting with prudence & discretion). . . . We cannot too much insist on the rights of Bishops on this point, as they are so often called in question, & the exercise of this right is essential to the discipline of the Church. . . .
>
> In view of recent experiences I think the H. See will be disposed to sustain the action of Bishops in a forcible removal from one place to another & in withdrawal of faculties, if the Bishops are careful to preserve in writing the charges on which they have acted, or when they can state the grounds on which they have decided ex informata conscientia.
>
> Although we are not obliged, I think it is desireable whenever the nature of the offense will admit of it, to give Pastors of mature years a trial before degrading them to an inferior place. It is well to have the clergy sustain an action when practicable. . . .[138]

The agitation over the rights of priests against their bishops was heightened a year later by the publication of a book entitled, *The Rights of Priests Vindicated; or a Plea for Canon Law in the United States.* Corrigan informed Gibbons that the New York publisher, James Sheehy, had recently told Father John Farley that the book was to appear with Gibbons' approval since he had "sanctioned verbally the author's design, etc."[139] Gibbons hastened to say that only a few days before he had

---

[137] 74-I-1, Corrigan to Gibbons, Newark, February 1, 1879.

[138] AAC, Gibbons to Elder, Baltimore, February 1, 1882.

[139] 77-D-8, Corrigan to Gibbons, New York, March 13, 1883, *Private.* The Mahoney volume appeared without author's name or *imprimatur* in a first edition in 1883 and ran to nearly 400 pages; a second edition in 1885 was longer and carried the author's name.

learned for the first time from Magnien that such a publication was in prospect and that the author was a Father William Mahoney, ordained for Baltimore in 1860 and presently living in Milwaukee. Mahoney had given trouble in Baltimore and his faculties had been withdrawn there by three successive archbishops. Gibbons continued, "So far from sanctioning or permitting such a publication, I was absolutely ignorant of the author, & even of the work till within the last few days, & when I heard of its author I had reason to believe that he would pour on my own head the vials of his wrath." Gibbons told Corrigan that if the latter advised he would gladly write a repudiation of this alleged approval to the publisher.[140] Corrigan did not think such a letter necessary, for as he said, "he knows perfectly well that you disapprove of the book." Mahoney had meanwhile written an impertinent letter to Cardinal McCloskey which the latter was not going to answer but rather send on to Archbishop Michael Heiss in Milwaukee.[141] The priest did not spare Gibbons personally, for the latter told Corrigan two months later, "Rev. Mr. Mahony [sic] will not let me alone. He is very angry with the criticism which appeared in the Freeman's Journal, & suspects either you or myself of being the author. It is an excellent article, whoever wrote it."[142]

The large number of appeals by priests to Rome over the heads of their bishops in these years excited the fears of the latter for the integrity of ecclesiastical discipline, particularly when a considerable number of these cases ended in vindication of the priests. While the instruction of July 20, 1878, sent out by the Holy See on the removal of priests from pastorates, made it clear that it was not at variance with the legislation of the Second Plenary Council of Baltimore, there were still a number of ill-defined points, such as the extent to which the bishop's council could exercise judgment in cases of removal of pastors. The fact of several particularly difficult cases in the early 1880's gave point to the need for clarifying legislation.[143] Questions such as these strengthened the view of some bishops that the Church

---

[140] AANY, Gibbons to Corrigan, Baltimore, March 15, 1883, *Private*.

[141] 77-E-2, Corrigan to Gibbons, New York, March 19, 1883.

[142] AANY, Gibbons to Corrigan, Baltimore, May 23, 1883.

[143] On this question of the bishops vs. priests and their rights, cf. the lengthy and detailed account of Frederick J. Zwierlein, *The Life and Letters of Bishop McQuaid* (Rochester, 1926), II, 171–208.

of the United States should hold another plenary council, and if such a gathering was to be held the attitude and views of the Archbishop of Baltimore in whose see city the two previous plenary councils had met would, of course, be of paramount importance.

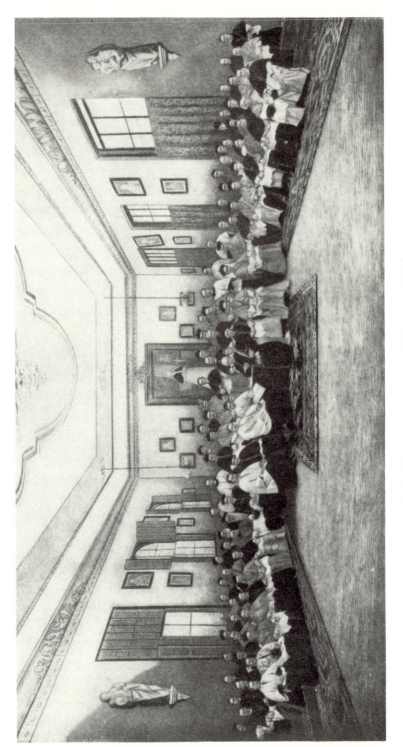

Third Plenary Council of Baltimore (1884).

CHAPTER VI

The Third Plenary Council

THE last time that the American hierarchy had assembled in a plenary council was in October, 1866. In the intervening years a number of new problems had arisen to command the attention of the bishops and to press for their solution. Besides the need for clarifying the relations between bishops and priests, mentioned previously, there was also the necessity of making provision for the thousands of Catholic immigrants who were now reaching American shores in increasing numbers as part of the New Immigration. The years after the Civil War witnessed a steady rise in the number of Europeans who sought to begin life anew in the United States, and a large percentage of these people were Catholics. For example, during the decade which closed in 1880 there had entered the United States 2,812,191 immigrants of whom an estimated 604,000 were Catholics, which raised the total Catholic population of the country for 1880 to 6,259,000.[1]

When it is remembered that during this decade and the one that followed immigration from Catholic countries such as Austria-Hungary, Italy, and Poland became really heavy for the first time it will be better understood what this influx of so many foreign-born Catholics meant to the American hierarchy. The vast majority of these people could not speak English, a fact which added greatly to the complexity of the problem of the American Church in furnishing religious ministrations for them. Moreover, the growth of secret societies, the increasing insistence of some bishops on the necessity for parochial schools, the improvement of religious facilities for the Negroes and Indians — all these and many similar questions suggested themselves for settlement in a national council of the Church. During the visit

---

[1] Gerald Shaughnessy, S.M., *Has the Immigrant Kept the Faith?* (New York, 1925), p. 161.

of Archbishop Gibbons to Rome in the spring of 1880 he had taken up with the officials of the Holy See a number of problems of importance to the Church in the United States, such as the inexpediency of sending an apostolic delegate, the best means to be used in collecting Peter's Pence, and the filling of vacant dioceses in the West about which he had been asked. After his departure from Rome he informed Archbishop Elder of Cincinnati of his action in these matters in a letter from Verona, and in alluding to Elder's recommendations to him concerning, as he expressed it, "the financial difficulty of which you write," Gibbons said, "Your suggestions would be good for the next Plenary Council."[2] This vague reference is the first mention found among Gibbons' papers to a plenary council, and no further move was made on the part of the Archbishop of Baltimore to inaugurate such a gathering.

It was characteristic of Gibbons not to initiate action in regard to a council since all through his life he showed a rather marked disinclination to launch ambitious projects of any kind. While this was true, it must be said that once he became convinced of the wisdom of action he did not hesitate to take it, and he could on occasion resort to surprisingly forceful moves in the direction of an enterprise and in urging co-operative action from others. In any case, Gibbons was not allowed to forget the question of a plenary council owing to the somewhat insistent demands for it arising from some of the bishops in the West. One of the strongest promoters of the idea of a council was Thomas L. Grace, O.P., Bishop of St. Paul. Grace had attended the consecration of Kilian C. Flasch as Bishop of La Crosse in Milwaukee on August 24, 1881. While there he had informed Michael Heiss, Coadjutor Archbishop of Milwaukee, that he had heard Gibbons had been asked if he would favor a council and that the latter had replied he would be ready to promote the work if a great majority of bishops would declare their wish for such a meeting. Heiss wrote Gibbons to say, therefore, that he wished to declare in favor of a council, and that he considered it not only "most useful" but in some respects "even necessary." Heiss cited the favorable opinions of six western bishops who told him he might quote them to that effect, and he added, "As far as I know the Western Bishops, I think there will be scarcely one opposed to

---

[2] AAC, Gibbons to Elder, Verona, June 8, 1880.

it." He said he realized that Gibbons would have to carry "the greatest burden in the holy undertaking," but he believed he could assure the Archbishop of Baltimore that the bishops of the country would be ready to assist him in every way they could.[3]

Nonetheless, Gibbons did not share the view of these western prelates. Late in 1881 he consulted Cardinal McCloskey and Archbishop Corrigan in New York, and he wrote the latter to say, "The more I think on the subject of the council, the more I incline to the Cardinal's view — that it is undesirable for years to come to hold a Plenary Council, & if his Eminence has not yet written, he might if he think proper express my views in connection with his own."[4] Early in the new year 1882 Corrigan, "at the instance of Cardinal McCloskey," came to Baltimore to see Gibbons in regard to the proposed council. Following the visit of the New York coadjutor, Archbishop Gibbons stated in his diary that some of the bishops and clergy had been urging a council on Cardinal Simeoni, the Prefect of Propaganda, and hence Simeoni had inquired of McCloskey what his views were. Gibbons noted that McCloskey was adverse to the gathering and he added:

> I gave as my opinion that it would not be expedient to hold a council for some time to come; but as a preliminary step, provincial councils might be held, or the Bishops of each province might assemble informally and consider what subjects might be discussed in a plenary council. The Bishops of the West seem to favor a national council, as some of them have intimated to me.[5]

Certain bishops in the West had, indeed, intimated their desire for a council, but there was almost a unanimous opposition to it from the leading prelates of the East. For example, Corrigan asked for the opinion of Archbishop Williams of Boston, outlining the reasons for opposition to be given by McCloskey to Simeoni, and over the top of the letter Williams wrote in, "*About a plenary Council. Ans.* unfavorable to it — from the Bps. of

---

[3] 76-C-7, Heiss to Gibbons, Milwaukee, August 26, 1881.
[4] AANY, Gibbons to Corrigan, Baltimore, n.d. Written in pencil on this letter is the date "1881." Gibbons' remark about quoting his opinion was most likely occasioned by Corrigan having indicated that McCloskey was going to write to Rome opposing the holding of a plenary council.
[5] Diary, January 4, 1882, p. 158.

this province. Jan. 27, 1882."[6] Moreover, in acknowledging Williams' reply a few days later, Archbishop Corrigan told him, "Abp. Gibbons, who is here now, and Abp. Wood, who was consulted recently, both agree with the Cardinal and yourself, that the time for another National Council has not yet come. A letter in this sense, but without particularizing names, etc. has been sent to the Propaganda, in reply to their letter."[7]

It is difficult to account for this difference of opinion along geographical lines. Certainly the immigrants and the problems which they created were more pressing in the dioceses along the Atlantic seaboard in these years than they were farther inland, and for that reason one might expect a greater eagerness on the part of the eastern bishops for the remedies which common consultation and regulation might offer through a council. One is prompted to wonder if the differences of view might possibly have reflected the venturesome spirit of the West in contrast to the more conservative influences of the older East. In any case, the western sentiment persisted, as was shown in a letter of Bishop Gilmour of Cleveland to Gibbons just about this time when he told him he felt the need, as he expressed it, for "more mutual and uniform action amongst us." He went on to say he believed the laws of the American Church needed remodeling. Gilmour wrote:

> The clergy need to be strengthened & protected against the people and the people also against the irresponsible ways of the clergy & the Bishop against both. I am convinced that we can not much longer rest where we are. What is really to be done is much harder to say than to recognize. The fact [is] that something must be done.[8]

During the course of the next year Gilmour made a trip to Rome where, as he related to Gibbons, he was consulted on the question of a plenary council and other matters. He told the archbishop that in regard to the council he had given his advice as follows: "That a Plenary Council was necessary but should not be held for at least three years to come, & before holding it that at least five Bishops should go to Rome & there with Rome prepare a schema to be submitted to all the Bishops here after which the Council could be called with profit."[9]

---

[6] AABo, Corrigan to Williams, New York, January 9, 1882.

[7] *Ibid.*, Corrigan to Williams, New York, January 31, 1882.

[8] 76-N-12, Gilmour to Gibbons, Cleveland, February 13, 1882.

[9] 77-E-7, Gilmour to Gibbons, Cleveland, March 26, 1883.

Although the Holy See had received conflicting opinions from the American bishops in response to its inquiries concerning a council, it is apparent that by the spring of 1883 the Roman officials had become convinced that such a gathering of the American hierarchy should be held. In this case the sentiment and reasoning of the bishops in the West must have appeared stronger to the Holy See than the opposition of the East. Late in May of that year Cardinal Simeoni addressed a letter to the heads of most of the ecclesiastical provinces in the United States inviting them to come to Rome the following November to prepare the ground for a plenary council through preliminary conferences with the officials of the Propaganda.[10] Referring to this invitation, Gibbons entered in his diary on June 21, "I wrote today promising to be present."[11] The task which lay ahead was, of course, an arduous one and it was probably with the idea of obtaining assistance that Gibbons at the same time wrote to Denis O'Connell asking him to come to Baltimore to see him. Father O'Connell was then pastor of Sacred Heart Church in Winchester, Virginia, and he hastened to reply that he was pleased to find that Gibbons, as he said, "still remembered me favorably." He added that he regarded the office as an honor and a kindness, and he told him, "I am truly grateful to you for it." O'Connell stated he would be in Baltimore to meet the archbishop on the date he had suggested.[12] Since O'Connell knew Rome so well, the archbishop found his assistance invaluable in making the preliminary preparations for the meeting, and when the time came for Gibbons to depart that fall for Rome he had the young priest accompany him.

Fortunately for Archbishop Gibbons one of his closest friends and most trusted advisers in the hierarchy was in Rome that summer. Bishop John J. Keane of Richmond wrote him two

---

[10] 77-G-11, Simeoni to Gibbons, Rome, May 22, 1883. John J. Keane, Bishop of Richmond, who was in Rome at the time, informed Gibbons in a letter of June 25, 1883, that he had learned, as he said, "that Abp. Alemany has not been invited, because he is always talking of resigning, — nor Abp. Lamy, because his province seems so *sui generis* & outside the ordinary circumstances of the country." Actually John B. Salpointe, Vicar Apostolic of Arizona, represented the Province of Santa Fe, but the Province of San Francisco, as Gibbons noted in his diary under date of March 13, 1884 (p. 173), was not represented at the Roman conferences.

[11] Diary, p. 169.

[12] 77-H-7, O'Connell to Gibbons, Winchester, June 21, 1883.

very lengthy letters in an effort to describe as accurately as he could for Gibbons the background to the Holy See's summons of the American bishops for consultation. There was obviously a certain misgiving on the part of some of the Americans as to why they had been called to the Eternal City. Following Keane's audience with Leo XIII and his conferences with Simeoni and Archbishop Domenico Jacobini of the Propaganda, and with Edward Cardinal Howard, an English representative in the Roman Curia, he endeavored to remove any lingering doubts in the mind of the Archbishop of Baltimore or his colleagues about Rome's motivation when he wrote:

> After my conversations with all these, it is perfectly clear to my mind that the summons has been issued in a spirit of the most entire friendliness towards the American Hierarchy, and through the desire to have all their relations with their priests & with the Holy See placed on the footing that will be the most advantageous & agreeable to our Hierarchy.

Keane stated that the Holy See had grown weary of receiving appeals from American priests against their bishops and that the Roman officials had likewise complained to him that the bishops often did not submit evidence to Rome for their side of these cases; consequently, "to their great regret," they sometimes had to decide against the bishops. There was grave need, therefore, for more personal consultation between the American prelates and the Holy See in order that the latter might obtain a more enlightened understanding of American conditions. The conferences scheduled for November would help to accomplish this objective. Cardinal Howard had told Keane he was delighted the Americans were coming and that for a long time he had been urging on the Holy See "some such action as this in regard to all countries." Pope Leo XIII, said Keane, had spoken most kindly to him about the Church of the United States, and he had said that through the conferences and the plenary council, which would follow, "the perfect unity of action which I desire among the Bishops & between them & the Holy See will be secured."

During his Roman visit Bishop Keane had himself become an ardent convert to the plan for the conferences and the council. He told Archbishop Gibbons, "I will only add in conclusion that I heartily rejoice that you are coming. Such consultation with the Holy See cannot but lead to the most beneficial results. . . .

And I sincerely hope it may prove a precedent for all future times & for all other countries."[13] A few days later from Florence, Keane wrote the Archbishop of Baltimore again regarding his final discussions on these matters before leaving Rome. He told him he found among the Roman officials "a sort of suspicion or dread that there was not a perfect disposition of concord & union on the part of the American Hierarchy towards the Holy See." Even Leo XIII had revealed that he was under some such apprehension. For this reason, said Keane, it was important that the American bishops "should come *cheerfully,* as any objections would surely be misunderstood." Near the end of his second letter Keane remarked:

> From these details I am sure Your Grace will understand just how the land lies in Rome, — & I trust you will be able to so direct the views & action of your colleagues that your conferences with the Propaganda & the Holy Father will be most agreeable to all, & the results highly beneficial to us.[14]

With these two lengthy explanations of the mind of Rome in his possession Gibbons was put in a better position to assume the leadership which would be expected of him when he reached the Holy See. The uncertain health of Cardinal McCloskey of New York precluded the possibility of his attending the conferences so that in his absence the American prelates would naturally look to the Archbishop of Baltimore to take the lead.

When the news of the summons of the Americans to Rome reached Canada, Archbishop John J. Lynch of Toronto wrote Gibbons to say, "I consider it a most providential thing, that the Archbishops of the United States are being called to Rome, and that one of the subjects is to be, the relation between bishops and priests." Lynch was annoyed by the success which unruly priests were meeting of late years in Rome when they made appeals against their bishops, and he was hopeful that the conferences of the American bishops might offer a remedy for what he considered a grave evil.[15] On September 12 the bishops who were going to Rome met in Baltimore at Gibbons' residence, and they agreed to engage the services of Dr. James A. Corcoran of St. Charles Seminary, Philadelphia, as a consulting theologian

---

13 77-H-8, Keane to Gibbons, Rome, June 25, 1883.
14 77-I-1, Keane to Gibbons, Florence, July 4, 1883.
15 77-K-2, Lynch to Gibbons, Toronto, September 3, 1883.

and each to pay him $150 for his assistance to them. Gibbons informed Elder of this decision and asked that he send his contribution to him since, as he said, "I am charged with handing the whole amount to Dr. Corcoran when we meet in Rome." Elder, who had not yet received his pallium as Archbishop of Cincinnati following the death of Purcell, was sensitive about going to Rome without an express invitation. Gibbons was strongly of the opinion that the Province of Cincinnati should be represented by either Elder or Bishop Chatard of Vincennes whether they got a direct invitation or not. He told Elder that he felt presumptuous as "one so young & inexperienced," in offering advice to a prelate of Elder's age and wisdom but, he added, "affection alone prompts me & your charity will forgive me."[16] Although Elder really wanted to go he did not feel he should do so without word from Simeoni, particularly since, as he told Gibbons, "In our case, the Cardinal expressly suggested Mgr. Chatard."[17] At length it was Chatard who represented the Province of Cincinnati in the Roman conferences.

Archbishop Gibbons left Baltimore on October 8 and sailed from New York two days later on the *Gallia*.[18] He reached the Eternal City on November 1, about two weeks in advance of the opening of the conferences at the Congregation of the Propaganda. Since the Church of the United States was still regarded in a canonical sense as missionary territory, its business was conducted through that congregation. The Propaganda officials were headed at this time by Giovanni Cardinal Simeoni, the prefect, who had as his associates Giovanni Cardinal Franzelin and Lodovico Cardinal Jacobini with Archbishop Domenico Jacobini, secretary of the congregation, and Bishop Luigi Sepiacci, O.S.A., who acted as a consultor. At the first meeting held on November 13 the American bishops were presented with a preliminary draft of thirteen headings by way of suggested agenda for discussion.[19] Simeoni made it clear at the outset that the American bishops were to feel entirely free in offering their observations on the

---

[16] AAC, Gibbons to Elder, Baltimore, September 27, 1883.

[17] 77-K-8, Elder to Gibbons, Cincinnati, September 30, 1883.

[18] Diary, March 13, 1884, p. 173.

[19] *Capita praecipua quae emi cardinales S.C. de Propaganda Fide censuerunt a rmis archiepiscopis et episcopis Foederatorum Statuum A.S. Romae congregatis praeparanda esse pro futuro concilio.* A photostat of this document was furnished to the writer through the kindness of Walter J. Leach, vice-chancellor of the Archdiocese of Boston, from the original in the AABo.

subjects proposed by the Propaganda and in suggesting additional matter for the agenda if they thought it necessary.[20] This opportunity for free discussion was fully employed by the Americans, with the result that there was a thorough canvassing of opinion before decisions were reached on the various topics. While it would be of interest to examine the views of the individual American bishops on the subjects as they arose in the conferences, this is not the place to tell the history of their meetings.[21] Suffice it to say that Archbishop Gibbons took the lead for the Americans in debating practically all the more important points, and on a number of occasions the record revealed him speaking, "in the name of all his other colleagues."

At the opening meeting on November 13 there were two subjects to which Gibbons took exception as they were framed by the cardinals of Propaganda. The first was the recommendation that summer villas for seminarians be instituted in the United States. He was opposed to villas being made a subject of general legislation and stated that their institution should be left to the discretion of individual bishops. Moreover, Gibbons gave it as his opinion that the summer vacation offered a good time to test the vocation of students for the priesthood, and that if a student were to change his mind about his vocation it were better it should happen before ordination.[22] While the Roman officials reemphasized the dangers to the vocation of young and inexperi-

[20] *Relatio collationum quas Romae coram S.C. de P.F. praefecto habuerunt arichiepiscopi pluresque episcopi Statuum Foederatorum Americae, 1883* (pp. 3–4). This document was published in Baltimore after the minutes of the conferences were received from Rome. It contained the minutes as held on the various subjects originally introduced by the *Capita praecipua* mentioned above. An English translation of the *Relatio collationum* was carried in *The Jurist*, XI (January through October, 1951), 121–132; 302–312; 417–424; 538–547. An intermediary document, entitled *Capita proposita et examinata in collationibus, quas coram nonnullis emis cardinalibus sacrae congregationis de Propaganda Fide ad praeparandum futurum concilium plenarium habuerunt rmi archiepiscopi et episcopi Foederatorum Statum Americae Septemtrionalis* [sic] *Romae congregati* gave the revised and enlarged version of the original *Capita praecipua* subjects after they had been submitted to the changes suggested by the American prelates. Only the *Relatio collationum* gives the individual views of the participating bishops.

[21] For a full treatment of the Roman conferences insofar as they pertained to education, cf. Francis P. Cassidy, "Catholic Education in the Third Plenary Council of Baltimore," *Catholic Historical Review*, XXXIV (October, 1948–January, 1949), 257–305; 414–436.

[22] *Relatio collationum*, p. 4. The result of the compromise on villas can be seen by reference to the language of the original *Capita praecipua*, p. 1, and the toned-down version in *Capita proposita*, p. 2.

enced clerics during the free months of the summer, they finally agreed that the coming council should not make the institution of villas obligatory, although it should strongly recommend them.

On the second topic, that of erecting cathedral chapters in the Church of the United States, Gibbons, speaking in the name of all his colleagues, gave it as his judgment that chapters would not be expedient for the American Church and that diocesan consultors would suffice.[23] With nothing definite decided on the subject at the first meeting, two days later on November 15 Gibbons returned to the question of cathedral chapters and read a communication in which he set forth why he and certain of his fellow bishops were opposed to them. The archbishop's reasons were that chapters would not conform to the customs of the American people; qualified priests could not easily be convened in chapter meetings due to the great distances and expense involved in traveling; some priests given the dignity of canons might, it was feared, become haughty in their attitude toward their bishops; finally, the system was conducive to contention and strife between a bishop and his canons as experience showed in places where that type of diocesan government was employed. Although the cardinals protested that they had suggested it only for those dioceses wherein conditions made it possible, citing England and the Netherlands to prove their point, the objection of Gibbons and his associates finally carried, and while cathedral chapters were not to be excluded, the system of diocesan consultors was to be made mandatory for all American dioceses.[24]

On two other matters at the first conference at the Propaganda the suggestions of the Archbishop of Baltimore were adopted. Agreeing at the outset with the Roman suggestion that a certain number of priests in each diocese be named irremovable rectors, he stated that he felt their selection should be governed by the bishop's judgment as to the fitness of a candidate, an examination to be satisfactorily passed, and for a priest to be eligible he should have spent ten years of praiseworthy work in the ministry. The three conditions outlined by Gibbons were accepted and the system of irremovable rectors was ordered instituted in the United States as it was then in England, namely, at least one

---

[23] *Ibid.*, p. 6.

[24] *Ibid.*, pp. 9–10. Again the compromise is reflected in the language of the *Capita praecipua*, pp. 1–2, and that of the *Capita proposita*, pp. 3–4.

pastor in ten to hold this status in every diocese. In the last major topic discussed at the meeting on November 13 the Archbishop of Baltimore, once more speaking for all the Americans present, gave his approval to the system outlined by the Propaganda for obtaining the votes of priests of a diocese in the case of a vacant see. The archbishop merely suggested the substitution of the metropolitan or one of the suffragan bishops instead of the administrator of the vacant see to preside at the priests' balloting, and the change was made as Gibbons had desired.[25]

At the opening of the meeting held on November 17 Archbishop Gibbons read a paper in which he outlined his ideas on the question of when a bishop should seek the consent, or merely the counsel, of the consultors on diocesan business. All admitted, said Gibbons, that their consent was required for the election of a new consultor and for the extra-synodal examiners, as well as for the imposition of new taxes for the bishop. In the matter of acquiring and alienating church goods by a bishop all but one of the American prelates felt, he said, that the consent of the consultors was necessarily required, but that once this consent was properly given the bishop should enjoy full liberty as to details and the manner of executing the transaction. In the case of dismembering parishes for the erection of new ones and of giving parishes over to the religious congregations, it was the opinion of the Americans, said Gibbons, that only the counsel of the consultors need be asked.[26] It was evident that Gibbons and his colleagues were anxious to set limits to the consultors' right of demanding their consent rather than their counsel for episcopal action. Although the cardinals gave their assent to all of Gibbons' suggestions and they were accepted by the conference, there were a number of aspects of this problem which remained unsettled and which provided material for one of the most closely debated subjects in the council itself.

When the question of the care of aged and infirm priests arose in the session of November 20, the Archbishop of Baltimore stated that in view of the differences of opinion among the bishops as to the best means of raising money for this purpose, he would suggest that the method of collecting funds be left to the discretion of the individual ordinaries rather than make it a subject

---

[25] *Ibid.*, p. 7; *Capita proposita*, p. 3.
[26] *Ibid.*, pp. 12–13; *Capita proposita*, p. 3.

of legislation, a suggestion with which the Propaganda officials agreed.[27] Later in the same session there was discussed the oath of secrecy imposed upon witnesses who gave testimony in ecclesiastical trials for the disciplining of priests. Gibbons proposed that there be added to the obligation of secrecy a clause which would state that the witness' oath did not impede him from giving testimony to the civil authorities if called upon to do so. The cardinals, however, were adverse to the insertion of such a clause in any instruction of the Holy See or in a decree of the council, although they conceded that bishops should warn witnesses in the clerical court that their oath of secrecy did not bar them from giving testimony to the legitimate civil authorities.[28]

The document which the Propaganda had prepared for the American bishops' consideration contained a separate section on the prohibition of certain offensive methods of collecting money for pious purposes. When this subject was raised in the session of November 22 Archbishop Gibbons again spoke for all his associates in giving full assent to the instructions of the Propaganda forbidding the collection of money at church doors, and ordering that space should be provided for those of the faithful who were not able or who did not wish to pay for the seats they occupied. However, Gibbons did not agree that picnics and fairs held for the purpose of raising money for church purposes need be entirely abolished as the cardinals had recommended. Instead the archbishop would have rules laid down governing these affairs in such a way as to remove the causes of scandal and sin. He suggested that these entertainments be forbidden on Sundays and feast days, that the use of liquor at picnics and fairs be abolished, and that functions of this kind be permitted only with the consent of the bishop. All the other Americans agreed with Gibbons in his stand, and it was the general consensus that it was impossible to eliminate entirely picnics and fairs in the American Church on account of the national customs and, too, because of the financial needs of the Church.[29]

The concern of the Holy See over secret societies was reflected in the cardinals urging the American bishops to impress once more upon the priests and the faithful the warning instructions

---

[27] *Ibid.*, p. 16.
[28] *Ibid.*, p. 17.
[29] *Ibid.*, pp. 19–20.

of Rome on these societies. On this question Archbishop Gibbons stated that he accepted fully the suggestion of the cardinals as outlined in the agenda. However, when Archbishop Charles J. Seghers of Oregon City, seconded by Chatard of Vincennes, mentioned the danger of Catholic workingmen belonging to labor unions (*societates operariorum*) due to their secret oaths, the predominantly non-Catholic personnel of the unions, and the tendency to use violence to prevent others from working, Gibbons and Archbishop Patrick A. Feehan of Chicago immediately came to the defense of the unions by saying that not all of the labor groups were of an evil character, and that many of them offered no reason for ecclesiastical authority to condemn them or to prohibit Catholics from belonging to them. The conclusion reached was that in the case of a doubtful society of any kind the bishop would have recourse to the Holy See if he could not clearly decide about its forbidden character.[30]

In the conference on November 29 the subject of parochial schools came up for discussion and Gibbons promptly gave his approval to the strong stand of the Propaganda for this type of school in the United States and the fulfillment of the previous instructions of the Holy See in this regard.[31] Before the close of this day's meeting the discussion turned to the subject of the improvement of religious facilities for the Negroes in the United States. Gibbons here gave his ready assent to the cardinals' recommendation of a collection to be taken up yearly in the American dioceses to further the Negro apostolate, and he added certain recommendations of his own. The Archbishop of Baltimore suggested that the Society for the Propagation of the Faith be instituted in all American sees, that bishops in prosperous circumstances who had no Negroes in their charge contribute to the missions in dioceses where Negroes lived in great numbers, and finally that the Prefect of the Propaganda be asked to help supply missionaries for work among the American colored population. These ideas of Gibbons met with general approval and were incorporated among the suggestions for the future council.[32]

When in the meeting of December 1 they reached the subject of religious aid for the Italian immigrants to the United States,

---

[30] *Ibid.*, p. 22; *Capita proposita*, p. 9.
[31] *Ibid.*, p. 25.
[32] *Ibid.*, p. 27; *Capita proposita*, pp. 10–11.

Gibbons agreed with the cardinals' proposal of committees to be organized in this country for that purpose, but he added that in his mind similar committees in Italy to work in conjunction with those in the United States would be of advantage. The archbishop stated the end would be better served, he believed, if Italian priests could be prevailed on to go out to America to minister to their fellow countrymen; these men could then supplement the labors of the Italian priests already employed in Italian parishes in the larger American cities. While on the subject of immigrants, Gibbons likewise suggested that the committees proposed for the Italians might well be extended to other nationalities due to the large numbers then emigrating from various countries in Europe.[33] On the final major topic of this session of December 1, namely, forms of holding church property, Gibbons read a lengthy document drawn up with a view to giving the Roman officials a clear understanding of the four principal ways in which American ecclesiastical property was held. He favored the second method, that is, holding temporal possessions of a diocese by the bishop, not absolutely in his own name, but in the name of all the Catholics of the diocese for whose welfare he administered these goods. The archbishop stated that this method conformed more closely to American customs than the others. Following the reading of Gibbons' paper, the cardinals acknowledged the impossibility of attaining uniformity in the method of property holding due to the differences in law, and they contented themselves with urging the bishops to discuss in the council the need for proper safeguards against alienation of the Church's properties by making their own wills and having the priests do the same.[34]

In the closing conference at Rome on December 10 Archbishop Gibbons, in the name of his colleagues, thanked the cardinals for their efforts in preparing and elucidating the points proposed and for their generous and patient responses to the questions which had been raised throughout the meetings. He assured them that the American bishops would do all they could in the coming council to carry out the recommendations of the Roman conferences and to conduct the council in such a way that it would redound to the usefulness and prosperity of the American Church.

---

[33] *Ibid.*, pp. 27–28.
[34] *Ibid.*, p. 29.

On the last day of the conferences at the Propaganda Gibbons cabled Cardinal McCloskey as follows: "Where do you wish the next plenary council to be held. All the archbishops decree Baltimore. Answer me and Simeoni."[35] Although McCloskey's answer was not available, he must have agreed to Baltimore because the decision for that city as the location of the council was made before the Americans left Rome.

One of the most delicate questions to arise in connection with the preliminary negotiations for the council related to the choice of an apostolic delegate to preside over its sessions. When Keane was in Rome the summer previous to the conferences of the American bishops, Pope Leo XIII had told him that when the consultations between the Roman officials and the American prelates had been completed he would send a representative to the United States to give the conciliar decisions, as he expressed it, "all the weight of my Apostolic authority." Keane quoted the Pope as saying:

> It would not do . . . to send a representative from here not thoroughly acquainted with your circumstances; but when he shall have repeatedly had conferences here with the Archbishops, he will be sure to understand them thoroughly & to act in union with them.[36]

The Americans, therefore, had foreknowledge of the fact that Rome was contemplating a representative from the Holy See to preside over their council. At the time Patrick A. Stanton, O.S.A., of Philadelphia was in Rome serving in the capacity of secretary to the Augustinian bishop, Luigi Sepiacci, who was consultor to the cardinals in the conferences with the Americans. Stanton revealed that it was Sepiacci whom the Holy See had in mind to send to the United States as apostolic delegate and the news of this was published in one of the Italian papers. Opposition was at once aroused among the American bishops to the Italian Augustinian being sent to Baltimore, and they did not fail to make their opposition known in Rome.[37] The result was that the Pope dropped the plan of sending Sepiacci and appointed Gibbons to preside over the council as apostolic delegate.

The news over the differences concerning the delegate was a

---

[35] AANY, Gibbons to McCloskey, Rome, December 10, 1883, cablegram.

[36] 77-H-8, Keane to Gibbons, Rome, June 25, 1883.

[37] Peter Guilday, "The Church in the United States (1870–1920). A Retrospect of Fifty Years," *Catholic Historical Review*, VI (January, 1921), 541.

matter of interest on both sides of the Atlantic. Young William
H. O'Connell, the future Archbishop of Boston, was a student at
the American College in Rome at the time. He wrote of the
episode to a friend and stated that Sepiacci had been set aside
for Gibbons, and in commenting on the various American prelates
who were attending the Roman conferences he said, "Archbishop
Gibbons is the conspicuous figure."[38] Two weeks after the close
of the conferences in Rome Abbé Magnien acknowledged a letter
from Gibbons in which he told him that the cable announcing his
choice as delegate had been received the previous Saturday.
Magnien continued:

> Personally I found almost ridiculous the idea of having a council
> of the American Church presided over by an Italian prelate. Nobody
> would have understood it; it would have been looked upon as a
> slur on the American episcopate & the results would have been
> unfortunate for the Church here & for Rome herself. I truly rejoice
> that your colleagues took this view & prevailed upon the Holy See
> to comply with it.[39]

Edgar Wadhams, Bishop of Ogdensburg, was of the same mind
as Magnien about an Italian friar as delegate,[40] and John J.
Kain, Bishop of Wheeling, told Gibbons that when word of the
Sepiacci appointment first reached this country, "all seemed to
feel really hurt. . . ."[41]

But if Magnien and others rejoiced at Gibbons' appointment
there were those who did not. Ella B. Edes, the unofficial agent
of Archbishop Corrigan in Rome, was greatly annoyed. She told
Corrigan that Gibbons, so she heard, had represented Cardinal
McCloskey as not being willing to be named delegate in any case.
She was of the opinion that had Corrigan remained in Rome the
appointment of McCloskey would have been made, but with him
gone and Hostlot of the American College ill she said, "Jacobi-
netto [probably Archbishop Jacobini of the Propaganda] and
Baltimore 'cooked up' the matter between themselves." Speaking
of Archbishop Gibbons, Miss Edes told Corrigan, "At the risk
of scandalizing you I say of His Grace 'Il est capable de tout'

---

[38] William Cardinal O'Connell, *The Letters of His Eminence William Cardinal
O'Connell, Archbishop of Boston*, I, 88. The statement was made in a letter
addressed to "Dear David" under date of December 20, 1883.

[39] 77-M-4, Magnien to Gibbons, Baltimore, December 28, 1883.

[40] 77-Q-4, Wadhams to Gibbons, Ogdensburg, March 26, 1884.

[41] 77-T-9, Kain to Gibbons, Wheeling, April 7, 1884.

where his own vanity or self-aggrandizement come in. It is provoking to see such intriguers succeed in their plans."[42] Through the next few weeks Edes continued to write Corrigan letters filled with tart comments on Gibbons and his Roman visit. When she learned that the archbishop had expressed a view regarding the time when the rectorship of the American College would be filled, she commented:

> I hope he is not going to be suffered to interject at will and have all the say. He is an intriguer and an ambizioso of the *first water* for all his pretended sanctity and he has fully conveyed that impression here though he and his Fidus Achates O'Connell were so clumsy that they were easily detected, though, no doubt assisted by French Sulpitian cunning he has succeeded pretty generally in securing his own ends.[43]

A week later the same correspondent expressed annoyance at the intrigues of "His Little Grace" who had succeeded in conveying the idea "that *he* is the leading *mind* and *man* in the American Episcopate and that *he* is the most devoted adherent of Rome among them all."[44] But the irritation of Edes had little influence on the final decision concerning the appointment of an apostolic delegate to the council, and so far as one could tell, her low opinion of Gibbons did not at the time seem to affect adversely the friendship between himself and Archbishop Corrigan.

Before leaving Rome the Archbishop of Baltimore was accorded a special honor by Leo XIII when the Pope appointed him to officiate on Christmas Day in the Basilica of Saint Mary Major. Magnien was encouraged by this news. "I hear many say," said the Sulpician, "that this is an omen of something else. I fondly hope it is."[45] Gibbons, of course, recognized how preoccupied he would be during the coming months and for that reason before leaving Europe he requested Bishop Northrop of Charleston to take a series of assignments for confirmation in the Archdiocese of Baltimore, and Northrop replied that he would be glad to be of assistance.[46] Word of the success of the Roman conferences had reached Archbishop Elder in Cincinnati and he

---

[42] AANY, Edes to Corrigan, Rome, January 8, 1884, *Private.*
[43] *Ibid.*, Edes to Corrigan, Rome, February 20, 1884, *Private.*
[44] *Ibid.*, Edes to Corrigan, Rome, February 26, 1884, *For yourself alone.*
[45] 77-M-4, Magnien to Gibbons, Baltimore, December 28, 1883.
[46] 77-N-6, Northrop to Gibbons, Charleston, January 29, 1884.

sent a hurried note to congratulate Gibbons on what he called "the great work you have inaugurated." However, Elder was of the opinion that the fall or winter of that year would not leave time for proper preparations for the council, and he, therefore, strongly urged that the date be left open until he could talk to Gibbons more fully on the subject. "All I ask now," he said, "is that you do not fix the time without hearing my explanation."[47] Unfortunately for the wishes of Elder, the date of the opening of the council had been fixed by Leo XIII in his letter of January 4, 1884, to Gibbons for the following November and there was little that the archbishop could do now to change it. The news of the good impression made by the American bishops in their meetings with the Propaganda officials was conveyed to his metropolitan by the Bishop of Hamilton, Ontario, who was in Europe that winter. Writing to Archbishop Lynch of Toronto he said:

> The Archbishops of the U. States worked well and harmoniously together. Their sitting continued over seven weeks. The programme was arranged between themselves and Propaganda. It was worked out by discussing a point between themselves, say on Monday, and the day after they had a Congresso at Propaganda being united as one man their arguments had great weight, thus they continued to the end. They made a most favorable impression with the S. Cong. So much so, that Monsig. Sepiacci who had been named as a Delegate Apostolic was set aside and the Archbishop of Baltimore appointed in his place. This is evidence of the great confidence of the Holy See in the wisdom of the American Bishops.
>
> There is a voce sottoranea in Rome that the Archbishop of Baltimore & Monsig. Corrigan in course of time will be created Cardinals. Both made their mark here.[48]

At length Archbishop Gibbons completed his business in Rome and left for home by way of the British Isles, sailing from Queenstown on the *Gallia* on March 2.[49] After an absence of over five months he returned to Baltimore on March 13, 1884, to face the most important and difficult task that had yet been assigned to him. He confided to his diary that he reached home

---

[47] 77-N-7, Elder to Gibbons, Cincinnati, January 31, 1884.

[48] Archives of the Archdiocese of Toronto, J[ames] J. Carbery, O.P., to Lynch, Cork, February 11, 1884. This letter was copied for the writer through the kindness of Henry J. Browne.

[49] AABo, Corrigan to Williams, New York, March 3, 1884.

in good health and that Denis O'Connell, who had accompanied him on his journey, had been of great service and comfort to him.[50] Mayor Ferdinand C. Latrobe of Baltimore wrote a note to welcome the archbishop home, to which he added, "The honor and respect with which you have been received abroad is fully appreciated by your fellow citizens."[51] On the Sunday following his return Gibbons preached in the cathedral when he took occasion to thank the people for their generous thought in preparing a public demonstration for his homecoming, an honor which he had declined. He stated that while receptions of this kind were appropriate on some occasions he felt that neither his age nor his merits deserved such and the fact, too, that it was Lent made a demonstration of this type seem improper to him. The archbishop paid a tribute in his sermon to the simple living and hard-working habits of the Roman cardinals, spoke of his three private audiences of Leo XIII, and added that the large standing armies of Europe had made him feel grateful to be back in peaceful America. He remarked, "The oftener I go to Europe, the longer I remain there, and the more I study the political condition of its people, I return home filled with greater admiration for our own country and more profoundly grateful that I am an American citizen."[52]

Archbishop Gibbons had not been at home more than a week when he began the work of preparing for the council. In the early stages he was assisted by his own chancellor, George W. Devine, his secretary, Alfred A. Curtis, several of the professors of St. Mary's Seminary, and others of his clergy. Moreover, he was also able to avail himself of the services of Denis O'Connell who soon joined the household on Charles Street to lend a hand in the preparations. In a letter welcoming him home the day after his arrival Patrick Ryan, coadjutor of St. Louis and soon to be named Archbishop of Philadelphia, told Gibbons, "We shall have something to do to defend our 'schemata' in the Council, but I do not see that we could have done better, especially when

---

[50] Diary, March 13, 1884, p. 173. In William O'Connell's Letters, I, 90, he made a comment to "Dear David" about Denis O'Connell under date of December 20, 1883. It read, "Doctor O'Connell, of Richmond, is with Archbishop Gibbons; as bright, intelligent, happy a face as you could see anywhere. He was in his time one of our very best students here. In fact, Doctor Ubaldi tells me he was a wonder in his way."

[51] 77-O-7, Latrobe to Gibbons, Baltimore, March 14, 1884.

[52] Catholic Mirror, March 22, 1884.

the result shall be compared with what the Cardinals submitted to us for adoption."[53] Evidently Ryan feared opposition to the work of the Roman conferences, an opposition which in the event did not prove too serious. Father James McCallen, S.S., who was to be the principal master of ceremonies at the council, informed the archbishop from Paris that he had taken up a number of doubtful points with the Roman authorities, and he suggested the printing of a booklet of rules governing the ceremonies which might be handed out as souvenirs. He then inquired of Gibbons if he did not think temporary galleries should be erected in the cathedral to accommodate the crowds. McCallen was worried about criticism on this score. "I fear so much that we may so disatisfy [sic] both Bishops and clergy so as to preclude the possibility of future councils being held in our Cathedral; or, at least, cause much unnecessary comment."[54]

One of the first tasks to be performed was to issue the formal letter of convocation to the American hierarchy. Gibbons did this on March 19, explaining the purposes for which the council was called, setting the date of opening for November 9, and explaining to the prelates that due to the illness of Cardinal McCloskey he had been named apostolic delegate.[55] A number of bishops were prompt to respond. Gross of Savannah sent congratulations on the work accomplished in Rome and said he believed "all the Church of our country" had been greatly pleased by the result. He added, "I hope also that dame rumor is telling the truth in regard to the report that a Cardinal's hat is soon to be tendered you."[56]

An important part of every council of the Church is played by the theologians. Gibbons exerted a serious effort, therefore, to obtain the best theological talent in the United States to come to Baltimore in the late summer to work on the preliminary schema of decrees so that they might be properly drawn up and submitted to the bishops in advance of the council's opening. With that end in view he inquired of a number of bishops if they would appoint a theologian to assist with the preliminary drafts. He stated to Archbishop Elder that he desired a representative

---

[53] 77-O-9, Ryan to Gibbons, St. Louis, March 14, 1884, *Private*.

[54] 77-P-4, McCallen to Gibbons, Issy, March 19, 1884.

[55] *Acta et decreta concilii plenarii Baltimorensis tertii* (Baltimorae, 1886), pp. xx–xxii.

[56] 77-R-3, Gross to Gibbons, Augusta, March 30, 1884.

of the Province of Cincinnati, but since Elder's seminary had been closed in 1879 due to the financial troubles of the archdiocese, Gibbons remarked that he supposed he would have to rely on Bishop Gilmour of Cleveland to supply a man. He asked Elder if he would confer with Gilmour and name the theologian who in his judgment would be most suitable for the work.[57] Gilmour ultimately named Nicholas A. Moes, rector of St. Mary's Seminary in Cleveland, and Gibbons accepted him.

The appointment of Moes to represent the Province of Cincinnati, however, came close to involving the archbishop in trouble. The misunderstanding arose through Gilmour letting it be known that Elder had told him he had no one to recommend.[58] Meanwhile Elder had inquired of Bishop McCloskey of Louisville, another of his suffragans, about a theologian to represent the province and McCloskey strongly recommended Aemilius Sele of Louisville. Gibbons promptly informed Elder how he had come to appoint Moes, and he hastened to add, "But owing to the warm tribute which the judicious Bp. of Louisville pays to Dr. Sele, I think it desirable that he should also serve."[59] This letter, doubtless intended to appease Elder, did not arrive in time to prevent the Archbishop of Cincinnati sending Gibbons a rather stiff note in which he said:

> I think if you wish a Theologian from this Province the Archbishop of the Province is the one who ought to designate the choice. And I decidedly adhere to the choice which I have expressed to you — of Revd Dr. Sele, of the Diocese of Louisville. I have mentioned this to Msg. Gilmour in a very friendly manner — but very decidedly and I hope that you will not reject my choice.[60]

Fortunately, the incident was closed without serious injury to to the feelings of the principals. The appointment of the other theologians, such as Sebastian G. Messmer of the Diocese of Newark and Peter M. Abbelen from the Archdiocese of Milwaukee, caused no difficulty. When Gibbons learned at a late date that the Archdiocese of San Francisco had a seminary under the Marist Fathers he sent a hurried note to Archbishop Alemany asking him to send a theologian immediately to assist in prepar-

[57] Letterbook, Gibbons to Elder, Baltimore, March 26, 1884, p. 40.
[58] 77-S-3, Gilmour to Gibbons, Cleveland, April 1, 1884.
[59] Letterbook, Gibbons to Elder, Baltimore, April 7, 1884, p. 53.
[60] 77-T-14, Elder to Gibbons, Cincinnati, April 8, 1884.

ing the decrees for the council. "Nearly every Archdiocese is represented by a theologian," he said, "& I desire one from the Pacific."[61] He likewise invited Father Stanton who had served as Sepiacci's secretary in Rome the previous winter. Gibbons told him, "You are already acquainted with the Schema, & would be a valuable acquisition to the ranks of the theologians." The archbishop informed Stanton that the theologians were to assemble on August 16 and during the first few weeks they would probably live at St. Charles College which, he said, "is a cool and pleasant place."[62] Stanton replied that due to his rheumatism and his wish to be present at Archbishop Ryan's installation in Philadelphia he could not be there on the appointed date, but he concluded that when these matters were cleared, "I will be at your service in any way in my power."[63]

While most of the bishops and priests who were asked by Gibbons to undertake a particular assignment relating to the coming council agreed to do so, he met with some refusals. For example, he requested Bishop Michael J. O'Farrell to join Keane of Richmond in writing the pastoral letter to be issued at the close of the council, but O'Farrell replied that he was booked for Rome in April and had many engagements to fill in the interim before sailing. He begged, therefore, to be excused with the promise that after his return from Europe he hoped he could be of help in some capacity.[64] Likewise Bishop James A. Healy of Portland had been asked to perform some special task in the council but he declined. He apologized to John S. Foley, one of the archbishop's secretaries, for his delayed reply, saying he had been balancing between his wish to please Gibbons and a desire to avoid any appearance beyond necessity in the council. Healy concluded, therefore, that unless Gibbons insisted he would wish them, as he expressed it, "[to] please consider the invitation as gratefully received and boorishly declined. . . ."[65] Although Bishop Becker of Wilmington did not refuse to preach the sermon on the Church and the promotion of learning he did tell Gibbons' secretary, "I could have wished my name to be left out of the list; or at least, that a different subject had fallen to me.

[61] Letterbook, Gibbons to Alemany, Baltimore, August 22, 1884, p. 114.
[62] Ibid., Gibbons to Stanton, Baltimore, June 11, 1884, p. 98.
[63] 78-K-1, Stanton to Gibbons, Philadelphia, August 13, 1884.
[64] 77-R-2, O'Farrell to Gibbons, Trenton, March 29, 1884.
[65] 78-B-7, Healy to Foley, Portland, May 8, 1884.

As it is, I shall not fail to say what I think on the matter, and leave the rest to Providence."[66]

With a view to obtaining representation of all elements in the hierarchy Gibbons asked Heiss of Milwaukee to preach one of the German sermons to be delivered at St. Alphonsus Church in Baltimore during the council. He assigned the subject, "The Councils of the Church," and told Heiss, "The selection of your Grace will be also gratifying to other Bishops of German nationality."[67] Archbishop Alemany was asked to preach in Latin on priestly zeal and when Gibbons got word of his acceptance he expressed his joy to learn that the Archbishop of San Francisco would attend. He told him, "Your presence will contribute to the dignity & wisdom of the Council, & when the Council is over, you may receive a red hat."[68]

All through the spring of 1884 Archbishop Gibbons kept in close touch with Archbishop Corrigan of New York and almost every important matter that arose was submitted to the judgment of the New York coadjutor. Corrigan, too, was asked to deliver one of the sermons during the council. Gibbons wrote:

I have a favor to ask, & I believe you will graciously accede to my request. It is that you preach at the Council the sermon on the deceased Prelates. I have many reasons for selecting you. On examining the list of Bishops, I find no one so well fitted for the task as Your Grace. You have an exactitude of mind & fact & feeling so essential for such a subject. Besides, the representative of the great Archdiocese of New York should be heard in the Cathedral, & I think you will deem the subject I propose more congenial than a sermon on one of the Sundays. His Eminence preached the opening sermon at the last Council. I know your labors are many. But you will have ample time to prepare, & the length & treatment of the subject is [sic] entirely in your hands.

I trust then that with your usual self-sacrifice & obliging spirit, you will gratify me by a favorable reply.[69]

Corrigan accepted the assignment and at the requiem Mass on November 13 he preached the sermon on the bishops who had

[66] 77-V-2, Becker to "Dear Rev. Fr.," Salisbury, Maryland, April 28, 1884.
[67] Letterbook, Gibbons to Heiss, Baltimore, April 6, 1884, p. 51.
[68] Ibid., Gibbons to Alemany, Baltimore, April 22, 1884, p. 67.
[69] AANY, Gibbons to Corrigan, Baltimore, April 8, 1884. The New York archives contain several dozen letters from Gibbons to Corrigan through these months on council affairs.

died since 1866, the date of the last plenary council. Not only did Gibbons frequently ask Corrigan for his opinion about important questions, but he likewise consulted one or more of the other archbishops before determining his own action in many particulars. For example, when it came time to select the conciliar officers he sought the approval of several of these leaders of the Church. He wrote the Archbishop of Boston:

> As it is necessary that the officials of the Council should receive some notice beforehand, in order to have time to prepare themselves for their functions, I wish to submit to Your Grace some names that I have selected after much consideration, and which, if they meet your approval, I would appoint to offices, subject to the approbation of the Bishops in the Preliminary meeting of the council.[70]

Williams replied that he thought Gibbons' proposals were excellent, except that he believed "some of the Western Bishops" ought to be on the list of officers.[71] Thus gradually — with the judgments of his fellow bishops — the Archbishop of Baltimore assembled the chief personnel who would have in hand the council's business when it opened in the autumn.

In the midst of his labors in choosing theologians, preachers, and officials for the council Gibbons received a considerable number of suggestions from various sources for legislative action at the coming meeting. Cardinal Simeoni wrote a strong letter urging that something be done for the Catholic immigrants going out to the United States from Europe, a plea which Gibbons assured the cardinal he would put before the fathers.[72] Gilmour of Cleveland was concerned about the question of rectors of churches, a matter which he felt needed to be "somewhat modified" by the council. Gilmour was generous with his offer of assistance to the Archbishop of Baltimore. As he put it, "Any help I can be personally or through others, will be at your disposal." A few days later he suggested to Gibbons other subjects on which he believed better legislation was needed, and he remarked, "I hope something will be done to establish a seminary in our midst for higher education, as I once suggested to

---

[70] AABo, Gibbons to Williams, Baltimore, April 16, 1884.

[71] 77-V-1, Williams to Gibbons, Boston, April 18, 1884.

[72] 77-O-2, Simeoni to Gibbons, Rome, March 6, 1884; Letterbook, Gibbons to Simeoni, Baltimore, April 4, 1884, p. 48.

you & also to the Propaganda when I was there."[73] Father Andrew A. Lambing, pastor of St. Mary's Church in Pittsburgh, called the attention of Gibbons to a recent item which appeared in a Catholic newspaper and he asked the archbishop if the question of Catholic papers and their freedom to print any news they liked could not be made a subject of conciliar legislation. Gibbons agreed, as he said, that "the advertisements to which you refer are indeed most offensive, & I think should not be tolerated in an official organ." Although the archbishop recognized the difficulty of the problem, he made Lambing no binding promise about the action he would take. Gibbons' caution on this subject of the editorial freedom of Catholic newspapers in relation to the bishops was made clear in his reply to his correspondent:

> It is difficult to legislate regarding so-called Catholic papers which are not official. They are sometimes started without Episcopal sanction & are even disrespectful to Episcopal authority. I do not see how any legislation can stop this evil. The last Plenary Council of Balto. (Cap. IV) enacted some wise decrees in regard to Catholic papers which unfortunately are not always observed. I think that the vigilance of the Ordinary is the most effective means of checking the evil of which you justly complain. I may however bring the subject to the attention of the Bishops.[74]

The council in fact did enact several lengthy decrees on the subject of the relationship of so-called Catholic newspapers to ecclesiastical authority. Besides suggestions for legislation which came unsolicited, the archbishop likewise received an occasional gratuitous offer of personal assistance. Placide L. Chapelle, pastor of St. Matthew's Church in Washington, recalled that he had been a secretary of the council in 1866, had succeeded Henry Coskery as president of the theological conferences of Baltimore, and was pastor of one of the "most important congregations in the country." Chapelle thought, therefore, he should be named to some office in the council,[75] a request which was rewarded with his being appointed one of the notaries of the gathering.

Archbishop Gibbons put forth in these weeks a serious effort to do justice to each group within the American Church which

---

[73] 77-Q-10, Gilmour to Gibbons, Cleveland, March 28, 1884; 77-T-6, same to same, Cleveland, April 6, 1884.
[74] Letterbook, Gibbons to Lambing, Baltimore, May 2, 1884, p. 74.
[75] 77-T-8, Chapelle to Gibbons, Washington, April 7, 1884.

might have a title to consideration. When Bishop Joseph Dwenger inquired, "Is it expected that a Bishop should invite such Religious Superiors as reside in his diocese or will it be done directly by Your Grace?"[76] Gibbons hastened to reply that he had already forwarded invitations "to all the Superiors & Heads of Religious Orders who jure vel consuetudine should be convoked."[77] Moreover, he suggested that Denis O'Connell write to Monsignor Corcoran at Overbrook and ask if he did not think "a distinguished member" of the Redemptorists and Jesuits should be added to the corps of theologians who would draw up the draft of the decrees since, as O'Connell told Corcoran, Gibbons felt they would "give greater solemnity and a greater evidence of fairness."[78] Archbishop Corrigan gave to the Archbishop of Baltimore information on the domestic prelates then living in the United States of whom he could think of only nine. He presumed most of them would be invited as theologians of their bishops, but he wanted to make sure in the case of Monsignor George H. Doane of Newark since he would not be likely to receive an invitation from his own bishop, "who knew not Joseph."[79] Corrigan approved of Gibbons' selection of Monsignor Robert Seton as chief notary of the council and in paying tribute to his good qualities he added, "He is odd, as you know, and peculiar in his ways, but knows how to maintain his dignity on occasion."[80] Gibbons first consulted Seton's bishop, Wigger of Newark, and after obtaining his consent he invited Seton whom he told, "Your exact knowledge, & zeal in what you undertake, as well as the title with which the H. See has honored you, eminently fit you, in my judgment, for the office."[81]

While these preparations were going forward John Gilmary Shea, the historian of the American Church, in the spring number of the *American Catholic Quarterly Review,* reviewed the legislation of the previous councils of Baltimore and pointed out the needs for additional legislation that would face the bishops

---

[76] 77-Q-6, Dwenger to Gibbons, Fort Wayne, March 27, 1884.

[77] Letterbook, Gibbons to Dwenger, Baltimore, March 29, 1884, p. 44.

[78] *Ibid.,* O'Connell to Corcoran, Baltimore, May 31, 1884.

[79] 77-Y-3, Corrigan to Gibbons, New York, April 28, 1884, *Private.*

[80] 78-A-5, Corrigan to Gibbons, New York, May 2, 1884.

[81] Letterbook, Gibbons to Seton, Baltimore, June 6, 1884, p. 97. Speaking of Gibbons' invitation years later Seton called it, "the only recognition in thirty-five years and a half of what Bishop Bayley had called my 'Merits.' " Robert Seton, *Memories of Many Years (1839–1922)* (London, 1923), p. 197.

when they assembled in Baltimore. He especially stressed the necessity of laws to define the position of bishops in the civil courts, the question of secret societies, the establishment of regular canonical parishes in the Church of the United States, and the need for Catholic schools and publication societies.[82] In a more strictly historical article Shea followed in the next number of the *Quarterly* with a survey of the progress made by the American Church from the time of the First Provincial Council of Baltimore in 1829 down to the present.[83] Through these articles the historian sought to give the American clergy and laity suitable background for the council which was scheduled for November.

Late in April Archbishop Gibbons sought the advice of the archbishops of the country concerning the introduction of new material for the council beyond that outlined in the Roman conferences. He suggested that such material might be entrusted to a committee of some of the archbishops for them to decide on its fitness. Williams of Boston replied, "I consider your plan excellent . . . ," but he urged that whatever new material was suggested should be put in print and distributed well in advance by the bishops who advocated it. He wrote, "We complained in Rome because we had not the schema more promptly to give us time for discussion before the conferences. There is more need for time to reflect before the Council if possible."[84] Elder found Gibbons' suggestion "very judicious," and he would have a time limit of August 1 placed on this suggested new material so that it would be in Gibbons' hands no later than that date.[85] Feehan of Chicago agreed to the committee but stated that he thought new material should be held to a minimum. He said, "Indeed I feel satisfied that when the Bishops look over the chapters of the Roman conferences they will feel convinced that in them and the development of them, there will be ample material for the work of a Council."[86] Ryan sent the approval of old Archbishop Kenrick and himself from St. Louis but suggested a

---

[82] John Gilmary Shea, "The Coming Plenary Council of Baltimore," *American Catholic Quarterly Review,* IX (April, 1884), 340–357.

[83] John Gilmary Shea, "The Progress of the Church in the United States from the First Provincial Council to the Third Plenary Council of Baltimore," *American Catholic Quarterly Review,* IX (July, 1884), 471–497.

[84] 77-W-13, Williams to Gibbons, Boston, April 25, 1884.

[85] 77-W-14, Elder to Gibbons, Cincinnati, April 25, 1884.

[86] 77-W-15, Feehan to Gibbons, Chicago, April 26, 1884.

broadening of the committee so "there could be no *oligarchical* suspicion in the minds of the majority."[87] In addition to some minor suggestions, Alemany of San Francisco said Gibbons' plan met his views entirely,[88] and Heiss of Milwaukee left the whole matter to Gibbons' judgment, saying, "I agree perfectly with your plan."[89] In this manner as each important decision arose for settlement the opinions of the prelates were sought by Gibbons and from the consensus of their answers he was able to frame a judgment that met with the approval of a majority among his colleagues in the hierarchy.

It had been decided by the archbishops that the best way to expedite the legislation suggested in the *Capita proposita* so that the bishops would have as finished a draft as possible to work on when the council opened, would be for each metropolitan and his suffragans to make themselves responsible for the analysis and comment on one or more chapters in advance. These were to be examined in the respective provinces and then forwarded to Baltimore where Archbishop Gibbons would have them printed and distributed to all the hierarchy. With this in view Gibbons himself took the chapter on the education of the clergy for the Province of Baltimore, but being so overwhelmed with work he turned to his suffragan, Becker of Wilmington, and asked him to assume the major responsibility for comment. He wrote:

> It was recommended to me by all the Prelates I could consult on the subject, to distribute the chapters of the schema among the different Archbishops of the country for close investigation before the Council, and as the plan besides seemed a good one, I adopted it and undertook the responsibility of the first chapter myself.
>
> I intimated to the Archbishops in my letter to them that they might associate some of their suffragans with them, in order to learn their views, but on account of my many cares I must look to you for more, and I must request you besides, as I intimated to you in my former letter, to make, if you please a thorough study of that chapter for me in all its bearings and to send me the result of your labors with a view to the decrees that must be framed.
>
> I know you are busy too but your familiarity with this kind of work makes it much easier for you than for me.
>
> I requested the Archbishops to send in their reports on or before

---

[87] 77-Y-12, Ryan to Gibbons, St. Louis, April 30, 1884.
[88] 78-A-1, Alemany to Gibbons, San Francisco, May 1, 1884.
[89] 78-A-9, Heiss to Gibbons, Milwaukee, May 3, 1884.

the 1st day of next August and I will request you to do the same, as I desire to have all the views collated and a digest of them sent to all the Bishops before they assemble in Council. I expect to consult some more of the Suffragans, but I will depend upon you to do the hard study.[90]

Becker did not welcome the assignment but he bowed to the archbishop's request as "equivalent to a command." The Bishop of Wilmington thought the subject "fraught with immense consequences," and although he was highly critical of many of the existing seminaries, he agreed to do his best in the work apportioned to him.[91] A few days after Becker's acceptance Gibbons wrote the other suffragan bishops of the Province of Baltimore and outlined for them the procedure. He said the metropolitans would soon be assembling their suffragans to learn their views on the schema, and he added, "In like manner, I desire to assemble mine, and I therefore invite you to meet me here in Baltimore on the morning of Wednesday the 28th day of next May to have an expression of your views and to examine with you and your fellow Bishops of the province the first Chapter of the Schema: 'De Clericorum educatione.' "[92] In the conference of the bishops of the Province of Baltimore with Gibbons in May only minor changes were suggested for the chapter on clerical education. They recommended that at least philosophy, theology, and canon law courses be given in Latin in the major seminaries; that courses in liturgy, sacred eloquence, and Hebrew be offered; and that in the minor seminaries the physical sciences, German, French, and when practicable one of the Slavic languages, mathematics, chant, and bookkeeping find a place in the curriculum.[93] With these and a few other verbal changes the original outline of the *Capita proposita* remained intact after the examination by the Baltimore prelates.

Most of the metropolitans accepted the chapters assigned to them without any difficulty. Ryan in St. Louis assured Gibbons that he would consider the portion of the work assigned

[90] 77-R-1, Gibbons to Becker, Baltimore, March 29, 1884, copy.

[91] 77-R-7, Becker to Gibbons, Wilmington, March 31, 1884.

[92] 77-S-8, Gibbons to his suffragan bishops, Baltimore, April 3, 1884, copy.

[93] *Relationes eorum quae disceptata fuerunt ab illmis ac revmis metropolitis cum suis suffraganeis in suis provinciis super schema futuri concilii praesertim vero super capita cuique commissa* (Baltimorae, 1884), pp. 3–4.

to him.[94] But before the bishops of the Province of St. Louis could be assembled Ryan himself was named Archbishop of Philadelphia. Referring to his transfer, he queried Gibbons, "What effect will it have on our portion of the Council work?"[95] Although Bishop John Hennessy of Dubuque, senior suffragan, was suggested in his place, an inquiry made of Hennessy in early July[96] failed to bring the report and in the final event only two brief expressions of views were received from the St. Louis bishops. Elder, who had been assigned the chapter on immigrants, thought the Province of Cincinnati an inappropriate place to discuss that subject since most of the immigrants settled in the seaports. He asked Gibbons, "Would you not obtain more satisfaction by referring to some one else than me, the matter De Colonis?"[97] But the Archbishop of Baltimore thought it too late to change since some of the provinces had already held their meetings. "Besides," as he told Elder, "there is very little to be said about it, & its study involves very little labor. I will make all the suggestions that occur to me on the subject."[98] Gibbons informed John B. Salpointe, Coadjutor Archbishop of Santa Fe, in answer to his question concerning what exactly he was responsible for, that all the Santa Fe bishops need comment on was the chapter on the election of bishops, but he added, "any comments which yourself & ven. colleagues may choose to make on the other chapters will be gratefully accepted."[99] The fact that Archbishop Seghers of Oregon City was in Europe that spring prevented a report being received on the chapter assigned to that province.

The most trying experience Gibbons had in relation to the reports from the various provinces was in the case of Archbishop Francis X. Leray of New Orleans. On March 29 he wrote Leray explaining the method of distribution as advised by all the prelates he could consult on the subject. He continued, "Anxious to comply in every way that I can with the wishes of the Bishops, I feel a pleasure in adopting this plan, which seems besides to recommend itself by many other reasons."

---

[94] 77-T-7, Ryan to Gibbons, St. Louis, April 6, 1884.
[95] 78-G-11, Ryan to Gibbons, St. Louis, June 17, 1884.
[96] Letterbook, O'Connell to Hennessy, Baltimore, July 3, 1884, p. 101.
[97] 78-B-4, Elder to Gibbons, Cincinnati, May 6, 1884.
[98] Letterbook, Gibbons to Elder, Baltimore, May 8, 1884, pp. 77–78.
[99] *Ibid.,* Gibbons to Salpointe, Baltimore, June 16, 1884, p. 100.

Gibbons, therefore, assigned the chapter dealing with the pastoral care of the Negroes to Leray and his suffragans. He closed his letter by saying, "I rely a great deal upon the cooperation of your Grace for the successful carrying out of this plan, and I further request you to aid me in any other way you can, to carry the burden that has been imposed upon me."[100] About a month later, Francis Janssens, Bishop of Natchez, a New Orleans suffragan, asked Gibbons for a copy of the *Capita proposita* which he had not received, a request with which Gibbons promptly complied, ending his letter with the remark, "My hands are full, but I am in good health, thank God."[101] When a similar request came from John C. Neraz, Bishop of San Antonio, also a New Orleans suffragan, Gibbons said he would send fresh copies in a few days and in his customary tactful way he adverted to Leray, "I have submitted a special chapter to each Metropolitan. Most of the Metropolitans are wisely calling a preliminary meeting of their suffragans some time before the Council."[102] Meanwhile he did not despair of Leray himself from whom no word had yet arrived. Gibbons wrote again on April 24, this time to say, "I would like to ask your advice in regard to the admission of new subjects into the deliberations of the council. . . . I most respectfully request Your Grace's views on this plan and a reply as early as convenient."[103] But no response was forthcoming from New Orleans.

A month later Gibbons transmitted the chapter on Negroes to Archbishop Leray with the request that he send his comments at his earliest convenience, "so as to enable me," he said, "to have them printed and distributed as soon as possible."[104] Neither was there a reply to this letter. By mid-June he had begun to feel that writing to the Archbishop of New Orleans might, indeed, be a waste of time. He told Janssens about sending the chapter on Negroes to Leray for examination and he added, "He has never replied to this letter, nor to any of the communications I have sent him. I presume he is very busy. He is certainly a poor correspondent."[105]

---

100 AUND, New Orleans Papers, Gibbons to Leray, Baltimore, March 29, 1884.

101 Letterbook, Gibbons to Janssens, Baltimore, April 7, 1884, p. 54.

102 *Ibid.,* Gibbons to Neraz, Baltimore, April 9, 1884, p. 60.

103 AUND, New Orleans Papers, Gibbons to Leray, Baltimore, April 24, 1884.

104 *Ibid.,* Gibbons to Leray, Baltimore, May 30, 1884.

105 Letterbook, Gibbons to Janssens, Baltimore, June 17, 1884, p. 99.

The suffragans of New Orleans were meanwhile growing restive, left in the dark as they were about the conciliar preparations by their own metropolitan. Bishop Fitzgerald of Little Rock maintained they had received "no correspondence whatever on the Council." He wondered if Leray was waiting for him — Fitzgerald — to take the initiative because, as he said, "I, not he was called to the conference of last Winter; but even then, if you have assigned any subject to our Province, it is strange that he has not given me notice."[106] Janssens continued to prod Gibbons with questions and suggestions in lieu of action from the metropolitan. He told him, "Archbp. Leray, I am sorry to notice, has not sent anything, — he will not either, I expect, — neither has he called his suffragans together."[107] The failure of Leray to reply to the communications addressed to him not only added to the troubles of Gibbons and forced him to write a good many unnecessary letters to these southern bishops, but what was more important, his inaction deprived the bishops in the council of the benefit of having in print the considered judgments of their southern colleagues on the serious subject of the spiritual care of the American Negroes. What prompted the Archbishop of New Orleans to take the attitude he did toward the council business it is impossible to say, unless it was the fact that Fitzgerald of Little Rock, and not himself, had been invited to Rome for the conferences to represent the province. Possibly this explanation, suggested by Fitzgerald himself, might account for the archbishop's peculiar conduct.

With Archbishop Ryan not yet installed in Philadelphia that province, too, was having its troubles keeping up with events. Bishop William O'Hara of Scranton, who had represented the province in the Roman meetings, told Gibbons that when he took leave of Simeoni in Rome the prefect made a remark that led O'Hara to believe he had no right, as senior suffragan, to assemble the bishops for the business of the council.[108] Another suffragan of Philadelphia, Tobias Mullen of Erie, wrote uneasily of his concern that no report had been sent from the province but he did not know how under the circumstances to remedy

---

[106] 78-I-5, Fitzgerald to Gibbons, Little Rock, July 9, 1884.
[107] 78-J-10, Janssens to Gibbons, Natchez, August 11, 1884.
[108] 78-I-7, O'Hara to Gibbons, Scranton, July 15, 1884.

the matter.[109] In the final event the council convened with no reports on the chapters assigned from Philadelphia, New Orleans, and Oregon City, and only two brief letters from bishops of the Province of St. Louis. While the omissions were regrettable, the work on the prospective decrees involved in these chapters would have to be made up by the theologians to the best of their ability without the guidance of the bishops.

By late July the reports had been received by Gibbons from several provinces and they were speedily prepared for the printer so that the whole could be mailed to the entire hierarchy with as little delay as possible. The reactions to the *Relationes*, once they reached the hands of the hierarchy, differed according to the individual bishops. Kain of Wheeling was "much pleased with many points in the 'Relationes' especially in those from Milwaukee and Cincinnati."[110] But Archbishop Heiss was not content, feeling there was need for much more specific proposals than merely to improve on the chapter headings as they came out of Rome. As he said, "in this way we would not come beyond generalities, not come to practical and effectual laws." Heiss went on at great length, giving Gibbons particular points which he believed needed emphasis, and in closing he apologized for what he called "this molestation," but he said he felt bound in conscience to give Gibbons his views, "for, I think, every bishop should do his best according to his abilities to make the Council a full success."[111]

Among the views of the bishops of the Province of Chicago as expressed in the *Relationes* there had been suggested the importance of some uniformity of textbooks in the schools in each diocese, "and especially the need of a Catechism, to be used everywhere."[112] This suggestion appealed to Janssens of Natchez as "a matter of great importance," and he, therefore, sent along further suggestions about a catechism. There was enough reaction to this matter of a uniform catechism for the Church of the United States from others to warrant Gibbons appointing a committee of bishops in advance of the council to report on the subject. He named Archbishop Alemany as chairman with de Goesbriand, Stephen Ryan, Dwenger,

109 78-J-8, Mullen to Gibbons, Erie, August 10, 1884.
110 78-J-11, Kain to Gibbons, Wheeling, August 11, 1884.
111 78-K-13, Heiss to Gibbons, Milwaukee, August 17, 1884.
112 78-K-7, Janssens to Gibbons, Natchez, August 15, 1884.

Spalding, Kain, and Janssens as members to serve under him.[113] In instructing the members of the committee the Archbishop of Baltimore asked them to consider especially three points: (a) the expediency of adopting a uniform catechism at the council; (b) naming the catechism which they preferred to have sanctioned; (c) whether translations into other languages should be made of the catechism adopted, or a separate catechism be prepared for Catholics in the United States who used languages other than English.[114]

Neraz of San Antonio approved the idea of a uniform catechism in English because of the constant moving about of so many Catholics in the country, but he was opposed to such being translated into Spanish for the Mexicans in his own Southwest. The bishop said they already had a Spanish catechism which they used generally, and if there was a change many of these Mexicans in the distant missions "would be unable to teach their children this new catechism and many Mexicans would grow ignorant of the rudiments of religion."[115] Elder was of the opinion that "A common catechism is certainly desirable, if there is any possibility of making one that will be generally acceptable."[116] Bishop Louis M. Fink, O.S.B., of Leavenworth told Gibbons, in a letter to which no reply was found, that he had for some time had a group of priests working on a catechism, and when he learned there was to be a committee of bishops assigned to the task he had ordered the work stopped; but since they were nearing the end of their efforts the priests wanted to go on; therefore, he inquired if Gibbons thought the result of their labors would be of any assistance to the council's efforts for a catechism.[117] Thus there was begun the project which eventually brought results in the form of the *Baltimore Catechism*, still so widely used in revised form throughout the Church of the United States.

Still another subject which entailed a good deal of correspondence on the part of Archbishop Gibbons in these weeks was that of the care of priests who were in need of discipline. It

---

[113] 78-L-11, Gibbons to Alemany, Baltimore, August 25, 1884, copy.

[114] 78-L-12, Gibbons to members of the catechism committee, printed circular, Baltimore, August 25, 1884.

[115] 78-O-10, Neraz to Gibbons, San Antonio, September 9, 1884.

[116] 78-P-1, Elder to Gibbons, Cincinnati, September 11, 1884.

[117] 78-P-7, Fink to Gibbons, Seneca, Kansas, September 21, 1884.

was his hope that in the decrees on this subject the names of specific institutions which would receive them might be given to guide the bishops. With that in mind he wrote to Archbishop Feehan concerning the possibility of the Alexian Brothers, whose mother house was in Chicago, receiving priests of this character.[118] Numerous letters were likewise dispatched by the archbishop to various religious houses at the same time making inquiry if they could provide for this need. In the nearly two-score replies which came in the idea of a house of refuge for priests in need of discipline was highly applauded by all Gibbons' correspondents, but only old Abbot Boniface Wimmer of St. Vincent's Abbey showed any disposition to accept these men. Wimmer told the archbishop that over the years around a hundred such priests had been received at St. Vincent's for whom the abbey had received no compensation, but if the bishops would undertake to help him he would be willing to look about for a building and get such a house for priests started.[119]

Amid the many arduous duties which preparations for the council entailed, Gibbons received from time to time encouraging comment from his colleagues on the procedure he was following. For example, Heiss at one point told him, "All the Bishops seem to be very much pleased by your way of preparing the schema for the Council."[120] Faced as he was by so many serious problems arising almost daily to test his judgment, a remark of this kind from a man almost twenty years his senior gave the young archbishop fresh courage to see the work through to the end. With so many persons involved in the enterprise it was natural that there would be found some who would not exercise prudence in regard to the plans as they matured. Bishop Wigger informed Gibbons in mid-August that the matters for discussion in the coming meeting had been spoken of freely by "a certain Provincial"; likewise Wigger had learned that one of the theologians, as he remarked, "has also freely spoken about the permission that is to be given certain Rectors, to vote for candidates for vacant Sees." Wigger was disturbed by

---

118 Letterbook, Gibbons to Feehan, Baltimore, August 24, 1884, p. 115.

119 78-M-12, Wimmer to Gibbons, St. Vincent's Abbey, August 30, 1884. The replies of the other religious superiors on the question are contained in Box 78.

120 78-C-6, Heiss to Gibbons, Milwaukee, May 17, 1884.

this news and he asked Gibbons if he did not think it would be well to inform superiors of religious houses and theologians that they were supposed to keep secret the matters to be proposed for discussion at the coming council.[121] Gibbons answered immediately:

> I regret to hear of the unwarrantable publicity given by certain persons, to the contents of the schema. A discreet silence on this subject is enjoined in the Pontifical, etc. I do [not] know how the mischief can be better checked than by a gentle admonition to those that have offended. Had I foreseen that the contents of the schema would be ventilated, I might have called the attention of the synodales to the secrecy imposed by the Pontifical. I suppose it is rather late to make a general reference to it now.[122]

When John Ireland sent on proposals for legislation on the observance of Sunday, temperance, and Indian affairs the Archbishop of Baltimore thanked him for his letter with its "excellent suggestions" and assured him he would place it in the hands of the theologians "now assembled, that it may receive their careful attention." He said he had requested the bishops who were drawing up the pastoral letter to make mention of the violation of Sunday and the evil of intemperance

---

[121] 78-K-9, Wigger to Gibbons, South Orange, New Jersey, August 15, 1884.

[122] Archives of the Archdiocese of Newark, Gibbons to Wigger, Baltimore, August 16, 1884. The *Tablet* of London carried an item from the New York *Sun* late in 1885 which revealed a leak to the press of the private *Acta* of the council. Bishop McQuaid was indignant and told Gibbons he had traced the leak to Baltimore where a correspondent there had sent the information to Dublin. McQuaid asked Gibbons if he knew who this Dublin correspondent was, and he added, "If not, then it is good for you to know that some one is betraying you and your secrets" (80-D-9, McQuaid to Gibbons, Rochester, January 28, 1886). A year later when more mysterious leaks of the Church's business were reaching the press, Elder wrote Gibbons while the latter was in Rome, asking if a way could not be found to avert the evil. He said, "You will remember that last year a New York paper published extracts from the Acta of the Balt. Council, giving portions of debates with the names of Bishops advocating various views. . . . On the occasion of the publication about the Council, I heard a suspicion that those things had been obtained by Count Soderini, correspondent of the Baltimore Mirror. And Your Eminence may remember that the Archbishop of New York told us he had learned privately but very positively that the New York paper had received it through the editor of the Baltimore Mirror. I mention names freely, to furnish a clew for inquiries. . . ." The document which the press secured and to which Elder here referred was the private edition of the *Acta et decreta,* issued after the council closed and intended only for the bishops.

which he believed, "ought to receive special attention from them."[123] Elder of Cincinnati suggested that Gibbons get out a circular telling the bishops what to bring to Baltimore in the line of ecclesiastical robes, and he took occasion to say, "I do wish you would reconsider that agreement to have a reception or entertainment given by Miss Harper — or any one else."[124] Elder continued for three pages outlining the reasons why the bishops should be free of all social engagements during the sessions of the council, but in spite of his protest there were at least two major receptions held for the visiting bishops in Baltimore that fall.

The silver jubilee of Archbishop Lynch of Toronto occurred on November 25, 1884. He inquired, therefore, on what day the council would close since he wished to avoid a conflict of dates. He was desirous "for the honor of the Church" to have some of the American bishops present in Toronto for his jubilee, believing, as he said, that it "would strengthen our position here."[125] Gibbons replied and invited Lynch to attend the closing session of the council in Baltimore, an invitation which he readily accepted and to which he added the suggestion that it would be well to invite some of the representatives of the Church in Lower Canada. Lynch prophesied, "The Council of Baltimore will be one of the most interesting & splendid manifestations of the progress & triumphs of the Catholic Church in America."[126]

As the time for the council neared rumors began to circulate that the health of Archbishop Gibbons was showing the strain of his labors. Corrigan wrote to caution him, "I have only one suggestion to offer, with all deference, and that is that you spare yourself as much as possible between now and the opening of the Council, as you will need all your strength at that trying time."[127] Wigger likewise had heard the rumors and he told Gibbons, "There is reason to fear that your health will be quite impaired by the time the Council will open." He, therefore, suggested that he take a week's holiday at Seton Hall College where everything would be made as pleasant as

---

123 Letterbook, Gibbons to Ireland, Baltimore, August 21, 1884, p. 112.
124 78-P-9, Elder to Gibbons, Cincinnati, September 25, 1884.
125 78-P-5, Lynch to Gibbons, Toronto, September 15, 1884.
126 78-P-11, Lynch to Gibbons, Toronto, September 30, 1884.
127 78-Q-11, Corrigan to Gibbons, New York, October 6, 1884.

possible for him.[128] Gibbons was grateful for this interest in
his health and for the invitation to South Orange of which, he
said, "I can hardly avail myself for want of time." He
further explained:

> With the increased labor & anxiety for the last seven months, I
> am now considerably enervated, but I am consoled by the fact that
> the preparatory work is now almost completed, & the rest of the
> work will be shared by my devoted colleagues. I pray God that our
> sessions will be marked by harmony & good will. Today we are
> mailing the new Schema to the Prelates. I trust you will be pleased
> with it.[129]

As he mentioned to Wigger, it was just at this time in mid-
October that the schema of the decrees came from the printer
and was mailed to the bishops for their scrutiny. By getting
the document into their hands three weeks in advance Gibbons
told Gilmour he believed they would have ample time to examine
it before the council met. He thanked the Bishop of Cleveland
for the services of Father Moes, who had shown himself
a master in theology, canon law, and Latin style.[130] It did not
take the Coadjutor Archbishop of New York long to go through
the schema and in a few days he sent word saying, "I beg to
congratulate you sincerely on the successful completion of
your labors." Corrigan thought the proposed decrees showed
throughout "marks of great zeal, good judgment and enlightened
wisdom," and that the distribution of matter was "remarkably
good, logical and judicious. . . ."[131] While the actual work on
the schema was done by the consulting theologians, the responsibility for its over-all preparation belonged to Gibbons, and for
that reason it was reassuring to receive the approval of so
exacting a critic as Archbishop Corrigan.

The first report from St. Louis had been that the old archbishop, Peter Richard Kenrick, who was then in his seventy-ninth
year would not attend. When word reached Baltimore that he

---

[128] 78-R-4, Wigger to Gibbons, Seton Hall College, October 13, 1884.

[129] Letterbook, Gibbons to Wigger, Baltimore, October 14, 1884, p. 122. Gibbons
added to the Bishop of Newark, "I avail myself of this occasion by thanking
you for the signal aid you have rendered me in sending me Father Messmer
whose zeal & ability cannot be too much admired."

[130] *Ibid.*, Gibbons to Gilmour, Baltimore, October 14, 1884, p. 123.

[131] 78-R-11, Corrigan to Gibbons, New York, October 17, 1884.

was coming Gibbons was delighted and he hastened to tell Kenrick that "the satisfaction will be shared by all our colleagues in enjoying the benefit of your wisdom & experience. I intend to invite your Grace to celebrate the Pontifical Mass at the opening of the Council, Nov. 9th. You will inaugurate the First Solemn Session, as your venerable brother did at the First Pl. Council."[132] Another distinguished person whom he was anxious to have in attendance was Isaac Hecker, founder of the Paulist Fathers. Augustine F. Hewit, Hecker's confrère, had written a strong letter to Gibbons deprecating Hecker's attempt to go to Baltimore since he feared his health would not stand the strain, and Hewit had reminded the archbishop that Hecker's life was more precious to the Paulists than it was to the council. Moreover, he feared proper accommodations for rest could not be found for Hecker in Baltimore during the meeting.[133] Gibbons promptly informed Hewit that he had that day made arrangements for Hecker to stay with Father William E. Bartlett, pastor of St. Ann's Church, who had a comfortable house; the archbishop would also see that a private carriage was placed at his disposal to take him to and from the council chamber. "We will do all we can," he said, "to prolong his valuable life. It is singularly proper that your Congregation should be represented, & Fr. Hecker or yourself is the most fitting representative."[134] At length the Paulists were satisfied with the arrangements made by Gibbons and Father Hecker did attend the council.

A few days later Gibbons received a request from Bishop Spalding of Peoria that since Miss Mary Gwendoline Caldwell intended to be present at the opening of the council, and, Spalding added, "as she is disposed to be very generous in aid of the project of founding *Unum Seminarium Principale,* I am anxious she should have a good seat in the Cathedral."[135] But it seemed at the time that provision would have to be made for more important guests than Miss Caldwell since the pastor of St. Matthew's in Washington told Gibbons that President

---

[132] Letterbook, Gibbons to Kenrick, Baltimore, October 11, 1884, p. 121. Gibbons was here referring to Francis Kenrick, Archbishop of Baltimore, presiding as apostolic delegate over the council in 1852.
[133] 78-R-9, Hewit to Gibbons, New York, October 15, 1884.
[134] Letterbook, Gibbons to Hewit, Baltimore, October 16, 1884, p. 125.
[135] 78-S-11, Spalding to Gibbons, Peoria, October 26, 1884.

Chester A. Arthur had indicated he might attend the opening session. Gibbons quickly dispatched the following invitation to the White House:

> Mr. President:
> I have learned with much satisfaction this evg. from Rev. Dr. Chapelle that Your Excellency intends, if no unforeseen circumstance occurs, to assist at the opening session of the third Plenary Council in our Metropolitan Church, Sunday, Nov. 9th.
> I heartily hope that Your Excellency will be present on that solemn occasion, & in that event, suitable seats will be provided for yourself & any members of the Cabinet, or friends who may accompany you.[136]

In the final event the President of the United States was not present, although Miss Caldwell and a party of friends were there.

By the last days of October all was in readiness and a printed circular was issued which stated that there would be three preliminary meetings before the first solemn session of the council to be held on Sunday, November 9, in the cathedral.[137] During the first week of November the bishops and their theologians began to arrive in Baltimore and to settle themselves in the various residences to which they had been assigned. The throng to be accommodated taxed every available bit of space in the city's religious houses, parish rectories, and the private homes of some Catholic families. When it is remembered that there were in attendance fourteen archbishops, fifty-seven bishops, seven abbots, thirty-one superiors of religious orders, eleven superiors of major seminaries, and eighty-eight theologians — to say nothing of other minor officials — it will be appreciated how difficult was the task of hospitality imposed on Catholic Baltimore during the month the council was in session. A brief preliminary meeting was held at Gibbons' residence on Thursday evening, at five o'clock, but the following morning at St. Mary's Seminary on Paca Street the apostolic delegate greeted the prelates in a formal way for the first time. It was evident from his address to the bishops that the

---

[136] Letterbook, Gibbons to the President of the United States, Baltimore, October 28, 1884, p. 132.

[137] 78-S-16, Gibbons' printed circular to the American hierarchy, October, 1884 (no day given).

thought uppermost in Gibbons' mind was the need for harmony and good will among themselves. He said:

> I bid you a hearty welcome to Balto. & I earnestly pray that you may be amply rewarded for the fatigues of travel & the labors of the Council by the wise & salutary legislation which you will enact under the guidance of the H. Ghost.
>
> For my part I must say in all candor & simplicity that since my return from Rome last March, I have labored in season & out of season in preparing the way for the C[ouncil] while I have studiously avoided to do any thing which wd. trench on the prerogatives of the Prelates or forestall their legitimate action. I hope that in what I have done I have interpreted yr. wishes. If I have in any way transgressed the bounds of propriety, I crave yr. indulgence, & I beg you to ascribe my shortcomings not to any want of regard for yr. sacred rights, but to my youth & inexperience.
>
> Not wishing to trespass on yr. valuable time permit me to close with one observation. A very large no. of Prelates & abbots will take part in the council. In so large a deliberative assembly it would [be] hard to expect perfect identity of sentiment & views, particularly in minor details.
>
> God grant that our deliberations may be marked by mutual forbearance, & good will & genuine charity. May we keep in view the golden maxim of St. Vincent Lerins: In necessariis unitas, in dubiis libertas, in omnibus caritas. May God bless our labors, & may His Holy Spirit so shape our thoughts & words that all our decisions may contribute to His glory & the exaltation of our Holy Religion.[138]

With this simple speech James Gibbons performed the first formal function of his office as apostolic delegate in the presence of his brother bishops. He was exceedingly nervous at first, a fact which he acknowledged years later in reminiscing on the experience. He said at that time, "When I started to read the prayer at the beginning of the first session, my hands trembled violently. I was a young man then and I might have been expected to stand the strain better. However, I felt my strength and buoyancy gradually rising as the Council proceeded until I was in good physical condition before the end."[139] On Saturday, November 8, Gibbons greeted the theologians in a brief speech in which he stressed their unity with the bishops, reminding

---

[138] 78-T-3, Gibbons' handwritten account of his greeting to the bishops, November 7, 1884.
[139] Will, *Life of Cardinal Gibbons*, I, 248, quoted without reference to the source.

them that their chief contribution would be made through the various committees of the council, but assuring the theologians at the same time that "we are all one though our functions vary."[140] With these preliminaries out of the way the apostolic delegate could turn his attention to the first solemn session of the council which convened in the Cathedral of the Assumption on Sunday, November 9, at ten o'clock.

The interest of the press was naturally attracted to the unusual gathering of churchmen in Baltimore. But since the sessions were held in secrecy it was difficult for them to find out what was really going on and to report it accurately. The *Freeman's Journal* of New York foresaw the trouble and warned its readers that "each and every pretention, — of which there will be many, in newspapers, of knowing what deliberations are going on, will be mere romance."[141] The New York editor was quite right in his warning, but that did not prevent some tall guessing by the newspapermen. Just five days preceding the formal opening of the council there had taken place the presidential election in which Grover Cleveland defeated James G. Blaine. Less than a week before the election, on October 29, the country had been electrified by the remark of a Presbyterian clergyman, Samuel D. Burchard, made in New York to Blaine when he acted as spokesman for a group waiting on the Republican candidate to assure him of their support. The minister had on that occasion stated that the group for which he spoke were Republicans and, as he said, "don't propose to leave our party and identify ourselves with the party whose antecedents are rum, Romanism, and rebellion."[142] The statement caused a

---

[140] 78-T-4, Gibbons' address to the theologians in his own handwriting, November 8, 1884.

[141] November 8, 1884. The writer is indebted to the article of Sister M. Augustine Kwitchen entitled, "Newspaper Comment on the III Plenary Council of Baltimore," *Jurist*, VIII (January, 1948), 3–12, for most of the references to the council and the press used here.

[142] "Samuel Dickinson Burchard," *Dictionary of American Biography*, III, 271–272. Several weeks before this incident Archbishop Corrigan wrote to Gibbons on council business and he added an interesting note on the presidential campaign. He said, "Several prominent Democratic politicians, some of them direct messengers from Gov. Cleveland, have called here during the past two weeks — much in the same sense as they waited upon Your Grace in Baltimore. The threat of persecution is ridiculous, and the insinuation that Catholics belong to the Democratic party and are not at liberty to vote otherwise is just as amusing" (78-Q-11, Corrigan to Gibbons, New York, October 6, 1884).

national sensation and was generally looked upon as contributing heavily to Blaine's loss of New York State and its decisive electoral votes. There was speculation, therefore, in the circles of the press if the Catholic bishops would show any reaction to the unfortunate incident, a matter which in actuality they entirely ignored.

With the sessions held in secrecy the press had to fall back upon descriptions of the public sessions of the council in the cathedral, comments on the leading personalities, and a few hints of action which they picked up here and there in Baltimore. The New York *Times* recognized the handicap in its issue of November 17 when it said the proceedings were in Latin; yet even those who knew that language, "but were not members of the Council," could gain no information as to what was going on. The New York *World* described the formal opening in the cathedral at some length and the procession which preceded it:

> Venerable princes moved along, their long trains supported by bright-faced boys; keen-faced and intellectual-looking men in the prime fit to rule and ready to obey, walked with modest mien. . . . Occasionally among the crowd of clean-shaven faces could be seen one with patriarchal beard and venerable look seeming as though he had stepped out of a stained-glass window. Slowly swinging his censer, and spreading round an odor of frankincense walked the censerbearer, and then bringing up the rear walked the Apostolic-delegate, Archbishop Gibbons.[143]

The New York *Times* of November 9 noted Gibbons' physical characteristics and stated that he was the center of attention on the opening day, although it remarked he was surrounded by his peers and, "in fact, some of them greater in the Council of the church and greater in public opinion." As the council progressed other news stories were carried by the press of Baltimore, New York, Washington, and cities in the West.

By the time the bishops and theologians were ready to begin the real work on Monday, November 10, they had already in their possession for a month's time a document of nearly 100 pages entitled *Schema decretorum concilii plenarii Baltimorensis tertii,* the product of the corps of theologians who had been

---

[143] November 10, 1884.

working under Gibbons' direction in Baltimore since mid-August. This document, which had printed in on the first page, "sub secreto servandum," now furnished the basis for the debates in the various sessions. The role of the apostolic delegate was that of presiding officer who, in the parliamentary rules drawn up to govern the debates, had the power to break a tie with his vote, to recognize each speaker who wished to enter the debate, to appoint all special committees in the council, to call members to order in case the rules were being violated, and to settle any doubts which might arise concerning the rules. In this way Archbishop Gibbons' functions were outlined for him in the regulations adopted for the debates.

The private edition of the *Acta et decreta,* which is the only extant record of the debates in council and of the roles played by individual bishops, would indicate that Gibbons used his powers as apostolic delegate very sparingly. In some instances, however, he interjected his opinion on the more important questions. When it came to a debate on the subject of irremovable rectors Bishop Ireland asked the apostolic delegate to tell the assembly his mind on the subject. Gibbons stated that it was the fixed opinion of the cardinals in Rome that there must be irremovable rectors in the Church of the United States, and that if the council failed to pass legislation on this point it would only invite action from Rome which would not be without embarrassment to the bishops in this country. He continued that it would be easier to remove unsuitable rectors from these posts under the proposed decree than it had hitherto been, nor could the inducements to priests to strive for irremovable rectorships be ignored. The apostolic delegate, therefore, indicated his view that the decree should be passed as it stood, and that was done.[144]

In the extended and rather heated debate on secret societies the voice of Gibbons was heard again on the side of moderation when he warned the bishops that it was the mind of the Holy See that, as he expressed it, "we condemn no society hastily," adding that he had received letters from the Ancient Order of Hibernians which stated they would fulfill the conditions laid down by the Church for approval.[145] On the subject of

---

[144] *Acta et decreta concilii plenarii Baltimorensis tertii* (Baltimorae), 1884, p. xlvii.
[145] *Ibid.,* pp. lxxvii–lxxviii.

round dances Gibbons told the assembly that this form of entertainment was not to be judged severely from the examples given of them at Rome.[146] In the proposed decrees on the Negroes special mention had been made of the fine work being done by the Josephite missionaries.[147] The particular mention of the Josephites prompted other bishops to mention the work of the Benedictines, and Gibbons himself to say that the Jesuits, too, had merited to be spoken well of in their efforts for the Negroes.[148] The matter of naming particular religious societies in praise apparently proved too troublesome to settle to the satisfaction of all and in the final decree no mention was made by name of any religious group working among the Negroes. Gilmour suggested that Mount Saint Mary's College in Emmitsburg was ready to convert itself into a center of training for missionaries to the Negroes and Indians, but Gibbons stated that he feared such might not prove a feasible plan since bishops might refuse to send their men there on account of the financial difficulties through which the college was then passing.[149]

The incidents cited above in relation to Gibbons' personal role in the debates are the only important instances in which the apostolic delegate played much of a public and official part, according to the private *Acta et decreta*. It is safe to say that Gibbons permitted the maximum of freedom of debate among the bishops, and that his natural inclination to take the judgment of older and more experienced men contributed to the silence of the record as far as he was concerned. Although he had passed his fiftieth birthday and had been an archbishop for seven years, he felt a certain reserve in the presence of men like Kenrick, Lamy, and Alemany who were much his seniors both in age and in their years as bishops. In any case, the apostolic delegate would seem to have interjected himself very little into the open debates, resting content to pilot the various sessions in such a way that more forceful debaters like John Ireland, John Lancaster Spalding, Richard

---

[146] *Ibid.*, p. lxxxvi.

[147] *Schema decretorum concilii plenarii Baltimorensis tertii* (Baltimorae), 1884, p. 71.

[148] *Acta et decreta*, private edition, p. lxxii.

[149] *Ibid.*, p. lxxv.

Gilmour, and others could be heard. While Gibbons was present in the cathedral at all the solemn sessions and at as many of the other ceremonies at possible, he preached none of the formal sermons delivered during the month of the council.

As the council neared its close and the newspapers found little in the realm of fact to report from Baltimore, speculation began to stir about the possibility of a red hat being born out of the gathering. The New York *World* of November 30 settled the question to its own satisfaction as follows:

> It can be stated now as an absolute fact that Archbishop Gibbons, of the metropolitan see of Baltimore and delegate apostolic to the third Plenary Council, will be a cardinal before the adjournment of the present council, or at least before January. This was determined upon at the Council of American Bishops held at Rome last November. After his elevation to the cardinalate it is likely that he will be given a coadjutor, on account of the increase of work in this archdiocese.

When the fathers of the council were tendered a reception at the residence of Miss Emily Harper — in spite of Archbishop Elder — and a civic reception at the Concordia Opera House, the press was given an opportunity for some colorful detail. Reporting the reception at the opera house in its issue of November 21 the New York *Times* said:

> The Reception was a representative gathering. . . . On the stage decorated with palm trees was the orchestra. The floor was crowded with ladies and gentlemen, many of whom were in full dress, and rich costumes of the former contrasted vividly with the purple robes and golden crosses worn by the ecclesiastics. In one corner could be seen a group of Bishops busily engaged in discussing some knotty question. Close by a smiling Archbishop was chatting merrily with a bevy of young ladies, and again an Abbot with corded gown, a pensive face, and patriarchal beard would pass slowly by. . . .

The solemn closing of the council took place on Sunday, December 7, in the cathedral with Archbishop Corrigan of New York the celebrant of the Mass, John L. Spalding the preacher, and Gibbons presiding as delegate. After the Mass there followed the customary *acclamationes,* the bestowal of the *pax* by Gibbons on each of the bishops, and then two brief speeches. Archbishop Kenrick of St. Louis, the patriarch of the council, expressed the thanks of the assembled prelates to Gibbons for the prudence and benignity he had displayed toward them in the council, for which he had earned, said Kenrick, their highest praise and their prayerful wishes for his future good fortune and happiness.[150] In his reply the apostolic delegate thanked the bishops especially for the good will they had shown toward one another during the sessions. He stated that in all the experience and observation he had of assemblies in both Church and State, in provincial and plenary councils, at the Vatican Council, in the Congress at Washington, and in the parliaments of France and Great Britain he had never seen truer concord and fraternal charity than he had witnessed during the previous four weeks. Varied nationalities there were among them with different personalities and scholastic backgrounds, but through it all they had remained one in faith and charity. Gibbons recalled the large portrait of Leo XIII which hung in the hall at St. Mary's Seminary where they had held their sessions, and he said had the Pope been present in person rather than in his portrait he would have cried out with a joyous heart, "Ecce quam bonum et quam jucundum habitare fratres in unum." The delegate stated that while many of the bishops present could not hope to be present at a future plenary council of the American Church, at least they could entertain the hope that some day in the future and immortal life they would have another reunion where they would be numbered among the heavenly throng of whom St. John wrote in the *Apocalypse,* that they were "standing before the throne and in sight of the Lamb. . . ."[151] With the intonement of the *Te Deum* the ceremony came to an end and the Third Plenary Council had finished its long and difficult work.

In all, the council passed 319 decrees, grouped under eleven major titles, which ranged over practically every problem touching on the Church in the United States. After a brief chapter on the Catholic faith the bishops defined the rights and authority of various classes of ecclesiastical persons, framed laws governing feasts and fasts in the yearly calendar, the administration of the sacraments, devoted a very lengthy section to Catholic education with provision for a university, passed

---

[150] *Ibid.,* p. cii.
[151] *Ibid.*

decrees on diocesan newspapers, secret societies, work for the Negroes and Indians, ways of holding church property, conducting clerical trials, and finally a brief chapter on Christian burial.[52] So thoroughly had they done their work that the decrees of this council remained as the law of the Church of the United States practically unchanged down to 1918 when the *Code of Canon Law* went into force for the Universal Church, and even after that date many of its laws continued in effect.[153] Before the decrees framed at Baltimore in 1884 could be declared in force they would have to be approved by Rome and that, of course, would take further time and effort on the part of Gibbons and the bishops whom he appointed to represent the hierarchy in the discussions with the Holy See.

For the time being, however, Archbishop Gibbons enjoyed a surcease from his labors. It was gratifying to him to be told by Archbishop Kenrick upon his return to St. Louis, "My first duty on arriving home is to address you my most grateful acknowledgement for the kindness and hospitality shown to me by your Grace while a guest at your Episcopal residence. My esteem for your Grace personally, always great, has been increased by the nearer opportunity of witnessing Your Grace's many virtues."[154] Ryan of Philadelphia was likewise complimentary when he said, "You must be deeply gratified with the result of the Council and with the favorable impression you made on the prelates as its presiding officer."[155] These expressions of approval for the course he had followed as apostolic delegate represented the general opinion of the hierarchy, and after carrying out so well the exacting duties of that office it is not difficult to see why speculation began to stir about Gibbons receiving the red hat of a cardinal. In the last days of the old year of 1884 the archbishop prepared the many documents that had to be transmitted to the Holy See, and after having dispatched

---

[152] Peter Guilday, *A History of the Councils of Baltimore (1791–1884)* (New York, 1932), has a chapter on the Third Plenary Council, pp. 221–249, which in the absence of a definitive history of the council is the best general treatment of its over-all aspects.

[153] Cf. John D. Barrett, S.S., *A Comparative Study of the Councils of Baltimore and the Code of Canon Law* (Washington, 1932), pp. 205–208, for a listing of the legislation of 1884 which remained in force after 1918 and the Baltimore laws that were abrogated with the publication of the code.

[154] 78-U-11, Kenrick to Gibbons, St. Louis, December 11, 1884.

[155] 78-V-6, Ryan to Gibbons, Philadelphia, December 20, 1884.

them he wrote a glowing over-all account of the council to Cardinal Simeoni. In this letter Gibbons emphasized the harmony which had marked the meetings, the generally friendly attitude of public opinion and the press, and the fact that the Post Office Department had established a special postal service for the bishops at the seminary. He told Simeoni that the President would have liked to have been present for the opening of the council but the pressure of urgent business kept him away. He concluded his description by saying:

> It is evident that everyone in our free America appreciates the important influence of the Catholic Church for the grandeur and prosperity of the nation and we can be only very grateful for the manifestations to which this sentiment has given rise. I am certain that your Eminence and His Holiness will be happy to learn this.[156]

---

[156] 78-Y-4, Gibbons to Simeoni, Baltimore, December 27, 1884, copy in French.

CHAPTER VII

Unfinished Business

WHILE the close of the Third Plenary Council on December 7, 1884, represented the completion of the most difficult labor for Archbishop Gibbons in that ambitious undertaking, the legislation which the bishops had passed during their month in Baltimore needed the formal approval of the Holy See before it could go into effect for the American Church. For this reason Gibbons as apostolic delegate had to give thought to the best means to accomplish that end. He decided to send Dr. O'Connell to Rome with the text of the decrees since O'Connell possessed the double advantage of having worked on the legislation from the outset and of having had considerable experience in the conduct of business with the Roman Curia. In addition to O'Connell it was thought proper to designate one or more of the American bishops to go to Rome so that they might offer explanations of the legislation and answer any inquiries that might arise in the minds of the cardinals of the Propaganda. With this in view Gibbons chose John Moore, Bishop of St. Augustine, one of his own suffragans, and Joseph Dwenger, C.Pp.S., Bishop of Fort Wayne.

The choice of Bishop Moore would seem to have been prompted in good measure by the fact that he had been educated in Rome and could speak Italian fluently. In the case of Dwenger, his German extraction made him a suitable candidate to represent the German Catholics of the United States, while the consideration that he was thought to enjoy close and cordial relations with a number of the Propaganda officials gave promise that his selection would prove a happy choice. Soon after learning that Dwenger was agreeable to undertaking the mission if the apostolic delegate advised, Gibbons expressed the wish to have the bishop stop in

Baltimore for a conference on his way to Rome, and he especially urged Dwenger to use all his influence when he reached the Eternal City to press for approval of the decree which required the bishops to seek only the counsel — rather than the consent — of their diocesan consultors in transactions pertaining to the purchase and sale of church property. Since up to this time there had been no strict clarification of the rights and duties of diocesan consultors in the United States, it was important that such should be definitely determined. This point was the source of great anxiety to Gibbons, knowing as he did that the council had substituted in its decree the word "counsel" for "consent" as originally recommended by Rome. He told Dwenger that the decree in question had been "passed almost unanimously, & its modification would be a great disappointment to the Prelates of the country."[1] In the selection of Dwenger as one of the bishops to represent the American hierarchy, Gibbons had sought the advice of Archbishop Elder, who informed the Bishop of Fort Wayne that when he was in Baltimore the apostolic delegate had told him he was considering Dwenger and Elder had encouraged him to do so.[2]

The appointments of O'Connell, Moore, and Dwenger to pilot the conciliar legislation through Rome, however, still left Gibbons with a certain uneasiness of mind regarding the success that might attend their efforts in securing approval without substantial change in the decrees. While it was apparent that he was entertaining the idea of strengthening the delegation to Rome, he was at the same time fearful that the officials of the Holy See might resent the presence there of too many Americans as giving the appearance of undue pressure from this side of the Atlantic. This case was one of many in which the archbishop had great difficulty in making up his mind about the best course to pursue. Gibbons had known Bishop Gilmour of Cleveland for a long time and he had come to admire the clear reasoning and forceful manner of the prelate in matters of church law, an ability which Gilmour had displayed to advantage during the recent council. The archbishop chose, therefore, to express his wish that Gilmour might join the Americans in Rome, but he was careful at first not to designate

[1] AUND, Fort Wayne Papers, Gibbons to Dwenger, Baltimore, February 9, 1885.
[2] *Ibid.,* Elder to Dwenger, Cincinnati, February 16, 1885.

him as an official representative in the hope apparently that if Gilmour would consent to go in a private capacity he could obtain the desired objective without arousing suspicions of pressure at Rome. Gibbons explained to the Bishop of Cleveland that O'Connell was sailing on the *Servia* on February 11 and that Moore and Dwenger would soon follow, to which he added, "I would be pleased if you could visit Rome in the spring. Your presence there would contribute much to obtaining the approbation of the decrees."[3] Gilmour, too, was intent upon the full approval by the Holy See of the Baltimore legislation, and although he confessed he would prefer to be spared the trip, he said he regarded the matter as so important that he would do "almost anything" to have the decrees approved as they came from the council.[4] For the present Gibbons contented himself with reiterating his wish that Gilmour would go, but he left the decision to the bishop himself and said that if he decided to make the journey he would like to have him visit Baltimore where he would then make a few suggestions.[5] In view of the uncertainty created in the mind of Gilmour and others as to what status Gibbons as apostolic delegate would give to the bishop in the Roman negotiations, it would have been far better if he had clearly designated the Bishop of Cleveland at the outset as one of the official representatives of the American hierarchy and provided him with proper credentials.

Meanwhile Bishop Dwenger made his plans to sail on the *Aurania* on March 4 and he assured Archbishop Gibbons that he would come to Baltimore before departing to receive his instructions. Dwenger promised to work hard to push through the legislation as the council had passed it, and even on points where his own views differed from the decrees he said, "my ideas will not be put forward. . . ."[6] Although recent word from Father August J. Schulte, acting rector of the American College in Rome, had assured Gibbons that Pope Leo XIII "never tires of speaking of the success of the Council,"[7] there was reason for believing that at least one of the cardinals of the Propaganda was not so favorably disposed. O'Connell had

[3] ADC, Gibbons to Gilmour, Baltimore, February 10, 1885.

[4] 79-D-18, Gilmour to Gibbons, Cleveland, February 13, 1885.

[5] ADC, Gibbons to Gilmour, Baltimore, February 16, 1885.

[6] 79-E-5, Dwenger to Gibbons, Fort Wayne, February 19, 1885.

[7] 79-E-8, Schulte to Gibbons, Rome, February 19, 1885.

reached Rome in late February and he recounted the approving attitudes of Cardinals Jacobini and Howard toward the council's work, but he added that Cardinal Franzelin had shown himself critical and Simeoni "as usual was quiet." Gibbons' confidant told him he would write regularly to report the progress of events and that he would try to mirror matters just as they happened, "coloring nothing and going rather under than over the mark in cases of doubt."[8] Through the ensuing months O'Connell was true to his promise and Archbishop Gibbons continued to receive lengthy letters wherein his agent described in detail the discussions of the American prelates as they progressed with the cardinals of the Propaganda.

The uneasiness upon the part of Gibbons and other American bishops over the Roman sanction of the council's decrees centered, as mentioned previously, in the question of the diocesan consultors' right to offer a bishop their consent or counsel in matters affecting church properties. Gibbons was intent that the American bishops' freedom of action should not be fettered by having to get the consent of their consultors for the purchase and sale of property, and he was determined, if at all possible, that the substitution made in the language of the decree in Baltimore should stand. Therefore, the repeated warnings from the Americans in Rome that Cardinal Franzelin was holding out for "consent" in the place of "counsel" only increased the misgivings of Gibbons and his colleagues on this side of the Atlantic. It was his worry over this and other important phases of the legislation that prompted Bishop Gilmour to reopen with Gibbons the necessity for strengthening the American delegation at Rome. He told the archbishop he did not feel confidence in the ability of Dwenger and Moore to stand up to Franzelin and others, and at the risk of seeming obtrusive he suggested that he and Bishop McQuaid of Rochester go to Rome after Easter. Gilmour reiterated his reluctance to make the trip but he felt no sacrifice was too great to bring back the council's laws intact. He apologized for his boldness in making the suggestion and asked Gibbons to believe that his forwardness was prompted entirely by the archbishop's kindness and confidence in him.[9]

---

[8] 79-F-9, O'Connell to Gibbons, Rome, March 8, 1885.
[9] 79-G-13, Gilmour to Gibbons, Cleveland, March 21, 1885.

To this suggestion Gibbons returned an immediate answer. Insofar as McQuaid was concerned, he agreed that Gilmour could not select "a stronger & more zealous companion." However, he was still fearful of Rome's reactions to so many Americans appearing there, believing it would be viewed as an attempt at pressure and coercion. Faced as he was by a practical suggestion for action, the archbishop sought to meet Gilmour's proposal, and at the same time safeguard his own position, by a counter suggestion that the two bishops announce they were going to Europe for reasons of health and relaxation. Gibbons was of the belief that:

> This and some other motives that may suggest themselves to you, while saving you from any suspicion of exercising any pressure, will not interfere with the exercise of your zeal and your aid in Rome. The authorities even will be glad to have you then for consultation.[10]

In the meantime Gilmour had consulted Elder, his metropolitan, about the projected trip and the latter said he desired that he should go, but he added, "especially if you go at the request of the Apostolic Delegate, to give you official position as representing the Council."[11] To be sure, no such official accreditation had either been offered or given by Gibbons and it was the lack of it which caused the Bishop of Rochester to show strong indignation at the course thus far pursued by the Archbishop of Baltimore.

McQuaid was noted for his plain speaking and to him Gibbons' conduct in this affair was entirely unsatisfactory. He told Gilmour that if he did not know what kind of a man Gibbons was he would feel disposed "to resent his proposition as an insult." McQuaid would be no party to any unofficial visit to Rome; either they would go as the accredited representatives of the apostolic delegate or he would not go at all. Alluding to Gilmour's proposal to Gibbons that the two bishops go to Rome after Easter, McQuaid said he believed the archbishop either did not appreciate it, or, as he expressed it, "what is more likely, he had not the courage to do what is required of him."[12] The Bishop of Rochester's annoyance did not abate and he told Gilmour two weeks later in a severely critical letter about Gibbons, "His

---

10 Letterbook, Gibbons to Gilmour, Baltimore, March 23, 1885, pp. 151–152.
11 ADC, Elder to Gilmour, Cincinnati, March 25, 1885.
12 *Ibid.,* McQuaid to Gilmour, Rochester, March 26, 1885.

Grace would be pleased if you could go to Rome on your own 'hook,' and save the American Church, without the possibility of his incurring any displeasure." He suggested further that Gibbons alone should not accredit agents for the council but that the co-operation of the other archbishops should be sought. "Thus united," he continued, "he need not fear adverse criticism for himself. But he will get plenty of it should there be radical changes through his default."[13] Meanwhile the disquieting news over the opposition of Franzelin and the danger to the council's legislation continued to reach Baltimore from the Eternal City.[14] While Gibbons relayed his mounting fears to Gilmour he could not bring himself to commission the Bishop of Cleveland to go as his official representative. He limited himself to saying, "You can draw yr. conclusions about going. I cannot take the responsibility of advising you to go, but I wish you were there. You must decide for yourself & quickly."[15]

The plain truth of the matter was that Archbishop Gibbons was sorely confused by the contradictory advice he was receiving from a number of sources, and as a result he did not know what action to take. Dwenger was by all odds the most optimistic of the Americans writing him from Rome and from his correspondence Gibbons might easily have been led to believe that the legislation would be approved without major changes. But then O'Connell informed the archbishop that he should take with some reserve what Dwenger wrote to him since the Bishop of Fort Wayne was, as he said, "very well pleased with himself" and showed a tendency to overrate his own ability to convert the Propaganda officials to his views.[16] To add to Gibbons' dis-

---

[13] *Ibid.*, McQuaid to Gilmour, Rochester, April 12, 1885, *Private*. McQuaid told Gilmour that as he drew to the close of this letter, "it struck me that the reading of it by his Grace might do him good. So, if you think well of it, you might send the letter, but not this postscript, to his Grace. It contains one sentence rather severe. If you take the same view of it, you might copy the letter, less the severity portion." There is no evidence in the AAB that Gilmour sent the McQuaid letter to Baltimore.

[14] 79-H-11; 79-I-2; 79-I-13 represent a few of the letters from O'Connell and Moore during these days of uncertainty in Rome.

[15] ADC, Gibbons to Gilmour, Baltimore, April 3, 1885, *Private*. Three days later Gibbons again wrote Gilmour saying he had meanwhile more reassuring word from Rome. He revealed in the letter of April 6 that he had not yet become aware of the difficulty with Dwenger when he told Gilmour, "The Bps. of Fort Wayne & St. Augustine are acting energetically & in concert." *Ibid.*

[16] 79-H-11, O'Connell to Gibbons, Rome, March 29, 1885.

comfort over the Gilmour appointment O'Connell, his most trusted adviser, expressed his own disapproval of Gilmour's coming to Rome. He told the archbishop he could not see "what other interpretation could be put upon it by the Propaganda than an intention to coerce."[17] This was precisely the fear that Gibbons had entertained from the outset. Meanwhile Gilmour's own growing impatience was reflected in a letter to Elder which the latter sent on to Baltimore. The Bishop of Cleveland summed up his mind to his metropolitan by saying:

> As it now stands I will not go. I did offer to go & see it out if properly & officially accredited. If this can not be done then those who have gone are simply officious intruders & will do harm by pretending to speak for the American hierarchy, & acquiescing will commit us all to what we never consented.[18]

This letter was forwarded to the Archbishop of Baltimore by Elder along with one of his own in which he strongly advised Gibbons to issue the credentials for Gilmour. He acknowledged that Gibbons might be hesitant since the matter had not been discussed in the council, but he suggested a course of action which ultimately broke the impasse. "If you feel a delicacy about assuming it," he wrote, "you might consult some of the Archbishops & some of the older Bishops; and I think their answers will reassure you."[19] Fortunately, the opportunity was at hand since a meeting of the bishops who composed the committee for the proposed Catholic university was scheduled to be held in Baltimore on May 7. At this meeting Gibbons consulted with Williams, Ryan, Corrigan, Ireland, and Spalding and they all agreed Gilmour should be sent officially. That day Gibbons telegraphed to Gilmour, "Look out for important letters mailed today."[20] He sent on a communication which outlined the agreement of the bishops about his mission and assured him that a Latin letter "signed by all of us," and addressed to Cardinal Simeoni would follow immediately. He concluded, "You had better prepare to start at once, & I hope you will please come to see me before you start."[21]

---

[17] 79-J-16, O'Connell to Gibbons, Rome, April 23, 1885.
[18] 79-J-21, Gilmour to Elder, Cleveland, April 28, 1885.
[19] 79-K-5, Elder to Gibbons, Cincinnati, May 4, 1885.
[20] ADC, Gibbons to Gilmour, Baltimore, May 7, 1885, telegram.
[21] *Ibid.*, Gibbons to Gilmour, Baltimore, May 7, 1885.

The succeeding months were anxious ones insofar as the Roman negotiations over the conciliar legislation were concerned. If Gibbons was encouraged in hearing from Gilmour shortly after the latter reached Rome that the prospects were good for the decrees to be returned "substantially as they left the hands of the council,"[22] this news was countered almost immediately by Dwenger. The Bishop of Fort Wayne related that the arrival of Gilmour had aroused the suspicion of coercion in the mind of Simeoni, as Gibbons had feared. He said, "Two weeks ago I felt sure that Bp. Moore and myself would obtain all we asked. I can give no such assurance now, in fact I feel a great deal discouraged."[23] To add to the troubles Moore and Gilmour found it increasingly difficult to work with Dwenger, and by the middle of July Moore bluntly told Gibbons that neither he nor Gilmour could get along with Dwenger because of what he called his "vanity and selfishness."[24]

Week after week the mail brought reports to Baltimore of the progress and setbacks suffered by the American representatives in Rome as the meetings with the Propaganda officials wore on through the hot summer months. In late August there arrived a cablegram from Gilmour which read, "Consensus reimposed. Telegraph Propaganda and instruct us." This alarming development forced Gibbons to get in touch quickly with the other archbishops to urge them to write Rome. He confided to his diary that he did this so that he might have the backing of his colleagues in preventing legislation which, as he said, "may hamper our administration, retard the progress of religion, and deprive the Bishops of power so necessary for them in the present condition of things."[25] Within a few days another cable arrived

---

[22] 79-M-7, Gilmour to Gibbons, Rome, June 7, 1885.

[23] 79-M-11, Dwenger to Gibbons, Rome, June 12, 1885.

[24] 79-O-11, Moore to Gibbons, Rome, July 15, 1885. Moore and Gilmour were working in close harmony and they prepared a document for the examiners of the decrees, a copy of which they forwarded to Gibbons. The archbishop called their report a "luminous document," sent his thanks, and said he believed that it would have "a decisive effect" in favor of the American views (ADC, Gibbons to Gilmour, Baltimore, August 18, 1885).

[25] Diary, August 20, 1885, p. 185. At the time of the crisis over "consent" or "counsel" for consultors the American bishops had an audience of Leo XIII during which they discussed the question. When they had finished with their business the Pope turned the conversation to the United States. Dwenger related to Gibbons that Leo spoke about "the President, the political parties — that he had heard the Democrats were as a rule more favorable to Catholics, asked

which read "Consilium restored — modified."[26] Gibbons sighed
with relief at the new turn of events in Rome and he promptly
informed Elder it would not now be necessary for them to write
the Holy See.

During the course of the Roman negotiations it became known
that only one American bishop had complained to the Holy See
about the management of the council in Baltimore. Gibbons
would naturally be sensitive on this point and he probably winced
a little when O'Connell told him, "Dr. Chatard was the only Bp.
that wrote a complaint about the management of the Council."[27]
O'Connell did not develop the matter beyond his brief postscript,
but a month later Bishop Moore particularized Chatard's complaint for the archbishop:

> A mischievous letter has been written to Propaganda by Bishop
> Chatard and put into the ponenza. It amounted to the charge that
> freedom of debate was not allowed in our council nor the authority
> of the Propaganda sufficiently respected. He complained that he was
> not allowed to read a letter from the Propaganda on secret societies.
> We explained that he had become very tiresome in the council, and
> that day the debate had worn everybody out and was deferred. It
> was reopened however another day and full liberty of opinion given
> to all, but Bp. Chatard did not offer to read his paper. What good
> object could he have had, we here ask ourselves, in writing such a
> letter which now remains in the official records of the council?[28]

There was not the slightest evidence from any other source of
interference with the freedom of debate by the apostolic delegate
in the council. The fact that the Bishop of Vincennes was the
only one to complain out of more than seventy bishops present

---

whether we were Democrats and was highly amused when he obtained an emphatic
democratic confession from Gilmour & Moore and learned that I passed for a
Republican; the Pope laughed heartily & Gilmour, I thought he could not go down
the stairs" (79-Q-11, Dwenger to Gibbons, Rome, August 24, 1884).

[26] AAC, Gibbons to Elder, Baltimore, August 25, 1885.

[27] 79-Q-3, O'Connell to Gibbons, Rome, August 11, 1885.

[28] 79-R-7, Moore to Gibbons, Villa Rufinella near Frascati, September 9, 1885.
When Corrigan heard of Chatard's complaint he expressed surprise that the Bishop
of Vincennes should have said he could not read Propaganda's letter about secret
societies, "when," as Corrigan told Gilmour, "we all remember that he *did*
read it, and the *Acta* duly record the fact (p. LXXVI)." He went on to say, "It
strikes me that if any opposition were manifested to Bp. Chatard in Baltimore,
during the Council, it was for a similar reason. We had not the *material time* to
enter into such discussions, nor the means at hand of pursuing the investigation"
(ADC, Corrigan to Gilmour, New York, September 4, 1885).

was not too serious, and the officials of Propaganda were probably not disturbed when they received the explanation of Moore and the other Americans concerning Chatard's grievance. The high opinion of Gibbons as presiding officer was, therefore, not seriously damaged by this single reflection upon his management of the council.

With the exception of the temporary flurry over Propaganda reimposing the "consent" of consultors which occurred in late August, the progress on the Baltimore legislation seemed to be fairly steady. By mid-September O'Connell could inform Gibbons, "The Council work is done, nothing remaining but the Pope's approval. I feel as if a mountain had been lifted off my mind."[29] On September 10 Leo XIII gave his approval to the legislation in an audience granted to Archbishop Jacobini and the formal documents were forwarded to Gibbons in a letter from Simeoni some days later. The troublesome question of the "consent" and "counsel" of diocesan consultors was settled by a special brief giving the American bishops permission to proceed for a ten-year period with property transactions without need of first winning their consultors' consent.[30] When the Roman conferences had closed Bishops Gilmour and Moore felt it of sufficient importance to write Gibbons a joint letter in which they stated it as their view that the appointment of Dwenger had been a serious mistake and that he was entirely unfitted for the work assigned to him. The two bishops said that he was prevented from acting alone only by their threats to inform Gibbons that he would not go along. Dwenger's vanity and desire to "curry favor for himself" were a constant source of irritation. Gilmour and Moore concluded with the hope that when American bishops "will have to undertake a similar labor after the next council [they] may have the good fortune to be able to work together harmoniously."[31] The appointment of Dwenger had not

---

29 79-R-10, O'Connell to Gibbons, Rome, September 11, 1885.

30 79-S-12, Simeoni to Gibbons, Rome, September 25, 1885. This decree pertaining to the consultors' consent was published in the *Acta et decreta* (Baltimore, 1886), p. ciii.

31 79-T-2, Gilmour and Moore to Gibbons, Rome, October 3, 1885. The appointment of Dwenger was unpopular with a number of other bishops besides Gilmour and Moore. The previous April Archbishop Ryan of Philadelphia had told Gibbons he believed great strength would be needed at Rome among the Americans. He hoped O'Connell, and Bishop James O'Connor of Omaha who was going to Rome, would "fight manfully for us," and he added, "& that Bishop Dwenger

been a happy one and the complaint of Gilmour and Moore must have made Gibbons regret his selection of the Bishop of Fort Wayne for the task.

Despite the reluctance he had shown at the outset to hold a council and the mistake of entrusting the decrees to Dwenger, the Third Plenary Council on the whole redounded to the personal fame of the Archbishop of Baltimore and his general management of its affairs during and after the sessions contributed greatly to its ultimate success. In fact, so well had the work been done and so generally favorable had been the impression created in Rome of this Baltimore council, that when Archbishop Elzear A. Taschereau of Quebec informed the Holy See that he was contemplating a provincial council, he was counseled by Simeoni to delay the meeting until the Baltimore decrees should be published.[32] Taschereau inquired, therefore, when they would appear and Gibbons informed him they should be out in February. The Archbishop of Quebec was grateful for this information as it enabled him to fix the date of his council for May when, following the advice of Simeoni, he said they would profit by the "wise decrees" of the Baltimore council.[33]

The high regard of the Roman Curia for the Baltimore legislation was soon shown a second time when the Archbishop of St. Andrews and Edinburgh told Gibbons that the Scottish bishops were making plans for their first provincial council, and he added, "Rome recommends to us your last Council of Baltimore as the best model for our imitation." Archbishop Smith wished to know likewise when and how he could secure the published volume of the legislation so that he might distribute copies among the Scottish hierarchy. He closed his letter by saying, "In Scotland we are far behind you in every way."[34] Word had reached Australia, too, of the success of the Baltimore council and Patrick

---

will help by some ponderous arguments. . . ." (79-I-9, Ryan to Gibbons, Philadelphia, April 6, 1885). Two weeks later John Ireland let Gibbons know of his disapproval of the Dwenger appointment. He said, "I do not expect, I must say, much good from Bp. Dwenger's presence in Rome; he does not like some of the decrees & it is his character to try to bring things down to his own liking" (79-J-9, Ireland to Gibbons, St. Paul, April 20, 1885). On the whole question of approval of the council cf. Zwierlein, *The Life and Letters of Bishop McQuaid*, II, 345–359.

[32] 79-W-12, Taschereau to Gibbons, Quebec, December 17, 1885.

[33] 79-Y-4, Taschereau to Gibbons, Quebec, December 23, 1885.

[34] 80-A-10, W[illiam] Smith to Gibbons, n.p., January 5, 1885.

Cardinal Moran, Archbishop of Sydney, sent the greetings of the Australian bishops, and he took occasion to praise Gibbons and his colleagues for what he called "your great Council, amongst the first in the history of the Church for its numbers and the extent of its territory, and for the importance of its deliberations. . . ."[35]

Archbishop Gibbons felt a natural gratification at these manifestations of approval by the Holy See and other hierarchies for the council over which he had presided. He told Bishop Gilmour about the letter from Taschereau and two weeks later he informed him that Scotland, too, was seeking the decrees. With pardonable pride he concluded, "Thus are they all marching into line."[36] By the end of March, 1886, the *Acta et decreta* of the council had been published and the large volume of over 300 pages was quickly dispatched to Rome and to the bishops of other nations who could thus examine in full the results of the long and trying labors of Gibbons and his associates. Among those to whom copies of the *Acta et decreta* were sent was Cardinal Newman who thanked Archbishop Gibbons for

a copy, not only splendid in its outward accompaniments, but which over and above its value and interest in itself, witnesses to what Holy Church has already done in your great cities, and perhaps what she will do in the vast spaces of which those cities are the centers, thus fulfilling the anticipation of Saints four centuries since, that in the bad days which threatened for Christianity, the new world, then recently discovered, would redress the balance of the old.[37]

The absorbing character of the work connected with the council occasioned the postponement of a number of other matters which otherwise would probably have found a solution long before they actually did. One of these was the filling of the vacancy in the rectorship of the American College in Rome caused by the death of Monsignor Louis E. Hostlot on February 4, 1884. Archbishop Corrigan, secretary of the executive com-

---

[35] 79-V-5, Hierarchy of Australia to the Hierarchy of the United States, Sydney, November 29, 1885, printed.

[36] ADC, Gibbons to Gilmour, Baltimore, February 17, 1886.

[37] 80-Y-13, Newman to Gibbons, n.p., May 28, 1886. Two years later Denis O'Connell told Gibbons that the legislation of the Baltimore council continued to be in "great demand" at the Propaganda, and he said Archbishop Jacobini had asked him if Gibbons would send about twenty more copies over for sale (84-I-12, O'Connell to Gibbons, Rome, April 17, 1888).

mittee of the college, arranged a meeting at the residence of Cardinal McCloskey in New York which was timed to permit Gibbons to be present since the latter had sailed from Queenstown on March 2. At the meeting in New York the committee drew up a *terna* consisting of the following names: William V. Kieran of the Archdiocese of Philadelphia, Henry Moeller of the Archdiocese of Cincinnati, and Denis O'Connell of the Diocese of Richmond.[38] Gibbons was strongly in favor of O'Connell and a few weeks later he entered in his diary that he had written to Simeoni, "recommending above others the name of Dr. O'Connell for Rector of the American College, while I spoke favorably of the other candidates."[39] The settlement of the problem was greatly complicated by the threat just at this time that the Italian government would confiscate the property of the college as belonging to the Congregation of the Propaganda. Archbishop Ryan informed Gibbons he thought they ought to give serious consideration to the appointment of the right kind of man. As he viewed it, "Until some regular representative of the American Bishops shall be selected, the Rector of the College will have to act — more or less — in that capacity and the Propaganda will consult him."[40] Gibbons was fully aware of the possibility of the rector of the American College acting as a representative of the hierarchy, and for that reason he was all the more anxious that the man selected should be O'Connell. The candidacy of O'Connell became known to Ryan after the meeting in New York, and he then told Gibbons, "I had not thought of him before, but the more I reflect on it the better I like the suggestion. He impressed me very favorably in Rome. . . ."[41]

Meanwhile Simeoni assured Archbishop Gibbons that the names submitted for the rectorship would be given careful consideration by the Propaganda,[42] although he let Cardinal McCloskey know that for the time being Father Schulte, who had been vice-rector under Hostlot, could be left in charge as acting rector since his management of the college had been to date quite satisfactory to the Propaganda. Corrigan informed

---

[38] Henry A. Brann, *History of the American College . . . Rome* (New York, 1910), pp. 91–92.

[39] Diary, April 4, 1884, p. 175.

[40] 77-O-9, Ryan to Gibbons, St. Louis, March 14, 1884, *Private*.

[41] 77-W-5, Ryan to Gibbons, St. Louis, April 22, 1884.

[42] 77-Y-8, Simeoni to Gibbons, Rome, April 29, 1884.

Gibbons of these details and asked the latter what he would advise. He said, "If you would have the kindness to give your opinion, and also Abp. Williams, we may be able to settle this question without the necessity of a formal meeting of the Board."[43] Gibbons was willing to accept the suggestion of Simeoni that Schulte be left temporarily in charge, but he felt that his youth and his lack of knowledge and experience in the affairs of the American Church would raise a question about his fitness for the position as permanent rector. The Archbishop of Baltimore cherished the idea of the Roman rector acting as the representative of the American hierarchy, and for that reason he should be a man who was, as he said, "well acquainted with our affairs . . . especially as he is the only representative that we have, & probably will have for some time in Rome."[44] When Schulte reported to Gibbons on the favorable conditions of the college and added that the only thing that was keeping them in a state of excitement was the uncertainty over who would be their next rector,[45] the archbishop told him he would be glad to learn that the committee of American archbishops were "so well pleased with your administration, that you will, in all probability, continue to act as Rector. . . ." While careful not to commit himself to Schulte's appointment, he did say that his continuing experience would help to remove the only objection which existed against him.[46] Under the circumstances it was hardly surprising that Schulte should feel that he had a good chance to be named permanent rector.

In the late summer of 1884 word reached the United States from Schulte that the bull for the canonical erection of the American College was then being prepared and that an old plan of making the Secretary of the Propaganda rector of the institution had been revived. Corrigan forwarded this information to Gibbons and stated that McCloskey, Williams, and himself were all opposed to it since an arrangement of that kind would make the college, as he said, "a mere annex of the Urban College, like the Greek and the Armenian College. . . ."[47] This danger to the

[43] 78-B-3, Corrigan to Gibbons, New York, May 6, 1884.

[44] Letterbook, Gibbons to Corrigan, Baltimore, May 7, 1884, pp. 75–76.

[45] 78-A-3, Schulte to Gibbons, Rome, May 1, 1884.

[46] Letterbook, Gibbons to Schulte, Baltimore, May 19, 1884, p. 81.

[47] 78-L-10, Corrigan to Gibbons, Montague City, Massachusetts, August 23, 1884. Seven years later a similar reaction was shown by Archbishop Janssens and

autonomy of the college did not materialize, however, and when Leo XIII issued his bull on October 25, 1884, the rector retained therein his powers as superior of the institution.[48]

At the time of the council in the fall of that year the American bishops pledged their support to the college, but nothing definite was done about the problem of selecting a rector. In the following spring, as we have seen, Bishop Dwenger went to Rome to hasten the approval of the conciliar legislation and he was not there many days before he informed Gibbons that Simeoni was anxious to have the rectorship filled. Simeoni was represented as well disposed toward Schulte but as regarding him as too young for the appointment. The Prefect of Propaganda thought the rector ought to be "a grand representative man," and Dwenger related that Simeoni openly complained that nothing was done in the definite appointment of a rector. He said, "they expect you not only to send three names — but to indicate definitely who you think should and ought to be appointed."[49] Gibbons hastened to recommend again Denis O'Connell, an opinion that Dwenger shared since he told the archbishop he thought there was none better for the job.[50] Dwenger was strong for O'Connell and continued to write Gibbons that he was backing his candidacy at the Holy See. Whether he urged Simeoni to cable Gibbons for his opinion or not there is no way of knowing, but at any rate, the Archbishop of Baltimore stated that in response to a cable of May 3 from the cardinal he had written "strongly recommending Dr. O'Connell for the post," to which the names of Kieran and Schulte had been added "without comment." Once again Gibbons had consulted his colleagues when they came to Baltimore for a meeting of the university committee on May 7, so

his colleagues who composed the committee appointed by Gibbons to supervise the affairs of the American College at Louvain. When Propaganda proposed that it be given the right to appoint the rector of the college, Janssens and his committee expressed their opposition. He told Gibbons, "I for one do not believe in this spirit of centralization, which paralyzes the real efforts of subalterns. The College has done well, no complaints have arisen about abuses, why then should it not be let alone?" (88-S-5, Janssens to Gibbons, Covington, July 9, 1891.) Gibbons agreed with the committee in their resistance to the absorption of the college by Propaganda and he remarked, "Centralization is being carried too far" (AANO, Gibbons to Janssens, Baltimore, July 28, 1891).

48 For the text of the bull cf. *Acta et decreta concilii plenarii Baltimorensis tertii* (Baltimore, 1886), pp. 193–196.

49 79-G-9, Dwenger to Gibbons, Rome, March 19, 1885.

50 79-J-11/1, Dwenger to Gibbons, Rome, April 21, 1885.

that he was able to back up his own recommendation of O'Connell with the endorsements of Williams, Ryan, Corrigan, Ireland, and Spalding.[51]

When the matter of O'Connell's appointment seemed at last assured a new complication arose. Early in 1885 William H. Gross, C.Ss.R., Bishop of Savannah, had been named Archbishop of Oregon City. This transfer created a vacancy in the Province of Baltimore for which the bishops were asked to suggest names at a meeting on May 28 at Gibbons' residence. Bishop Becker of Wilmington asked to be transferred to Savannah, a request which his fellow bishops agreed to second in their letter to Rome. In the final voting for Wilmington, should Becker be sent to Savannah, O'Connell's name was placed second, and if Becker's desire was not honored at Rome then the bishops put O'Connell on the list as first for Savannah.[52] The day following the meeting of the bishops in Baltimore Gibbons wrote to Dwenger. He made no mention of the fact that O'Connell had been put on the lists for Wilmington and Savannah, but he did say, in reference to the opinions of the bishops at the university meeting, "We have unanimously recommended Dr. O'Connell for Rector of the American College, and I am desirous to hear of his appointment."[53] By this time O'Connell himself had learned of Gibbons' action in his behalf and he said the first feeling he wanted to express was his deep sense of gratitude for the kind manner, as he expressed it, "in which you put my name forward for the rectorate of the American College and equally so for the warm love and joy with which you wrote the tidings to me." While he was still uncertain as to the outcome in high Roman quarters it was said, as he remarked, that probably the candidate recommended by the American bishops would be named.[54]

The cardinals of the Propaganda at length made the nomination of O'Connell to the Pope on June 8, a circumstance which incidentally brought keen disappointment to Schulte.[55] At the very time of his appointment O'Connell became dangerously ill, but after a week in bed he was able to announce formally Leo

---

[51] Diary, May 8, 1885, p. 182.

[52] *Ibid.,* May 28, 1885, p. 183.

[53] AUND, Fort Wayne Papers, Gibbons to Dwenger, Baltimore, May 29, 1885.

[54] 79-L-15, O'Connell to Gibbons, Rome, May 28, 1885.

[55] 79-M-8, O'Connell to Gibbons, Rome, June 8, 1885.

XIII's approval of his nomination and to tell Gibbons that his first act was to declare, as he said, "my indebtedness and my gratitude to you for the same and also to add (what I presume you already well know) my readiness to serve you in my new capacity."[56] The general reception given to his appointment in Rome was favorable with the students showing enthusiasm and O'Connell meeting at the Propaganda and other offices in the Roman Curia with nothing "except what was most gracious & encouraging."[57]

Gibbons was pleased at this news, but he was concerned lest his desire to see O'Connell as rector in Rome go unfulfilled were the Holy See to appoint him to either of the American sees for which his name had gone into the curia. Gilmour was still in the Eternal City and Gibbons used the presence there of the forceful Bishop of Cleveland to work against O'Connell's being changed to Wilmington or Savannah. He told Gilmour, "I regard his selection as not only a great blessing to the College, but also as a signal advantage to the American Bishops who will find in him a wise and discreet intermediary between them & the Holy See. He will discharge with zeal & ability whatever commission may be entrusted to him." He recounted for Gilmour the meeting of the suffragans of Baltimore and told him he had informed them of O'Connell's name being up for rector. But one of the bishops had insisted on putting him on the *terna* for Savannah and the others acquiesced. He then made his plea for Gilmour's intervention in Rome:

> He is of far more use to the Church as Rector in Rome, than as Bishop in Savannah, & I am informed that his appointment is singularly opportune for the well-being of the College which needed an experienced man.
>
> I earnestly hope therefore that the thought of making him a Bishop will not be entertained, & I beg you to urge his retention as Rector, if the question arises; but the question I trust will not come up at all.

---

[56] 79-N-3, O'Connell to Gibbons, Rome, June 19, 1885. Bishop Moore told Gibbons that O'Connell's illness was caused by inflammation of the bowels and it became serious when — at the suggestion of Bishop Gilmour — he took "a dose of laudanum" (79-M-14, Moore to Gibbons, Rome, June 15, 1885).

[57] 79-N-13, O'Connell to Gibbons, Rome, June 28, 1885.

He was the unanimous choice of all the Archbishops, & I do not know where we would find another such man for such a position.[58]

As it turned out it was not necessary for Gilmour to make efforts in Rome to keep O'Connell out of Savannah, and the rectorship, once approved by the Pope, was allowed to stand. Gibbons had worked hard for the appointment of this favorite priest friend to the post in Rome, not only for what he believed would be the good of the college, but, too, because he was convinced that O'Connell could best fill the need for a representative of the American hierarchy at the Holy See, a service to which Gibbons attached the greatest importance. With his intimate friend in that role the Archbishop of Baltimore would have every reason to believe that the questions in which he took a special interest would receive from O'Connell the attention they deserved. In this he was not disappointed, for during the next ten years Gibbons' Roman interests were watched over and guided through the offices of the Roman Curia with great care and effort. O'Connell had promised his patron that he would be a loyal liaison man for him and in the years which followed he fulfilled that promise faithfully.

Another item of business which arose at this time concerning the American College was the threatened sale of its property by the Italian government. Word of this danger reached McCloskey by cable from Simeoni the first week of March, 1884, while Gibbons was still on the high seas returning from Europe. Corrigan, acting for Cardinal McCloskey, took the initiative in approaching President Arthur to use the good offices of the United States government in preventing the seizure of the property and its sale by the government of Italy. The pretext under which the confiscation was to be made was found in the law of 1866 ordering the sale of all church property held in *mortmain* throughout Italy, and a second law of 1873 which had applied the former measure to the city and district of Rome. On January 29, 1884, the Court of Cassation, Italy's supreme tribunal, had handed down the decision that the properties of the Congregation of the Propaganda came under the laws of 1866 and 1873. Although the deed to the property on which the college stood

---

[58] ADC, Gibbons to Gilmour, Baltimore, July 5, 1885.

actually was held by the Propaganda, the cost of its upkeep and repair had been borne for years by the American hierarchy. They could, therefore, legitimately protest against this seizure of property upon which they had expended so much money and in the buildings of which their students resided during their studies for the priesthood. The prompt action of Cardinal McCloskey and the favorable reception given to his appeal by the President, Secretary of State Frederick T. Frelinghuysen, and the American minister in Rome, William W. Astor, saved the property. Astor energetically represented to Pasquale S. Mancini, Minister of Foreign Affairs, the rights of the American bishops, and by March 25 the decision was given to exempt the property of the American College from those marked for confiscation.[59]

The credit for the favorable outcome in this case belonged to Cardinal McCloskey and Archbishop Corrigan of New York, although upon his arrival in the United States Archbishop Gibbons was quick to associate himself with their efforts. About ten days after reaching Baltimore from Rome the archbishop wrote a pastoral letter covering the case of the threatened loss of the Propaganda's properties in which he set before his priests and people the injustice involved. He made special mention of the American College and its close connection with the American Church and he sought to marshal the opinion of his people behind the action which the bishops were taking to prevent the seizure. Speaking of the United States government's role, Gibbons said, "It cannot be that our government, jealous of the rights of the least of its citizens, could allow ours to be violated without a protest, and we look for protection from it." Copies of the pastoral were forwarded to Rome where Eduardo Soderini, who often acted as unofficial agent for Baltimore with the Roman press, said the *Moniteur de Rome* had already published part of it and the *Osservatore Romano* had promised to do so. Soderini

---

[59] In regard to Astor's part in the case, L. M. Montgomery a reporter in Rome for the New York *Sun*, told Gibbons, "I must speak of Minister Astor's admirable energy & promptness in behalf of the American College. If President Arthur wanted a trump card to play for the Presidency his Minister here has given him one for the Irish Catholic vote in America by his energy & promptness. He stood out against Mancini's lawyer for three quarters of an hour and convinced him of the tenor of the law" (77-U-2, Montgomery to Gibbons, Rome, April 9, 1884). Cf. Brann, *op. cit.*, pp. 149–196, for further details on this case and for the texts of a considerable amount of the correspondence between the New York prelates and the officials of the United States government.

told his correspondent, "I can assure you that both the documents have been highly appreciated by all those to whom I have given them to read."[60] From Ghent, Archbishop Seghers informed Gibbons that he had read the pastoral and, he added, "Amidst the silence of those that should speak in Europe, the voice of an American Prelate resounded all the louder; and, if I am well informed, the protest of Your Grace has not been without effect."[61]

When James Fullerton, one of the leading Catholic lawyers of Washington, asked Gibbons if he would approve a protest meeting in the capital, as he said, "to express opinion upon the action of the Italian government towards the Propaganda at Rome,"[62] the archbishop promptly gave his assent to such a protest. The meeting was to be sponsored by the Young Catholics' Friend Society, and Gibbons told Fullerton that he would be pleased if the society would hold its contemplated meeting at as early a date as possible. He suggested that they secure as many prominent names as they could to act as vice-presidents, and he concluded with the hope that the meeting would be a credit alike to the society, to the archdiocese, and, as he put it, "to the great cause which it proposes to vindicate."[63] The meeting was held on June 17 at the National Theater when printed resolutions were issued in thanks to President Arthur, Secretary Frelinghuysen, and Minister Astor for their help in saving the property of the American College, and in protest against the Italian government considering the properties of Propaganda as Italian, whereas they were supported by money raised by the faithful of all nations for the spread of Catholicism everywhere in the world.[64] Shortly after the meeting Gibbons sent to Simeoni a copy of the

---

[60] 77-V-7, Soderini to "Dear Friend," Rome, April 20, 1884. The text of Gibbons' pastoral was published in the *Catholic Mirror*, March 29, 1884.

[61] 78-A-12, Seghers to Gibbons, Ghent, May 3, 1884. In his pastoral letter Gibbons made the mistake of saying that the American College had been purchased with money sent to Rome from the United States, whereas actually it was bought with money furnished by the Holy See. Bishop Chatard called the error to his attention and said, "I have thought it well to notify your Grace of the mistake, as the real facts must come out, and it were better the statement be made by you before anyone else makes it" (77-Q-9, Chatard to Gibbons, Indianapolis, March 28, 1884).

[62] 78-B-5, Fullerton to Gibbons, Washington, May 15, 1884.

[63] Letterbook, Gibbons to Fullerton, Baltimore, May 17, 1884, p. 80.

[64] 78-G-9, printed resolutions of meeting of the Young Catholics' Friend Society, Washington, June 17, 1884. For the story on the meeting cf. the *Catholic Mirror*, June 21, 1884.

proceedings of the Washington meeting so that the Holy See would know of the effort made to save the properties of the Propaganda.[65] When Cardinal Simeoni had been given an opportunity to examine the pastoral of Archbishop Gibbons and to learn of his efforts to support the Holy See in this emergency, he wrote his thanks and told him that the Holy Father was sad and weary with the struggle but the manifestation of loyalty from the Catholics of the United States had heartened him greatly.[66]

A further problem which had been submitted to Archbishop Gibbons for action and which had to be delayed until after the plenary council involved the administrative difficulties of Archbishop Leray of New Orleans. We have already had occasion to see how oddly Leray had acted in regard to the business of the council in not answering communications on the subject nor holding meetings of his suffragans. One of the suffragans, Francis Janssens of Natchez, a conscientious man, had more than once mentioned to Gibbons the peculiar conduct of the Archbishop of New Orleans. He told the Archbishop of Baltimore confidentially that he distrusted anything that Leray said or promised to do, and he added, "He has a way of talking and acting, which to me does not inspire confidence."[67] Due to Gibbons' personal experience with Leray over the council, he doubtless felt some sympathy with Janssens' view. It must, therefore, have come as an unpleasant surprise when Simeoni in the middle of the summer of 1884 asked him to undertake an investigation of some of the difficulties in New Orleans.[68] The request arrived at a time when the archbishop was in the midst of his preparations for the council. Consequently he told the Prefect of Propaganda that he would investigate the situation but it would have to be delayed as the pressure of council business was too great just then to leave home, and he reminded Simeoni that the distance between Baltimore and New Orleans was about the same as that from Rome to London; the prefect would, therefore, appreciate the reasons for delay.[69]

The trouble in New Orleans was by no means all of Leray's own making. His predecessor, Napoleon J. Perché, had accumu-

---

[65] Diary, June 29, 1884, p. 177.
[66] 78-G-13, Simeoni to Gibbons, Rome, June 18, 1884.
[67] 78-H-3, Janssens to Gibbons, Natchez, June 21, 1884.
[68] 78-H-14, Simeoni to Gibbons, Rome, June 30, 1884.
[69] Letterbook, Gibbons to Simeoni, Baltimore, July 26, 1884, pp. 107–110.

lated a staggering debt of over $590,000 of which more than
$250,000 represented bonds due in France.⁷⁰ This was the situa-
tion when Leray arrived as coadjutor in the fall of 1879.
Through the imposition of heavy taxes and the working out of
personal compromises with some of the creditors, the debt was
reduced by over $140,000 in three years, but the amount still
outstanding was great. As time passed a number of the creditors
became increasingly impatient and pressed Leray for settlement
and when the archbishop found no other remedy at hand he
began to entertain the idea of declaring bankruptcy and of putting the archdiocese in the hands of a receiver. In the emergency
Gibbons was soon the recipient of requests for advice from
several of the clergy. The Archbishop of Baltimore was well
known in New Orleans where his family was still living and
where he visited annually. The regard in which he was held
was reflected in the words of Anthony Durier, Bishop-elect of
Natchitoches, who told him at this time, "Here in Louisiana
we all know and feel that you love Louisiana, and our priests
and our missions; and we are proud of you, and we cherish you
as if you were a son of Louisiana."⁷¹ Although it was gratifying
to be held in affection by the clergy of Louisiana, it was quite
another matter to offer a solution to their difficulties.

When Father Eugene Fraering, pastor of St. Joseph's Church
at Gretna and a member of the corporation of the Archdiocese
of New Orleans, wrote of the threatened bankruptcy and begged
for advice, Gibbons answered at once and deplored the thought
of bankruptcy which, as he said, he hoped could be averted
"even at the eleventh hour." But he confessed, "I feel a delicacy
in interfering in your affairs, or even in giving any advice."⁷²
Up to this time he had been merely asked by Rome to gather
information, but he had not been given any commission to act
in the name of the Holy See. His prudence in responding to
Fraering was, therefore, altogether justified. The priest returned
a second time, however, to inform Archbishop Gibbons that he
had since been summoned to court when Father Andrew Cauvin
took his case against Leray into the civil tribunal. Fraering had
induced them to delay the trial for eight days until he could ask

⁷⁰ Roger Baudier, *The Catholic Church in Louisiana*, pp. 462–467.
⁷¹ 79-F-3, Durier to Gibbons, New Orleans, March 2, 1885.
⁷² Letterbook, Gibbons to Fraering, Baltimore, March 13, 1885, p. 147.

Gibbons' advice on the question of what he should say in court about the bankruptcy. Fraering maintained that it was his belief that bankruptcy could be avoided and the Archdiocese of New Orleans pay its debts if matters were properly managed. This testimony would be damaging to Archbishop Leray, and the distracted priest pleaded with Gibbons, "Please, let me know what I shall do, and I shall be ever sincerely grateful to you."[73] But with no word from Leray himself to Gibbons, the latter told Fraering he would consider it unwarrantable on his part to volunteer any counsel unless asked by the archbishop. He assured Fraering, however, that he had informed Simeoni in Rome of the financial condition in New Orleans so the Holy See was at least in possession of the facts.[74]

Meanwhile the receipt of confusing reports from Rome in the case made it difficult for Gibbons to see his way clearly. O'Connell stated that Simeoni was cabling Leray that he must absolutely avoid bankruptcy,[75] and two weeks later Dwenger told Gibbons in confidence that the Pope had given his approval to a request that Leray resign the See of New Orleans.[76] It was, indeed, a situation in which a false step could lead Gibbons into serious personal trouble and only complicate further the difficulties in New Orleans. If he was going to act at all it was necessary to obtain more specific powers from Rome. Fortunately, these were forthcoming from Simeoni by late May when the cardinal forwarded broad faculties of investigation for Gibbons as apostolic commissary *in temporalibus* for the Archdiocese of New Orleans with the statement that he could fix his own time for doing the work.[77] With these documents in his hands he proceeded at a leisurely pace to inform Archbishop Leray of his approaching visit. He told Leray that the Holy See had permitted him to name his own time and he proposed, therefore, to go to New Orleans sometime in the fall. He added:

I think you have adopted the most judicious measures for collecting funds to reduce the debt, in the contracting of which you had no

---

[73] 79-G-2, Fraering to Gibbons, Gretna, Louisiana, March 14, 1885.
[74] Letterbook, Gibbons to Fraering, Baltimore, March 17, 1885, p. 149.
[75] 79-H-11, O'Connell to Gibbons, Rome, March 29, 1885.
[76] 79-I-15, Dwenger to Gibbons, Rome, April 13, 1885.
[77] 79-L-10, O'Connell to Gibbons, Rome, May 24, 1885, with enclosures from Simeoni.

share. I trust, please God, that my labors will not be burdensome or unpleasant; & it will be a satisfaction to me to aid you every way in my power in lightening your burden which I believe can be best accomplished by giving an impulse to the plans already inaugurated by Your Grace.[78]

This tactful announcement of the coming investigation seemed to meet with Leray's approval, for he replied, "I can only say that I am glad that you have been selected for that purpose, my only regret is, that it has not been done sooner." But the Archbishop of New Orleans let it be known that he did not feel as well disposed toward Simeoni, the man who had requested the investigation. "This does not prevent me, of course," said Leray, "feeling and that deeply, the unkind and unjust treatment meeted to me by Card. Simeoni. When you come I will have all ready to show what I have done and also the circumstances against which I had to contend."[79] The sensitive feelings of Archbishop Leray would require diplomatic treatment if the investigation was not to cause them further hurt.

In order to prepare himself properly for his task Gibbons engaged the assistance of Father Placide L. Chapelle, pastor of St. Matthew's Church in Washington, as his secretary. Chapelle was French-born and felt thoroughly at home in that language which was still so widely used in the Church of Louisiana. Late in the summer Simeoni forwarded two more New Orleans cases to Gibbons for investigation and report during his visit there, one involving a dispute between Leray and Father Francis X. Ceuppens, one of his priests, and another between the Marianite Sisters of the Holy Cross and their provincial.[80] The time of the archbishop during his stay in New Orleans would, therefore, be greatly occupied in trying to bring a settlement to all these vexing problems.

Gibbons arrived in New Orleans in the company of Chapelle on November 18. He spent over two weeks investigating the financial disorders of the archdiocese, inquiring into the details of the controversies between Archbishop Leray and several of his priests such as Cauvin, Ceuppens, and Anthony Borias, and visiting a number of religious houses like the Marianite Sisters

---

[78] AUND, New Orleans Papers, Gibbons to Leray, Baltimore, July 15, 1885.
[79] 79-P-6, Leray to Gibbons, New Orleans, July 21, 1885.
[80] Diary, August 25, 1885, p. 185.

of the Holy Cross and the Sisters of Mercy where trouble had arisen. During the visit Leray and Gibbons discussed the question of a coadjutor for the Archbishop of New Orleans and the latter, impressed with Chapelle, expressed his desire to have Gibbons' secretary for that post.[81] After he had been on the spot two weeks Gibbons sent a brief account of his mission to Simeoni with the information that after his arrival home he would forward a more detailed report. Upon his return to Baltimore on December 10 he confided to his diary the following entry:

> My visit was most satisfactory. The Abp. of New Orleans afforded me every facility in making the various investigations. Dec. 3rd I wrote from New Orleans to Card. Simeoni a brief report of the result of my investigations promising on my return home to send him a full & detailed statement of my labors. I trust D. V. that my visit will result in inspiring greater confidence in the financial condition, & in promoting harmony between the ordinary & his clergy & Religious.[82]

Gibbons was optimistic about the success of his visitation of New Orleans and a week after his return home he told Archbishop Elder, "my mission, thank God, was, as far as I can judge, very satisfactory."[83] There is no evidence to show what he recommended either to Leray or to the Roman authorities in his report, but Cardinal Simeoni was enthusiastic in his thanks for a job well done and told Gibbons, after receiving the report, that he hastened to extend to him his gratitude and to signify to him his "full satisfaction" at the manner in which he had conducted the mission entrusted to him by the Holy See.[84] The Marianite Sisters of the Holy Cross were likewise pleased with his efforts in their behalf and the provincial wrote her thanks for his part in obtaining the papal approval of their congregation and she assured Gibbons, "we will make it a duty of gratitude to pray for you unceasingly, as being the one to whom our humble congregation is, in a great measure, indebted for the greatest of all blessings, the august sanction of the Vicar of Christ."[85]

---

[81] AANO, Chapelle to Leray, Washington, December 23, 1885, copy.

[82] Diary, December 10, 1885, p. 190.

[83] AAC, Gibbons to Elder, Baltimore, December 19, 1885.

[84] 80-C-4, Simeoni to Gibbons, Rome, January 13, 1886.

[85] 80-D-8, Sister Mary of St. Magdalen to Gibbons, New Orleans, January 28, 1886.

While it was doubtless gratifying to learn of the favorable reception given to his efforts in behalf of the Church of New Orleans, Gibbons' very success was the reason for further assignments of a like nature from the Holy See. In the absence of an apostolic delegate in the United States, Rome was bound to look to the leaders of the hierarchy for assistance in adjusting troublesome cases which reached the curia from the American Church. Gibbons' position as Archbishop of Baltimore and as apostolic delegate to the recent plenary council, together with his success in New Orleans on the first important mission entrusted to him by Rome, prompted Cardinal Simeoni to turn to him again when new cases arose for settlement. The spring of 1886 brought another such appeal from Simeoni. He apologized for bothering Gibbons, but he said that recently letters had reached the Propaganda containing facts which, if true, would indicate that Archbishop Leray was incapable of properly governing his see. Simeoni asked, therefore, if he would investigate and report his opinion to him.[86] As previously mentioned, Leray had expressed his desire to have Chapelle for his coadjutor. If the proper man could be found for the position it might, indeed, offer a remedy to Leray's troubled administration.

But when it became known that Chapelle was a candidate, opposition arose against him in different quarters. Bishop Keane of Richmond urged Denis O'Connell, "If Providence gives you a chance, work against Archbishop Leray's mistaken plan as to the N.O. succession. Last week I was at Emmitsburg and Father Mandine [Alexius H. Mandine, C.M., director of the Daughters of Charity], intimately acquainted with things and persons, declared emphatically that Bishop Janssens is the man for the place. Insist on that, all you can."[87] For the time being Gibbons contented himself with telling Leray that he had "long since" told the Holy See of Leray's desire for a coadjutor, but he warned the archbishop that no nomination could be made until Rome had approved the step and he had conferred with his suffragans. When these formalities were observed Leray's wishes would be more securely consummated if, as Gibbons remarked, he could go to Rome.[88] After Leray had got around to presenting his

[86] 80-U-14, Simeoni to Gibbons, Rome, May 7, 1886.
[87] ADR, Keane to O'Connell, Richmond, May 20, 1886.
[88] AUND, New Orleans Papers, Gibbons to Leray, Baltimore, August 12, 1886.

petition to Rome in the fall of 1886 Simeoni told Gibbons that before presenting it to the Pope he [Simeoni] would wish to know if Gibbons thought the coadjutor for New Orleans ought to be of French nationality.[89] In his reply Gibbons insisted on the urgency of a coadjutor for Leray who would be given full powers of administration. Insofar as candidates were concerned, he recommended Chapelle as the man who, in his judgment, would be best qualified for the position. Chapelle had been born in France and had come to the United States as a boy of seventeen. Ordinarily, said Gibbons, he believed it was far better to choose native-born priests for the American episcopate, or at least those who had been reared and educated from their early years in this country. But in the present case he believed Chapelle would answer the needs in New Orleans better than others.[90]

In the meantime someone had suggested to Simeoni the propriety of naming Bishop Janssens of Natchez as coadjutor of New Orleans, and this suggestion was now forwarded to Baltimore with a request for Gibbons' judgment.[91] He responded by telling the Prefect of Propaganda that he was happy to speak "in high terms of praise" of Janssens, but he informed Simeoni that the Bishop of Natchez was "a persona ingrata to the Abp. of N. Orleans." He could add that Archbishop Perché had desired Janssens as coadjutor in New Orleans some years before, and the fact that Janssens was a good administrator, had a firm will, and knew French would be added reasons to recommend him.[92] This letter of recommendation of Janssens brought great joy to Keane who was then in Rome on the university question. He told the Archbishop of Baltimore:

I was very glad to be thus enabled to put your Eminence in a proper light in the Propaganda on the N. Orleans question. You were there identified with the advocacy of Dr. Chapelle's nomination; and as he is sure to be the losing man, you were going down with him on the losing side. Your present advocacy of Bishop Janssens puts you once more on the winning side, where you ought to be.[93]

---

[89] 82-B-8, Simeoni to Gibbons, Rome, October 9, 1886.

[90] 82-F-5, Gibbons to Simeoni, Baltimore, November 24, 1886, copy in Latin.

[91] 82-F-10, Simeoni to Gibbons, Rome, November 30, 1886.

[92] Diary December 22, 1886, p. 212; 82-I-1, Gibbons to Simeoni, Baltimore, December 22, 1886, copy in Latin. It was Gibbons' suggestion that, given Leray's aversion for Janssens, the latter should have the title not only of coadjutor but he should likewise be made apostolic administrator of the archdiocese.

[93] 82-J-4, Keane to Gibbons, Rome, December 29, 1886.

Although Gibbons' recent recommendation of Janssens might have put him on "the winning side," his earlier approval of Chapelle was known and in his apparent effort to please all parties the archbishop was running the risk of serious misunderstanding.

In his request for a coadjutor Leray had not observed the regulations governing such appointments. Simeoni, therefore, told Gibbons he should inform the Archbishop of New Orleans that before Rome would act in the case he must consult his irremovable rectors and consultors, as well as his suffragans, submit three names to Rome, and inform the other archbishops of the United States.[94] Gibbons dutifully complied with the request and outlined the procedure for Leray to follow, telling him that Simeoni had sent the instructions in a reply to his letter recommending as Leray's coadjutor the one whom the Archbishop of New Orleans desired to have.[95] Presumably he must have had in mind Chapelle, since he had already made it clear that Leray did not wish Janssens. Once Leray learned what he must do he summoned meetings of his consultors and suffragans to obtain their votes for the coadjutor. Several of the suffragans communicated their views to Gibbons with the reasons governing their choice of names.[96] In general they favored Janssens over Chapelle. News of their meeting soon became known and Magnien told Chapelle he had word from a priest in New Orleans that four of the suffragans had "voted solid" against him.[97] Gibbons, who was by this time in Rome, informed Chapelle that Simeoni had stated to him that the report was not yet in from the New Orleans voting but, he added, "I could easily infer that he was in possession of private letters giving information regarding the result of the meeting."[98] Beyond this Gibbons himself did not comment, which prompted Magnien to tell Chapelle that Gibbons' letter left matters vague and that it was apparent his appointment would not be as easily made as had first appeared.[99]

---

[94] 82-I-2, Simeoni to Gibbons, Rome, December 22, 1886.

[95] AUND, New Orleans Papers, Gibbons to Leray, Baltimore, January 6, 1887.

[96] 82-M-8, Jeremiah O'Sullivan to Gibbons, Mobile, January 20, 1887; 82-N-1, Edward Fitzgerald to Gibbons, Little Rock, February 14, 1887.

[97] AANO, Magnien to Chapelle, Baltimore, February 20, 1887.

[98] *Ibid.*, Gibbons to "My Dear Doctor," Rome, March 15, 1887.

[99] *Ibid.*, Magnien to Chapelle, Baltimore, March 29, 1887. Gibbons left Rome on April 18. A few days before he reaffirmed his preference for Janssens in answer

Bishop Janssens was fully aware of Leray's dislike for him. He told Gibbons, "He has taken it into his head that I have opposed him." While Janssens was not in favor of Chapelle as coadjutor and did not desire the position for himself, he did say, "I will do whatever I may be ordered to do, and will not consult my own pleasure or comfort."[100] Bishop Fitzgerald of Little Rock, another suffragan of New Orleans, warned Gibbons to proceed slowly on Janssens because of Leray's dislike and the fear of scandal if their differences should become known.[101] With all this confusing evidence reaching him in Rome, Gibbons' own position in the matter did not improve. With the arrival of Archbishop Leray in the Eternal City early in the summer of 1887 he took the matter of his coadjutorship up directly with the Propaganda.

In a conference with Simeoni the Archbishop of New Orleans was informed that Gibbons had preferred Janssens to Chapelle. The ambiguous position of the Archbishop of Baltimore was accounted for, in the opinion of Leray, by the fact that Gibbons had allowed himself to be swayed by Keane of Richmond into championing Janssens' cause after having previously written a letter of recommendation of Chapelle. As Leray told Chapelle from Rome, "Then I explained this preference in spite of his [Gibbons'] former letter of the 25th Nov. 1886 and his engagements with me. I insisted upon the influence which K. of R. exercised over him.[102] Leray was probably not far wrong since on a number of important questions the eloquent Bishop of Richmond spoke out forcefully to Gibbons and was successful in winning him to his point of view. But it did leave the Archbishop of Baltimore in a rather bad light in the minds of Leray, Chapelle, and their sympathizers, and the chancellor of New Orleans, L. A. Chassé, confided to Chapelle that he was forced

---

to the request of Propaganda and said he felt his candidature should prevail over Leray's inclination toward Chapelle. The archbishop likewise remarked the lack of foundation for the suspicions and prejudiced impressions of some who were opposed to Janssens as coadjutor. The writer is indebted for a summary of this letter of Gibbons of April 12, 1887, to Propaganda to Monsignor Giuseppe Monticone, general archivist of Propaganda, who copied the summary from the Acta of the Congregation of the Propaganda, 1887, Vol. 257, pp. 498–501, which carried the minutes of the meeting of the congregation on September 7, 1887.

[100] 82-R-10, Janssens to Gibbons, Natchez, May 30, 1887.
[101] 82-S-7, Fitzgerald to Gibbons, Little Rock, June 9, 1887.
[102] AANO, Leray to Chapelle, Rome, July 1, 1887.

to conclude that Gibbons was a politician.[103] The entire case of the coadjutor for New Orleans became so involved that Rome hesitated to make the appointment. Archbishop Leray himself died at Chateau Giron, France, on September 23, 1887, and not until the following July was Janssens named Archbishop of New Orleans. Gibbons had not escaped serious criticism in the affair for his failure to stand by Chapelle, his original candidate, although in the light of subsequent events his shift to Janssens would seem to have been warranted.

The case of Archbishop Leray and his difficulties, which dragged on for over two years, entailed the expenditure of a great amount of labor, time, and anxiety for the Archbishop of Baltimore. It has been thought worth while to relate the facts in some detail to illustrate the outside activity which in these years often distracted Gibbons from the business of his own jurisdiction. Moreover, this case was only the beginning of such assignments made to him by the Holy See in the interest of the Church in various parts of the country. For example, at the very time he was appointed apostolic commissary *in temporalibus* for the Archdiocese of New Orleans, he received from Simeoni a similar task to perform in the Vicariate Apostolic of Colorado where Bishop Joseph P. Machebeuf had gotten into serious debt through faulty administration.[104] It was impossible for Gibbons to go to Denver immediately so he entrusted the preliminary investigation to Archbishop John B. Salpointe of Santa Fe, asking him at the same time if he could suggest the names of any priests fit to be named coadjutor to Machebeuf.[105] After his examination of the situation Salpointe reported the facts in detail to Gibbons and told him Machebeuf was reluctant to ask for a coadjutor because he believed it would reflect on his ability to pay his debts.[106] With Simeoni pressing Gibbons to submit names for the coadjutor for Colorado,[107] and Machebeuf pleading that until he was named Bishop of Denver he be spared "the *humiliation* of a *coadjutor* under such circumstances,"[108]

---

[103] *Ibid.*, Chassé to Chapelle, New Orleans, May 21, 1887.
[104] Diary, June 8, 1885, p. 183.
[105] Letterbook, Gibbons to Salpointe, June 11, 1885, *confidential*, pp. 155–157.
[106] 79-Q-8, Salpointe to Gibbons, Santa Fe, August 20, 1885.
[107] 79-R-2, Simeoni to Gibbons, Rome, September 5, 1885.
[108] 79-R-8, Machebeuf to Gibbons, Denver, September 10, 1885.

Gibbons must have been hard put to know what to recommend.

Despite the desire of Bishop Machebeuf, however, Gibbons was so convinced of the need of a coadjutor that he submitted to Simeoni three names for the position and sent along a strong recommendation that the choice be made of a priest from the West who would better understand the local conditions.[109] Machebeuf continued to press his point of view on Gibbons and to urge him to use his influence in Rome to have the vicariate erected into a diocese to coincide with Machebeuf's golden jubilee.[110] After submitting additional names to the Holy See for coadjutor at Simeoni's request and discussing the matter personally with the cardinal during his visit to Rome in the spring of 1887, the Archbishop of Baltimore had the satisfaction of learning that the Holy See had appointed to the position the western priest whose name was second on Gibbons' original *terna,* namely, Nicholas C. Matz. The long drawn-out case was finally brought to a solution when Rome raised the vicariate to the status of the Diocese of Denver on August 16, 1887, and named Machebeuf as its first bishop. The jurisdiction would now have the assistance of the firm administrative hand of Matz while the feelings of Machebeuf would suffer no serious injury. In fact, when the bishop received two cables from Rome with news of the coadjutor and the new diocese he wrote the following day to Gibbons in an appreciative vein for the part the archbishop had played in bringing about the results.

> I thank you most sincerely for the great interest you have taken in the affair. It was no doubt at your request that the question was decided so soon after your departure. Fr. Matz, although a very worthy man, may meet with some little opposition for not being an American or Irishman but I am confident that by his usual kindness, piety, prudence and good sense, he will overcome it & become very popular.[111]

Missions of the character he was asked to undertake for New Orleans and Colorado were fairly frequent in the life of Archbishop Gibbons during the ensuing years, and the long journeys and exacting labors which he was at times compelled to undergo must have taxed considerably his strength and patience.

---

[109] 79-T-7, Gibbons to Simeoni, Baltimore, October 6, 1885, copy.
[110] 80-O-10, Machebeuf to Gibbons, Denver, March 8, 1886.
[111] 82-T-11, Machebeuf to Gibbons, Denver, June 14, 1887.

Nearer home there were other problems affecting the welfare of the Church of the nation which had been left unsolved at the time of the plenary council. One of these had to do with the management of the affairs of the Catholic Indians. As early as January, 1873, a bureau had been set up in Washington for this purpose with Father J. B. A. Brouillet as director and the general supervision placed under the auspices of Archbishop Bayley, Gibbons' predecessor in Baltimore. Unfortunately, in the minds of some the bureau became involved in the controversy stirred up over President Grant's policy of extermination of Indian resistance to the white man in the West, and Catholic papers like the *Freeman's Journal* of New York charged the director with being a mere cat's-paw of the Grant administration. When Gibbons came to Baltimore in 1877 he was appealed to by various parties in the controversy. He sought to quiet the stormy opposition of James A. Corcoran, editor of the *American Catholic Quarterly Review*, to the Bureau of Catholic Indian Missions by asking General Charles Ewing, who was serving as Catholic Indian commissioner, to write an article for the *Review* that would put the facts before the Catholic public.[112] But beyond this the archbishop was able to accomplish little to bring a satisfactory solution to the question of the care of the Catholic Indians until the plenary council met in November, 1884.

Some months before the council the name of Father Joseph A. Stephan had been recommended to Gibbons by Martin Marty, Vicar Apostolic of Dakota, as director of Catholic Indian affairs at Washington in place of Brouillet.[113] Before taking any action the archbishop sought the judgment of a number of western bishops in whose dioceses there were Indians living and who might know Stephan and his ability.[114] Having received satisfactory replies, Gibbons then informed Marty that as chairman of the Bureau of Catholic Indian Missions he would appoint Stephan temporarily and if he gave satisfaction his appointment, as he said, would be made permanent on the occasion

---

[112] 73-V-9, Ewing to Gibbons, Washington, August 21, 1878. For background cf. Peter J. Rahill, *Catholic Indian Missions and Grant's Peace Policy* (Washington, 1952).

[113] 77-N-8, Marty to Gibbons, St. Paul, February 22, 1884.

[114] 77-N-11, Thomas L. Grace to Gibbons, St. Paul, February 29, 1884. Gibbons wrote in over this recommendation of Stephan by the Bishop of St. Paul, "Before ratifying his choice I desire the views of some of the other Bps. concerned. J.G." Box 77 contains a considerable number of recommendations from bishops in the West of the appointment of Stephan.

of the plenary council.[115] When the council convened in November a committee of bishops consisting of Riordan of San Francisco, Brondel of Helena, and Healy of Portland was appointed by Archbishop Gibbons. This committee ratified the choice of Stephan and instructed Gibbons to inform him that he was to act as their agent in all matters pertaining to Catholic Indians with the United States government.[116] Further trouble occurred, however, when the members of the board of control of the old bureau existing before the council found themselves at cross purposes with Stephan.[117] In the new emergency Gibbons sounded out the bishops of the committee and found that they wished the old board to retire and to make way for Stephan as their sole agent. It became, therefore, the unpleasant duty of the archbishop to inform Captain John Mullen, the commissioner, as follows:

> I conferred again with the Board of Bishops to ascertain strictly their views regarding the personnel of the Indian Bureau.
> They have replied unanimously that the Washington Board henceforth will consist of only one responsible member, viz, Father Stephan. I discharge my duty in informing you of this fact.[118]

Two months after this letter was written Captain Mullen and the board of control of the Bureau of Catholic Indian Missions founded in 1873 submitted their resignations to Gibbons since, as they said, many of the bishops who had Indians under their control no longer approved or supported them and had come to regard their office as "an obstacle in the way of the prompt and satisfactory settlement here at the capital of affairs regarding the temporal interest of said Indian missions."[119] With Father Stephan in sole control of the bureau, and acting on the authority of Gibbons and the committee of bishops, the administration was simplified and rendered more efficient. Gibbons fulfilled another directive of the plenary council on the Indians when in October, 1886,

---

[115] Letterbook, Gibbons to Marty, Baltimore, April 5, 1884, p. 49.

[116] 78-V-7, Gibbons to Stephan, Baltimore, December 20, 1884, copy.

[117] 79-A-8, Stephan to Gibbons, Washington, January 7, 1885; 79-B-11, Marty to Gibbons, Yankton, South Dakota, January 21, 1885; 79-K-2, Brondel to Gibbons, South Orange, New Jersey, May 3, 1885.

[118] Letterbook, Gibbons to Mullen, Baltimore, May 19, 1885, p. 154.

[119] 79-P-5, Commissioner and Board of Control of Catholic Indian Missions to Gibbons, Washington, July 20, 1885.

he held a meeting with Kain of Wheeling and Curtis of Wilmington as the commission provided for by the conciliar legislation to direct the national collection for funds for the Negro and Indian missions.[120] A circular letter was dispatched by Gibbons as chairman of the commission to all the bishops of the United States who were directed to have the collection taken up on the first Sunday of Lent and to make the returns to Edward R. Dyer, S.S., of St. Mary's Seminary in Baltimore who had been appointed secretary of the commission and who would distribute the funds to needy missions under the general supervision of the Archbishop of Baltimore.[121] In this manner a chronic difficulty over the management of the affairs of the Catholic Indians of the United States was to some extent remedied with the bureau in Washington under more efficient administration and a more certain income provided by the national collection for the furtherance of the missions among the Indians.

In the midst of the many demands on his time Archbishop Gibbons managed to carry on the business of his own arch-diocese and to fulfill the increasing calls for his services from men in both Church and State. On December 28, 1884, he dedicated the new church for St. Patrick's Parish in Washington when Bishop Keane, as he noted, preached a fine sermon.[122] A week later he traveled to Philadelphia where he invested his friend, Archbishop Ryan, with the pallium.[123] On the day that Grover Cleveland was inaugurated as President the arch-bishop presided at the funeral in his cathedral of the sister of the former Secretary of State, James G. Blaine,[124] and two weeks later he called on the new President at the White House in the company of two Washington Catholic lawyers, Richard

120 Diary, October 20, 1886, pp. 210–211.

121 AANY, Gibbons to "Most Rev. Dear Sir," printed circular, Baltimore, December 3, 1886. The composition of this committee did not meet with the approval of Bishop McQuaid of Rochester. He told his friend, Gilmour of Cleveland, "Note how his Eminence constituted the Commission for the dis-tribution of the moneys to be raised on the First Sunday of Lent. All are Sulpitians: Gibbons, Kain and Curtis. Here in the North we don't propose to be tied to the chariot wheel of Baltimore" (ADC, McQuaid to Gilmour, Rochester, February 20, 1887).

122 Diary, December 28, 1884, p. 179.

123 Ibid., January 4, 1885, p. 180.

124 Ibid., March 4, 1885, p. 181.

T. Merrick and George E. Hamilton. Gibbons noted that their conversation lasted about a half hour and that the President expressed the hope that his visits would be renewed from time to time during his administration.[125] President Cleveland was the first chief executive with whom Gibbons enjoyed close personal friendship and during the next four years the archbishop was a fairly frequent caller at the White House.

On the day after his visit to Cleveland the archbishop received a letter from Anthony M. Keiley, former Mayor of Richmond, whom he had known well during his years in that city. Keiley desired a diplomatic post from the new administration and he asked if Gibbons would write in his behalf, providing it would cause him no embarrassment.[126] Gibbons complied with a letter to Thomas F. Bayard, the new Secretary of State, in which he recommended Keiley for a diplomatic assignment. The recommendation called forth Keiley's thanks who said he had the unanimous backing of the congressmen and electors of Virginia and he believed he was the only man from the state seeking such an appointment.[127] At any rate, the appointment was soon thereafter made of Keiley as United States Minister to Italy.[128] However, the naming of Keiley to the Roman legation gave rise to serious objection on the part of the Italian government, since it had become known that at the time of the seizure of Rome from the Pope in 1870 the Richmond mayor had been outspoken in his criticism of the government of Victor Emmanuel II. As a result of the opposition Keiley was compelled to submit his resignation before ever taking up the work. News of this reached Rome and O'Connell told Gibbons he believed the resignation would not prove "an unmixed evil" for Keiley. He said:

A strong part of Americans here were opposed to him. He has not the family traditions nor the wealth they desire. I heard they telegraphed to Mr. Cleveland against the appointment as soon as they learned it. How news travels! Nearly a week ago I heard a letter read of an American Bp. in which he said he thought you gained him the appointment.[129]

---

[125] *Ibid.*, March 19, p. 181.
[126] 79-G-10, Keiley to Gibbons, Richmond, March 20, 1885.
[127] 79-G-16, Keiley to Gibbons, Richmond, March 24, 1885.
[128] 79-H-13, Keiley to Gibbons, Richmond, March 31, 1885.
[129] 79-J-18, O'Connell to Gibbons, Rome, April 27, 1885.

Gibbons' own view of the matter was related a few weeks later to Dwenger. The archbishop commented:

> I am glad that Mr. Keiley is not going to Rome. He would be out of a place there. He would be not acceptable either at the Quirinal or at the Vatican. Before leaving Richmond he compromised himself by some extravagant praise of the Italian government. I was I think in a great measure instrumental in getting him an embassy, but I did not ask for Rome. He was first appointed to Rome in deference to the supposed wishes of the hierarchy.[130]

Interestingly enough the *Catholic Mirror* of Baltimore was vigorously opposed to the Keiley appointment and openly attacked the ex-mayor as unfit for the position. He was naturally pained at these attacks and when the New York *Herald* carried a disclaimer of Gibbons' for any responsibility for the policy the *Mirror* was pursuing toward Keiley, the latter expressed his thanks that "a prince of the Church should graciously volunteer the statement that he has no part or lot in them. . . ."[131] The episode with the *Mirror* was an interesting example of Gibbons' relations with the Baltimore Catholic paper, about which there were a considerable number of complaints at this time over the policies it pursued in questions affecting both Church and State.[132] A later attempt to have

---

130 AUND, Fort Wayne Papers, Gibbons to Dwenger, Baltimore, May 29, 1885. Gibbons made a curious error in saying Keiley had compromised himself by "extravagant praise" of the Italian government. Actually he had criticized the government of Victor Emmanuel II for its conduct toward the Holy See. In a letter of April 18, 1885, from Richmond, Keiley told Bayard that at a public meeting of Catholics in Richmond on January 12, 1871, he had served as chairman when a set of resolutions were adopted criticizing the Italian government. Keiley informed Bayard that the meeting had been called "at the request of the bishop of this diocese" and that the resolutions of protest had been "prepared by the bishop." Cf. *Papers Relating to the Foreign Relations of the United States* (Washington, 1886), p. 549. The bishop in question was John McGill, predecessor of Gibbons in the See of Richmond.

131 79-P-16, Keiley to Gibbons, Geneva, Switzerland, July 31, 1885.

132 AUND, McMaster Papers. These papers contain an unsigned document inserted at August, 1885, which criticizes severely the management and policy of the *Catholic Mirror* of Baltimore. The writer stated that the newspaper was published by the Baltimore Publishing Company, composed of five members of whom three were Protestants and two Catholics. The Catholics were William J. O'Brien and Hugh P. McElrone. It referred to the attacks of the *Mirror* on Keiley and on Secretary of State Bayard, and it cited the issue of August 14 ["This week's issue"] as containing an unjust editorial on Bayard and also some reflections on the *"Pestilent Freemans Journal."* The document went on to relate

Keiley named American minister to Austria-Hungary likewise met with failure due to the fact that Mrs. Keiley was a Jewess and to the tension at the moment between the dual monarchy and Italy over the irredentism along their common frontier. President Cleveland's biographer called the appointment of Keiley to Rome the President's "one bad error in the diplomatic field," but he was wrong in believing that the revoking of the appointment was made "to the chagrin of Archbishop Gibbons, who had urged it upon Cleveland."[133] Gibbons had, it is true, written to Secretary Bayard in Keiley's behalf but he had not specified the post in Rome for his friend, and his later statement of Bishop Dwenger revealed relief rather than chagrin that Keiley was not going to Rome.

On April 19, 1885, Gibbons consecrated his fourth bishop in the person of Alphonsus J. Glorieux, Vicar Apostolic of Idaho.[134] Six weeks later the archbishop met with his suffragans at his residence to select names to fill the See of Savannah, vacated by the promotion of Bishop Gross to Oregon City. The *terna* of names was headed by John S. Foley, pastor of St. Martin's Church in Baltimore, and a close friend of the archbishop's. When the news of the nomination of Foley got out someone informed Cardinal Simeoni that he was not fitted for the episcopacy. This prompted the cardinal to inform Gibbons of the serious criticisms against Foley which he had received from one whom he described as "a persona fide digna" and to ask for the archbishop's confidential judgment in the case.[135]

---

that the Catholic community of Baltimore did not know "who are the real owners." The writer felt the *Mirror* deserved "a severe castigation" from McMaster, the editor of the *Freeman's Journal,* for its policies in general and for copying stories from the secular press "without even correcting their silly blunders as regards Catholic matters." The differences between the *Mirror* and *Freeman's Journal* were, of course, of long standing, but there were enough complaints in these years against items appearing in the *Mirror* to indicate that Gibbons' supervision of the policy of the newspaper was exercised — if at all — in a very remote way. For that reason the *Mirror's* editorial policies could not be said to reflect the official views of the Archbishop of Baltimore.

[133] Allan Nevins, *Grover Cleveland, A Study in Courage* (New York, 1932), p. 209. Another work which carried this version of the event is Charles Callan Tansill, *The Foreign Policy of Thomas F. Bayard, 1885–1897* (New York, 1940). Tansill stated, "It was also true that Archbishop Gibbons supported the nomination of Anthony M. Keiley to the post in Rome" (p. xxi).

[134] Diary, April 19, 1885, p. 182.

[135] 79-Q-7, Simeoni to Gibbons, Rome, August 20, 1885.

Gibbons was extremely loyal to his friends, at times one is led to believe too loyal. His attachment to Foley occasioned a reply to Simeoni in which, as he related in his diary, he "wrote stating that the charges were unfounded, & the opposite of the truth. The charges were of a vague & general character, no special instance being cited. My answer was a warm commendation of his sincerity & virtues."[136] It so happened that Bishop Becker of Wilmington was transferred to Savannah, but the bishops of the province had suggested Foley's name in second place for Wilmington should Becker be changed. The matter dragged on for over a year but Gibbons remained steadfast and when the prelates met again on May 11, 1886, Foley's name headed the list with Alfred A. Curtis, Gibbons' secretary, in second place.[137] Opposition to Foley now arose in the Diocese of Wilmington, and Benjamin J. Keiley, one of the priests of Wilmington and a brother of the ex-Mayor of Richmond, told Denis O'Connell he understood Gibbons had stood by Foley. He further related that the priests had held an informal meeting and talked about writing Gibbons a letter of protest against Foley but nothing had come of it. Keiley, who did not care for Archbishop Gibbons, concluded to O'Connell, "I am heart sick at the thought of wire pulling by high dignitaries — Basta!"[138] Moore of St. Augustine, who had just been to Baltimore, let O'Connell know that the news was out that Foley had been rejected for Wilmington and Moore thought he was to be pitied. Said Moore, "He had intended to refuse Wilmington, but would have been glad to have the refusal as a vindication of his character."[139] Meanwhile O'Connell protested he was doing all he could for Gibbons' candidate at Rome where, he said, the Propaganda had made inquiries of him and "I have put in a strong reply against the letter written about Fr. Foley."[140] As it turned out Curtis was appointed

---

[136] Diary, September 12, 1885, p. 185.
[137] *Ibid.*, May 25, 1886, p. 204.
[138] ADR, Keiley to O'Connell, Wilmington, June 9, 1886.
[139] *Ibid.*, Moore to O'Connell, St. Augustine, July 21, 1886.
[140] 79-T-19, O'Connell to Gibbons, Rome, October 22, 1885. A year and a half later when Bishop Borgess of Detroit resigned Foley was put first on the priests' *terna* and also on the bishops' list. Gibbons again wrote to Rome recommending Foley and saying he was glad the chance had come up to refute the false accusations made against him when he was nominated for Wilmington (83-B-7, Gibbons to Jacobini, Baltimore, July 11, 1887, copy).

as Bishop of Wilmington in August, 1886, although two years later Foley was named Bishop of Detroit.

In the recommendation of another of his pastors for the episcopacy at this time Archbishop Gibbons had more success. In June, 1885, he received a cable informing him that Jeremiah O'Sullivan, pastor of St. Peter's Church in Washington, had been named Bishop of Mobile. The archbishop spoke in glowing terms of this priest in relaying the news to Archbishop Elder of Cincinnati. He called O'Sullivan "a learned, pious & zealous priest, a first class disciplinarian & financier & a temperance man by example & precept, like the Archbp. of Cincinnati. I do the precept part."[141] O'Sullivan thanked Gibbons for his congratulations and stated, "The appointment is due to the too favorable opinion you have formed of my works and myself."[142] The archbishop consecrated O'Sullivan on September 20 in the latter's parish church in Washington, the fifth in a long line of American bishops who received episcopal consecration at his hands.[143]

As James Gibbons came to the close of 1885 and his eighth year as Baltimore's archbishop he could look back upon those crowded years with considerable satisfaction as he viewed the generally prosperous growth of the archdiocese under his administration, the finished work of the Third Plenary Council, and the increasing stature which he was gaining in the esteem of the American people of all faiths. He had now reached the point where he was easily among the three or four top leaders of the Church in the United States, a position to which he had risen not only by virtue of his office as Archbishop of Baltimore but, as well, through the exercise of his talents and natural virtues which recommended him strongly to the affection and regard of his associates. To his friends and admirers the rumors which had been circulating for some time to the effect that greater honors were in store for him seemed altogether fitting, and when in October, 1885, the only cardinal of the United States died the speculations on the possibility of Gibbons' merits being rewarded with the red hat took on more immediate significance.

141 AAC, Gibbons to Elder, Baltimore, June 12, 1885.
142 79-M-12, O'Sullivan to Gibbons, Washington, June 12, 1885.
143 Diary, September 20, 1885, p. 186.

CHAPTER VIII

The Red Hat

THE highest honor that can come to a Catholic churchman, aside from the Papacy itself, is to be named a member of the College of Cardinals. Not only is the cardinal's office regarded as a great personal distinction for him who is selected by the Pope, but in the case of prelates who reside outside of Rome it is viewed as an honor bestowed upon their country and their diocese. Moreover, the conferring of the cardinalate upon a citizen of a particular nation is often interpreted to mean, and rightly so, that the Holy See wishes to signalize by this act its favorable opinion of that nation and its government in relation to the Church, as well as to give public testimony of the fact that the branch of the Universal Church thus honored has reached a status of maturity.

With the Catholic Church of the United States numbering well over six million members by 1880 and growing rapidly with each succeeding year, it was not surprising that there should have been repeated rumors about the likelihood of a second cardinal for this country. Furthermore, the relations existing between the government of the United States and the Church, although entirely unofficial, were cordial and there was every prospect that the Church's progress in the Republic would continue unimpeded by any hampering action of the civil power. The first American prelate to be raised to the dignity of a cardinal was John McCloskey, Archbishop of New York, who received the red hat in the consistory of September, 1875. In the intervening years Cardinal McCloskey's health had failed and by the year of the Third Plenary Council he had become so enfeebled that he was not able to preside over its sessions. Naturally this situation quickened the pace of rumor that the Church of the United States would soon have another cardinal. The successful manner in which Archbishop Gibbons had handled the affairs of the council as apostolic delegate, together with the fact that he occupied the premier see of the country, focused the attention of many on him as the most probable candidate for such honors.

The favorable impression created by Gibbons in Rome in 1883 as the leader of the American bishops who had come to prepare for the council, was enhanced by the rather marked attentions of Leo XIII to the Archbishop of Baltimore in his audiences and in his designation of him to preside at the Christmas Mass in the Basilica of St. Mary Major. These courtesies were not lost upon observers and, as we have seen, Gibbons began to receive even at that early date hints from various sources that he would in all likelihood be made a cardinal. When Denis O'Connell arrived in Rome in the early spring of 1885 with the decrees of the plenary council he informed the archbishop that he heard contradictory reports about a second American cardinal, although it seemed certain there would be no action until the decrees had been examined and approved.[1] A week or so later O'Connell had an audience of Leo XIII in which the Pope inquired for the health of McCloskey and told O'Connell that after McCloskey's death there would be a new cardinal for the United States. The Holy Father closed the audience with a reference to Gibbons and, as O'Connell put it:

> He spoke of you with an air of great acquaintance and affection, and tho he did not say so in so many words, I am satisfied that he intended to convey to me the impression that he intended to create a cardinal in Balto. to succeed the one of New York, and I think you know from experience with me that I am not one disposed to commit myself to the promises of hope.[2]

We have no way of knowing what train of thoughts this Roman news may have unloosed in the mind of Gibbons, but it was at least evident that long before the event numerous premonitions had reached him.

In the autumn of 1885 the condition of Cardinal McCloskey had grown steadily worse, and by the first week in October it was clear that his death was at hand. With this in mind

---

[1] 79-F-9, O'Connell to Gibbons, Rome, March 8, 1885.
[2] 79-G-15, O'Connell to Gibbons, Rome, March 23, 1885.

his coadjutor, Archbishop Corrigan, sent a hurried message to Baltimore in which he asked Gibbons to adjust his engagements in order that he might preach the funeral sermon. Gibbons readily agreed to Corrigan's request, although he stated that he was surprised to be asked since he had thought Archbishop Ryan of Philadelphia would be invited to deliver the eulogy. He told Corrigan, "I will do the best I can but what is that for such a subject! I had engagements extending for two weeks, but as soon as I hear of the Cardinal's death, I will give them up, & attend to the sermon."[3] Three days later Cardinal McCloskey died and the funeral was held on October 15. In his sermon Gibbons first developed the theme of what constituted a prelate's office and function after which he spoke of the deceased cardinal. In the Catholic Protectory and the new St. Patrick's Cathedral, said the preacher, McCloskey had left to New York two great monuments of his zeal, just as in his unsullied life and the person of his gifted successor New York had inherited two precious legacies of his love. "After spending upwards of half a century in the exercise of the ministry," said Gibbons, "he goes down to his honored grave without a stain upon his moral character."[4]

The news of the death of Cardinal McCloskey was promptly cabled to Rome where O'Connell was entrusted with the task of obtaining faculties for the new Archbishop of New York. He informed Gibbons that when he called at the Propaganda he had a talk with Archbishop Jacobini, the secretary, on the subject of a new cardinal for the United States, and Jacobini had said, "I think it will be Baltimore."[5] The rumors continued and by late January of 1886 Bishop Gilmour of Cleveland was in possession of information which he considered reliable enough to warrant giving the news to his diocesan paper, the *Catholic Universe*. Without stating the "reliable authority" from which he had obtained the news, he told Gibbons of his action in authorizing the statement and sent him his congratulations.[6] Although no official word had reached him, the archbishop accepted the congratulations of his friend in Cleveland and told him, "I would be more than human not to be moved by

---

[3] AANY, Gibbons to Corrigan, Baltimore, October 7, 1885.
[4] 79-T-14, printed copy of Gibbons' sermon at McCloskey's funeral.
[5] 79-T-12, O'Connell to Gibbons, Grottaferrata, October 13, 1885.
[6] 80-D-12, Gilmour to Gibbons, Cleveland, January 29, 1886.

the apparently impending honor, & I shall continue to hold in affectionate regard him who gave me the first direct information on the subject."[7]

Ten days later Archbishop Gibbons received a telegram from the Archbishop of New York which read, "It is authentic. Biglietto will arrive about the twenty second."[8] Corrigan, convinced of the authenticity of a cablegram he had received from Rome, released the news in New York and within a few hours Gibbons began to receive congratulations from many friends and admirers. The Baltimore *American* of February 11 promptly picked up and published the Associated Press dispatch from New York which read, "Archbishop Corrigan has a cablegram from Rome announcing that Archbishop Gibbons, of Baltimore, will be created a cardinal at the coming consistory." A reporter on the *American* rushed to the archbishop's residence that night and was told by John Foley that private telegrams received by the archbishop confirmed the authenticity of the news and that "there was no longer any doubt about the appointment."

On the day that the Corrigan telegram reached Gibbons he wrote an entry on the subject in his diary which he closed with the words, "Should the report be verified may God give me as He gave to His servant David a humble heart, that I may bear the honor with becoming modesty & a profound sense of my unworthiness. . . ." To this comment he added on the following day, "Telegrams & messages of congratulation are pouring in from all parts of the country."[9] Bishop McQuaid of Rochester joined with dozens of others in sending their felicitations to Gibbons at the news which they had read in the papers,[10] and among them was Charles F. Deems, president of the American Institute of Christian Philosophy. Deems said he wondered if a "heretic" might venture the expression of honest admiration he had for the archbishop; he told him he had been watching his course ever since "the days before the war" and Gibbons' growing power and usefulness had given him much pleasure. Therefore, he was really glad in his heart "that (if

[7] ADC, Gibbons to Gilmour, Baltimore, February 1, 1886.

[8] 80-F-3, Corrigan to Gibbons, New York, February 10, 1886, telegram.

[9] Diary, February 10–11, 1886, p. 197.

[10] 80-G-12, McQuaid to Gibbons, Rochester, February 11, 1886.

there must be cardinals), you are to be made a cardinal."[11] Meanwhile Gibbons acknowledged Corrigan's announcement of the news to him and related the commotion it had caused over the country. He told Corrigan he hoped the day was not far distant when he would be "sweetly revenged" upon him by being able to communicate a similar message to the Archbishop of New York. "Then what a hurricane there will be! The present storm will be mild in comparison to it."[12] It was just at this time that Corrigan fixed March 4 as the date for receiving his pallium and he asked Gibbons to confer it, a request to which the latter gladly assented, adding that he hoped later on to witness "another ceremony" of which Corrigan would be the principal figure.[13]

During these days of mid-February, 1886, Archbishop Gibbons was the recipient of hundreds of congratulatory messages. Their authors ranged through all ranks of the hierarchy and priesthood, officials of the United States government, officers of the state and municipality and on down to little children in the parochial schools. Among the more interesting of these letters was one from Father Sylvester Malone, pastor of SS. Peter and Paul Church in Brooklyn. Malone, who was destined to play the role of a partisan in the McGlynn case in New York a year or two later, was a priest of strong views. He told Gibbons that ever since he had first met him at the plenary council of 1866 he had been pleased by his "independent mind" and his "honesty & fine sense of justice." Malone conceived of Gibbons' role as a cardinal as one that would enable him to perform a greater good by making himself felt outside of the sanctuary and among his fellow citizens who were not of the Catholic faith. He believed American non-Catholics would be brought to honor the Church more from the fact, as he expressed it, that "the Most Rev. Archbishop Gibbons does not forget he is a citizen of a free republic, though Cardinal in the Holy Catholic Church."[14] Most of the reaction shown to the news of Gibbons' new honor was in a similarly complimentary vein, although discordant voices were not lacking. For example, the arch-

---

11 80-H-13, Deems to Gibbons, New York, February 12, 1886.
12 AANY, Gibbons to Corrigan, Baltimore, February 12, 1886.
13 *Ibid.*, Gibbons to Corrigan, Baltimore, February 13, 1886.
14 80-J-6, Malone to Gibbons, Brooklyn, February 13, 1886.

bishop's old friend of Richmond days, Anthony M. Keiley, wrote him that he had visited with Father Thomas Conaty in Worcester some days before and he had inquired of Conaty if he knew who had inspired "the scurrilous article" that appeared on Gibbons in the Springfield *Republican* when the news was first announced. Conaty was unable to enlighten Keiley, but he agreed that the article in question was entirely unjustified in calling into question Gibbons' fitness and ability to wear the red hat with distinction.[15]

Amid all these notices in the public press and the numerous letters received by the archbishop from his admirers, there had been no official word from the Holy See concerning the subject. It often happened that news of the action of Rome concerning the American Church was cabled through various agencies long before the official information reached this country. For that reason it was probably not thought exceptional that nearly two weeks should pass without official word to Gibbons from the Holy See. But then a registered letter to Archbishop Corrigan from Miss Edes in Rome revealed to him that by publishing the news about Gibbons' honor he had unwittingly committed, as he expressed it, "an awful blunder." Corrigan's mistake was quite understandable and had come about in the following way. With the approach of Lent the Archbishop of New York and his consultors had discussed the subject of permitting the Catholic people the use of meat on Saturdays of the lenten season. Corrigan knew that an indult had been requested by Gibbons to dispense from the law of abstinence and with that in mind he asked Ella Edes to inquire of Propaganda if Gibbons' request had been granted or not, and he instructed his agent that if time pressed she should cable the answer. Following out Corrigan's orders Edes cabled him on February 10 in these words, "Granted, Official letter Baltimore, Feb. 8th." Since, as

---

[15] 80-I-2, Keiley to Gibbons, New York, February 12, 1886. The Springfield *Republican* of February 1, 1886, under "Note and Comment" had said that Gibbons "graduated near the foot of his class in college, and was in no wise a brilliant student, nor is he noted as a pulpit orator." The *Republican* credited him with a keen insight into human nature and said he had taken a strong hold on the people of North Carolina and Virginia; that he knew how "to eat a hoe-cake meal spread on the ground," etc. It seemed evident from the several items in this paper at the time on the subject of new American cardinals that they were anxious that Williams of Boston should receive the honor since they invariably mentioned him in a way that would indicate his superiority to Gibbons.

Corrigan explained to Gibbons, reports had been circulating about the cardinalate for Baltimore, reports which seemed to him to have been authenticated by Gilmour's announcement and a letter from Miss Edes to the same effect, the Archbishop of New York received the cable on February 10 with the assurance that it pertained to Gibbons' red hat and nothing else. He confessed that he had meanwhile entirely forgotten about the lenten indult, and that when he read the word "Baltimore" in Edes' cable he "did not know what other interpretation to give." Corrigan felt further excused on the ground that the *Catholic Mirror* of February 13 had made a front-page announcement and when this was added to the other indications, as he told Gibbons, "I was satisfied that what we had hoped for, was really true."[16]

The episode proved painful, of course, to the two principals. Corrigan told Gibbons that he was "mortified beyond measure," but if the information were kept secret probably no harm would be done. The mistake would hasten the consummation if Corrigan himself could wield any influence and, as he remarked, meanwhile the good will of the entire community had been called out and made manifest. He confided to Gibbons in strict confidence that an added factor in making him believe that the cable of February 10 related to the red hat was that Miss Edes had told him in her letter of January 20 that Archbishop Williams of Boston had written to Rome requesting the cardinalitial honor for Baltimore. The Archbishop of New York craved the forgiveness of Gibbons for his error; as he put it, "I *meant* to do a kind act, and on the contrary have only covered myself with confusion."[17]

The state of mind of Archbishop Gibbons was well revealed in his prompt reply to the Archbishop of New York's explanation and apology. He wrote:

> Your letter came just as I was going down to breakfast with Bp. Kain & Bp. Dwenger. You may well realize its effect on me. I tried with great difficulty to maintain my composure at the table. It has of course unnerved me. But I am praying earnestly to God to give me grace & strength to bear the humiliation & drink the chalice. I am sorry also my Dear Friend, for your sake. I know how distressed

---

[16] 80-M-10, Corrigan to Gibbons, New York, February 23, 1886, *Private.*
[17] *Ibid.*

you must feel, & all on my account, in your friendly eagerness to send me what you naturally supposed would be a joyful message. I will keep the secret, but I cannot stop the congratulatory messages that are coming in every day. I can only say to them in reply, as I have been saying, that I have no communication from Rome on the subject. I heard the Mirror professed to have direct news. I did not read it, & did not believe it had; for, if so, I would have been shown the Despatch. Its article was of course, based on your cablegram though it had not the courtesy to acknowledge it.

I am confused & annoyed by the fulsome paragraphs in the papers, & by the titles they give me, but I have no means of stopping their pen. I shall keep the last paragraph a profound secret [about Archbishop Williams writing to Rome]. The main portion I have revealed to Dr. O'Connell in whom I can safely rely.

I have about a hundred letters and telegrams still unanswered. I may send an answer, but such as will reveal nothing.

What I dread most will be the circulation of the American papers through Europe. This A.M. I had a congratulatory cable message from Ireland.

Pray my Dear Friend that I may have grace to bear this confusion, & may joyfully do God's will, & I beg you not to be distressed on my account.[18]

Dr. O'Connell was then in Baltimore with Gibbons and he sent a clipping from the Baltimore *News* to Corrigan which O'Connell had written with a view to calming the excitement. He stated that Gibbons was feeling somewhat better but he was still experiencing embarrassment from the congratulations of friends meeting him "especially on the street."[19] Meanwhile McQuaid learned of Corrigan's mistake, probably from the

---

[18] AANY, Gibbons to Corrigan, Baltimore, February 24, 1886, *Private*.

[19] *Ibid.*, O'Connell to Corrigan, Baltimore, February 24, 1886. Shortly after Corrigan's death in May, 1902, his brother, Dr. Joseph F. Corrigan, informed Arthur Preuss, editor of the *Review* of St. Louis, that the archbishop had told him that the red hat had been suggested for him by Cardinal Simeoni in 1886. He was quoted as having declined because of his youth at the time, that it might give rise to jealousy on the part of others, and that New York already had had a cardinal. For these reasons, it was said, he had suggested that it be given to either Williams or Gibbons. The archbishop was quoted as having remarked in Florida the winter before he died that his friends in Rome still wished him to be made a cardinal and some of them had stated that the red hat would yet come if he would give some indication of wishing it, but Dr. Corrigan stated that his brother refused to be moved by his friends' promptings (Archives of the Central Bureau, St. Louis, Arthur Preuss Papers, Corrigan to Preuss, New York, June 29, 1902; same to same, St. Leo, Florida, July 22, 1902. The writer is indebted to Colman J. Barry, O.S.B., for copies of these letters). Several weeks later Preuss

archbishop himself, and he told Gilmour that while it would likely come out all right in due time, he added, "The Archbishop may have the mortification of waiting longer than he expected."[20]

The tension under which Gibbons lived during these days of the late winter of 1886 must have been exceedingly trying to him. In an effort to give the public an explanation of the lack of official information and at the same time not reveal Corrigan's error, O'Connell prepared several paragraphs for the press which the Baltimore *Evening News* and the *American* carried. They had the hoped-for result of causing the excitement to die down in Baltimore but, as Gibbons confessed to Corrigan, he dreaded the gauntlet he would have to run in New York when he came for the conferring of the pallium, although he would be careful not to commit himself in any way to the newspapermen. He was fearful that the strong emotion under which he had written his first letter to Corrigan would convey the impression that he was thinking more of himself than of his friend in New York, for as he expressed it, "You needed more sympathy than I did." Gibbons was especially uneasy lest the Roman correspondent of some American secular or religious paper would secure the original announcement from a New York paper and then seek authentication of the news from either the Cardinal Secretary of State or the Cardinal Prefect of Propaganda. In that case there might well be an official contradiction cabled from Rome to the United States. For that reason, Gibbons remarked, it had occurred to him that Corrigan might forestall such a contingency by writing an explanation of what had really happened to the two cardinals in question. He did not press the point but contented himself with saying, "I leave the whole matter to your better judgment." He revealed his own relations with the *Catholic Mirror* of Baltimore when he said he would have O'Connell see the editor and prevent another *faux pas* on his part, confessing that he had not seen the man himself in months. "He is a good young man, but imprudent & impulsive & I believe is sore with me for the public rebuke I gave him in re Keiley."[21]

---

used Corrigan's remarks to publicize the fact that Gibbons was indebted for his red hat to Archbishop Corrigan. Cf. *The Review,* IX (July 17, 1902), 447–448.

[20] ADC, McQuaid to Gilmour, Rochester, February 25, 1886, *Private.*

[21] AANY, Gibbons to Corrigan, Baltimore, February 26, 1886. The previous year when Anthony Keiley was refused acceptance by both the Italian and

During the ensuing weeks the announcements of a consistory to create cardinals were repeated in the press to the point where they became almost monotonous. From time to time the newspapers drew up lists of names for the honor of the red hat and Gibbons was invariably among the names, although the Holy See continued to maintain an official silence. Archbishop Corrigan meanwhile communicated to the Secretary of the Propaganda, Jacobini, the story of his own blunder and had accompanied it with a request — in the name of the entire American hierarchy — that if the Pope should see fit to confer the hat on Gibbons it would be gratifying to all the American bishops. Jacobini informed Leo XIII of Corrigan's error which the Pope took good-naturedly and said that no harm had been done.[22] Gibbons was grateful to his friend in New York for his action and told him that he never dreamed he would carry his atonement "for a most pardonable & magnanimous mistake to such a length of noble generosity." He wondered how Corrigan learned so correctly the sentiments of the American hierarchy, but it was a fact, as he said, that all the provinces of the country with the archbishops at their head had written him letters of congratulation, although, as he added, "these letters are locked in my drawer — & in my heart."[23] Actually Corrigan had spoken without authority for the hierarchy, taking, as he said, the will for the act and becoming the interpreter of what they would have said had they been given the opportunity.[24]

At length the official silence was broken when a cablegram arrived in Baltimore from Lodovico Cardinal Jacobini, Secretary of State, informing Gibbons of his designation by the Pope for the cardinalate in the forthcoming consistory.[25] The painful suspense had lasted from the middle of February until the first week in May, and it must have been with a feeling of

Austro-Hungarian governments as United States minister, the *Catholic Mirror* had said some very harsh things about him. Fearing the views of the *Mirror* might be taken as his own, Gibbons permitted Keiley's brother, John D., to publish a statement made in a letter to him from the archbishop as follows: "I beg to state that I have no official organ, and that I do not hold myself in any wise responsible for the editorials which have appeared in a Baltimore paper reflecting on your brother, Mr. A. M. Keiley" (New York *Herald*, July 16, 1885).

[22] 80-S-5, Corrigan to Gibbons, New York, April 12, 1886, *Private*.
[23] AANY, Gibbons to Corrigan, Baltimore, April 17, 1886.
[24] 80-S-18, Corrigan to Gibbons, New York, April 19, 1886.
[25] 80-U-7, Jacobini to Gibbons, Rome, May 4, 1886.

immense relief that the archbishop could now speak freely about the matter without fear of compromising himself or the few persons who knew of the misunderstanding. O'Connell cabled three times within as many days giving further details,[26] and he followed the cables with a letter in which he outlined for the cardinal-elect information concerning the ceremonies of the consistory, the purchase of robes, etc. He was plainly elated at the successful termination of the question and said he thanked God from the bottom of his heart. He added, "Gibbons 'are trumps' now, and everyone will try to play them."[27]

The official letter of Cardinal Jacobini arrived in Baltimore on May 18. In it the Secretary of State stated that Leo XIII had chosen him to be a cardinal for his personal virtues and merits, as well as to increase the luster of the See of Baltimore, "first among all the churches of the vast Republic of the United States. . . ."[28] The customary letter of thanks from the bishops of the Province of Baltimore for the honor which had come to their metropolitan was written to the Pope by Bishop Becker,[29] and Gibbons himself sent a lengthy message of gratitude to Leo XIII.[30] He soon received word that Monsignor Germano Straniero, secretary of the nunciature in Vienna, had been appointed to bring the red biretta to him from Rome, and that Archbishop Kenrick of St. Louis had been chosen by the Holy See to confer it upon him. Gibbons informed Corrigan of these details, expressing at the same time his surprise that it was Kenrick rather than Corrigan or Williams who had been selected. He chided Archbishop Corrigan for the reports he had received of late of his incessant labors and urged him to slacken his pace; if he did not relax a little, said Gibbons, he would get his crown before the red hat. "I want the latter to come first."[31]

The cardinal-elect chose the date of June 30 for the imposition of the red biretta in Baltimore. It was the silver jubilee of

---

[26] 80-U-10, 11/1, and 13, May 5, 6, and 7, cablegrams from O'Connell to Gibbons from Rome.

[27] 80-V-3, O'Connell to Gibbons, Rome, May 14, 1886.

[28] Diary, May 18, 1886, p. 201.

[29] 80-W-16, Suffragans of the Province of Baltimore to Leo XIII, Savannah, May 26, 1886, copy.

[30] Diary, May 23, 1886, pp. 203–204.

[31] AANY, Gibbons to Corrigan, Baltimore, June 2, 1886.

his ordination as a priest which he had received on this date
in 1861 at the hands of Archbishop Francis P. Kenrick, the
brother of the man who had now been appointed to confer
upon him the scarlet biretta. There were numerous details to
be attended to for the ceremony in the cathedral on June 30,
and Gibbons' time, as well as that of his household, was largely
absorbed in this business through most of that month.

On the afternoon of June 29 the official letter of notification
and the red zucchetto were presented to Gibbons in the parlors
of his residence by Count Stanislaus Muccioli, the noble guard
who had come from Rome with Straniero. On the following
morning the Cathedral of the Assumption was filled to over-
flowing for the unusual ceremony of the imposition of the red
biretta. The solemn procession into the cathedral found twenty-
four bishops and ten archbishops in the line of march. Archbishop Williams said the Mass, the sermon was preached by
Archbishop Ryan, and at the end of the Mass Kenrick of St.
Louis imposed the biretta on the new cardinal. Straniero, the
papal ablegate, made a brief speech and the long ceremony
was concluded by three brief addresses by Gibbons, the first
to Kenrick in which he gracefully recalled the event of a quarter
century before when the Archbishop of St. Louis' brother had
ordained him, and the second to Straniero in which Gibbons
called attention to the thriving state of Catholicism in this
country and urged the ablegate to picture it before the eyes
of the Holy Father on his return to Rome. The third address,
directed to the prelates, clergy, and laity, afforded Gibbons an
opportunity to recall the historic importance of the See of
Baltimore, the mother of so many flourishing dioceses, and the
councils of the American Church which had been held within
its cathedral. He paid a special tribute to Leo XIII and the
high moral influence exercised by the reigning Pontiff, particularly in relation to his encyclical, *Immortale Dei,* on the
relations of Church and State. The new cardinal struck a
favorite note in praise of his own country when he said:

> In no country of all the nations of the earth does he find more
> loyal and devoted spiritual children than among the clergy and laity
> of this free republic. And I am happy to add that our separated
> brethren, while not sharing in our faith, have shared our profound

admiration for the benevolent and enlightened statesmanship of the present Supreme Pontiff.[32]

The Baltimore *Sun* for July 1 issued a special supplement on the occasion and the press of other cities carried lesser notices of the event. The American press reaction to the reception of the biretta found favor in Rome where the tokens of respect expressed by the American newspapers for Leo XIII and Gibbons were used as a lesson in contrast to the anti-papal attitude of the Italian government and press. Count Eduardo Soderini, Roman correspondent of the *Catholic Mirror,* had the article from the *Osservatore Romano,* the Vatican newspaper, translated and sent to Baltimore. In the article the writer paid high praise to the United States for the friendly reception given to its new cardinal, and he wrote, "To those proud republicans, citizens of the greatest and best constituted republic the earth has ever known, the Pope is something higher than any other man, and they laugh at and scorn and cannot understand those who seriously pretend to consider the Pope a simple citizen of Italy."[33]

The press reactions in the United States brought comment from others besides Soderini. Miss Kathleen O'Meara, a friend of Cardinal Manning's, had recently come to this country for a visit bearing a letter of introduction from Manning to Gibbons. While she could not get to Baltimore for the ceremony, she wrote her congratulations and told the cardinal how deeply impressed she had been by the respectful, "in some cases the sympathetic," tone of the American non-Catholic press on the subject. She commented, "How different from the spirit of our miserable sham Republic in France where every man's hand is raised to strike at the Church & her representatives!"[34] In providing Miss O'Meara with her introduction to Gibbons the

[32] 81-I-6, printed pamphlet of addresses delivered at the biretta ceremony of June 30, 1886. For an English translation of the report made to the Holy See by the ablegate, Monsignor Straniero, of the Baltimore ceremonies, cf. Joseph J. Murphy's "A Papal Ablegate in America. Report of Mgr. Gennaro [*sic*] Straniero's Mission for the Presentation of the Red Biretta to Cardinal Gibbons," in *Records of the American Catholic Historical Society of Philadelphia,* XXVI (December, 1915), 361–370.
[33] *Catholic Mirror,* August 28, 1886.
[34] 81-L-9, O'Meara to Gibbons, Cohasset, Massachusetts, July 8, 1886.

Cardinal of Westminster took occasion to tell him that it was in no official phrase that he expressed his joy in knowing that the Holy Father had united them in the College of Cardinals.[35]

Although Cardinal Gibbons had received on June 30, 1886, several of the symbols of his new office, the principal ceremony was yet to come in the consistory at Rome where he would receive the red hat itself. When O'Connell inquired at the Holy See concerning the consistory date he could learn nothing definite and was told that Gibbons would be notified in due time. O'Connell learned that the Pope had been pleased with Gibbons' letter of description of the ceremony on June 30, and the papal secretary for letters to princes seemed impressed by the fact that "even the President wrote him [Gibbons] a letter."[36] In the meantime the new cardinal attended to certain formalities, such as addressing letters of greeting to all other cardinals in the world and to the Catholic sovereigns which, in turn, brought him the felicitations of the King and Queen of the Belgians, the Emperor and Empress of Austria-Hungary, the Emperor and Empress of Brazil, and the Queen of Portugal.[37] The fall and early winter of 1886 found Gibbons preoccupied with the increasingly serious problems of the German question and the secret societies, the story of which we shall see in another connection. These matters, together with diocesan business, absorbed his attention while he was waiting for the summons to Rome. In late September Gibbons held a diocesan synod, following a retreat preached by Bishop Gilmour, and at the synod the diocesan administration was strengthened by the appointment of consultors, synodal examiners, and the personnel of the matrimonial court and the court for disciplinary causes.[38]

At length there arrived a cablegram from Cardinal Jacobini, the Secretary of State, informing Gibbons that the consistory would be held at the end of February or in early March and that the Pope desired him to come to Rome.[39] In the interval since the Third Plenary Council there had arisen in the Church of the United States a number of problems which called for

---

[35] 81-D-5, Manning to Gibbons, Westminster, June 10, 1886.
[36] 81-S-3, O'Connell to Gibbons, Rome, August 20, 1886.
[37] AAB, Boxes 81 and 82 contain these letters.
[38] Diary, September 20, 1886, p. 209.
[39] 82-L-13, Jacobini to Gibbons, Rome, January 17, 1887, cablegram.

settlement. Some of these questions had grown out of the council itself and, although preliminary action had been taken in this country, it was obvious that a final solution could not be given to them until they had been examined by the Roman curial officials. One such question was the university projected in the council and on which a number of preliminary meetings had been held through the years 1885 and 1886; another was the troublesome matter of secret societies in the United States and the enrollment in them of Catholic men. The bishops were particularly concerned at this time about Catholic membership in the Knights of Labor. Still another problem was that of the German Catholics in the United States, among whom there was an articulate minority who were urging upon the Holy See their rights for separate parishes and a larger representation in the American hierarchy. All these problems were of a sufficiently important nature for Gibbons as the ranking dignitary of the Church in this country to warrant separate treatment, but it is necessary to mention them here to make it clear that the journey on which the new cardinal embarked late in January, 1887, had implications for his personal career and the future of the American Church far beyond his reception of the red hat.

In view of the importance and gravity of these issues Cardinal Gibbons showed his customary desire for the fullest consultation with his colleagues in the hierarchy before he departed for the Eternal City. The day following the cablegram from Jacobini he sent a hurried letter to Archbishop Elder in which he informed him of his plan to sail from New York on January 29 and to spend the two days previous in that city as the guest of Archbishop Corrigan. He told Elder that it was likely that one or two other of the "Atlantic Abps." would be there, and he would like Elder to come on to New York to meet with them. As he expressed it, "We could discuss the points likely to come up when I go to Rome, & an interchange of views would be an advantage to me."[40]

A week before leaving Baltimore the cardinal received a letter from Secretary of State Thomas F. Bayard which enclosed a circular to the diplomatic and consular officers of the United States in Europe, in which the secretary requested

---

[40] AAC, Gibbons to Elder, Baltimore, January 18, 1887.

for Gibbons of these American officials abroad, "such official aid and courtesies as it may be in your power to bestow."[41] The cardinal decided to pay a farewell visit to President Cleveland, and, since the day fixed for the appointment coincided with a reception which Mrs. Cleveland was giving, the President suggested that possibly the cardinal might wish to attend and meet the First Lady.[42]

With all preparations finally attended to Cardinal Gibbons set out from Baltimore for New York on January 26 in the company of Father Patrick J. Donahue, chancellor of the archdiocese, who would act as his secretary on the journey. They remained over in New York for two days as the guests of Archbishop Corrigan where Gibbons was given an opportunity to consult with several of his fellow archbishops on the problems that would be examined in Rome. On Saturday, January 29, he sailed on the *Bourgogne* for France where he had as a fellow passenger Elzear Cardinal Taschereau of Quebec who was also to receive the red hat in the consistory. Taschereau, as we shall see, had already taken a strong stand against the Knights of Labor, and in the coming weeks the work of his fellow passenger from Baltimore was destined to undo in good measure the efforts so far put forth by the Archbishop of Quebec against the labor organization. On his way to Rome Cardinal Gibbons stopped in Paris, Genoa, and Pisa for short visits and finally arrived in the Eternal City on February 13 where he found a warm welcome awaiting him at the American College from his trusted friend, Denis O'Connell, who was then in the second year of his rectorship of that institution.[43] Likewise in Rome at the time, and that primarily on business for the future university, were Bishops John Ireland of St. Paul and John J. Keane of Richmond. These American prelates, along with Bishop John A. Watterson of Columbus, formed a pleasant company for Gibbons during a good part of the two months he was in residence at the American College.

Having arrived a month before the secret consistory which had been set for March 17, Gibbons was able to devote his

---

[41] 82-M-7, Bayard to diplomatic and consular officers, Washington, January 19, 1887, enclosed in a letter of Bayard to Gibbons, Washington, January 19, 1887, *Personal* (82-M-6).

[42] 82-M-9, A. A. Wilson to Gibbons, Washington, January 20, 1887.

[43] *Catholic Mirror*, February 19, 1887.

Views of the Basilica of Santa Maria in Trastevere, the titular
church of Cardinal Gibbons in Rome, 1887–1921.

time to the questions affecting the American Church at the Congregation of the Propaganda and to fulfill a large number of social engagements to which he was invited with the other cardinals by various persons and institutions anxious to honor the new princes of the Church. On St. Patrick's Day the colorful ceremony of the consistory was held in which the seven new cardinals went through the ceremony of the sealing and opening of the lips, the reception of their red hats, the assignment of their places on the various congregations, and the designation of their titular churches. The other members of the College of Cardinals who received their honor with Gibbons were Elzear Taschereau of Quebec, Benoît Langénieux of Rheims, Charles Place of Rennes, Victor Benardou of Sens, and the curial officials, Augusto Theodoli and Camillo Mazzella, S.J. Gibbons was assigned by the Pope to a place on the Congregations of the Propagation of the Faith, Religious, Indulgences, and Studies.[44]

To Cardinal Gibbons there was assigned by Pope Leo XIII as his titular church the ancient Basilica of Santa Maria in Trastevere which dated in its original foundation from the time of Julius I (337–352), an edifice which had undergone a number of restorations since the twelfth century, the most recent during the pontificate of Pius IX. It was on March 25, a week after the consistory, that Gibbons took possession of the church in a memorable ceremony which found him surrounded by a large gathering of friends, among them his colleagues in the American hierarchy, Bishops Ireland, Keane, and Watterson. Up to the present the public pronouncements which he had made since the announcement of his cardinalate had all been of either a routine character in his capacity as Archbishop of Baltimore or of a brief and formal nature as a cardinal. On the present occasion, however, it was the advice of Denis O'Connell that he should go beyond the expression of polite generalities in his sermon and deliver a major address which would carry a serious message, not only to his Roman audience but to the United States and to the world at large. The counsel was given by O'Connell only a few days before the event and the cardinal decided to adopt it.[45]

---

[44] 82-N-9, Mario Mocanni to Gibbons, Rome, March 17, 1887.
[45] Will, *op. cit.*, I, 308.

In the opening remarks of the sermon Cardinal Gibbons spoke of the antiquity of his titular church and alluded to the fact that both this basilica and his own cathedral in Baltimore were dedicated to the Virgin Mary. He then traced rapidly the growth of the Church in the United States from its humble beginnings in the Diocese of Baltimore to the numerous and flourishing dioceses stretching over the vast expanse of the continent. The present prosperous state of the American Church, the cardinal maintained, was owed under God and the vigilance of the Holy See "to the civil liberty we enjoy in our enlightened republic." Citing the encyclical of Leo XIII entitled *Immortale Dei [On the Civil Constitution of States]* which had been issued a year and a half before, Gibbons noted the fact that the Pope had insisted that the Church was not committed to any particular form of government and that it adapted itself to all. The Church grew and expanded under absolute or constitutional monarchies and under free republics; only despotism and the invasion of its rights had hampered its growth, but wherever the Church enjoyed what Gibbons termed, "the genial atmosphere of liberty," it blossomed like the rose.

These general remarks on the relations of Church and State provided the cardinal with the proper introduction for what was the principal point in his sermon, namely, a tribute to the cordial relations existing between the Church and the State in his own country. He then continued:

> For myself, as a citizen of the United States, without closing my eyes to our defects as a nation, I proclaim, with a deep sense of pride and gratitude, and in this great capital of Christendom, that I belong to a country where the civil government holds over us the aegis of its protection without interfering in the legitimate exercise of our sublime mission as ministers of the Gospel of Jesus Christ.
>
> Our country has liberty without license, authority without despotism. Hers is no spirit of exclusiveness. She has no frowning fortifications to repel the invader, for we are at peace with all the world! In the consciousness of her strength and of her good will to all nations she rests secure. Her harbors are open in the Atlantic and Pacific to welcome the honest immigrant who comes to advance his temporal interest and to find a peaceful home.
>
> But, while we are acknowledged to have a free government, we do not, perhaps receive due credit for possessing also a strong govern-

ment. Yes, our nation is strong, and her strength lies, under Providence, in the majesty and supremacy of the law, in the loyalty of her citizens to that law, and in the affection of our people for their free institutions.

There are, indeed, grave social problems which are engaging the earnest attention of the citizens of the United States. But I have no doubt that, with God's blessings, these problems will be solved without violence, or revolution, or injury to individual right.[46]

The cardinal concluded his address with the statement that in naming him to his new dignity Leo XIII had given evidence of his good will toward the United States as a nation as well as his consideration for the American hierarchy and the premier See of Baltimore. For this striking manifestation Gibbons thanked the Pope in the name of the hierarchy, clergy, and Catholic laity of the United States, and he added:

I presume also to thank him in the name of our separated brethren in America, who, though not sharing our faith, have shown that they are not insensible — indeed, that they are deeply sensible — of the honor conferred upon our common country. . . .

Given the circumstances, it is hardly an exaggeration to say that the sermon of Gibbons delivered in Santa Maria in Trastevere on that March day of 1887 was, indeed, unusual. It was spoken at a time when the relations between Church and State in Italy had reached an acute crisis, with the government of Agostino Depretis steadily deepening the gulf between them by its anti-clerical legislation. In France matters were not much better for the Church. The ministry was presided over by René Goblet, a strong anti-clerical, who a few months before, as Minister of Education and Worship, had proposed to parliament the bill secularizing primary education. In the German Empire the long and cruel struggle of the *Kulturkampf* waged by Bismarck against the Church was only then coming to a close, and even in Spain and Portugal there were signs of increasing tension between the Church and the State as the liberal anti-clerical spirit spread to the Iberian peninsula. The atmosphere of a large part of western Europe at the time was charged with bitterness engendered by the attacks of liberals upon the Catholic Church, and since they were in

---

[46] *Catholic Mirror*, April 2, 1887.

possession of a number of the governments, their attitude was often translated into action in the form of laws which seriously restricted the freedom of the Catholic religion. For this reason the Gibbons address with its strong emphasis upon the liberty of the Church in the United States had an importance and significance quite beyond the ordinary sermon of this kind.

If European Catholics, so accustomed to union of Church and State, experienced some surprise at the forthright approval given by the new American cardinal to the harmonious relationship existing between the two great institutions on a basis of separation, Americans themselves were delighted with Gibbons' pronouncement. Bishop Kain of Wheeling expressed what was in the minds of many when he told Gibbons of the joy which all Americans — Catholic and non-Catholic alike — experienced in reading the favorable accounts in the press of the cardinal's prestige in Rome. It was Kain's belief that a native American enjoying such distinguished favor near the Pope would help to dissipate prejudice against the Church in the United States. As he expressed it, a native American cardinal, "voicing with clarion tones beneath the very shadow of the Vatican the sentiments so dear to all lovers of our free institutions, is the strongest refutation of the grievous charges by which our loyalty has been so long impugned."[47]

The address in Santa Maria in Trastevere called forth an enthusiastic response in both the secular and religious press of the United States. The New York *Herald* of March 26 carried the text of the sermon, a news article on the ceremony, and an editorial on the address which they said would be "read with interest by Catholic and Protestant alike." The Baltimore *Weekly Sun* of April 2 applauded the patriotic sentiments of the sermon as well as Gibbons' allusions to American shortcomings. They said, "Those who heard it pronounced the address magnificent." The New York *Independent* of March 31 believed the sermon proved Leo XIII's wisdom in making Gibbons a cardinal. This Protestant weekly called the address "one of singular spirit and tact," and they were especially gratified at Gibbons' references to American non-Catholics as "our separated brethren" which the *Independent* said bespoke the gentleman and the Christian. The editorial closed in a hearty agreement with

---

[47] 82-P-5, Kain to Gibbons, Wheeling, April 4, 1887.

Gibbons that Protestants in the United States recognized in Leo XIII one whose wisdom had scarcely had an equal in the chair of St. Peter. An editorial in the *Catholic Mirror* of April 2, 1887, stated:

> No such words have ever been uttered to the world by an American bishop since Archbishop Carroll founded our See of Baltimore, nor ones to make every true American citizen thank God he has such a representative at the Eternal City. . . .

Father Isaac Hecker, editor of the *Catholic World,* made Gibbons' sermon the subject of an article in his journal in which he stated that the sentiments expressed in the sermon had animated the entire life of the cardinal as a Catholic and a citizen. Hecker believed that all Gibbons' countrymen would rejoice that he had spoken these words "with so much emphasis and bravery," and they would thank him for them and accept him as a true representative of their ideas at Rome, since he was fitted, as he said, by his "thorough-going American spirit to interpret us to the peoples and powers of the Old World." Hecker concluded with the statement that it was entirely fitting that what he characterized as "the best expression of the good of civil freedom as a favorable human environment for the development of the religious character," should have been made by an American cardinal in the center of Christendom.[48]

The happy sequel of the sermon of March 25 proved the wisdom of O'Connell's suggestion to the cardinal that he avail himself of the opportunity to make a major pronouncement on the relations of Church and State. In this, as in so many other important decisions in Gibbons' life, he probably needed the stimulus of his friend to undertake the work. The cardinal often manifested during this period of his life a timidity about taking strong stands on grave public questions, and, as we shall have occasion to see, he was frequently nerved to do this only after the urging of friends like O'Connell, Ireland, and Keane who displayed a more venturesome spirit in these matters. But regardless of the fact that the original suggestion for the sermon had come from O'Connell, the actual doing of the deed was Gibbons' and

---

[48] I. T. Hecker, "Cardinal Gibbons and American Institutions," in *Catholic World,* XLV (June, 1887), 330–337. The quoted passages occur on pages 331, 335–336.

full credit should be given to him for the accomplishment. It was Gibbons' reputation — not O'Connell's — that was risked and it was on the cardinal that the ultimate responsibility would rest.

Given the hostile attitude of many of the European governments of that time against the Church, and remembering as well the teaching and tradition of the Church on the question of union of Church and State, the sermon in Santa Maria in Trastevere was at once a striking reminder to governments such as those of Italy and France that the United States was not impeded in any way in its strength and prestige by allowing full liberty to the Church, while it was a bold affirmation of the favorable results which could accrue to the Church in a land where there was no union of Church and State. In Leo XIII's encyclical of November, 1885, which Gibbons took as the text of his speech, the Pope had defended the thesis of Catholicism as the one true religion but, as he said, the Church did not condemn "those rulers who for the sake of securing some great good or of hindering some great evil, allow patiently custom or usage to be a kind of sanction for each kind of religion having its place in the State."[49] The cardinal employed this passage of the encyclical, as well as Leo's statement that the right to rule was not bound up with any special form of government, to advance the American position and to detail for his audience the happy harmony that obtained in the United States between the civil and ecclesiastical powers. The generally favorable reception given to the sermon on Church and State probably emboldened Gibbons on the subject since in the years ahead he never changed his position and he returned to the theme more than once. For example, in an important article which he published in 1909 he was at pains to explain the Church's theological doctrine on the ideal union of Church and State. He made the distinction, however, that such an arrangement was not always the happiest solution in all countries since, as he expressed it, "while the union is ideally best, history assuredly does not prove that it is always practically best." Gibbons concluded his article with a paragraph that made his position quite clear. He wrote:

> American Catholics rejoice in our separation of Church and State;
> and I can conceive no combination of circumstances likely to arise

---

[49] John J. Wynne, S.J. (Ed.), *The Great Encyclical Letters of Pope Leo XIII* (New York, 1903), p. 127.

which should make a union desirable either to Church or State. We know the blessings of our present arrangement; it gives us liberty and binds together priests and people in a union better than that of Church and State. Other countries, other manners; we do not believe our system adapted to all conditions; we leave it to Church and State in other lands to solve their problems for their own best interests. For ourselves, we thank God we live in America, 'in this happy country of ours,' to quote Mr. Roosevelt, where 'religion and liberty are natural allies.'[50]

Reminiscing on the subject of the Roman sermon of 1887 a quarter of a century later the cardinal remarked to Archbishop Ireland,

But times have changed since I commended that policy (with your cordial adhesion) in Rome in 1887. Those who were then opposed to us, were afterwards eager to join our band wagon, as experience has taught them that it is the only sound policy, & the sooner the Xtian nations adopt it, the better it will be for the Church, & for the invigorating of its members.[51]

Following the installation ceremonies at Santa Maria in Trastevere Cardinal Gibbons was the guest of honor at a number of social functions in Rome during the remaining weeks of his stay in the Eternal City. At last his official business with the Holy See was concluded and on April 18 he left Rome for visits to Florence and Turin on his way to France. A large delegation of friends accompanied the cardinal to the station on his departure. When O'Connell saw the Pope some weeks later Leo XIII remarked, "So the Cardinal is gone. Why didn't you hold him?" To the question O'Connell replied that Gibbons' health was beginning to show the strain.[52] In Paris he was the guest of the Sulpicians at their mother house whence he made a number of short trips to points of interest such as Orléans and

---

[50] "The Church and the Republic," *North American Review*, CLXXXIX (March, 1909), 336. Later statements of the same theme may be found in Gibbons' sermon, "Will the American Republic Endure?" which was preached in the cathedral of Baltimore on November 3, 1912, and was printed in *A Retrospect of Fifty Years*, II, 212–213; cf. likewise a sermon of December 7, 1913, on "Civil and Religious Liberty" delivered in the same cathedral and printed in excerpts by Will, *op. cit.*, I, 318–319.

[51] AASP, Gibbons to Ireland, Baltimore, December 25, 1912 (Private), copy. The writer is indebted to the kindness of Patrick H. Ahern for all the copies of Gibbons' letters in this archives.

[52] 82-Q-10, O'Connell to Gibbons, Rome, May 18, 1887.

Rheims.[53] After a few days in Belgium and the Netherlands in mid-May the cardinal and Father Donahue crossed to England where they visited Cardinal Manning, Bishop Vaughan of Salford, and the missionary seminary of the Mill Hill Fathers. After some days in Ireland Gibbons sailed on the *Umbria* for New York on May 29.[54]

For some weeks previous to his arrival in the United States the cardinal's friends in Baltimore had been making plans for a public reception in his honor when he would reach home. Plans for the home-coming were in the charge of Father John Foley who consulted frequently with Abbé Magnien, president of St. Mary's Seminary. The outline of events was made out and published in the Baltimore *Sun* of May 14. Magnien informed the cardinal that the public demonstration would be held as closely as possible to a canonical character with only the Catholic societies taking official part. This had been determined on, he remarked, so that "all partisan interpretation will be prevented." The Sulpician superior told Gibbons that the laboring men in both New York and Baltimore were anxious to join the demonstration in his favor out of gratitude for what he had done in their behalf while at Rome in his memorial on the Knights of Labor. Since Foley and Magnien feared "a wrong interpretation" being put on the participation of the workers in their status as members of the unions, these men would be given a chance to join the demonstration under another guise so they could show their gratitude for what Magnien termed, "the forcible and truly eloquent way in which you defended their cause in Rome. . . ."[55] The severe tension existing just at the time in New York over the Henry George-Edward McGlynn difficulties with Archbishop Corrigan prompted Foley to warn Gibbons against allowing any demonstration in that city on his arrival. He told the cardinal that in all their plans they had been at pains to exclude anything that might suggest the appearance "of a partisan, political or class nature."[56]

The preparations made by Foley met with the approval of

---

[53] The Roman correspondent in the *Catholic Mirror* of May 7, 1887, described Gibbons' last days in the Eternal City and said everyone was sorry to see him leave.

[54] *Ibid.*, June 4, 1887.

[55] 82-Q-2, Magnien to Gibbons, Baltimore, May 14, 1887.

[56] 82-Q-3, Foley to Gibbons, Baltimore, May 15, 1887.

Gibbons and he cabled that on his arrival in New York he would go directly to Corrigan's residence.[57] The strain of the busy months in Rome and the traveling in Europe apparently did not tell on the cardinal since Corrigan remarked to Elder shortly after Gibbons landed, "He is very well, and in excellent spirits."[58] After a day or two in New York as the guest of Archbishop Corrigan the cardinal and his party, which included Bishop John Moore of St. Augustine, left for Baltimore on the morning of June 7.[59] They were greeted there by an immense throng at the station headed by the official committee of welcome where Mayor James Hodges and Charles J. Bonaparte, prominent Catholic lawyer, made the speeches of welcome to the cardinal. The Catholic societies of the archdiocese then formed in line and marched to the cathedral where Monsignor McColgan, the vicar-general, was the spokesman to greet Gibbons. The cardinal in reply expressed his gratitude to everyone for their enthusiastic welcome home to him, and speaking of the sentiments which had been expressed to him by various groups, he said, "They will bind me still more strongly, if that is possible, to my fellow-citizens, and to this city of Baltimore, where I was born, where Providence has cast my lot, and where I hope to die."[60]

The week after his return home Gibbons wrote a letter to Pope Leo XIII in which he described for the Pontiff his home-coming to Baltimore. He said that 8,000 men and boys of the Catholic societies had preceded him in the procession from the station to the cathedral and that it had been estimated that they marched through a crowd of 100,000 onlookers. Gibbons cited this as evidence of the interest which the American people took in religious matters and, too, in the Pope himself since these people saw in Gibbons not only one whom they wished to honor as a cardinal, but as the representative of the Holy Father.[61] The home-coming reception called forth more messages of congratulation from friends out over the country and Bishop O'Connor of Omaha cautioned the cardinal to take care of his health since,

[57] AANY, Foley to Corrigan, Baltimore, May 31, 1887.
[58] AAC, Corrigan to Elder, New York, June 5, 1887.
[59] Archives of the Diocese of St. Augustine, Moore to Edward A. Pace, New York, June 6, 1887. This item was copied for the writer through the kindness of Henry J. Browne.
[60] *Catholic Mirror*, June 11, 1887.
[61] 82-T-8, Gibbons to Leo XIII, Baltimore, June 13, 1887, copy in French.

as he said, "Cardinals are hard to raise, and even when in bloom, need careful nursing."[62] Father John Farley of New York, always a warm admirer of Gibbons', contrasted the outpouring of affection and loyalty on the part of Baltimore's clergy and laity with the dissension over McGlynn then prevalent in the Archdiocese of New York. He expressed the fear that many souls would be lost because of the unhappy trouble in the Church of New York and he concluded, "In the midst of it all Your Eminence is looked up to as the man of providence."[63]

The role which Gibbons had played while in Rome in the McGlynn case had caused Archbishop Corrigan to cool in his feelings toward the Cardinal of Baltimore. A few months after Gibbons' home-coming the papers carried a report that Archbishop Williams of Boston would be named a cardinal. Corrigan told his friend, Bishop McQuaid, that Williams was deserving of any honor Rome could give him, and he added that the report of a cardinal for Boston made him wonder if it was not intended to save the Roman purple from falling into discredit, "by conferring it on one whose head would not be turned by the compliment."[64] Smarting as he was under what he believed to be Gibbons' interference in the affairs of his archdiocese, Corrigan's early enthusiasm for the honors which had come to Baltimore was now pretty well dissipated. Fortunately, as time passed the archbishop's resentment wore off and cordial relations were once more established between Baltimore and New York.

Thus at the age of fifty-three James Gibbons had attained the highest rank in the American hierarchy, a position which he was to hold as the only cardinal in the United States for the next twenty-four years. Apart entirely from his winning personal manner with men of all religious faiths and social classes, it is not surprising that when a representative of the Catholic Church was sought for important public functions that attention should be directed to Cardinal Gibbons. And it was no time at all after his return from Rome before the new prince of the Church received an invitation of this kind which caused him some concern. In September, 1887, the United States government was scheduled to celebrate the centennial of the federal Constitution

---

[62] 82-S-8, O'Connor to Gibbons, Omaha, June 9, 1887.

[63] 82-U-3, Farley to Gibbons, New York, June 16, 1887.

[64] AABo. Transcript file, 1846–1914, Corrigan to McQuaid, New York, December 29, 1887, from ADRo.

at a three-day celebration in Philadelphia. Hampton L. Carson, secretary of the Constitutional Centennial Commission, wrote to Gibbons the first week in August to say that the commission had instructed him to request the kind offices of the cardinal, "for one of the services of prayer, to form part of the exercises on the 17th of September."[65] Gibbons answered immediately to express his gratitude for the courtesy of the invitation and to tell Mr. Carson that he would send a formal reply before the end of the month.[66]

From the outset it was clear that the cardinal wished to accept the invitation, but the novelty of his position as a member of the College of Cardinals and the sensitiveness of the Holy See about Catholic prelates participating with ministers of other faiths in public exercises having a religious significance, made Gibbons uneasy of mind. For that reason he sent off a hurried note to Archbishop Corrigan in which he explained the circumstances, offered what he believed to be precedents for his going to Philadelphia, and told the archbishop he would like to have his opinion regarding the propriety of his accepting the invitation.[67] The same day Gibbons wrote to Denis O'Connell telling him to inquire of the Holy See if there would be any objection to his offering a prayer at the celebration and asking O'Connell to cable the answer since there would be no time for a reply by mail. After advancing all the arguments in favor of his acceptance, he concluded with a postscript, "My presence on the occasion would, I am sure, give great joy to the Catholics of this country; they wd. rejoice to see our Church represented."[68] Archbishop Ryan was also interrogated for further details on the religious aspects of the celebration and for his opinion concerning the answer which Gibbons ought to give. Moreover, John Foley was sent to Philadelphia to confer with Ryan and Carson and then to report to the cardinal what he had been able to learn about the affair.

The results of these precautionary moves were, in the main, reassuring. Corrigan believed that the invitation could be accepted and that genuine good would come from Gibbons' presence at the celebration, providing that there be no prayers offered by ministers of other religions on the same occasion. The Archbishop of New York noted the natural disposition on the part of those planning the celebration to please all parties and the lack of understanding among non-Catholics of the position of the Catholic Church on these mixed gatherings. But Corrigan believed that with the exercise of prudent precaution a mistake could be avoided and in the end, as he put it, "only good results would follow from your attendance."[69] Ryan confessed he could learn little about the religious part of the program, but he assured Gibbons he need have no misgiving about his own feelings in the matter as the cardinal's position would render any unfavorable reaction on his part unreasonable, and his personal friendship for him would preclude such even independent of that position.[70] Foley told Gibbons after his trip to Philadelphia that he found Carson a first-rate gentleman and that when he had asked for an assurance that the cardinal would not be immediately preceded or followed by any other clergyman Carson had promptly told him that Gibbons would be entirely alone.[71]

It was not as easy for Denis O'Connell to give an answer. Upon receipt of Gibbons' request he had sought out Cardinal Simeoni, Prefect of the Propaganda, but the prefect felt the matter was so grave that he could not assume the responsibility for a decision and recommended that he go to Raffaele Cardinal Monaco, the head of the Holy Office. Monaco, too, showed alarm at the prospect of Gibbons engaging in what seemed to the Roman cardinals as *communicatio in divinis,* and all the persuasion which O'Connell was able to use would not bring them to change their minds. Finally Monaco agreed to ask Leo XIII, and the Pope assented to Gibbons participating on the opening day of the celebration with the precaution that on the subsequent days of the affair no Catholic clergy should assist at prayers offered by the ministers of other religions.[72] Although O'Connell's cablegram and letter had specified the first day at Philadelphia, the cardinal did nothing to change the plans of Carson and his committee who had set Gibbons' appearance for the last day when he was to give the closing prayer and pro-

---

[69] 83-F-4, Corrigan to Gibbons, New York, August 5, 1887.
[70] 83-F-5, Ryan to Gibbons, Philadelphia, August 6, 1887.
[71] 82-G-3, Foley to Gibbons, Baltimore, August 8, 1887.
[72] 83-H-3, O'Connell to Gibbons, Grottaferrata, August 19, 1887.

nounce the benediction.[73] Instead he sent off to Carson his
acceptance with an expression of thanks and said he would
cheerfully comply with the committee's wish in performing "the
sacred duty" assigned to him. To his letter of acceptance the
cardinal added a tribute to the Constitution itself which is worthy
of record. He said:

> I heartily rejoice in common with my fellow citizens in the forth-
> coming commemorative celebration. The Constitution of the United
> States is worthy of being written in letters of gold. It is a charter
> by which the liberties of sixty millions of people are secured, and
> by which, under Providence, the temporal happiness of countless
> millions yet unborn will be perpetuated.[74]

The celebration in Philadelphia in September, 1887, brought
a large gathering of prominent persons to the city for the three
days filled with festivities of all kinds. It was the type of ceremony, honoring the finest traditions in American history, which
Cardinal Gibbons thoroughly enjoyed. When it became known
that he would be present, he was asked if he would permit the
Catholic Club of Philadelphia to give a reception in his honor
on the evening of September 15. The cardinal agreed and the
event turned out to be brilliant beyond the anticipation of any
of those who had planned it. The distinguished guests who came
to honor the cardinal were headed by President Cleveland with
Secretary of State Bayard and Secretary of the Treasury Charles
S. Fairchild, ex-President Hayes, several justices of the Supreme
Court, a large number of senators and representatives from Congress, and the governors of seventeen states. Besides these dignitaries of the federal and state governments, Archbishop Ryan
and Bishops Keane of Richmond, Ryan of Buffalo, and O'Farrell
of Trenton were present at the reception to pay tribute to the
cardinal.[75] On September 17, the final day of the celebration,
John A. Kasson, president of the Constitutional Centennial Commission, was in the midst of his speech in Independence Square
when Cardinal Gibbons and his party arrived. After Gibbons
had made his entrance he extended his greetings to President and
Mrs. Cleveland and was then introduced to the Protestant Epis-

---

[73] 83-G-2, Carson to Gibbons, Philadelphia, August 8, 1887.
[74] 83-H-5, Gibbons to Carson, Baltimore, August 23, 1887, copy.
[75] Philadelphia *Public Ledger,* September 16, 1887; 83-N-15, Gibbons to Simeoni, Baltimore (n.d.), copy.

copal Bishop of New York, Henry C. Potter. The churchmen shook hands, "while fully fifteen thousand people looked on," as the New York *World* expressed it, "at the unusual sight of the meeting of the two American heads of the Romish and Anglican churches."[76] At the close of the program, in the words of the *World*

> Silence came over the assemblage as Cardinal Gibbons raised his hand and opened the words of the closing prayer. He, too, had been cheered until he found it necessary to step to the front and quiet the people with a bow.[77]

Gibbons chose as his prayer a combination of Archbishop Carroll's prayer for civil authorities, the Our Father, and a final general blessing.

The visit of Cardinal Gibbons to Philadelphia for the centennial of the Constitution, his first public function of that kind as a prince of the Church, proved to be a decided success. The courtesies extended to him were marked and the impression which Gibbons made upon men of all ranks of society and upon Catholic and non-Catholic alike was altogether happy. The officers of the centennial commission sent him their written thanks for the part he had taken in the program and asked him for a copy of the prayer he had delivered.[78] The cardinal described the affair in a letter to Cardinal Simeoni in which he told him about the reception at the Catholic Club with its distinguished roster of guests, the closing ceremonies where he had said the prayer, and the circumstances surrounding the presence of Bishop Potter and himself on the same platform. Gibbons said the entire program indicated the value placed on religion in public life in the United States, and he cited especially the speech of President Cleveland which, as reported in the Philadelphia *Public Ledger* of September 19, did, indeed, have a strong religious tone throughout. He explained that a Protestant minister, a grandson of one of the signers of the Constitution, was present at the closing meeting and spoke at the end of the session, although his appearance was accidental and not a part of the formal program. In honoring Gibbons, said the cardinal to Simeoni,

---

[76] New York *World*, September 18, 1887.
[77] *Ibid.*
[78] 83-N-7, Kasson, Little, and Carson to Gibbons, Philadelphia, September 21, 1887.

the government officials were honoring the Church and the Pope himself.[79]

One might very well ask why Gibbons took such unusual pains in ascertaining the mind of the Holy See in this matter before he accepted the invitation to participate in the ceremonies at Philadelphia. The novelty of the cardinalate, as has been mentioned, was, of course, a factor, but it could hardly have been the principal factor. Behind Gibbons' anxiety lay the well-known opposition of Rome toward the participation of Catholic churchmen in mixed religious gatherings. It was an attitude born of the teaching of the Church that Catholicism was the one true religion and to make it appear that it was only one among a group of equal religious bodies was, in the Catholic position, to run the danger of religious egalitarianism and ultimately of religious indifferentism. That, in brief, was and is the cause of the Holy See's sensitiveness in situations of this kind. To be sure, to the vast majority of non-Catholic Americans such an attitude might seem narrow and intolerant. Yet given the fundamental principle of Catholic belief on the question, the Church could not be expected to take any other view.

However, the certainty of the Catholic Church regarding its own uniquely true character as the Church of Christ was not a warrant for holding its faithful aloof from participation in the noble and inspiring celebration of their country's splendid heritage. Gibbons was patently sincere in the love and veneration he had for the United States and all that made it great. At the same time he realized the delicacy of his position at Philadelphia, and the misinterpretation that might easily be put upon it if the mixed religious character were too strongly emphasized. For that reason he took the necessary precautions to safeguard his appearance from being given a false interpretation in Rome. But as it happened the general effect was everything that could be desired. The cardinal represented the Church before the Philadelphia audiences in a manner which called forth the highest respect and esteem for his person as well as for the Church which he represented, and at the same time he demonstrated in the happiest light to his non-Catholic fellow citizens the moving loyalty he felt as an American for the Republic which had given him birth. The love of Gibbons for his Church and its doctrines

---

[79] 83-N-15, Gibbons to Simeoni, Baltimore (n.d.), copy in French.

was beyond question; his love for his country and its institutions never showed to better advantage than when he saluted the century of the American Constitution and joined so wholeheartedly in its commemoration.

Any misgivings that Gibbons might have entertained concerning the Roman reactions to his role in Philadelphia were quickly dissipated when word reached him from Monsignor O'Connell, Eduardo Soderini, and others. O'Connell told the cardinal, "They feel proud in Rome now of your presence at the Philadelphia feast, seeing how imposing it became."[80] Soderini said he could assure him that the incident had produced "an excellent impression not only at the Vatican but all over Italy." The Roman correspondent of the *Catholic Mirror* went on to say that, "Certainly to-day, there is not a Cardinal so well known in Europe as you," and he was glad of it because he believed it would be profitable for the increase of faith in the United States. He said Vladimir Cardinal Czacki and Placido Cardinal Schiaffino both congratulated Gibbons on the event and sent him their regards.[81] Simeoni a month later thanked Gibbons for his letter of description and told him of the lively satisfaction which he experienced in hearing of the religious sentiments of the American people expressed at Philadelphia; it led Simeoni to hope that events such as these would help to attain happy results for the welfare and prosperity of the Church in the United States.[82] The favorable reaction at the Holy See to Gibbons' participation in the centennial of the Constitution was an interesting contrast to the reluctance which some of the cardinals had shown when the subject was first mentioned to them.

Not long after his return to the United States the Cardinal of Baltimore took the lead among the American hierarchy in drawing up plans for their participation in the golden jubilee of Leo XIII's priesthood. The Pope would be a priest for fifty years on December 31, 1887, and since the hierarchies of England, Ireland, the Netherlands, and other countries had begun to take action, Gibbons decided to have a congratulatory letter composed, printed, and distributed among the American bishops for their signatures. He asked the metropolitans to have the signed

---

[80] 83-N-4, O'Connell to Gibbons, Grottaferrata, September 18, 1887.
[81] 83-P-1, Soderini to Gibbons, Rome, October 10, 1887.
[82] 83-R-7, Simeoni to Gibbons, Rome, November 15, 1887.

letters sent to him and he would forward them to Rome along with a "special copy beautifully engrossed."[83] The letter itself made mention of the Pope's encyclicals and the troubles he had experienced of late at the hands of the governments of Europe, and it ended with a word of gratitude for all the benefits with which the Pontiff had enriched the American Church, and the expression of a desire on the part of the hierarchy of the United States to associate themselves with their brethren of other lands in felicitating Leo XIII on the completion of a half century in the priesthood.[84]

As the date of the jubilee approached Gibbons received a letter from President Cleveland in which he stated that he presumed the cardinal would be sending his congratulations to the Pope. The President then added, "Remembering with proud gratitude and satisfaction the kind words you brought from the Holy Father upon your recent return from Rome, I should be very much pleased if you could without impropriety on your part, convey to him my congratulations and felicitations."[85] The President's suggestion prompted the cardinal to visit Cleveland and, in turn, to suggest that he send the Pope a copy of the Constitution as a souvenir of his jubilee. Cleveland was pleased with the idea and requested Gibbons to write for him the inscription which he thought ought to accompany the document.[86] Complying with the President's wish, the cardinal suggested the following wording: "Presented to His Holiness, Pope Leo XIII, as an expression of congratulation on the occasion of his sacerdotal Jubilee, with the profound regards of Grover Cleveland, President of the United States. Through the courtesy of Cardinal Gibbons."[87] The cardinal conveyed the President's good wishes to Leo XIII and told the Pontiff that Cleveland had been profoundly touched

---

[83] 83-F-1, Gibbons to the archbishops of the United States, Baltimore, August 4, 1887, copy.

[84] 83-F-3, Hierarchy of the United States to Leo XIII, n.d., printed copy.

[85] 83-S-1, Cleveland to Gibbons, Washington, November 17, 1887. William R. Grace, Mayor of New York City, told Gibbons that he had written Cleveland saying some recognition of the papal jubilee should be taken by the United States and that he had gone to Washington to speak to the President about the matter. Therefore, when Grace read of Cleveland's action in the papers he told the cardinal, "It is a source of real pride & gratification to me to feel that I may have contributed to the bringing about of the result" (83-V-10, Grace to Gibbons, New York, December 24, 1887).

[86] 83-S-10, Cleveland to Gibbons, Washington, November 24, 1887.

[87] 83-T-1, Gibbons to Cleveland, Baltimore, November 24, 1887, copy.

at the words which Leo had expressed through him to the President. He likewise informed the Pope that he would soon send a specially designed copy of the Constitution of the United States to him as an expression of the President's veneration for him on his jubilee.[88]

The American participation in Leo XIII's jubilee was keenly appreciated in Rome. O'Connell informed the cardinal that when he presented the letter of the hierarchy, along with the letter and offering of Gibbons and his clergy, the Pope "received them all with unmistakable signs of deep gratification," and said he would write the cardinal personally. Moreover, the news about the letter of President Cleveland on the jubilee gave Leo great pleasure and he told O'Connell that he could bring along a small delegation so that the President's letter would be presented with some solemnity.[89] The special copy of the Constitution was sent by Cleveland to Gibbons who gave it into the hands of John T. Morris, a reporter for the Baltimore *Sun,* to take to O'Connell in Rome.[90] The gift arrived safely and was presented at a special audience late in January, 1888. O'Connell told the cardinal, "I do not know of any presentation of the jubilee as cordial or genial and gratifying as this one, nor anyone that elicited more real, genuine feelings of pleasure on all sides." He said he could not exaggerate the gratification of Leo XIII at receiving Cleveland's gift, "nor the warm glow with which he spoke of the President and of our country." O'Connell was led to believe that by this incident "the Church and democracy stand nearer than ever together now the world over."[91] The episode was closed when Leo XIII wrote to Cardinal Gibbons and charged him with thanking President Cleveland for his letter and gift at the time of the jubilee. In this letter the Pope paid tribute to the American Constitution when he said:

> In fulfilling this duty We desire that you should assure the President of Our admiration for the Constitution of the United States, not only because it enables industrious and enterprising citizens to attain so high a degree of prosperity, but also because under its protection, your Catholic countrymen have enjoyed a liberty which has so confessedly promoted the astonishing growth of their religion in the

[88] 83-U-1, Gibbons to Leo XIII, Baltimore, December 1, 1887, copy in French.
[89] 83-U-4, O'Connell to Gibbons, Rome, December 4, 1887.
[90] Diary, January 12, 1888, p. 221.
[91] 84-B-6, O'Connell to Gibbons, Rome, January 31, 1888.

past and will, We trust, enable it in the future to be of the highest advantage to the civil order as well.[92]

In the circumstances it was not strange that President Cleveland should turn to Cardinal Gibbons to act as the intermediary of his message and gift to the Holy Father since he knew the cardinal personally and the latter's rank would naturally suggest him as the most fitting medium for the task. This episode, which came so early in Gibbons' life as a cardinal, was only the first of a series in which the Archbishop of Baltimore was to figure from that time to his death as the principal channel of communication between the United States government and the Holy See. The transmitting of the Cleveland jubilee greeting required, of course, the exercise of tact on the cardinal's part, yet the years ahead would bring duties of a far more delicate character to test the prudence and diplomacy of Gibbons as a successful intermediary between Rome and Washington.

But the sense of duty of the new prince of the Church was directed to the people as well as to presidents and popes. A year before the news was announced that Gibbons had been named a cardinal he lost, as previously mentioned, one of his suffragan bishops of the Province of Baltimore when William Gross, Bishop of Savannah, was appointed in February, 1885, as Archbishop of Oregon City. Gross and Gibbons had been born

---

[92] 84-B-11, Leo XIII to Gibbons, Rome, February 4, 1888. Across the top of this document Gibbons wrote in his own hand the following, "Copy. I left the original with the President at his special request. J. Card. Gibbons." Upon receipt of the letter from Leo XIII the cardinal asked the advice of Bishop Gilmour about publishing it, saying he would first ascertain the President's wishes in the matter (ADC, Gibbons to Gilmour, Baltimore, April 5, 1888). Meanwhile he had an interview with Cleveland who apparently gave permission for its publication after an interval in the Catholic papers. At any rate, Gibbons wired Gilmour on April 9 from Washington, "Publish the Pope's letter in Universe" (ADC). The cardinal then had the letter translated into German for a German Catholic paper and sent a copy to the *Catholic Mirror*. He instructed his secretary, however, to see that the copy did not leave the *Mirror's* office. But the Baltimore daily papers secured a copy and published it. President Cleveland was upset at the premature publication and when Gibbons tracked down the source through which the secular press got the letter he found the UP dispatch had come from Cleveland, Ohio. That discovered for him that it was through the *Catholic Universe* of Cleveland the news had become known, and this he explained to the President, saying Gilmour had wired for permission to publish which, as he told Cleveland, "I granted him only after my interview with you" (LC, Cleveland Papers, two letters from Gibbons to Cleveland, Baltimore, April 10, 1888).

three years apart in the same neighborhood in Baltimore and the latter's intimate association with Father Mark Gross, the bishop's brother, while Gibbons was a missionary bishop in North Carolina had drawn him more closely to the Bishop of Savannah. When, therefore, Gross was transferred to Oregon he asked his friend if he would confer the pallium on him at Portland. The idea of getting Gibbons to make the trip to the Far West was enthusiastically shared by John Ireland, Bishop of St. Paul. When Gross stopped over in St. Paul on his way to Oregon in May, 1885, Ireland gave him a glowing description of the accommodations he would make for the bishops to travel to the ceremony from his see city.[93]

Meanwhile Gross was content to delay fixing the date until the Archbishop of Baltimore could fit it in to his schedule. When the news of the red hat broke, it was decided to postpone the trip until after the ceremonies in Baltimore and Rome, but in the summer of 1887 the cardinal informed Archbishop Gross that he could be with him in Portland on Sunday, October 9. Gross was delighted at the news and wrote to say that his people felt "immensely big" over the honor which was in store for them. He said it would be the first time that a cardinal had visited the Pacific coast and Portland felt proud to be the host for the occasion. The Archdiocese of Oregon City was at the time still missionary territory, embracing the entire State of Oregon with over 96,000 square miles and having only thirty-two priests to administer the thirty churches and chapels scattered over wide distances. It was not surprising, then, that Gross should feel that Gibbons' visit would do good for the Church in that region, and that the Catholics who were few in number and without social standing would be heartened by his presence. As he expressed it, "The visit of Your Eminence will give a tone to Catholicity."[94]

When the news was announced that Cardinal Gibbons was going to Portland there soon reached him a number of invitations to receptions and banquets in various cities along the route of his journey. Plans were made for four principal stops between Baltimore and Portland and before long in each of these cities committees of welcome were busy preparing the program for the time that the cardinal would spend with them. He invited

---

[93] 79-K-16, Gross to Gibbons, St. Paul, May 17, 1887.
[94] 83-H-9, Gross to Gibbons, Portland, August 27, 1887.

Placide L. Chapelle, pastor of St. Matthew's in Washington, to accompany him, and they left Baltimore on September 26 for Chicago. In Chicago the following day a reception was held in Gibbons' honor at Cathedral Hall where Archbishop Feehan and several other speakers greeted their guest in a public welcome.[95] From Chicago he traveled on to Milwaukee where Archbishop Heiss headed a similar committee at a banquet and reception. Large throngs of people turned out in all these places to see Gibbons, and the secular press everywhere gave a wide coverage to the events staged in his honor.

News of the enthusiastic manner in which the Middle West was receiving Gibbons was, of course, sent back to Baltimore and it caused the editor of the *Catholic Mirror* to glow with pride at the attentions shown to Baltimore's cardinal. In a rather flambuoyant editorial in the issue of October 1 he wrote, "Reports from points *en route* indicate that the beloved head of the Church in America has been everywhere received with the strongest tokens of affectionate respect and esteem by all classes of citizens without regard to creed." While it was true that the reception given to Gibbons had been extremely cordial, the form which the Baltimore editor took to express himself caused irritation in some quarters. Bishop McQuaid had apparently seen the editorial and he told his friend, Archbishop Corrigan, "This everlasting talk about *head* of the *American church* annoys me. The good little man can't see that he is making himself ridiculous. He will go so far that somebody will have to call him to order."[96] There is little doubt that the cardinal was enjoying the experience to the fullest extent, but he could hardly be blamed for the incautious language employed by the editor of the Catholic paper in Baltimore.

The reception in St. Paul outdid Chicago and Milwaukee, and it was evident that the resourceful mind of John Ireland had

---

[95] When Gibbons arrived in Chicago he was met at the station by Feehan and a committee of welcome. The newspaper reporters had gathered, too, in the hope that they could get from him a statement on McGlynn of New York. However, the cardinal, "mildly but firmly refused to be interviewed on the subject of his alleged instrumentality in preventing the delivery to the Pope of the papers containing Dr. McGlynn's defense." Gibbons stated only that McGlynn's star was waning, that he was a good man, and that it was his [Gibbons'] wish that he might be brought to a realization of his indiscretions and ask the Pope's pardon (Chicago *Tribune*, September 28, 1887).

[96] AANY, McQuaid to Corrigan, Rochester, October 9, 1887.

seized upon the occasion to show off the cardinal of the United States to the best advantage and to the largest number of prominent citizens. Here, too, the familiar pattern of the banquet and the public reception was followed where many complimentary speeches were made. When one of the speakers in St. Paul alluded to Gibbons' role as an American citizen, the cardinal took up the point in his response and replied, "You were pleased to mention my pride in being an American citizen. It is the proudest earthly title I possess."[97] After the party left St. Paul the only other major stop was at Helena, Montana, where they were greeted by Bishop John B. Brondel on October 5. From Helena they traveled on to Portland where on Sunday, October 9, the ceremony of the conferring of the pallium on Gross was held in the Church of the Immaculate Conception. Governor Sylvester Pennoyer of Oregon led the large group of civil officials who attended the Mass, and Gibbons, at the request of Gross, preached the sermon.[98] After a few days in Portland the cardinal went on to San Francisco where he was the guest of Archbishop Riordan and then to Los Angeles where Lieutenant Governor Stephen M. White extended the greetings of southern California to the distinguished visitor. By the first week in November Gibbons had reached New Orleans, and at a reception for him in Grunewald Hall he had the pleasure of meeting again old Mr. Raymond in whose grocery store he had worked as a clerk over thirty years before. On the following Sunday Gibbons presided at the high Mass and preached at St. Joseph's Church, the parish wherein he had heard the sermon as a young man which had set his feet on the path to the priesthood.[99]

By the middle of November the cardinal had returned to

---

[97] *Catholic Mirror,* October 8, 1887.

[98] The Portland *Oregonian* for October 11, 1887, reported the civic reception at the Casino Opera House the evening before and carried the text of the speeches.

[99] New Orleans *Picayune,* November 6, 1887. The visit of Gibbons to New Orleans happened at the same time as the meeting of the suffragan bishops to choose a successor to Archbishop Leray. This circumstance was the subject of unfavorable comment on the part of someone to the Holy See. O'Connell told Gibbons, "There were not wanting charitable persons to call attention to the coincidence of your visit to New Orleans with the meeting of the suffragans, nor I suppose would you be surprised to hear that while the American West was receiving you with the honors of a triumph, there were others busy here trying to make you appear small indeed" (83-U-4, O'Connell to Gibbons, Rome, December 4, 1887).

Baltimore from his extended trip across the continent. This first visit of Gibbons to the Northwest and the Far West aroused a great deal of interest and enthusiasm among the Catholic people of those regions. It was their first glimpse of a prince of the Church, and their pride in playing host to a member of the College of Cardinals was heightened when they observed the generally friendly manner in which their non-Catholic friends and neighbors greeted the visitor. For Gibbons himself it was a bracing experience. It would have taken a dull spirit, indeed, not to respond to the outpouring of respect and affection shown by the large crowds that met him at all his stops. The cardinal was quick to sense the value of these demonstrations for the Church, and in the many speeches which he was called on to give he did not fail to take in the local scene and to capitalize on it for the welfare of the Catholic Church in that particular region. Gibbons had shown care in each of the cities he visited to pay courteous tribute to the local bishops, to the governors and mayors, as well as to make special calls at the leading Catholic institutions, and the effect of his gracious presence was not lost upon his hosts.

Cardinal Gibbons' trip across the continent in the first year of his cardinalate enabled him to become acquainted at first hand with the personnel and problems of the Church in those distant areas. Monsignor Bernard O'Reilly, the biographer of Pius IX and Leo XIII, was in Dublin that fall but he was following the cardinal's progress weekly through the accounts in the *Catholic Mirror*. O'Reilly was especially impressed by the speeches of Gibbons and Gross at the evening reception in Portland, and it was his opinion that, "These manifestations of the American mind and heart do immense good in Italy and France."[100] O'Connell from the Eternal City told the cardinal that his "march of triumph through the West" was written up in the *Moniteur de Rome* and that a good impression had been created by it. As O'Connell put it, "The Church in America had never before such an ovation."[101] Although the reactions of O'Reilly and O'Connell were probably written in pardonable exaggeration, it was surely true that the western trip of the cardinal did call forth an unusual manifestation of interest on the part of Americans of all classes and creeds. The ranking dignitary of the Catholic Church

---

[100] 83-S-5, O'Reilly to Gibbons, Dublin, November 18, 1887.
[101] 83-S-11, O'Connell to Gibbons, Rome, November 23, 1887.

in the United States had now been seen and heard in almost all sections of the country and the experience was one which helped to fit him for the larger role which he was destined to play as the acknowledged leader of American Catholicism in the years that lay ahead.

The commanding position of Cardinal Gibbons by 1887 brought to him, as was to be expected, repeated requests to give his judgment on public questions. In the fall of this year he published one of the first of a large number of articles in Amercan secular journals on issues of general interest to the American public. In the *North American Review* for October, 1887, Gibbons had an article in which he set down what he believed to be the outstanding defects in the political and social life of the United States. He maintained that the dangers which threatened American civilization, in his judgment, could be traced for the most part to the family. Under this heading he made some severe strictures on Mormonism and the growing prevalence of divorce. The desecration of the Christian Sabbath, fraudulent use of the ballot, an insatiable greed for gain, the dilatory character of administering justice in the courts, and the co-existence of colossal wealth and abject poverty with the extravagance of the rich, all met his criticism and condemnation. Another major defect Gibbons saw in the United States was what he termed "an imperfect and vicious system of education, which undermines the religion of our youth." He emphasized especially the dangers inherent in a system of education conducted without reference to God and devoid of a religious motivation, and as a remedy for this he suggested that the denominational plan which then obtained in Canada might well be applied to the public schools of the United States.[102] No one who knew anything about Cardinal Gibbons could question his patriotism or loyalty to his country, and while this sentiment was always one of the distinguishing characteristics of the man, the article in the *North American Review* was proof for the fact that Gibbons' patriotism did not blind him to the dangers he perceived in American public life. America's new cardinal loved his country, but not to the extent of abdicating his position as a guardian and leader in the realm of morals when he felt his voice should be raised in warning to those whom he might expect would heed his advice.

---

[102] "Some Defects in Our Political and Social Institutions," *North American Review*, CXLV (October, 1887), 345–354.

CHAPTER IX

Nationalities in Conflict

BY THE time Cardinal Gibbons received his red hat in March, 1887, the Catholic Church of the United States had been experiencing for some years the throes of what was, perhaps, the most troublesome period in its history. While it would be an oversimplification to attribute the many vexing problems of the last two decades of the nineteenth century solely to the increase in Catholic foreign immigration, it would be true to say that it lay at the root of some of these difficulties and that it definitely aggravated others. When it is remembered that during the 1880's immigration accounted for an increase of 604,000 to the American Church and that in the decade of the 1890's' this source was responsible for a further increase of 1,250,000 foreigners to the Catholic population,[1] it will be readily seen how grave a responsibility was thus placed on the American hierarchy to provide religious care for the immigrants, many of whom did not even speak English.

While all of these foreign-born Catholics shared a common religious faith their traits of similarity often ended there. From the late 1840's when the volume of Catholic immigration to the United States became really heavy it was the Irish and Germans who predominated among the newcomers. The Irish, of course, possessed an advantage over the Germans from the outset in the fact that English was their mother tongue. It enabled them to become assimilated with the native population much faster than the Germans, and it probably was accountable for the fact that more Irish priests than Germans were selected for the episcopacy at a time when native-born American clergy were still few in numbers. In the years before the Civil War the intensely anti-Catholic nativist movements had a tendency to draw all Catholics

---

[1] Shaughnessy, *Has the Immigrant Kept the Faith?*, pp. 161, 166.

of the United States together in self-defense regardless of their national origins. But in the second half of the century with nativist sentiment relatively quiet, the growing prosperity and constantly increasing numbers of the various Catholic foreign-born groups contributed to an added sense of strength with less dependence upon one another. Although it is true that the years after 1880 witnessed the coming of thousands of Catholic Poles, Italians, Bohemians, and other eastern European peoples — who from time to time were the cause of friction with the older Catholic nationalities in the country — the leadership of the American Church remained clearly with those of Irish and German extraction and it was between these two groups that the principal trouble arose.

From the very beginning of their residence in the United States the Catholic Germans held tenaciously to their mother tongue, whether it was in the rural areas such as northern Ohio where they formed solidly Catholic communities that were models of thrift and exemplary living, or in the crowded neighborhoods of the cities on the eastern seaboard and in the great German centers of the Middle West such as Cincinnati, St. Louis, and Milwaukee. Wherever they settled in any numbers the familiar pattern of church, parish school, parish clubs and societies, and the German language newspaper soon appeared. Confronted as they often were by hostile forces which resented their foreignism and their religion, the German Catholics quite naturally clung all the more closely to their German priests, schools, and press as the best media through which to preserve their faith. No one with even a passing knowledge of these German-American parish units would deny that they made a magnificent contribution to the development of the Catholic Church in the United States, nor could the fair-minded fail to appreciate the lofty motives that lay behind the insistence of many of the German Catholics on the preservation of their native language in the different aspects of their parochial life.

But regardless of the undoubted merit of many features of the life of these Catholic Germans, their adherence to the German language for church services, school instruction, and the press appeared to many non-German Catholics as an excessive fondness for old world customs, as well as a lack of appreciation for the language and customs of the country that had given them a haven and a better life. By the last quarter of the nineteenth century there was abroad in the United States a marked growth of national feeling which had the inevitable result of making all variations from the American pattern seem out of harmony with the national trend, and which by the 1880's, as one historian has expressed it, "was rushing at full torrent through all the channels of American thought and action."[2] In this kind of environment, of course, many American Catholics became more sensitive about their German coreligionists' holding to their native language, for with good reason did they remember that the charge of "foreignism" was one of the most constant refrains against Catholics in former times. It made little difference that some of the most vociferous among the Catholic critics of the Germans were themselves either born in or only one generation removed from Ireland. Their exclusive use of the English language gave them, or so they thought, at least the appearance of belonging, even though in the matter of time they might not possess any margin over their German brethren.

Added to the difference of language there were profound differences in temperament between the Catholics of German and Irish origin. As one authority has said the contrast in temperament between the Irish and Germans was so sharp that for several generations American vaudeville and variety stage audiences were entertained by exaggerated versions of the contrasting characteristics of the stage Irishman and the "Dutch" comedian.[3] To the phlegmatic German his mercurial Irish neighbor often appeared fickle and unstable, while the somewhat volatile Irishman viewed the more somber and plodding German as a respectable but generally dull companion. These differences, of course, showed up among the clergy as well as the laity and when the two groups were thrown together in the realm of church government the result frequently was friction and trouble. Apart from differences of language and temperament there were sore spots, such as the German parishes of the Archdiocese of St. Louis, of which we shall speak more in detail later, being held in a dependent relation to the so-called Irish parishes. Another contention of the opposing parties was the nationalist representa-

---

[2] Arthur Meier Schlesinger, *The Rise of the City, 1878–1898* (New York, 1933), p. 410.

[3] Carl Wittke, *We Who Built America. The Saga of the Immigrant* (New York, 1939), p. 187.

tion in the hierarchy. For example, in 1886 of the sixty-nine bishops in the United States the distribution according to nationalities, either born in a particular foreign country or of that extraction, was as follows: Irish, thirty-five; German (including Austrian and Swiss), fifteen; French, eleven; English, five; and Dutch, Scotch, and Spanish, one each. Many German Catholics felt with considerable justification that their numbers and strength in the American Church warranted a higher proportion of bishops than the over two to one advantage enjoyed by the Irish in 1886. Again the fiery advocacy of the Catholic temperance movement, by prelates of Irish blood such as Ireland and Keane, aroused little besides ridicule and resentment among the Germans who felt that they knew how to use liquor with moderation, something they believed the Irish had yet to learn.

With the German Catholics thus feeling aggrieved at their failure to win a higher proportion of posts in the hierarchy and to gain untrammeled control of their parish units in places like St. Louis and with the Irish showing little disposition to yield to these demands, it is not difficult to see how a situation of this kind led to mutual opposition in the many serious national questions that beset the Church in the late years of the nineteenth century. If only the growing differences between the Catholics of German and Irish extraction could have remained in the hands of moderates in both camps most of the trouble could have been avoided. But, unfortunately, a minority of extremists among the Irish were intent upon compelling the Germans to step into line with the increasing tempo of Americanization, and to accomplish their ends they did not scruple to resort on occasion to violent and abusive language which left behind it wounds that were long in healing. On the other hand, a minority of leaders among the Catholic Germans were themselves extremely untactful in the way in which they urged what they regarded as their rights in the matter of their parishes, and especially their parish schools. The result was that the great majority of both groups who deplored the bitterness and the damage being done to Catholic fraternal sentiment were powerless to check the extremists and to heal the breach before the storm had run its course.

In the early years of his life as a bishop Gibbons had experienced little or no worry on the score of foreign-born Catholics since in neither North Carolina nor Virginia was the immigration at all heavy and, in any case, exceedingly few of the immigrants who were found in those states in Gibbons' time were Catholics. Upon his entrance to Baltimore in 1877, however, the situation was somewhat different. Baltimore, with its population of 332,313 in 1880, was the sixth largest city in the United States, a position it held down to 1900 when it counted 508,957 people.[4] Since it was one of the principal ports of the Atlantic seaboard, it was not surprising to find that over 600,000 immigrants landed in Baltimore between 1870 and 1900, although "the overwhelming majority . . . did not tarry long but continued westward."[5] While most of the immigrants moved on after their entrance to the city, nonetheless, the foreign-born composed thirteen and one-half per cent of the total population in 1900 when they numbered 68,600. All through the last thirty years of the century the Germans were by far the most numerous of Baltimore's foreign-born residents, constituting in 1880 and again in 1890 approximately sixty per cent of the total. The Irish ranked second up until the closing years of the century when they were passed by the Russians, and the new immigration from eastern Europe reflected itself in Baltimore as elsewhere in the nation when in 1900 those born in the Austro-Hungarian Empire (including the Bohemians) had risen to over five and one-half per cent and those born in Poland to over four per cent of Baltimore's foreign-born.[6]

To be sure, not all these immigrants who settled in Baltimore in the late nineteenth century were Catholics, but considerable numbers of those coming from Germany, Austria-Hungary, Poland, and Italy were of that faith. One can see the evidences of this growth in the parishes of the city. In 1886, a key year in this discussion, there were in Baltimore five parishes for the Germans, one for the Poles, and one for the Bohemians, figures which had been increased by 1897 to six parishes for the Germans, two for the Poles, and one each for the Bohemians and Lithuanians. In Washington, the only other large city in the Archdiocese of Baltimore, there were in 1886 two parishes designated for the Germans which by 1897 had dropped to one. The only really numerous group of foreign-born Catholics in

---

4 *Sixteenth Census of the United States: 1940. Population*, I, 464.
5 Charles Hirschfeld, *Baltimore, 1870–1900: Studies in Social History*, p. 23.
6 *Ibid.*, table on page 24.

Baltimore in these years — aside from the Irish — were, therefore, the Germans who had five parishes out of a total of
twenty-eight in the city in 1886, to which they had added a sixth
by 1897.

The German Catholics of Baltimore had established a thriving
parochial life long before the advent of James Gibbons as archbishop. Their parishes, mainly under the direction of the Redemptorist Fathers, had shown steady growth, and since 1859
the German-speaking Catholics of the city had their own weekly
newspaper, the *Katholische Volkszeitung,* which kept them abreast
of the activities of their fellow countrymen in other parts of the
United States while giving them news of developments in the
fatherland. The German Catholic community of Baltimore gave
no cause for uneasiness to the archbishop and his relations with
both priests and people were of a friendly nature.

But if there was an absence of tension among the national
groups of Catholics in Baltimore, such was not the case elsewhere, and Gibbons was not Archbishop of Baltimore much
longer than six months when he was made keenly aware of the
fact. In early May of 1878 the archbishop received a lengthy
letter from Father George L. Willard, pastor of St. Joseph's
Church in Fond du Lac, Wisconsin, who laid before him what he
regarded as a serious threat to the welfare of the Church in the
Archdiocese of Milwaukee. Willard explained that he was a convert of American — rather than Irish — blood and that he spoke
the German language. These facts had prompted the German
priests to confide in him the plans discussed in their frequent
meetings, "the principal and ulterior object" of which was,
according to Willard, "to perpetuate a young Germany here."
He told Gibbons that one of their ambitions was to secure a
German successor in the See of Milwaukee to the aging Archbishop John M. Henni, and he set forth in an objective manner
his reasons for believing that a German successor to Henni would
have grave consequences for Catholicism in Wisconsin.[7] The
Willard letter was but the first of a series which reached Gibbons
on the Milwaukee coadjutorship during the ensuing weeks. Six
priests of Milwaukee joined in a petition to the Archbishop of
Baltimore asking him to exercise the influence which, they said,
belonged to him "by right and law." These men were confident

---

[7] 73-S-1, Willard to Gibbons, Fond du Lac, May 7, 1878.

that Gibbons' authority could put an end to the excessive nationalism in Wisconsin's Church which they regarded as not only un-Catholic but also un-American.[8]

Meanwhile Archbishop Henni had acted on his own to secure a coadjutor by submitting to the Prefect of Propaganda in Rome the names of Bishops Michael Heiss of La Crosse, Joseph Dwenger of Fort Wayne, and Francis X. Krautbauer of Green Bay. This *terna* of German names was sent on to Gibbons by Henni with the request that he forward to the Holy See his judgment on the three men selected by the Archbishop of Milwaukee.[9] Gibbons decided to consult the Archbishop of Boston before he wrote to Rome. He told Williams that while he wished to gratify Henni by recommending his selection, he felt the memorial of the Milwaukee priests was worthy of some consideration. At the time that he wrote to Williams Bishop Thomas Foley of Chicago was in Baltimore and Gibbons cited him as one who ought to be conversant with the situation in Milwaukee, and he added that Foley had spoken approvingly of the English-speaking priests' memorial. He further told Williams that Archbishop Wood of Philadelphia was strongly in favor of putting Dwenger's name first since he was thoroughly familiar with English. To this Gibbons added that, perhaps, Bishop Spalding of Peoria, who knew German well, might be placed second or third on the list.[10] The other American archbishops had, like Gibbons, received the *terna* and the protests from Milwaukee, and when he was consulted by the Archbishop of Baltimore, Wood of Philadelphia let it be known that he felt very strongly about the perpetuation of what he termed the *"germanising* process" in the Province of Milwaukee which, he believed, would be a calamity for the English-speaking Catholics of that region.[11] Williams, who confessed he had written to Rome before the protest of the priests had reached him, was not so explicit, contenting himself with advising Gibbons to put the case clearly before the Holy See so that someone would be appointed coadjutor who would be satisfactory to the Germans, but who

---

[8] 73-S-2, P. F. Pettit *et al.* to Gibbons, Milwaukee, May 8, 1878. Cf. also 73-S-13, H. F. Fairbanks to Gibbons, Whitewater, Wisconsin, May 23, 1878.

[9] 73-S-3, Henni to Gibbons, Milwaukee, May 10, 1878, in Latin.

[10] AABo, Gibbons to Williams, Baltimore, May 16, 1878.

[11] 73-S-15, Wood to Gibbons, Philadelphia, May 25, 1878.

would likewise, as he said, "take an interest in others not German."[12]

Archbishop Henni's action in selecting names for the co-adjutor without reference to his suffragans caused Rome to instruct him to consult the bishops before the Holy See would seriously consider the question. In the early autumn of 1878 the meeting was held in Milwaukee and the same Father Willard, who had written Gibbons the previous spring, promptly informed him that the name of Dwenger had been dropped from the list and Spalding's name put in its place. He added, "This would be a selection giving universal satisfaction here."[13] Within a day or two Archbishop Gibbons received a detailed account of the meeting of the bishops in Milwaukee from Thomas Grace, Bishop of St. Paul, and the only non-German bishop in the Province of Milwaukee. He told the archbishop that it was only "with the utmost difficulty" that he succeeded in obtaining the consent of his colleagues to have the name of Spalding placed on the *terna*.[14] Another petition from four Milwaukee priests followed within two weeks in which they earnestly begged Gibbons to use his influence to have Spalding chosen, since in their opinion, "he would be just the man for the place."[15]

Keeping in mind the strong American sentiments of the Archbishop of Baltimore, it is not difficult to imagine how disturbed he must have been by these unmistakable signs of nationalist antagonism in the Church of Wisconsin. His sentiments were probably re-enforced by the petitions of the priests of Milwaukee, the judgment of Foley of Chicago, and the cogent reasoning of Grace of St. Paul. The combined evidence was sufficient for Gibbons to cast his vote for the American. He noted in his diary that he had written to Cardinal Simeoni in regard to the Milwaukee *terna* and, he added, "I have recommended the Bp. of Peoria as the most worthy in my estimation."[16] Unfortunately for those who desired John Lancaster Spalding in Milwaukee, he

---

[12] 73-T-4, Williams to Gibbons, Boston, June 7, 1878.

[13] 73-W-2, Willard to Gibbons, St. Francis, Wisconsin, September 7, 1878.

[14] 73-W-3, Grace to Gibbons, St. Paul, September 8, 1878.

[15] 73-W-10, Martin Kundig *et al.* to Gibbons, Milwaukee, September 23, 1878. Cf. also 73-W-11, Thomas Fagan to Gibbons, St. Francis, September 25, 1878, and 74-F-5, E. J. Fitzpatrick to Gibbons, St. Francis, December 23, 1878, for evidences of disagreement among the professors of St. Francis Seminary on the coadjutor question and their efforts to influence Gibbons' action.

[16] Diary, September 28, 1878, p. 118.

refused to be considered for the coadjutorship, as was likewise true of Krautbauer of Green Bay. When a year later Henni submitted a new list consisting of Heiss; Father Kilian C. Flasch, rector of St. Francis Seminary, Milwaukee; and Bishop James O'Connor of Omaha in that order Gibbons stated that he had recommended the names to the Holy See, but that he had put O'Connor in second place.[17] Rome took its time in making the appointment but when it finally came in the spring of 1880 the first choice of Henni, Michael Heiss, Bishop of La Crosse, was chosen and thus one of the earliest contests of this kind between the German element and their coreligionists resulted in a victory for the Germans.

The experience of Archbishop Gibbons in the case of the Milwaukee coadjutorship doubtless quickened his interest in the matter of Catholic immigrants of all nationalities. Some time before he submitted to the Holy See his judgment on the second *terna* for Milwaukee, Gibbons requested Father Joseph L. Andreis, an Italian priest stationed at St. Vincent's Church in Baltimore, to make a survey of the Italians in the city. Andreis reported that there were then only about 500 Italians in Baltimore who were in permanent residence, although numerous Italian seamen were coming and going as crew members of the many Italian ships in the port. The priest recommended to the archbishop that a church for the Italians be opened, stating that he believed that this would be more effective than the Mass and special instruction for them each Sunday at St. Vincent's.[18] Andreis' suggestion was acted upon without much delay, and on September 18, 1881, Gibbons dedicated the new St. Leo's Church at Stiles and Exeter Streets for the Italians.

As time passed the number of Italian immigrants entering the United States greatly increased and with it the Holy See showed a growing concern for their spiritual welfare in the new world. When the American archbishops and their representatives were in Rome in the fall of 1883 for the conferences preparatory to the Third Plenary Council, it had been one of the subjects which the cardinals of the Propaganda proposed for their discussion. Gibbons at that time had approved the setting up of committees in the United States for the Italian immigrants. He went further

---

[17] *Ibid.,* October 25, 1879, p. 129.
[18] 74-R-4, Andreis to Gibbons, Baltimore, September 11, 1879.

and suggested that corresponding committees be established in Italy, that Italian priests be secured to minister to their country-men in the United States, and he added that in his judgment it would be highly expedient to have committees for other nation-alities who were then emigrating in large numbers.[19] Gibbons' colleagues at the Roman conferences supported him unanimously in his suggestion of appointing groups who would interest them-selves in behalf of the immigrants, and the St. Raphael Society for German immigrants was singled out for special praise as a model to be followed.[20]

Archbishop Gibbons was not allowed to forget the subject, for he had hardly reached home when Simeoni wrote him an urgent plea that he give the plight of the immigrants his close attention and suggest any and all means to remedy it.[21] Although the arch-bishop replied a month later, we have no way of knowing what practical suggestions he advanced and his brief diary entry merely noted that he would refer Simeoni's letter to the coming council.[22] When Archbishop Elder of Cincinnati complained to Gibbons that he thought the chapter of the schema for the council dealing with Italian immigrants should be referred to an arch-bishop who had more experience than himself, the Archbishop of Baltimore stated it was then too late to make a change, and, besides, he believed very little needed to be said on the subject.[23] Actually, the chapter on Italian immigrants raised so many dif-ferences of opinion in the council that it was finally dropped entirely, and Gibbons, in his role as apostolic delegate, appointed a committee which rewrote the chapter with no special reference to the Italians. The new version contained words of praise for

---

[19] *Relatio collationum,* pp. 27–28.

[20] Letterbook, Gibbons to Elder, Baltimore, May 8, 1884, pp. 77–78. On this entire question, insofar as it relates to the Italians, cf. Henry J. Browne, "The 'Italian Problem' in the Catholic Church of the United States, 1880–1900," *Historical Records and Studies,* XXV (1946), 46–72.

[21] 77-O-2, Simeoni to Gibbons, Rome, March 6, 1884.

[22] Diary, April 4, 1884, p. 175. The copy of Gibbons' letter of this date to Simeoni failed to make an impression in his Letterbook, p. 48. In any case, Simeoni found Gibbons' reflections on the subject satisfactory and some weeks later he stated that since the conditions among the Italian immigrants were worse than those of other immigrant groups they were, therefore, in greater need of assistance; he thought the coming council offered a good opportunity to do something for them (77-Y-8, Simeoni to Gibbons, Rome, April 29, 1884).

[23] 78-B-4, Elder to Gibbons, Cincinnati, May 6, 1884; Letterbook, Gibbons to Elder, Baltimore, May 8, 1884, pp. 77–78.

the German and Irish immigrant societies, as also an emphasis on the need for priests in the seaboard cities to care for the newcomers, the necessity of special protection for women immigrants, and the desirability of directing the foreign-born from the cities to the rural areas.[24]

It had been decided in the council that the apostolic delegate should write a letter to the Holy See in the name of all the American bishops concerning the conditions obtaining among the Italians who had come to the United States in recent years. Gibbons entrusted the drafting of the letter to Bishop Thomas A. Becker of Wilmington, one of his suffragans, who informed the archbishop that he had been supplied with statistics on the Italians in New York and elsewhere by Archbishop Corrigan. Showing his strong feeling on the subject, Becker told Gibbons:

> My letter shall be carefully worded, yet quite as firmly as usual. It is a very delicate matter to tell the Sovereign Pontiff how utterly faithless the specimens of his country coming here really are. Ignorance of their religion and a depth of vice little known to us yet, are the prominent characteristics. The fault lies far higher up than the poor people. The clergy are sadly remiss in their duty.[25]

The letter, which was addressed to Cardinal Simeoni, spoke frankly of the Italians' neglect of Mass, the sacraments, and the support of their parish priests once they arrived in the United States. Gibbons, speaking in the name of his colleagues, urged that the bishops of Italy bestir themselves to see that the immigrants were provided with religious instruction before they left their native land since the number of priests speaking Italian in this country was altogether inadequate to care for their people reaching these shores. The letter further urged the appointment of priests both in Italy and the United States for this special task. The tragic squalor of many of these people caught in the meshes of the *padrone* system was described for Simeoni, and the control of certain Italian societies in New York by apostate priests was adduced as further evidence of the need of remedial action. Gibbons' letter closed with the statement, "These things briefly are what is to be said in

---

[24] *Acta et decreta concilii plenarii Baltimorensis tertii* (Baltimore, 1886), pp. 130–132.
[25] 78-V-1, Becker to Gibbons, Wilmington, December 17, 1884.

the matter, and we have thought them significant to Your Eminence."[26] While the statements made in the letter were true, nothing was said of the fact that the Italian immigrants to the United States often met an unfriendly reception from some of their fellow Catholics of other nationalities, and for this reason were not drawn toward the Church. At any rate, for the time being the question of the Italians rested there.

But the problem of the Germans had by this time become even more urgent. In August, 1883, there arrived in the United States Peter Paul Cahensly, the secretary-general of the St. Raphael's Society for the Care of German Catholic Emigrants. Cahensly spent several months visiting the German Catholic centers and conferring with both priests and lay leaders, but the available records do not reveal what was discussed in these conferences or what recommendations, if any, the visitor might possibly have made. There is no evidence that there was any connection between Cahensly's visit and what followed, but, at any rate, about two months after his departure from St. Louis a German Catholic monthly journal of that city, the *Pastoral-Blatt,* published an article called "Clerical Know-Nothingism in the Catholic Church of the United States," in which it criticized the system of maintaining a number of German Catholic churches in St. Louis under the jurisdiction of English-speaking parishes. This system of succursal churches or chapels of ease had been introduced in St. Louis in 1845 by Bishop Peter Richard Kenrick with a view of serving exclusively the Germans in large parishes like St. Vincent, St. Patrick, and St. Francis Xavier. While the German Catholics could fulfill all their religious duties in such succursal churches as that of Our Lady of Victory, they were still within the general parish boundaries of St. Louis Cathedral and their priest did not enjoy the full privileges which were accorded to other pastors. The system led, as one might expect, to friction and the *Pastoral-Blatt* condemned the practice as discrimination and called for a grant of full

---

[26] 79-B-2, Gibbons and Becker to Simeoni, Wilmington, Idibus Januariis [*sic*], 1885, Latin copy. Ten years later when Gibbons went to Rome the New York *Tribune* of June 14, 1895, reported that he was going to make an effort to get more Italian priests to take care of the Italian immigrants in the United States. The *Tribune* said, "Cardinal Gibbons will make a strong representation on the subject to the Roman officials." Cited in Browne, *op. cit.,* p. 72. This is the only evidence the writer has found for this Gibbons effort of 1895 in behalf of the Italians.

autonomy to these German congregations.[27] The question was aired in both the German- and English-speaking Catholic journals,[28] and by the summer of 1884 the German priests of St. Louis had framed a protest to the Holy See against their churches being continued in a dependent relation to the English-speaking parishes.

The attention of Archbishop Gibbons was drawn to the situation in St. Louis by a letter from Cardinal Simeoni in which the latter transmitted the views of the St. Louis priests and suggested the matter be made a subject for discussion at the Third Plenary Council.[29] Father Henry Muehlsiepen, Vicar-General of the Archdiocese of St. Louis for the German, Bohemian, and Polish Catholics, likewise informed Gibbons of the petition which had been sent to Rome. He stated he hoped it would not be regarded as "any kind of accusation," and he was at pains to tell Gibbons of the satisfaction of the German element in St. Louis with Archbishop Kenrick. Muehlsiepen, too, hoped that the question might be settled at the council.[30] Archbishop Ryan of Philadelphia, who had only recently terminated a residence of many years in St. Louis, explained to Gibbons the background to the situation there. He stated that while it was true the German churches were regarded as succursal, Archbishop Kenrick had said that he wished all German Catholics to attend their own churches and receive the sacraments from their own priests, "so that *practically* they

---

[27] *Pastoral-Blatt* (November, 1883), 121–131. On the German Catholics in the United States, cf. the two articles of John J. Meng, "Cahenslyism: The First Stage, 1883–1891," and "Cahenslyism: The Second Chapter, 1891–1910," *Catholic Historical Review*, XXXI (January, 1946), 389–413; XXXII (October, 1946), 302–340, also John Rothensteiner, *History of the Archdiocese of St. Louis* (St. Louis, 1928), I, 834–835; II, 562–568. The entire question has been investigated by Colman J. Barry, O.S.B., under the title of *German Nationality and American Catholicism* (to be published, Milwaukee: 1953). Father Barry's work is a definitive treatment of the subject from both the German and American points of view.

[28] Cf. "Sohin wir gehen und was uns noth thut, oder Unsere Befürchtungen und Hoffnungen," *Pastoral-Blatt* (April, 1884), 37–49; John Gilmary Shea, "Converts — Their Influence and Work in This Country," *American Catholic Quarterly Review*, VIII (July, 1883), 509–529.

[29] 78-Q-4, Simeoni to Gibbons, Rome, October 2, 1884. Gibbons informed Corrigan of the arrival of the petition of the St. Louis priests forwarded by Simeoni, and he told the New York prelate, "I consider the complaint at least exaggerated" (AANY, Gibbons to Corrigan, Baltimore, October 21, 1884).

[30] 78-R-18, Muehlsiepen to Gibbons, St. Louis, October 20, 1884.

were parish churches." Nonetheless, Ryan likewise felt the council might help to clarify matters and to prevent what he termed "collisions in the future."[31]

In his reply to Simeoni's letter the Archbishop of Baltimore deplored the publicity which this question had received in the German language newspapers. It would have been better, said Gibbons, to have the Propaganda informed and the matter then referred to the bishops in council so that a remedy might be applied without exciting odium and spite. He stated that from what he knew of his own and other dioceses he strongly feared that quarrels of this kind in public would exaggerate the situation and make a peaceful settlement all the more difficult. Gibbons promised Simeoni that as soon as Kenrick would arrive in Baltimore for the council he would confer with him on the best means to be pursued and that he would make it his business, insofar as he was able, to have the council provide everything by which the Germans and Catholics of other nationalities would be treated justly and have their desires satisfied.[32] Actually during the council the question of independent parishes for the Germans did not arise, nor did the bishops of German nationality make any effort to introduce it. About ten days before the close of the council Gibbons wrote to Simeoni again and at this time he told him that he had discussed the German protest from St. Louis with Archbishop Kenrick and other prelates to whom the problem pertained and that he found these bishops were aware of the situation and would decide on what was best for religion.[33]

The agitation aroused on the German question in the Church of the United States prompted two of the prelates who had been sent to Rome to win approval of the council's decrees, to prepare a memorial on the subject for the Propaganda during their stay in the Eternal City. Bishop John Moore informed Gibbons that he and Gilmour were drawing up a document in which they intended to show the effort being made, as it was

---

[31] 78-S-3, Ryan to Gibbons, Philadelphia, October 22, 1884.

[32] Letterbook, Gibbons to Simeoni, October 23, 1884, pp. 127–129. Gibbons was then sorely pressed for time with the opening of the council only two weeks away. He answered Vicar-General Muehlsiepen but confined himself to saying he was glad that the former had spoken "in such high terms" of Archbishop Kenrick and if Muehlsiepen should stop in Baltimore he would be pleased to see him (*ibid.*, October 24, 1884, p. 130).

[33] *Ibid.*, Gibbons to Simeoni, Baltimore, November 27, 1884, p. 137.

said, to "germanize the Church," and to register a complaint at the "undue influence" which the Germans in the United States were permitted to exercise at the Propaganda in the appointment of bishops and similar questions.[34] The Gilmour-Moore memorial was at length submitted to the Propaganda under date of October 2, 1885, in which the German Catholics were charged with egotism in resisting the request that they attend church with other nationalities. This attitude, the bishops maintained, threatened to lead to a conflict between the German and Irish Catholics in the United States and if it were not stopped there would ensue scandal to religion and injury to souls. In the opinion of Gilmour and Moore the German-Americans were responsible for encouraging a spirit of nationalism in the American Church which would do untold harm if not checked.[35]

Although Archbishop Gibbons might take satisfaction in the generally favorable conditions obtaining among the German Catholics of his archdiocese, he was compelled to direct his efforts to the settlement of the question in less peaceful quarters. Not only did Gilmour and Moore keep him closely informed of their moves in Rome, but Cardinal Simeoni, probably confused by the contradictory reports reaching him, continued to seek his advice. Simeoni told him about two months after the Gilmour-Moore memorial that he had received a letter from a certain bishop in the United States who asked if he might establish more than one parish in the same area to care for persons of a foreign nationality, and second, whether a bishop would offend against the laws of the Church if he demanded that the sons and daughters of families of a particular parish — and who were still living in their parents' home —

---

[34] 79-O-11, Moore to Gibbons, Rome, July 15, 1885. The differences that arose in Rome between Gilmour and Moore and their colleague, Dwenger of Fort Wayne, probably had an influence on their attitude. Moore told Gibbons that before he was in Rome two weeks he had said Dwenger was working to become Archbishop of St. Louis, and he added, "I am now convinced of it more than ever that should be prevented."

[35] *Memoriale sulla questione dei Tedeschi nella chiesa di America (Denkschrift über die deutsche Frage in der Kirche Amerikas)* (n.p., 1885). The Italian and German texts appear on facing pages. Ella Edes wrote Gibbons from Rome on October 24, 1885 (79-T-20) to say she was glad to learn that he had approved of her article against the Germans and in defense of the Irish as it appeared in the *Osservatore Romano* of November 28, 1884. She stated that the editors had accepted it "a little unwillingly, but I *insisted. . . .*"

remain restricted to the same parish until they had left home
or contracted marriage. Before he would answer the bishop
Cardinal Simeoni asked Gibbons if he would please consider
these questions "with all possible prudence, wisdom, and
experience," and let the Propaganda have the benefit of
his judgment.[36]

In his reply Gibbons stated that he could answer in the
affirmative generally to the first question since in his own archdiocese and in other dioceses there already existed such separate
parishes for language groups in the same neighborhood. If
parishes of this kind did not exist it would be difficult to care
for the foreign-born and there would be danger of their neglect.
The second question, however, was more difficult to answer
since the children of immigrants showed a tendency to take up
English and to attend English-speaking parishes. Gibbons cited
the practice in Baltimore where, he said, the children of immigrant parents were free to be baptized or married in either a
German or an English parish when one or the other parent
was German, but it was not possible to bind them strictly in
the matter. He thought that if both parents of a child were
Germans the child should be baptized in a German church,
but if later they wanted their child to go to an English-speaking
Catholic school they should not be prohibited from sending
it there.[37]

The anxiety experienced by the Archbishop of Baltimore
concerning the care of the foreign-born in the Church was not
limited by his desire for their proper spiritual ministration. He
was worried as well at the evident signs of radicalism and
violence which had begun to manifest themselves among the
foreign-born laboring classes. Like every other decent American
Gibbons was horrified when in Chicago on May 4, 1886, there
occurred the riot in Haymarket Square caused by the hurling
of a bomb and the subsequent deaths of eleven persons including
seven policemen. The archbishop seized the opportunity of the
dedication of Holy Cross Church in Baltimore for the German
Catholics on the following Sunday to utter a strong note of
warning to the foreign-born of his own flock against the dangers

[36] 79-W-10, Simeoni to Gibbons, Rome, December 15, 1885.
[37] Letterbook, Gibbons to Simeoni, Baltimore, n.d., pp. 164–167. Gibbons' Diary
(p. 195) stated that he answered this letter on January 9, 1886.

of these radical movements. Gibbons emphasized that the United States welcomed foreigners, but he lashed out against the turbulent minority of anarchists in their midst who preached the gospel of socialism and nihilism and whose favorite weapon was dynamite. He said, "Instead of strengthening the hands of the government that upholds and protects them, they are bent upon its destruction. Instead of blessing the mother that opens her arms to welcome them, they insult and strike her." He made it plain that while the citizens of the United States enjoyed the amplest liberty it was, as he expressed it, "a liberty of law, of order and of authority."[38] In this salutary warning Gibbons joined his voice to those of responsible citizens everywhere in deprecating the tragic events in Chicago which had implicated a number of the foreign-born.

Early the following autumn Cardinal Gibbons received a letter which heralded a chain of events that would involve him deeply in the conflict between the Catholics of German birth and ancestry and their coreligionists in the United States. Father Peter M. Abbelen, spiritual director of the School Sisters of Notre Dame in Milwaukee, had served on the commission of theologians in Baltimore two years before in preparing the schema for the plenary council.[39] In this capacity he had done good work and had earned the admiration of the Archbishop of Baltimore. Abbelen now recalled to Gibbons' mind the agitation which had troubled the German Catholics for several years in their efforts to secure what they regarded as their rights. The burden of Abbelen's complaint was what he termed the tendency on the part of a "great many Irish priests" to hold that the German churches were subordinate to their own, and that the German priests attached to such congregations as the succursal churches or chapels of ease in St. Louis had no true parochial rights, that there was but one parish so called in any one district and that was the English-speaking parish while others such as the Germans were dependencies of the former. Abbelen stoutly defended the right of the Germans to enjoy full parochial rights while just as strongly he condemned the undue haste with which some were trying to

---

[38] *Catholic Mirror,* May 15, 1886.
[39] Cf. 78-F-12, Heiss to Gibbons, Milwaukee, June 9, 1884, wherein the Archbishop of Milwaukee recommended Abbelen to Gibbons for the work of the council.

Americanize the Germans and to deprive them of their language and culture. He quite correctly pointed out that the Germans — unlike the Irish — were surrounded by fellow countrymen who were often infidels and members of secret societies who did everything in their power to lure the Catholic Germans away from the Church. He advanced the argument that if these non-Catholic Germans could taunt their Catholic country-men with being only second-rate Catholics it would have serious consequences for the Church.

The Milwaukee priest admitted that in the course of time Americanization would come through a gradual amalgamation, but he did not seem to appreciate the danger which other Ameri-can Catholics saw, namely, that the tenacious holding to the German language might end in his countrymen being considered not second-rate Catholics but second-rate citizens. At any rate, Abbelen calmly outlined the case for the Germans and stated that he had been appointed to go to Rome to lay the matter before the Holy See. Cardinal Simeoni knew of his mission and had made it known that he was willing to receive him. Abbelen asked Gibbons if he would be agreeable to writing a personal recommendation for him to Simeoni "as being a trustworthy person and sufficiently Americanized not to be a one-sided partisan in this question."[40] The priest sailed for Europe on October 13 on the *City of Rome,* having previously received at New York the letter of recommendation from the Cardinal of Baltimore. Not long after his arrival in the Eternal City he wrote to thank Gibbons, and he stated that the fact he could point to the cardinal as one who had not only personally, but officially, done justice to those whom Abbelen represented would greatly assist him in obtaining a decision that would be for the lasting honor and welfare of the Church in the United States.[41]

It was not long before Cardinal Gibbons had reason to regret his letter of recommendation of Abbelen. Bishops Keane and Ireland, who were in Rome that winter on business for the proposed university, soon got wind of the Abbelen mission. Keane informed the cardinal that Ireland had secured a copy of the Abbelen document handed in to the Propaganda and,

---

[40] 82-B-1, Abbelen to Gibbons, Milwaukee, October 4, 1886.
[41] 82-E-13, Abbelen to Gibbons, Rome, November 15, 1886.

he added, "a more villainous tissue of misstatements I have seldom read." Ireland had the document printed and was awaiting permission to send it to the bishops of the United States, but for Gibbons' benefit Keane enclosed a section showing Abbelen's criticism of the synodal decrees of Baltimore insofar as they related to the Germans. Keane did not hesitate to tell Gibbons of their amazement in learning, as he said, that "this secret emissary of a clique of German Bishops among us" had come with a letter of recommendation from the cardinal. "No wonder the Propaganda is puzzled!" The Bishop of Richmond closed his letter by urging Gibbons to hasten a strong message to the Holy See regarding these alleged injustices to the Germans, a step which he felt was warranted since the question to his mind, involved "the most vital interests" of the American Church.[42]

The document which had unduly excited Bishops Ireland and Keane when they learned of it in Rome had been presented by Father Abbelen to the Prefect of Propaganda in November, 1886, shortly after his arrival in the Eternal City. Abbelen's petition, which bore the approval of Archbishop Heiss of Milwaukee, dwelt particularly on the succursal parishes for the Germans in St. Louis, as well as the unfair treatment which this minority was receiving in Albany and New Orleans. While Abbelen praised Cardinal Gibbons personally for his fairness to the Germans in the Archdiocese of Baltimore, he did take exception to the diocesan synodal legislation there on the foreign-language groups, and he added that Gibbons' kindness toward the Germans did not prevent, as he expressed it, "Irish rectors from acting against the letter of the law, and meddling in various ways with the rights of the Germans."[43] But the language of the Abbelen petition was on the whole mild and judicious and there was substantial justice behind the claims which he made concerning the inequality of treatment in certain places between the German and Irish parishes.

Ireland and Keane did not wait for the approving support of the bishops in the United States before they lodged a protest with Cardinal Simeoni against the Abbelen petition. On

---

[42] 82-G-4, Keane to Gibbons, Rome, December 4, 1886.
[43] The full texts in Latin and in English of the Abbelen petition and the Ireland-Keane memorial were published in the New York *Freeman's Journal*, December 24, 1892.

December 6 they handed into the Propaganda a memorial which repudiated the idea of there being any "Irish" question in the American Church. In a lengthy communication the two bishops answered Abbelen's contentions point by point in order, as they said, that Propaganda might know that "there is also a non-German side, which, in all justice, should not fail to be heard." As for conditions in the Archdiocese of Baltimore, they said they knew Abbelen was mistaken, for Bishop Keane himself had been resident there for a number of years and he could assure Simeoni that the German pastors enjoyed the same rights as the others, "and that the latter never invade the rights of the former." Keane and Ireland warned the Prefect of Propaganda that when this secret move would become known the hierarchy of the United States would be "exceedingly indignant," and they stated that they had evidence to prove that there was a conspiracy among certain German bishops and priests to extend the German episcopal power over the entire country.[44]

In their anxiety over the matter Ireland and Keane sent cables to a number of the American prelates warning them of what was afoot and urging them to write Rome in protest and they did this in such a way that they doubtless gave an exaggerated impression of the danger. Gibbons immediately got in touch with Corrigan, quoted the text of the cable, and said he would not write Rome until he heard from the Archbishop of New York.[45] The cables at once alerted the American bishops and Cardinal Gibbons began to receive urgent pleas for action. Among the most thoroughly aroused was Bishop Gilmour of Cleveland who told his friend, Bishop Moore of St. Augustine, "If you can influence the Cardinal to active opposition we would have a large gain, but aid must come from the Archbishops."[46] Corrigan

---

[44] *Ibid.*

[45] AANY, Gibbons to Corrigan, Baltimore, December 9, 1886; 82-H-1, Corrigan to Gibbons, New London, Connecticut, December 11, 1886. Corrigan, in turn, quoted for Gibbons the text of the cable he had received.

[46] 82-G-8, Gilmour to Moore, Cleveland, December 10, 1886. Moore told Gibbons he could not do better than to send Gilmour's letter on directly to the cardinal, and he added that he was in entire agreement with the Bishop of Cleveland (82-H-6, Moore to Gibbons, St. Augustine, December 19, 1886). Ryan of Philadelphia also was in favor of action; he said he feared that they would have "a conflict of nationalities," and, therefore, they must be prepared to act prudently and firmly (82-G-10, Ryan to Gibbons, Philadelphia, December 10, 1886).

of New York was visiting in New London, Connecticut, when the cable arrived from Rome, but he hastened to acknowledge Gibbons' own telegram to him by saying that he would advise him to call a meeting of the Archbishops of Boston and Philadelphia, himself, and Gibbons early the following week so that they could draft a letter in time to have it reach Rome before the next meeting of the Congregation of the Propaganda. He said Dr. O'Connell had recently told him that the Holy See was not properly informed on the true state of affairs relating to this German question, and that if the archbishops could get off a letter "by next *Saturday's Steamer*" it would arrive in time to be of use for the meeting of the Propaganda on January 3, the probable date of the next session.[47]

Once the four eastern archbishops had agreed upon a place and time for convening, Cardinal Gibbons sent off the following wire to Archbishop Elder of Cincinnati, "Archbishops Williams, Ryan, Corrigan, and myself hold important meeting at Philada on Thursday the 16th at noon. If possible by all means be present."[48] Although Elder was not able to go east he did send a letter associating himself with any action the others might take. With Gibbons as chairman and Corrigan acting as secretary they drew up the outlines of a letter to Cardinal Simeoni which was put in final form by Corrigan after he reached home. In the communication the archbishops stated that they knew of the Abbelen petition to the Holy See. They denied any unfair treatment of the Catholics of any national group in the American Church and they stated that only in the Archdiocese of St. Louis did there exist the system of succursal parishes for the Germans. They acknowledged that they knew of trouble there on this score, but as they emphasized to Simeoni, there had been ample opportunity in the Third Plenary Council for discussion of this question when a special committee for "new material" was appointed with Archbishop Heiss himself a member; yet the German bishops had remained silent. Therefore, the archbishops asked in what way had they offended.

---

[47] 82-H-1, Corrigan to Gibbons, New London, Connecticut, December 11, 1886. Denis O'Connell had also told Bishop O'Sullivan of Mobile, "The German question comes before the Congregation in Jan." (Archives of the Diocese of Mobile, O'Connell to O'Sullivan, Rome, December 16, 1886).

[48] AAC, Gibbons to Elder, Baltimore, December 13, 1886.

The eastern metropolitans recognized, too, the folly of trying to uproot customs in a sudden and violent manner, and for that reason they had made provision for the Catholics who were not English-speaking in their respective sees. But their efforts had not resulted in the manner which Abbelen had envisioned. Three examples were cited. In Philadelphia the Church of St. Mary Magdalen dei Pazzi had been given over to the Italians by Ryan after they became numerous in frequenting it, but when the archbishop told the English-speaking people to remain away from it the pastor protested that without them he could not find means to sustain the church. In Gibbons' jurisdiction St. Joseph's Church of Washington had been tried as a mixed congregation for Germans and non-Germans, but when German sermons were delivered the people got up and left, although they remained for the English sermons. These people, so it was stated, were second-generation Germans. In New York the parish of Holy Innocents had two German churches within it, one Franciscan and the other Capuchin, but Holy Innocents got most of the people, and the superior of the Capuchin church had told Corrigan that he had heard confessions through many hours one day and only a single German came to him. The letter gave the numbers of six of the leading foreign groups in New York City along with comments on others. They then asked Simeoni, "Are Vicars to be set up for these individual tongues?" The Prefect of Propaganda was warned, therefore, that there were two sides to this question and it would be dangerous to the welfare of Catholicism in the United States if the Holy See were to act precipitously on the demands of the Abbelen petition.[49]

The day following the meeting in Philadelphia the Cardinal of Baltimore gave an account of their conference to Archbishop Elder, assuring him that his views had been embodied in the communication sent to Simeoni. Gibbons said:

> In our letter we deny in general terms that there is any grievance, & we answer categorically the statements that are made. If they (the Germans) get what they ask, other nationalities will claim similar priveleges [sic], & we will have a war of races, the charges of our enemies that we are a religion of foreigners will be vindicated. . . .

---

49 82-H-5, Corrigan to Simeoni, New York, December 17, 1886, copy in Latin.

I hesitate to remonstrate directly with the Bps. concerned. I think our strong but dignified reply will answer the purpose.[50]

But Gibbons was not content to let the matter rest there insofar as his personal effort was concerned. Ireland and Keane had won a stay of proceedings in Rome and had requested the American prelates to lend them support before the Holy See. Beyond the joint letter drawn up in Philadelphia, to which he affixed his signature, the cardinal wrote another letter which was intended to reinforce the memorial that Ireland and Keane were preparing for the Propaganda.

In his second communication Gibbons deplored the division that was threatened in the Catholic Church of the United States and he stated frankly, "The only way to correct the evil at the beginning is to absolutely refuse to recognize any distinctions in our government of the Church, for if any one nationality is accorded special privileges, other nationalities will thereafter demand the same." He remarked he was glad Keane was on the scene so that he could answer from his personal experience the charges made by Abbelen against the treatment of the Germans in the Archdiocese of Baltimore. The cardinal repudiated the personal compliment paid him by Abbelen and said he did not care for any honor of this kind in which his clergy were not allowed to share. As for the charge that the Irish clergy of Baltimore were guilty of mistreatment of the Germans, Gibbons stated that only fifteen of the English-speaking priests of the archdiocese were born in Ireland and even these were Americans by reason of their education and their manner of thought. He acknowledged the ambiguity in the synodal decree of 1875 which might seem to discriminate against the Germans, but he stated that the synod of September, 1886, had corrected this to give the German priests "exclusive jurisdiction over children of German parents" insofar as it related to baptism, first communion, and marriage as long as they continued to live under the parental roof. Finally Cardinal Gibbons touched on the point of his recommendation of Abbelen to Simeoni. He maintained that he had written the letter under

---

[50] AAC, Gibbons to Elder, Baltimore, December 17, 1886. Four days later Gibbons told Corrigan he had received an admirable letter from Bishop Camillus Maes of Covington vindicating the American hierarchy from the charges of the Abbelen petition (AANY, Gibbons to Corrigan, Baltimore, December 21, 1886).

the impression that Abbelen was going to Rome in the interests
of some local conflict between German- and English-speaking
missions, and that he had no idea his objective embraced
questions of so universal a character. He closed by saying, "My
letter simply recommended him as a priest who had rendered
us good and faithful services at the Plenary Council; I did not
make any allusion to any other subject."[51]

There were few questions affecting the welfare of the Church
in the United States about which the Cardinal of Baltimore
was more sensitive than that of harmonizing the Catholic
body with the spirit and institutions of the country. For that
reason it was to be expected that he would assume a position
of leadership in the threatening situation occasioned by the
Abbelen petition in Rome. When he dedicated the new St.
Wenceslaus Church for Bohemians in Baltimore on Sunday,
December 19, 1886, he seized the chance to give public expression again to a favorite theme. He reminded the congregation
that they had come from the shores of the Danube to the
shores of the Chesapeake to find a new government, language,
and customs, but not a new religion. He urged them to be
faithful to their church and pastor, and he did not fail to add,
"You have not only a duty of religion to discharge, but also
of loyalty to your adopted country and to this city, in which
you have cast your lot. Strive to be law-abiding citizens. Study
and obey the laws of the country. Be always in harmony with
the spirit of its institutions."[52] The cardinal ended his remarks

---

[51] AABo, *La question allemande dans l'église des Etats-Unis* (Roma, 1887).
This brochure of twenty-eight large pages is almost entirely in French except for
a few items in Latin. It reprints in whole or in part the letters of protest against
the Abbelen petition from thirteen American bishops and ends with Ireland and
Keane's own summary of the case. The Gibbons letter of December 22, 1886, to
Ireland and Keane quoted above is found on pages 13–14.

[52] *Catholic Mirror*, December 25, 1886. A certain Alfred A. Adams of Chicago
read Gibbons' sermon and wrote him appreciatively of it. He said, "It is only to
be deplored that such wise counsel could not be addressed to congregations in
cities where the apostles of disorder are more aggressive and dupes more numerous, and where so many of the latter are of the nationality whom you addressed"
(82-I-8, Adams to Gibbons, Chicago, December 27, 1886). The cardinal's experiences during this year 1886 from restive national groups made him chary
of efforts to enlist his support, e.g., in a letter to Bishop Borgess of Detroit
he said, "Some weeks ago a delegation of Poles came here with an appeal. I sent
them back with a severe admonition to obey & reverence their Bishop" (Archives
of the Archdiocese of Detroit, Gibbons to Borgess, Baltimore, October 30, 1886).

with an exhortation to industry and sobriety on the part of the Bohemian families of this new parish.

Two bishops with whom Gibbons was very closely in touch on the German question were Elder of Cincinnati and Gilmour of Cleveland. The former had accepted the cardinal's judgment that it would be better for the time being to avoid a direct protest to the bishops of German nationality in this country over the Abbelen affair, but he believed that some time in some form, as he put it, "they should be made aware of how unfair has been their conduct in this matter, and how grievous injury it threatens to our peace & unity, & consequently to the deepest interests of religion."[53] In reply Gibbons told the Archbishop of Cincinnati about the number and firm tone of the letters which had been forwarded to Rome during the previous week and he expressed the hope that these protests would end the matter. He added, "It would be an unfortunate day for the Church of America, if class legislation were established, & that a Cardinal Protector were set over a section of our faithful."[54] When he received a lengthy and stormy protest from Gilmour on the Abbelen document and the forces that lay behind it, Gibbons gave the bishop an account of the action of the archbishops in Philadelphia, enclosed a clipping of his sermon to the Bohemians from the Baltimore *Sun,* and he said, "I think it would do no harm if you write a strong letter to the Bishops now in Rome, for the cardinal's eye."[55] Elder was gratified by the explanation of the Philadelphia conference and he thanked Gibbons, as he expressed it, "in the name of all, for the prompt & efficient measures you have taken to avert the very grievous calamity that was threatening us."[56]

While the conduct of Cardinal Gibbons in this German question was not lacking in vigor once he understood the grave issues involved, the fact that he had given the letter of recommendation to Father Abbelen before he left for Rome produced a disquieting effect on the mind of Bishop Keane. During his Roman visit of the winter of 1886–1887 Keane was confronted with a number of knotty problems over and above the approval of the university which had taken him to the Eternal City.

[53] 82-H-9, Elder to Gibbons, Cincinnati, December 20, 1886.
[54] AAC, Gibbons to Elder, Baltimore, December 23, 1886.
[55] ADC, Gibbons to Gilmour, Baltimore, December 23, 1886.
[56] 82-I-7, Elder to Gibbons, Cincinnati, Christmas, 1886.

It was during these same months, as we shall have reason to see, that the difficult matters of the Knights of Labor and the case of Dr. McGlynn were pressing for solution. Each question called for the utmost care and study lest a blunder be made, and the naturally cautious temperament of Gibbons, combined with his desire to give satisfaction to the many conflicting elements who sought his support, convinced Keane that Gibbons' seeming vacillation on these important issues was endangering his reputation in Rome for forceful and enlightened leadership in the American Church. It was with this thought firmly rooted in Keane's mind that he wrote the cardinal some days after Christmas, 1886, a letter which was in every sense admirable for its candor and for its revelation of genuine bravery in offering counsel to his friend in Baltimore.

At the outset Keane thanked Gibbons for his communication of December 17 which had just come with its welcome paragraphs on the German question, the coadjutorship of New Orleans, and the Knights of Labor. Keane had translated them into Latin and handed them into the Propaganda that morning where, as he said, he felt sure they would have great weight. However, he begged the cardinal to pardon him if he now mentioned certain things which were exceedingly painful to say, and which only his high regard for him personally and for the exalted office he held could induce him to write. The bishop said he recognized what a hard and risky task it was to write painful truths to a friend, especially when he was a superior, and only real friendship could nerve one to the duty. Keane then proceeded:

> I find, to my intense regret, that an impression has taken shape in Rome to the effect that your Eminence is changeable in views, weak and vacillating in purpose, anxious to conciliate both parties on nearly every question; that it is hard to know, therefore, upon which side you stand concerning any important question, or what weight to attach to your utterances. Hence I find a growing inclination to look elsewhere than to your Eminence for reliable information & judgments, — a tendency, not only here but among the Bishops of the United States, to look to New York rather than to Baltimore for the representative & leader of our Hierarchy.

Keane said he had protested earnestly against these opinions, but certain curial officials had instanced the cardinal's change of mind on the candidate for the coadjutorship of New Orleans, the fact that he had sent a letter of recommendation with Abbelen, and that Bishop Dwenger, who was believed to be a prime mover in the German agitation, had been chosen by Gibbons as a representative of the hierarchy to win approval of the decrees of the plenary council. As Keane explained, the accusations against Gibbons' integrity were not always made in so many words, but "in meaning shrugs, and smiles, and insinuations." Even Leo XIII had intimated he had a kind of apprehension that the cardinal was uncertain and vacillating in his views on the location of the university.

While Bishop Keane was prompt to say he knew that whatever truth there was in all this had its real source in Gibbons' kindness of heart and in his anxiety to be as gracious and yielding to everyone as he could, he felt the situation was serious enough to remind the cardinal that a lack of determination on his part would lead to a widespread mistrust of his consistency and strength of character and cause men to look elsewhere for leadership in these important questions. Keane closed his remarkable letter with these words:

> It galls me to the heart to think that such injustice should be done to our Cardinal, to the leader whom Providence has given to us, — and it is this thought that has given me courage to write so plainly on so painful a subject. Let me hope that you will not be offended, that you will appreciate the affectionate devotedness which, next to my desire for the Church's best welfare, has been my only motive in thus writing; and let me hope that henceforth your Eminence will more than regain the lost ground, by showing such singleness, such consistency, such firmness, such nobleness, in every word and act, as to fully realize the grand ideal of your position in the fore-front of the foremost Hierarchy of the world.[57]

A letter such as this could have been written only by a character possessed of the forthrightness and transparent honesty of John Keane; it could have been received with profit and equanimity only by a man whose lofty position in life had not robbed him of the spirit of humility that he might view in their true light the personal criticisms lodged against him. The extant evidence does not permit one to say what were the cardinal's reactions to the Keane letter. The only written

---

[57] 82-J-4, Keane to Gibbons, Rome, December 29, 1886.

notice of it from Gibbons himself was the unrevealing sentence which he entered in his diary under date of January 14, 1887, "Wrote to Bp. Keane in reply to his letter from Rome of Dec. 29."[58] But this much we do know, that the friendship between the two prelates was in no way impaired by Keane's candor, and when one considers the bold and risky public stands which the cardinal was to assume on some very delicate problems within the next few years, it does not seem too farfetched to suggest that Keane's plain talking may, indeed, have had a salutary effect upon the cardinal's stamina.

Meanwhile the agitation over the German question did not cease. When Elder expressed sympathy with some of the Abbelen demands, while at the same time reprobating the secret method employed by the priest, Gibbons agreed that the objectionable feature of the petition did not lie so much in what it contained as in the manner in which it had been carried out. He told Elder, "I think the Bishops of the country are disposed to deal fairly with the Germans, & the grievances, if any exist, are magnified by this formal representation to the H. See."[59] Bishop McQuaid, who was likewise interested in the question, was not greatly consoled when Denis O'Connell told him that Cardinal Gibbons was soon coming to Rome and that Leo XIII would then discuss this and other questions with the Archbishop of Baltimore. As he remarked to Gilmour, "Alas, the Cardinal is weak in the face of those above him."[60]

But despite McQuaid's misgivings, Gibbons was able to demonstrate effective results on the German issue when he reached the Holy See. The cardinal departed for Rome in January, 1887, and after he had been gone for some weeks he wrote encouragingly to Elder that the American bishops had, as he expressed it, "gained immensely lately in Rome." Not only were their petitions granted, but the Propaganda officials had conceded that in the future nothing would be decided on vital matters affecting the American Church until the bishops had been heard from. Gibbons said, "The German question will come up pro forma, Easter Monday, but I have no fear of the result. I have prepared another paper for the congregation

---

[58] Diary, p. 213.

[59] 82-J-6, Elder to Gibbons, Cincinnati, December 30, 1886; AAC, Gibbons to Elder, Baltimore, January 3, 1887.

[60] ADC, McQuaid to Gilmour, Rochester, February 20, 1887.

at which I will attend."[61] The meeting of the congregation to which he referred was held on April 11 and on this occasion Gibbons was able to present his case in person before his colleagues of the Propaganda.

The decision gave sanction to the practice of accommodating the foreign language groups in more than one parish in the same neighborhood, the designation of certain of these pastorates as irremovable rectorships, and the restriction of the children of families of a foreign nationality within the limits of that nationality's parish, so long as they lived in their parents' home and providing it be understood that the parents were free to send their children to any Catholic school of their choice. Aside from these points of the original Abbelen petition, the other demands concerning separate vicars-general for the foreign-born, the desire that bishops and priests be warned to make provision for the German language, etc., were rejected.[62] Gibbons was

---

[61] AAC, Gibbons to Elder, Rome, March 31, 1887.

[62] 82-S-5/1, Simeoni to Gibbons, Rome, June 8, 1887, printed. Simeoni requested Gibbons to distribute copies of the decision to the other archbishops. Through a slip the answer to the second question, viz., whether the bishops would offend against the laws of the Church if they restricted children living under the parental roof to the limits of the parish of their parents, the answer was given as "affirmative," whereas it should have been "negative." Gibbons called attention to the mistake in writing O'Connell and said he thought the answers to questions two and three were transposed and, therefore, should be reversed (ADR, Gibbons to O'Connell, Baltimore, August 14, 1887). The Germans noted the error, of course, once the Propaganda document was distributed to the bishops and they began to make inquiries (e.g., 83-F-8, Bede Maler, O.S.B., to Gibbons, St. Louis, August 8, 1887). Gibbons attempted to give Maler an explanation of the Propaganda's intent (83-G-11, Gibbons to Maler, Baltimore, August 16, 1887, copy), although his answer was not very clear. Meanwhile Denis O'Connell was trying to get the matter straightened out in Rome (83-J-2, O'Connell to Gibbons, Grottaferrata, August 29, 1887), and he was able to secure from Propaganda the decision that the response to question two in the instruction of June 8 should read, "Negative, salvo iure parentum mittendi filios ad quascumque Scholas catholicas" (ibid.). By a misunderstanding in correspondence between Baltimore and Rome O'Connell admitted he was "lost" when Gibbons wrote saying nothing should be changed in the original wording of the instruction (83-N-4, O'Connell to Gibbons, Grottaferrata, September 18, 1887). The Pastoral-Blatt (October, 1887), 109–110, published the corrected version with "negative" for the answer to the second question. Unfortunately, Bishop Gilmour had not been kept abreast of the changes with the result that his Catholic Universe of December 22, 1887, took the Pastoral-Blatt to task for printing the wrong answers to the questions submitted to the Propaganda. William Faerber, editor of the St. Louis paper, then quoted O'Connell's letter of August 29, 1887, to Gibbons by way of vindication of the Pastoral-Blatt's version (January, 1888), 1–6; this move brought a somewhat ungenerous confession of error from the Catholic Universe in its issue

quick to inform interested parties in the United States such as Corrigan, Gilmour, and Elder. Corrigan thanked the cardinal for his cable containing the good news and said he was sure that all the American bishops were grateful that Gibbons was, as he expressed it, "on the spot to defend their interests."[63] In relating the success of his efforts in this and other questions that had arisen during his visit to Rome the cardinal confessed to Elder that the confinement, constant employment, and nervous tension had impaired his health, and he added, "I felt the responsibility of my position, & worked hard."[64]

Bishop Gilmour was generous with his thanks to Cardinal Gibbons for what he had done on the German question and other problems while at Rome, but he wisely cautioned that the struggle was only temporarily lulled for, as he said, "the end is not yet."[65] The end, indeed, was not yet since in the previous February at a meeting in Chicago there had been organized the Deutsch-Amerikanischer Priester-Verein which laid plans for holding a national meeting in September. This activity, of course, stimulated the non-Germans to renewed efforts, and in the spring of 1887 there appeared the first in a lengthy series of scolding pamphlets which attacked the German Catholics in very harsh terms.[66] It was written by Father John Gmeiner of the Diocese of St. Paul. Gmeiner charged the Germans with being a stubborn foreign group who refused to accept the customs of their adopted country, and he stated that if they continued their opposition to Americanization they would bring about a new wave of prejudice against the Church

---

of January 12, 1888. Gilmour was embarrassed. He told Gibbons he had published the changed version with the facts after getting from Cincinnati the latest information and he thought that had the *Pastoral-Blatt* done the same originally he [Gilmour] "would not have been caught" (84-C-7, Gilmour to Gibbons, Cleveland, February 15, 1888). O'Connell told Gibbons later that Gilmour had written him complaining very strongly of the "bungling about the German document" (84-F-7, O'Connell to Gibbons, Rome, March 25, 1888).

[63] 82-P-12, Corrigan to Gibbons, New York, April 12, 1887.

[64] AAC, Gibbons to Elder, Florence, April 20, 1887. In telling him that "all the claims" of Abbelen had been rejected Gibbons was not entirely accurate since the demands for separate parishes and irremovable rectorships had been approved by the Propaganda.

[65] 83-C-6, Gilmour to Gibbons, Cleveland, July 16, 1887.

[66] *The Church and the Various Nationalities in the United States. Are German Catholics Unfairly Treated?* (Milwaukee, 1887). For the activities of the yearly German Catholic congresses and further details on the pamphlet war, cf. Meng, *op. cit.*, p. 397 ff.

in this country. In sometimes intemperate terms he set out to blast the thesis that the German Catholics were unfairly treated in the Church of the United States. The Gmeiner pamphlet was naturally painful to the Germans and they answered the attack.[67] The result was that the excitement grew more intense as time passed with the newspapers, both German and English, airing in their columns the nationalist strife in Catholic circles. This is not the place to follow the developments in this conflict of views which filled the American Catholic press; suffice it to say that it continued at a steadily mounting pace through the next three years to the point where, as has justly been said, by the autumn of 1890 the problem had become "a keg of ecclesiastical gunpowder."[68]

The flow of complaints to Rome from German sources did not abate with the Propaganda's decision of the previous April, and O'Connell let it be known that Paul Cardinal Melchers of the Congregation of the Propaganda, to whom much of this correspondence was directed, had sent to him for further information on the question.[69] Gibbons was, of course, circumspect in his public utterances on the matter, but when the question arose of a possible softening of the decision of Propaganda he let O'Connell know privately that he was opposed to the least sign of backing down or weakening of the decision since, as he said, he believed this "would only make the Germans more insolent & aggressive."[70]

Further trouble arose late that summer when Archbishop Heiss on August 17 gave an interview to a reporter of the Milwaukee *Sentinel* in which he said that the approaching meeting of the Priester-Verein at Chicago would probably discuss the need for more German bishops in the United States. Heiss was likewise quoted as saying that the Germans predominated in the Provinces of Milwaukee, Cincinnati, and St. Louis, and although he could not predict the action of the

---

[67] 82-W-8, Abbelen to Gibbons, Milwaukee, June 30, 1887. Abbelen thanked the cardinal for informing him of the Roman decision of which he had not previously heard. He took occasion to deplore the publicity given to the question in the newspapers and in the pamphlet of Gmeiner, and he said he now felt justified in defense of himself and his supporters, in publishing at least the Latin text of his original petition to Rome.

[68] Meng, *op. cit.*, p. 400.

[69] 83-D-12, O'Connell to Gibbons, Grottaferrata, July 31, 1887.

[70] ADR, Gibbons to O'Connell, Baltimore, August 14, 1887.

Chicago assembly, he presumed that the question of keeping up the German language, which was of vital importance to the Germans of the country, would also be treated.[71] Prompt protests against the Heiss interview were sent to Gibbons by Archbishops Gross of Oregon City and Elder of Cincinnati.[72] Both prelates were of the opinion that Gibbons should inform Rome of the serious indiscretion of the Archbishop of Milwaukee, and Elder at the same time expressed the fear that an effort would be made to secure the appointment of a German to the vacant Diocese of Detroit. Although Gibbons was vitally interested he was not disposed to interfere in the affair of the Heiss interview unless Rome asked for his opinion. Acting according to his customary procedure, he consulted a number of other bishops as to what should be done, and he then informed Elder that if any remonstrance was to be made to Heiss it should come from Elder himself; if the Holy See should thereafter ask his [Gibbons'] opinion it would under these circumstances carry more weight. He expressed the hope that the coming Chicago convention of Germans would pass without doing further harm since he did not feel it was likely to do good, and the cardinal revealed his mistaken optimism on the question when he gave it as his opinion that after the Chicago meeting he looked for "a reaction in the right direction."[73]

The fears which Cardinal Gibbons had expressed more than once, that this agitation among the German Catholics for special legislation in their behalf would incite other nationalities to request the same, proved to be well founded. In the fall of 1887 Father Ignatius Barszcz, pastor of St. Anthony of Padua Church in Jersey City, appealed to the Holy See for a separate diocese to be erected for the Catholics of Slavic origin in the United States.[74] When the priest called on Gibbons in early January, 1888, with his request the cardinal told him that he was not in favor of the plan. The Polish pastor then carried

[71] Milwaukee *Sentinel,* August 18, 1887.

[72] 83-J-6, Gross to Gibbons, Portland, August 30, 1887; 83-K-1, Elder to Gibbons, Cincinnati, September 2, 1887.

[73] AAC, Gibbons to Elder, Baltimore, September 7, 1887.

[74] 83-P-4, Barszcz to "Eminenza," Rome, October 29, 1887, printed. Presumably this was addressed to Simeoni and forwarded by him to Gibbons. Over the top Gibbons wrote in a note concerning the interview of Barszcz in Baltimore on January 3, 1888, with the statement that the cardinal had opposed his request.

his case to President Cleveland who was obviously puzzled by it. Cleveland decided to forward Barszcz's request to Gibbons for his advice, characterizing it "as a specimen of the queer letters" he received.[75] The cardinal composed an answer for the President to Barszcz in which he stated that the Church was opposed to placing bishops over people of different nationalities, although it provided ample services for them by supplying priests of their native country, or at least priests who spoke their language. Gibbons sympathized with Cleveland for the annoyance he had experienced and told the President that the priest was something of a crank and no further attention should be paid to him.[76]

While it proved relatively simple to dispose of the proposal of the Polish priest from Jersey City, the continuing pressure of the Germans to increase their number among the American bishops did not admit of so easy a solution. In the spring of 1887 Bishop Borgess of Detroit resigned his see and the name of John S. Foley of Baltimore was advanced for the position. A year before Gibbons had failed in his attempt to secure the appointment of Foley as Bishop of Wilmington, but he now came strongly behind Archbishop Elder and others by writing to Rome in Foley's behalf.[77] However, the Holy See had begun to receive conflicting advice about the proper candidate for Detroit and as a consequence there developed a long delay. Almost a year after Gibbons' recommendation of Foley he learned from his friend Elder that Bishop Katzer of Green Bay was trying to have a German appointed to Detroit.[78] Elder felt this interference in the affairs of his Province of Cincinnati warranted him in writing a letter of protest to Rome. The archbishop, however, was fearful of giving offense so he sent the letter on to Gibbons for the cardinal's perusal and judgment as to whether it ought to be forwarded to the Holy See. The record of Gibbons' reaction is not available, but meanwhile other interested parties like Moore of St. Augustine furnished Simeoni with recommenda-

---

[75] 84-A-7, Cleveland to Gibbons, Washington, January 20, 1888.

[76] LC, Cleveland Papers, Gibbons to Cleveland, Baltimore, January 21, 1888, *Personal*. Gibbons kept a copy of the answer he drafted for Cleveland to send to Barszcz (84-B-7).

[77] ADR, Gibbons to O'Connell, Baltimore, August 14, 1887.

[78] 84-S-9, Elder to Gibbons, Cincinnati, July 18, 1888.

tions of Foley, and at length in the late summer of 1888 he was appointed Bishop of Detroit.[79]

More serious than Detroit in this respect was the filling of the Archdiocese of Milwaukee left vacant by the death of Michael Heiss on March 26, 1890. Gibbons was informed that at a meeting of the bishops of the Province of Milwaukee on April 16 the prelates had drawn up a *terna* to submit to Rome consisting of three bishops all of German extraction: Frederick X. Katzer of Green Bay, Kilian Flasch of La Crosse, and Henry J. Richter of Grand Rapids.[80] John Ireland got wind of the first choice and immediately urged Gibbons that the American metropolitans delay sending their judgments until he could be heard from. As for Katzer, the Archbishop of St. Paul felt he was "thoroughly unfit to be an archbishop." Ireland had received a protest from the English-speaking consultors of Milwaukee against the bishops' list and he was anxious that the facts should be fully known before action was taken.[81]

Gibbons, too, was in favor of delay until the first annual meeting of the American archbishops, scheduled for Boston in July, would afford an opportunity for a full discussion of the Milwaukee candidates. With this in mind he requested Simeoni to delay the appointment until after that date.[82] The cardinal was encouraged to hear from John P. Farrelly, spiritual director of the American College, that Archbishop Jacobini of the Propaganda had given assurances nothing would be done until the archbishops had met, and Farrelly added that Jacobini had likewise intimated that their choice would decide the matter.[83] A month later Farrelly advised the cardinal that Archbishop Corrigan who was then in Rome had no hope of reaching

---

[79] 84-S-10, Moore to Simeoni, Baltimore, July 19, 1888, copy in Italian.

[80] 87-J-2, Katzer to Gibbons, Green Bay, April 18, 1890.

[81] 87-J-5, Ireland to Gibbons, St. Paul, April 21, 1890. Ireland, of course, was always one of the most forceful advocates of Americanization of the immigrants. A year and a half before he had told Gibbons he hoped the latter would be successful in persuading the officers of the Irish Catholic Benevolent Union to drop the word "Irish" from the name of their organization which, he thought, would be an example to the Germans. "My conviction grows daily," said Ireland, "that the Church cannot prosper in America so long as she seemingly persists in draping herself in foreign un-Americanism garbs . . . " (85-G-9, Ireland to Gibbons, St. Paul, October 27, 1888).

[82] 87-M-3, Gibbons to Simeoni, Baltimore, May 13, 1890, copy in Latin.

[83] 87-M-8, Farrelly to Gibbons, Rome, May 19, 1890.

Boston for the meeting and had already spoken his preference for Milwaukee at the Propaganda and Farrelly had reason to conjecture that his choice was Katzer. The spiritual director counseled that if the archbishops were to favor someone not on the list of Milwaukee bishops, it would be well to have a decided number of votes in his favor with a document explaining why they had not voted for those on the Milwaukee *terna*.[84]

The first annual meeting of the archbishops of the United States convened in Boston on July 23–24, 1890, and the first item of business was the Milwaukee case. Following a discussion of the candidates, the name of Katzer was unanimously set aside by the metropolitans and in his place as the first on the list they chose John Lancaster Spalding, Bishop of Peoria.[85] Gibbons promptly sent off the choice made by himself and his colleagues to Simeoni with a strong recommendation of Spalding, an approving nod for Bishop Marty of Sioux Falls, and the expression of a doubt that Richter of Grand Rapids would prove a suitable candidate due to the peculiar circumstances of the Church in Milwaukee.[86] While for a time hopes were high that the vote of the metropolitans would tip the scales in Spalding's favor with Bishop Foley of Detroit reporting that the Bishop of Peoria's chances were improving, it proved to be false optimism.[87] Shortly before Christmas, Katzer, first on the original list from Milwaukee, was named archbishop of that see.

The appointment of the Bishop of Green Bay to Milwaukee was a severe disappointment to Gibbons, but it was characteristic of him to accept defeat in good grace and to endeavor to make the best of it. He quickly sent his congratulations to the archbishop-elect who, in turn, thanked him for his kindness while at the same time assuring the cardinal that he had been most reluctant to allow his name to be put forward and that the appointment had come to pass against his will.[88] Not only did Gibbons congratulate Katzer, but in the interests of peace in the Church of the United States he counseled Archbishop Ireland to do the same. Ireland confessed he found it difficult

---

[84] 87-P-9/1, Farrelly to Gibbons, Rome, June 17, 1890.
[85] 87-R-4, Minutes of the Meeting of the Archbishops, Boston, July 23–24, 1890.
[86] 87-R-5, Gibbons to Simeoni, Boston, July 25, 1890, copy in Latin.
[87] 88-D-2, Ireland to Gibbons, St. Paul, November 19, 1890.
[88] 88-F-3, Katzer to Gibbons, Green Bay, December 24, 1890.

to comply with the request and that without Gibbons' direct appeal he would not have done it, but he had finally brought himself around and written the letter. Now that it was done the Archbishop of St. Paul saw that it was the proper thing to do. "I see," he wrote, "the good in having a wise friend to advise me."[89] The aspect of the whole affair which Ireland found most galling was the slight put upon the archbishops by the Holy See.

The year that opened with the victory of the Germans in the matter of the Milwaukee candidacy was destined to be one of the most crucial in the controversy over their status in the American Church. Denis O'Connell wrote ominously of a few intransigent cardinals in the Propaganda who were determined to teach the American bishops a lesson on docility toward the Holy See. Secretary Jacobini and Donato Sbarretti, the *minutante* of the congregation, were represented as regretting what had happened in the Katzer case, and Sbarretti did not hesitate to say that the German influences in Rome were invoked to win the miter of Milwaukee for the Bishop of Green Bay. Sbarretti was quoted as having told O'Connell concerning the Germans in Rome, "There are some of them in the congregation and you have no voice there at all. We should have Gibbons here."[90]

But by this time Gibbons had his hands more than full in Baltimore. The German question had been further complicated in July, 1890, when Archbishop Ireland addressed the National Education Association in St. Paul and in a ringing speech which was open to misunderstanding gave added offense to the Germans on the score of his attitude toward parochial schools.[91] Ireland, who was no friend of the Germans, gave his enemies a handle to use against him and they did not fail to employ it in the struggle they were then waging for their cause. We shall have occasion later to speak of Gibbons' attitude in the school controversy; suffice it to say here that he backed Ireland strongly

---

[89] 88-G-1, Ireland to Gibbons, St. Paul, January 2, 1891.

[90] 88-H-2, O'Connell to Gibbons, Rome, January 19, 1891.

[91] On this question cf. Daniel F. Reilly, O.P., *The School Controversy (1891–1893)* (Washington, 1943), p. 47 ff. This is the best work on the subject, although it would have taken on a more definitive character had the archives of the Archdiocese of New York been consulted for the Corrigan side of the case. The O'Connell Papers in the archives of the Diocese of Richmond, which are now available for research, also shed further light on this question.

in his fight with the Germans and other adversaries over the issue of the parochial school.

A further source of bitterness arose when Bishop Gilmour of Cleveland died on April 13, 1891, and the names of three German bishops were advanced by the consultors to fill the vacancy. Here again Gibbons was appealed to for advice by Foley of Detroit who told him he had no one else to whom he could speak confidentially on a question of this kind.[92] The cardinal was ill at the time but he regarded the matter as of such importance that he undertook to write his views on the Cleveland vacancy to Archbishop Elder from his sickroom even, as he put it, "at the risk of overtaxing my strength." Gibbons urged Elder to confer with his suffragans and to agree on two or three strong names. He said he regarded their meeting as exceedingly important and that in his mind an American bishop, by reason of his position as a property holder and a citizen, should be a man possessed of a deep love not only for his Church, but as he said, "also for his country, & a thorough acquaintance & sympathy with our political institutions."[93] But despite all the efforts to prevent the appointment of one of the German party to Cleveland the attempt failed and in December of that year Ignatius F. Horstmann of Philadelphia was named Bishop of Cleveland.

In May of 1891, however, there broke a new storm over the German question which for the fierce excitement which it aroused made all other aspects of the problem appear almost trivial. The previous September there had been held at Liège, Belgium, a general European Catholic congress during which a paper by Father Alphonse Villeneuve, pastor of Assumption Church in Albany, New York, was read purporting to show that out of twenty-five million Catholic immigrants who had entered the United States, twenty million had lost the faith. This startling figure naturally alarmed the leaders of the various immigrant societies in Europe and when in December the delegates of the national branches of the European St. Raphael's Society assembled in Lucerne, Switzerland, for an international conference, the Villeneuve report was made the subject of further discussion.

As a consequence of the conference in Lucerne a memorial was drawn up to be submitted to the Holy See recommending

---

[92] 88-P-5, Foley to Gibbons, Detroit, May 14, 1891.
[93] AAC, Gibbons to Elder, Baltimore, June 3, 1891, *Private*.

remedial action. The document was dated February, 1891, and was ultimately presented to Leo XIII on April 16 by Peter Paul Cahensly who eight years before had given cause for uneasiness when he visited the German immigrant groups in the United States. The suspicion which still attached to Cahensly was really quite unfounded, for, as was later made clear, he was a man of genuine integrity whose zeal for the immigrants' welfare prompted him to sacrifice part of his personal fortune in their behalf. Although the Villeneuve figure of twenty million lost was now cut in half, the document which emerged from Lucerne urged upon the Holy Father certain remedies which could scarcely avoid stirring resentment among the non-German leaders of the Church in the United States. It asked for separate parishes for each nationality, the appointment of priests of the respective nationality to these parishes, the provision of priests who understood the language in those areas where there were foreign-born Catholics but not in such numbers as to enable them to form a parish, parish schools to be erected and as far as possible separate schools for each nationality, priests who served the immigrants to be given equal rights and privileges with other priests, Catholic confraternities, mutual aid and protection societies to be formed for the immigrants, and, said the document, it would be desirable as often as judged feasible for the immigrant groups to have in the hierarchy some bishops of their own race.[94]

Although the so-called Lucerne memorial was presented to the Pope on April 16 the American Catholic public was not made aware of its existence until a brief news item appeared in the New York *Herald* of May 9. On May 28 the same paper published the full text. Immediately there arose an outburst of indignation in American Catholic circles, and Cardinal Gibbons was at once besieged by demands for action from a number of his fellow bishops. Kain of Wheeling urged the preparation of a counter-memorial while awaiting the annual meeting of the archbishops.[95] Ireland of St. Paul inquired of the cardinal if Cahensly was to be permitted to tell Rome how the Church of this country was to be ruled amid the silence and apparent ap-

---

[94] The full text is given in John T. Reily, *Collections in the Life and Times of J. Card. Gibbons* (McSherrystown, 1895), III, Pt. III, 7–9, and the second memorial of Cahensly, dated June 30, 1891, will be found on pages 9–13. The pagination in this work is not consecutive.

[95] AAB, unclassified, Kain to Gibbons, Wheeling, May 18, 1891.

proval of the American hierarchy. He said he knew Gibbons' "delicacy of sentiment" which might tempt him not to act lest jealous minds should complain. This delicacy Ireland said he honored; yet there were times when delicacy must yield before stern duty. For that reason he asked if Gibbons would not summon the archbishops to meet with him to plan a reply to Cahensly's memorial. The Archbishop of St. Paul stated he knew Gibbons would say he was hasty and needed to be repressed, but this time he felt he was right. "We are American bishops," said Ireland, "an effort is made to dethrone us, & to foreignize our country in the name of religion."[96] Bishop Foley added his voice to those demanding action from the metropolitans. Foley was worried after recently reading in the Baltimore *Sun* of the illness of the cardinal, which prompted him to say, "We need you more than ever. For to your Eminence we must look for salvation from the wicked wretch, Cahensly, who is striving to undo the work of the Church in our country."[97]

In the midst of the excitement there came a request from Archbishop Katzer of Milwaukee that Gibbons confer the pallium on him, and he took occasion to remark that in spite of his name being mentioned in connection with "this deplorable Cahensly affair," he knew absolutely nothing of it.[98] Monsignor O'Connell, who was depended upon by Gibbons and others to keep them informed of developments in Rome, let it be known that the vehement American reactions to the Lucerne memorial had given pause to some elements in the Eternal City. As he expressed it to the Abbé Magnien, "The explosion of the Cahensly movement shatters the foundations of one of the supports of the new departure that some here contemplated making towards America."[99] It was known, of course, that O'Connell

---

[96] *Ibid.,* Ireland to Gibbons, St. Paul, May 30, 1891.

[97] 88-Q-1, Foley to Gibbons, Detroit, June 2, 1891.

[98] 88-Q-4, Katzer to Gibbons, Milwaukee, June 5, 1891.

[99] ASMS, O'Connell to Magnien, Rome, June 15, 1891. O'Connell's letter dealt in the main with the prospects of Placide Chapelle's appointment as coadjutor of Santa Fe which Gibbons and others had been trying for some time to accomplish. When Chapelle was mentioned for New Orleans nearly three years before, O'Connell revealed a mistaken optimism when he wrote to Bishop O'Sullivan of Mobile, "I suppose the time is pretty well over now when it will ever be urged again in the question of New Orleans episcopal candidate that it is a French See. The new blood infused into that Province has done it good service" (Archives of the Diocese of Mobile, O'Connell to O'Sullivan, Grottaferrata, September 22, 1888). The appointment of Francis Janssens, Bishop of Natchez,

exercised a strong influence on Gibbons. For that reason Ireland told the Roman rector he was still working on the Archbishop of Baltimore in the hope he would call a meeting of the archbishops so they could send out "a fierce protest" against Cahensly. He said Gibbons was waiting to hear from O'Connell so he hoped that by now the rector would have cabled the cardinal "to move forward."[100]

But Cardinal Gibbons did not "move forward" in this matter during the next few weeks with anything like the open and speedy manner which John Ireland so earnestly desired. On May 18 Gibbons had sent the Peter's Pence of $5,000 from his archdiocese to the Pope through O'Connell,[101] and at that time it is more than likely he expressed himself on the Cahensly memorial, the news of which had reached the United States just ten days before. More than that, there is no record of his communicating with Leo XIII during the next month, except to send a letter of congratulation on the Pontiff's encyclical, *Rerum novarum*.[102] But that the cardinal felt keenly about the matter we know. At the time that he recommended to Elder a meeting of the bishops of the Province of Cincinnati to name candidates for Cleveland, he attached great importance to their meeting as the first to take place, as he said, since the revelation of the "Americo-European conspiracy which has inflicted so deep an insult on the Episcopate & the Catholics of the U. States, & seems to regard the Sees of America as fit to [be] filled by the first greedy ecclesiastical adventurer that comes to our country."[103] It would seem, therefore, that Gibbons had determined upon the plan of communicating his views privately to Monsignor O'Connell who, in turn, would make them known at the Holy See. In any case, for the time being he held his peace even though he continued to be importuned by others who were calling for action.[104]

---

to New Orleans some weeks before proved in time to be the cause of considerable opposition from the French clergy on the score of his Dutch background. Cf. Baudier, *The Catholic Church in Louisiana,* p. 477.

[100] ADR, Ireland to O'Connell, St. Paul, June 16, 1891.

[101] Diary, May 18, 1891, p. 252.

[102] *Ibid.,* June 22, 1891, p. 253. Cf. I, 529–531, 589–590, for Gibbons' comment on the encyclical.

[103] AAC, Gibbons to Elder, Baltimore, June 3, 1891, *Private.*

[104] 88-R-8, Gross to Gibbons, Portland, June 28, 1891. Archbishop Gross hoped

That the true opinion of Gibbons and his colleagues on the proposals of Cahensly had been made known to the Pope became evident when Mariano Cardinal Rampolla, the Secretary of State, addressed a letter on June 28 to the Archbishop of Baltimore which stated the Holy See was aware of the trouble caused by the suggestion of national bishops in the United States. Rampolla made it clear that the proposal was not viewed with favor in Rome and he said the Pope had commissioned him to have Gibbons reassure his colleagues on that score.[105] Two days later when Denis O'Connell presented the Peter's Pence of the Archdiocese of Baltimore to Leo XIII the latter repeated his determination not to allow national bishops in the American Church, although he affirmed his view that in those areas where there were enough German immigrants to constitute a parish they should have a priest who understood their language.[106]

While he had up to this time maintained silence insofar as the public was concerned Cardinal Gibbons decided on June 28, before the letter was received, to take public cognizance of the issue. Preaching at the dedication of the new St. Mary's Church for the Germans in Washington, the cardinal stated that the vast number of churches provided throughout the United States for the spiritual benefit of various European nationalities was evidence that the Catholic Church was a family of many peoples. He instanced the fact that almost every Sunday saw the dedication of a church somewhere in the country for the use of Poles, Lithuanians, Bohemians, Germans, or Italians. The cardinal ventured the statement that no hierarchy in the world paid more attention to the spiritual needs of the foreign-born Catholics than the bishops of the United States, and he named Paris, Vienna, Berlin, and Rio de Janeiro as cities with large immigrant colonies where, as far as he could learn, little or no provision was made for the foreign Catholic populations. Then directing his remarks to Cahensly and his supporters, Gibbons said:

> With these facts before us we cannot view without astonishment and indignation a number of self-constituted critics and officious gentlemen in Europe complaining of the alleged inattention which

---

the cardinal would "devise some means" to destroy the threat to peace from the Lucerne memorial.

[105] 88-R-9, Rampolla to Gibbons, Rome, June 28, 1891.

[106] 88-S-1, O'Connell to Gibbons, Rome, July 1, 1891.

is paid to the spiritual wants of the foreign population and to the means of redress which they have thought proper to submit to the Holy See.[107]

The principal parts of Gibbons' sermon were published in the New York *Herald* and other papers and attracted wide and generally favorable attention.[108] When the papers on July 2 published a notice that Gibbons had been informed a letter was on its way to him from the Pope on the subject of the German question,[109] Archbishop Ireland was pleased, but he pointedly asked, "Are we, however, to stop there?" He furnished the cardinal on this occasion with the text of a second memorial to the Holy See from Cahensly and the more he wrote the more excited he became. He ended by saying he was going to see Gibbons in July whether the latter convoked a meeting of the archbishops or not. In Ireland's opinion a crisis was upon them in which the American bishops must either sink or swim, and he believed they were then sinking and he thought they ought to sink if they did not "struggle for life."[110] In spite of all the pressure from St. Paul, the Cardinal of Baltimore held fast to his view that the situation did not call for a special meeting of the metropolitans of the country before the time set for their annual session in St. Louis in November.

Meanwhile another flurry of nationalist feeling showed itself in a renewed effort to secure a bishop for the Polish Catholics of the United States. A small group were reported circulating

---

[107] New York *Herald*, June 29, 1891. Gibbons' words were reprinted in an editorial of the *Catholic News* of New York on July 11, 1891, which was entitled, "His Eminence, the Cardinal."

[108] Cf. newspapers cited in Meng, *op. cit.*, p. 409, n. 54. The New York *Freeman's Journal* of July 4 had a long editorial defending its own strong stand against Cahenslyism in which they said Gibbons' interview gave emphasis to its position. It was items like the one in the Washington *Post* of June 28, 1891, that made uneasy reading for both Catholic and non-Catholic Americans on this subject. In a front-page news story from Brussels on June 27 the reporter spoke of the Cahensly demands on the Holy See and he concluded, "The political character of the movement is inadvertently manifested by the statement that the European governments cannot longer regard the matter with indifference and that it is of the utmost importance to retain their influence on their people in America."

[109] 88-T-1, Corrigan to Gibbons, New York, July 13, 1891.

[110] 88-S-3, Ireland to Gibbons, St. Paul, July 2, 1891. The New York *Herald* of July 1, 1891, carried the text of the second Cahensly memorial under a date line of June 30 from Berlin, and the next day the same paper had an editorial "The Pope Refuses," in which Leo XIII was praised for his gift of "abundant common sense."

prominent citizens of Philadelphia and seeking their signatures to a petition to this effect. When two representatives of this party from Brooklyn came to solicit support among the alleged 12,000 Poles of Baltimore they got slight consolation from the pastors of the two Polish parishes. Fathers Peter Chowaniec of the Holy Rosary Church and John Rodowicz of St. Stanislaus rebuked the nationalist representatives. Rodowicz urged them to go to the cardinal which he knew they would not dare do. The priest was then quoted as saying, "We are too much attached to the Cardinal to think of any other to take his place. None could consult our spiritual and moral interests and our material welfare as well as he."[111]

Early in July Archbishop Katzer informed the cardinal that he had set August 20 as the date for conferring the pallium at Milwaukee and he hoped Gibbons' health would permit him to fulfill his promise to do him that honor.[112] The cardinal, of course, realized the key position occupied by Milwaukee in the present controversy, and he doubtless welcomed the opportunity of a visit to this center of German influence to express his views on the subject that was uppermost in the minds of so many Catholics. Gibbons had not been well of late so about this time he decided to take a holiday at Cape May, New Jersey, to regain his health. On July 11 while taking a walk with Abbé Magnien the cardinal met President Benjamin Harrison who invited him into his cottage for a visit. The President brought up the subject of the Cahensly memorial and expressed himself as very pleased at Gibbons' strong condemnation of the movement. He said he had thought of writing to compliment him but he feared it might be misinterpreted by some as an effort to interfere in Church matters. Harrison informed the cardinal that he was free to make any use he thought proper of the remarks he had made on the subject.[113] Gibbons had the satisfaction of being able to tell the President that on that very morning he had received the Rampolla letter in which the Holy Father had rejected the Cahensly proposal regarding the appointment of national bishops. He sent off an account of the interview with Harrison to Elder of Cincinnati in which he said he regarded the remarks of the President

---

[111] *Catholic News* (New York), July 11, 1891.

[112] 88-S-4, Katzer to Gibbons, Milwaukee, July 3, 1891.

[113] Will, *Life of Cardinal Gibbons*, I, 524–525, which reprinted a letter of Gibbons from Cape May of July 12, 1891, to Denis O'Connell.

as "very significant," coming spontaneously as they did from the head of the nation.[114] When the newspapers got word of the interview, curiosity was aroused as to the authenticity of the story; in these circumstances Gibbons was happy to tell Bishop Keane that the report was entirely correct, to which he added, "I was delighted with his [Harrison's] words."[115]

Cardinal Gibbons remained opposed to any joint effort of the American archbishops against the Cahensly memorials. In mentioning the interview with Harrison to Archbishop Janssens of New Orleans, he said the President's rebuke to the German nationalists would have more weight in Rome against foreign inter-

---

[114] AAC, Gibbons to Elder, Cape May, July 16, 1891. Aside from the interview with Harrison there is no evidence that Gibbons made any approach to government officials on this question. However, just at this time Archbishop Ireland was in touch with Senator Cushman Kellogg Davis of Minnesota who told him that the Senate Committee on Immigration was determined to air the Cahensly affair at the next session of Congress. Ireland wished Denis O'Connell to have this information for use in Rome (ADR, Ireland to O'Connell, St. Paul, July 14, 1891). When O'Connell hinted that a word from Secretary of State James G. Blaine might help, Ireland replied that he had been thinking of that for some time. He said Senator Davis urged delay, however, until the opening of Congress when Blaine would be interrogated as to what course the administration intended to pursue and a "studied document" would then be secured from Blaine, the result of which the Archbishop of St. Paul thought would be "a solemn warning to Rome, and the deathblow to foreignism in the American Church" (*ibid.*, Ireland to O'Connell, St. Paul, n.d., but from internal evidence it would be in the summer or early autumn of 1891). It is interesting to note that Gibbons was not informed about this political angle by Ireland as far as the extant evidence shows, although O'Connell advised the cardinal to let the question go before Congress (88-U-2, O'Connell to Gibbons, August 3, 1891). The same summer the cardinal was apprised of the political aspects of Cahenslyism on the international scale when O'Connell related the substance of an audience he had with Cardinal Rampolla. O'Connell told Rampolla of the resentment in the United States against the Holy See listening to Europeans on matters pertaining to the Church in this country; to this the Secretary of State replied that when it was a matter of the spiritual concerns of the fellow countrymen of these people the Holy See must listen, particularly when men of great merit interposed their influence as, e.g., Ludwig von Windthorst, leader of the Center Party in the German Reichstag, who was, said Rampolla, "deeply interested" in Cahensly's plan. O'Connell told Gibbons that he hastened to insist with Rampolla that this was precisely what offended public sentiment in the United States (88-U-2, O'Connell to Gibbons, Rome, August 3, 1891, *Private*). Actually in April, 1892, the Cahensly memorials were the subject of debate on the floor of the United States Senate in connection with Chinese immigration and at that time Senator Davis maintained that Cahenslyism was a more serious threat to the country than oriental immigration would be for a long time to come. Cf. Meng, *op. cit.*, p. 322.

[115] ACUA, Keane Papers, Gibbons to Keane, Cape May, July 21, 1891.

ference in American ecclesiastical affairs than "the combined protests of the hierarchy."[116] He persisted in this policy, too, when Elder of Cincinnati suggested that the archbishops should join in trying to prevent the succession of a German in the Diocese of Green Bay to replace Katzer. That the cardinal was smarting under the rebuff which the archbishops had received in their attempt to keep Katzer out of Milwaukee was evident. He told Elder that he favored each archbishop writing individually to Rome in the matter of Green Bay and that he felt a concerted action on their part was undesirable, coming, as he said, so soon "after the treatment we recd. in regard to Milwaukee."[117]

Although the wisdom of Gibbons' course of action was doubtless seriously questioned at the time by some of his fellow archbishops, he remained adamant in his stand. The cardinal often revealed a sensitiveness over what might appear undue pressure on the Holy See and this reluctance, plus the failure of their efforts in the Katzer case, made him turn aside all suggestions for a joint protest. But this did not mean that he slackened his correspondence with Rome. In fact, some weeks after meeting Harrison at Cape May Gibbons recounted the incident in full to Rampolla. He told the Secretary of State of the profound satisfaction which the President had shown at Gibbons' public condemnation of the nationalists and the pleasure which he had manifested in learning that the cardinal had just received word from Rome that Cahensly's proposals were not found acceptable.[118]

Less than a month after the report to Cardinal Rampolla there occurred the conferring of the pallium on Frederick X. Katzer in St. John's Cathedral in Milwaukee. Gibbons prepared himself for a major pronouncement. Passing through Chicago the day before the ceremony, he was interviewed by the secular press on the Cahensly troubles. The cardinal was quoted as having said, "The efforts of foreigners to change the existing condition of affairs will meet with strenuous opposition, and I am satisfied

---

[116] AANO, Gibbons to Janssens, Baltimore, July 28, 1891. On July 11 the cardinal had told Corrigan that a hasty perusal of the Italian text of Rampolla's letter to him seemed to intimate that the Holy See felt a special meeting of the bishops just at that time was undesirable and might revive excitement (AANY, Gibbons to Corrigan, Cape May, July 11, 1891).

[117] AAC, Gibbons to Elder, Cape May, July 24, 1891.

[118] 88-T-7, Gibbons to Rampolla, Baltimore, July 29, 1891, copy in Italian.

will prove utterly futile." The interview was widely copied and appeared, among other papers, in the *Church News* of Washington on August 23. The Milwaukee *Daily Journal* of August 19 announced the cardinal's arrival in that city in company with Bishop Foley of Detroit, and stated that he had been so weakened by the heat and the fatigue of travel that he had to abandon the idea of celebrating the pontifical Mass and would confine himself to presiding and giving the sermon. In his sermon Gibbons first called attention to the "streams of immigrants" who had flowed into Wisconsin to enrich the life of the Church of that region and the solicitude which the Church had shown for their spiritual welfare. He cited the large number of nationalities represented in the Catholic body of the United States, united, as he said, by the precious bond of Christian brotherhood. Instancing the splendid harmony of the American bishops displayed at the Third Plenary Council and the hierarchy's centennial celebration of 1889 in Baltimore, the cardinal then came to the heart of the warning he had determined to utter:

> Woe to him my brethren, who would destroy or impair this blessed harmony that reigns among us! Woe to him who would sow tares of discord in the fair fields of the Church in America! Woe to him who would breed dissension among the leaders of Israel by introducing a spirit of nationalism into the camps of the Lord! Brothers we are, whatever may be our nationality, and brothers we shall remain. We will prove to our countrymen that the ties formed by grace and faith are stronger than flesh and blood. God and our country! — this our watchword. Loyalty to God's Church and to our country! — this our religious and political faith.[119]

Gibbons then developed the double loyalty that should motivate American Catholics, love of God and of country, and he exhorted his audience to glory in the title of American citizen. There was but one country to which American Catholics owed allegiance and that was the United States, and it mattered not whether it was the land of their birth or their adoption. Directing his remarks to the Catholic foreign-born, the cardinal stated that when they decided to cross the Atlantic to seek a new home in this country they should be animated by the spirit of Ruth in the Old Testament when she determined to join her husband's

---

[119] Gibbons, *A Retrospect of Fifty Years,* II, 151–152; the full text of the sermon is given here, pp. 148–155.

Cardinal Gibbons at the age of fifty-seven in 1891.

kindred in the land of Israel. Gibbons would have the Catholic immigrant say in the words of Ruth:

> Withersoever thou shalt go, I will go: and where thou shalt dwell, I also will dwell. Thy people shall be my people, and thy God my God. The land that shall receive thee dying, in the same will I die: and there will I be buried.[120]

Reactions to the Gibbons sermon in Milwaukee were both widespread and favorable. Although the Milwaukee *Daily Journal* of August 20 gave generous space to a front-page story on the ceremony with a paraphrase of some of the Gibbons points in the most general terms, its complimentary editorial in the same issue on Archbishop Katzer made no allusion whatever to the burning question of the hour. But the Chicago *Tribune* of August 21 was less restrained and pronounced Gibbons' sermon "patriotic in every sense," and said if it had not been delivered before the altar it would undoubtedly have been frequently applauded. In an editorial of the following day entitled, "Cardinal Gibbons' Wise Words," the *Tribune* felt that the cardinal's remarks were not just for Katzer and his immediate audience but for all American Catholics, and to the writer's mind the place was well chosen due to the part played during the previous year in Wisconsin by some of the churchmen in the Cahensly agitation. No one, said the *Tribune* editorial, could for a moment question Gibbons' sincerity because of his thoroughly American background. There were Americans who, it was true, feared the Catholic Church and the silly utterances of Cahensly enhanced that fear, but the cardinal was the "real" representative of American Catholicism and they, therefore, need not be alarmed by the un-American talk of European sympathizers. The Washington *Post* of August 24 had an editorial on the Gibbons sermon which it called, "Cardinal Gibbons' Americanism," in which his words in Milwaukee were pronounced "wise and patriotic." The *Post,* too, thought the place and occasion well chosen, for although everyone knew the cardinal's position, it was desirable that he should have spoken publicly and authoritatively in Milwaukee so soon after Cahensly's approach to the Vatican. The *Post* editorial writer saw significance as well in the sermon coming soon after Katzer's appointment to Milwaukee which

---

120 *Ibid.,* I, 153; Ruth 1:16–17.

had been regarded by some "as a distinct triumph for the German-American element in the Catholic Church of America." The New York *Freeman's Journal* of August 29 had high praise for the sermon in an editorial on "Milwaukee's Great Day," and stated that if the Church were governed by the principles laid down by Gibbons there need be little fear for its unity.

Archbishop Ireland had to admit, if a bit begrudgingly, that the Germans were on their best behavior during the visit of the cardinal to Wisconsin, although he would have Gibbons know that it sprang from a determination to make a favorable impression upon their distinguished guest. Ireland wished Gibbons would listen to his warning to conserve his health. He maintained he spoke thus out of personal devotedness as well as for the interests of the Church which needed the cardinal so much.[121] Denis O'Connell was more generous in his appreciation of the cardinal's performance, saying that he had converted his dangerous position at Milwaukee into a "very pedestal of glory." O'Connell thought the speech was truly masterly and that only extremists could take any exception to what had been said.[122] Over twenty years later Gibbons himself said the Milwaukee sermon was one of the most audacious things he ever did, and he remarked at the time, "When I finished they were aghast, but I think the lesson had its effect."[123]

There was little doubt in the minds of all who heard or read the sermon that it was a bold and offensive move into the camp of the enemy, but the cardinal's hope that it might bring peace proved vain. Not only had Cahensly returned to the subject by a second memorial to the Holy See earlier that summer which stirred further resentment by repeating the old charges,[124] but the bitterness engendered over the Faribault-Stillwater school plan of John Ireland intensified the conflict. In November the archbishops of the United States assembled in St. Louis for their annual meeting and the golden jubilee of Archbishop Kenrick. They did not fail to discuss at length the Cahensly memorials

---

[121] 88-V-3, Ireland to Gibbons, St. Paul, August 24, 1891. Neither the *Pastoral-Blatt* of St. Louis nor the *Katholische Volkszeitung* of Baltimore made any comment on the speech, although the latter carried a news item on the ceremony in its issue of August 29.

[122] 88-W-3, O'Connell to Gibbons, Grottaferrata, September 10, 1891.

[123] Will, *op. cit.*, I, 530.

[124] Reilly, *op. cit.*, III, Pt. III, 9–13. This second memorial bore the date of June 30, 1891.

and to single out two points for special condemnation, namely, Cahensly's exaggerated and unjustifiable statements of the losses to the faith in the United States and the interference of the subjects of foreign governments in the ecclesiastical affairs of the American Church. Cardinal Gibbons presided at the meeting which unanimously adopted a resolution to send a letter to the Holy See firmly protesting against "the utterly false representations" made by Cahensly.[125]

As much as Cardinal Gibbons might yearn for a quieting of the agitation of nationalist elements in the Church of the United States he was destined to disappointment, and the problem, in one aspect or another, would be with him through the remaining thirty years of his life. Even while he was in St. Louis attending the meeting in November, 1891, Cardinal Simeoni was preparing an inquiry for him based on a complaint from one of the German pastors of that city. Simeoni requested Gibbons to investigate the case of Father William Faerber, pastor of Our Lady of Victory Church in St. Louis, who had protested to the Propaganda that Archbishop Kenrick would not allow him to build a church for the Germans.[126] The cardinal was furnished with data from the provincial of the Vincentians, Thomas J. Smith, who explained that at St. Vincent's Church, on whose territory Faerber wished to impinge, they had two priests for the Germans and two schools in which both German and English were taught. Another parish in the neighborhood would wreck St. Vincent's, so Smith told the cardinal.[127] The Vincentian's testimony was corroborated by Father Philip P. Brady of St. John's Church in St. Louis,[128] and on the basis of these reports Gibbons made up his reply to Simeoni. He named Faerber and Muehlsiepen, the two German priests who were pushing the project of the new church, as disturbers of the peace and he said that in his judgment Archbishop Kenrick's action in withdrawing a previously granted permission for the new church should be sustained for the good of religion in St. Louis.[129]

[125] 89-D-5/1, Minutes of the Meeting of the Archbishops, St. Louis, November 29, 1891.

[126] 89-D-7, Simeoni to Gibbons, Rome, November 30, 1891.

[127] 89-F-7, Smith to Gibbons, Perryville, Missouri, December 23, 1891.

[128] 89-G-2, Brady to Gibbons, St. Louis, December 28, 1891.

[129] 89-G-6, Gibbons to Simeoni, Baltimore, December 29, 1891, copy in Latin; ten days later when he had further information on the case Gibbons wrote Simeoni again on January 8, 1892, copy in Latin (89-H-6).

When Cardinal Gibbons addressed Leo XIII in the name of the American hierarchy early in 1892 he thanked the Pontiff for his continuing benevolence as displayed on the occasion of Kenrick's jubilee, and he made special mention of their gratitude for the Pope's repelling the demand for national bishops. Gibbons stated that they had done all they could to quiet the disturbance, particularly when they witnessed the storm to which it had given rise in the newspapers. But it had been to no avail until Leo's own voice was heard. The Pope's words closed the mouths of all and showed with what wisdom and prudence His Holiness handled the Church's affairs.[130]

It is difficult to attribute Gibbons' message to Leo XIII to more than wishful thinking, for the controversy deepened during this year 1892 when the added factor of Ireland's school plan heaped more coals upon the fire. In fact, the cardinal himself told Archbishop Ryan three months after his letter to Leo that the unpleasant business was giving him real pain and he confessed, "I am praying and sighing for peace."[131] But of peace there was to be little in American Catholic circles during 1892 and when Father John Conway, editor of the *Northwestern Chronicle* of St. Paul, made a slashing attack on the Germans in the August issue of the *Review of Reviews,* Gibbons received an indignant letter from Katzer trying to clear his good name of the imputations which Conway made concerning him in rela-

---

[130] 89-J-7, Gibbons to Leo XIII, Baltimore, January 14, 1892, copy in Latin. A very free translation of this letter appeared in the *Catholic Mirror* of April 9, 1892, with Leo XIII's reply couched in general terms. Six weeks after Gibbons' letter to Leo XIII he urged on Ireland, who was then in Rome, that he impress on the officials of the Holy See that there was now a golden opportunity to bring the sentiment of the United States to the side of the Church ("and public sentiment is Emperor here, more powerful than the Kaiser"). But this opportunity, said the cardinal, would be lost if "the German or any other foreign element" was sustained at Rome. He fairly distinguished among the German groups in the American Church when he told Ireland, "The German movement is the work of a small but desperate clique. The saner part of the German priests and people see that the English language is fast becoming the language of the country" (AASP, Gibbons to Ireland, Baltimore, February 26, 1892, copy).

[131] 89-T-9, Gibbons to Ryan, Baltimore, April 11, 1892, copy. When a few weeks later Miecislaus Cardinal Ledochowski, Prefect of the Propaganda, wrote condemning the intrigues and agitation in the United States over appointing foreigners to episcopal sees, Gibbons told Corrigan that in order to provide a wide circulation for the prefect's letter of May 15 he was going to give it to the Associated Press (AANY, Gibbons to Corrigan, Baltimore, June 6, 1892).

tion to the Cahensly memorials.[132] The cardinal was probably by this time more than weary of the whole affair so he contented himself with telling Katzer he had not yet read the article but the archbishop's disavowal was evidence enough for him that he had had no participation in the Lucerne conference and its subsequent acts.[133] When the archbishops assembled under Gibbons' chairmanship at New York in November of that year they once more repudiated the false statements of Cahensly about the loss of faith of the immigrants in the United States and they again informed Leo XIII to that effect.[134]

When Cardinal Gibbons endeavored to show his good will toward the German Catholics in one of their societies' activities he was left in doubt about the wisdom of his effort. Alfred Steckel, recording secretary of the Deutscher Roemisch-Katholischer Central-Verein von Nord-Amerika, sent the cardinal a detailed report on the thirty-eighth annual convention of the society in which he outlined the size of membership, the amount of benefits derived from insurance for the widows and children of members, and the spiritual diligence which the society exercised over its members.[135] Gibbons congratulated the society on its progress and said it was accomplishing among the faithful of German descent what the Catholic Legion was doing for the English-speaking Catholics, and he concluded by expressing the prayerful wish that the Lord would continue to bless its work.[136] Steckel, of course, did not fail to publicize the blessing of the Cardinal of Baltimore in his paper, *Excelsior*. Whereupon the editor of the *Sternenbanner*, another German paper in Logansport, promptly warned Gibbons of what he considered a danger. This Peter Wallrath said he was a delegate to the Central-Verein's meeting in St. Louis where he heard the cardinal,

---

[132] 90-B-4, Katzer to Gibbons, Milwaukee, August 3, 1892. Cf. John Conway, "'Cahenslyism' Versus Americanism," *Review of Reviews*, VI (August, 1892), 43–48. The problem was treated at this time in France, too, when Vicount de Meaux contributed an article, "La question allemande dans l'église catholique aux Etats-Unis," to *Le Correspondant*, CLXVII (April 25, 1892), 273–283, in which he concluded that if the Germans would become good Americans there would be less trouble.

[133] 99-B-9, Gibbons to Katzer, Baltimore, August 14, 1892, *Personal*.

[134] 90-9-3, Minutes of the Meeting of the Archbishops, New York, November 16–19, 1892; Diary, November 19, 1892, p. 263.

[135] 92-U-8, Steckel to Gibbons, Milwaukee, December 7, 1893.

[136] 92-V-2, Gibbons to Steckel, Baltimore, December 10, 1893, copy.

Ireland, and the "liberal" bishops roundly denounced. Wallrath said he had been born and brought up in Germany, and he could talk, therefore, as one who knew Steckel and his crowd from the inside. He begged Gibbons to suggest some line of action to prevent this German nationalist element from continuing their activities.[137] The lack of evidence of any reply on the part of the cardinal may possibly suggest that he concluded under the circumstances that silence was his best policy.

While Cardinal Gibbons had by no means seen the end of the problem of German nationalism in the episode of the two editors, he had already made his position clear both in public pronouncements and in private correspondence. It would, therefore, be of little profit to pursue the course of the movement itself through the succeeding years. It will be sufficient to state here that the animus aroused over this question pervaded the atmosphere of American Catholicism through the closing years of the century, and in the other main movements of the period in which Gibbons was a principal actor one will encounter it again under various aspects. The strife and dissension occasioned in the early years of the Catholic University of America, the school controversy of Ireland, the temperance movement, and the struggle over the alleged heresy of Americanism as the century was closing would have been robbed of much of their bitterness had not the atmosphere been poisoned years before by the unfortunate differences between German- and English-speaking Catholics of the United States.[138]

In the case of the Irish there had been a great slackening in the number of immigrants to the United States toward the end of the century, although they were still coming in considerable

---

[137] 92-W-5, Wallrath to Gibbons, Logansport, December 25, 1893.

[138] In September 1910, Cahensly, who had been one of the most controversial figures during the troubles of the 1880's and 1890's, paid another visit to the United States. On this occasion he noted a great improvement of conditions among the German Catholics and other immigrants. In Washington he was cordially received at the Catholic University of America by the rector, Monsignor Shahan, and Cahensly remarked that at Baltimore he found a most friendly welcome from Cardinal Gibbons who invited him to dine with him (*St. Raphaels-Blatt*, XXV [October, 1910], 734–742). Two years after Gibbons' death the Central-Verein met in St. Paul where Archbishop Messmer was present. Messmer was quoted as having said, in reference to the controversy of years before, "I know that Cardinal Gibbons and Archbishop Ireland positively understood that they had made a mistake." Max Groesser, S.A.C., "Die deutschamerikanischen Katholiken in Kampf mit den Nativisten," *Gelbe Hefte*, V (1928–1929), 295.

numbers. Early in 1897 the cardinal published an article in Ireland on Irish immigration to the United States in which he reviewed the history of the movement from colonial times and assessed in a general way the contributions which the Irish had made to American life. On the point of advising the Irish about further immigration, he said he was in no position to offer counsel on the economic aspects of the problem. But in the moral sphere he would wish prospective Irish immigrants to know that if they intended to come to the United States they should be models of the natural virtues and practice thrift, perseverance, honesty, and fidelity to contracts, all of which Americans admired so much. Moreover, they should realize that the American people, regardless of some external evidence to the contrary, were a religious people. But above all Gibbons stressed the obligation of incoming Irishmen to be good citizens. In trying to resolve the grave question about whether they should come or stay at home he paid tribute to the extraordinary contributions of the Irish in spreading the Christian religion and in conclusion he said:

> I would not, therefore, discourage Irish immigration, because there are at stake more than economic considerations. There are at stake the interests of the Catholic religion, which in this land and this age are largely bound up with the interests of the Irish people.[139]

But four years later the cardinal had apparently changed his mind. He finished his journey to Europe in 1901 in Ireland and at Wexford he gave the only public address of his trip. When he reached New York on August 24 in an interview to the press he alluded to the Wexford speech and, according to the New York *Herald* of August 25, he said, "I urged the Irish people to stay at home and told them that the same activity displayed there, which they would need to use here, would result in bettering their conditions." The New York *Times* of the same date quoted Gibbons as having said, "The country, it seems to me, is overrun with immigrants, and a word of caution should be spoken to them."

As time passed the acute character of the German problem passed with it, but the new century, with its greatly accelerated immigration from eastern Europe, created for Gibbons and his

---

[139] "Irish Immigration to the United States," *Irish Ecclesiastical Record*, I, Fourth Series (February, 1897), 109.

colleagues further difficulties in relation to the eastern European Catholics. In Gibbons' own see city the recently organized schismatic Independent Polish Catholic Church attempted in 1898 to make inroads upon Baltimore's Catholic Poles. In February of that year a lawsuit was decided in the cardinal's favor when a clique of rebellious parishioners of Holy Rosary Church endeavored to gain control of the parish on the grounds of their having paid money in to its support. The court decided that there was no evidence of the money having been exacted from the defendants by either direct or indirect means. Five months later when a church was dedicated for the schismatic Poles, Gibbons addressed a lengthy letter to the pastors and congregations of the Polish parishes urging them to remain loyal to the Roman Church and pointing out the condemnation of the schismatics by Leo XIII. Although the rebels formed a congregation in Baltimore they did not draw off large numbers of the Catholic Poles and the loyalty of these people to the old faith was manifest at the time that the remodeled Holy Rosary Church was rededicated by the Cardinal in February, 1899.[140]

Likewise agitation for a greater representation in the hierarchy for the Poles became especially noticeable. The executive committee of the Polish Catholic Congress, for example, in April, 1902, circulated Gibbons and other American prelates with a respectful request that there be named an auxiliary bishop in Cleveland of Polish descent.[141] Three years later Archbishop Sebastian G. Messmer of Milwaukee informed Gibbons of the newspaper stories concerning the Polish effort to secure a bishop in his province, a move which Messmer felt would prove "a dangerous experiment" due to the fact that the Poles were not yet sufficiently Americanized.[142] When a group of Poles in Rochester defied Bishop McQuaid and the name of Gibbons was used ambiguously in the newspapers in connection with this episode, the cardinal hastily wrote to McQuaid to tell him that two

---

[140] Reily, *op. cit.,* V, 331, 381–386; VI, 201. There had been some difficulty with the Poles in Baltimore a few years earlier, for in a letter to Bishop Keane, Gibbons told him, "I have many things to annoy me just now, especially are the Poles giving me trouble" (ACUA, Keane Papers, Gibbons to Keane, Baltimore, March 28, 1890).

[141] 99-P-3, printed circular addressed to Bishop Ignatius F. Horstmann of Cleveland from the executive committee of the Polish Catholic Congress, Chicago, April 10, 1902, with a notation that copies were sent to Gibbons and others.

[142] 102-A, Messmer to Gibbons, Milwaukee, January 19, 1905.

months before a delegation of Poles from Rochester had waited on him at Southampton, Long Island, but he had sent them word that under no circumstances would he even see them.[143]

With the early years of the twentieth century the number of eastern European Catholics of the Greek Ruthenian rite coming to America likewise began to constitute a problem. The Apostolic Delegate to the United States, Diomede Falconio, asked Gibbons to bring to the attention of the archbishops at their meeting in the spring of 1905 the inquiry of the Prefect of Propaganda whether it would be advisable for the Holy See to appoint a bishop of that rite for these people in the United States. Although the metropolitans gave their assent to such an appointment at this meeting, it was only on certain conditions, one of which was that it should not be regarded as a precedent for other nationalities making similar claims.[144] A year later they reversed their stand and suggested that a vicar-general be named in all dioceses that had a number of the Greek Ruthenian Catholics since it would appear, said the archbishops, that a vicar-general would answer the desired purpose better than the appointment of a bishop.[145]

The final concern which Cardinal Gibbons was made to feel on the question of the foreign-born Catholics in the United States came, however, from the Poles. Six months before he died Archbishop Bonzano, the apostolic delegate, sent him a group of documents which revealed that Joseph Wierusz Kowalski, the Polish minister to the Holy See, had intervened at the Vatican in behalf of the appointment of bishops of Polish descent to the American hierarchy. In reply the cardinal told Bonzano he would bring the matter to the attention of the bishops' meeting about to convene, but as for himself, he had always followed the practice of recommending to vacant sees the most suitable candidates without consideration of nationality.[146] At the meeting of

---

[143] AAB, Unclassified, Gibbons to McQuaid, Baltimore, September 1, 1905, copy.

[144] 102-H, Falconio to Gibbons, Washington, April 5, 1905; 102-K, Minutes of the Meeting of the Archbishops, Washington, May 4, 1905.

[145] 103-E, Minutes of the Meeting of the Archbishops, Washington, April 26, 1906. On May 28, 1913, a diocese of the Byzantine rite was established in the United States for the Ukrainian Greek Catholics and on February 25, 1924, the Greek rite Diocese of Pittsburgh was erected by the Holy See to embrace all Greek Catholics in the United States of Russian, Hungarian, and Croatian nationality.

[146] 129-E, Gibbons to Bonzano, Baltimore, September 12, 1920, copy.

the hierarchy Gibbons delivered a strong speech against recognition of any national groups within the American Church. He recalled his fight of years before when the Germans had made a similar effort and he stated that he would oppose this latest move with his last breath. "Ours is the American Church," said the cardinal, "and not Irish, German, Italian or Polish — and we will keep it American." He was enthusiastically applauded by his fellow bishops who were in unanimous agreement with him, and one bishop who was present later wrote of Gibbons' remarks, "He was at his best, and seemed only about fifty years [of age]."[147] The deep resentment which the hierarchy felt toward this renewed attempt at what was termed "foreign intermeddling" in the affairs of the Church of the United States[148] was shown when a committee consisting of Archbishops George W. Mundelein of Chicago and Dennis J. Dougherty of Philadelphia was appointed to draft a protest to the Holy See against the interference of the Polish minister to the Vatican. The two archbishops communicated their ideas to Gibbons along with the texts of the protest,[149] and the cardinal incorporated their statements along with his own and affixed his signature to the document sent in the name of the entire hierarchy.

Four months before his death the Archbishop of Baltimore forwarded to Pietro Cardinal Gasparri, Secretary of State, this very strongly worded protest against the action of the Polish legation at the Holy See. Gibbons quoted the two pertinent resolutions passed unanimously at the meeting of the American hierarchy in September, which condemned the interference of any foreign government in the affairs of the Church of the United States, as well as the conduct of any body of clergy who

---

[147] Archives of the Diocese of Rockford, Diary of Bishop Peter J. Muldoon, September 23, 1920.

[148] 129-N, Dougherty to Gibbons, Philadelphia, October 4, 1920. Insofar as his own archdiocese was concerned Gibbons, in answer to an inquiry of Cajetan Cardinal de Lai concerning the Catholic immigrants in his jurisdiction late in 1912, replied that there were around 20,000 Poles, 8,000 Bohemians, 2,500 Lithuanians, and 4,000 Italians among the immigrant groups then in the archdiocese. The first three were reported to be making out quite well, but the Italians were not so easily cared for by reason of their being scattered in different areas, having so little instruction in religion, and giving no support to the Church (109-B, Gibbons to De Lai, Baltimore, February 5, 1913, copy in Italian).

[149] 130-M, Mundelein to Gibbons, Chicago, November 16, 1920.

would appeal to laymen or a foreign government with the idea of coercing the episcopate in the selection of candidates for vacant sees. Gibbons, speaking in the name of the entire hierarchy, repudiated the charges of neglect of the Catholic Poles in this country, and said there was no disposition on the part of the bishops to "Americanize" any of the existing Polish parishes. He stigmatized the move for Polish bishops as a step toward isolating the Polish Catholics from the rest of their coreligionists, and he branded the attempt to preserve a distinct and separate Polish nationality in the United States as something that would be "absolutely injurious both to the Church and to the Country."[150]

Although wonderful progress had been made in assimilating the thousands of foreign-born Catholics who had come to the United States since the days of Gibbons' youth, their numbers had been so great, their knowledge of English so meager, and the spirit of their fatherland so strong in the hearts of many of these people that even the lengthy episcopate of fifty-three years during which James Gibbons served the American Church was not enough time to see the task to completion. Yet the cardinal in his public avowal of love for the country and its institutions, his tactful handling of the foreign-born and their peculiar problems, and the role of leadership which he assumed when Cahensly-ism was at its peak made a lasting contribution to the settlement of what John Gilmary Shea in 1883 had called "a canker eating away the life of the Church in the United States."[151] And a later generation appreciated his effort. Referring to the conflict of nationalities within the American Church, André Siegfried stated in 1927:

> Thirty years ago that great statesman, Cardinal Gibbons, steered the Catholic Church into a very different path. He wished it to take its place among the national institutions of the country, not as an Irish or German influence, but as simply and essentially American.[152]

Still more recently in alluding to Gibbons' work in behalf of the foreign immigrants, a leading Protestant historian wrote, "It was particularly fortunate that the American Catholics should

---

[150] 130-N, Gibbons to Gasparri, Baltimore, November 18, 1920, copy.
[151] John Gilmary Shea, "Converts — Their Influence and Work in This Country," *American Catholic Quarterly Review,* VIII (July, 1883), 525.
[152] *America Comes of Age* (New York, 1927), p. 50.

have had such wise and patriotic leadership at the time that Catholic immigration was pouring into the country in such unprecedented streams."[153]

---

[153] William Warren Sweet, *The Story of Religion in America* (New York, 1939), p. 537.

CHAPTER X

The Early Years of the University

THERE must have been many times during the last twenty years of the nineteenth century when the Archbishop of Baltimore longed for an opportunity to devote himself uninterruptedly to the administration of his archdiocese. The constant pressure of vexing national problems would have taxed the strength and energies of a far more robust man than Gibbons. But however much he might have desired a respite from worries of more than a local nature, he was not destined to enjoy it. In the years after 1880 it seemed that hardly had one question affecting the welfare of the Church of the nation been settled before another appeared. Not until the opening of the twentieth century did there descend upon the Catholic Church of the United States a period of relative peace and quiet which enabled Cardinal Gibbons and his associates to relax their vigilance and to concentrate more fully upon their diocesan affairs.

Apart entirely from the prominence which his office as ordinary of the premier see of the country gave to Gibbons, his personal graciousness and a growing confidence in his qualities of leadership inspired other members of the American hierarchy to turn more and more to him for advice and counsel. In a number of matters submitted to his judgment Gibbons was ill prepared by reason of knowledge and experience to offer direction. But his extraordinary wisdom afforded him remarkable assistance in such cases. In matters of dubious merit Gibbons unfailingly fell back on the technique of sounding out others more familiar than himself with the business in hand. Meanwhile he would study the problem more closely and put out tentative opinions of his own while awaiting the verdict of his advisers. For the most part this was the procedure he followed, although on occasion the cardinal had fixed ideas on a question from the outset, and in cases of that kind he took his stand and held to it in the face of opposition from any quarter. Where Cardinal Gibbons' services proved particularly useful was in circumstances that permitted free play to his genius for the arts of conciliation. More than any of the other American bishops of the time, Gibbons seemed to be able to hold together opposing factions, and where he was unable to keep them together, he at least proved to be the best medium through which differences could be ironed out and erstwhile opponents reconciled. Such was the type of service which Gibbons rendered in a special way to the Catholic University of America in its formative period.

While Gibbons as a young priest and minor official of the Second Plenary Council of Baltimore in 1866 probably heard mention of the question of a national university for the Church of the United States, it most likely meant little or nothing to him at the time.[1] Moreover, the agitation which was carried on in certain Catholic journals after that date might very well have engaged his attention as a passing reader, but there is no evidence that he took any part in the discussion during the years when he served as a bishop in North Carolina and Virginia. It was only in the period immediately preceding the Third Plenary Council of 1884 that the proponents of the idea of a university grew more insistent and practically forced the new Archbishop of Baltimore to give the plan some consideration. This was the type of question in which Gibbons would feel his own inadequacy and would be inclined to seek the guidance of others. He had never been an academic man nor had he ever experienced any training in a university. True, he had made a very superior showing as a student at St. Charles College and St. Mary's Seminary, but his formal education had been limited to the professional training given to candidates for the priesthood, and about the only contact Gibbons had maintained — aside from social visits — with educational institutions above the secondary level was to sit in occasionally as an examiner of students who

---

[1] For the background to the conciliar action on the university in 1884, cf. the writer's volume, *The Formative Years of the Catholic University of America* (Washington, 1946), pp. 15–86. Through the 1870's there was considerable agitation among the German Catholics for a Catholic university in the United States for their own people. Cf. *Monsignor Joseph Jessing, 1836–1899* (Columbus, 1936), by Leo F. Miller *et al.* for the part played by Jessing in this movement (p. 162).

were giving a defense of their theses at St. Mary's in Baltimore.[2]

But regardless of his lack of university training, something which Gibbons shared in common with practically all his fellow bishops, he would soon have to face the university problem. By far the most prominent protagonist in behalf of a university in the early 1880's was Bishop Spalding of Peoria. So eager was he to make a start that he seized on the financial embarrassment of Mount Saint Mary Seminary of the West in Cincinnati, occasioned by the Purcell bankruptcy, to suggest that the seminary there be taken over by the hierarchy. The Coadjutor Archbishop of Cincinnati, William Henry Elder, welcomed the proposal as a partial solution to his troubles, and with that in mind Elder urged the Archbishop of Baltimore that he use his influence to push Spalding's idea without delay.[3] The extant records do not reveal Gibbons' reaction to Elder's prompting in this and several subsequent letters relating to a university project.[4] Meanwhile Spalding continued to agitate the question and in the silver jubilee sermon at St. Francis Seminary in Milwaukee on June 30, 1881, he outlined more fully his ideas. The sermon was later published in a volume of essays by Spalding, and when Gibbons acknowledged receipt of the book it gave the Bishop of Peoria a chance to urge a university upon the Archbishop of Baltimore and to pledge his personal services to such an institution.[5] During the year 1882 the Catholic journals were writing pro and con on the university question, and that year also brought the adumbration of opposition in the form of a pastoral letter of August 20 from one of the future university's stoutest opponents, Bishop McQuaid of Rochester.

Meanwhile no action was taken and if the friends of the university idea were hopeful when they learned that the arch-

---

[2] For example, the *Catholic Mirror* of July 14, 1866, spoke of Gibbons as one of the public examiners of a certain William O'Brien at St. Mary's. Gibbons was represented as having presented the student "with arguments that would sadly puzzle a less skillful opponent," in his endeavor to prove that "historical testimony is incapable of giving us real certainty."

[3] 75-M-9, Elder to Gibbons, Cincinnati, November 19, 1880. On August 8, 1881, Elder proposed to Gibbons that a beginning for a future university might be made at Woodstock College (76-B-2).

[4] The archives of the Archdiocese of Cincinnati were searched in vain for Gibbons letters in these early years of Elder's administration as coadjutor.

[5] 76-A-8, Spalding to Gibbons, Peoria, July 18, 1882. Spalding's Milwaukee sermon appeared under the title, "The Catholic Priesthood," in his volume, *Lectures and Discourses* (New York, 1882).

bishops were going to Rome in November, 1883, to prepare for a plenary council, their hopes were due for a disappointment. The Roman conferences, as we have seen, did embody a good deal of discussion on matters relating to Catholic education but the project of a university found no place in the conversations of the American prelates with the cardinals of the Propaganda. Although a university had not entered into the discussions for the council in Rome, it continued to be mentioned in the spring of 1884 as plans went forward for the gathering. Bishop Gilmour expressed the hope that something would be done to make provision for the higher education of the clergy, an idea which, as he recalled, he had mentioned previously to Gibbons and to the Propaganda on his last visit.[6] In reply to Gilmour's suggestion Gibbons said he agreed with him that "a seminary for higher education" should be established in this country. The archbishop mistakenly told the Bishop of Cleveland that such was commended in the schema for the council, and he added that in the Baltimore seminary they already had a class in cosmogony and physical science with two years devoted to moral and natural philosophy.[7] This early assent of Gibbons to the idea of an institution for the higher education of the clergy was given, it would seem, more out of support for what he believed to be contained in the schema than from a deep personal conviction of the need. Actually there was no such provision in the schema, although Gibbons persisted under that impression for the next two and a half years until he was corrected by Archbishop Corrigan.[8]

In the months before the opening of the council the Archbishop of Baltimore continued to receive arguments for and against a university from various bishops. During that time he was deeply absorbed in council business and probably gave the matter little thought. The pace of developments, however, was quickened when four days after the formal opening of the council Miss Mary Gwendoline Caldwell, a wealthy young heiress of New York City, gave written expression of her intention to donate $300,000 toward the beginning of a university.[9] The Caldwell offer, followed three days later by the powerful sermon of Spalding for a university delivered in the cathedral, definitely

---

[6] 77-T-6, Gilmour to Gibbons, Cleveland, April 6, 1884.

[7] ADC, Gibbons to Gilmour, Baltimore, April 7, 1884.

[8] AANY, Gibbons to Corrigan, Baltimore, November 4, 1886.

[9] 78-T-6, Caldwell to Gibbons, Baltimore, November 13, 1884.

put the idea in a new light. Ten days after Spalding's sermon the subject arose for discussion in the council and a heated debate ensued with Gibbons presiding as apostolic delegate. On the day after the debate the deputation of theologians recommended that the university question be referred to a special committee. When Bishop Tobias Mullen of Erie made a motion for the chapter on a university to be expunged or referred to a future council, it mustered only twenty-three votes. It left the way clear for Gibbons to appoint the suggested committee which he did in the persons of Corrigan, Kenrick, Alemany, Ryan, and Spalding. This committee studied the problem further and on December 2 reported to the council that Miss Caldwell's gift should be accepted and plans begun for a university. The council accepted the special committee's report and embodied the plan in the decrees to be sent to Rome for approval. The Holy See approved the decree with a few minor changes, and the American hierarchy was thus committed to a university for the American Church.

There was no feature of the legislation of the Baltimore council which caused more comment in the press than the decree on the university. Speculation was rife and critics of the scheme were not lacking. In the meantime the Archbishop of Baltimore held his peace, although two days before the close of the council he had been named chairman of the committee for the university at the request of Miss Caldwell. A month later Gibbons endeavored to persuade the young lady to make the actual transfer of the money she had promised, but Miss Caldwell was not disposed to do so until the business had taken a more definite shape. The archbishop was not too pleased with her response, and he suggested to Archbishop Corrigan in communicating the Caldwell reply that he have Spalding make another attempt. As Gibbons told the New York coadjutor, they could take no further steps until the money was in their hands.[10]

On the occasion of the dedication of the Church of St. Paul the Apostle in New York on January 25, 1885, an informal meeting of the university committee was held at which Gibbons was not present. At that time the members discussed the possibility of buying Seton Hall College at South Orange, New Jersey, and the discussions of this informal gathering were duly reported to Gib-

---

[10] AANY, Gibbons to Corrigan, Baltimore, January 11, 1885.

bons. Miss Caldwell did not approve of the New Jersey site nor of putting her money into an old institution. She, therefore, informed Gibbons that she would favor Washington as the site for the university and she asked him to support her choice.[11] However, it would be quite some time, and only after very animated argument, that the question of a site would finally be settled. Gibbons did not seem at this time to have any strong prepossessions regarding the site to be chosen, and he told Father John M. Farley of New York, secretary of the committee, that he would be in accord with any location which a majority of the committee desired to select. The archbishop seemed to favor Seton Hall over Washington and the only misgiving he expressed regarding the college at South Orange was that it might be invaded by "the terrible Jersey mosquitoes."[12]

As plans progressed the inevitable opposition to so large an undertaking manifested itself in various quarters. This opposition was called to the attention of Gibbons by the publishers of the *American Catholic Quarterly Review* who believed that if the archbishop would write an article on the proposed university for their journal it might have a good effect in stilling criticism.[13] Although Gibbons did not avail himself of the offer, it may have had something to do with hastening his action for a formal meeting of the committee of which he was chairman. The Bishop of St. Paul was growing restive at the long delay and he pointedly reminded Gibbons that two members of the original committee had already died, that interest in the project was endangered by further delay, and that as far as the meeting in New York in January was concerned, nothing was settled because of Gibbons' absence.[14] Just two days previous to Ireland's letter the Archbishop of Baltimore decided to consult Archbishop Corrigan on the advisability of convening a meeting of the committee. He confessed that if there was any blame for delay it rested principally on him, but since the money of Miss Caldwell had not yet arrived he had not seen his way to acting sooner. However, if Corrigan advised a meeting he would send out the invitations.[15] Corrigan answered that while Cardinal McCloskey declined to

---

[11] 79-D-6, Caldwell to Gibbons, New York, February 6, 1885.
[12] Letterbook, Gibbons to Farley, Baltimore, March 3, 1885, p. 145.
[13] 79-F-11, Hardy & Mahony to Gibbons, Philadelphia, March 10, 1885.
[14] 79-H-5, Ireland to Gibbons, St. Paul, March 26, 1885.
[15] AANY, Gibbons to Corrigan, Baltimore, March 24, 1885.

assume any responsibility for the Archdiocese of New York in the question of a university, he had left his coadjutor free to act as he thought best and, therefore, Corrigan would advise a meeting of the committee.[16]

The coolness of Cardinal McCloskey was a source of discouragement to Archbishop Gibbons. He revealed his own lack of enthusiasm for the university when he told Corrigan that he had almost given up the idea of calling a meeting of the committee after receiving his letter since, as he expressed it, "yr. views coincide with my own." Apparently Corrigan had undergone a change of mind since his letter of the previous week recommending a meeting. However, the strong pressure of Spalding and Ireland had decided Gibbons to make a new start and he set May 7 for the date of the meeting in Baltimore. He was still hoping that the Bishop of Newark would sell Seton Hall College, and when Miss Caldwell had called on him unexpectedly the previous Monday he had spoken very plainly to her about her duty to fulfill her obligation in turning over the money regardless of the site of the university.[17] When the Archbishop of Cincinnati reiterated his objections to the selection of Washington as a site, Gibbons assured Elder that his opinion would be given due consideration, and he added that he would not care to have Baltimore selected since it might interfere with the work of the Sulpicians in the seminary there, whereas Philadelphia was a central place and would be, Gibbons thought, a desirable locality.[18]

When James Gibbons took the chair at the meeting of the university committee in his residence on May 7, 1885, he little realized that this was the first of a very lengthy series of meetings on university business over which he would preside during the next thirty-five years. From this time on no step of any consequence was taken without previous consultation with the chairman of the committee and, after the formal constitution of the university was approved, Gibbons acted in all important matters in his capacity as chancellor of the institution. On May 7 the leading item of business was the selection of a site and when Bishop Spalding put the motion for Washington it carried with-

---

[16] AAB, unclassified, Corrigan to Gibbons, New York, March 25, 1885.
[17] AANY, Gibbons to Corrigan, Baltimore, April 1, 1885.
[18] AAC, Gibbons to Elder, Baltimore, April 22, 1885.

out any difficulty. The choice was not to the liking of Gibbons since he expressed his regret at the decision to Elder, but he explained that when he saw the strong preference of Spalding and Ireland for the national capital and knew that it was also the wish of Miss Caldwell, he did not urge his own views. He told the Archbishop of Cincinnati, who had been the strongest opponent of Washington, that he would still have preferred Philadelphia.[19] The news of the selection of Washington was greeted with favor by both the Catholic and secular press, and the New York *Times* of May 11 stated in an editorial that the choice was an evidence that the American hierarchy recognized the promise which Washington gave as a cultural center. Gibbons may have been more reconciled to Washington when he learned that it met with the pleasure of his favorite, Dr. O'Connell in Rome, although O'Connell let it be known that the entire project of a university for the Church of the United States had given rise to misgivings among some of the Roman prelates, and he cautioned that it would not be wise to proceed much further without consulting the Holy See about the plans.[20]

In the early fall of 1885 Bishop Spalding completed the text of a circular which was to be sent out to all interested parties in an effort to enlist support for the university. Gibbons gave his approval to the document, and later that autumn he received a letter from Cardinal Newman to whom a copy had been sent by an anonymous friend. Newman stated that at a time when the Catholics of the old world had so much to depress and trouble them the circular on the prospective university for the new world had rejoiced the hearts, as he said, "of all well-educated Catholics in these Islands."[21] Before the next meeting of the committee scheduled for November 11 the Holy Father had shown his interest in the question when he addressed a private letter on October 22 to the Archbishop of Baltimore in which he expressed his gratification that the American bishops were planning a university for their country.[22]

The arrival of Leo XIII's letter in Baltimore in time for the

[19] *Ibid.,* Gibbons to Elder, Baltimore, May 7, 1885.
[20] 79-L-15, O'Connell to Gibbons, Rome, May 28, 1885; 79-N-13, same to same, Rome, June 28, 1885.
[21] 79-T-11, Newman to Gibbons, n.p., October 10, 1885, copy. The original of this letter is in the ACUA.
[22] *Acta et decreta* (1886 edition), pp. lxiv–lxv.

committee meeting on November 11 enabled Gibbons to read it to the members as an encouragement to their efforts. On that occasion the principal item of business was the authorization to be given to Bishops Spalding, Ireland, Keane, and Marty as collectors of funds throughout the dioceses of the United States. It was decided that Gibbons should write a letter to the American hierarchy explaining the authorization of the collectors and inviting the support of the bishops for their work. When three months had passed and the Archbishop of Baltimore had not yet written the letter, Bishop Keane, who was meeting with a rather cool reception in New York, suggested to Farley that he remind the archbishop of the obligation.[23] Gibbons had evidently not yet warmed to the business in hand since his activity up to this time had been held to a minimum. For example, when he had the Pope's endorsement of the university idea printed for the hierarchy, he distributed it to them with the bare statement that it had been written in reply to his own letter of the previous December. In other words, Gibbons did not expand in any way on the question himself.[24] But Keane did not hesitate to prod the archbishop from time to time. After he had been on the job collecting in New York for some time he informed him that New York was claiming most of what had been accomplished thus far, and he asked pointedly, "Does it not seem time for Baltimore to speak out & act?"[25]

The caution of Archbishop Gibbons found support in the spring of 1886 from several factors. While Denis O'Connell was personally enthusiastic about the university, the impression gained from his correspondence in these months would suggest that the idea had not taken too well with a number of the officials of the Roman Curia. Irresponsible stories in the American press were the occasion for embarrassment to all parties interested in the project when, for example, the Washington *Sunday Herald* carried a story in the latter part of March that dissension had broken out in the committee and that sectional rivalry had arisen.[26] But a matter that was calculated to give Gibbons more

---

[23] 80-D-11, Farley to Gibbons, New York, January 29, 1886.

[24] AAC, printed circular of Gibbons to the American hierarchy, Baltimore, November 12, 1885.

[25] 80-S-9, Keane to Gibbons, Richmond, April 13, 1886.

[26] *Catholic Mirror,* March 27, 1886, quoting the Washington *Sunday Herald.* A search of the Library of Congress files of this paper revealed that the run begins with the issue of March 22 and the item was not in that issue.

serious concern was the resignation of Archbishop Heiss from the university committee. Heiss pleaded his many duties in Milwaukee, the great distance he would have to travel to meetings, and the little he could contribute to the university work.[27] Although there was no reason to question the sincerity of the Archbishop of Milwaukee, his resignation was a rather serious matter since it removed from the university project the leading representative of the German Catholics in the United States. It did not add to Gibbons' comfort to be told some time later by O'Connell that the Heiss resignation was made to look "ominous" in Rome.[28] But whatever his private feelings may have been, Gibbons prepared himself for the meeting at his residence on May 12 when the important subject of a rector for the future university would come up.

When the committee was able to dispose of an item of business pertaining to the clearing of the title to the Washington property at the meeting in Baltimore on May 12, a motion was made and carried that the Archbishops of Baltimore, Boston, New York, and Philadelphia should be constituted a special committee to choose a rector. Gibbons stated that the success of the venture depended entirely upon selecting a rector who would devote all his energies to the work in the way that President Daniel Coit Gilman was doing for the Johns Hopkins University.[29] The first choice of the four archbishops was John Lancaster Spalding, but when he refused the post they then chose John J. Keane, Bishop of Richmond. After expressing his reluctance to undertake a position for which he had no previous training or experience, Keane was at length prevailed on to accept the rectorship, it being understood that the matter would be kept confidential until it had received the approval of the Holy See.[30]

It was then decided that Gibbons should make a full report in writing to Rome on all that had been done thus far on the university question. At this point Keane insisted that Rome be requested to withhold its approval for any other university in the United States for twenty-five years. This request puzzled Gibbons. Knowing nothing of the fact that the previous winter in New York Archbishop Corrigan had told Keane he felt a

---

[27] 80-S-17/1, Heiss to Gibbons, Milwaukee, April 17, 1886.
[28] 81-R-10, O'Connell to Gibbons, Rome, August 14, 1886.
[29] ADR, Keane to O'Connell, Richmond, May 20, 1886.
[30] *Ibid.*

university in New York under the Jesuits should be established, Gibbons pressed Keane in the meeting to give his reasons for this demand of the Holy See. But since Archbishop Corrigan was present and remained silent Keane naturally did not feel free to speak. He later explained in private to the Archbishop of Baltimore what lay behind his request, at which, said Keane, "he was not a little astonished."[31]

Before the meeting adjourned it was decided that Bishop Keane should personally go to Rome in the autumn to lay the plans before the officials of the curia. John Ireland was going at that time to make his *ad limina* visit and it was the view of the committee that the two bishops should travel and work together. Corrigan had stated he had information which indicated that the university was looked on with disfavor by the Holy See, which prompted Gibbons to instance Leo XIII's letter of encouragement in opposition to this view; whereupon the Archbishop of New York narrowed his original assertion of Roman disfavor to the Congregation of the Propaganda. But if the opposition was there it was all the more reason why it should be met honestly and energetically by the delegation to Rome, and that was the view that prevailed among a majority of the committee. Keane and Ireland were not to depart until the fall and in the meantime the former feared there might be a good deal of private opposition expressed in Rome. He, therefore, begged his friend, Denis O'Connell, to be on his guard and watch to protect the university project against what he termed "petty undermining."[32]

In the interval between the meeting on May 12 and the following autumn Bishop Keane busied himself with visits to educational institutions in New England and Canada, the details of which he described in full for the Archbishop of Baltimore. While awaiting the move of the Holy See, Gibbons withheld further action other than to furnish various correspondents with answers to their inquiries about the university insofar as he was able. When a generous layman of Currie, Minnesota, offered $500 toward the endowment of a chair of philosophy in honor

---

[31] ACUA, "Chronicles of the Catholic University of America from 1885," p. 10. This is a typed report by Keane bearing the date of January 9, 1894. Hereafter it will be referred to as "Chronicles."

[32] ADR, Keane to O'Connell, Richmond, May 20, 1886.

of Orestes Brownson, Gibbons replied he thought the idea an admirable one and he knew of no better way to pay tribute to the memory of the illustrious convert.[33] Quite unknown to the chairman of the university committee, Cardinal Simeoni, Prefect of the Propaganda, informed Corrigan that he had heard there were differences among the bishops on the proposed university and he would, therefore, appreciate a confidential statement of the Archbishop of New York's opinion on the matter.[34] Corrigan had recently sought the judgment of Father Robert Fulton, provincial of the New York-Maryland Province of the Jesuits, who had opposed the university so strenuously in the Third Plenary Council. Fulton complied with a detailed statement of objections to the university on September 17.[35] Three weeks later the Archbishop of New York informed his friend, Bishop McQuaid, of Simeoni's request and he outlined for McQuaid the substance of his reply to the Prefect of Propaganda. It is interesting to note that Corrigan's summary of objections to the university followed almost exactly the points of opposition given to him by the Jesuit provincial three weeks before.[36] When Keane and Ireland arrived in Rome later that fall it was not too difficult for them to spot the source of the opposition to the university which had been reaching the Holy See from the United States.

It was in this same autumn of 1886 that the committee of archbishops of the country, constituted by the Third Plenary Council for the investigation of secret societies, had reached a point where, on Rome's suggestion, they were ready to hold a joint meeting on the Grand Army of the Republic, the Ancient Order of Hibernians, and the Knights of Labor. The occasion offered a favorable time for a further meeting on university business. With that in mind Gibbons fixed October 27 as the date for the university committee to convene, to be followed the next day by the meeting on the secret societies. The principal business of October 27 in relation to the university had to do with approving the texts of two lengthy letters drawn up for Leo XIII and Simeoni to which there would be affixed the signatures of all members of the committee. After the letters

---

[33] Letterbook, Gibbons to John Sweetman, Baltimore, October 13, 1886, p. 181.
[34] AANY, Simeoni to Corrigan, Rome, September 11, 1886.
[35] *Ibid.*, Fulton to Corrigan, New York, September 17, 1886.
[36] ADRo, Corrigan to McQuaid, Newark, October 9, 1886.

had received the approbation of all the university committee, allowing for some minor modifications suggested by Archbishop Corrigan, the documents were signed. Since the Archbishops of St. Louis, New Orleans, Cincinnati, Santa Fe, and Chicago were then in Baltimore to discuss the problem of the secret societies these five metropolitans were invited to affix their signatures as well, although they were not members of the university committee. The letters to the Pope and the Propaganda prefect, outlining what had been done to date and stating the desires of the American prelates in regard to a university, thus bore the names of nine of the twelve archbishops of the United States.[37] Armed with these documents, Bishops Keane and Ireland sailed on the *Aurania* three days later to lay the question before the Roman authorities.

While the university was uppermost in the minds of Keane and Ireland in making their journey to Europe, it so happened that upon their arrival in the Eternal City they soon discovered that the troublesome questions of the Knights of Labor, the Abbelen petition in behalf of the German Catholics, the agitation over the single tax doctrines of Henry George, and the prospect of a nuncio for the United States would distract their attention from their principal objective. However, they would not have to carry the entire burden of these problems themselves as the time was approaching when they would be joined in Rome by the Archbishop of Baltimore. Gibbons had received official notification of his nomination as a cardinal the previous May and it would, therefore, be necessary for him to cross the Atlantic to receive the red hat at the consistory which Leo XIII would call early in the new year. While the two bishops were still on the high seas Gibbons was made aware of his mistake in thinking the university had been included in the original schema of 1883 of the Third Plenary Council. Corrigan apprised him of his error, and in acknowledging his mistake Gibbons revealed the motive which had thus far governed his attitude toward the university project. He told Corrigan:

> Whilst I feel bound to labor for this work as emanating from the Council, I must confess that my zeal for the undertaking was stimu-

---

[37] 82-D-3, Gibbons *et al.* to Leo XIII, Baltimore, October 27, 1886, copy; 82-D-5, Gibbons *et al.* to Simeoni, Baltimore, October 27, 1886, copy.

lated by the strong impression resting on my mind that it had
originated with the Holy See & that it recommended [it] to us
in Rome.[38]

This letter would indicate that up to this time the chairman
of the university committee was not very ardent in his support
of the project.

As was to be anticipated, Keane and Ireland were not long
in Rome before they encountered resistance to the university.
So seriously did they regard this opposition that they composed
a very strong answer to all the objections made to them by
the Propaganda officials.[39] A copy of this lengthy document,
along with private letters from Keane and O'Connell, kept
Gibbons posted on developments in Rome. When the opposition
went so far as to impugn the sincerity of the signatures affixed
to the letters to the Pope and Simeoni as drawn up in Baltimore,
Ireland and Keane were sufficiently alarmed to have a letter
printed exposing the effort to discredit the signatures and asking
the American bishops to write Rome in defense of their own
sincerity.[40] In their conferences with the officials of the Roman
Curia, Keane and Ireland found that the Vatican was far more
friendly to the university idea than was the Propaganda, and
when the secretary of the congregation, Archbishop Jacobini,
told the two bishops that the whole question was to be laid
aside until the arrival of Gibbons and then "laid on the table
indefinitely," that proved too much for the Americans. They
demanded and received an audience of Leo XIII the next day
during which they were treated very kindly. They were able
to answer several inquiries of the Pope and the Holy Father
told them he had not yet made up his mind about the
university, but he asked the two bishops to remain in Rome
until Gibbons arrived.[41]

In the meanwhile the Archbishop of Baltimore took no action
on the university matter. The failure of Gibbons to come out
strongly in behalf of the question had proved to be a source
of embarrassment to the Americans in Rome. Naturally the

---

[38] AANY, Gibbons to Corrigan, Baltimore, November 4, 1886.

[39] 82-G-6, Animadversiones quaedam de universitate in America fundanda, Rome,
December 6, 1886.

[40] AABo, printed letter of Ireland and Keane to John J. Williams, Rome,
December 14, 1886.

[41] ACUA, "Chronicles," pp. 13–14.

Holy See would look to Gibbons as the highest dignitary of the Church of the United States and chairman of the university committee, to give it guidance and direction, particularly so when reports containing objections to the university were reaching the Roman Curia from bishops in the United States. The reaction of the Pope and the Roman officials to Gibbons' attitude was conveyed by Keane in an extremely candid letter which we have already seen in connection with the Abbelen petition of this same autumn of 1886. Regarding Gibbons' conduct on the university, Keane told the Archbishop of Baltimore:

> We have lately been pouring out our honest indignation at the charge that the signatures of the Prelates to the University petition could not be implicitly trusted as giving the real sentiment of the signers; but I cannot help recognizing with what crushing force they can say to us: "Why look, even your Cardinal puts his name to statements & recommendations which he will afterwards take back or modify; if even he can send us important documents, not because he believes them best for the interests of the Church, but in order to please this one or that one, what confidence can we repose in any of these signatures?" . . . Even the Holy Father himself has thus intimated his apprehension that your Eminence was uncertain & vacillating in your views as to the University's location, etc.[42]

Once in possession of the Keane letter it would be obvious to Gibbons that he would have to declare himself once and for all on the university when he reached the Eternal City. Meanwhile the opposition party did not relax its efforts, and McQuaid told Corrigan that the American bishops in Rome might or might not know that his letters to the Holy See on the university question were "blocking their game," although he suspected that they knew since he had made no secret of his views.[43]

---

[42] 82-J-4, Keane to Gibbons, Rome, December 29, 1886.

[43] AANY, McQuaid to Corrigan, Rochester, January 22, 1887. Ireland was meeting this opposition as well as he could from Rome. He wrote Corrigan on the German question and the McGlynn case, and in regard to the university, he said he would stop in New York long enough on his way home to give the archbishop "a good talking" on his opposition. He stated frankly he did not think Corrigan's conduct had been fair in not revealing his opposition openly since they had left the United States feeling that he was in accord with them. Miss Edes, said Ireland, had never ceased in Corrigan's name to poison the mind of Propaganda against the university, "with arms furnished by you." Had it not been for Leo XIII's interest the affair would have dragged on so long at Propaganda on account of Edes' efforts that Ireland confessed he would have

Cardinal Gibbons arrived in Rome early in February, 1887, and was soon plunged into a busy round of events which more than filled his days before the consistory scheduled for March 17. Keane and Ireland, of course, brought the cardinal up to date on all the current questions that had occupied their time during the nearly three months they had already spent at the Holy See. Gibbons was especially irked at the secrecy of the opposition to the university reaching the Roman officials from the United States. He informed Archbishop Elder of this after he was in Rome only a few days and he made it clear that honest opposition dictated by conscience met his full approval, but he did not like opposition to measures of this kind to be put in what he called "a covert way." He told Elder that the Propaganda had informed him some of the bishops signed the petition for the university out of complacency but that they were really opposed to it. Under the circumstances Gibbons intended to advise the Holy See to consult the bishops directly and find out their true sentiments. In closing the cardinal remarked to the Archbishop of Cincinnati, "Till then I will have nothing to do with the enterprise. Liberavi animam meam. We can afford to wait as the matter is not pressing."[44] While Keane and Ireland probably thought they had waited long enough, the course suggested by Gibbons was wise, for the university could not hope for any real success if it did not have the genuine support of the American hierarchy. In the end the cardinal's delaying tactic proved worth the prolonged strain.

In a conference which Cardinal Gibbons held with Simeoni, the Prefect of Propaganda made known the fact that he had received a lengthy protest against the university from a leading American prelate, and it was unofficially disclosed that it had emanated from Archbishop Corrigan. With this Gibbons became so discouraged that he proposed to Keane that they abandon the enterprise and let the responsibility for its failure fall where it belonged. Keane, wearied by the long and trying ordeal, readily consented. It appeared for a moment that the university was doomed. But then Ireland, who had been out of Rome for a few days, returned and was informed of what had happened.

---

gone home without waiting for the end (AANY, Ireland to Corrigan, Rome, February 5, 1887).

[44] AAC, Gibbons to Elder, Rome, February 19, 1887.

The fighting blood of the Bishop of St. Paul was thoroughly aroused, and he protested to Gibbons and Keane that he would be no party to what he termed "so cowardly a surrender to so unworthy an opposition." Ireland insisted they go forward with their original plan for winning papal approval, and then if the university committee later felt it necessary the entire matter could be dropped. Ireland's energy once more galvanized Gibbons and Keane into action and they began the preparation of a lengthy document in French which Gibbons would sign for the Holy Father in an effort to meet all the objections that had been raised by Corrigan.[45]

In his letter to Leo XIII the cardinal rehearsed the story of the university idea from the time of the Third Plenary Council, the support it had met in that body, the favorable reaction of the laity to the proposal, and the work which had thus far been done by the university committee. Gibbons alluded to the Pope's knowledge of opposition by some bishops to Washington as the site, and he suggested that the Pontiff consider the question of site as secondary until he could circulate the American hierarchy and get their votes on the question. Gibbons then proposed that the time had now arrived when a formal approbation by the Holy See of the university was due, and in granting such an approval the Pope would be giving cause for joy to the American Catholics who regarded the projected university as in harmony with the various instructions on Christian education which the Holy Father had more than once given to the world during his pontificate.[46]

In less than three weeks Gibbons received the assurance of favorable action and he was able to tell Archbishop Corrigan that a papal brief would soon be issued authorizing the university and granting Gibbons' request that the question of a site be reconsidered.[47] The tone of the cardinal's correspondence on the university now began to grow a bit more animated and three days after the letter to Corrigan he told Elder that the Pope's heart was set on a university and, as he expressed it, "We must not disappoint him."[48] The clouds of discouragement were lifting and Easter Sunday of that year brought additional

---

[45] ACUA, "Chronicles," p. 19.
[46] AABo, printed copy of letter of Gibbons to Leo XIII, Rome, March 9, 1887.
[47] AANY, Gibbons to Corrigan, Rome, March 28, 1887.
[48] AAC, Gibbons to Elder, Rome, March 31, 1887.

joy to the Cardinal of Baltimore when Leo XIII signed the papal brief giving his hearty approval to a Catholic university for the United States. The Pope addressed his letter to Gibbons in which he urged that he go forward with his colleagues in fulfilling their plans. He told them to take courage from the assured hope that they would be laying the foundations of an institution which would redound to the glory of both the Church and the Republic, and Leo XIII counseled them not to be deterred by any difficulty or labor which they might encounter.[49]

With his Roman business concluded the Cardinal of Baltimore set out upon his return journey, arriving home on June 7 where an enthusiastic reception greeted the city's first prince of the Church. During the late spring and summer the replies of the bishops to Gibbons' circular on the site for the university were gradually assembled in his office. The Bishop of Rochester used the occasion to send a lengthy communication on the university question in which he went over again the ground of his opposition and set before Gibbons a series of questions which he wished answered before he would commit himself on the matter of a site. The cardinal's reply patiently outlined the committee's intentions, assured McQuaid that there was no intention of taxing the poor for the university's support, and made plain once more that he did not care to have the university in Baltimore or anywhere else in his archdiocese. He ended by saying the next meeting of the committee was scheduled for September 7 and that it was the mind of all the members that they should proceed slowly and cautiously and take no steps without careful deliberation.[50] The week following Gibbons' reply to McQuaid, the Archbishop of New York told his friend in Rochester that he was disposed to resign from the university committee since he had lost confidence in the good faith of some of the members. "What would you advise me to do?" asked Corrigan.[51] The response from McQuaid was immediate. He advised Corrigan by all means to sever his connections with the university project and to have nothing further to do with it. "You have been shabbily

---

[49] 82-P-10/1, Leo XIII to Gibbons, Rome, April 10, 1887.
[50] ADRo, Gibbons to McQuaid, Baltimore, June 15, 1887.
[51] *Ibid.*, Corrigan to McQuaid, New York, June 22, 1887.

treated . . . ," said McQuaid, and he ended by stating that in reply to his inquiries of Gibbons the latter had not answered them. "He dodged them adroitly, or ignored them."[52]

Any fair-minded observer would find it difficult to agree with McQuaid that the university committee had treated Archbishop Corrigan "shabbily." The Archbishop of New York had been present at all the meetings and could, if he chose, have presented his objections to the body. The fact that he remained silent and concealed his own plans for a Jesuit university in New York would naturally put the committee at a disadvantage in knowing the archbishop's real mind in the matter. Moreover, with the university plans held to only a tentative status until after the papal approval of April 10, some of the questions which McQuaid put to Gibbons could not be answered. In all the aspects of the problem where he could give a direct answer Gibbons did so, and the reading of his reply to the Bishop of Rochester revealed no attempt to dodge or ignore his questions as McQuaid charged.[53] It is perfectly true that Gibbons had wavered in his attitude toward the university, and for this he received, as we have seen, a rather sharp rebuke from Keane; but once Leo XIII had acted the cardinal showed a firmer resolve, and considering how undeveloped plans for the university were in the early summer of 1887, his answers to McQuaid's questions were as direct and candid as could reasonably be expected.

The committee assembled in Baltimore on September 7 for another of its series of meetings. Several resignations were accepted and replacements made in the personnel of the committee, and the rector posed a series of questions which he wished the committee to decide. Before taking up Keane's proposals, Gibbons stated that he had sent an answer to the Holy See covering all the points raised in a recent letter he had received treating objections to the university. The cardinal emphasized that Leo XIII had not only approved the project but he was really enthusiastic about it and had taken several occasions to speak of it, with the result that his words had been quoted all over Europe. Gibbons then made it known that he had received fifty-three replies to his circular on the

---

52 AANY, McQuaid to Corrigan, Rochester, June 23, 1887.
53 Cf. Ellis, *op. cit.*, pp. 231–232, for the full text of Gibbons' reply to McQuaid.

site. Of these, thirty-three bishops had voted for Washington while the other twenty votes were scattered for New York, Philadelphia, Baltimore, and Chicago while five bishops had declined to give their opinion but left it to the judgment of the committee. The long-disputed question was, therefore, finally decided by a large majority of the bishops who voted. Plans had now advanced far enough so that the next meeting could be scheduled to coincide with the laying of the cornerstone of the university's first building in May, 1888. The meeting in September, 1887, drew the customary spate of stories in the press, one to the effect that the entire project would ultimately cost eight million dollars. The *Catholic Mirror* of September 17 was at pains to correct some of the inaccuracies of this type in an editorial entitled, "Sensational Newspaper Stories," and the New York *Tribune* of October 10 in a more sober editorial congratulated the hierarchy on the choice of Washington and stated that the new university "deserves all the success which will undoubtedly come to it."

Another item of business at the meeting on September 7 was the formal announcement of the appointment of Bishop Keane as the first rector, and from this time on the active management of affairs passed almost entirely into his capable hands. Keane kept closely in touch with Gibbons in all matters of importance, and the cardinal gave his active assistance to the rector by writing a letter to the hierarchy begging their support for the bishops who would come into their dioceses to collect.[54] It was to Gibbons likewise that there were directed all through the preparatory stages various communications about the university from the hierarchy.

To the cardinal there was sent, for example, the woeful intelligence that Archbishop Corrigan could not see his way to permit the collectors in the Archdiocese of New York and that he was resigning from the committee.[55] It was a major blow to the hopes of all who had the university's interests at heart. Gibbons was deeply affected by the news, and he told Corrigan that he had thought over the matter for several days

---

[54] AAC, printed circular of Gibbons to the American hierarchy, Baltimore, November 11, 1887.

[55] 83-T-6, Corrigan to Gibbons, New York, November 28, 1887; 83-T-6/1, same to same, New York, November 28, 1887.

and had determined to ask him to reconsider his action.[56] Corrigan replied that he would give the cardinal's request careful consideration, but in ten days time he followed with another letter in which he stated that he regretted he could not change his mind.[57] To this Gibbons answered in a restrained manner, noting the receipt of Corrigan's final determination and dismissing the subject with the words, "Fiat voluntas Dei."[58] He had done what he could to save the work from suffering this reverse, but since he had failed there was nothing to do but make the best of it and try to go along without the Archbishop of New York. Corrigan's resignation eventually became known and the Chicago *Tribune* of February 1, 1888, carried a sharply critical editorial on the archbishop's action, imputing it to jealousy of Gibbons, Ireland, and Keane. When Gilmour of Cleveland told Gibbons that he prayed for the success of the university, even though he wished it had gone to Philadelphia,[59] the cardinal revealed that he believed it was the duty of all to support the undertaking wholeheartedly. He said that the bishops were committed to it before the American public and a half-hearted support would not suffice. As he put it, "Many a noble enterprise has perished for want of generous cooperation at the proper time." Then the cardinal revealed to the Bishop of Cleveland his personal attitude on the university. He said:

> If I were to consult my feelings & personal comfort I would have the project abandoned. It has been to me a source of anxiety and care since the close of the council. If the enterprise succeeds, as I hope it will, it will redound to the glory of God & of our faith in this country.[60]

[56] AANY, Gibbons to Corrigan, Baltimore, December 3, 1887.

[57] 83-U-6, Corrigan to Gibbons, New York, December 6, 1887.

[58] AANY, Gibbons to Corrigan, Baltimore, December 23, 1887. Ireland, too, begged Corrigan to reconsider, saying he could understand that he was not pleased with all the committee had done and might not feel inclined to unlock the resources of the archdiocese to the collectors. "But an open rupture with us will do no good, and I trust it may be prevented" (AANY, Ireland to Corrigan, Baltimore, January 22, 1888). Ireland tried to cheer Gibbons by telling him that the West remained enthusiastic about the university and the resignation of Corrigan had not done "a particle of harm" (84-D-6, Ireland to Gibbons, St. Paul, February 26, 1888). O'Connell, too, sent consoling word from Rome that some of the curial officials did not see the wisdom of Corrigan's act, and he concluded, "You still rule" (84-G-2, O'Connell to Gibbons, Rome, March 27, 1888).

[59] 84-C-7, Gilmour to Gibbons, Cleveland, February 15, 1888.

[60] ADC, Gibbons to Gilmour, Baltimore, February 17, 1888.

As the time neared for the laying of the cornerstone, Gibbons sent out letters to all the hierarchy urging their attendance and stressing again the interest which Leo XIII took in the university. Keane was meanwhile pursuing his collection tour and the success he had met in Philadelphia gave him a chance to prod Gibbons again to enlist the financial support of the wealthy Catholics of Baltimore like Michael Jenkins; otherwise, as he expressed it, "Baltimore will be far passed in the race by Phila."[61] The committee on arrangements for the cornerstone ceremony used Gibbons' prestige to secure the attendance of President Cleveland. In a call at the White House on April 9 the cardinal invited Cleveland to be present and the President let it be known that he would give the matter serious consideration. When the event took place on May 24 the President was in attendance with several members of his cabinet, who mingled with thirty-some bishops to make a distinguished audience to hear the oration of Bishop Spalding of Peoria. Cardinal Gibbons blessed the cornerstone and presided at the affair, after which the committee held a meeting at St. Matthew's Rectory to which Gibbons invited all the bishops present whether they were members of the committee or not.[62] In inviting the archbishops of the committee on secret societies to sign the documents to Rome in October, 1887, in circulating the entire hierarchy on major matters, and in inviting the bishops attending the cornerstone laying to meet with the university committee, Gibbons was acting wisely, for the entire undertaking would certainly fail if the American bishops were not won to it in good numbers.

A cheering bit of news reached Gibbons in early July when John Farley let it be known confidentially that he and Eugene Kelly, treasurer of the university committee, had prevailed on Archbishop Corrigan to return to the committee.[63] The cardinal was delighted and he lost no time in thanking Farley for his intervention and that of Mr. Kelly in bringing about this happy result.[64] Archbishop Ireland had recently called on Corrigan in New York and he told Gibbons that he found him "in every respect a changed man." Ireland repeated the informa-

[61] 84-K-10, Keane to Gibbons, Philadelphia, May 11, 1888.
[62] Ellis, *op. cit.*, pp. 284–293.
[63] 84-R-10, Farley to Gibbons, New York, July 8, 1888.
[64] AANY, Gibbons to Farley, Baltimore, July 9, 1888.

tion about the archbishop rejoining the committee and said it was no longer a matter for secrecy.[65] The Archbishop of Baltimore told Ireland that the news had filled him with consolation. He remarked that the university had had an uphill fight in struggling against the opposition of a great archdiocese, to say nothing of the opposition of what he termed "intangible agencies" in Rome. Gibbons felt that Keane would have particular reason to rejoice since it was he who had borne "the brunt of the battle with heroism." The cardinal alluded to the unfriendly statements on the university in the pastoral letter of August 20 issued by Bishop McQuaid, and he said, "I would have to use very strong language if I were to express my mind on that uncalled-for document."[66]

Bishop Keane spent most of the summer of 1888 giving addresses in various cities on the university. In August he settled down at the University of Notre Dame to draw up the preliminary draft of the statutes that would govern the new university. The rector sent Gibbons frequent reports of his work with occasional requests for action on the part of the cardinal. For example, Keane was anxious that Gibbons should communicate with Father Henri Icard, the Superior-General of the Sulpicians in France, about appointing several of his men to take care of the discipline of the priest students in the university. Gibbons complied and told Keane he had just mailed a letter to Icard embodying the request and that Abbé Magnien believed there would be no difficulty about securing the Sulpicians.[67] At the same time the cardinal suggested a tentative date for a fall meeting of the committee so that the members could approve Keane's statutes before he sailed for Rome to win papal sanction for the regulations that would govern the institution.

The meeting was held at Baltimore on November 13 with Archbishop Corrigan in attendance, and four days later Keane sailed on the *Gascoigne* with two main objects in mind, namely, to win the Holy See's approval for the statutes and to engage professors. During the absence of the rector the general supervision of the university business was left in the hands of Father Philip J. Garrigan, the vice-rector, who consulted frequently

[65] 85-B-6, Ireland to Gibbons, St. Paul, September 14, 1888.

[66] AASP, Gibbons to Ireland, Baltimore, September 17, 1888, copy.

[67] AUND, Gibbons to Keane, Baltimore, September 3, 1888, photostat.

with the cardinal. Matters had gone very well at the meeting on November 13 and ten days later Ireland with understandable pride reminded Gibbons, "I trust you now pardon me for having when in Rome with you insisted that you should not abandon the project."[68] Meanwhile the Roman skies likewise seemed to be brightening and Gibbons was happy to be told by Denis O'Connell that Keane would receive a "royal welcome" in the Eternal City and that the influence of the opposition did not now amount to much.[69]

Meanwhile Gibbons gave the university business a considerable amount of his time in regard to details like the alien contract labor law, which threatened to bar the foreign professors being hired by Keane, and the arrangements for a library committee for the purchase of books. It was while Keane was still absent in Europe that application was received by Gibbons from the first religious community for a house of studies at the university. Father Augustine F. Hewit, Superior-General of the Paulists, inquired of the cardinal about his view of the matter. Gibbons told the Paulist superior to make application first to the Prefect of the Propaganda, and when Hewit did so Simeoni inquired of the Archbishop of Baltimore about his opinion. This gave Gibbons an opportunity to say that he would not only give permission to the Paulists to open a house in his archdiocese, but that he would be highly pleased to have them at the university and within his jurisdiction.[70]

On March 7, 1889, Pope Leo XIII issued his apostolic letter, *Magni nobis gaudii,* to Cardinal Gibbons and the American hierarchy in which he placed his final approval on the university at Washington. With this attained the rector could inform the Cardinal of Baltimore that one of his main objectives had been secured, and he could now devote his remaining time in Europe to a search for professors.[71] With the formal approval of the

---

[68] 85-I-6, Ireland to Gibbons, St. Paul, November 23, 1888.

[69] 85-I-7, O'Connell to Gibbons, Rome, November 23, 1888.

[70] 85-R-1, Hewit to Gibbons, New York, February 13, 1889; 85-R-3, Gibbons to Hewit, Baltimore, February 18, 1889, copy; 85-U-12, Simeoni to Gibbons, Rome, March 28, 1889; 85-W-7, Gibbons to Simeoni, Baltimore, April 12, 1889, copy.

[71] 85-T-3, Keane to Gibbons, Rome, March 12, 1889.

Holy Father the Catholic press in the United States stepped up the tone of its enthusiasm for the undertaking, and one editor who had been friendly from the outset used the opportunity to say that the time for criticism was now passed and any "what?" or "why?" would be a childish impertinence. As he concluded, "Enthusiasm in word and act is now demanded."[72]

The formal opening of the university was scheduled to coincide with the celebration of the centennial of the American hierarchy to be held in November, 1889. In view of these events it was suggested as early as the previous March by Henry F. Brownson of Detroit, son of Orestes Brownson, that a Catholic lay congress be held at the same time. Gibbons was doubtful about the wisdom of attempting such a congress, and gave as his excuse that a lack of time and the absorbing character of the events already planned would seem to make it preferable to postpone the lay congress until another time.[73] But other bishops were less cautious and Ireland reported a month later the names of five prelates who had already commended the plan. Ireland stated that when asked he had declined to commit himself until he first learned what Cardinal Gibbons thought of the proposal, but he believed that if the arrangements were prudently managed the congress would do good.[74] At any rate, Gibbons finally gave his consent, a committee of leading Catholic laymen was organized, and an outline of the topics for the addresses was circulated.[75] At a meeting of the congress committee in Detroit it was decided to have a paper on the position of the Papacy in relation to the Italian government, although it was agreed that this delicate subject would have to be treated with extraordinary tact.[76] Archbishop Ireland suggested the names of a committee of bishops to be appointed

---

[72] [Daniel Hudson, C.S.C.], "A Word Concerning the New University," *Ave Maria*, XXIX (August 3, 1889), 109.

[73] 85-U-8, Gibbons to Brownson, Baltimore, March 27, 1889, copy.

[74] 85-W-13, Ireland to Gibbons, St. Paul, April 20, 1889. The plans of the American bishops to commemorate the centennial of the inauguration of George Washington on April 30 delighted Ireland who told Gibbons, "In Abp. Carroll's time the Church was truly American. Later the flood of Catholic foreign immigration overpowered us, and made the Church foreign in heart & in act. Thank God we are recovering from this misfortune."

[75] 86-A-7, circular letter of William J. Onahan, Chicago, May 20, 1889.

[76] 86-E-6, Foley to Gibbons, Detroit, July 11, 1889.

by Gibbons to supervise the papers,[77] a list which the cardinal accepted with one addition of his own.

Although Gibbons viewed with considerable misgiving the holding of the lay congress, he was given encouragement when O'Connell told him that the struggle between the Vatican and the Italian government had brought a deep sadness to all at the Holy See, but they were looking with comfort "to the Congress announced to be held next November. . . ." He added that he had been interrogated regarding reactions in the United States to the antislavery campaign of Charles Cardinal Lavigerie, Archbishop of Algiers, and he had replied that the subject could well be introduced into the coming lay congress.[78] A week later O'Connell reported to Gibbons that a considerable rivalry had arisen among several of the Roman curial officials as to who would represent Leo XIII at the centennial and the opening of the university, and he cautioned the cardinal in several subsequent letters to be exceedingly careful how his invitation for a papal representative read so that no offense would be given. The main contenders for the honor were Francesco Satolli, professor of theology in the College of the Propaganda, Donato Sbarretti, *minutante* of Propaganda, and Domenico Jacobini, Secretary of the Propaganda. Gibbons followed the directions of his Roman agent and on August 12 addressed a letter to Leo XIII asking him to send a representative and at the same time inviting the three churchmen through O'Connell.[79] In the end the Pope chose Satolli, consecrated the previous year as Archbishop of Lepanto, to be his representative at the celebrations in Baltimore and Washington.

The knowledge that there would be a lay congress in connection with the centennial and the opening of the university, did not meet with universal favor. Old Archbishop Kenrick of St. Louis informed Cardinal Gibbons that he declined to take

---

[77] 86-E-9, Ireland to Gibbons, St. Paul, July 16, 1889.

[78] 86-E-10, O'Connell to Gibbons, Rome, July 16, 1889.

[79] 86-H-7, Gibbons to Leo XIII, Baltimore, August 12, 1889, copy; Diary, August 12, 1889, p. 235. In the matter of these invitations both O'Connell in a letter from Rome of July 23 (86-E-14) and Ireland in one from St. Paul on August 9 (86-G-10) were insistent that Gibbons act ahead of Corrigan who was reported to have already invited Archbishop Jacobini. As Ireland told Gibbons, "Now whoever is to come, should come on *your* invitation. This is a most important point. Mgr. Corrigan is not to be allowed to appear as the leader of the hierarchy."

part in the proposed celebration in consequence of what he called "the mixed character" of the convention to be held on that occasion.[80] As the date for the festivities approached the press carried some misleading stories and in one such tale Miss Caldwell was reported to have decided to withdraw the money she had given for the university. The young woman was upset when she learned this and wrote to the cardinal, asking if he would not please issue a denial as chairman of the university committee since such a thought had never entered her mind.[81] Three months before the celebration Gibbons had issued invitations to the hierarchy of the United States, as well as to the bishops of other countries, to attend. A large number sent in their acceptances, among them Cardinal Taschereau of Quebec,[82] while others offered their congratulations but stated that they could not be present. Bishop McQuaid of Rochester begged, as he expressed it, "most respectfully to be allowed to be absent," and wished abundant success to the occasion.[83] The pressure of business on Cardinal Gibbons had been heavy that summer and it would be even greater during the autumn. For that reason he took a holiday at Cape May with a further brief period of rest at Deer Park where he dined with President Harrison.[84] With the pressure of official business increasing in the fall, Gibbons declined the invitation of the congress committee to give an address and suggested that they ask either Ireland or Gilmour. The cardinal's secretary informed William J. Onahan that every moment of Gibbons' time was then taken up with work in preparation for the centennial and at the time of the celebration he would have to entertain his guests.[85]

A month before the date scheduled for the centennial the Cardinal of Baltimore published a pastoral letter on the significance of the coming celebrations. He devoted the first part of it to a eulogy of Archbishop Carroll and the role he had played in establishing the hierarchy of the United States

---

[80] 86-H-6, Kenrick to Gibbons, St. Louis, August 12, 1889.

[81] 86-N-12, Caldwell to Gibbons, St. Regis Lake, September 21, 1889.

[82] 86-I-2, Taschereau to Gibbons, Quebec, August 16, 1889.

[83] 86-J-1, McQuaid to Gibbons, Rochester, August 20, 1889.

[84] Sarah Lee Collection, Washington, Gibbons to Miss Rebecca S. Hayward, Woodstock, Maryland, August 23, 1889.

[85] AUND, Onahan Papers, John T. Whelan to Onahan, Baltimore, September 5, 1889.

and in reconciling the Catholic Church of that day to the new American milieu. The cordial relations of Church and State in the days of the early Republic were proof, said Gibbons, that the Catholic religion adapted itself to all times and places and circumstances, and this without any compromise of principle. Alluding to Carroll's outstanding Americanism and what it had meant to the nascent Church, the cardinal said the first Archbishop of Baltimore knew the mischief which national rivalries bred and for that reason he had been intent that both priests and people, from no matter what country they came, should be thoroughly identified with the land in which they had cast their lot. Gibbons made mention of the opening of the university when he said:

> We hail it as an auspicious omen that the new century will be inaugurated by the opening of the Catholic University, just as the closing century was ushered in by the founding of Georgetown College.[86]

Archbishop Ryan congratulated the cardinal on the pastoral which he had read that morning in the Philadelphia *Ledger*. He thought the holding of the lay congress was an excellent idea, although he regretted to see that the news had leaked out that the papers to be read had first to be submitted to the bishops of the advisory committee. Ryan suggested to Gibbons that the Archbishop of New York be invited to celebrate the Mass at the centennial since he believed he had not been assigned any role in the opening of the university. As Ryan expressed it, "Not to assign him to any position will, I fear, give rise to remark. . . ."[87]

As the plans matured Gibbons showed an increasing cordiality toward the lay congress. He confessed to Bishop Wigger of Newark that he had at first opposed its being held during the

---

[86] *Catholic Mirror*, October 5, 1889.

[87] 86-P-4, Ryan to Gibbons, Philadelphia, October 3, 1889. A young American woman who said she owed her conversion to Gibbons' *The Faith of Our Fathers*, wrote him from Paris in commendation of the pastoral which she said had been published in extracts in several English and French newspapers which she read. She liked especially its American tone. She closed by saying, "Nearly all the priests in Europe are royalists, & so to you has fallen the noble task of demonstrating to the world that a good Catholic can be & should [be] a patriotic citizen of the Republic" (86-T-3, Mary Beach to Gibbons, Paris, November 3, 1889).

centennial week due to lack of time to prepare, his own very crowded schedule, and the fear that much of the labor would devolve on him. But he yielded to the urgent wishes of some other bishops, and he now believed that while the coming congress would be necessarily crude and imperfect in details it would serve a good purpose as a preparation of the Catholic community for a future and better organized congress.[88] But the belated good will of the cardinal did not come in time to avoid the suspicion on the part of Peter L. Foy, a prominent Catholic layman and one of the committee, that Gibbons and his entourage were at heart opposed to the idea. Foy confided to Brownson that he believed if it were not felt that so many prominent laymen would add *éclat* to the centennial, the lay congress committee would experience "open hostility from his Eminence."[89]

The centennial of the American hierarchy brought many beautiful messages of congratulation and good wishes to Cardinal Gibbons and his colleagues. Cardinal Manning forwarded the formal greetings of the English hierarchy in which he gracefully alluded to the spiritual bonds which knit the English-speaking Catholics of the two countries. As Manning expressed it, "In the greatest Commonwealth, and in the greatest Empire of the world, the Church Catholic and Roman, deeply-rooted and daily expanding, calls the freest races of mankind to the liberty of Faith, the only true liberty of man."[90] Herbert Vaughan, Bishop of Salford and Superior-General of the Mill Hill Fathers, used the occasion for a lengthy and inspiring appeal to the American Church to bestir itself in the new century now opening before it in behalf of the foreign missions.[91] Greetings poured in to the cardinal's residence from Ireland, France, Canada, and South America and the day before the great events began Pope Leo XIII cabled his congratulations and blessing to the American Church.[92]

---

[88] Archives of the Archdiocese of Newark, Gibbons to Wigger, Baltimore October 7, 1889.

[89] AUND, Henry Brownson Papers, Foy to Brownson, St. Louis, October 20, 1889.

[90] 86-R-6, Manning to Gibbons, Westminster, October 20, 1889.

[91] 86-S-8, Vaughan to Gibbons, Mill Hill, October 28, 1889. This long letter was published in full in the *Catholic Historical Review*, XXX (October, 1944), 290–298.

[92] 86-T-8, Leo XIII to Gibbons, Rome, November 9, 1889, cablegram.

The centennial celebration was opened with pontifical Mass in the Cathedral of the Assumption in Baltimore on Sunday, November 10, at which Cardinal Gibbons presided. Archbishop Williams was the celebrant and Ryan of Philadelphia preached. In the evening at pontifical vespers Gibbons again presided with Heiss the celebrant and Ireland of St. Paul the preacher. In his powerful and stirring sermon the Archbishop of St. Paul made special mention of the university when he said:

> In love, in reverence, in hope I salute thee, Catholic University of America! Thy birth — happy omen! — is coeval with the opening of the new century. The destinies of the Church in America are in thy keeping. May heaven's light shine over thee and heaven's love guard thee. . . .[93]

On the next two days there were held at the Concordia Opera House the sessions of the Catholic Congress during which thirteen major papers on a variety of subjects, along with many brief and informal speeches, were heard. The formal addresses ranged over many subjects such as the Church's relations to the press, labor, social order, temperance, the state, education, and the position of the Holy See. On the opening day Gibbons addressed the delegates. After extending to them in the name of his clergy and people a warm welcome to Baltimore, the cardinal confessed his early skepticism concerning the congress but said he had been forced to yield before the pressure of some of his friends from the West who, as Gibbons remarked, were absolutely irrepressible when they were under the leadership of the great Archbishop of St. Paul! But he now saw the congress as an excellent means for drawing the clergy and laity closer together in a land where they should correspond and co-operate with one another more than in any other on the face of the earth. He paid a generous tribute to the Catholic laity for their support of the Church in the United States where churches and schools were built and maintained by their free-will offerings and where the salaries of the clergy were handed to them, "not on a silver salver of the government, but from the warm hands and hearts of the people themselves."[94] The ceremonies in Baltimore were con-

---

[93] John Ireland, *The Church and Modern Society* (St. Paul, 1906), I, 92–93.

[94] *Souvenir Volume of the Centennial Celebration and Catholic Congress* (Detroit, 1889), p. 24. The text of all the addresses and proceedings are given

cluded on Tuesday evening, November 12, with a gigantic torchlight procession through the streets which was viewed by thousands of onlookers headed by two cardinals, nearly twenty archbishops, and over seventy bishops representing the United States, Canada, England, and Mexico with hundreds of priests and laity from all over the country and many from foreign lands.[95]

On Wednesday, November 13, the hierarchy and their guests moved to Washington for the opening of the university. Once more, as on the day of the cornerstone ceremony, it rained the entire day which, of course, detracted somewhat from the enjoyment of the occasion. In the morning before the Mass Cardinal Gibbons, as chancellor of the new university dedicated Caldwell Hall and there then followed the solemn pontifical Mass in the chapel celebrated by Archbishop Satolli with the sermon by Bishop Gilmour. After the Mass a dinner was served to the guests at which President Harrison and three members of his cabinet were present with the distinguished prelates headed by Gibbons and Cardinal Taschereau of Quebec. The afternoon witnessed the formal presentation of several gifts to the university such as the marble bust of St. Thomas Aquinas from the Catholics of the British Isles residing in Rome, the reading of a number of letters of congratulation from foreign universities, and several more addresses. At the end of the day the original band of thirty-seven priest students entered upon a retreat preached by Father John B. Hogan, S.S., and Bishop Keane, the rector, and on Monday, November 18, the first classes were held.

This second week of November, 1889, had been an exhausting one for the Cardinal of Baltimore, but the general success and enthusiasm attendant upon the festivities proved a recompense for all the anxiety and labor they had cost him. The entire program had delighted Archbishop Ireland and a week after the university inauguration he informed Gibbons that brief visits to New York, Philadelphia, and Washington convinced

---

in this volume. Cf. also Vincent J. Donovan, "The First American Catholic Lay Congress held at Baltimore, November 11–12, 1889," an unpublished master's thesis, The Catholic University of America (1940).

[95] The full details concerning the celebrations in Baltimore and Washington are given in the *Catholic Mirror* of November 16, 1889, which published a special supplement for the occasion.

him of how much interest had been awakened by the events even among Protestants. He felt that never before did the Catholic Church stand so well in the United States as it did then, and in one of his typically flamboyant passages he attributed it all to Gibbons:

> We have to thank you for all this. You have the ear of the American public as no other man in the Republic. Your words are heeded by all & God be thanked, they are always the words that are needed.[96]

While the cardinal's modesty would probably shrink from taking the lion's share of the credit, there was little doubt that Gibbons did, indeed, enjoy a rare prestige among Americans of all classes and creeds. Apparently the impression created by Gibbons' performance during the celebration must have been a very happy one, for even Bishop James A. Healy of Portland, who was not in the habit of extending compliments to Baltimore, was high in his praise of the cardinal's management of the events.[97] From far-off Australia the cardinal received the greetings of Patrick Cardinal Moran, Archbishop of Sydney, who had read of the solemnities as they were cabled to the Australian press. Moran rejoiced at the growth of the Church in the United States where it enjoyed such full liberty, and he said the Australian Church, enjoying a similar liberty, would endeavor to follow in its footsteps. The Archbishop of Sydney feared it would be a long time before they could begin to think of a Catholic university, but in the meantime he wished the institution at Washington every success.[98]

But as was to be expected of so ambitious an undertaking involving so many persons not all were content with the Baltimore-Washington celebrations. Bishop William G. McCloskey of Louisville told his friend, Gilmour of Cleveland, that the period was too short for the lay congress to do more than shake hands and take dinner, and the ecclesiastics were kept in such a whirl that there was no time for the personal exchange of views which bishops like to have on such occasions. One thing McCloskey felt was certain, and that was that a definite declaration coming from the entire assembly on the

---

[96] 86-U-5, Ireland to Gibbons, Washington, November 20, 1889.

[97] 86-V-2, Healy to Gibbons, Portland, December 3, 1889.

[98] 86-W-4, Moran to Gibbons, Sydney, December 24, 1889.

necessity of the temporal power of the Holy See, in view of the spoliation of papal properties by the Italian government and the growing crisis between the Church and State in that country, was expected at the Vatican, and if Bishop Chatard's view was correct there would not be, as he expressed it, "so much 'J'aime Gibbon' in future." Moreover, McCloskey did not like the presence of Satolli which he thought took the Americanism out of the celebration since, regardless of what some might say, "from top to bottom, in prelates of high & low degree, caution rather than frankness was the order of the day."[99]

But despite McCloskey's predictions the Holy See reacted very favorably. Gibbons wrote a lengthy description of the entire celebration to Leo XIII in which he detailed the program, the presence of the President and government officials at the university inauguration, and the courtesies shown to his delegate at the various events. The cardinal told the Pope:

> The President of the United States, the Vice-President, the Secretary of State, and several members of the Cabinet made it a point to honor this festivity with their presence, and the applause which burst forth when Your health was proposed and which followed the answer of Mgr. Satolli to this toast, as well as that which greeted the President, manifest greatly that the love of the Church and the love of the country are indissolubly united in the hearts of the faithful. . . .[100]

In less than a month Gibbons received an acknowledgment of

[99] ADC, McCloskey to Gilmour, Louisville, December 2, 1889.

[100] 86-V-7, Gibbons to Leo XIII, Baltimore, December 7, 1889, copy in French. On the occasion of the centennial in a conference of the archbishops it was suggested that they convey to Cardinal Manning their congratulations on his silver jubilee, and they asked Gibbons to write in their name. Gibbons told Manning that he had seldom been assigned a more grateful duty than to be chosen as the medium for extending this message of brotherly affection and esteem. He maintained that he was certainly unconscious of any disposition to flatter when he said that the American hierarchy held Manning in the highest admiration. "Your private virtues and apostolic life, your public discourses delivered in season and out of season, your prolific writings in defense of religion and sound morals, your untiring zeal in the cause of temperance, your readiness, at the sacrifice of health, to co-operate in every measure affecting the interests of humanity, are a source of constant edification to one and all, and an incentive to emulate so bright an example." Gibbons enclosed a gift of $540 made up among eight of the American prelates to which the cardinal, Ireland, Feehan of Chicago, and Foley of Detroit each contributed $100 (86-W-14, Gibbons to Manning, Baltimore, 1889, n.d., copy).

his letter to the Pope from Cardinal Rampolla, Secretary of State, who said Leo XIII wished to extend to him the highest praise for the success of the celebrations and at the same time his full approval for the prudent line of conduct which Gibbons had followed in every endeavor directed to the promotion and greater development of the young and illustrious Church of the United States. Moreover, Rampolla wished to add that the Pontiff had shown himself very grateful to Gibbons for the welcome and affectionate attentions which the cardinal had displayed toward his envoy, Archbishop Satolli.[101]

Once the university had opened Cardinal Gibbons generally confined himself in his role as chancellor of the institution to acting at the instance of the rector on matters requiring attention in the interval between meetings of the board of trustees. He likewise made himself available at all times for advice and counsel to the rector, the trustees, and the professors on the institution's business. Gibbons gave the prestige of his name to the university as chancellor, and he was always faithful in attendance upon the principal functions of the academic year and at meetings of the trustees where he presided. It meant a tremendous amount to Bishop Keane and his successors in the office of rector to have the strong support of one who by the closing decade of the century had attained a national and even an international fame in both Church and State. The university had experienced real travail in its formative stages and in the first twenty years of its life it would become involved in controversies, both within and without its own halls, which at times were serious enough to call in question the fact that the institution would ever be established on a solid and enduring foundation. Through all this trying time the cardinal remained steadfastly loyal. Although his steps had faltered several times during the difficult and painful process of launching the project, once the Holy See had given the university its final blessing Gibbons responded to every call of duty in its behalf, even when it cost him heavily in time, labor, and peace of mind.

The type of service rendered to the university by its chancellor was well illustrated in the spring of 1890 when he gave his approval to the rector for the purchase of ten additional acres of land for future buildings in the belief that a delay until

---

[101] 87-A-3, Rampolla to Gibbons, Rome, January 3, 1890.

A picture of the faculty and student body of the Catholic University of America taken in front of Caldwell Hall, October 26, 1893, on the occasion of a reception honoring Cardinal Gibbons on the twenty-fifth anniversary of his episcopal consecration.

Sitting (left to right): Philip J. Garrigan (vice-rector), Joseph Schroeder (professor of dogmatic theology), George M. Searle, C.S.P. (of St. Thomas College), Thomas O'Gorman (professor of modern ecclesiastical history), Charles P. Grannan (professor of scripture), Donato Sbarretti (of the Apostolic Delegation), Hector Papi (of the Apostolic Delegation), Francesco Satolli (Apostolic Delegate), James McMahon (New York priest, donor of McMahon Hall), James Cardinal Gibbons (Chancellor of the University), Joseph Pohle (professor of apologetics), John J. Keane (rector), Georges Péries (professor of canon law), John B. Hogan, S.S. (spiritual director and president of Divinity College), Edward A. Pace (professor of experimental psychology), Thomas Bouquillon (professor of moral theology), Alphonse L. Magnien, S.S. (provincial of the Sulpicians).

Standing (left to right): Charles Warren Stoddard (lecturer in English literature) Daniel Quinn (professor of Greek philology) Joseph F. Smith (New York), Arthur Vaschalde (Toronto Basilian, subdeacon), Nathaniel P. McCaffrey (St. Paul), George V. Leahy (Boston, deacon), Tiburtius A. Goebel (Columbus), James P. Foy (Syracuse), John D. McGuire (Philadelphia, subdeacon), Peter W. Mundy (Philadelphia, deacon), John A.

Tennissen (Cleveland), Lawrence J. McNamara (Baltimore), James F. Mackin (St. Paul's Church, Washington), Peter H. McClean (Hartford, deacon), James A. Bruen (Omaha), Edward J. Fitzgerald (Springfield, Massachusetts), George F. Hickey (Cincinnati), Philip J. O'Ryan (San Francisco), John F. Lunney (Springfield, Massachusetts, subdeacon), Edward J. Rengel (Buffalo, in minor orders), John A. Cull (San Francisco) Francis W. Maley (Boston, deacon), Patrick J. Hayes (New York), William J. Kerby (Dubuque), Alexis Orban, S.S. (assistant to Father Hogan), Lawrence J. Enright (Davenport), Florence J. Halloran (Boston, deacon), George J. Reid (Pittsburgh, subdeacon), Thomas J. Shahan (professor of early ecclesiastical history), Timothy M. Donovan (Springfield, Massachusetts, deacon).

Missing: Henry Hyvernat (professor of oriental languages and biblical archaeology). The student enrollment was then at an all-time low of twenty-five with Father Mackin coming out from the city and Father Thomas E. Shields (St. Paul) over from Johns Hopkins on occasion. Credit and gratitude for the identifications are extended to the Reverend Joseph McSorley, C.S.P. (S.T.L., 1897), and the Right Reverend George V. Leahy (S.T.L., 1895).

the next meeting of the trustees would endanger the success of the transactions.[102] Gibbons had to listen, too, to the complaints of all regarding their real or fancied grievances against the university administration. Bishop Foley, for example, grew indignant at Keane for refusing entrance to a subdeacon from the Diocese of Detroit, and he poured out his troubles to the chancellor and said that at the next meeting of the trustees he hoped there would be appointed "a Professor of common sense."[103] Not infrequently the intervention of the cardinal was sought to secure appointments to the faculty, as was the case when Robert Underwood Johnson, associate editor of *Century Magazine,* detailed the qualifications of his friend, Maurice Francis Egan, for the chair of English literature in the university.[104] When the board of trustees at its meeting in April, 1891, approved the rector's request to have the hierarchy circularized in an effort to increase the student body, Gibbons complied with a letter which urged the bishops to send at least one student from their dioceses so that the ends envisioned by the Holy Father for the institution might be fulfilled.[105] At times the cardinal found it difficult because of the scarcity of priests to maintain a proper representation at the university from the Archdiocese of Baltimore. Keane asked Garrigan, the vice-rector, to remind Gibbons that he ought to have more than one student enrolled, and when the subject was brought to his attention the cardinal stated that in view of his trouble in freeing more of his priests for higher studies, he had given one of his burses to Bishop John Shanley of Jamestown, South Dakota, but he promised that if he could find another available priest in his archdiocese he would send him.[106]

---

[102] ACUA, Keane Papers, Gibbons to Keane, Baltimore, April 17, 1890.

[103] 87-Y-1, Foley to Gibbons, Detroit, September 26, 1890.

[104] 88-H-1, Johnson to Gibbons, New York, January 17, 1891.

[105] AAC, Gibbons to Elder, Baltimore, May 1, 1891, printed circular. Gibbons repeated this action on several occasions during the early years of the university when he endeavored to rally the bishops to a greater effort in sending students to Washington. Cf., e.g., AANY, Gibbons to Corrigan, Baltimore, September 1, 1896; AAC, Gibbons to Elder, Baltimore, September 7, 1897.

[106] ACUA, Garrigan Papers, Keane to Garrigan, Queenstown, Ireland, July 7, 1892; 90-C-6, Garrigan to Gibbons, Washington, August 19, 1892; ACUA, Garrigan Papers, Gibbons to Garrigan, Baltimore, August 20, 1892. That spring Michael Jenkins of Baltimore gave Gibbons $5,000 to be applied in the cardinal's name and right for the education of a student at the university. He turned over the money to the institution for the establishment of a perpetual scholarship in the interests of the Archdiocese of Baltimore (Diary, April 28, 1892, p. 260).

By the time the university had become a reality Cardinal Gibbons had won a reputation among all who knew him for his ability to act as a conciliator, and it was a talent which was put to excellent use in his capacity as chancellor. When the Dominicans began to consider opening a house of studies near the university in 1890 it was to Gibbons that they first turned, and during the prolonged negotiations which ensued he more than once used his good offices to smooth over the rough spots that had arisen between the rector and the superiors of the order. Eventually the difficulties were overcome and the new house of studies opened in 1903.[107] The cardinal chancellor was likewise able to calm the fears of Cardinal Satolli, Prefect of the Congregation of Studies, when the Roman prelate grew apprehensive over locating a women's college within a few blocks of the university. Gibbons explained that Trinity College would not be a part of the university proper and that its courses would be taught almost entirely by the Sisters of Notre Dame of Namur. He made known to Satolli that the rumors reaching Rome about the relationship of the two institutions were, as he expressed it, "utterly false or grossly exaggerated, & are the offspring of ignorance or malice."[108] And in the case of a rumored threat to close the house of studies of the Congregation of Holy Cross on the part of some of the members of that religious community, Gibbons responded to Keane's request to write the superior-general and the provincial deploring such action. The cardinal's appeal met the hearty co-operation of Father John A. Zahm, the provincial, and the Congregation of Holy Cross not only retained their house of studies at the university but laid the cornerstone of a new building in the next year.[109]

If the authority and prestige of the Cardinal of Baltimore

---

[107] For the story of the Dominican foundation, cf. Patrick H. Ahern, *The Catholic University of America, 1887–1896. The Rectorship of John J. Keane* (Washington, 1948), pp. 84–88, and Peter E. Hogan, S.S.J., *The Catholic University of America, 1896–1903. The Rectorship of Thomas J. Conaty* (Washington, 1949), pp. 92–95. The writer is indebted to these two volumes for Gibbons' role in the history of the university during the early years. The cardinal acted in a similar way to the Dominican case when in 1897 the negotiations were begun for the Franciscan house of studies. Cf. Hogan, *op. cit.*, pp. 88–90.

[108] 95-S-9, Gibbons to Satolli, Baltimore, September 5, 1897, copy. Cf. Hogan, *op. cit.*, pp. 95–98.

[109] 96-A-10, Keane to Gibbons, Rome, January 24, 1898; 96-C-3, Zahm to Gibbons, Notre Dame, February 18, 1898.

were employed to good advantage in the business dealings of the university with the neighboring and affiliated institutions, they were probably of even greater assistance in the personal controversies which sorely beset its first two decades of life. In 1891 there broke over the Church of the United States the famous school controversy of Archbishop Ireland, the further story of which, insofar as it affected Gibbons, we shall see in another connection. The university professors were divided on the matter with Bishop Keane and Thomas Bouquillon, professor of moral theology, taking the side of Ireland while Joseph Schroeder, professor of dogmatic theology, gave his support to the German Catholics and the Jesuits who were opposed to the Ireland position. Naturally a situation such as this caused serious dissension within the faculty and both factions frequently appealed to Gibbons for support. The cardinal's sympathies were clearly with the Archbishop of St. Paul, yet as chancellor of the university he tried to moderate the vehemence of both parties. But when the attacks on the university grew particularly sharp in quarters like that of the *Civiltà Cattolica* of Rome, Gibbons did not hesitate to protest to Cardinal Rampolla against the attacks and to tell the Secretary of State of the profound pain which this criticism caused him.[110] So aroused had Gibbons become that he indicated he was ready if need be to make a trip to Rome to explain in person to Leo XIII the background to the campaign against the university and to answer the charges of "liberalism" which were being directed against some of its professors. The cardinal was stayed at the time from executing his plan by the advice of Monsignor O'Connell that he saw no need for the trip.[111]

A year later, however, Gibbons made his *ad limina* visit to the Holy See where he had three lengthy audiences of Leo XIII during which he defended the university's cause against its critics and successfully pleaded for a letter from the Pontiff renewing

---

[110] 92-R-2, Gibbons to Rampolla, Baltimore, November 14, 1893, copy in French. In this same letter Gibbons also protested against the attacks in the *Civiltà Cattolica* on St. Mary's Seminary in Baltimore which he regarded as unjust and containing grave and gratuitous charges against the Sulpicians.

[111] ADR, Keane to O'Connell, Washington, April 13, 1894. For an insight into student life in the university at this time, cf. Henry J. Browne, "Pioneer Days at the Catholic University of America," *Catholic Educational Review*, XLVIII (January and February, 1950), 29–38; 96–103, which is based in good measure on the reminiscences of two surviving members of the class of 1895.

his benediction on the institution. He told the rector that the Pope was, as he expressed it, "if possible more interested than ever" in the university and that as chancellor he had not failed to sound its praises to both Leo XIII and Rampolla. In his letter on the university the Pontiff had referred, said Gibbons, to the Catholic colleges as feeders for the institution. Gibbons explained to the Pope about the invitations extended to Keane to visit and speak in some of the leading colleges, and the cardinal made it known to the rector that Keane was more indebted to Leo XIII than he imagined for these invitations to visit the Catholic colleges.[112]

In a more positive vein the cardinal gave his hearty approval to the plan of a group of the professors to found a learned journal,[113] and when the first issue of the *Catholic University Bulletin* appeared in January, 1895, it carried a leading article by Gibbons entitled, "The Church and the Sciences." The university's chancellor defended the Church against the mistaken idea that Catholics were not free to pursue scientific research, and he outlined the duties of Catholic scholars to take a leading part in the promotion of science by original investigation and to keep a watchful eye on systems and theories wherein by prudent criticism they could sift hypothesis from certainty and established fact from erroneous deduction.[114] Moreover, in the continuing difficulties surrounding Professor Schroeder on the German question and the Americanism controversy, the cardinal asked and won the promise of Schroeder that he would cease his attitude of aloofness toward the *Bulletin* and write for its pages.[115] As chancellor he gave every encouragement to the advancement of research within the university, and when Thomas Bouquillon sent him a copy of the latter's new book, *Theologia moralis fundamentalis* (Bruges, 1890), Gibbons congratulated him and remarked, "I rejoice to see that the Professors of our

---

[112] ACUA, Keane Papers, Gibbons to Keane, Rome, June 29, 1895. Six years later when support of the university was still at a low ebb, Gibbons once more appealed to Leo XIII and secured a letter in which the Pope made known to the American hierarchy his desire that they contribute more interest and support to the institution (ACUA, Leo XIII to Gibbons, Rome, June 13, 1901, English translation).

[113] ADR, Thomas O'Gorman to Ireland, New York, April 15 [1894].

[114] *Catholic University Bulletin*, I (January, 1895), 1–7.

[115] 94-L-10, Gibbons to Schroeder, Baltimore, April 23, 1896, copy; 94-L-13, Schroeder to Gibbons, Washington, April 26, 1896.

Cath. University are already adding to the prestige of the Institution by becoming authors as well as teachers."[116]

A good example of Gibbons' contribution to the university was seen, too, in his ability to assist the rector in recruiting suitable men for the faculty. An attempt had been made in 1894 to secure the release of Father William J. Kerby from his duties in the Archdiocese of Dubuque but his superior, Archbishop John Hennessy, had refused. An appeal was then made to Gibbons to intervene with the result that Hennessy waived his objections and told the cardinal, "what I certainly would have done neither for the Rector nor the University I shall now do most cheerfully."[117] A further example of Gibbons' personal intervention in behalf of a solution for difficulties within the university was seen in the spring of 1894 when trouble arose over the appointment of John B. Hogan, S.S., to the chair of apologetics. The faculty opposed the appointment for various reasons after the rector had made the nomination. They appealed to Gibbons, and it was his conclusion that the nomination should be allowed to stand until the next meeting of the trustees when the informality of the rector's action could be rectified without further trouble. Gibbons gave as his reasons that if any other course was pursued it would afford joy to the enemies of the university in discovering internal dissension and, too, the Sulpicians of Montreal, Boston, and Baltimore should be considered lest antagonism arise in these quarters over what might seem unfair treatment of Hogan. The result was that the cardinal made a personal trip to the university on June 2 to help settle the difficulty, and it was there agreed to accept Hogan's own disinclination to take the appointment. In this way the dissension was quieted and Charles Aiken of the Archdiocese of Boston was finally appointed as the professor of apologetics. Gibbons likewise enhanced the dignity of all the major academic functions at Washington by his personal presence. The inauguration of the School of Philosophy and the School of Social Sciences on October 1, 1895, found the chancellor on hand to bless and dedicate the new McMahon Hall which was to house the offices and classrooms of these new divisions of the university.[118]

---

[116] ACUA, Bouquillon Papers, Gibbons to Bouquillon, Baltimore, May 31, 1890.

[117] 93-Q-5, Hennessy to Gibbons, Dubuque, January 20, 1895.

[118] ACUA, Faculty Records, November 15, 1889–May 31, 1901, pp. 128–129; Ahern, *op. cit.*, pp. 55–56, 108–109.

While it was true that the Cardinal of Baltimore had been helpful to the religious orders in establishing their houses of studies around the university, to the individual professors in seeking a solution to their personal problems and at times in calming their ruffled feelings, to the Holy See in periodically explaining the aims and purposes behind certain policies of the university administration, it was especially to the early rectors that Gibbons proved a tower of strength in these years. Bishop Keane, the first rector, was a close personal friend of the cardinal's, and in every important development he leaned heavily on the prudent judgment, the tactful management, and the national prestige of the chancellor. That the cardinal gave this support in no narrow personal spirit was proven after Keane had left office, for his successor, Thomas J. Conaty, not previously well known to Gibbons, experienced a co-operation from the chancellor that left nothing to be desired. It was, indeed, by reason of his strong support of the rectors that Gibbons suffered in these early years some of his keenest anxiety over university affairs. Little did the chancellor of the university realize when he presided at the seventh annual commencement on June 16, 1896, that it would be the last for the institution's first rector. Gibbons spoke in an optimistic vein of the prospects that lay ahead, and he referred approvingly to the introduction during the past year of the lay students and of two new schools. The cardinal mentioned that the new schools and their courses had demanded certain adjustments on the part of the older School of Theology in order to effect the proper co-ordination, but he was happy to say that the changes had been made without serious difficulty. He continued:

> Indeed, there is a gratifying evidence of such harmonious relations in the fact that to-day, for the first time in the history of the University, degrees have been conferred upon students from these several schools; that the laity have taken their place at the side of the clergy, thus initiating on the noble plane of intellectual effort that helpful co-operation in the matters of practical life which the Church so earnestly desires.[119]

Bishop Keane was a forthright man with pronounced views on controversial subjects such as the German question in the Ameri-

---

[119] John T. Reily, *Collections in the Life and Times of Cardinal Gibbons,* IV, 995.

can Church and the attempted condemnation of the Knights of Labor and of the writings of Henry George. Moreover, he felt an especially strong compulsion to urge upon American Catholics at all times that they show an open and uncompromising loyalty to their country. Naturally those of a more conservative turn of mind resented what they sometimes regarded as the unduly liberal philosophy of the university rector. Occasionally the bishop gave his enemies an opportunity to make capital by certain actions which seemed to them indiscreet as, for example, when he delivered the Dudleian lecture in Appleton Chapel at Harvard University in October, 1890, in his episcopal robes and closed the ceremony by imparting his blessing to the audience.[120] In an atmosphere which was growing tense with criticism from abroad on the score of a false Americanism among some of the leaders of the Church in the United States, episodes of this kind were seized upon to render more insecure the position of the university rector in certain circles of the Roman Curia. In addition, the internal disturbances which had arisen during his administration over Georges Périès, professor of canon law, Joseph Schroeder, professor of dogmatic theology, and the appointment of John B. Hogan, S.S., to the chair of apologetics also became widely known and were undoubtedly reported to the Holy See.[121] The cumulative effect of all this evidence damaged Keane's reputation in the Eternal City and suddenly in September, 1896, the rector was relieved by the Pope of his office.[122]

It was to Gibbons that the letter of dismissal was sent and it was he who had the unpleasant task on September 28 of breaking the news to the unsuspecting bishop. In the crisis which was now upon the university there was none who grieved more sincerely than its chancellor. Not only did Gibbons deeply regret this disruption of the temporary peace that had settled over the

---

120 New York *Sun,* October 24, 1890.

121 Ahern, *op. cit.,* pp. 55–56, 136–142, 152–156.

122 *Ibid.,* pp. 162–163. A biography of Keane by Patrick H. Ahern has recently been completed. Less than two years later Monsignor Jean B. Abbeloos, rector of the Catholic University of Louvain, resigned. Four months before his resignation Abbeloos had told Bishop Spalding, his classmate, the trouble he was having when the latter visited Louvain. In the opinion of Spalding the Louvain rector had been driven to resign by what the Bishop of Peoria termed "intrigues, originating in the University and fostered at Rome, Satolli being the chief offender" (AUND, Hudson Papers, Spalding to Daniel Hudson, Peoria, August 26, 1898, photostat).

institution, but he was chagrined and embarrassed by the storm which soon broke loose over the Keane affair in the Catholic and secular press of the nation. Seldom in the history of the American Church, either before or since, did the press react so universally and so unfavorably to an action of the Holy See affecting this country. But Gibbons saw nothing to be gained by idle laments, so on the day after the news reached Baltimore he quickly summoned a meeting of the trustees to face the emergency.[123] At the meeting on October 21 the trustees selected the names of three priests to be sent to Rome as a *terna* for the rectorship, and in the order of the trustees' preference they were: Thomas J. Conaty of Worcester, Massachusetts, Daniel J. Riordan of Chicago, and Joseph F. Mooney of New York. Before adjourning their session the board tried to stem the sensational newspaper stories by issuing a statement which repudiated the rumors of dissension, sectional rivalry, and the existence of liberal versus conservative factions in their own ranks.[124] But their efforts in this regard proved singularly futile and, in fact, as the weeks wore on the press became even more irresponsible and by mid-November it was being reported that Cardinal Gibbons and Archbishop Ireland, friends of the deposed rector, had been summoned to Rome with the possibility that they would be removed from their sees.[125]

Gibbons bore the tension with as much equanimity as he could summon. He had been present for the formal opening of the academic year in Washington on October 4 when, in the presence of Keane, he addressed the students and revealed the deep emotion under which he labored. The New York *Irish World* of October 10 reported the cardinal as saying, "I am a hard man to move, but to-day I am moved with the most profound sorrow I have ever felt in a long life full of sorrow." Amid all the hue and cry in the press Gibbons had held his peace until a week after the opening of the university, when the Baltimore *Sun* presumed to give its readers the party alignment of the board of trustees; this proved too much for the cardinal's forebearance and he issued a public denial of any disagreement or antagonism in their ranks.[126] At the end of that month he set his signature

---

[123] AANY, Gibbons to Corrigan, Baltimore, September 29, 1896.
[124] New York *Tribune,* October 23, 1896.
[125] Hogan, *op. cit.,* pp. 10–11.
[126] Ahern, *op. cit.,* p. 173.

in the name of the trustees to a splendid letter of appreciation to Keane for his services, and on the same day he sent a similar expression of gratitude to Garrigan, the vice-rector, in which he pleaded with him to remain at his post until a new rector had been appointed by Rome.[127]

In the days of trial and sorrow that lay ahead for Bishop Keane his friend, the Archbishop of Baltimore, proved his sterling loyalty at every turn. Not only did Gibbons inform Cardinal Rampolla of events as they touched Keane in several letters clearly breathing his sympathy for the bishop,[128] but after Keane went to Rome the cardinal urged upon Rampolla the necessity of avoiding delay in the appointment of the bishop to an honorable position in the Roman Curia so that criticism might be stilled.[129] Two years later when the proposal was made to have Keane return to the United States to collect money for the university, Gibbons seconded the idea energetically in a lengthy communication to Rampolla, and in the spring of 1899 there was none happier than the chancellor when the former rector returned to his native land to take up this work.[130] Nor did the cardinal rest with this temporary leave of absence for Keane from his Roman exile. He remained on the alert for a permanent and dignified American post for his friend, and at the time of the death of Archbishop Gross of Oregon City in November, 1898, Gibbons recommended Keane for the vacancy.[131] This effort proved unsuccessful, but about a year and a half later the Archdiocese of Dubuque opened with the death of Hennessy on March 4, 1900, and Gibbons then sent strong recommendations in Keane's behalf to Rampolla and Miecislaus Cardinal Ledo-

---

[127] ACUA, Keane Papers, Gibbons to Keane, Baltimore, October 31, 1896; 94-S-6, Gibbons to Garrigan, Baltimore, October 31, 1896, copy. The letter to Keane had been drafted by Archbishop Ireland and Bishop Maes at Gibbons' suggestion. Cf. Ahern, *op. cit.*, pp. 175–176.

[128] 94-T-7, Gibbons to Rampolla, Baltimore, November 24, 1896, copy in French; 94-T-11, same to same, Baltimore, November 30, 1896, copy in French. In regard to the letter of November 24, the cardinal entered in his diary under that date the following, "I sent a letter to Card. Rampolla about Bp. Keane's resignation, & I took occasion to refer to rumors regarding the forced resignation of some of the Professors of the University, saying that their enforced resignation under existing circumstances wd. be for many reasons disastrous" (Diary, p. 281).

[129] 95-B-10, Gibbons to Rampolla, Baltimore, January 15, 1897, copy in French.

[130] 96-S-1, Same to same, Baltimore, November 1, 1898, copy in French. Cf. Hogan, *op. cit.*, pp. 39–44.

[131] 97-B-9, Gibbons to Ledochowski, Baltimore, January 24, 1899, copy in French.

chowski, Prefect of the Propaganda.[132] Late in July the Holy See acted favorably in the case by naming Keane as second Archbishop of Dubuque and Cardinal Gibbons rejoiced heartily at the vindication of his old friend.

On January 19, 1897, the cardinal chancellor installed Father Thomas J. Conaty who had been named by the Holy See as second rector of the university. Gibbons used the occasion for a pronouncement on the relations of Church and State in the United States which is worthy of record. He said:

> Let the watchword of the Catholic University be: Revelation and science; religion and patriotism, God and our country. If I had the privilege of modifying the Constitution of the United States, I would not expunge or alter a single paragraph, a single line, or a single word of that important instrument. The Constitution is admirably adapted to the growth and expansion of the Catholic religion, and the Catholic religion is admirably adapted to the genius of the Constitution. They fit together like two links in the same chain. There are no hereditary privileges in the republic of the United States; there are no hereditary privileges in the republic of the Church. The Constitution declares all citizens are equal before the law, that all are equally subject to the law, all equally protected by the law. The Catholic religion proclaims that all her children, whatever may be their race or color or condition of life, have an equal right to the sacraments and other spiritual treasures of the Church.
>
> According to the Constitution, every citizen is eligible to the highest position in the gift of the people, and we all know that the highest post in the hierarchy is open to the humblest son of the Church. In Church and State fitness and availability, and not pedigree, is the paramount aim to office.[133]

At the time of his appointment the papal brief had indicated that the Pope would be agreeable to giving Conaty a higher ecclesiastical honor if such were requested. Gibbons took several months to judge the qualities of the new rector and to sound out other members of the board of trustees, whereupon he asked Pope Leo XIII through his Secretary of State to elevate Conaty to the episcopal dignity. The cardinal told Rampolla that for the position of the university and for the Church of the United

---

[132] 98-D-6, Gibbons to Ledochowski, Baltimore, April 15, 1900, copy in Latin; 98-D-7, Gibbons to Rampolla, Baltimore, April 15, 1900, copy in French.

[133] *Catholic Mirror*, January 23, 1897. Cf. Hogan, *op. cit.*, p. 28 ff. for Conaty's first days at the university.

States no less a rank would be fitting.[134] However, the officials of the Holy See felt it was a bit premature to grant Conaty the rank of bishop, but they did respond to Gibbons' request by bestowing on the rector the honor of a domestic prelate with the title of monsignor. Four and a half years later he was named titular Bishop of Samos, and Gibbons consecrated him in the cathedral of Baltimore on November 24, 1901.[135]

During the years of Conaty's administration several unpleasant incidents arose over individual professors, the most celebrated of which was that involving Monsignor Joseph Schroeder.[136] In all these troublesome cases the cardinal gave Conaty the benefit of his advice and counsel, and where he felt the rector's course of action was right he backed him with his support. In the Schroeder affair there was bitter resentment against the professor on the part of some of his colleagues and of certain bishops for the role he had played in the Cahensly question, and for the share they believed he had taken in the dismissal of Bishop Keane. Nothing short of a removal of Schroeder from the university faculty would content Archbishop Ireland, but Gibbons was reluctant to approve such drastic action if it could be avoided. With Gibbons' attitude in mind, Ireland asked Monsignor O'Connell in Rome to urge upon the cardinal that Schroeder must go since the Archbishop of St. Paul said Gibbons was "the obstacle" and talked of letting Schroeder off with only a warning.[137] Charles P. Grannan, professor of Scripture, was another who appealed to O'Connell to bring the cardinal into line. Grannan feared the unfavorable reaction of some of the trustees to a motion for dismissal of Schroeder, but most of all he feared Gibbons because in his opinion he lacked backbone. "Can't you strengthen it?" asked the professor.[138]

While it was obvious in the Schroeder case that the interested parties felt Denis O'Connell could do more than anyone else to influence Gibbons' course of action, it was not at all obvious that his hesitation was prompted by lack of courage. The cardinal rightly regarded the dismissal of the professor as a very

---

[134] 95-M-1, Gibbons to Rampolla, Baltimore, April 1, 1897, copy in French.

[135] Hogan, *op. cit.*, pp. 113–115.

[136] *Ibid.*, for the case of Richard Henebry, professor of Gaelic, pp. 116–124; and that of Daniel Quinn, professor of Greek, pp. 104–107.

[137] ADR, Ireland to O'Connell, St. Paul, September 13, 1897.

[138] *Ibid.*, Grannan to O'Connell, Washington, October 1, 1897.

serious matter which should be done only after it had become evident that such a step alone would restore peace to the university faculty. In the final analysis Gibbons' caution was vindicated when four days before the date set for the trustees' meeting a cable was received from Rampolla by Sebastiano Martinelli, the apostolic delegate, saying the Holy Father wished the case referred to him for final adjudication. This action had a somewhat moderating influence on the trustees, although they voted in a majority to recommend to the Pope that Schroeder sever his connections with the university. Cardinal Gibbons executed his part of the business by composing for Rampolla a lengthy explanation of the action of the trustees, in which he supported in temperate and measured words the majority and the rector in urging Schroeder's removal from Washington. Schroeder himself indicated his willingness to resign if the Pope thought best, and an opening for him at the Catholic Academy of Münster a few weeks later made his exit from Washington easier for all concerned.[139] The Schroeder case, inherited in good measure from the Keane administration, was by all odds the most trying experience Conaty had to face as rector, and in its final settlement the calm and judicious action of the chancellor proved a source of strength and comfort.

As the years passed the interest taken by Gibbons in the Catholic University of America deepened and he never lost an opportunity to place its cause before the general Catholic public, and especially before wealthy Catholics whose sense of generosity he thought he could arouse in its behalf. When he was visiting in Bavaria in 1895 the cardinal met accidentally Judge Myles P. O'Connor of San Francisco who some years before had helped to endow a chair of canon law in the university. Gibbons hastened to inform Keane that O'Connor was disposed to give

---

[139] Cf. Hogan, *op. cit.,* pp. 153–158, for the Schroeder case. Gibbons' letter of November 15, 1897, to Rampolla is published here in an appendix, pp. 188–190. One of the reasons for Gibbons' caution in this case may very well have been that he knew how powerful an influence Schroeder had in some circles in Rome. O'Connell made it clear that the action of the trustees met with strong disapproval on the part of these sympathizers when he told Archbishop Chapelle of Santa Fe, "When the news first reached Rome of the action of the Board some here were actually wild, but sober reflection deemed it better not to provoke a whole hierarchy & nation to save one pet. Now the whole future wears another aspect for the American Church and the Bishops know their strength" (AANO, O'Connell to Chapelle, Rome, November 30, 1897).

the university $500,000 and he wanted to communicate this good news, he said, before it escaped his memory. The cardinal outlined the conditions of the grant and told the rector he thought the proposal should be accepted.[140] Gibbons' own brother John had by the closing years of the century made a fortune in the grain business in New Orleans and in May, 1897, he sent a check for $150,000 to help this favorite institution of his distinguished brother.[141]

While benefactions of this kind were of great help to the university, the business management of the institution was not conducted in an efficient manner and by the opening of the century there had grown up a widespread discontent with Conaty as rector. The appointment of a special investigating committee of the trustees at their meeting on November 21, 1901, revealed very serious disorders in the finances, as well as a spirit of opposition to the rector among a group of trustees and professors which made it appear that it would be better for all concerned if Bishop Conaty would retire at the end of his first term of office. As these facts became more widely known in the spring of 1902 talk naturally turned to a successor. Monsignor O'Connell, who had been forced to resign in 1895 from the rectorship of the American College in Rome, had continued to live in the Eternal City as the vicar of Gibbons' titular church of Santa Maria in Trastevere, a post in which the cardinal kept his friend in an effort to minimize his embarrassment. In the intervening years O'Connell regained the favor of Cardinal Satolli, Prefect of the Congregation of Studies, who let O'Connell know his dissatisfaction with Conaty as rector and intimated to the monsignor that he might be the next rector. When this news was sent to Gibbons it filled his heart with joy and he told O'Connell that the only obstacle that stood in the way as far as he could see was some suitable provision for Conaty. Gibbons asked the monsignor if he would be willing to serve as vice-rector should the trustees hesitate to remove Conaty until such time as a place were found for him. He assured O'Connell, "Between now & the date of the meeting I will profit by every occasion to strengthen your appointment."[142]

---

140 ACUA, Keane Papers, Gibbons to Keane, Munich, July 8, 1895.
141 AAB, unclassified, Gibbons to Gibbons, New Orleans, May 11, 1897.
142 ADR, Gibbons to O'Connell, Baltimore, September 1, 1902.

Meanwhile Satolli indicated to O'Connell the manner in which the *terna* should be drawn up by the trustees and when it reached Rome he said that he would see to it that O'Connell's name was sent to the Pope for approval.[143] The meeting of the trustees was held on November 12 and Conaty received a unanimous vote of the ten members present for first place, O'Connell got six out of ten for second place, and Thomas J. Shahan, professor of church history, received eight votes for the third place on the *terna*.[144] O'Connell's friend Ireland was in a state of high expectancy as a result of the balloting and he remarked to the monsignor, "The Cardinal was told by me that unless he has you near him he can never get along in his relations with Rome."[145] The return of Archbishop Riordan of San Francisco from Rome brought to Gibbons the reassuring word that the Holy See would appoint Conaty to the vacant Diocese of Monterey-Los Angeles, and in communicating this intelligence to O'Connell the cardinal said, "Now we have done our part. I hope that Rome will ratify our action by sending you to us."[146]

The action of Rome was delayed for a few more weeks but on January 7, 1903, Cardinal Satolli informed Gibbons that the Holy Father had commissioned the Congregation of Studies to name a rector of the university and, therefore, as he expressed it, "thinking to please to [*sic*] Your Eminence," he had selected O'Connell.[147] O'Connell himself cabled the cardinal and expressed his joy over the appointment, at the same time revealing his anxiety that Bishop Conaty should be taken care of. Gibbons replied that the apostolic delegate, Diomede Falconio, had assured the cardinal the previous evening at dinner that he would urge Conaty's appointment to the California see, and that, thought Gibbons, was a virtual approval of their program. Gibbons told O'Connell, "I believe that in the Providence of God you have a great & glorious career before you which will atone for your dark days & will compensate me for my many sorrows on account of your distress."[148] On the following day, Patrick C.

---

[143] 100-B-3, O'Connell to Gibbons, Rome, October 6, 1902.

[144] 100-D-3, Maes to Gibbons, Washington, November 12, 1902. Bishop Maes was secretary of the board of trustees.

[145] ADR, Ireland to O'Connell, St. Paul, November 28, 1902.

[146] *Ibid.*, Gibbons to O'Connell, Baltimore, November 29, 1902.

[147] 100-F-6, Satolli to Gibbons, Rome, January 7, 1903.

[148] ADR, Gibbons to O'Connell, Baltimore, January 11, 1903.

Gavan, Gibbons' chancellor who was also a close friend of O'Connell, told the rector-elect that when the news of his appointment reached Baltimore the cardinal was as happy as a child. Gavan added, "I never saw him so elated before."[149]

O'Connell quite naturally was pleased that his seven years of living under a shadow were over and that the cloud had finally lifted. He told Gibbons of the exceedingly cordial audience he had of Leo XIII, that Bishop Conaty's appointment to Monterey-Los Angeles was expected soon, and that he would not think of leaving Rome for the United States until it was known everywhere that suitable provision had been made for the outgoing rector. This intimate friend of Gibbons closed his letter by saying, "It often comes to my mind to say to you in these circumstances what once in other circumstances you said to me: 'Vos estis qui permansistis mecum in tentatione mea.' "[150] The bond between the two men was exceedingly close, and it was a comforting thought to the Cardinal of Baltimore to know that in the days ahead he would have his dear friend at the head of the university and within close reach for agreeable companionship and for his consultation on important business affecting the Holy See upon which Gibbons set such a high value.

With the appointment of Thomas Conaty as Bishop of Monterey-Los Angeles on March 27, 1903, plans could be definitely made for the inauguration of Monsignor O'Connell as third rector of the university. This event took place on April 22 in conjunction with the meeting of the trustees. The university was by now in its fourteenth year of life. Many difficulties had been met and overcome but the years immediately ahead would have their own share of troubles. Cardinal Gibbons had meant much to the young institution in the interval since it was first projected in 1884, but his service to the institution was by no means ended, and during the administrations of its third and fourth rectors he continued to manifest the same devoted loyalty and strong support that Keane and Conaty had experienced in its infancy. The hesitancy of earlier days had long since departed and each new crisis found the cardinal exercising ever stronger leadership in behalf of an institution which he had grown to love. In financial assistance, in enthusiastic appeals to the American hierarchy,

---

[149] *Ibid.*, Gavan to O'Connell, Baltimore, January 12, 1903.
[150] 100-G-9, O'Connell to Gibbons, Rome, January 31, 1903.

and as the arbiter of differences Gibbons' contribution to the university excelled. Above all the prestige of his name and the love of his person sustained the university cause before the American Catholic community when the vicissitudes of its fortune might otherwise have accomplished its ruin.

CHAPTER XI

The Secret Societies

ONE of the most striking phenomena in the social history of the United States in the late nineteenth century was the growth of secret societies. The suspicion and dislike of secret organizations, which had been characteristic of Americans generally when the century was young, had long since passed by 1880, and by the year 1900 the vogue enjoyed by secret fraternal groups had registered the names of over six million Americans on their membership lists.[1] In the midst of the rapidly urbanizing movement of the large industrial areas, the secret society presented an organized medium through which social intercourse could be established with more ease. Likewise the egotistic impulses in many obscure Americans were served by their enrollment in groups to which all could not belong and which permitted them, too, the romantic extravagance of wearing elaborate regalia on occasion. In the more practical order, most of the secret societies made provision for sickness and death benefits for their members, a factor which held a strong attraction for many. While the older and still flourishing secret societies had been imported from abroad, such as the Freemasons and Odd Fellows from England and the Ancient Order of Hibernians from Ireland, the trend in the late century was toward indigenous groups. The tremendous growth of these new and native-born secret lodges is strikingly illustrated by the fact that between 1880 and 1900 there were approximately 490 such societies established in the United States.[2]

In view of a development of this magnitude in American life

---

[1] Arthur Meier Schlesinger, *The Rise of the City, 1878–1898*, pp. 289–290. The earlier opposition to secret societies in the United States during the 1820's and 1830's is treated in Carl Russell Fish, *The Rise of the Common Man, 1830–1850* (New York, 1927), pp. 39–40.

[2] Schlesinger, *op. cit.*, p. 289.

it is not surprising that large numbers of American Catholics should have found their way into one or other of the secret groups. From the very outset of the organized life of the Catholic Church in the United States the problem of Catholic membership in these societies had been present. As early as 1794 Bishop John Carroll of Baltimore had been asked by a layman concerning Catholic membership in the Freemasons, and when the first meeting of the American hierarchy took place in 1810 the bishops issued a ban against any Catholic receiving the sacraments who was publicly known to belong to the Masons.[3] The opposition of the Church to the Masons had been stated as early as 1738 in the bull *In eminenti* of Pope Clement XII where the two main objections advanced had been the tendency of Masonry to undermine belief in Christianity by setting up a religious cult based on deistic principles and the oath of secrecy exacted of members. In the intervening years the papal condemnation of Masonry was repeatedly renewed, although it would seem that it was not too widely known for a considerable time by many Catholics since as late as the closing years of the eighteenth century there lingered some doubt in the minds of a number on the question of Catholic membership in this group.

The American bishops, of course, followed the directives of the Holy See on the Masons. But what complicated the matter was the periodic emergence of new secret societies in the United States on which Rome had not given a decision and the nature and purposes of which were so hidden in secrecy that it was almost impossible to gain an exact knowledge of their character. While the principles governing the Church's condemnation, such as secrecy of aims and purposes, a secret oath, a semi-religious cult, and the danger of conspiracy against Church or State might appear clear in the abstract, it was quite another matter to apply them against a particular society when knowledge of these factors was so difficult to ascertain. For this reason the Holy See showed a great deal of caution before condemning societies by name, and the prudence and good sense of the American hierarchy likewise received a prolonged testing in all these

---

[3] Fergus Macdonald, C.P., *The Catholic Church and the Secret Societies in the United States* (New York, 1946), p. 4. This work gives a thorough treatment of the problem down to 1895 and will be used throughout the present chapter for background material.

cases lest they be guilty of an injustice and a consequent injury to souls.

Sometimes there was little reason for hesitancy, as in the case of the Know-Nothings of the 1850's with their violently anti-Catholic bias. But in the matter of the fairly numerous Irish societies it was not so clear. For example, for a long time the bishops of the United States were concerned about the Fenians until the Holy See in January, 1870, finally condemned them.[4] Hardly had the Fenians been disposed of when other Irish societies gave cause for alarm by the secret manner in which they pursued their goals for the freedom of Ireland or the alleviation of their own lot here in the United States. A bewildering variety of these Irish groups intensified their activity during the 1870's, and the rising tempo of violence in places like Schuylkill County, Pennsylvania, where the Molly Maguires led the campaign for redress of their very real grievances against the coal operators, became a source of acute anxiety to those who were responsible for the spiritual guidance of the Catholic laity. Mysterious names like the Ribbonmen and the Emeralds were intertwined with the excesses of the Molly Maguires, and the Ancient Order of Hibernians itself did not escape the suspicion of many of the Catholic clergy that it was a secret society which ought to be condemned.[5]

All during these years there were repeated condemnations of secret societies in general from the provincial and plenary councils of the American bishops, with constant admonitions against membership in the pastoral letters issued at the close of the councils or by individual prelates. Yet these warnings failed to stem the tide of Catholic advance into the secret orders, with the result that by the year 1884 it had become evident that it was a question which demanded more organized and consistent action on the part of the bishops in the plenary council sched-

---

[4] Macdonald, op. cit., pp. 46–47. In the period of the Civil War Archbishop John Hughes of New York took a somewhat lenient attitude on the question when he was interrogated by Father Thomas J. Mooney of the 69th Regiment. While Hughes advised the priest to work against the membership of Catholics in the secret societies, he added that discretion and all the charity which religion afforded should be used in dealing with the subject (AANY, Hughes to Mooney, New York, May 22, 1861, copy).

[5] Macdonald, op. cit., pp. 54–55, where there is reprinted from the New York Freeman's Journal of October 10, 1874, the declaration of seven pastors of the Pennsylvania coal region against the Ancient Order of Hibernians.

uled for the end of that year. The loose and disorganized manner in which the problem had been handled up to this time had become a source of confusion and even of scandal. A pastor here and a bishop there periodically thundered against a particular society while their neighbors in near-by parishes or dioceses often remained silent. It was evident that a uniform practice based upon accepted criteria was long overdue.

Although James Gibbons could not have been unaware of the increasing seriousness of the situation created by the secret societies in the years of his priesthood, he did not, of course, have any direct responsibility for settling the problem. The fact that he doubtless heard the matter discussed among his elders in such gatherings as the Second Plenary Council of Baltimore in 1866 would not occasion any responsibility. But after his appointment as a bishop the question necessarily had a greater pertinence for him as a shepherd of souls. The earliest evidence of Gibbons' attitude toward secret societies came as a result of the activities of the Ku Klux Klan in North Carolina. Late in the year 1870 Governor Holden was impeached by the votes of the conservative majority of the state legislature. During the trial in 1871 the issue of the Ku Klux Klan came prominently to the fore and, as we have seen, Edward Conigland, one of the lawyers for Holden and a friend of Bishop Gibbons, made a lengthy speech in which he detailed the outrages committed by the klan and the dangers to society which arose from these secret associations.[6] Conigland sent a copy of his speech to the bishop who in two letters expressed his satisfaction with it. Gibbons remarked to his lawyer friend with a rather obscure figure, "It is not often that I can praise public speeches. I think that without the 'Jew of Verona,' you brought to light the horrors of secret societies, which may effect some good."[7] It was the klan, too, that furnished several years later the first recorded problem of a disciplinary character brought before the young bishop when his vicar-general in Charlotte inquired if he might grant absolution to a member of the hooded order. Father O'Connell said he knew the party was bound by oath to obey its leaders and, he added, "There are plenty of them on my

---

[6] J. G. de Roulhac Hamilton, *Reconstruction in North Carolina,* p. 551.

[7] University of North Carolina Library, Conigland Papers, Gibbons to Conigland, Wilmington, March 5 and 10, 1871.

mission."[8] What answer Gibbons gave to the question is not known.

After the transfer of Bishop Gibbons from North Carolina to the See of Richmond the question of secret societies did not cease to engage his attention. In October, 1874, the Irish Catholic Benevolent Union held its convention in Baltimore, and at a Mass in the cathedral Archbishop Bayley preached to the delegates and took the opportunity to condemn Catholics joining secret societies as injurious to their faith as well as to their citizenship. The Bayley sermon[9] was telegraphed to Richmond where it appeared the following day in the local papers. Gibbons congratulated the archbishop and stated that he was very glad he had given a thrust to the secret societies. He went on to say that in Richmond there was a branch of the Ancient Order of Hibernians composed largely of Catholics and which was suspected of secrecy, although, as he expressed it, "it tries to wear an honest face." Gibbons confessed he was unwilling to take any directly hostile action against them until he had consulted more experienced bishops, but meanwhile he was throwing as much cold water on the A.O.H. as he could and wishing he could freeze them out quietly.[10] Just a month before he left Richmond to become Archbishop of Baltimore, he addressed the convention of the Irish Catholic Benevolent Union in St. Peter's Cathedral. Gibbons developed the idea of strength in the union of many within a single organization. He likened it to the power of a great river composed of countless drops of water; but occasionally, said the preacher, the Mississippi overflowed its banks and then there was havoc. The moral he would wish to leave with the delegates of the I.C.B.U. was that they should strive to live within the boundaries fixed by their constitution. This is as close as the bishop came in his sermon to touching on the subject of the societies.[11]

At the time that Gibbons became Archbishop of Baltimore in the fall of 1877 one of the societies whose status was most controverted among the authorities of the Church was the Ancient

---

[8] 72-O-15, O'Connell to Gibbons, Charlotte, October 26, 1873.

[9] The principal portions of Bayley's sermon are quoted in Sister M. Hildegarde Yeager's *Life of James Roosevelt Bayley,* pp. 386–388.

[10] 41-S-6, Gibbons to Bayley, Richmond, October 22, 1874.

[11] 73-E-11, Gibbons' handwritten copy of the sermon delivered on September 19, 1877.

Order of Hibernians. As mentioned previously, Gibbons felt
uneasy about the A.O.H. and had expressed his hope three years
before that the order might be kept at a distance insofar as
Catholics were concerned. A number of American bishops, however, were more forceful in their opposition to the A.O.H. than
Gibbons and for that reason it was not surprising that when
the order met in Boston for their convention in May, 1878, they
should take steps to remedy this unfavorable reaction from the
clergy. With that in mind, the convention framed a set of resolutions which they had printed with a view to making it perfectly clear that there was nothing in the constitution of their
organization which should trouble the conscience of a Catholic.
Copies of these resolutions, along with the revised constitution,
were sent to Archbishop Gibbons with the information that they
were "respectfully submitted" for his inspection.[12] There was
nothing in the documents of the A.O.H. to which the archbishop
could take exception, since even the oath binding members to
keep the secrets of the order was explicitly stated not to apply
when it related to the Catholic clergy. Again there is no evidence
to show what answer, if any, Gibbons returned to the communication from the A.O.H.

In the late summer of that same year Cardinal Simeoni, Prefect of the Propaganda, sent Gibbons a clipping from the New
York *Herald* of May 6 which had been forwarded by someone
to the Holy See.[13] The clipping contained a bitter attack on the
Catholic religion by Edwin Cowles, president of the Order of
the American Union and editor of the Cleveland *Leader*. Simeoni
asked that investigation be made of this society and that Catholics be warned against it. The archbishop apparently knew nothing about the O.A.U. so he inquired of Bishop Gilmour of
Cleveland, only to be told that he had tried in vain to secure a
copy of the order's constitution but that since it was a secret
society his failure was not to be wondered at. Gilmour reassured
Gibbons that the organization was so notoriously anti-Catholic
that he felt safe in saying no practicing Catholics held membership, and he paid his respects to the Cleveland *Leader*, edited
by Cowles, by saying that it was a sheet in which there was

---

[12] 73-T-7, John Hart to Gibbons, Jersey City, June 21, 1878, enclosing the
printed documents.
[13] Diary, September 7, 1878, p. 115. Simeoni's letter which Gibbons transcribed
in his diary was dated Rome, August 22, 1878.

"nothing too vile nor too false for its columns." The inquiry of the Archbishop of Baltimore prompted Gilmour to raise the question of the need for more unity of action among the bishops in regard to the secret societies. As the bishop put it: "Our diversity of actions on these points are [sic] surely not to edification, & gravely tend to weak [sic] our status before the people & the non-Catholic world."[14] While the reply of Gilmour enabled Gibbons to quiet the fears of Simeoni on the Order of the American Union,[15] its greater importance lay in its suggestion for united episcopal action. But for some time the situation continued to drift without any concerted plan of attack by the hierarchy to unify their efforts.

The general uneasiness among the Catholic clergy in these years on the score of secret societies reflected itself occasionally in the sensitive attitude displayed by the more conservative-minded toward Catholic fraternal groups. When, for example, in the summer of 1880 the Knights of St. John held a convention in Cincinnati and conducted a night festival on one of the hilltops in spite of the wishes of Archbishop Elder, their action aroused the indignation of Father Francis X. Weninger, S.J., the famous missionary. Weninger was especially outraged at the knights electing Archbishop Gibbons as an honorary chaplain, and he urged Elder to inform Gibbons of their conduct so that he might, as the priest expressed it, "rebuke their folly. . . ."[16] Word of the trouble in Cincinnati reached Gibbons and he told Elder that before he would accept the chaplaincy he wished to know what the difficulty was and if an adequate reparation had been made for the offense. It afforded Gibbons an opportunity to elaborate a bit on his own attitude toward these societies. The archbishop told his friend in Cincinnati that he was disposed to be very indulgent toward Catholic societies since they were generally actuated by a proper spirit of loyalty toward the Church. Gibbons revealed his awareness of the current trend when he stated that it was the tendency of men then to belong to some organization, and so long as Catholic men belonged to authorized societies it would help to keep them secure from the dangerous and condemned groups. As he expressed it, "if they

---

[14] 73-W-9, Gilmour to Gibbons, Cleveland, September 21, 1878.

[15] Diary, September 24, 1878, p. 117, copy of Gibbons' answer to Simeoni.

[16] AAC, Weninger to Elder, Marquette, Michigan, July 9, 1880.

withdraw from our organizations, they are exposed to be absorbed by some secret society."[17] Archbishop Elder explained the episode of the Knights of St. John in Cincinnati in a manner that did not reveal too great chagrin at their conduct and he expressed approval of their having chaplains. However, Elder was strongly opposed to the national unification of the knights for fear that they might give the appearance of a Catholic army because of their commander in chief and their use of military terms for divisions and officers.[18]

While the episode of the Knights of St. John showed something of the attitude of Gibbons on the question of the societies, the preliminary investigations concerning the Grand Army of the Republic revealed his mind more clearly. The G.A.R. had been organized in 1866 by the veterans of the Civil War and it grew steadily until by 1881 it had enrolled over 87,000 members. Naturally the Catholic veterans were anxious to join with their former comrades in arms and General William S. Rosecrans sought the approval of Gibbons, taking care to stress the fact that the Catholic members did not have to participate in the ceremonies of the ritual.[19] What answer, if any, Gibbons gave is not known, but a year later Archbishop Elder had an exchange of correspondence with the G.A.R. commander at Carthage, Ohio, in which the prelate exposed to the latter the Church's objections to the religious ceremonies and acts of worship practiced by the organization.[20] Elder sent on the correspondence to Baltimore and asked for Gibbons' judgment in the case of the G.A.R. Gibbons was of the opinion that Elder had put the Church's case on this delicate subject very well. He was hopeful that all the obnoxious features might be revoked by the G.A.R. as he felt loath to place the Catholic Church in antagonism to such an organization if it could possibly be avoided. He said he was anxious to concede all that could possibly be conceded in order to make it possible for Catholic veterans to join. The archbishop then added:

> I may be wrong, & too liberal, when I say that I would not hastily make the saying of a prayer by a non-Catholic before exercises a

17 *Ibid.*, Gibbons to Elder, Baltimore, n.d., but Elder answered this letter on November 19, 1880.
18 75-M-9, Elder to Gibbons, Cincinnati, November 19, 1880.
19 75-H-4, Rosecrans to Gibbons, Washington, July 25, 1880.
20 Macdonald, *op. cit.*, p. 93.

cause for excluding Catholics from the society, provided the obligation of assisting at them were not enforced as a sine qua non. Such prayers are said in Congress & other deliberative assemblies in this country. The presence of a Catholic congressman is not considered, I think, a communicatio in divinis. It is looked upon as a civil function. To refuse to allow a Catholic to *be present* at these exercises would involve our exclusion from all participation in our legislative assemblies.

I hope I do not shock you by these remarks which are hastily made.[21]

However hasty the remarks of the archbishop may have been, they sprang from a conviction that was very deeply rooted. The whole mentality of James Gibbons reacted against harsh and unnecessary condemnations of any kind at any time. As we shall have reason to see, he fought some of his most notable battles in an effort to ward off condemnations by the Holy See and American ecclesiastical authorities of both men and movements. He did this in the belief that they were either innocent of the charges brought against them, or of so transitory a character that the Church's ban would only help to keep them alive and lend to them an emphasis and importance which they did not deserve. It was Gibbons' way to win men if at all possible through persuasion and kindliness, not to alienate them through hasty and unsympathetic use of ecclesiastical authority. This reasonable approach was in entire consonance with the man's nature. Gibbons was comfortable in the atmosphere of conciliation, but he felt estranged when the discussion of differences lost that spirit and assumed the air of uncompromising dogmatism. It was this same trait which in the heated controversies of these years more than once led to accusations of vacillation, lack of courage, and even a false liberalism being lodged against the Archbishop of Baltimore. True, he did at times waver and hesitate, but beneath his uncertainty of action there lay fundamental strength. When a situation called for condemnation Gibbons could give it, and his sermon at the ceremony of Archbishop Katzer's pallium in Milwaukee, of which we have already spoken, will stand as an example of what is meant when it is said that James Gibbons was not a weak man.

At the time of the conferences of the American metropolitans

---

[21] AAC, Gibbons to Elder, Cincinnati, October 12, 1881.

in Rome in November-December, 1883, held in preparation for the Third Plenary Council, the subject of secret societies arose in the discussions with the cardinals of the Congregation of the Propaganda. Archbishop Gibbons let it be known that he accepted without question the general regulations which had been proposed in the schema governing condemnation of the secret societies. However, as has been stated, when Archbishop Seghers of Oregon City and Bishop Chatard of Vincennes showed a disposition to include labor unions in the same category with the suspected societies, Gibbons and Archbishop Feehan of Chicago quickly came to the defense of the workers and said that not all associations of laborers were of an evil character and that many of them offered no reason for condemnation or prohibition by ecclesiastical authority.[22] After his return from Rome early in 1884 the Archbishop of Baltimore continued to receive communications of one kind or another calling for action on the societies. Chatard complained to him of a St. Patrick's Day celebration of the A.O.H. in Indianapolis, where an unknown Scotch priest by the name of Agnew was engaged to address the society without previous permission from the bishop. Chatard remarked, "We seem to be drifting towards a lay episcopate. I merely mention the fact to draw attention to the existing state of things."[23]

Meanwhile the concern of General Rosecrans for approval of the G.A.R. by the Church prompted him to direct repeated pleas to Gibbons at this time for sanction of that organization. Rosecrans endeavored to remove all grounds for suspicion against the veterans' society by informing the archbishop that the commander in chief had appointed him and four other Catholic members as a committee to establish the liceity of the G.A.R. for Catholics.[24] The repeated requests of the general made it clear that he was receiving no satisfaction from Gibbons, and the latter was probably employing a delaying tactic in the hope that the coming council might settle the problem. Actually the archbishop was not in a position to give a judgment independently of his colleagues in council, as the whole question on the

---

[22] *Relatio collationum quas Romae coram S.C. de P.F. praefecto habuerunt archiepiscopi pluresque episcopi Statuum Foederatorum Americae. 1883,* pp. 21–22.

[23] 77-P-1, Chatard to Gibbons, Indianapolis, March 17, 1884.

[24] 77-R-6, Rosecrans to Gibbons, Washington, March 30, 1884; 78-Q-2, same to same, Washington, October 2, 1884.

suspected societies had been referred to that body by the Roman schema. Rosecrans did not know, of course, that the G.A.R. had been discussed by the bishops of the Province of New York who were assigned that portion of the schema by Gibbons as apostolic delegate of the council. Nor did he know that they had not been able to arrive at a unanimous agreement about the G.A.R. and so had ended by expunging from the record all reference to the society by name.[25] The inability of the New York prelates to reach a decision doubtless heightened the sense of caution with which Gibbons approached the whole question of the G.A.R. which was bothering Rosecrans and others at the time.

In the Third Plenary Council over which Gibbons presided as apostolic delegate he intervened, as we have seen, very little in the debates themselves. When on December 1 the long and heated discussion on secret societies was held, revealing as it did a wide divergence of opinion as to the nature of certain societies and the method of procedure in their regard, the official minutes show that Gibbons spoke only once. He broke his silence on this occasion when a proposal of Archbishop Williams to permit individual bishops to speak their minds on the Ancient Order of Hibernians received fifty-seven votes. At this point Gibbons warned the bishops that it was the mind of the Holy Father that no society should be condemned too hastily.[26] Knowing as he did the feeling of certain prelates toward the A.O.H., Gibbons doubtless foresaw rash action if this proposal was allowed to stand. After further discussion and a dramatic speech in behalf of the A.O.H. by Feehan of Chicago, the council finally adopted a decree which took the matter entirely out of the hands of the individual bishops and gave over the question of judgment of the secret societies to a committee composed of all the metropolitans of the United States.[27] The mechanism had at last been

---

[25] 78-I-13, Corrigan to Gibbons, New York, July 24, 1884.

[26] *Acta et decreta concilii plenarii Baltimorensis tertii* (private edition), p. lxxvii.

[27] *Acta et decreta concilii plenarii Baltimorensis tertii* (Baltimore, 1886), pp. 143–144. This legislation of 1884 gave back closer control of the matter to the American bishops and was an improvement over that of the Second Plenary Council of 1866 wherein the bishops had been forbidden to condemn any society by name and, at the instance of the Holy See, all cases were to be referred to Rome for final judgment. It was a stipulation which was accepted by the council of 1866 with some reluctance since it effectively tied the hands of the hierarchy in their efforts to eradicate the evil according to their own judgment. For discussion of this legislation of 1866, cf. Henry J. Browne, *The Catholic Church and the Knights of Labor* (Washington, 1949), pp. 13–16.

established for giving a solution to the problem. Now a unanimous decision of the American archbishops would settle the fate of a given society one way or another insofar as the Catholic Church was concerned, and if they could not reach unanimity then the case was to be referred to the Holy See for judgment.

In the days after the council the two societies that gave the bishops the most anxiety were the Grand Army of the Republic and the Ancient Order of Hibernians. General Rosecrans persisted in his efforts to win approval for the G.A.R. and near the close of the year 1884 he informed Gibbons that the commander in chief was a practical Catholic, and that out of the million and a half members enrolled he believed that probably one fifth were Catholics. Since, in Rosecrans' opinion, a continued silence on the part of the bishops would cloud the consciences of many good Catholic veterans, he pleaded once more that a decision be rendered.[28] The A.O.H., too, continued to press for a settlement of their status in relation to the Church. When a local division of the order at Galesburg, Illinois, was refused permission by their pastor to appear in church in their regalia until they had been approved, their secretary sought the counsel of the ordinary, Bishop Spalding of Peoria. Spalding, however, side-stepped the issue by forwarding the correspondence to Gibbons and informing his inquirer that it was to the Archbishop of Baltimore, as chairman of the committee of archbishops, that his questions should be addressed.[29] While it was true that the problem would ultimately have to reach Gibbons it would have been of some help to him had Spalding conducted an investigation of the case

---

[28] 78-U-1, Rosecrans to Gibbons, Washington, December 2, 1884. When Jeremiah O'Donovan Rossa revived the Fenian Brotherhood early in 1885 and they resorted to violence in England to win the freedom of Ireland, an outraged English Protestant by the name of William Kirkus wrote Gibbons indignantly at the support being given to the Fenians by the *Catholic Mirror*. He said that Gibbons and other Catholic prelates could, if they would, stop this sort of thing. The archbishop sent to Kirkus a copy of Leo XIII's recent encyclical, *Humanum genus,* against the Masons along with a copy of the pastoral letter of the Third Plenary Council to show that the Church was not abdicating its responsibilities in this regard. At this Kirkus was quite appeased and stated that he believed all would come right in the end (79-C-1, Kirkus to Gibbons, Baltimore, January 24, 1885; 79-C-9, Kirkus to Denis J. O'Connell, Baltimore, January 30, 1885). For the Fenian revival in 1885 and the sudden *denouement* of the society, cf. William D'Arcy, O.F.M.Conv., *The Fenian Movement in the United States: 1858–1886* (Washington, 1947), pp. 406–407.

[29] 79-L-3, John McLernan to Spalding, Galesburg, May 23, 1885; 79-L-16, Spalding to McLernan, Peoria, May 28, 1885.

and given his judgment on it, but he chose to pass it on without comment. Meanwhile the legislation of the Baltimore council had reached Rome for approval and Denis O'Connell informed Gibbons that Bishop Sepiacci of the Propaganda had expressed himself as well pleased with the procedure outlined for handling the secret societies through the archbishops' committee.[30]

When Archbishop Elder made inquiry of Gibbons about the A.O.H. in the summer of 1885 the latter told him that he had never given them an approval of any kind, although he confessed that he may have said the plenary council had manifested a benevolent disposition toward them. Gibbons' lenient attitude toward the order was revealed in his informing Elder that while he thought the bishops should watch them with vigilance, their recent good deportment inclined him to believe that the A.O.H. was moving in the right way to gain the confidence of the hierarchy.[31] On the other society which was foremost in the bishops' minds at the time, the G.A.R., Gibbons told his friend in Cincinnati that while he had not given them any formal sanction, he had spoken kindly of them and would be sorry to see them harshly treated without due cause. The only cloud that the archbishop could see hanging over the G.A.R. was the charge that they had a ritual, and if the ritual were suppressed or not made obligatory on Catholic members Gibbons was of the opinion that, as he expressed it, "we could shake hands with them. . . ."[32]

Even the Odd Fellows, who had been condemned many years earlier, elicited a certain sympathy from Gibbons. When Archbishop Elder queried him on this society at the instance of a Catholic man who held membership, he stated clearly the condemnation of the Church on the Odd Fellows. He further pointed out that until it was removed or modified it must stand, although it was his belief, as he said, that "the H. See would deal more leniently with said society if the subject came before it in our days."[33] Few bishops were more active on this question than Elder, and his repeated inquiries to the Archbishop of Baltimore had the effect of drawing Gibbons out on the individual societies

---

[30] 79-I-13, O'Connell to Gibbons, Rome, April 12, 1885. O'Connell remarked that Sepiacci had told him that some bishops "see Freemasons in everything and some never see them anywhere."

[31] AAC, Gibbons to Elder, Baltimore, July 6, 1885.

[32] *Ibid.*, Gibbons to Elder, Baltimore, July 7, 1885.

[33] *Ibid.*, Gibbons to Elder, Baltimore, May 22, 1886.

as well as on points of procedure. In the summer of 1886 he told Elder that it was the function of the committee of archbishops to act as a standing tribunal to take cognizance of cases as they arose, but it was not intended that the committee should take the initiative. Gibbons believed it would be impossible for the archbishops to resolve themselves into an investigating committee that would pry into the affairs of other dioceses, and he showed his mind clearly when he said to Elder, "I believe that more good will result from a vigilant, masterly inactivity than by any hasty legislation."[34] This generally favorable attitude of Gibbons was in striking contrast to his cautious distrust of ten years before. He had now attained an attitude of liberality on the question of the societies and in some cases even of approval.

Although Cardinal Gibbons might be content to follow the policy of "masterly inactivity" in regard to the suspected societies, there were those among his colleagues who were not at all disposed to allow matters to take their course. All through the year 1886 a number of the bishops were busy conducting private investigations of the societies and counseling with one another concerning them. While Elder was concerning himself with the Odd Fellows, Archbishop Corrigan of New York was concentrating on the A.O.H. Corrigan made as conscientious an investigation of this group as he possibly could, strongly supported by his suffragan, Bishop McQuaid of Rochester. He prepared a letter with which he circulated the metropolitans of the United States, outlining to them what he had learned about the A.O.H., and asking if the archbishops would approve Catholic chaplains being assigned to the order. As it turned out, only two of the twelve metropolitans — Ryan of Philadelphia and Kenrick of St. Louis — were opposed to chaplains for the Hibernians, and no one of the archbishops was more positive in his approval than the Archbishop of Baltimore. Gibbons told Corrigan, "I most emphatically believe that the A.O.H. should have recognition, and have a chaplain." He went on to outline his fears that if this recognition was withheld numbers of the A.O.H. might be alienated from the Church and tempted to join societies that were hostile to religion. It was Gibbons' view that granting the privilege of chaplains would afford the bishops the best guarantee that the conduct of the A.O.H.

---

[34] *Ibid.*, Gibbons to Elder, Baltimore, July 20, 1886.

would be directed along the right lines. The society's officers had given satisfactory statements about their constitution and by-laws, and any objectionable features, if such should be discovered, could then be removed by judicious advice from the chaplains. Gibbons hoped Archbishop Corrigan, who had told him there were 50,000 members of the A.O.H. in his see city, would lead the way in appointing the chaplains. His view was succinctly expressed when he said, "If we want to preserve these thousands of souls to the faith, let us show sympathy for them."[35]

By the late summer the failure of the American committee of archbishops to take definite action for or against some of the societies had prompted certain parties to lodge complaints and pleas for action with the Holy See. Among these was Bishop Chatard of Vincennes who had pursued the subject relentlessly ever since the time before the plenary council. Chatard was apparently restive that no decision had been made and he probably hoped to force the issue by appealing to the Prefect of Propaganda, a tactic in which, it would seem, he attained at least a partial success. At any rate, Monsignor O'Connell informed the Cardinal of Baltimore that Chatard was again trying to get a condemnation of the A.O.H., and — an even more disquieting fact — O'Connell likewise suspected it was the Bishop of Vincennes who had lately sought a condemnation of the Knights of Labor by Rome.[36] Since we shall treat the case of the Knights of Labor and Gibbons' relation to it later, it will suffice here to mention the fact that by this same summer the labor organization's status was being called seriously into question by some bishops in the United States, stimulated no doubt by the fact that the K. of L. in Canada had already been condemned by the Holy Office. Prompted doubtless by the prodding of men like Chatard, Cardinal Simeoni on August 28 finally asked Gibbons through Archbishop Corrigan to summon a meeting of archbishops to consider the standing of those societies about which there was suspicion. Gibbons quickly complied with the wish of Simeoni and announced October 28

---

[35] AANY, Gibbons to Corrigan, Baltimore, April 21, 1886. The answers to Corrigan's inquiry sent to the various archbishops are detailed in Macdonald, *op. cit.,* pp. 127–139.

[36] 81-Q-3, O'Connell to Gibbons, Rome, August 1, 1886.

as the date for a meeting of the metropolitans to be held at his residence in Baltimore.[37]

In the intervening weeks the interested parties among the American hierarchy were busy holding conferences and exchanging views by mail on the subject of the societies.[38] When the meeting convened on the scheduled date nine of the twelve archbishops of the United States were present with Michael Heiss of Milwaukee, Patrick W. Riordan of San Francisco, and William H. Gross of Oregon City unable to attend. The three societies discussed by the metropolitans were the Knights of Labor, the Grand Army of the Republic, and the Ancient Order of Hibernians. On the K. of L. they could not reach agreement and, therefore, following the directive of the plenary council, the case had to be referred to the Holy See. On the G.A.R. the archbishops unanimously decided that since the only serious doubt related to the use of prayers at their meetings and at funerals for which Catholic members were not required to be present, the order should be left undisturbed. The point on the prayers was intended, of course, to preclude the possibility of Catholics having to join in prayers which might embody expressions contrary to their religious beliefs. The same lack of any condemnatory action was to be noted in the case of the A.O.H. after the deliberations of the archbishops on that group.[39] The G.A.R. and the A.O.H., therefore, stood untouched, even if there was no formal and public blessing given to Catholics in their ranks.

Even before the meeting of the metropolitans in Baltimore in October, 1886, there had risen again the question of Catholic membership in the Odd Fellows. As long ago as 1850 the Congregation of the Inquisition had declared this society included among the forbidden lodges and the Second Plenary Council of 1866 had restated the condemnation. However, in the intervening twenty years the Odd Fellows had shown a growth of almost 400 per cent, and in 1886 their numbers stood at 530,000.[40] Inquiries were made of some of the arch-

---

[37] 81-V-5, Gibbons to the archbishops of the United States, Baltimore, September 17, 1886, copy. Gibbons informed Simeoni a month in advance of the coming meeting scheduled for October 28 (Diary, September 25, 1886, p. 209).

[38] Cf. Macdonald, *op. cit.*, pp. 144–147, for these preliminary preparations.

[39] *Ibid.*, pp. 147–149, which is based on the minutes of the meeting as found in 82-D-8.

[40] Macdonald, *op. cit.*, p. 151.

bishops concerning the society's standing, as well as that of the Knights of Pythias, with the result that a round of investigations was begun and finally by March, 1889, it became necessary for Gibbons to circulate the metropolitans for their views.[41] The answers, as in previous cases, revealed considerable differences of opinion. Since it was the Archbishop of Cincinnati who had placed the problem before Gibbons as chairman of the committee, it was to Elder that he sent the replies along with his own judgment.

Once more Gibbons enlisted himself on the side of moderation and leniency. He alluded to the Odd Fellow condemnation by Rome in 1850 but then referred to the more liberal interpretation of Pius IX issued in 1869 which had declared all societies were to be tolerated which were not hostile to Church or State. Gibbons then took note of the tendency of the age to join organizations and said that often the intentions of the members were harmless and even praiseworthy. He instanced the failure of ecclesiastical condemnations in the past to arrest the growth of such societies in Catholic countries, and he pointed especially to Italy where repeated condemnations of that sort had been issued yet, as he expressed it, "that country is honeycombed with secret societies." As a practical measure in the present case of the Odd Fellows and Knights of Pythias, the Archbishop of Baltimore was in favor for the time being of tolerating both, with the proviso that the members should express themselves as willing to honor any future action which the Church might take in their regard. The cardinal believed that a special committee of bishops might meanwhile be appointed to study the constitutions of the two societies and report to the archbishops; if the latter then agreed "almost unanimously" on action one way or another that would end the matter, whereas a wide divergence of opinion would make it a fitting case to refer to the Holy See.[42] In the end, however, the advice of Gibbons in regard to the two societies, as we shall see, was not followed.

[41] Diary, March 5, 1889, p. 234. When several months before Elder reported criticism of the archbishops' committee from some quarter, Gibbons explained again the procedure as it was enacted at the council and he said this should make it clear that the metropolitans had not been wanting in the duty assigned to them and, he added, "The strictures or criticism to which you call my attention is not just" (AAC, Gibbons to Elder, Baltimore, December 19, 1888).

[42] AAC, Gibbons to Elder, Baltimore, March 28, 1889, copy.

In all this discussion in regard to secret societies Cardinal Gibbons kept constantly before him the danger of alienating the masses from the Church. It was a theme to which he returned again and again in his correspondence with his fellow bishops. Keen observer as he was of public opinion, he sensed that severe measures against the societies on the part of the Church would run the risk of doing more harm than good and, as he remarked to Elder, he was not impressed by the record in Italy where repeated condemnations had been tried. Gibbons wished above all to prevent the masses of the people from regarding the hierarchy as unsympathetic and hostile to their interests. As he told Elder about the societies, "It is better for us to win their confidence, & then we can succeed in eliminating what is bad or suspicious from their constitution."[43]

While the cardinal's view may well have shown an optimism that at times was unwarranted, he held unshakably to his position except where he was confronted by the virtually unanimous opposition of his colleagues or where a given society's aims and conduct were unmistakably evil. When a society resorted to acts of violence the cardinal quickly showed alarm and stiffened his attitude. Such a case occurred in the spring of 1889 with the United Brotherhood of Clan-na-gael. This Irish revolutionary society, which had recently been reactivated, was torn by internal strife which a temporary truce, effected at their Chicago convention in June, 1888, had not overcome. In May, 1889, the body of Patrick H. Cronin, leader of one of the opposing factions, was found in a catch basin in Chicago and the light of national publicity was turned on the society and reprobation of their deeds was general. Gibbons fully shared in this reprobation, and a few weeks after the murder of Cronin he told Archbishop Elder that he thought the Clan-na-gael needed investigation. The cardinal said he believed there was "something mysterious & sinister" about the order, but he hoped the stern action of the civil authorities toward them would render any movement on the part of the hierarchy unnecessary.[44]

---

[43] *Ibid.*

[44] *Ibid.*, Gibbons to Elder, Baltimore, June 12, 1889. Insofar as Gibbons was concerned the present writer has found no evidence that would justify Zwierlein's judgment in speaking of the Clan-na-gael to the effect that, "The curse was not taken off all this by the countenance given to such men as Alexander Sullivan

The Cronin murder in Chicago was the subject of comment months later among some of the bishops who felt that the metropolitans' committee was neglecting its duty. Bishop McQuaid of Rochester was especially irked at the inaction. He told the Archbishop of New York that he intended to send copies of the ritual of the Clan-na-gael to the bishops of the country, but he was not very hopeful that anything would happen since, as he expressed it, "it might hurt one's popularity to check anything wrong in an Irishman."[45] Nearly three months later the archbishops assembled in Boston on July 23–24 for their first annual conference under the chairmanship of Cardinal Gibbons. The Clan-na-gael was the subject of a special discussion but it was decided to take no action against them awaiting subsequent developments. As for the other societies, with the exception of the Masons, the minutes merely stated that while Catholics should be discouraged from joining them, as far as it was known to the archbishops there seemed to be no absolute certainty of any positive evil in them and for that reason no general mandate could be issued forbidding them.[46] Precisely who and what lay behind this surprisingly moderate judgment within the meeting it is impossible to say. The secretary of the meeting was Archbishop Ireland and the version of the action of the metropolitans as given above reached the public. The impression created was, of course, that societies like the Odd Fellows, Sons of Temperance, and Knights of Pythias were now to be tolerated by the Church. Conservative prelates like McQuaid were aghast at the news, and the situation, more confused than before, was not relieved until the next annual conference in St. Louis in November, 1891, corrected the view given out in Boston.

Meanwhile Cardinal Simeoni himself became concerned over the reported leniency of one of the American bishops toward the Freemasons. He informed Gibbons some months after the Boston meeting that a bishop had sent him a copy of the *Colorado Catholic* for October 18, 1890, a weekly paper

---

and Michael Davitt by Archbishop Feehan and Cardinal Gibbons." Frederick J. Zwierlein, *Life and Letters of Bishop McQuaid*, II, 386.

[45] Zwierlein, *op. cit.*, II, 436, citing AANY, McQuaid to Corrigan, Rochester, May 6, 1890.

[46] 87-R-4, Minutes of the Meeting of the Archbishops, Boston, July 23–24, 1890.

published in Denver. It contained a quotation from John J. Kain, Bishop of Wheeling and one of Gibbons' suffragans, in which he was supposed to have said upon his return from Europe that the Masons in France and Italy were, indeed, the enemies of Christianity, but those in the United States and England, Kain believed, were essentially Christian. Simeoni regarded the matter as of grave moment and he asked Gibbons to make inquiries and then inform him of what he had learned.[47] The cardinal did as he was bid and a month later he told the Prefect of Propaganda that Kain had repudiated the words ascribed to him concerning the Masons, to which Gibbons added that the Bishop of Wheeling was a prelate who never compromised Catholic doctrine and interests.[48]

When the archbishops convened in St. Louis in the autumn of 1891 for their second annual conference the subject of forbidden societies again came up for discussion. Archbishop Katzer of Milwaukee presented a paper in which he stated that the wording of the minutes of the Boston meeting was open to serious misunderstanding and was, therefore, objectionable. Katzer believed that the resolution as made known would cast the mantle of toleration over societies which he thought were dangerous for Catholics to join. The same division of opinion obtained among the metropolitans in St. Louis as was previously the case, with some arguing for strictness of interpretation and others deprecating what they called arbitrariness in the exercise of ecclesiastical authority. They were all agreed, however, that the wording of the Boston resolution was somewhat inexact, and they now changed the phrase that left the question of leaving or remaining in a given society to the conscience of each individual, to read that the decision should be made "by the conscience of each individual under the direction of his confessor." With a further resolution that the Boston statement had not altered the rules of the Third Plenary Council governing secret societies, the conference passed to other business.[49]

Two weeks before the St. Louis conference the Archbishop of Milwaukee had written a lengthy report to Rome which in

[47] 88-E-9, Simeoni to Gibbons, Rome, December 17, 1890.

[48] Diary, January 16, 1891, p. 250.

[49] 89-D-5/1, Minutes of the Meeting of the Archbishops, St. Louis, November 29, 1891.

substance was a charge of neglect on the part of the American committee of archbishops to do its duty in regard to the suspected lodges. It was represented that numerous Catholics were joining societies of a dangerous character and what was to be deplored most of all, said Katzer, was that scarcely any effective remedy was being offered to protect Catholic men from these groups.[50] While it is not possible to assess the real motives which lay behind this independent action of Katzer, it is not at all difficult to picture the effect which a letter of this kind would have on the Roman curial officials. The archbishop's move was made just a few months after the uproar occasioned by the Cahensly memorial and the heated discussion that had begun over the Faribault-Stillwater school plan of John Ireland in the Archdiocese of St. Paul. Katzer knew, of course, the feelings of Gibbons and Ireland on these major questions and he realized that they were on the side opposite to his. He knew as well that the cardinal and Ireland were opposed to a condemnation of the Odd Fellows, Knights of Pythias, and Sons of Temperance; yet he did not hesitate to name these three societies in his communication to the Holy See as worthy in his judgment of prohibition. Whether or not Katzer's attitude was colored by his conflicting views on other major questions it is not possible to say, but at least we know that his letter was calculated to arouse serious concern in Rome and to accentuate the differences existing among the American hierarchy on secret societies.

The spring of 1892 brought an article in the *American Ecclesiastical Review* from Archbishop Katzer in which the more conservative point of view on the societies was set forth, and two months later Francis Janssens, Archbishop of New Orleans, in the same journal came out against the Knights of Pythias as a forbidden society, although, as he was careful to state, it was not condemned under pain of excommunication.[51] The lines were being drawn more closely, therefore, between those who favored condemnation and those who opposed. One of Janssens' suffragans was sorely puzzled by

---

[50] Macdonald, *op. cit.*, pp. 164–167.

[51] Frederick X. Katzer, "Societies Forbidden in the Church," *American Ecclesiastical Review*, VI (April, 1892), 241–247; Francis Janssens, "Are the Knights of Pythias a Forbidden Society for Catholics?", *ibid.*, VI (June, 1892), 450–455.

the confusion and turned to Gibbons in the hope of enlighten-ment. Bishop Thomas Heslin of Natchez revealed his anxiety and embarrassment when he said that his priests were asking him what they were to do about Catholic men joining societies like the Odd Fellows and the Knights of Pythias. He stated that all he could say to them was that he did not know, since he was forbidden to interfere and he did not know the mind of the archbishops or even of Rome. He pleaded with Gibbons to refer all the information available to the Holy See so that they might be relieved of what he termed "this distressing uncertainty." Heslin put it sharply but truthfully when he said that "while the Pastors are contending the flocks are roaming about in the dark without a guide."[52] In reply Gibbons joined Heslin in deploring the difference of opinion among the bishops. He was hopeful that at the next meeting of the metropolitans they could reach some definite arrangement. "Otherwise," he said, "the only remedy is to have recourse to Rome." He did not feel warranted in condemning the two societies in his own archdiocese, and when he was asked about them the cardinal said he pursued the following course of action:

> I advise the clergy that consult me, to urge those who are anxious to become members not to join the society. If they are already mem-bers, they are admonished to abandon the society, & I believe the admonition is usually obeyed. If they are unwilling to yield after all possible efforts are employed, absolution is not denied them, pro-vided that they express their willingness to abide by any future decision of the Church.

Gibbons concluded by telling the Bishop of Natchez that the prelates of the Province of Baltimore had recently assembled in Wheeling and had agreed to follow the procedure he outlined above until a final decision had been rendered on these societies.[53] Even some of the more liberal bishops were beginning to despair of finding a satisfactory solution to the vexing problem on this side of the Atlantic. Bishop Moore of St. Augustine, one of Gibbons' suffragans, told the cardinal that he was still of the opinion that hasty condemnations ought to

---

[52] 89-V-5, Heslin to Gibbons, Natchez, May 9, 1892.

[53] Archives of the Diocese of Natchez, Gibbons to Heslin, Baltimore, May 12, 1892, copy. The writer is indebted for a copy of this letter to the kindness of Bishop Richard O. Gerow of Natchez.

be avoided, although the refusal of the Knights of Pythias to give their ritual to Archbishop Janssens for examination had "staggered" him a little. Moore, like Heslin, believed that the American hierarchy should gather all the data possible concerning the societies and then refer the matter to Rome for decision.[54]

This was one instance where Gibbons' policy of "masterly inactivity" was not working to his advantage. By their forthright public stands the Archbishops of Milwaukee and New Orleans had taken the lead from the other metropolitans, and in view of the silence of Gibbons as the chairman and the inaction of the committee as a whole, the decisive moves of Katzer and Janssens were bound to attract recruits to their side. In fact, Bishop Ignatius F. Horstmann of Cleveland, a prelate who, it is true, was usually on the conservative side of most questions, told Archbishop Corrigan that his views were those publicly expressed by the two archbishops.[55] Meanwhile further attempts at settlement were made in a number of the ecclesiastical provinces of the United States. The bishops of the Provinces of Cincinnati, New Orleans, Santa Fe, and Milwaukee in their meetings held between August and October, 1892, reached varying degrees of agreement on what should be done in the case of the Odd Fellows, Knights of Pythias, and Sons of Temperance, although in no instance was there a definite demand for condemnation in these provincial meetings. But in the Provinces of New York and Philadelphia the affair took a more definite turn. On September 14 the New York bishops adopted a unanimous resolution which stated that in their opinion the Odd Fellows, Knights of Pythias, and Knights Templar were prohibited societies in the sense of the decrees and pastoral letter of the Third Plenary Council. Six weeks later their colleagues of the Province of Philadelphia reached a similarly unanimous decision on these three societies, to which they added the Sons of Temperance.[56]

The action of these provincial meetings was taken in view of the approaching third annual conference of the archbishops scheduled to open in New York on November 16. In preparation

---

[54] 90-D-5/1, Moore to Gibbons, St. Louis, August 30, 1892.

[55] Macdonald, *op. cit.*, p. 173, citing AANY, Horstmann to Corrigan, Cleveland, May 16, 1892.

[56] *Ibid.*, pp. 174–182.

for the meeting Cardinal Gibbons did not choose to assemble his suffragans for consultation but he did ask the advice of the noted Jesuit theologian, Aloysius Sabetti, professor of moral theology at Woodstock College, on the question of the Odd Fellows and the Knights of Pythias. In reply Sabetti stated that he was opposed to a formal condemnation of the Odd Fellows since its danger to Catholics differed according to the circumstances of persons and places and he believed, therefore, that it might be left for each confessor to decide in particular cases. Sabetti enclosed for the cardinal a copy of a study on secret societies that had been made by Salvatore M. Brandi, S.J., when he was on the faculty at Woodstock. Brandi reached the conclusion after close examination of both the Roman directives and the Baltimore decrees, that no society except the Masons must be held as condemned under censure in the United States unless it was proven that it worked against Church or State.[57] Gibbons would seem, therefore, to have had support for his lenient attitude on this question from one of the leading moral theologians of the United States at the time.

By the time the archbishops met in New York in November, 1892, it was obvious to all who took any interest in the subject that bishops, priests, and people were expecting some kind of decisive action on the secret societies. But they were doomed to disappointment. The same diversity of opinion appeared as at previous conferences so that no unanimous judgment could be rendered on groups like the Odd Fellows and the Knights of Pythias. The result was that a new approach was resolved upon in the appointment of a committee consisting of Archbishops Corrigan, Riordan, Ryan, Ireland, and Katzer who were to gather all available material on the disputed lodges and send the data to Cardinal Gibbons who, in turn, would communicate them to the Holy See for a final decision.[58]

This action of the conference was a confession that the mechanism devised by the Third Plenary Council had failed. And yet the failure of the metropolitans was understandable. The Baltimore decree's stipulation of the necessity for a unanimous decision of the archbishops on the case of each

---

[57] 90-P-2, Sabetti to Gibbons, Woodstock, November 7, 1892.
[58] 90-Q-3, Minutes of the Meeting of the Archbishops, New York, November 16–19, 1892.

society, instead of allowing a two-thirds or simple majority, laid down a condition that proved impossible of fulfillment. Moreover, the obtaining of complete and authentic data of a number of the secret lodges on which to base a fair judgment was likewise almost an impossibility. It is small wonder, then, that after eight years of well-nigh futile effort to give a lasting solution to the difficulty the archbishops should ultimately have determined that the only hope lay in an appeal to the Holy See. Whether or not the result would have been different had Gibbons, as chairman of the committee, assumed a more aggressive attitude in behalf of his favorite policy of leniency, cannot be stated with certainty. In the light of the strong feelings of men like Katzer, Corrigan, and Janssens, however, it is unlikely that he could have brought them over to his way of thinking even if he had tried. At any rate, his delaying tactics and his hope that the situation might right itself within the societies failed in the end. Knowing his mind on the subject as we do, the cardinal doubtless viewed with considerable reluctance and misgiving the transfer of the responsibility out of American hands. Yet given the circumstances there seemed to be no other course to follow and there is no evidence that Gibbons protested the judgment that the societies' case should be heard in Rome.

During the course of the next few months the special committee of five archbishops gathered all the data they could on the societies, urged on by prelates like McQuaid and Janssens who were restive at the long delay. Cardinal Gibbons, however, refused to be hurried and in informing the apostolic delegate, Francesco Satolli, that the Knights of Pythias was one of the lodges then under investigation, he said he thought the matter could well be deferred until the conference of the archbishops scheduled for Chicago in September. For the same reason Gibbons told Satolli he was not in favor of the delegate distributing a document on the societies recently drawn up by the bishops of the Province of New Orleans.[59] At the Chicago conference, which opened on September 12, the metropolitans re-enacted the familiar scene of the secret societies after hearing the individual reports of the special committee. Archbishop Ireland framed a resolution to the

---

[59] 91-K-7, Gibbons to Satolli, Baltimore, May 9, 1893, copy.

effect that Catholics should not be forbidden to join the Odd
Fellows under penalty of loss of the sacraments but should
be strongly exhorted not to belong to the society. The vote
was eight in favor of the resolution, five opposed, and one
blank ballot. When a similar resolution on the Knights of
Pythias was put to a vote of the archbishops there were nine
in favor, four against, and one blank ballot. This latest failure
to reach a unanimous agreement was then clearly set forth
in the final item of the minutes:

> It was finally ordered that the reports of the aforesaid Committee
> be sent to the Holy See together with these minutes as there was
> a serious divergence of opinion. However, all agreed in the hope
> that in view of our circumstances, the Holy See would exercise
> leniency in its final decision.[60]

The Roman Curia proceeded in the matter in the leisurely
pace to which it was accustomed and it was not until late in
the summer of 1894 that the judgment was given. Bishop
Keane, rector of the university, went to Europe that summer
and after he had left Rome in late July he took the pains to
give Gibbons an extended account of his visit to the Holy See
insofar as it related to the secret societies and other important
questions. Keane stated that in an audience he had of Leo XIII
the Pontiff expressed his serious concern about societies which
showed a tendency toward socialism and he believed they ought
to be condemned. The bishop explained that he had spoken
earnestly to the contrary, "especially," he said, "as to our labor
organizations, & even as to Odd Fellows, etc. . . ." He quoted
for the Pope the conviction of Gibbons that there should be
no condemnations, that they were unnecessary, and that they
would do more harm than good. But Keane confessed to the
cardinal, "He listened, but seemed not convinced." On the
following day the bishop saw Rampolla and went over the
same ground, telling the Secretary of State the disastrous
results that would follow condemnation of the societies and
begging him to suspend all action until Gibbons could come
to Rome. Keane said that Leo XIII had remarked rather
complainingly that it had been a long time since the Archbishop

---

[60] 91-V-1/1, Minutes of the Meeting of the Archbishops, Chicago, September
12–13, 1893.

of Baltimore had been to Rome, but he had assured the Pope that Gibbons intended to make the trip in the coming autumn or winter. Rampolla, too, was anxious that Keane should urge Gibbons to come as he wished to make his acquaintance and the sooner he came the better. This gave Keane a chance to add his own word of counsel that Gibbons should visit the Holy See. The university rector ended on a note that would be likely to stir a sympathetic reaction in Baltimore when he remarked, "Card. Rampolla was very emphatic in saying that the importance of American affairs made it very desirable that your visits to Rome should be frequent and long, so that you might be indeed 'consiliarius Papae.' "[61]

Nonetheless, the persuasive eloquence of the rector of the university had apparently little effect on the Roman officials, for about a month after his departure from the Eternal City Raffaele Cardinal Monaco of the Congregation of the Holy Office forwarded, on August 20, 1894, a decree to Archbishop Satolli in Washington in which the three disputed societies of the Odd Fellows, the Knights of Pythias, and the Sons of Temperance were condemned by the Church. The decree directed that the American bishops be notified of the action of the Holy Office and their people warned against the societies; if Catholic members persisted in the ranks after being warned, they were to be deprived of the sacraments. After receiving the decree Satolli was asked by Rampolla in the name of the Pope if there were any observations to be made in regard to its execution. Satolli forwarded his ideas on the subject to Rome to which, as he told Cardinal Gibbons, the Secretary of State replied on September 22 to the effect that the decree should be communicated to the archbishops assembled in their annual conference in Philadelphia in early October. At the same time Rampolla told Satolli that the carrying out of

---

[61] 93-J-7, Keane to Gibbons, Pegli, July 31, 1894. Four days later Keane wrote to Thomas Bouquillon, professor of moral theology in the Catholic University of America, a very similar letter in which he said Thomas O'Gorman, professor of church history in the university who had been in Rome at the same time, and Denis O'Connell both thought that Leo XIII's tendency to condemn the societies arose from the fact that "the mind of the Pope has been influenced by recent protests that he was encouraging socialism." Keane said both O'Gorman and O'Connell thought it might be useful for Bouquillon to go to Rome and discuss the matter thoroughly with Rampolla, the two Cardinals Vannutelli, and others (ACUA, Bouquillon Papers, Keane to Bouquillon, Pegli, August 3, 1894).

the decree should be committed to the prudence and conscience of the metropolitans. Three days before the meeting due to open on October 10 at Philadelphia the apostolic delegate, therefore, sent the decree and the summary of his correspondence with Rome to the cardinal in Baltimore for presentation to the metropolitans at their meeting.[62]

Although the judgment of the Holy Office had been mailed only to Satolli, in some way or other the news leaked out since Archbishop Riordan in San Francisco learned of it and wrote in alarm to Gibbons at the unfortunate effects which he believed would follow publication. Riordan regarded the danger of publication as so great that he said it would produce "incalculable mischief to thousands." In the emergency that was now upon them Riordan looked to Gibbons to avert what he anticipated would be a catastrophe. He felt the cardinal should go to Rome and that Archbishop Ireland should accompany him. He said, "You are our only hope in this crisis, and I hope that God will aid you to prevent a great mischief."[63]

The terse language of the official minutes of the Philadelphia meeting gives no direct evidence of the role played by Gibbons as chairman, but in the action taken on the decree it is not difficult to detect his hand. After relating that the decree was read and the decision to promulgate it or not was left to the bishops to decide, the minutes stated:

> The Most Reverend Prelates were unanimous in their opinion that it was inopportune under the present circumstances to publish said condemnation; they moreover agreed not to communicate this condemnation even to their suffragans; and in fine they resolved that no individual Archbishop or Bishop should promulgate it, unless its promulgation were expressly ordered by the Holy See or by the Archbishops in convention assembled.[64]

There could hardly be plainer evidence for the fact that the moderates had carried the day at Philadelphia. The surprising tone of these resolutions, in view of the known opinions of a number of the archbishops present, was accountable by the fact that at the very time of their meeting the American

---

[62] Macdonald, *op. cit.,* pp. 190–191.

[63] 93-L-1, Riordan to Gibbons, San Francisco, October 2, 1894.

[64] 93-L-4, Minutes of the Meeting of the Archbishops, Philadelphia, October 10, 1894.

Protective Association was waging a bitter campaign against the Catholic Church, and the strength of the organization had swelled within recent months to the point where the leaders of the Church were seriously concerned. The A.P.A. agitation was growing noisier with each passing day in anticipation of the congressional elections less than a month away.[65] In the face of this situation even the most conservative of the archbishops took pause lest the publication of the decree against the three societies give further weapons into the hands of the Church's enemies. The current wave of bigotry, therefore, did more to prevent temporarily the promulgation of the Roman decree by a unanimous vote than the arguments of Gibbons and the party of moderation.

The resolution for a stay of proceedings in the case was destined, however, to be nullified when in early December, 1894, the apostolic delegate communicated to the archbishops the wish of the Pope that the condemnation of the societies should be promulgated and communicated at once to their suffragans. When this news reached St. Paul, Archbishop Ireland was indignant and he wrote Gibbons a detailed account of his opposition. Ireland wondered if Leo XIII had reached this decision after hearing of their Philadelphia action and, if not, why had the Pope referred the subject to their conference at all? The Archbishop of St. Paul said that few things in the past decade had amazed and saddened him more than this action of the Holy See, and the disregard of what Ireland believed was the larger portion of the American hierarchy irritated him. He would make no move until he had word from Baltimore. "Please tell me," he wrote, "what if anything may yet be done. I will say nothing to my suffragans until I shall have heard from you."[66] Cardinal Gibbons answered at once and told him he was startled the previous week when Satolli had communicated to him verbally the latest directive from the Holy See. Gibbons expressed his distress at the whole affair, especially since the bishops would have to bear the odium and responsibility without being able to give a reasonable answer to those who would ask them for their motives. He said the

---

[65] Gustavus Myers, *History of Bigotry in the United States* (New York, 1943), p. 219 ff.

[66] 93-N-3, Ireland to Gibbons, St. Paul, December 7, 1894.

delegate was likewise surprised and disappointed, but when the cardinal asked Satolli if he could not withhold distributing the command of Rome for promulgation until he had written again to the Holy See, the delegate had replied that he would not undertake to decide that. Gibbons himself was not going to let it pass without a protest and he urged Ireland to make the same. He said he realized that most of the bishops would fail to act, feeling that it would be of no avail, even if they were opposed to condemnation. But as for his own position, regardless of the outcome he had made up his mind. He told Ireland, "I wish to put myself on record. Let the responsibility rest on them that brought about the condemnation."[67]

Several weeks later the Cardinal of Baltimore addressed a strong communication to Cardinal Rampolla, the Secretary of State, on the subject of promulgation of the decree. It contained none of the customary expressions of thanks for the Holy See's solicitude for American Catholic affairs, and as for the decree of condemnation itself, the cardinal dismissed the point summarily with the words, "without calling in question the wisdom of this decision;" whereupon he proceeded at once to his arguments against publication. Gibbons told Rampolla that he felt it would not be opportune to publish the decree in his archdiocese since the Catholics who belonged to the banned societies saw nothing evil in them and the Protestant members had shown no hostility to the Catholic Church. He went on to say that he feared the decree's publication would only irritate the Protestants and submit the Catholics to a serious temptation to disobedience because of the financial losses they would sustain should they abandon their membership. The cardinal pointed out that the influence of confessors could be used effectively to withdraw the Catholics from the forbidden societies in a gradual and quiet manner; therefore, since promulgation in Baltimore would have only harmful results he hoped the Holy See would weigh these reasons and approve his course of action in accepting the judgment of Rome but not officially publishing it.[68]

---

[67] AASP, Gibbons to Ireland, Baltimore, December 19, 1894, copy.

[68] 92-W-6, Gibbons to Rampolla, Baltimore, December 26, 1893 [sic], copy in French. The incorrect date on this copy as "1893" instead of "1894" threw Macdonald off at this point and occasioned a certain confusion in his narrative, op. cit., p. 189 ff.

On the same day Gibbons informed Ireland of the action he had just taken and he urged the Archbishop of St. Paul to write a similar protest to the Holy See. He said Riordan and his suffragans on the Pacific coast agreed with them and that he had suggested that Riordan, too, write Rome and have his suffragans join with him. The cardinal was of the opinion that ten out of the fourteen metropolitans in the United States regretted the decision for publication, and if they would all likewise communicate their views to Rome he was hopeful that they might yet, as he expressed it, "be saved the scandal of a promulgation," to which he added, "Do all you can in that direction & act promptly." Gibbons expressed himself as especially anxious that the subject be kept out of the Catholic papers, and as far as he could learn the decree had been promulgated only in the Archdiocese of New York and the Diocese of Brooklyn.[69] About two weeks later the cardinal quoted for Ireland a cablegram just in from Monsignor O'Connell in Rome which read, "I believe the decree of condemnation practically abortive." He thought the foreshadowing of the reply he was awaiting from Rampolla could be seen in what he termed "this comforting dispatch."[70] But Gibbons had guessed wrongly, for the Rampolla answer which arrived three weeks later did no more than thank the cardinal for giving his reasons against the publication of the decree and then refer him to Satolli who, said Rampolla, had been furnished with particular instructions and who would be ready to give opportune suggestions.[71]

---

[69] AASP, Gibbons to Ireland, Baltimore, December 26, 1894, copy. The speech of Bishop McQuaid on November 25, 1894, delivered in his cathedral against Archbishop Ireland's participation in the politics of New York State irritated Gibbons. He told the archbishop he had read an account of it in the London *Tablet* which also carried an editorial sympathetic to McQuaid. He said, "I was indignant. . . . I intend soon to drop the paper." For the McQuaid speech and its aftermath, cf. Zwierlein, *op. cit.,* III, 216–225.

[70] *Ibid.,* Gibbons to Ireland, Baltimore, January 12, 1895, copy. The original of the cablegram read: "Censeo decretum damnationis practice abortivum." When Leo XIII addressed his encyclical, *Longinqua oceani* of January 6, 1895, to the American hierarchy, William Henry Thorne, convert editor of the *Globe,* thought he saw in the letter a condemnation not only of those who encouraged mixed religious gatherings and neglected to establish parochial schools, but also of "those prelates who so long failed to promulgate the Papal decree against certain secret societies . . ." (*The Globe,* VI [February, 1896], 97).

[71] 93-Q-4, Rampolla to Gibbons, Rome, January 18, 1895.

The confusion over the status of the Odd Fellows, the Sons of Temperance, and the Knights of Pythias in relation to the Catholic Church became more confounded in the public mind during the early days of 1895. Unknown to Gibbons at the time he informed Archbishop Ireland that only New York and Brooklyn had promulgated the decree, the Archbishop of Cincinnati had acted similarly on January 6. Ten days after the Cincinnati publication the Coadjutor Archbishop of St. Louis, John J. Kain, told Gibbons, however, that he would not make known the Roman condemnation until. he had received further instructions. Kain rightly complained that the Sons of Temperance had not even been discussed by the archbishops, and he did not think it fair that the odium for securing the decree should fall on the metropolitans when as a matter of fact, as Kain remarked, "the majority of us were opposed to the condemnation of those societies."[72]

The anxiety which Gibbons was experiencing was naturally enhanced when he learned that the news concerning the ban on the three societies was threatening to do damage to the Catholic Indian mission schools. He informed Bishop Keane that he had this report from Father Joseph A. Stephan, the director of the Bureau of Catholic Indian Missions in Washington, who feared that undue agitation on the part of the hierarchy against the societies would prompt their members to wreak vengeance upon the Church's schools among the Indians.[73] Gibbons said he had talked with Stephan and given him instructions to write a letter to the bishops warning them against unnecessary notice being given to the Roman decree.[74] The cardinal then forwarded a copy of the Stephan letter to Rome to be used by Monsignor O'Connell as evidence of the

---

[72] 93-Q-3, Kain to Gibbons, St. Louis, January 15, 1895.

[73] ACUA, Keane Papers, Gibbons to Keane, Baltimore, January 24, 1895.

[74] When Archbishop Elder received Stephan's letter he sensed the danger and told him, "I agree with you perfectly that it is not wise to excite any agitation against the prohibited societies. And there is no reason for doing so. All the object of the decree is to keep Catholics away from these societies and this needs no agitation but only the publication of the decree. Its operation must be left to the conscience of the individual Catholics interested" (Archives of the Commission for Catholic Missions among the Colored People and the Indians, Elder to Stephan, Cincinnati, February 12, 1895). For a copy of this letter the writer is grateful to John B. Tennelly, S.S., director of the commission.

potential danger to the Church's interests in the United States that might come from insistence on the decree's publication and emphasis.[75]

Acting on the suggestion given in Rampolla's letter of January 18, the Cardinal of Baltimore got in touch with the apostolic delegate. Satolli's secretary, Dr. Frederick Z. Rooker, came to Baltimore and explained to Gibbons the sense in which the decree was to be interpreted. As soon as he was in possession of the facts the cardinal hastened to inform Ireland and others how the case stood. He told the Archbishop of St. Paul that the apostolic delegate had been besieged by letters from bishops, some clamoring for a public promulgation, others advocating milder measures. Several Catholic laymen had also called on Satolli strongly deprecating the condemnation with the result that the delegate had drawn up the following points as a practical guide for all concerned. Catholics were not to be allowed to join the three societies, but this ban would be lifted in the future if the societies would modify their constitutions so as to remove all grounds for suspicion; second, those Catholics who already belonged were not to be obliged to leave the societies if it would entail a serious injury to their interests. Since in practically every instance a grave injury to the financial interests of Catholic members would be suffered by their withdrawal, they need not take such action. Third, Rooker told Gibbons that no public promulgation of the Roman decree was necessary or desirable and that private instructions concerning the decree could be given to the clergy by the bishops. The secretary of the apostolic delegate had also stated that the documents sent to Rome against the societies by the committee of three archbishops had been prepared with great skill and had justified Rome's action, whereas the statements against condemnation by the full conference of the metropolitans had shown signs of haste. The cardinal told Ireland that he hoped to go to Rome early in the summer and that it had been his original intention to reopen the case of the condemned societies, but Rooker had advised that it was too soon. What Gibbons referred to as the "partial ban" would be entirely lifted, he said, if they could induce the societies to revise their constitu-

---

[75] Diary, January 31, 1895, p. 274.

tions and submit them to Archbishop Satolli who was described by the cardinal as well disposed.[76] Gibbons had further confirmation of his view a week later when Satolli came to see him. The cardinal then told Ireland:

> He is fully alive to the situation & in entire sympathy with us. His interpretation of the Decree takes the sting out of it & practically puts us where we were before. He has his mind & heart set on having the whole question reopened in Rome & I strongly advised him to do so. . . .[77]

When Gibbons made known the interpretation of Archbishop Satolli prelates like Feehan of Chicago and Riordan of San Francisco were happy and relieved. John Ireland was, of course, overjoyed and he told the cardinal:

> Without your efforts, we should have been obliged to publish it and incalculable harm would have been done to Church and to souls. . . . It is a blessing that Mgr. Satolli listens to you and adopts your views.[78]

But in the final analysis the optimism of Cardinal Gibbons and his friends was shown to have rested on a false foundation.

The Archbishop of Baltimore meanwhile made preparations for his Roman visit where he hoped to win from the officials of the Holy See a nullification of the decree against the secret societies. Ireland was jubilant when he got word that the cardinal was going. He said that he intended to withhold any further action in St. Paul and to await the result of Gibbons' visit. He counseled him to go armed with plenty of documents and courage, and he urged the cardinal on with the words, "You are needed there. Go to conquer, and return having conquered."[79] There was still fresh in the minds of Gibbons' admirers the triumph which he had won some years before in prevailing on the Holy See to reverse itself on the ban against the Knights of Labor. They were hopeful now that he could repeat the performance. Some months before, feeling keen distress over the recent condemnation of the three societies, Archbishop Riordan had expressed the anticipation that was

---

[76] AASP, Gibbons to Ireland, Baltimore, February 9, 1895, copy.
[77] Ibid., Gibbons to Ireland, Baltimore, February 17, 1895, copy.
[78] 93-S-2, Ireland to Gibbons, St. Paul, March 4, 1895.
[79] 93-S-4, Ireland to Gibbons, St. Paul, March 14, 1895.

probably in the minds of all these close associates when he
told Gibbons, "I pray you for the sake of the Church to take
up the matter and do again what you did for the Knights
of Labor."[80] Doubtless Gibbons himself hoped that what he
had accomplished in 1887. could be done again. At any rate,
he was prepared to try.

The cardinal attended the golden jubilee of Archbishop
Williams in Boston on May 16 and two days later he sailed
from New York on the *Touraine* with a party of clergymen
which included the Bishops of Detroit and Harrisburg and
Father Cornelius F. Thomas of his own cathedral household.
Among the large group gathered to see the cardinal off were
Archbishop Corrigan of New York and Archbishop Chapelle
of Santa Fe.[81] After three days in Paris as guests of the
Sulpicians, Gibbons and his party reached Rome on May 31
where, as Ireland had told him some time previous, "There
is work before you."[82] There was, indeed, work before him and
the month of June was filled with long and exhaustive conferences with various officials of the Holy See on the question
of the condemned societies and other important business which
Gibbons had to transact at the Roman Curia.

It so happened that Bishop Charles E. McDonnell of
Brooklyn, former secretary to Archbishop Corrigan, was in
Rome at the same time. Toward the end of June, McDonnell
informed Corrigan that in a private audience the previous week
Leo XIII had asked him several pointed questions on the secret
societies and had implied that he knew the decree of condemnation had not been published in the Archdioceses of
Baltimore and St. Paul. McDonnell quoted the Pope as saying
that Gibbons was leaving Rome early in July but that he would
have another audience of the Holy Father before his departure
and at that time, as the bishop expressed it, "he would tell His
Eminence to publish the Decree." Corrigan's correspondent
related that he had heard recently of Gibbons' attempts to win
over several of the cardinals to a withdrawal of the decree, but
they had replied that the matter was settled. The questions
which Pope Leo XIII put to McDonnell prompted the latter

80 93-N-10, Riordan to Gibbons, San Francisco, December 29, 1894.

81 John T. Reily, *Collections in the Life and Times of J. Card. Gibbons,* III,
242-244.

82 93-S-4, Ireland to Gibbons, St. Paul, March 14, 1895.

to believe that the argument of the danger of persecution to the American Church had been advanced against promulgation of the ban on the societies, but if this was so the bishop was inclined to believe the argument may have "overreached the mark," since Leo XIII had asked him very seriously if the Church was making progress. in the United States. Bishop McDonnell informed his friend that on the previous day Gibbons had given a dinner for about sixty guests at the American College where there were present three cardinals of the curia as well as a large number of lesser dignitaries.[83] It was apparent that McDonnell's sympathies on the question of the decree were not with Gibbons, and that he believed the cardinal had failed in his efforts to have it rescinded.

The news which the Bishop of Brooklyn had picked up around Rome regarding the Cardinal of Baltimore and the case of the societies soon proved to be authentic. Four days before his departure from the Eternal City on July 2 Gibbons informed Bishop Keane that he had secured a very fine letter from the Pope urging support of the university by the American Catholics. He said that he had had a very busy time in Rome, but on the subject of the secret societies the cardinal could report only failure. He told Keane:

> The H. Office is inflexible, & a few days before I arrived a letter was sent to the Delegate urging more explicit promulgation. Interested parties were working with H. Office before I arrived, & representing some Prelates as neglectful in this regard. But those high in authority suggest an interpretation which moderates the severity of the decision. I will have much to say to you viva voce.[84]

The allusion of Gibbons to instructions being sent Satolli calling for more explicit promulgation referred to a directive which Cardinal Monaco of the Holy Office had communicated to the delegate. Monaco had learned that certain American newspapers were stating that the publication of the decree was not obligatory; as a consequence he instructed Satolli to send out a circular to the hierarchy making it clear that the Holy Office wished the decree to be promulgated and enforced. Satolli added his own advice when he sent the instruction of Monaco to

---

[83] AANY, McDonnell to Corrigan, Rome, June 24, 1895. *Riservatissima.*
[84] ACUA, Keane Papers, Gibbons to Keane, Rome, June 29, 1895.

Monsignor Edward McColgan, administrator of the Archdiocese of Baltimore in Gibbons' absence. He told McColgan that Monaco's letter put beyond all question the obligation of the decree and of its publication and it was no longer lawful for any Catholic newspaper to express doubt about the matter.[85] Meanwhile, however, McColgan took no action awaiting the return of the cardinal from Europe. After leaving Rome Gibbons stopped at Wörishofen near Munich for a rest, and from there he explained further his failure in Rome on the secret societies' decree by saying that the new directive had been issued before he reached the Holy See and that it had been industriously circulated there that he was to plead strongly for the societies. "Hence," he remarked, "I was forestalled."[86]

The effort made by Cardinal Gibbons in Rome in the summer of 1895 in behalf of the condemned societies was one of the first major reverses which he had suffered in his guidance of the Holy See on American Church questions. Up to this time Gibbons had enjoyed extraordinary success in preventing action that he felt would do injury to the cause of religion in the United States, or in modifying the policies and directives of Rome in such a manner that they would be received with respect and effectively executed in this country. The confidence which he had won as the spokesman and leader of a large majority of the American hierarchy had come to him by reason of the role he had played in the Roman conferences of 1883 preparatory to the Third Plenary Council, the vigorous leadership he had displayed in the Cahensly affair, and the triumph he had gained in the Knights of Labor case. True, a certain group of the American bishops did not agree with Gibbons' ideas on some of these questions, and in those cases they made their opposition felt in Rome. But in the main he had defeated the opposition and had experienced the satisfaction of bringing the Holy See around to his point of view, and of knowing that he was supported by the great majority of his colleagues in the episcopacy. It was for these reasons no doubt, as well as for his deep and sincere conviction concerning the harm that might result in the public condemnation of groups

---

[85] Macdonald, op. cit., pp. 205–206.

[86] ACUA, Keane Papers, Gibbons to Keane, Wörishofen near Munich, July 12, 1895.

like the Odd Fellows and the Knights of Pythias, that he felt disappointment at not being able to persuade Rome to his way of thinking in the present case.

In several ways Cardinal Gibbons' European journey in the summer of 1895 proved to be an unpleasant experience. It was while he was in Rome on this occasion that he suffered a keen personal sorrow in the forced resignation of his close friend, Monsignor O'Connell, as rector of the American College. We shall have reason to refer to it elsewhere, but it should be mentioned here as an added source of disappointment to the cardinal at this time. Moreover, he was greatly annoyed at the false and misleading stories appearing in various papers concerning the motives for his trip and the policies which he had been pursuing in Rome. Gibbons had grown somewhat accustomed by this time to distorted versions of ecclesiastical affairs in the public press, but during the summer of 1895 they proved particularly irksome and caused the cardinal to refer to them with a good deal of feeling. He told Keane that "various wild misstatements," as he called them, had been circulating in regard to the purpose of his visit. He was comforted to read in a recent issue of the Baltimore *Sun* which had reached him a flat contradiction of the statement that he had protested in Rome against the mission of Archbishop Satolli to the United States. The fact that a number of these misleading stories were originating in Europe and were being cabled to the United States prompted the cardinal to say, "On this side of the Atlantic intrigue and deceitful diplomacy are reduced to a science."[87] It was not often that Gibbons spoke in such sharp tones even to his intimate friends. It was evident that his patience with the embarrassing and clumsy news items appearing about him was wearing thin.

After a second visit to Paris and several weeks spent in Ireland the Cardinal of Baltimore returned to the United States on August 23 and to a home-coming reception in his see city which was attended by Archbishop Satolli and other dignitaries.[88] After reaching home the cardinal did nothing further about the

---

[87] *Ibid.* The New York *Tribune* of June 14, 1895, reported Gibbons as treating with the Holy See of the problem of the Italian immigrants to the United States, although there was no other evidence found to show that this was one of the objectives of his Roman visit.

[88] Reily, *op. cit.*, III, 309–311.

secret societies, nor did he take any steps to promulgate the decree in the Archdiocese of Baltimore. About six months later Satolli communicated to Gibbons the latest instructions from Rome in regard to the condemned societies. He stated that Catholic men who were members of the three societies might be allowed to continue their membership for the purpose of receiving the benefits of their payments, provided that there was no formal co-operation with the societies. The conditions attached to the privilege of retaining passive membership evidenced the Church's recognition of the practical aspects of the members' financial investment, although the spiritual factors were naturally given the greater emphasis.

Satolli's instructions also stated that passive membership might be retained on condition that those who had joined the society had done so in good faith, not knowing that it was forbidden; that their retention of membership would not prove a scandal to others, or at least that a statement be made to the effect that membership was retained solely with a view to obtaining the benefits to which members were entitled in equity, and that they had no intention of participating in the activities of a given society by attending its regular meetings; that a complete withdrawal would impose a serious hardship on the members; and finally, that there would be no danger of Catholic men who held such membership being forced to accept non-Catholic burial services. When differences arose over the interpretation of the Latin text concerning the necessity of applying in each individual case to the apostolic delegate for permission to hold passive membership, they were resolved by the delegate himself in December, 1896, in the *American Ecclesiastical Review* where he stated that the application must be made in each individual case to the Apostolic Delegation.[89]

Although Cardinal Gibbons had striven now for some years to moderate the Church's attitude toward the secret societies in his belief that condemnation in the end did more harm than good, he had, as we have seen, failed to prevent the ban from being laid upon a number of societies then flourishing in the United States. Not only did he try to check what he regarded as useless and harmful condemnations by the Holy See and by some American prelates, but he showed every inclination as

---

[89] Macdonald, *op. cit.*, pp. 207–208.

well to bury the issue as far as that was possible. However, in spite of Gibbons' efforts the question of membership of Catholics in secret societies would not die and through the remaining years of his life the Archbishop of Baltimore was periodically compelled to face the unpleasant subject. At times it would seem, insofar as the records reveal, the cardinal simply ignored requests for his judgment on particular societies. For example, ten days before the annual conference of the archbishops in Washington in November, 1901, the secretary of the Catholic Order of Foresters inquired of Gibbons concerning the correctness of some of his members in Missouri joining the Modern Woodmen of America. He asked the cardinal to submit the question to the archbishops, assuring Gibbons that it was hardly necessary to say that the C.O. of F. would cheerfully accept any decision which the archbishops might render.[90] Since the minutes of the meeting of the metropolitans show no mention of any secret society, it would appear that Gibbons did not bring the question of the Modern Woodmen before his colleagues at all.[91]

During the early years of the twentieth century the problem of societies, both Catholic and otherwise, continued to come before the metropolitans. In the fall of 1902 the Archbishop of Cincinnati presented a communication to the archbishops from the prelates of his province in which they inquired concerning the expediency of a pronouncement from the metropolitans' conference on the Knights of Columbus, the Catholic Order of Foresters, and similar Catholic societies. Following a discussion on the matter, it was decided that it was not advisable to take any action at the time regarding the Catholic organizations mentioned.[92] Precisely what lay behind this reluctance of the archbishops to give their formal blessing to these Catholic societies it is not possible to say but, at any rate, they declined a public endorsement.

---

[90] 99-F-1, Theo. B. Thiele to Gibbons, Chicago, November 11, 1901.

[91] 99-F-8, Minutes of the Meeting of the Archbishops, Washington, November 21–22, 1901.

[92] 100-D-4, Minutes of the Meeting of the Archbishops, Washington, November 13, 1902. The annual meeting held on April 23, 1903, took no action on the secret secular societies, and, in regard to the federation of Catholic societies, it was stated that after mature discussion it was decided that no action by the metropolitans was either necessary or desirable at present (Minutes of the Meeting of the Archbishops, Washington, April 23, 1903, copy).

A year later Gerolamo Cardinal Gotti, Prefect of the Propaganda, informed Diomede Falconio, the apostolic delegate in Washington, that the Holy Office had recently received a denunciation of the Modern Woodmen, the Knights of the Maccabees, and the Improved Order of Red Men. Gotti stated that the wide divergence of opinion obtaining among the bishops of the United States on these societies was known in Rome and he asked, therefore, that the delegate call the matter to the attention of the archbishops who, in turn, should discuss the question with their suffragans and then report their judgment on the three societies to the Holy See.[93] When the archbishops assembled for their next annual conference in April, 1904, Gibbons presented the problem to them and it was treated at length. It was the decision of the metropolitans and of most of their suffragans, however, that in view of the facts then known to them about the three societies and the obscurity still surrounding some of their activities, it would be inadvisable for any condemnatory action to be taken either by the Holy See or the American hierarchy. The conference authorized Cardinal Gibbons to communicate this judgment to Rome with the reasons that supported it. Meanwhile he appointed a special committee of Archbishops Ireland, Keane, Glennon, and Messmer to secure all the necessary information they could from the officers of the three societies and to report back to the metropolitans' conference at their next meeting.[94] Gibbons followed up this action by informing Cardinal Gotti of the steps taken at the conference where, as he said, all the archbishops and all but two of their suffragans had stated they felt it would be inopportune to issue any condemnation of the Modern Woodmen, Knights of the Maccabees, and Improved Order of Red Men.[95]

In pursuance of their assignment the committee of four archbishops held a meeting in Dubuque on April 4, 1905,[96] a month in advance of the conference of the metropolitans. At the meeting in Washington on May 4 the Archbishop of Dubuque spoke for his colleagues of the committee and stated that it was their judgment that the three societies were not of so secret a character as to exclude investigation by the authorities of the Church,

[93] 100-W-3, Falconio to Gibbons, Washington, December 22, 1903.
[94] 101-E, Minutes of the Meeting of the Archbishops, Washington, April 14, 1904.
[95] 101-G, Gibbons to Gotti, Baltimore, May, 1904 (n.d.), copy.
[96] 102-G, Ireland to Gibbons, St. Paul, March 22, 1905.

that the officers had shown an eagerness to please the prelates, and, therefore, under the circumstances the committee wished to report that they would regard it as "unwise, undesirable and, from a standpoint of Catholic Theology, apparently unnecessary to condemn them." The report was accepted unanimously and Gibbons was asked to communicate their judgment to the Holy See. At this meeting Archbishop Ireland raised the question of the Knights of Pythias to which there belonged, he said, a great number of Catholics who would not leave them and these men were, therefore, cut off from the sacraments. Ireland stated that some of the K. of P. desired to have their society investigated and were willing to have their activities approved by the Church. The conference thereupon moved to have the present committee of four archbishops investigate the Knights of Pythias and report back, and should their report be favorable to the K. of P., Gibbons stated that he would be pleased to urge reconsideration of the society by the Roman officials.[97] What action, if any, was taken on the society during the ensuing year the minutes for 1906 did not say.

In the spring of 1907 the archbishops once more discussed the Woodmen, Maccabees, and Red Men and repeated again their favorable judgment of two years before on these societies. Their report was unanimously accepted and a motion was carried that it should stand as the "united judgment" of the archbishops of the United States.[98] Ireland then raised again the question of a rehearing for the Knights of Pythias and the Odd Fellows. He said that in a recent interview he held with Cardinal Gotti the latter had expressed himself as not adverse to a reopening of the case provided sufficient reasons could be advanced. Ireland had given as his reasons to Gotti that Catholics in their ranks found nothing to injure their consciences, and that some of these men complained rightly that their society was condemned without a hearing. Archbishop Keane seconded Ireland's point of view and added that an examination of the rituals and other literature had revealed nothing in them that was worthy of condemnation. Moreover, said Keane, these documents had been freely turned over for examination by the officers, although previous reports from the United States to Rome had declared

---

[97] 102-K, Minutes of the Meeting of the Archbishops, Washington, May 4, 1905.
[98] 104-G, Minutes of the Meeting of the Archbishops, Washington, April 10, 1907.

that the bishops had been refused access to them. For these reasons Keane felt they deserved a reconsideration. Their colleagues agreed with Ireland and Keane, and it was decided to forward a report on the subject to the delegate and to urge him to send the judgment of the archbishops to the Holy See.[99] During the ensuing year further reports were gathered on other societies by the committee but no response was received from Rome on reopening the case of the Odd Fellows and the Knights of Pythias. Since Archbishop Messmer was soon going abroad it was decided at the conference in May, 1908, that he should act in their name in trying to secure a lifting of the ban on these societies.[100]

After a prolonged delay the Holy See finally issued a directive to the American hierarchy regarding the Woodmen, Maccabees, and Red Men. The Holy Office stated that it did not have enough evidence to condemn these three societies; consequently it left to the individual bishops the cases of Catholics who were members or about to become members in good faith. The bishops might permit membership, providing the Catholic men would abstain from any formal communication *in divinis* and that every danger of perversion of their faith be removed. When this instruction was laid before the metropolitans at their meeting in April, 1909, they again held a lengthy discussion and arrived at the judgment that the letter of the Holy Office was ample for their purposes and that it should be communicated to all their suffragan bishops. The archbishops' resolution added that in passing on the information to their suffragans the latter should be warned that it should in no way be made a subject for public discussion.[101]

But the request for lifting the ban on the Odd Fellows, Sons of Temperance, and Knights of Pythias, originally imposed in 1894, did not meet with the same benevolent treatment at the hands of Rome. When the archbishops met in Washington under the chairmanship of Gibbons in the spring of 1910, he communicated to them a letter that had been received by the apostolic delegate from Rampolla in which it was stated the Holy Office regretted that the request of the archbishops for lifting the condemnation

---

[99] *Ibid.*

[100] 104-Y, Minutes of the Meeting of the Archbishops, Washington, May 8, 1908.

[101] 105-L, Minutes of the Meeting of the Archbishops, Washington, April 22, 1909. The information from the Holy Office was contained in a letter from Cardinal Rampolla of March 28, 1909, which was read at the meeting.

against the three societies could not be granted. Rampolla suggested that the archbishops work for a change in the rules and practices of the societies and only then would the Holy See entertain a request for their approval. There was nothing further the American metropolitans could do at this point than to recommend to their committee that they try to induce the officers of the societies to make the necessary changes.[102] Whether they made any effort along these lines is not known, but if they did they apparently failed to convince the leaders of the three societies, since a year later the annual conference passed a motion to take no further action in regard to these groups.[103] Meanwhile the necessity of applying to the apostolic delegate for permission to allow passive membership in the three societies had proven difficult by reason of the great distances in the United States and the need at times for immediate action. For this reason Gibbons requested in the name of his colleagues that the individual bishops be given faculties for passing on such cases rather than referring them to Washington.[104] This concession Rome granted to the American hierarchy, it being understood that the delegate still held his present faculties and that all the necessary conditions be exacted by the bishops for passive membership in the societies in question.[105]

Although the discussion on various secret societies which took place in the annual conferences of the archbishops during the later years of the life of James Gibbons reveal that the issue continued to be a live one, as far as the evidence shows the cardinal for the most part confined his personal activity in that regard to appointing the committees, presiding at the discussions, and reporting the findings to the apostolic delegate or to the Holy See. Knowing his mind as we do, it is safe to say that he

---

[102] 106-E, Minutes of the Meeting of the Archbishops, Washington, April 7, 1910.

[103] 107-F, Minutes of the Meeting of the Archbishops, Washington, April 27, 1911.

[104] 108-G, Gibbons to Rampolla, Baltimore, May 15, 1912, copy. Minutes of the Meeting of the Archbishops, Washington, April 18, 1912, copy.

[105] 108-J, Rampolla to Gibbons, Rome, July 2, 1912. At the meeting of the metropolitans on April 23, 1914, a committee consisting of Archbishops Messmer and Glennon reported their investigation of the National Grange of Husbandry, the Farmers' Educational and Co-operative Union, and the American Society of Equity, which had been investigated at the request of the apostolic delegate. Without saying what the committee had reported, the minutes read that Gibbons would forward the report to Archbishop Bonzano (Minutes of the Meeting of the Archbishops, Washington, April 23, 1914, copy).

supported every measure which sought a lifting of the ban on the societies already condemned or a moderate and benevolent attitude toward those lodges which had more recently come under suspicion. Gibbons had made his supreme effort in behalf of the societies in 1895 in Rome and he had failed. From that time on it would seem that he said as little about the subject as possible. The attitude of the cardinal should not be interpreted, however, as lax and negligent. He accepted the Roman condemnation reluctantly, it is true, and he did not publish the decree against the Odd Fellows, Knights of Pythias, and Sons of Temperance in his own archdiocese. But that did not mean that he was indifferent to the danger which secret lodges of a quasi-religious character might hold for the Catholic faith of men who were attracted to them. Gibbons felt the remedy lay through a general attitude of discouragement of the societies on the part of ecclesiastical authority and a careful counseling of the men by their confessors. He was convinced that the policy of public condemnations as he had observed it in countries like Italy had failed, and that an unnecessary antagonism would be aroused in the United States toward the Church if it followed such a policy. Moreover, the difficulty of securing exact information on the societies made the cardinal and others uneasy about condemnations when all the facts were not known.

Nonetheless, when Cardinal Gibbons was convinced that there were enough facts to prove the evil character of a secret society he was not slow to condemn it. For example, in the closing days of the presidential campaign of 1916 the sergeant at arms of the Republican National Committee, William F. Stone, sent him in confidence some information on a secret group which was called the "P's." In response to a request for his judgment on this organization Gibbons said he regarded it as "one of the most infamous, unchristian, and un-American" that had come to his notice since the days of Know-Nothingism and he could not understand how any man with self-respect could give countenance or encouragement to it.[106] A year before this inquiry there had been founded the second Ku Klux Klan which by 1920 had undergone new management and this quickened its growth to the extent that nearly 100,000 members were enrolled. The ugly

---

[106] 114-A, Stone to Gibbons, Baltimore, November 1, 1916; Gibbons to Stone, Baltimore, November 3, 1916, copy.

campaign of bigotry and hatred of the hooded order that darkened many American communities in the last days of the cardinal's life was, however, so patently anti-Catholic that there was no danger of sincere Catholics being attracted to it.[107] However, the anti-social activities and character of the K.K.K. were such as to give pointed emphasis to the evil influence which secret societies of a certain type exercised in American life.

All during these years, therefore, the peril to the faith of American Catholics — whether real or imaginary — from secret societies which manifested hostility toward the Church was a serious concern felt by Gibbons and his fellow bishops. The anxiety which they experienced at times prompted some of the prelates to view even Catholic societies a bit uneasily. They were watched carefully and in order that the general aims and undertakings of these groups should be kept within proper bounds, the archbishops at their meeting in 1917 passed a resolution to the effect that no priest might serve as chaplain of a Catholic society of any kind unless he had first been confirmed by his bishop for the position.[108]

Two years later the same archbishops gave their approval to the formation of a Catholic Young Men's Association after investigation and a favorable report of two prelates on them, the idea being expressed that such approbation might have the desired effect of keeping Catholics from joining non-Catholic societies.[109] To these measures Gibbons, of course, gave hearty support in the belief that a quiet vigilance exercised in regard to Catholic societies would help to keep them out of dangerous territory. At the same time the growth and prosperity of Catholic groups under clerical supervision would afford a channel of profitable enterprise for the zeal of the Catholic laity, as well as a safeguard against the dangers of those secret societies which were unfriendly to the Church and to organized religion. But during the lifetime of the cardinal there was no further change in the legislation of the Church concerning the secret lodges, and three

---

[107] Cf. John M. Mecklin, *The Ku Klux Klan* (New York, 1924). Mecklin stated that the motive which had gained the most members for the Klan and took precedence over all others in the strength and universality of its appeal was "undoubtedly anti-Catholicism" (p. 157).

[108] 115-G, Minutes of the Meeting of the Archbishops, Washington, April 18, 1917.

[109] 120-L, Minutes of the Meeting of the Archbishops, Washington, February 21, 1919.

years before his death when the new *Code of Canon Law* was published for the Universal Church in May, 1918, the regulations as they were enacted in the agitated era we have reviewed were brought over into the code and made applicable to the Catholics of the entire world.[110]

---

[110] Joseph A. M. Quigley, *Condemned Societies* (Washington, 1927), pp. 47–48. Canons 684, 693, 1240–1241, and 2335 of the *Code of Canon Law* treat of secret societies.

CHAPTER XII

The Knights of Labor

IT WAS in the guise of a problem directly related to the secret societies that James Gibbons earned one of his most striking claims to fame and to an enduring place in the esteem of his fellow Americans of all religious beliefs. In the years after the Civil War the national labor movement in the United States was struggling to be born against the greatest odds. It was not surprising to find, therefore, that some of the workmen should have resorted to secrecy in an effort to safeguard their activities from a hostile and powerful management that was as yet unreconciled to dealing with its employees joined in effective unions. But the very fact that the workingmen's organizations operated in secret had a tendency to cast over them a sinister shadow in the minds of conservative men of both Church and State. If those outside the ranks of labor felt a certain uneasiness at developments among the industrial masses, their fears were more than confirmed during the decade of the 1870's. As a consequence of the panic of 1873 thousands of American laborers were thrown out of employment, and as the distress deepened and widened throughout the land there ensued widespread violence which reached a major national crisis in the great railway strikes of 1877. The period was, indeed, as a recent historian of labor has called it, "an era of upheaval," and decent-minded citizens of all walks of life were horrified by the loss of life and destruction of property which accompanied these outbreaks.[1] To be sure, the worst excesses committed were the work of a minority misguided by revolutionary agitators, but the impression left in the minds of Americans generally was seriously damaging to the interests of all members of the laboring class.

---

[1] Cf. Foster Rhea Dulles, *Labor in America. A History* (New York, 1949), Chapter VII, "An Era of Upheaval," pp. 114–125.

To all this unrest and dissatisfaction in the world of labor the authorities of the Catholic Church could not remain indifferent, even if they had been disposed to do so. With each succeeding year the number of Catholic immigrants to the country was increasing, and a large majority of these people found employment in the expanding factory system which was then rapidly converting the United States into one of the leading industrial nations of the world. The presence of thousands of Catholic men enrolled as hands in the factories, mines, and railroads heightened the anxiety of the American hierarchy when they witnessed the violence of the 1870's and the renewed disturbances of the next decade that brought tragedies like the Haymarket Square riot at Chicago in May, 1886. Not only were the bishops eager to keep their spiritual charges from indulging in violence and being misled by radical demagogues, but they were desirous as well of shielding the religious faith of these men from the dangers of secret societies, to which their position in the laboring world seemed more and more to expose them.

Apart, however, from an alertness on the part of some of the American bishops to the threat of labor groups as secret societies, they had made no close study of the labor movement and its relation to the Church prior to the Third Plenary Council of Baltimore. True, here and there a bishop would voice his opinion for or against the workingmen's groups, but not until the plenary council of 1866 was the subject even mentioned in the national legislation of the Church and then only by way of granting an exception to "associations of workmen" from the familiar prohibition against the secret lodges.[2] In the hectic labor strife of the 1870's the worry of the churchmen was particularly concentrated in the northeastern and east central sections of Pennsylvania where the Molly Maguires, a secret organization, were raising havoc in the coal regions. The extremes to which this group carried their warfare against the coal operators called down upon them severe condemnation from bishops and priests who were alarmed over the moral and material damage being done to the numerous Catholic miners and their families.[3] While the problem posed by the Molly Maguires was of immediate concern to

---

[2] *Concilii plenarii Baltimorensis II . . . acta et decreta* (Baltimore, 1868), p. 263.
[3] On the Molly Maguires, cf. J. Walter Coleman, *Labor Disturbances in Pennsylvania, 1850–1880* (Washington, 1936).

the Archbishop of Philadelphia and the Bishops of Scranton and Harrisburg, the affair caused a national sensation and became a subject for comment among their brother bishops in distant dioceses.[4]

All the circumstances of the early life of Cardinal Gibbons were calculated to make him sympathetic to the cause of the workingman. He had been born into a family of modest means, the father of which knew from personal experience the problems that beset the wage earner trying to provide for the needs of a wife and six children. Moreover, the death of Gibbons' father at an early age had necessitated his going to work to help support his widowed mother and her younger children. In fact, it was economic necessity that had caused the delay in the education of young Gibbons as a candidate for the priesthood. He was twenty-one years of age when he entered St. Charles College and had he not made such rapid progress in his studies in the preparatory seminary, he would have been considerably older than his classmates at the time of his ordination. As a priest, it is true, he never wanted for the necessities of life, although his four years as a pastor afforded him no very comfortable living in the poor neighborhoods of Canton and Locust Point in his native Baltimore. It was during these days of parochial experience that Gibbons received a further insight into the hardships of the working class, for his parishioners were composed for the most part of the families of the dock workers and shipbuilders who earned their living along the quays that lined the Patapsco River leading into Chesapeake Bay.

When the young Vicar Apostolic of North Carolina went South in 1868 to assume his episcopal duties he entered upon a renewal of his previous experiences with poverty, steady toil, and an uncertain economic status among those with whom he lived. Gibbons' own life was filled with hardship and worry over the lack of resources to carry on the Church's work, and the vast majority of his small and scattered flock in North Carolina were at the time suffering from the severe dislocations of the reconstruction era. He knew, therefore, at close range the lot of those

---

[4] For a full discussion of the Church's relation to the labor movement in the years before the council of 1884, cf. Henry J. Browne, *The Catholic Church and the Knight of Labor* (Washington, 1949), pp. 1–33. This scholarly and definitive work will be used throughout this chapter for background to the role played by Cardinal Gibbons in labor and social questions.

who had to toil for a living and his sympathies were with them. Three years after his arrival in Wilmington, North Carolina, the young bishop preached a sermon on the subject, "Man Born to Work: or, Necessity and Dignity of Labor." He paid tribute to the useful and beneficent role of the laborer and he showed his sentiments when he said, "I would rather grasp the soiled hand of the honest artisan, than touch the soft, kid-gloved hand of the dandy." He stated that he had three admonitions to give to the men who composed his congregation. He would have them avoid idleness and be as much ashamed to be called an idler as they would a thief; second, the preacher urged his listeners to take an active and personal interest in the business of their employers; and third, he counseled the laborers to be content in the state and city where Providence had placed them and not to be beguiled into moving from place to place since, as he said, "a strolling family gather very few coins or greenbacks in their perambulating wheel of fortune."[5] Nor were the experiences of Gibbons, insofar as they related to labor, essentially different during the five years from 1872 to 1877 that he spent as Bishop of Richmond, for the same sermon which he had preached in his pro-cathedral in Wilmington in 1871 was repeated five years later in the capital of Virginia.

It was during the years that Gibbons spent in the South that there was born the labor organization that would bring him into prominence in the movement. In 1869 at Philadelphia there was organized by a small group of the Garment Cutters' Union the secret order called the Noble and Holy Order of the Knights of Labor. From the outset their activities were closely guarded by means of a ritual, hand clasp, and password. Moreover, many of the features of speculative Masonry were brought into the ritual and the first master workman, Uriah S. Stephens, was himself a Mason, an Odd Fellow, and a Knight of Pythias.[6] At first the knights grew but slowly, although within a few years they had gained sufficient strength and were attracting enough Catholic members for certain prelates and priests in Pennsylvania to manifest uneasiness and even hostility toward them. During these

---

[5] 72-G-5, this sermon is preserved in Gibbons' handwriting and is noted as having been given a third time in the Cathedral of the Assumption, Baltimore, January 13, 1878.

[6] For a description of the character and early history of the knights and their relation to the Church, cf. Browne, *op. cit.*, pp. 34–69.

first years when there were occurring periodic brushes between the knights and the Catholic clergy over the hidden character of the order's activities, there was gradually rising to prominence within the knights' organization a Catholic, Terence V. Powderly, who in February, 1878, had been elected Mayor of Scranton. Powderly's star continued in the ascendant until the Chicago meeting of the K. of L. general assembly in September, 1879, elected him grand master workman. He had been active for some years in trying to allay the suspicions of the Catholic clergy concerning the labor group, and now the chief responsibility for the policies and conduct of the organization devolved upon him.

Two years before Powderly assumed the leadership of the Knights of Labor Gibbons had been promoted from Richmond to become Archbishop of Baltimore. By this time the K. of L. had spread far beyond their birthplace and about six months after the archbishop's arrival in Baltimore the first local assembly was organized there in May, 1878, although the existence of the knights in the city was not publicly admitted until 1881.[7] But it was not from his see city that the first recorded question concerning the K. of L. would be presented to the new archbishop. By 1878 the knights had invaded the coal regions of western Maryland, and it was not long before the local pastors were registering their concern about Catholics joining the organization. Father Valentine F. Schmitt, pastor of St. Michael's Church at Frostburg, described the situation which confronted him and Father James O'Brien in nearby Lonaconing. He told Gibbons of the increasing number of Catholic miners who were joining the K. of L., and he was not impressed by the fact that the knights stated they were allowed to reveal the business of their closed meetings to their confessors. Schmitt considered this "a catch in order to gain the good will of the clergy." The priest was obviously unsympathetic, but as yet he said that none of the pastors had spoken plainly against the order. Therefore, he asked Gibbons what they should do in the future. As Schmitt put it, "Shall we let them continue or denounce the organization?"[8]

---

[7] R. T. Crane, "The Knights of Labor in Baltimore," *Johns Hopkins Circulars,* XXII (April, 1903), 39.

[8] 74-J-6, Schmitt to Gibbons, Frostburg, February 19, 1879. If three years later Schmitt had not been won over to the K. of L., he at least was not then sympathetic to the mine operators. For a highly interesting account of the evils existent in these years in the company towns of the coal region of western

Unfortunately, no answer of the archbishop to this inquiry could be found.

Meanwhile Powderly was making some progress in his efforts to remove the obstacles to clerical approval of his organization. Convinced as he seemed to be that the best interests of the K. of L. would be served by lifting the veil of extreme secrecy which enshrouded the order, Powderly succeeded at the Detroit general assembly of September, 1881, in having the name made public, and the secret oath replaced by a word of honor. A short time later certain of the ritualistic features were dropped from the initiation ceremony. While these were steps in the right direction, they did not altogether quiet criticism from some of the clergy since the order retained secrecy regarding the private work of the various assemblies and prohibited members from revealing the name of anyone who was enrolled as a fellow member without the latter's permission. In the meantime, of course, the hostility of the managers of industry did not abate, and this opposition, coupled with the criticism of churchmen, prompted Powderly to tell one correspondent, "Between the men who *love* God and the men who don't believe in God I have had a hard time of it."[9]

Regardless of the difficulties which the grand master workman encountered from capitalists and clergy, the organization he headed continued to grow. The depression of the years 1883–1885 swelled the ranks of the knights and by September, 1884, the membership rolls showed a total of 71,326.[10] It was at this very time of expansion of the K. of L. that there occurred two events which would have an important bearing on the relations of the Church to the order. First the decision was made to hold a plenary council of the bishops of the United States. In preparation for this gathering the American archbishops, as we have seen, were summoned to Rome in November, 1883. As has already been noted, during the discussions which took place between the officials of the Propaganda and the American prelates on the subject of secret societies, Archbishop Seghers of Oregon City, strongly seconded by Bishop Chatard of Vincennes, showed

---

Maryland and how adversely they affected the Catholic miners of the community, cf. his description to Gibbons (76-R-9, Schmitt to Gibbons, Frostburg, June 8, 1882).

[9] Powderly to [   ] Tecker, July 26, 1882, cited in Browne, *op. cit.*, p. 69.

[10] Browne, *op. cit.*, p. 105.

a critical attitude toward labor unions and a disposition to have them prohibited to Catholic workers. But at this point Archbishop Gibbons and Archbishop Feehan of Chicago interposed a sympathetic explanation of the workmen's groups and stated that many of them offered no reason for ecclesiastical condemnation or prohibition.[11] We have already reviewed the action taken by the Third Plenary Council a year later, over which Gibbons presided, insofar as it related to the secret lodges and the labor organizations. It was significant that in the decrees on the prohibited societies, the exception made in favor of *bona fide* labor unions in 1866 should have been repeated word for word in the legislation of the council of 1884. It was at this time, too, that the American archbishops were constituted a standing committee to investigate and pass judgment on suspected societies. The duty of this committee, of which Gibbons was chairman, was to try to reach a unanimous decision on each case that came before it, and if they failed to attain unanimity the matter was to be referred to Rome.

The second event of these days which affected the Knights of Labor and the Catholic Church occurred in the neighboring Dominion of Canada just three weeks before the opening of the council in Baltimore. The growth of the K. of L. in Canada had alarmed Archbishop Taschereau of Quebec and in consequence he had solicited in October, 1883, a judgment from the Holy See on the organization. The decision was long in coming but a year later a directive of the Holy Office was sent out to the clergy of the Archdiocese of Quebec to the effect that the knights were a society that "ought to be considered among those prohibited by the Holy See."[12] The adverse action against them in Canada soon became known, of course, among the bishops in the United States, and it was not long before the more conservative prelates were pointing to it as a precedent which the American hierarchy should follow. This was particularly true of Bishop James A. Healy of Portland, Maine, whose border diocese lay close to the area where the knights had fallen under the ban.

In the midst of the discussion aroused by the decree of the Holy Office in Canada, there was no indication that the Archbishop of Baltimore had veered from his benevolent policy toward

---

[11] Cf. p. 215 of this study.
[12] Quoted in Browne, *op. cit.*, p. 108.

the workingman.[13] In fact, it became known through Father Peter C. Manning, pastor of St. Mary's Church at Lonaconing, Maryland, that Gibbons had examined the ritual and constitution of the knights and had raised no objection to them.[14] The sudden and almost startling growth of the K. of L. just at this time was reflected in Gibbons' see city which reported an increase of over 11,000 members for the year 1886 to bring the Baltimore knights to a total of 13,052 in 111 local assemblies, and when they demonstrated on Artisan's Day, September 6, 1886, it was said that over 25,000 marched through the streets of Baltimore in parade.[15] Early in 1886 the Baltimore car drivers and conductors went on strike for shorter hours, and the Baltimore *American* of February 27 carried a letter from Gibbons in which he said that if the report were true that the workers had to labor sixteen or eighteen hours a day, he believed their cause was deserving of public sympathy and called for redress. Some weeks later the strike was settled and on April 2 a twelve-hour day went into effect for the drivers and conductors on the city's street railway system.[16]

Later that spring when the disastrous strike of the K. of L. on the Southwest railway system of Jay Gould was in progress the *Catholic Review* of New York for April 3 published a news item to the effect that the Archbishop of Baltimore had been invited to attend a meeting looking toward a remedy for certain wrongs that the workingmen were suffering. It was stated that Gibbons was not able to attend the meeting, but he directed his secretary to assure the laborers that any and every movement

---

[13] The case had not yet advanced to the point where Gibbons was to suggest the policy of "masterly inactivity" as he did a year and a half later to Elder. (AAC, Gibbons to Elder, Baltimore, May 6, 1886.)

[14] Browne, *op. cit.,* p. 127.

[15] Crane, *op. cit.,* p. 39.

[16] *A History of the City of Baltimore* (Baltimore, 1902), p. 33. No name of the author is given. Over a half century later Professor Richard T. Ely of the Johns Hopkins University published his memoirs in a volume entitled *Ground Under Our Feet. An Autobiography* (New York, 1938). He spoke of having worked at the time with Gibbons to avert the strike of streetcar employees in Baltimore who were then working seventeen hours a day. A bill was introduced for a twelve-hour day which was bitterly fought by the railway interests. Ely stated, "I fought as strongly as I could for the passage of the legislation. More effective, perhaps, than all I could do was the work of Cardinal Gibbons, who wrote, at this critical time, a strong article on behalf of the streetcar employees." The bill was later passed and the strike thus averted (pp. 78–79).

consistent with justice and fair dealing toward their employers and having for its end the amelioration of the conditions of the laboring class deserved encouragement. Gibbons was quoted to the effect that all such efforts met with his "cordial approval" as they did with that of the bishops generally throughout the country.

While these cautious but sympathetic indications of Gibbons' attitude were appreciated by the knights, and by the same token probably reprobated by more conservative ecclesiastics, they did little to clarify the status of the American branch of the order in view of the Canadian condemnation. It was to be expected that curiosity should arise concerning the stand that would be taken by the American bishops, and Archbishop Elder of Cincinnati was apparently among the first to be sought out by the newspaper reporters for a statement on the question. Elder wisely declined to commit himself due to his lack of knowledge of the situation, but the questions of the reporters prompted him to tell Gibbons that he felt the answer of the Holy Office to Taschereau could not be entirely ignored. Elder suggested that Gibbons request the Congregation of the Propaganda to await information from the United States, and in the meanwhile the Archbishop of Baltimore and the other metropolitans could furnish Rome with all the data they were able to gather. The archbishop then alluded to an alternative of having the metropolitans consult together and send a joint statement if they could agree on one. Elder confessed he knew little about the knights but he would proceed to learn at once all he could on the subject.[17] The inquiry of the Archbishop of Cincinnati called forth the most complete statement on the knights which had up to this time come from the Cardinal of Baltimore. He said:

> With regard to the Knights of Labor it is not easy to determine what action if any should be taken. A masterly inactivity & a vigilant eye on their proceedings is perhaps the best thing to be done in the present junction. If the Holy See has disapproved of the society in Quebec, as has been represented — the decision was *juxta exposita*. My impression is that the metropolitans of the United States will be almost, if not unanimous in not condemning them. The society

---

[17] 80-U-3, Elder to Gibbons, Cincinnati, May 3, 1886.

cannot be held responsible for the acts of individual members. There are however some features of this organization that ought to receive an official rebuke:

1. Their persecution of non-unionmen, forbidding employers to employ them &

2. The custom of boycotting. . . .

It has occurred to me to propose to the Abps. that a formula of paternal exhortation (calling attention also to the irregularities which I have referred to) be drawn up, that the draft be submitted to each of the Abps., published in the name of all the metropolitans after they have approved of it.

But we should be careful not to be too hard on them, otherwise they would suspect us of siding with the moneyed corporations & employers.[18]

It was apparent that Gibbons was not to be stampeded by the action which Quebec had evoked from Rome and that his sympathies lay on the other side. His prediction concerning the reaction of the American archbishops was borne out in time, and the exceptions which he took to the practices of the K. of L. were shared by the vast majority of his fellow citizens in a day that knew little of the closed shop. What appeared at first to be a public affirmation of the cardinal's position came the same week as his letter to Elder when on May 10 the *Journal of United Labor,* the official organ of the K. of L., carried a story to the effect that in the opinion of Gibbons, Taschereau's action had most likely been based on local conditions, that although he admitted no full knowledge of the order, the cardinal would infer from the information which he had gleaned from newspapers and Powderly's public statement that the knights had praiseworthy objectives which were in no way opposed to the Church. Gibbons was quoted as having said, "The Catholic prelates will to a man declare in favor of the organization of labor." The cardinal was represented as having distinguished between those societies which were anti-social and blindly oath-bound, to which the Church was opposed, and organizations that exacted secrecy concerning their activities but with the proviso that nothing therein was contrary to the laws of the country or to the member's conscience and religious beliefs. The supposed

---

[18] AAC, Gibbons to Elder, Baltimore, May 6, 1886.

interview concluded with the statement that it was in accordance with the ideas which the cardinal had outlined that the constitution of the K. of L. would be re-examined in Rome.[19]

Although this interview was repudiated three months later in the Baltimore *Sun* of August 18 as having arisen from hearsay, it was picked up at the time it first appeared and was widely reprinted during the early summer. The Catholic press of the United States became quite articulate in contradicting the belief that the decree addressed to Taschereau by the Holy Office applied to the knights in the United States. In addition to these views emanating from south of the border, the Archbishop of Quebec found that there were members of his own hierarchy, notably Archbishops John J. Lynch of Toronto and Edouard Fabre of Montreal, who were not enthusiastic about enforcing the ban against the K. of L. In these circumstances it was understandable that Taschereau should seek clarification from the Holy See concerning the application of the decree of 1884 so that what he called "this scandal" might be terminated as speedily as possible.[20] Further interest was directed just at this time to the ecclesiastics who would be the two principals on opposite sides of the labor question when it was announced that Gibbons and Taschereau had been named cardinals and that there would soon follow the ceremony of imposing the red birettas in their respective see cities. As the summer wore on the uncertainty over the knights in clerical circles continued, and when Taschereau received no answer from Rome to his request of the previous May, he gathered further documentary evidence of the current confusion and sent it off to Cardinal Simeoni in a letter of August 18. The Archbishop of Quebec was unaware of the Baltimore *Sun's* correction of the Gibbons interview, so a French version of that story was dispatched to Simeoni along with other data in an effort to convince the Holy See of the urgent need of action to halt these widely varying interpretations.[21] It was apparent

---

[19] Quoted in Browne, *op. cit.,* p. 166.

[20] Cited in Browne, *op. cit.,* p. 168, from a letter of May 13, 1886, of Taschereau to Simeoni. Fabre had prepared a document for Rome in the knights' behalf, but before sending it he consulted Archbishop Corrigan of New York who answered on August 20 that in his judgment the order was *"undoubtedly forbidden"* and he made the application universal. In view of Corrigan's strong reply Fabre did not forward his document to the Holy See. Cf. Browne, *op. cit.,* pp. 179–180.

[21] *Ibid.,* pp. 179–181.

that events were gradually shaping toward a definite decision one way or another.

While speculation was rife over the Church's next move regarding the Knights of Labor, the investigation of other suspected societies went forward. It was in consequence of Archbishop Corrigan's negotiations with Simeoni on the Grand Army of the Republic that the Prefect of Propaganda expressed the wish that Corrigan should tell Cardinal Gibbons to call a meeting of the committee of archbishops. It was Simeoni's desire that the metropolitans should render a judgment on the G.A.R. for the guidance of the Holy See.[22] It was some weeks, of course, before the Roman directive became known and in the meantime Elder had again approached Gibbons in a spirit of "deep uneasiness" about the Canadian condemnation and the failure of the American hierarchy to do anything about it.[23] This time Gibbons was able to tell his friend in Cincinnati, "I have not been idle on the subject." The cardinal explained he had inquired of Rome if a copy of the K. of L. constitution should be sent and he had also asked Powderly's pastor to forward one to him. Since Bishops Keane and Ireland were going to Rome after the meeting of the university committee on October 27 Gibbons believed this would afford a good opportunity to have the case placed before the Roman Curia. The university committee would draw to Baltimore the Archbishops of Boston, Philadelphia, and New York and for that reason he thought it an excellent opportunity to discuss the entire question. The cardinal revealed what he had already done, as well as the policy he had decided to follow when he said:

> A distinguished professor of Woodstock who is personally adverse to any condemnation of the Knights without better grounds than we have at present tells me that an eminent member of the Society informed him that he lived in Canada and the States, and that he knows the working and aims of the society in both countries. The sentiment of Woodstock and of a distinguished moral professor from Montreal who is here, is that the action of Quebec does not apply to us.
>
> In my judgment, our plain duty is to submit the matter to the Holy See and be guided by its supreme decision.[24]

---

22 *Ibid.*, p. 188.
23 81-S-12, Elder to Gibbons, Cincinnati, August 31, 1886.
24 AAC, Gibbons to Elder, Baltimore, September 3, 1886. The professor referred

But while awaiting such action as Rome or a meeting of the metropolitans might take, Gibbons decided to move forward a step or two on his own. He was aided in his endeavor by a communication from Father Francis Carew, pastor of St. Rose of Lima Church at Carbondale, Pennsylvania, which included not only a copy of the constitution of the knights but a letter from Powderly which breathed, as Gibbons told Elder, "a truly Catholic spirit of obedience and respect for the voice of the Church, and a willingness to amend the constitution if anything faulty is found out."[25] With these documents in his possession, and with the outline of the case made up for him by Aloysius Sabetti, S.J., of Woodstock College, the cardinal quickened his pace and on the same day that he wrote to Elder he forwarded to Simeoni a letter in which he deprecated a hasty condemnation of the K. of L. and set forth his reasons against it.[26] Gibbons gave a favorable picture of the knights in the United States and stated that there were widespread fears that the promulgation of the decree of the Holy Office by Taschereau might prompt the Holy See to extend the ban to this country. The cardinal explained that the purpose of the knights was in no way evil, that their sole aim was to strengthen themselves by united effort within the law so that they could better protect their members against what he termed "the tyranny with which many very rich

---

to at Woodstock was most likely Aloysius Sabetti, S.J., who, as we shall see, advised Gibbons on the matter. Paulinus F. Dissez, S.S., professor of moral theology at St. Mary's Seminary, Baltimore, also gave an opinion on the knights for the cardinal in which he stated that certain expressions in the constitution of the K. of L. indicated a "communistic or socialist spirit" as, e.g., "a share, for use of, the soil" and the claim to a full enjoyment of the wealth they created by the laborers with no regard for the capitalist (86-Y-1, n.d., n.p.). That Gibbons was soliciting opinions about the K. of L. in many quarters was evident. He paid a visit around this time to Mount Saint Mary's College in Emmitsburg and, as the historians of the college stated, "inquiring who was the professor of moral theology, asked him and the other members of the Faculty what we thought of the great question" (Mary M. Meline and Edward F. X. McSweeny, *The Story of the Mountain* [Emmitsburg, 1911], II, 221). In all likelihood this visit took place in the late summer or early autumn of 1886 and not, as stated here, in 1887. Up to June, 1887, McSweeny himself was the professor of moral theology and when he left for a year his classes in that subject were taken by Father John J. Tierney (*ibid.*, II, 227).

[25] AAC, Gibbons to Elder, Baltimore, September 3, 1886, the second letter of the same date.

[26] Diary, September 3, 1886, p. 209. The entry concluded, "Today I recd. a copy of the constitution of the order with a letter from its president, Mr. Powderly."

corporations, and especially those controlling the railroads, inhumanly oppress the poor workers." He pleaded against a condemnation that would expose the Catholic Church of the United States to serious losses, and he was at pains to explain the nature of the secrecy of the K. of L. as in no sense intended to hide its aims from legitimate authority.

Furthermore, the knights had made frequent offers to institute whatever changes the Church might recommend. For the few evil men in their ranks the whole order should not be blamed since their evil character did not arise from their K. of L. membership. Near the end of his letter Gibbons emphasized the argument that a condemnation would prove a detriment to religious growth and he said that since the government did nothing to protect the workers, the latter — in good part Catholics — looked to the Church for sympathy and counsel. If instead of sympathy they encountered penalties and condemnation, it would be only natural for them to give a willing ear to agitators who babbled about the Church favoring the strong and leaving the weak to their fate. The pertinent decree of the Third Plenary Council was called to Simeoni's attention concerning the archbishops' committee, but he was told that up to that time no bishop had had recourse to the metropolitans for a canonical judgment in the matter of the societies. Referring to the K. of L., Gibbons stated that as far as he knew all the American archbishops were, as he expressed it, "entirely of the opinion that it should not be condemned."[27]

Cardinal Gibbons had, therefore, put himself on record against a condemnation of the knights nearly two months in advance of the meeting of the committee on secret societies. His strong stand was intended to avert an application of the ban to the United States, and though his stricture against the government's lack of protection to the workers was later to change, more than once in the coming months he used the other arguments which he had outlined to Simeoni in this communication of September 3. His opinion that all the metropolitans of the United States were against condemnation was advanced without evidence of the source of his information, and in the end it was proved that on this point the cardinal was wrong. Gibbons was kept informed of developments in Rome by his agent, Denis O'Connell, who

---

[27] 81-U-2, Gibbons to Simeoni, Baltimore, September 3, 1886, copy.

wrote encouragingly that the action against the American knights had been temporarily stayed and he believed the matter would be dealt with in a spirit of great caution.[28] Therefore, when Corrigan informed Gibbons in mid-September of Simeoni's wish for a meeting of the committee on the G.A.R., the cardinal added the K. of L. and promptly sent out the invitations to the archbishops to convene at his residence on October 28. If any of the metropolitans should have to absent themselves Gibbons asked that they forward to him their views on the G.A.R., the K. of L., and any other suspected society in their province.[29]

In all the details pertaining to the case of the knights, as in other important questions of these years, the Archbishop of Baltimore followed faithfully the advice of Monsignor O'Connell. When, for example, O'Connell suggested that he secure a copy of the old constitution of the K. of L. so that it might be compared with the revised edition, Gibbons again appealed to the pastor at Carbondale for this document and asked that he send it on as soon as possible.[30] It was probably a bit disconcerting to be told by his Roman agent just at this time that O'Connell had withheld the cardinal's defense of the knights to Simeoni in the belief that it might be more prudent to await a further turn of events. O'Connell was under the impression that only the G.A.R. was up for scrutiny at the Baltimore meeting on October 28, which was perfectly understandable since that was the only society originally specified by Simeoni. Moreover, O'Connell had gotten wind of the objections of some American bishops to the K. of L. lodged with the Propaganda, and for this reason he was a trifle uneasy when he read Gibbons' statement to Simeoni implying virtual unanimity against condemnation. The rector of the American College had grown suspicious that the attitude of Archbishop Corrigan was unfavorable. He noted, for example, that the previous friendliness of James McMaster, editor of the New York *Freeman's Journal,* toward the knights had now changed and he observed, too, the opposition to the order which Ella Edes, Corrigan's Roman agent, showed in speaking against them and saying that Gibbons was altogether on the knights' side.

---

[28] 81-U-3, O'Connell to Gibbons, Rome, September 8, 1886.

[29] 81-V-5, Gibbons to the archbishops, Baltimore, September 17, 1886, copy.

[30] Letterbook, Gibbons to Francis Carew, Baltimore, September 27, 1886, p. 177.

For these reasons O'Connell did not want to risk Gibbons' reputation at the Propaganda by handing in his document and thus giving rise to the possible charge that he had misrepresented the state of mind of the American prelates.[31] But before this message arrived in Baltimore the cardinal informed Simeoni of the step he had taken in convening the committee to hear the case of the knights, the A.O.H., and any other society whose good standing had been questioned. No mention was made of the G.A.R., and he was saved any hesitancy he might have felt about Rome's reaction to his moves by reason of the fact that O'Connell's cautionary hint was not yet in his hands. Simeoni received a promise of full information on the opinions of the metropolitans, and Gibbons told the Roman cardinal that even before his suggestion for a meeting had arrived he had intended to obtain the advice of many of the archbishops on the suspected societies.[32]

As preparations went forward for the archbishops' meeting in Baltimore on October 28 and the bishops continued their private discussion of the subject by mail, plans were also maturing for the annual convention of the knights which was scheduled to convene in Richmond the first week in October. The knights, too, were alert on the matter of ecclesiastical approval of their order and were making it the topic of correspondence in these fall days of 1886.[33] It was fortunate for the cause of the labor organization that the preliminary work of bringing the two groups around the conference table should have fallen to the lot of the Bishop of Richmond, John J. Keane, who acted as a liaison man between the hierarchy and the K. of L. Keane was definitely sympathetic to the workers' interests and the assembling of the order in his see city at a time when it was at the peak of its growth and power gave him an opportunity to show his good will. During the first days of the convention Powderly attended the high Mass in St. Peter's Cathedral and on the evening of October 7 the bishop and the labor leader met. A few days later Keane reported the conference to Cardinal Gibbons, and he said that while there seemed to be a rather general fear of some of the elements that made up the K. of L., he agreed with the view that the churchmen had better let such things correct them-

---

31 81-W-1, O'Connell to Gibbons, Rome, September 25, 1886.
32 81-W-2, Gibbons to Simeoni, Baltimore, September 25, 1886, copy.
33 Browne, *op. cit.,* pp. 199–201.

selves.[34] Before the grand master workman left Richmond he held a second meeting with Keane and the latter wrote out the text of an address to the K. of L. which, if circumstances favored, he would deliver to the convention. Although the address was never given it was through the contacts of Powderly and Keane in Richmond that the arrangements were made for the labor leader to confer with Gibbons in Baltimore at the end of that month.[35]

At last the time for the meeting of the metropolitans arrived and the morning of October 28 found nine of the twelve archbishops of the United States gathered at the cardinal's residence. The three missing metropolitans were Riordan of San Francisco, Heiss of Milwaukee, and Gross of Oregon City, the first two of whom sent statements against a condemnation of the society, while Gross contented himself with some general observations on the dangerous character of the question of capital and labor but said he would concur with Gibbons' views as he had read them in the newspapers. The cardinal opened the meeting with a statement that there were about a half million Catholic members of the Knights of Labor and that Powderly had declared against the boycott and the refusal to allow non-union men to work. He most likely had these facts fresh in his mind from the conference he held that morning with the grand master workman.

After the preliminary remarks of the cardinal the archbishops were all given a chance to express themselves on the subject, which they did with varying degrees of sympathy or hostility according to their convictions. It became evident that Archbishops Kenrick of St. Louis and Salpointe of Santa Fe were in favor of condemnation while the Archbishop of New York's unfriendliness to the order fell short of asking for this serious penalty. After the metropolitans had been given ample opportunity to air their opinions Gibbons concluded the session by restating his benevolent attitude toward the organization. The rough draft of the minutes revealed his position:

[34] 82-B-9, Keane to Gibbons, Richmond, October 12, 1886.

[35] Cf. Browne, *op. cit.,* pp. 205–211, for a discussion of the evidence — or lack of it — on the Powderly visit to Baltimore, and the doctored character of some of the Powderly correspondence on this point. After a critical sifting of the documents Father Browne arrived at the conclusion that Powderly probably went unaccompanied to the meeting with Gibbons, although there are some indications that two other knights were with him. For the text of the Keane statement prepared for the knights, cf. *ibid.,* pp. 363–364.

Labor has rights as well as capital. We should not condemn labor and let capital go free — would regard condemnation of K. of L. as disastrous to the Church — We should send documents to Rome and if objectionable features are eliminated K. of L. should be tolerated, should not be condemned — We have controlling influence over them; if they are condemned, a secret organization will follow in their wake and over that we will have no control.[36]

On the final vote all but two of the archbishops — Kenrick and Salpointe — gave their judgment against condemnation, but since it lacked unanimity the canonical procedure laid down by the Third Plenary Council demanded that the case be referred to Rome for ultimate decision.

Gibbons had thus made his second major effort in behalf of the Knights of Labor with only partial success. His plea to Simeoni in early September had been held up by Denis O'Connell, and now his endeavor to settle the issue in the knights' favor on this side of the Atlantic had been balked by the two adverse votes in the meeting of the metropolitans. The cardinal would have to gird himself for a more strenuous exertion of his influence at Rome. He fulfilled his promise to the Prefect of Propaganda by giving him a summary of the action taken at the meeting and informing him that Bishop Keane was then on his way to Rome with a copy of the knights' constitution.[37] Gibbons had great confidence in the Bishop of Richmond, and he probably felt relieved at this point that the case of the K. of L. would be presented in person by one who was disposed in so friendly a way to the workers and so opposed to the Church's condemnation of their organization. During this month of November, 1886, the labor question in its relations to the Church was further enlivened — if not clarified — by the faulty interpretations put upon the archbishops' meeting at Baltimore by the Catholic press and by certain developments that had arisen in the Archdiocese of New York.

We shall have occasion to see later the role played by Cardinal Gibbons in the case of Dr. Edward McGlynn, pastor of St.

---

[36] 82-D-8, Minutes of the Meeting of the Archbishops on the Secret Societies, Baltimore, October 28, 1886. It was on the same day that the G.A.R. was discussed and given a vote of toleration and the question of the Ancient Order of Hibernians was examined but left undecided.

[37] 82-E-12, Gibbons to Simeoni, Baltimore, November 12, 1886, copy.

Stephen's Church. Suffice it to say here the priest had become deeply involved, much to the chagrin of his archbishop, in the single tax movement of Henry George and the latter's campaign to win the mayoralty election in New York. Corrigan's annoyance led ultimately to his suspension of McGlynn and to the publication of a pastoral letter on the subject of private property at the close of the archdiocesan synod on November 18. The archbishop's known unfriendliness toward the Knights of Labor was doubtless enhanced when he found some of the order giving support to George's single tax proposals and to the latter's political ambitions. In the pastoral he acknowledged that abuses had been practiced against the workingmen, but in a cryptic fashion he maintained their redress could never be brought about through the denial of a fundamental right or the perpetuation of a radical wrong. The knights were not mentioned by name but it was evident to all that the pastoral was, nonetheless, a frontal attack on the teachings of Henry George. Gibbons congratulated the archbishop on his pronouncement and stated that his remarks on land and property were timely and a good counter-balance to the evil effect of loose utterances on the subject.[38] Although the Corrigan pastoral was accorded a generally favorable reception in the Catholic press, the whole McGlynn-George incident had now become intertwined with the case of the Knights of Labor, and in the end it contributed to the further division and even embitterment of those who had taken opposite stands on the K. of L. question.

With the transference of the knights' case to the Holy See the conduct of its business passed temporarily into the hands of Bishops Keane and Ireland who arrived in the Eternal City in November with their main objective that of winning papal approval for the university.[39] We have already referred to the major questions which distracted the two bishops from the university question, and the Knights of Labor was one of these. Keane and Ireland worked in close co-operation with Denis O'Connell on all these matters and through them Cardinal Gibbons was kept informed of the latest moves made at the Roman

[38] AANY, Gibbons to Corrigan, Wilmington, November 20, 1886.
[39] For the Roman negotiations on the university, cf. Ellis, *The Formative Years of the Catholic University of America*, pp. 198–253.

Curia.[40] The cardinal had sent a further statement of his views on the knights, the German question, and the coadjutorship of New Orleans to Keane, and these the bishop immediately translated into Latin and handed in at the Propaganda where, as he told Gibbons, he was sure they would have great weight.[41] It was in acknowledgment of this letter of December 17 from the Cardinal of Baltimore that Keane, as mentioned previously, wrote his candid criticism of the lack of consistency which Gibbons had shown on some of the problems then engaging their attention. While he adduced evidence of Gibbons' hesitation in the German and New Orleans questions, no mention was made of the knights which was not surprising since on this matter the cardinal had taken a strong position at the outset and had held to it without wavering.

In the first days of 1887 there reached Baltimore the summons from the Holy See that Gibbons should come to Rome to receive the cardinal's hat. He quickly informed Archbishop Corrigan of his plans and indicated that he wished to confer with him on a number of problems before sailing. The cardinal had several engagements scheduled for New York but he promised Corrigan the "lion's share" of his time for a whole day, before they would give over the evening to a dinner at Major John Keiley's home in Brooklyn where Cardinal Taschereau of Quebec would share the honors with them.[42] The press followed the movements of the prelates closely in these days, sensing as they did the news value in the coincidence of Gibbons' and Taschereau's presence in New York. The burning question of McGlynn was just then very much to the fore in the papers, to say nothing of the agitation over Irish freedom attendant upon the American visit of Michael Davitt, and the relation which Powderly and his knights had to both of these questions. It was small wonder that the reporters should have been on the alert for a statement from the churchmen. Gibbons succeeded in

---

[40] 82-G-4, Keane to Gibbons, Rome, December 4, 1886; 82-G-9, O'Connell to Gibbons, Rome, December 10, 1886.

[41] 82-J-4, Keane to Gibbons, Rome, December 29, 1886. An effort to find the letter of Gibbons to Keane of December 17 as well as his reply of January 14, 1887, to Keane's letter of December 29 was unsuccessful.

[42] AANY, Gibbons to Corrigan, Baltimore, January 7, 1887; same to same, January 20, 1887.

eluding the reporters and maintaining silence during the days before he sailed, but the New York *Daily Tribune* of January 29 had better luck with Taschereau who was quoted as saying he would join Gibbons in asking the Holy See for a pronouncement on Henry George's doctrines, but as for the K. of L. he remarked, "I shall do what I can to have it denounced."[43]

The two cardinals sailed on January 29 on the *Bourgogne* and after a few days in Paris Gibbons arrived in Rome on February 13 and three days later he had his first private audience of Pope Leo XIII. The ground for the cardinal's effort in behalf of the K. of L. had already been laid by Keane and Ireland who before Gibbons' arrival had entered their "respectful protest" against an extension of the decree of the Holy Office to the United States until the American bishops could be heard from.[44] Moreover, Keane had sought the support of Cardinal Manning several days in advance of Gibbons' coming, in order that he might uphold the Americans in preventing a hasty decision in regard to the labor and social questions then agitating the Church of the United States.[45] Knowing as he did that Cardinal Taschereau would exert all his influence to prevent a rescinding of the decree against the knights, it now became incumbent on Gibbons to avail himself of all the help his colleagues could lend in the supreme effort that was before him.

The cardinal called upon all the key officials in the Congregations of the Holy Office and Propaganda in the hope of persuading them through personal conferences of the inadvisability of condemning the American knights, and in what an earlier

---

[43] Cited in Browne, *op. cit.*, p. 234. The newspapers were often misled or published items on the strength of mere rumor. For example, two weeks before Gibbons sailed the New York *Herald* of January 16 printed a dispatch from Baltimore announcing that the cardinal was writing a book which would treat "chiefly of the labor questions." This information was supposed to have come from a secretary of Gibbons. The *Herald* account went on, "The Cardinal hesitated a long time about undertaking the task, since his duties allow him scarcely an hour daily for literary work, but when he observed how the Church was suffering because of the wrong impressions as to its attitude on labor questions he resolved, as the head of the Church in America, to given an authoritative statement on the subject." There was not any foundation at all for this rumor of a book on labor from Gibbons.

[44] ACUA, John J. Keane, "Chronicles of the Catholic University of America from 1885," p. 16.

[45] MP, Keane to Manning, Rome, February 10, 1887.

biographer described as a "heated interview" with Vincenzo
Sallua, O.P., Archbishop of Chalcedon and commissary of the
Holy Office, he went so far as to say he would hold him
responsible for the loss of souls in the United States if the
knights were condemned.[46] But he did not rest his case solely
on personal interviews. He determined to fortify his position
with an elaborate statement for Cardinal Simeoni, the Prefect
of Propaganda, and in this he turned to Keane and Ireland
for assistance.

The part played by Gibbons' famous memorial on the knights
by the two bishops was stated by Keane nine years later when
he wrote, "He had us prepare a memorial on the whole labor
question & on the Knights of Labor in particular, which he
signed & urged with all his influence."[47] The day before Gibbons
signed the document he told Archbishop Elder that he was
preparing a paper that would show the injustice, danger, and
folly of denouncing the knights. Alluding to the excitement
caused by the suspension of McGlynn who was regarded as
the friend of the workingman, he said, "what a tumult would
be raised if we condemned the laborers themselves."[48] Since
the original memorial was written in French, and the cardinal
was not accustomed to that language, it is probably safe to
conclude that the actual composition was Keane's or Ireland's
or both since the two bishops were quite familiar with French.
Allowing full credit to Keane and Ireland for their work on
the memorial, nonetheless, the only signature it bore was that
of James Gibbons and, more important, the responsibility before
the Roman Curia for the arguments it advanced was his alone.

The memorial, which the historian of this question has called
"the most important single factor in the settlement of the
case,"[49] was dated February 20, 1887, and opened with a quick
review of the action of the American archbishops the previous
October. It then proceeded in orderly fashion to outline the
case against condemnation. First Gibbons insisted that the
American knights could not be classed as a society condemned
by the Church since they were free of any oath, extreme
secrecy, or blind obedience. As evidence that they were not

[46] Will, *Life of Cardinal Gibbons*, I, 332–333.
[47] Keane, *op. cit.*, p. 16.
[48] AAC, Gibbons to Elder, Rome, February 19, 1887.
[49] Browne, *op. cit.*, p. 239.

hostile to the Church the cardinal cited Powderly's pledge of devotion. Nor was the order of the type which intrigued against the State, since President Cleveland had told Gibbons of a long conference he had with Powderly in which they had canvassed the various aspects of the labor question and possible legislative remedies to meet it. As for the laborers organizing themselves, this was only "natural and just," and if Catholic workingmen avoided, as Powderly had stated, the protection afforded by Masonry because it was banned by the Church, were they now to find themselves hindered from what the cardinal called "their only means of defense" by a condemnation of their organization?

In the next section of the memorial the Archbishop of Baltimore answered some objections that had been raised against organizations such as the K. of L. To the charge that Catholics would suffer by contact with Protestants in groups of this kind, he replied that it was truer to say that Protestants were admitted to share in an organization many of whose members and officers were Catholics. True, there were men of all religious beliefs or of none at all in the knights, but to suppose that the faith of the Catholic laborers was endangered by this contact was to reveal that one did not know the Catholic workingmen of the United States. Admitting that Catholics were thrown in with radical elements at their work, Gibbons maintained that this was merely another test of their faith, and he stated that Powderly and the press were agreed that they had stood up well under this trial to their religious beliefs. To the question of whether the laborers could be united in confraternities under the direction of the clergy and the influence of religion, the cardinal replied, "I answer frankly that I do not believe this either possible or necessary in our country." Gibbons then spoke with pride of the happy relationship in the United States between the Church and its faithful, and he said the only serious danger he would fear would be a cooling of this affection which, he added, "nothing would more certainly occasion than imprudent condemnations."

At this point Gibbons showed his awareness of the current trends when he explained to Simeoni that this was an age wherein social questions were to the forefront, especially those questions which concerned the improvement of the condition of the working people. He quoted Cardinal Manning to the effect that the Church had no longer to deal with parliaments and princes but rather with the masses, and from this he educed a warning against the danger to the Church of alienating the working classes. As he put it, "To lose the heart of the people would be a misfortune for which the friendship of the few rich and powerful would be no compensation." There would follow from a condemnation of the knights, in the judgment of Gibbons, a threat to the Church's right in popular estimation to be called a friend of the people, of incurring the hostility of the political power in the United States, and of having the Church regarded as un-American. The risks were emphasized on all these scores. To them Gibbons added the danger that the American Catholic laboring class might not obey a condemnation, for as he said, "it is necessary to recognize that, in our age and in our country, obedience cannot be blind." If this were to happen Simeoni was reminded that the revenues of the Church, emanating entirely from the free-will offerings of the people in the United States, would suffer and the same thing would happen to Peter's Pence. Furthermore, many keen observers predicted that the knights would not endure long and if the Church now condemned them it would embitter the faithful and in so doing accomplish no lasting good. Alluding to the suspension of McGlynn by Archbishop Corrigan, the cardinal then instanced the "sad and threatening confusion" that had arisen over the case of a single priest who was regarded as a friend of the laboring people. If consequences so deplorable for the peace of the American Church had occurred in this instance would not, the cardinal asked, a condemnation that fell on the people themselves bring even more disastrous results?

In all of this Cardinal Gibbons made it plain that he was speaking solely for the Church of the United States. He said he had not mentioned Canada since he would regard it as an impertinence to meddle in the ecclesiastical affairs of another country that had its own hierarchy. However, insofar as the United States was concerned, out of seventy-five archbishops and bishops only about five desired the condemnation of the knights. As he approached his concluding summary the cardinal set down for the Prefect of Propaganda a pointed counsel that was probably not lost on Simeoni. He said:

And, to speak with the most profound respect, but also with the frankness which duty requires of me, it seems to me that prudence suggests, and that even the dignity of the Church demands that we should not offer to America an ecciesiastical protection for which she does not ask, and of which she believes she has no need.[50]

In every respect the Gibbons memorial on the Knights of Labor was a remarkable document. Not only did it display a deep sympathy with the just claims of the workingman to organize and for Catholics to join such organizations, but it showed as well that the cardinal understood thoroughly the temper of the age in which he lived. His shrewd observations about the strength of the masses — even if he did exaggerate the power which the laboring class then wielded at the polls — his keen insight into the psychology of the American people in their dislike for orders given by simple fiat, which he shared with his collaborators, Ireland and Keane, his correct judgment that the knights had already shown signs of a short life, and the manner in which he drew out the implications of all these factors for the future welfare of the Catholic Church in the American Republic, stamped Gibbons as a man who possessed a knowledge and understanding of his country and its conditions that was truly admirable. No less remarkable was the courage which he showed in practically telling the highest officials of the Holy See that they had made a mistake two and a half years before in condemning the knights in Canada and that he would not wish to see the mistake repeated in his own country. The situation before him called for firm leadership and guidance of the Holy See by the American cardinal and he risked the displeasure of the Roman officials to give it to them, knowing that it ran counter to their previous judgments. This risk he took in the determination to insure that the Church and the Republic he loved so deeply should not suffer injury.

With the major statement of the American case for the knights in Simeoni's hands the Cardinal of Baltimore did not relax. A week later he held a conference with the principal officials of the Holy Office with what Keane described to Manning as "most gratifying results." Keane believed that in Gibbons' words the Roman prelates felt the weight of the whole American Church and that his sentiments had already produced

---

[50] For a critical edition of the memorial giving the variant readings of the original French and later English editions, cf. Browne, *op. cit.*, pp. 365–378.

what he saw as "an evident change of front."[51] Gibbons, too, was breathing a more confident air when he forwarded a copy of the memorial to Bishop Gilmour in Cleveland with the words:

I feel strongly on this subject. We must prove that we are the friends of the working classes; if we condemn or use them harshly we lose them, and they will look on us with as much hatred and suspicion as they do in the Church of France. They commit excesses now and then. Let us correct them, but they have also real grievances. Let us help them to redress them. I would regard the condemnation of the Knights of Labor, as a signal calamity to the Catholic Church of America.[52]

Through an altogether unexpected medium Cardinal Gibbons was soon to learn that the America of which he spoke largely concurred with his judgment. The memorial to Simeoni was, of course, a confidential document. But through some means, the exact nature of which has eluded historians, a Roman correspondent of the New York *Herald* secured an abbreviated version of it, including the text of the final nine points made in summary by Gibbons and on March 3, 1887, this appeared in the paper. Various explanations of the "leak" were advanced and John Ireland's surmise may have been the correct one when he told Gilmour, "the 'Herald' man evidently got it, as he indeed hints, by bribing some secretary."[53] At any rate, the news was out and the first intimation that Gibbons received that the story had appeared in the United States reached him in the form of a cable of congratulations.[54]

Other papers, as was to be expected, picked up the item from the *Herald,* and soon the American press buzzed with comment favorable and otherwise on the cardinal's action. The reactions of some editors were enthusiastic. For example, the *Catholic Herald* of New York carried an editorial on March 19 entitled "Light at Last," in which it said that Gibbons had won many claims in his honorable and useful life to the high regard of the American people, but his latest presentation of popular rights before the Holy See "outranks all of his former claims and

[51] Keane to Manning [Rome], February 28, 1887, quoted in Shane Leslie, *Henry Edward Manning, His Life and Labours* (London, 1921), p. 361.
[52] ADC, Gibbons to Gilmour, Rome, March 3, 1887.
[53] *Ibid.,* Ireland to Gilmour, Rome, March 6, 1887.
[54] AANY, D. J. O'Connell to Charles E. McDonnell, Rome, April 14, 1887.

makes us feel that in his person American Catholics have a representative of whom they may well be proud." The opposite extreme was found in the *Nation* of March 17 and 31 and in the New York *Times* of March 30. The editorial writer in the *Times* maintained that if Gibbons was a politician looking for votes he could understand his conduct, but for the cardinal to talk about "hard and obstinate monopolies," he regretted to say, made him feel that Gibbons ought to be ashamed of himself for repeating it. Since no political motive could be seen in his catering to labor, the writer was forced to the conclusion, as he expressed it:

> that he is a man of weak judgment, and that the church will make a terrible blunder if it permits him to persuade it into taking the side of an organization which is trying to substitute brute force and intimidation for law, reason, equity, and the precepts of the Christian religion.

While there were differences of press opinion on the wisdom of Gibbons' policy, the general reaction was favorable and the early spring of 1887 was enlivened with news items and editorial opinion on the subject. In Protestant circles the Episcopalian *Churchman* of New York on March 9 thought they saw the inroad of Rome into the social and political affairs of the United States through this move of "the wily Cardinal Gibbons"; whereas the *Independent* of the same city a month later pointed out in a friendlier vein that Gibbons had done better by going to Rome than McGlynn who had remained at home. The *Independent* believed the Church of Rome was now ready to patronize a mild form of socialism since its hold upon the dynasties and civil power had been lost.[55]

The publicity given to his memorial at first disturbed Cardinal Gibbons greatly. He was quick to assure Taschereau that he knew nothing of the circumstances in which the document had reached the press, although this in no way prevented the Archbishop of Quebec from renewing his campaign against

---

[55] New York *Independent,* April 7, 1887. For a wide coverage of the press on this incident, especially of the Catholic newspapers, cf. Browne, *op. cit.,* pp. 243–255. Reflecting upon the conservative character of the French Catholic press at that time, a recent writer stated that he recalled in 1887 the Catholic press of Paris did not have enough courage to mention the memorial of Gibbons. Félix Klein, *La route du petit morvandiau. Souvenirs* (Paris, 1948), III, 55.

the knights with Simeoni.[56] The apprehension which Gibbons at first entertained gradually subsided, however, when telegrams and newspaper comment "of a most cheering character" began to reach him with proof of the good the publication was doing in the United States.[57] Archbishop Ryan of Philadelphia had read the synopsis of the memorial in the papers and he thought the reasons given against condemnation by Gibbons were convincing, even if he regretted the publication of the names of the Archbishops of St. Louis and Santa Fe as the minority who had voted against the knights in Baltimore.[58] Another private document which reached the press about this time and was extensively — although inaccurately — quoted on both sides of the Atlantic helped to solidify the impression created in the public mind by Gibbons' memorial. On March 11 Cardinal Manning had written to Bishop Keane and expressed his "great assent" with Gibbons on the knights. He said he thanked the American cardinal for allowing him to share in the argument and if he could find a copy of his lecture on "The Dignity and Rights of Labor" he would send it as requested by the Archbishop of Baltimore and it would, he thought, qualify him for knighthood in the order. Manning concluded, "The Church is the mother, friend, and protector of the people. As the Lord walked among them, so His Church lives among them. The Cardinal's argument is irresistible."[59]

Needless to say, Gibbons was deeply grateful for the powerful endorsement of the Archbishop of Westminster. He promptly told Manning:

> I cannot sufficiently express to you how much I felt strengthened in my position by being able to refer in the document to your utterances on the claims of the working-man to our sympathy, and how I am cheered beyond measure in receiving from your own pen an endorsement of my sentiments and those of my American colleagues now in Rome. God grant that the Church of America may

---

[56] Browne, *op. cit.*, p. 254.

[57] MP, Keane to Manning, Rome, March 14, 1887. Keane asked Manning's permission to make public the latter's two letters on the American Catholic social questions if that should prove advantageous, a permission which Manning granted (*ibid.*, Keane to Manning, Rome, Easter Tuesday [1887]).

[58] 82-N-8, Ryan to Gibbons, Philadelphia, March 15, 1887.

[59] The full and authentic text of Manning's letter to Keane was published in the *Tablet* of London on May 7, 1887.

escape the dire calamity of a condemnation which would be disastrous to the future interests of religion among us. . . . We are indebted more than you are aware to the influence of your name in discussing these social questions and in influencing the public mind. We joyfully adopt your Eminence into the ranks of our Knighthood; you have nobly won your spurs.

I shall certainly D.V. call on Your Eminence when I visit England which will probably be in May.[60]

Encouragement came likewise from Archbishop Lynch of Toronto who wanted Gibbons to know that he was in "most hearty accord" with the cardinal's position.[61] To be sure, those who disagreed with Gibbons' sentiments did not cease their attempts to influence the mind of the Holy See against accepting his judgment on the knights. Men like Taschereau and Healy of Portland, Maine, were not the type to retreat from the field of battle. Nor did Father Charles E. McDonnell, the secretary of Archbishop Corrigan, fail to bring to the attention of Gibbons the unfavorable impression of his conduct created in some quarters. McDonnell forwarded to Denis O'Connell a caustic editorial that had appeared on March 17 in the *Nation,* the conservative and influential weekly edited by Edwin L. Godkin. The *Nation* capitalized on the garbled text of an interview given by Gibbons in Rome wherein he was quoted as considering himself an "enemy of plutocracy and of corporations of men with no souls." The editorial writer referred to the cardinal as "partaking freely of the labor beverage" and sarcastically lamented the loss sustained by politics when he entered the Church.[62]

Amid all these varying expressions of opinion the negotiations on the knights' case continued in Rome. With the approach of the period for Catholics to fulfill their Easter duty by receiving the sacraments, Cardinal Taschereau was anxious to secure permission to absolve those members of the K. of L. in his jurisdiction who would pledge themselves to abide by

[60] MP, Gibbons to Manning, Rome, March 14, 1887.

[61] Lynch to Gibbons, Toronto, March 23, 1887, quoted in Browne, *op. cit.,* p. 257. Keane reported Gibbons' departure from Rome to Manning and he said, "The most lasting result, though the one least anticipated, will probably be that produced by his labor document" (MP, Keane to Manning, Rome, April 23, 1887).

[62] AANY, O'Connell to McDonnell, Rome, April 14, 1887. The interview in question appeared in the New York *Herald* of March 10, 1887.

the final decision of the Holy See regarding their society. With that in mind, prior to his departure from Rome on March 20 he obtained the promise of Gibbons to inform him by wire of the answer of the Holy Office. Ten days later the decree was issued permitting the Canadian knights to be admitted to the sacraments upon their declaration that they would honor the decision of the Holy See when the case was fully decided. True to his promise Gibbons promptly wired Taschereau, "Pope grants your petition fully."[63] Before leaving the Eternal City the Cardinal of Baltimore filed another report with the Holy Office in which he stated that the American bishops had not followed the Canadian decree of 1884 since they had found not even a "reasonable suspicion" against the order in the United States. Gibbons pictured the innocent character of the organization, the danger that they might drift into other secret groups if they were condemned, and he ended with an assurance that while the American hierarchy would continue their vigilance in this question they were almost unanimous in their belief that nothing should be changed in the status of the K. of L. in the United States.[64]

During a short holiday at Anzio the Cardinal of Baltimore sent a report on the state of all the major American questions then before the Holy See to Archbishop Corrigan. He explained that he knew nothing of how his memorial on the knights had reached the press, remarked that it had given him "exceeding pain," and expressed his grief that the names of Archbishops Kenrick and Salpointe should have been mentioned. He stated that a fuller edition of the memorial had appeared in the *Moniteur de Rome*.[65] The cardinal made no allusion to the omission from

---

[63] Gibbons to Taschereau, Rome, March 31, 1887, telegram, quoted in Browne, *op. cit.*, p. 261.

[64] AAB, unclassified, "Draft. Petition to Holy Office. Knights of Labor. Filed April/87."

[65] AANY, Gibbons to Corrigan, Anzio, March 29, 1887. Keane reported to Cardinal Manning that Monsignor Eugène Boeglin, a German Alsatian, editor of the *Moniteur de Rome,* was completely on their side. The Pope, said Keane, had sent for Boeglin some days previous and stated that complaints had been made against his evident advocacy of Gibbons' views as tending to coerce the Holy Office. Boeglin had discounted the complaints as absurd since all Europe approved Gibbons' labor memorial, to which Leo XIII replied that he agreed with Boeglin but it would be prudent to keep silence for a few days. Keane said he thought Boeglin suspected Cardinal Parocchi as the source of the complaint, but Keane himself was more inclined to think it was Simeoni who had protested.

the *Moniteur* version of his reference to the McGlynn case. Gibbons, of course, was unaware that this was already known in New York, for McQuaid had called to Corrigan's attention the text in the *Moniteur* which, as he said, had omitted the cardinal's "reference to your affairs." The Bishop of Rochester concluded, "His Eminence put his foot in it badly."[66] Nor did Gibbons know that a week before he wrote Corrigan the Archbishop of Philadelphia had commented to the New York prelate on the memorial and had implied that Gibbons was responsible for disclosing the names of the two archbishops. Ryan said, "It was not necessary for his purpose, and was unfair to these prelates."[67] Considering their serious difference over the McGlynn case just at this time, it is not difficult to see how these remarks deepened the misunderstanding under which Corrigan labored in regard to the Archbishop of Baltimore.

On April 5 Cardinal Taschereau issued a circular to his clergy which embodied the conditions under which the ban against the Knights of Labor might be lifted for their reception of the sacraments. This document, together with the *Moniteur de Rome's* version of March 28 of the Gibbons memorial, continued to furnish copy for the press in keeping the question before the public. Much of the old ground was covered again and the *Catholic Herald* of New York, which had already incurred the ire of Corrigan and was soon to be extinguished, editorialized in a flippant manner on the mistakes of some of its Catholic rivals and ended triumphantly, "God reigns, Cardinal Gibbons lives and Labor thrives."[68] To all of this, of course, Gibbons was no party and he could do little to stop the newspaper stories which greeted him everywhere as he left for home by way of Paris, London, and Ireland. At Paris the cardinal made a further attempt to explain to Archbishop Corrigan the part of his Roman transactions that touched the Metropolitan of New York. He said the paragraph on McGlynn in the memorial had been omitted from the *Moniteur's* text, "not because it contained any argument against your Grace," but

---

"*The Vatican,*" said Keane, "seems open to living ideas, — but the Propaganda & Holy Office keep doors & windows closed to the new light" (MP, Keane to Manning, Rome, April 23, 1887).

[66] AANY, McQuaid to Corrigan, Rochester, April 12, 1887.

[67] *Ibid.,* Ryan to Corrigan, Philadelphia, March 23, 1887.

[68] May 21, 1887.

because he feared enemies might distort it. He agreed that boycotting by the workers was worthy of condemnation, and, in referring to the trouble which the archbishop was having with some Knights of Labor in Calvary Cemetery, Gibbons remarked that it was evident "there are some bad Knights in New York."[69]

From Paris the cardinal traveled to London where he visited with Manning and exchanged notes on the struggle they had just come through at Rome. It gave Gibbons an opportunity to thank the Archbishop of Westminster in person for the splendid support he had given to the cause of the American workers and to talk over in further detail the case of Henry George in which, as we shall see, Gibbons was again to appeal for Manning's assistance. As the time neared for the home-coming of the Archbishop of Baltimore plans were launched for his reception in Baltimore. Abbé Magnien, the Sulpician superior, was one of the directing hands and he made it known to Gibbons that they were taking pains to have the demonstration kept to "as canonical a character as possible." Magnien knew of the enthusiasm in laboring circles for the returning prelate, but he feared "wrong interpretations" if the workers took part as such.[70] Magnien may or may not have heard of the rumors then current in New York that the rebellious Knights of Labor in Calvary Cemetery were assessing their members for a demonstration in favor of McGlynn and for the chartering of a steamer to escort Gibbons up the bay and later to bring him to St. Patrick's Cathedral.[71]

After an absence of over four months from home the Cardinal of Baltimore reached New York on June 5 and went immediately from the ship to the residence of Archbishop Corrigan. What transpired during their visit we do not know, although the K. of L. was not discussed since Corrigan in speaking of the cardinal's visit remarked to Elder, "He made no allusions to the Knights of Labor, directly, and I did not like to ask questions."[72] Gibbons traveled to Baltimore on June 7 and

---

[69] AANY, Gibbons to Corrigan, Paris, April 30, 1887.

[70] 82-Q-2, Magnien to Gibbons, Baltimore, May 14, 1887.

[71] AAC, Corrigan to Elder, New York, June 2, 1887. An even more ridiculous twist to the story had reached the ears of Corrigan to the effect that he was to be thrust out of his see and that McGlynn was to be installed by Gibbons as vicar-general and rector of St. Patrick's Cathedral!

[72] *Ibid.*, Corrigan to Elder, New York, June 5, 1887.

there he expressed in the cathedral his gratitude for the warm reception they had given him and his happiness to be home again. In his informal talk he made only a passing reference to the labor question in remarking on the far happier state of American workers in comparison to those he had seen in Europe, and he concluded with a warning against anarchists who would, as he said, "pull down the fabric of our constitution."[73] With his main effort behind him Gibbons could for the time being leave the knights' case at Rome in the capable hands of his lieutenants, Keane and O'Connell, who had recently been re-enforced by Archbishop Williams of Boston, a prelate who was in entire sympathy with the cardinal's views.[74]

At the very time that Gibbons was receiving the congratulations of his friends for his work in Rome, the Knights of Labor themselves had begun the decline from which they were never to recover. Several ineptly handled strikes contributed to their disruption and, as one historian expressed it, "the knights were already deeply involved in that decisive struggle with the emerging forces of the new unionism that was to complete their downfall."[75] Nonetheless, the K. of L. was in the main grateful for the cardinal's help even if a few cranks among them affected indifference. As Thomas O'Reilly, a prominent Catholic knight, said in sending congratulations to Powderly on the publication of the Gibbons memorial, "The Cardinal has stood our brave friend to the end!"[76] Some months later Powderly sent his personal thanks to Gibbons, apologizing for his tardiness with the excuse that it was only diffidence in addressing him that had so long delayed the expression of his gratitude. They all felt their order was in the safest hands, said Powderly, when the cardinal undertook to champion their cause and, as he put it, "our hearts — a million hearts, went out to you on reading your lucid and forcible report in which you stated our real aims and objects. . . ." The grand master workman believed that Gibbons had placed the knights under

---

[73] New York *Freeman's Journal,* June 18, 1887.

[74] 82-Q-1, Keane to Gibbons, Rome, May 14, 1887; 82-Q-10, O'Connell to Gibbons, Rome, May 18, 1887; 82-V-4, O'Connell to Gibbons, Rome, June 24, 1887.

[75] Dulles, *op. cit.,* p. 147.

[76] O'Reilly to Powderly, Macon, Georgia, received March 7, 1887, quoted in Browne, *op. cit.,* p. 276.

many lasting obligations to him, and he expressed the hope that they would continue to merit his good will and favorable opinion as well as the toleration of the Church.[77] A few days later Cardinal Gibbons, in turn, thanked Powderly for his letter, expressed his continuing interest in the K. of L., and the hope that the leader would exert every effort to purge their ranks of all dangerous affiliations. The cardinal realized the enemies of the order were assiduous in playing up every disloyal sentiment or breach of law, and for that reason he would be happy if Powderly would use all his power to abolish or reduce to a minimum the strikes which paralyzed labor and nearly always ended disastrously for the workmen. He closed on a note of exhortation: "God grant that your order may contribute to the material and moral well-being of the laboring classes who are so dear to my heart."[78] Bishop Gilmour, too, was grateful to Gibbons for his work in the knights' behalf. He thought all had reason to thank him even if the question was not yet finally resolved, since he had given them something until, as he said, "we see farther ahead."[79] On July 14 the cardinal had a long conversation with President Cleveland during which they discussed the knights and the President expressed his sympathy for Gibbons in the attacks which the New York *Times* had made on him some months before and told him he regarded them as unwarranted and unjust.[80]

By midsummer of 1887 the decline in the Knights of Labor had become a source of alarm to its leaders with a drop in membership of nearly 200,000 from the maximum of 700,000 of the previous year. In light of this fact the responsible officials were naturally anxious to bolster the order's falling fortunes in every possible way. In the emergency which faced them a further encouraging word from Gibbons was sought in the hope that it might be read before the annual convention of the knights scheduled for Minneapolis in early October. Thomas

---

[77] 82-W-10, Powderly to Gibbons, Scranton, June 30, 1887. Powderly took the occasion to compliment Gibbons for his sermon in Santa Maria in Trastevere the previous March. He said, "The patriotic words you spoke have won, not alone for yourself, but for our Church, the respect and esteem of Protestant Americans everywhere."

[78] 83-B-4, Gibbons to Powderly, Baltimore, July 9, 1887, copy.

[79] 83-C-6, Gilmour to Gibbons, Cleveland, July 16, 1887.

[80] ADR, Gibbons to O'Connell, Baltimore, July 15, 1887.

O'Reilly, leading knight and close friend of Powderly, went to Baltimore on September 20 where he persuaded Gibbons to oblige with a statement of his views on the K. of L. In this instance the cardinal referred to his defense of the laboring man's rights when he was in Rome; now that he was at home he wished to speak in a friendly spirit of the workingmen's duties and responsibilities. Gibbons warned of the evil effects of strikes and the danger to the good name of the order that would come from any association with anarchists and nihilists. His advice closed with the assurance that his only motive in offering these suggestions was his sincere affection for the laboring classes and his ardent desire for their moral and material welfare.[81] In all probability the K. of L. would have appreciated a stronger emphasis on their rights, but on this occasion they did not get it, and they could hardly quarrel with Gibbons in his profession of friendship for them when they recalled his Roman labors of some months before. The cardinal's statement of September 21 was read at Minneapolis along with a doctored version of his memorial to Simeoni and Manning's assent to the same. In the end the general assembly voted approval of Powderly's handling of the order's business insofar as it related to the Catholic Church.[82]

Just a few days before the opening of the K. of L. convention in Minneapolis Cardinal Gibbons had passed through that city on his way to Oregon to confer the pallium on Archbishop Gross. At a public reception in his honor on October 10 in Portland M. G. Munly, editor of the *Catholic Sentinel*, had saluted Gibbons as the friend of the laboring man. In reply the cardinal acknowledged the compliment but said he was the friend of both the laborer and the capitalist. He developed the idea of the necessity of mutual assistance of the two and, as he said, "by means of these brains and these arms our country will be so developed as to surpass any other nation on the face of the earth."[83] That fall Henry George was defeated in his effort to become Mayor of New York and four of the

[81] 83-N-10, Gibbons to Powderly, Baltimore, September 21, 1887, copy.

[82] Cf. Browne, *op. cit.*, pp. 287–303, for developments within the K. of L. at this time and Powderly's ambiguous conduct in regard to the dating and editing of the documents bearing on the Church's relation to the order, as well as press reactions to Powderly and the Church in the fall of 1887.

[83] Portland *Oregonian*, October 11, 1887.

men convicted for the Haymarket murders in Chicago were hanged. These events gave renewed courage to conservative minds, and the defeat of George especially was looked upon by some as a rout of the knights. With this in mind Bishop McQuaid gleefully asked Archbishop Corrigan:

> How does his Eminence feel now about his pets, the Knights of Labor?
> They are evidently breaking to pieces and are getting many more kicks than kisses. . . . For the countenance his Eminence gave them, he will have to suffer. He exceeded his instruction and must bear his burden.[84]

Far from feeling any burden, His Eminence was just at this time concluding his triumphal tour across the continent during which he had received everywhere the plaudits of enthusiastic crowds in the Far West and South who gathered to see for the first time a member of the College of Cardinals.

During the intervening months since Gibbons had left Rome the officials of the Holy See had been examining the evidence submitted by the Americans on the Knights of Labor and were slowly moving toward a decision. In June, 1888, Monsignor O'Connell sent the cardinal what proved to be a premature report that the Holy Office had arrived at a judgment of *tolerari possunt* on the order.[85] This news reached the press and set the editors off on another round of dispatches and editorials in which Gibbons got his customary share of praise and blame. The unfriendly *Protestant Standard* of July 26 in an item entitled "Mr. Leo and the Knights of Labor," in crediting the victory to the "bland, insinuating, persuasive power" of the cardinal, thought "the blarney of Gibbons was an over-match for the Italians in the Vatican."[86] But the blandishments of Cardinal Gibbons had not won quite so clear-cut a victory as had been originally reported by O'Connell. The final judgment rendered on August 16 was communicated two weeks later by Cardinal Simeoni to the Archbishop of Baltimore. The knights were to be tolerated, true, but only on condition that

> whatever in its statutes is improperly expressed or susceptible of wrong interpretation shall be corrected. Especially in the preamble

---

[84] AANY, McQuaid to Corrigan, Rochester, December 28, 1887.
[85] 84-P-7, O'Connell to Gibbons, Rome, June 17, 1888.
[86] Quoted in Browne, *op. cit.*, p. 323.

of the constitution for local assemblies words which seem to savor of socialism and communism must be emended in such a way as to make clear that the soil was granted by God to man, or rather the human race, that each one might have the right to acquire some portion of it, by use however of lawful means and without violation of the right of private property.[87]

The decree, therefore, gave no outright approval to the K. of L., but instead what might be called a conditional toleration. It adhered to the principles framed years before on secret societies, and its emphasis was anti-socialistic in tone rather than positively sympathetic toward labor's organization.

But Gibbons had his own way of handling the attached condition. A week after receiving the decree he announced the news to Archbishop Ireland and told him his plans for sending a circular to the hierarchy. Some days before there had come a request from Powderly that the cardinal use his good offices in behalf of a certain James Lonergan.[88] Gibbons seized this opportunity to inform the general master workman of the Holy Office's decision and to suggest that he visit him in Baltimore and bring with him a copy of the latest constitution of the K. of L.[89] He explained all this to Ireland and told him he wanted to be able to announce in his letter to the metropolitans the willingness of Powderly to make the changes demanded by Rome. "This," said the cardinal, "will put a quietus on the subject." As for the demands made by the Roman officials, Gibbons was not impressed. He said, "I attach little or no importance to the conditions imposed by the H. Office. They do not specify a single sentence for animadversion but simply demand some verbal changes. Something had to be done to save them from the charge of inconsistency."[90] In the same vein Denis O'Connell was informed of Gibbons' anticipated moves and he emphasized that he did not wish the decree to be given any publicity, even among the bishops, until he had taken "the little sting" out of the document with Powderly's pledge of co-operation. The cardinal was in a

---

[87] 84-Y-3, Simeoni to Gibbons, Rome, August 29, 1888.

[88] Powderly to Gibbons, Scranton, September 7, 1888, copy, quoted in Browne, *op. cit.*, p. 325.

[89] 85-B-2, Gibbons to Powderly, Baltimore, September 11, 1888, copy.

[90] AASP, Gibbons to Ireland, Baltimore, September 17, 1888, copy.

contented mood when he told O'Connell, "I now breathe freely, thanks to God, & to your vigilance."[91]

The second meeting between Gibbons and Powderly took place in a cordial atmosphere on September 24, and the following day the cardinal was able to assure his fellow metropolitans that the labor leader had cheerfully promised to make the emendations required by the Holy Office and to comply at all times with the wishes of the authorities of the Church.[92] The promise of Powderly was likewise duly reported to Simeoni, along with a vindication of Gibbons' prediction of February, 1887, that the knights would decline, for he was now able to tell the Prefect of Propaganda that of the order's 700,000 members scarcely 350,000 were left.[93] But he was not alone in adverting to the perspicacity of his forecast of a year and a half before. O'Connell was glad to let him know that Camillo Cardinal de Rende, Archbishop of Benevento, had recently spoken of the American cardinal's "rare judgment" and how everything had turned out "exactly as he foretold" when de Rende had discussed the question with Gibbons in Paris.[94] The reports of the rector of the American College at this time would indicate that Gibbons had, indeed, made a deep impression on the Roman officials by his handling of the knights' case. Archbishop Satolli had compared the alertness and skill of the American bishops to the disadvantage of the Irish hierarchy in the latter's presentation of the land question before the Holy See, and in speaking of Gibbons as the "great statesman he is" he gave him the main credit for saving Rome from what he called "the commission of a great mistake." O'Connell dutifully recorded Satolli's opinion for the cardinal, to which he joined his own flattering judgment in saying, "You never did anything that so added to your prestige in Rome as that action of yours in regards to the Knights."[95]

There is no reason to believe that O'Connell was exaggerating the esteem which Gibbons had gained as a consequence of his championing of the Knights of Labor. The testimonies he received afforded ample evidence that this was so. From one

[91] ADR, Gibbons to O'Connell, Baltimore, September 20, 1888.

[92] 85-D-2, Gibbons to the archbishops, Baltimore, September 25, 1888, copy.

[93] 85-D-10, Gibbons to Simeoni, Baltimore, September 28, 1888, copy.

[94] 85-C-3, O'Connell to Gibbons, Grottaferrata, September 17, 1888.

[95] 84-V-6, O'Connell to Gibbons, Rome, August 14, 1888.

of the most highly placed friends of the Catholic social movement in France there came praise for the role Gibbons had played when Charles Cardinal Place, Archbishop of Rennes, extended his congratulations and said the only salvation for the workingman was the liberating doctrines of the divine Worker of Nazareth, "doctrines," said Place, "which you have explained so correctly and eloquently in your work."[96] And Cardinal Rampolla, Leo XIII's Secretary of State, met a reproach on the leakage of such documents as Gibbons' memorial with the retort, "Oh, but that did a great deal of good."[97] From far-off India the cardinal received the felicitations of Archbishop George Porter in Bombay who said he had been following the progress of the case of the Knights. "May God guide your Eminence in settling it," said Porter, "as he has done so far."[98] When a year later the proposal for an international conference on labor legislation was taken up by Leo XIII and Emperor William II of Germany it put the aging Cardinal Manning in a reminiscent mood with Baltimore:

We little thought when we were writing about the Knights of Labour in Rome, a few years ago, that every word would be so soon published to the world by an Emperor and a Pope.

This is surely the New World over-shadowing the old, and the Church walking with its Master among the people of Christendom. Were we prophets?[99]

Archbishop Ireland, upon being shown Manning's letter by Gibbons, reacted with a typical flourish:

The words are cheering, and to you who staked your name on the outcome of the problem, then rather obscure, they must have been very gratifying.

You were a prophet! The people are the power, and the Church must be with the people. I wish all our own bishops understood this truth![100]

But even before this time Gibbons' accomplishment had

---

[96] 85-I-1, Place to Gibbons, Rennes, November 21, 1888.

[97] 85-I-7, O'Connell to Gibbons, Rome, November 23, 1888.

[98] 85-U-9, Porter to Gibbons, Bombay, March 27, 1889.

[99] 87-G-8, Manning to Gibbons, n.p., March 31, 1890; also quoted in Leslie, op. cit., pp. 365–366.

[100] 87-J-5, Ireland to Gibbons, St. Paul, April 21, 1890; also quoted in Leslie, op. cit., p. 366.

won him an international fame. It was on his trip in 1887 that the Archbishop of Baltimore came in contact with a number of the leaders of the European Catholic social movement, and by his memorial on the knights earned in their eyes the right to be regarded as the leader of the American Church in social questions. It was during this journey that the cardinal met men like Eduardo Soderini of Italy, the friend and biographer of Leo XIII and a close student of these matters. In France he became acquainted with Léon Harmel and visited his model factory at Val-des-Bois which was conducted along strictly Christian lines. Count Albert de Mun, influential member of the Chamber of Deputies, was present on the occasion and helped to explain to Gibbons the various workers' clubs, co-operatives, and pious associations which had offered, in Harmel's mill, patterns for many other French factories to follow. His host on this visit was Benoît Cardinal Langénieux, Archbishop of Rheims, to whom Gibbons later remarked that his visit to the French factory was "among the most precious memories" of his eventful journey.[101] Langénieux had been deeply impressed by the American cardinal's work for the knights and when there reached him a rumor that Leo XIII was preparing an encyclical on labor, he told Gibbons that he had been on the attack at the first hour and, as he expressed it, "your word is a preparation for that of the Supreme Pontiff." That the influence of Gibbons' reputation had already gone far in labor circles was evidenced when Langénieux related that the mention of his name at a conference on social questions at Liége had brought unanimous applause from an audience representing several nations.[102]

Some months before the convening of the Third International Social Congress in his see city in September, 1890, Victor Doutreloux, Bishop of Liége, sought a message for the congress from Cardinal Gibbons and, if possible, a priest to represent him. Doutreloux was encouraged to make this request, he said, because of the high consideration which attached to Gibbons' name in Europe on social questions.[103] The cardinal obliged

---

[101] 83-U-3, Gibbons to Langénieux, Baltimore, December 3, 1887, copy. For these developments in France at the time cf. Parker T. Moon, *The Labor Problem and the Social Catholic Movement in France* (New York, 1921).

[102] 83-N-9, Langénieux to Gibbons, Rheims, September 21, 1887.

[103] 87-Q-6, Doutreloux to Gibbons, Liége, July 17, 1890.

with a letter of good wishes to the congress and its work. The memorial on the Knights of Labor had begun, too, to enter the literature on the subject. Gibbons was told by the author of *Les Américains chez eux* (Paris, 1890), that she owed the real merit of her book to the cardinal's permission to use what she called "your beautiful chapter on the Labour Classes."[104] When Count de Mun wrote an article for the *Revue d'association catholique* in answer to accusations against him and his colleagues for urging the necessity of an accord among Catholics on social and labor problems, he asked and won an endorsement of his article from Gibbons.[105] Not only did the cardinal approve the article, but he wrote de Mun in praise of his efforts to mitigate the hardship of the laboring classes and called it "a sad reflection" that one who had consecrated his time and talents to the best interests of society should have to defend his actions which eloquently spoke for themselves.[106]

Meanwhile the promise made to Cardinal Gibbons by Terence Powderly in their conference of September, 1888, that he would make the changes in the constitution of the K. of L. requested by the Holy Office, was not kept. In fact, Powderly came out even stronger for the single tax theories of Henry George and amid further criticism of him by his own members for truckling to the Church, he was in no mood to urge the revisions suggested by the Roman officials. When the K. of L. met, therefore, in their convention at Atlanta in November, 1889, they approved a statement on land which George declared was the "most important event" that his newspaper had been able to record.[107] The attempt of Gibbons to secure a full execution of Powderly's promise and an exact conformity to the will of the Holy See consequently ended, through no fault of his own, in failure. The old adversary, Bishop McQuaid, was keeping a close eye on the matter and some time later he quoted Simeoni's necessary conditions for the Church's

---

[104] 87-G-4, Madame de San Carlos de Pedroso to Gibbons, Chambly, Oise, March 26, 1890.

[105] 88-G-9, de Mun to Gibbons, Paris, January 15, 1891. On de Mun cf. Sister Miriam Lynch, *The Organized Social Apostolate of Albert de Mun* (Washington, 1952).

[106] 88-K-5, Gibbons to de Mun, Baltimore, February 21, 1891, copy.

[107] Quoted in Browne, *op. cit.*, p. 339. For details of Powderly's conduct in this matter of revising the constitution and his growing testiness toward the Church, cf. Browne, *op. cit.*, pp. 332–339.

toleration of the knights and pointedly asked Gibbons, "Will your Eminence be pleased to inform me if these conditions required for tolerance of the Knights of Labor have been complied with, and where I am to get a copy of the amended Constitution?"[108] To the embarrassing question the cardinal replied in an unruffled manner:

> I beg to say that I have not at hand a copy of the Constitution of the Knights of Labor. I may be permitted to add that as the Archbishops of the country were constituted with approbation of the H. See a standing committee on societies, that subject is now in their hands.[109]

The extent to which his inquiry had caused discomfort in Baltimore the Bishop of Rochester could only guess.

Despite the failure of Powderly to live up to the conditions which Rome had required for complete toleration and which he had promised Gibbons to fulfill, the reputation of the cardinal as the champion of the workingman remained undiminished. From time to time his views on labor were asked and frequently they appeared in the press in the form of interviews, quotations from his public addresses, or occasionally as reprints of letters. While they unfailingly revealed his sympathy with the workers, these statements were ordinarily couched in rather general and hortatory language which showed the cardinal's desire to adhere to his role as a guide of morals rather than to essay any competence in the province of the economist where he was not at home. In one such statement that appeared in the New York *Herald* of February 20, 1891, Gibbons went beyond his customary generalizations on the need for amicable relations between capital and labor to urge a sympathetic understanding of the workers by churchmen. He was quoted as having written:

> The toiling masses should be practically convinced that they possess the sympathy of the Church. Mistakes are, indeed, made and sins sometimes committed by labor organizations; but these faults are usually exaggerated by timid souls and selfish capitalists. If ministers of religion are to continue to exercise a salutary influence over the workman and to keep him within the bounds of moral duty, they must convince him of their sincere affection by earnest efforts to better his material condition.

---

[108] 88-G-7, McQuaid to Gibbons, Rochester, January 12, 1891.
[109] 88-H-6, Gibbons to McQuaid, Baltimore, January 23, 1891, copy.

The statement was particularly gratifying to Marc F. Vallette, secretary of the United States Catholic Historical Society of New York, who felt that the bishops in Europe had given real leadership to the laboring classes. But as for the United States, he remarked to Gibbons, "You are the only one in this country who has taken an open and decided stand in their behalf."[110] The compliment was doubtless sincere, even if it did overlook the contributions of other American prelates like Keane and Ireland.

Despite the pressing problems which faced the American Church in the closing decade of the nineteenth century, in all of which as we shall see Cardinal Gibbons was deeply involved, his interest in the labor question did not flag and he found time for a considerable amount of writing on the subject. On the occasion of the centennial of the American hierarchy in November, 1889, he published a volume entitled *Our Christian Heritage* in which he included a chapter on "The Dignity, Rights and Duties of the Laboring Classes." He strongly supported the worker's right to organize and to receive what he termed "a fair and just compensation for his services." Moreover, he condemned child labor and the greed that motivated the monopolies, although he was careful to say that from his study of the condition of the laboring classes in Europe and the British Isles he was persuaded that the American workman was much better off than his brother across the Atlantic. Gibbons likewise outlined what he regarded as labor's duties, such as keeping its organizations clear of socialists and anarchists, opposing the boycott, and holding strikes to an absolute minimum. In closing his chapter the cardinal counseled the workingmen to cultivate industry, thrift, sobriety, and above all the virtue of religion in their lives.[111]

A year and a half later Gibbons repeated a number of these same points in an article in the *North American Review* on the obligations of wealth in which he took occasion to emphasize the tremendous service rendered by the Catholic Church in the United States through its numerous agencies of charity for the poor and the downtrodden. The growth of colossal fortunes and a deepening spirit of greed in American life were signs which, he said, filled him with disquiet. He was severe on the rich who

---

[110] 88-K-4, Vallette to Gibbons, New York, February 20, 1891.
[111] *Our Christian Heritage* (Baltimore, 1889), pp. 438–455.

neglected their duty to their less fortunate brethren, and he maintained that it could safely be affirmed that "one sanctimonious miserly millionaire" in a community worked more deadly harm to Christianity than a dozen isolated cases of burglary or drunkenness.[112] In his familiar exhortation to employers and employees to co-operate in amity with one another for the common good, the cardinal gave as an example the factory of Val-des-Bois which he had visited and the work of de Mun whom he characterized as "that great Christian socialist."[113]

Just a few weeks after Gibbons' article in the *North American Review* appeared, there was published on May 15 the most famous of the social encyclicals of Pope Leo XIII entitled *Rerum novarum*. Three years before in the midst of his anxiety over the teachings of Henry George and the aftermath of the Knights of Labor case, the cardinal had suggested to Archbishop Ryan that they solicit the Holy Father to issue an encyclical on social questions for the guidance of Catholics.[114] The publication of *Rerum novarum*, therefore, filled Gibbons with joy, and on June 22 of that year he wrote the Pope his congratulations. He stated that Cardinal Manning had furnished him with an official translation of the encyclical and he hastened to thank the Pontiff for the great service which he had rendered to the Church and to society by this act of his supreme authority. Leo XIII's word, always heard with respect even outside the Church, had in this case made a very notable impression. The encyclical, precise, complete, and clear as it was, said Gibbons, had shed rays of light on the questions of property, of capital and labor, of workers' associations, and on the relations between the rich and the poor, and it was these questions which now preoccupied all serious men and which the Church alone was able to resolve in safeguarding the rights of truth, justice, and charity. Gibbons then stated:

You spoke to all the Catholic universe, but Your word, Holy

---

[112] "Wealth and Its Obligations," *North American Review*, CLII (April, 1891), 388. In his diary under the date of March 19, 1891, the cardinal wrote as follows: "Fr. Donahue deserves the chief credit for this article, as I simply furnished him with some leading thoughts & hints. He arranged & wrote the whole article" (p. 251). Patrick J. Donahue was at the time chancellor of the Archdiocese of Baltimore.

[113] *Ibid.*, p. 394.

[114] 84-H-2, Gibbons to Ryan, Baltimore, April 3, 1888.

Father, in the present circumstances is wonderfully opportune for the United States. More than anywhere else, perhaps, the workers among us sense the need of association and nowhere is honest labor more honored. But on the other hand, in our country the power of capital is enormous and it is important for the public peace and prosperity of our nation that not only all conflict be avoided, but moreover that a cordial understanding, founded on the recognition of reciprocal rights, exist between these two forces — of labor which produces and of capital which, to a certain degree, determines labor.

The cardinal went on to say that the encyclical taught the doctrine which Catholics ought to believe and indicated as well the direction which they ought to follow. He informed Leo XIII that immediately after he received the official translation he had it reprinted and sent to the most influential newspapers in the country as well as to all the bishops of the United States and of English-speaking Canada.[115]

In acknowledging Gibbons' letter a few weeks later the Pope made no allusion to the influence which the cardinal's role in the Knights of Labor may have had upon the encyclical.[116] Although an historian of fairly recent date has maintained that the conversations of men like Manning and Gibbons were welcomed by Leo XIII in the period before the encyclical as giving support to his ideas,[117] there can be advanced no clear proof that the Pope was directly influenced by Gibbons and his memorial on the Knights of Labor. True, the encyclical condemned the monopolies and called for the state to take a part in the protection of the workers as the memorial had done. Leo XIII, like Gibbons before him, recognized that the laborers were often driven to strikes to gain their just dues and both agreed on the right of workers to organize. But Leo XIII's ringing condemnation of socialism was no echo of Gibbons' remark that socialistic views in the United States were an importation from Europe,

---

[115] Vatican Archives, Gibbons to Leo XIII, Baltimore, June 22, 1891, photostat. The writer is indebted to the Right Reverend Domenico Tardini, Secretary of the Congregation for Extraordinary Ecclesiastical Affairs, for this photostat.

[116] 88-S-7, Leo XIII to Gibbons, Rome, July 9, 1891. The only evidence the writer has seen of Leo XIII's personal reaction to Gibbons' memorial on the K. of L. was contained in a letter of Bishop Keane to Cardinal Manning. Keane said, "The Pope himself has said that he had read it with pleasure, and the Cardinals say the same quite emphatically" (MP, Keane to Manning, Easter Tuesday [April 12, 1887]).

[117] Joseph Schmidlin, *Papstgeschichte der neuesten Zeit* (München, 1934), II, 371.

although the Pope's general description of the type of organization labor should take left room for Gibbons' earlier endorsement of the nonreligious associations of workmen along American lines. Yet aside from the omission of any specific credit for his work, Cardinal Gibbons was grateful for *Rerum novarum* and a quarter century later in reviewing the case of the knights he said the encyclical had been "a great consolation" to him.[118]

Regardless of the lack of any specific credit for the encyclical, the reputation of Gibbons in social questions was firmly established and continued to endure. In the fall of 1891 he was honored with Cardinal Manning in being named a member of the International Social Committee of European Catholics. In reply to the invitation to attend their meeting the cardinal regretted his inability to be present, but they were told that more than ever before the social question was "the great question" and he felt it was the Church alone that could solve the difficulties which it embraced. He was happy to say that he had asked Archbishop Ireland to represent him at their reunion and that he had accepted. He needed to furnish no introduction of Ireland since his competence in social questions, said Gibbons, was as well known in Europe as in the United States.[119] Some months later when he had to refuse a similar invitation of the Catholic Workmen's Benevolent Union in New York he sent a letter in which he praised them for commemorating Leo XIII's birthday and referred to the encyclical as "your safe and sure guide" in urging the members to spread the doctrines of *Rerum novarum*.[120] Austin Ford, editor of the *Freeman's Journal,* told Gibbons of the enthusiasm which his letter had aroused and that when the reader finished "the cheers that followed could not have been more mighty."[121]

On the occasion of Cardinal Gibbons' silver episcopal jubilee

---

[118] *A Retrospect of Fifty Years* (Baltimore, 1916), I, 190. When John Ireland preached in Baltimore on October 18, 1893, at the silver jubilee of Gibbons as a bishop he gave credit to the cardinal for a share in *Rerum novarum*. He said, "And the historic incident of the Knights of Labor, whose condemnation by the Roman Congregations Cardinal Gibbons was able to avert, exercized, I am sure, no small influence upon the preparation of the encyclical 'The Condition of Labor' " (*The Church and Modern Society*, I, 128).

[119] 89-A-5, Gibbons to Count Frederick L. Waldbottele Bassenheim, Baltimore, October 10, 1891, copy.

[120] *Catholic Review* (New York), March 12, 1892.

[121] 89-S-2, Ford to Gibbons, New York, March 19, 1892.

in 1893 the Knights of Labor of Montreal remembered their benefactor and wired their good wishes that he might live long to enable him "to continue the work of emancipation of the laboring classes."[122] Two months after the jubilee the cardinal was quoted in an interview by Raymond Blathwayt of the London *Daily Chronicle*, in which Gibbons was alleged to have said that he thought the condition of labor was improving and that public opinion was growing more favorable.[123] In view of the bloody Homestead strike of the previous year in which labor was roundly beaten and public opinion outraged, it is doubtful if Gibbons was correctly quoted. In fact, the United States was then in the throes of one of its worst outbreaks of industrial warfare, and only six months later the Pullman strike of the summer of 1894 made evident to all that peace between capital and labor was still far in the distance. When Archbishop Ireland gave an interview condemning the lawlessness of the workers in the Pullman strike, it met with Gibbons' approval. Ireland stated that he was at first puzzled as to just what he ought to say and do in the circumstances but the blessing from Baltimore had relieved him. "When you are satisfied," said Ireland, "I have no alarm about the part I may have taken." He was concerned at the number of Catholics involved in strikes and riots and it was Ireland's view that socialistic ideas had made headway with the Catholic laity and even with many priests. "We have been siding with labor in its grievances," he said, "the unthinking ones transgress the golden mean, & rush into war against property." For these reasons the archbishop told Gibbons, "I wish you would say something soon."[124] In distant France Alfred Vicomte de Meaux was alarmed at the accounts he had read of the disorders in Chicago but he viewed the situation more calmly when Gibbons sent him some additional data. De Meaux felt that the same struggle was menacing the old world as well as the new and

---

[122] 92-J-11, J. A. Rodier to Gibbons, Montreal, October 18, 1893.

[123] Reily, *Collections in the Life and Times of J. Card. Gibbons*, III, 138, quoting the London *Daily Chronicle* of December 23, 1893.

[124] 93-J-4, Ireland to Gibbons, St. Paul, July 31, 1894. Among other things Ireland had said, "Labor, too, must learn the lesson that the liberty of the citizen is to be respected. One man has the right to cease from work, but he has no right to drive another man from work." The text of the Ireland interview was reprinted by Reily, *op. cit.*, III, Part II, 120.

he was warning of the danger ahead in an article he had recently written for *Le Correspondant*.[125]

In the first year of the new century a strike was threatened among the anthracite coal miners in Pennsylvania. By this time Terence V. Powderly was commissioner general of immigration under President William McKinley. The former master workman of the Knights of Labor turned to Cardinal Gibbons in the plea that he exert himself to avert the strike which, thought Powderly, would end in sure failure for the miners. While he did not presume to tell the cardinal what to do, he only knew that in the "dark days gone by" when labor stood in sore need of justice Gibbons' voice was never silent. He offered the suggestion that the cardinal might prevail on Bishop Michael J. Hoban of Scranton to act as arbiter between the contending parties.[126] Gibbons stated that should an opportunity present itself for him to use his influence in the anthracite region he would gladly exert himself against the strike, although he did not then see his way as to the method of acting in the interest of peace.[127] Two years later when a serious strike actually occurred among the anthracite miners, the cardinal had a copy of his memorial on the Knights of Labor forwarded to President Theodore Roosevelt in the thought, as his representative said, that the President would find it of interest "at this particular moment."[128]

In the autumn of 1907 Cardinal Gibbons once more set forth his views on labor, this time in *Putnam's Monthly*. He asserted

---

[125] 93-K-4, de Meaux to Gibbons, Monbrison, Loire, August 23, 1894.

[126] Powderly Papers, Department of Archives and Manuscripts, The Catholic University of America, Powderly to Gibbons, Washington, August 29, 1900, confidential, copy.

[127] *Ibid.*, Gibbons to Powderly, Southampton, August 31, 1900. A year later when Gibbons returned from Europe and was interviewed in New York, he inquired of a reporter about the general strike in the United States Steel Corporation which had broken out on August 10, and he remarked, "I am deeply interested in this. . . . I deplore a strike of any kind, and such a one as this which unsettles business affairs, is very unfortunate. It injures the country, and before all interested have again placed themselves on a stable basis the loss is tremendous" (New York *Herald,* August 25, 1901).

[128] LC, Roosevelt Papers, D. J. Stafford to Roosevelt, Washington, November 3, 1902. For the part played by Bishop John L. Spalding in Roosevelt's commission for settling this strike, cf. Sister Mary Evangela Henthorne, "Bishop Spalding's Work on the Anthracite Coal Strike Commission," *Catholic Historical Review,* XXVIII (July, 1942), 184–205.

again the natural right of the workingman to organize for his own protection and he encouraged unions in the belief that they would lessen the dangers of the workers joining secret societies. In the main the article repeated the arguments he had used before against monopolies, with a balancing of the scales by the familiar warning to the workers of their duties and obligations to their employers. Gibbons concluded with his customary exhortation to the laboring men, inspired as he said he was by his affection for "the hardy sons of toil." Industry, economy, and law observance were urged with a special emphasis on the need for sobriety. "Intemperance," said the cardinal, "has brought more desolation to homes than famine or the sword, and is a more unrelenting tyrant than the most grasping monopolist."[129] In spite of the fact that Gibbons had said these same things over and over again they seemed to be welcomed, for years later the editor told him that his article on labor, with possibly one exception, "attracted more attention than any other article that magazine, during the few years of its publication, was privileged to print."[130]

But probably the most specific statement made by the cardinal in relation to the problems of the laboring man was spoken in a sermon delivered in his cathedral sometime before November, 1908, and entitled "Am I My Brother's Keeper?" The principal theme was man's obligation in conscience to exercise charity toward his fellow man. By way of illustrating his point, he said he wished to set before his hearers the sad plight of men and women working in the sweatshops of a number of large clothing establishments in Baltimore of which, he said, there were eighteen in one section of the city. Gibbons maintained that after careful investigation he had learned that these people were laboring for ten or twelve hours a day for six days a week and receiving as compensation only six or eight dollars a week. The shops in which they labored were contracted in size, poorly lighted and ventilated, and the preacher declared that men compelled to live on starvation wages and to labor in conditions such as these would in a few years become incapacitated for work entirely. The cardinal insisted that they did not ask for alms; all they demanded was to obtain living wages for the work they performed. They appealed to the public of Baltimore for compassion

---

[129] "Organized Labor," *Putnam's Monthly,* III (October, 1907), 67.
[130] 129-K, Joseph B. Gilder to Gibbons, New York, September 27, 1920.

and consideration and, he added, "They are our own flesh and blood." At this point Gibbons outlined for the congregation how they might help. He urged them to agitate the question and to appeal to the conscience and humanity of the employers. If they proved deaf to such an appeal then he suggested that they have recourse to more drastic measures. There were in Baltimore some clothing-house proprietors who treated their employees with justice and charity. "In making your purchases," he advised, "you can discriminate in favor of these establishments. You will thus exercise a moral pressure on the oppressors, by appealing to their self-interest." And as a final remedy he suggested that his listeners encourage and co-operate with the Consumer's League which he called an excellent society for improving conditions among the oppressed toilers. Thus in this very practical manner did Gibbons drive home the lesson of how his cathedral audience could show themselves to be their brother's keeper.[131]

In the years around the turn of the century the Catholic Church was seriously concerned about the advance of socialism. The Archbishop of Baltimore frequently spoke against the movement in addressing himself to labor questions in which, of course, he was only following the directives of Pope Leo XIII. Thus in 1911 when it was reported to Gibbons that the Labor Party in Australia was sponsoring legislation that would give the government power to take over and operate business and industry, and that in this endeavor the party enjoyed the support of the Australian Catholics, the Cardinal of Baltimore was puzzled. In his perplexity he made inquiries of Cardinal Moran, Archbishop of Sydney, and gave as a reason for American fears that if the proposed measure passed it might affect legislation in this country.[132] Moran deferred his answer until he could tell Gibbons the result of the referendum which had been greeted by the elec-

---

[131] *Discourses and Sermons for Every Sunday and the Principal Festivals of the Year* (Baltimore, 1908), pp. 19–21, for the pertinent passages. An effort to date the sermon more exactly was unsuccessful. It may have been preached during the strike of over a thousand Baltimore clothing workers in 1892 who struck for a ten-hour day, weekly payment of wages, and abolition of the task system. Although the union won no contract at this time, better conditions were obtained in general and many laborers had their working time reduced from eighteen, sixteen, or fifteen hours a day to ten hours a day and weekly payment of wages became in many instances the rule, although the sweatshops were not abolished. Cf. Hirschfeld, *Baltimore: 1870–1900. Studies in Social History*, pp. 71–72.

[132] 107-D, Gibbons to Moran, Baltimore, March 11, 1911, copy.

torate, as he said, "with a triumphant vote of *No.*" Thus the friends in whose name Gibbons had written, said Moran, could remain quite satisfied.

While the Cardinal of Sydney had welcomed the defeat of the socialist proposal, he was at pains to clear the Labor Party of any serious taint of socialism. He admitted there were a few socialists and communists among them, but the leaders who formulated policy confined their program to the principles of Christian socialism which, remarked Moran, "I consider to be quite orthodox." The Laborites, as he explained, were as a rule more friendly to Catholic interests than the Liberal Party which had leagued itself with the Orangemen and for that reason the Labor Party got many Catholic votes.[133] The person who had called the Australian situation to the attention of Gibbons was Thomas Fortune Ryan, the New York Catholic financier, who was reassured by Moran's explanation.[134] Gibbons never lost a chance to give a thrust to the evils of socialism and when a copy of the *Home Defender* containing an article on this subject was sent to him he declared the journal deserved the thanks of all friends of order in disclosing what he termed, "the dangerous tendencies of this widespread economic heresy."[135]

But if the evils of socialism and communism were to be effectively combated it would demand more than condemnations. With a view to offering a positive program of Catholic social reform modeled along the lines of the encyclical *Rerum novarum,* an enterprising priest of the Archdiocese of Cincinnati, Peter E. Dietz, was instrumental in gathering a group of Catholics interested in labor and social questions into an organization which was called the Militia of Christ for Social Service. This group was formed by Dietz in November, 1910, during the convention of the American Federation of Labor in St. Louis and had the blessing of Archbishop John J. Glennon.[136] The Militia of Christ

---

[133] 107-G, Moran to Gibbons, Sydney, May 1, 1911. In concluding his letter Cardinal Moran recalled a walk which he and Gibbons had taken in Dublin in 1869 and he remarked the many changes which had since transpired in Rome, the United States, and Ireland. For an interesting account of Moran and the Australian Catholics in their relation to the Labor Party, cf. James A. Murtagh, *Australia: The Catholic Chapter* (New York, 1946), pp. 133–184.

[134] 107-J, Ryan to Gibbons, New York, June 10, 1911.

[135] Howard-Tilton Memorial Library, Tulane University, William Beer Papers, Gibbons to Albert B. Walmsley, Baltimore, July 29, 1912.

[136] Henry J. Browne, "Peter E. Dietz, Pioneer of Catholic Social Action," *Catholic Historical Review,* XXXII (January, 1948), 448.

was disconcerted by the varying interpretations of and indifference shown by many of the clergy to *Rerum novarum,* and for that reason they sought from the hierarchy an authoritative statement that would make clear "once for all the Catholic position in the organized labor movement of this Country." Their plea was addressed to Cardinal Gibbons who assured them of his "great personal interest" in their work.[137] In pursuance of this request for an official statement from the hierarchy, Gibbons turned to William J. Kerby, professor of sociology in the Catholic University of America. Father Kerby gave it as his judgment that in view of President Wilson's anticipated appointment of a commission on industrial relations which was to study the question thoroughly, it would be preferable to postpone the hierarchy's pronouncement until the facts were uncovered by the government in order that the bishops could speak with knowledge and certainty in this very complex problem.[138] To all of this Gibbons gave his endorsement and consequently there was no statement from the hierarchy at this time.

However, the matter was given serious consideration by the American archbishops. In their meeting of April, 1911, the need for a pastoral pronouncement of the hierarchy that would offer guidance concerning the bearing of present-day movements on faith and morals was expressed, and Gibbons appointed a committee, of which Archbishop William H. O'Connell of Boston was the chairman, to draw up a draft.[139] The extant records are not entirely clear as to precisely what was intended in the pastoral but, at any rate, O'Connell worked out a lengthy statement on the relations of the Church to labor which he submitted for Gibbons' approval. The Archbishop of Boston confessed that he found it no easy task and that the more he studied the question the more complex and involved it proved to be. O'Connell protested his unwillingness to have the statement he was forwarding published as the official position of the Church, and he said he frankly believed it would be a mistake to give out a letter to the public over the name of anyone occupying the office of an archbishop. His only intention at the moment was that the enclosed paper might serve as rough material from which to draft a state-

---

137 *Ibid.,* p. 455.
138 109-G, Kerby to Gibbons, Washington, June 10, 1913.
139 107-F, Minutes of the Meeting of the Archbishops, Washington, April 27, 1911.

ment that could later be submitted to the archbishops for their approval.[140] Meanwhile the difficulties involved in framing an official pronouncement of the American Church on labor, together with the distractions occasioned by World War I, deferred the fulfillment of the desire of the Militia of Christ until early in 1919.

Shortly before the entry of the United States into the European conflict the Union Pacific Railroad adopted a system of life insurance and insurance for sickness and accidents for its thousands of employees. The Railway Executives' Advisory Committee sent Ballard Dunn to Baltimore to interview the cardinal on the new plan of the Union Pacific. Gibbons gave his hearty approval to the scheme, and what especially impressed him was the stimulation it would offer to the workers to put forth their best efforts in the interest of themselves and their company. As he expressed it, "The employee will work more eagerly if he has a stake in the final goal for which the industry is striving."[141] Gibbons used the opportunity to condemn in vigorous language the suggestion of government ownership of the railroads which, he thought, would be contrary to the spirit of the American people. Such a move, said the cardinal, would build up a central power that would use the employees for political purposes and would bring about corruption of the worst character. In closing the interview he referred to his constant friendliness to the laboring men and their organizations, but he added, "I oppose them when they overreach themselves." In recalling his work for the Knights of Labor thirty years before he said, "My attitude then and now and the many things which I have written and preached along these lines, I feel, give me the right to voice these opinions."[142]

Late that same year a Montreal lawyer by the name of Bernard Rose said that in a discussion recently held in that city on the subject of labor unions and the right of women to organize, Cardinal Gibbons had been represented as favoring unions even for women, but that an opponent had as emphatically declared that the cardinal was against unions and was especially opposed to organizing women wage earners. Since it was stated that Gibbons' views might influence the action of those who contemplated

[140] 109-Q, O'Connell to Gibbons, Boston, February 17, 1914.
[141] "A Human Side of the Railways. An Authorized Interview with Cardinal Gibbons," *The Outlook*, CXV (February 28, 1917), 354.
[142] *Ibid.*, p. 354.

the unionizing of women in a Montreal industry, he was asked to give his opinion.[143] The cardinal's secretary replied in his name that he had approved the organization of labor more than thirty years before and the laboring man or woman had, in his mind, the same right to unite in the promotion of their material welfare as the capitalist had to better his business interests.[144]

To the very end of his life the Archbishop of Baltimore continued to interest himself in the affairs of labor and to respond to the requests that were frequently made of him for an expression of his views. On Christmas Eve of 1918 he gave out an optimistic interview to a reporter of the Baltimore *Sun* in which he rejoiced that for the first time in five years the world would celebrate Christmas at peace. Gibbons said he realized that many were concerned about the labor situation in the United States during the period of adjustment to peacetime living that lay ahead. As for himself, he entertained no fears on that score. He had every confidence in the intelligence and common sense of the American workers; they knew their lot was better than that of the workingman in other countries and they knew, too, that a social upheaval would bear more heavily upon them than upon any other class in the community. As for the spread of socialism in the United States, the cardinal now assumed a more assured tone than he had shown in previous years. He said, "I feel no apprehension whatever." Every socialist in the land knew in his heart that the grievances in this country warranted no revolution and the workers knew it, too. For that reason Gibbons had no fear that the laboring classes would be led astray to their own undoing by the specious doctrines of socialism. The shift in his thought was reflected in the sole fear which he expressed regarding the future, namely, what he called "the consolidating of control of the great public interests of the country in the authorities of the Government itself." On this point the cardinal felt some misgiving, and he closed his interview with a strong statement against government control of railroads, the telegraph, and other public utilities. As he said, the American government had made provision for a system of checks and balances and it had proved a good one; therefore, it should be allowed to stand.[145]

---

[143] 116-E, Rose to Gibbons, Montreal, November 1, 1917.
[144] 116-E, Eugene J. Connelly to Rose, Baltimore, November 4, 1917, copy.
[145] Baltimore *Sun*, December 25, 1918.

The attack on government ownership drew favorable comments from several sources. Clarence H. Mackay, president of the Postal Telegraph-Cable Company, was gratified at Gibbons' warning against what he regarded as the tendency toward socialism, a movement which he believed was advocated by those whose motives were insidious and whose only supporters were the unthinking.[146] A non-Catholic lawyer in Philadelphia shared these views and wanted Gibbons to know how much he appreciated what he termed "the splendid and statesmanlike address" of Christmas Eve. Many feared the swing of the pendulum too far in the direction of radicalism, and for that reason the cardinal's warning word about the evil of government control of industries and utilities would prove most helpful.[147]

With the end of World War I and the pressing problems which confronted the United States as it returned to a peacetime basis, there were a number of social-minded American Catholics who felt there was an imperative need for an official statement from the American bishops that would offer guidance in these matters. The request of the Militia of Christ of seven years before had gone unfulfilled but the necessity for an authoritative pronouncement seemed now to be even more urgent. Through the authorship of Father John A. Ryan, professor of moral theology in the Catholic University of America, and the management of Father John O'Grady, secretary of the Committee on Special War Activities of the National Catholic War Council, such a statement was produced and submitted to the administrative committee of bishops of the War Council. These bishops had been named by Cardinal Gibbons at the time the United States entered the war and their activities were still in progress during the first years of peace. The prelates made their own the text submitted to them, and on February 12, 1919, there was issued what was officially entitled, "Social Reconstruction: A General Review of the Problems and Survey of Remedies."[148] The statement contained a set of proposals for solving social and labor questions which at that date were thought very advanced. It called among other things for minimum wage legislation, public housing for the working

146 119-W, Mackay to Gibbons, New York, December 27, 1918.

147 119-XYZ, Ira J. Williams to Gibbons, Philadelphia, December 28, 1918.

148 For the details concerning the origin and contents of the document, cf. John A. Ryan, *Social Doctrine in Action. A Personal History* (New York, 1941), pp. 143–158.

classes, effective control of monopolies, progressive taxes on income, inheritance, and excess profits, the establishment of co-operatives, and the participation of labor in management with a wider distribution of ownership through co-operative enterprises and worker ownership in the stock of corporations.

For such far-reaching proposals to be made over the signatures of four Catholic bishops was regarded in 1919 as little short of revolutionary. In all that led up to the publication of the statement Gibbons had played no direct part, except that he had appointed the bishops to the committee two years before and had shown every confidence in the way they had handled their difficult assignment. At any rate, when it came time to protest it was to Gibbons that a number of people turned in the hope that he would offer some kind of brake upon what they viewed as a dangerous departure on the part of these prelates. Among those who registered their surprise with the cardinal over the bishops' statement on social reconstruction was Stephen C. Mason, president of the National Association of Manufacturers. Mason wanted to know if the document had come to Gibbons' attention and received any detailed consideration from him. He felt the treatment accorded business problems was not impartial in nature, conciliatory in phraseology, and not entirely accurate in fact. The worried official of the N.A.M. stated that it was generally assumed that the Catholic Church was opposed to socialism, but he believed a careful reading of the bishops' statement would lead Gibbons to the same conclusion he had reached, namely, that it involved what might prove to be a covert effort to disseminate what he termed "partisan, pro-labor union, socialistic propaganda under the official insignia of the Roman Catholic Church in America." For that reason Mason would appreciate an expression of opinion from the cardinal on the subject.[149] But he was destined to be disappointed, for over the back of his letter a secretary wrote in, "Not yet read article & so knows nothing of it except what he has heard."

Another correspondent expressing concern was Vincent Wehrle, O.S.B., Bishop of Bismarck, who urged Gibbons to appoint soon

---

[149] 120-N, Mason to Gibbons, New York, February 25, 1919. An effort to find Gibbons' reply to Mason was unsuccessful. Vada Harsch of the staff of the N.A.M. offices in New York answered the writer's inquiry on April 25, 1949, to say, "I . . . can find no mention of any exchange of correspondence between Mr. Stephen C. Mason and Cardinal Gibbons. . . ."

a committee of the hierarchy that would make public a declaration that the Church was opposed to that type of capitalism which was nothing more than naturalism and rationalism carried into commercial life, but likewise to socialism in all its diverse forms. Wehrle said that the people of his diocese were being misled by agitators who declared that the bishops of the N.C.W.C. were in favor of their own program, namely, a socialistic state. For that reason the bishop wanted an authoritative pronouncement that would meet this assertion.[150] There is no evidence that Gibbons ever sought to have an additional statement issued by the hierarchy either to give further interpretation or to offset in any way the program which the bishops had published in February, 1919.

The last recorded utterance of Cardinal Gibbons on the subject of labor was addressed to the wage earners of his own State of Maryland. It had been solicited by one of the staff of the Baltimore *Trades-Unionist,* the official organ of the Baltimore Council Building Trades Department of the American Federation of Labor, in the belief that it would prove beneficial for their use on Labor Day.[151] In responding to this request less than a year before his death, the cardinal employed parts of previous statements he had made on the subject in deploring the technique of the strike to win labor's goals and in advocating a fair and impartial tribunal to examine and decide upon differences between employers and their workers. He urged again a living wage for labor, a wage, as he expressed it, "which will keep the workingman and his family in comfort." What the country needed then, in the cardinal's mind, was more production — mechanical, industrial, and agricultural — but there would not be more production, he said, without a full day's labor. The spiritual note of Christ's example was not forgotten when he told the Maryland laborers, "I cannot conceive any thought better calculated to ease the yoke and to lighten the burden of the Christian toiler than the reflection that the highest type of manhood has voluntarily devoted Himself to manual labor."[152]

---

[150] 121-M, Wehrle to Gibbons, Bismarck, May 8, 1919. An effort to find Gibbons' reply to Wehrle was not successful. William F. Garvin, chancellor of the Diocese of Bismarck, in answer to an inquiry replied on August 11, 1949, "Bishop Wehrle did not keep a complete record of his correspondence at that time and, therefore, I am afraid we must presume the records were destroyed."

[151] 127-N, William Sweiger to Gibbons, Baltimore, June 4, 1920.

[152] 127-W, Gibbons to the A. F. of L., Baltimore, June 28, 1920, copy.

At the time Cardinal Gibbons penned his message to the Maryland members of the A. F. of L. he was eighty-six years of age and could look back upon more than thirty years of effort in labor's behalf. It had been by a somewhat fortuitous circumstance that he had found himself the central figure of a crisis in the relations between the American Church and the most powerful labor organization of that day. Although Gibbons brought to his task no professional or technical knowledge of labor economics, he was endowed with a heart that warmed to the workers' cause and a burning conviction that the Church must never be isolated from the interests which justice accorded to the sons of toil. To these qualities were added an uncommon ability to sense the drift of current trends and a happy instinct that guided him in directing the course of the Church's action so that its function as an arbiter of morals would be played to the fullest possible advantage. In a day when monopolies were tightening their grip upon the lives of thousands of American workers, when the so-called "Gilded Age" was revealing some of the worst aspects of an unrestrained capitalism, to abet the condemnation of the Knights of Labor would have brought the cardinal the plaudits of the rich and the powerful. Moreover, at a time when *Rerum novarum* had not yet appeared and many Catholic bishops and priests were highly conservative in their social views, such a policy on Gibbons' part would have earned the praise of a large number within his own Church. Judging the case solely on the grounds of the canonical measures enacted to ferret out secret societies, plausible reasons could have been found — as they were in the case of the Canadian knights — for a condemnation. But the signal character of Gibbons' contribution was that he refused to be bound by any narrow canonical interpretation and insisted upon viewing the case in the broadest possible manner in the implications it would have for the future of American Catholicism.

To have assumed the stand he did on the Knights of Labor in 1887 required courage of the first order. Gibbons fully recognized the significance of his action. Writing of it thirty years later he remarked that at the time it seemed to many that he and the bishops who agreed with him were destroying the reputation of the Church as a conserver of society, that, as he expressed it, "we Bishops of the Church of God were making of ourselves demagogues and the harbingers of the 'Red Revolution.' "[153] But he adhered tenaciously to his policy, and on the subject of the knights, as on few other things in his life, this ordinarily mild man displayed an unrelenting firmness that withstood every effort, no matter from what quarter, to deflect him from his goal. Nor did he change his mind about his policy on the knights in after years. Near the end of his life Gibbons was asked to write some of his reminiscences for the *Dublin Review*. From a rich life of over eighty years that had been crowded with actions of a striking character he chose to speak of three of his experiences that were most memorable. They were the Civil War, the Vatican Council, and the Knights of Labor. Referring to the knights he said:

> I can never forget the anxiety and distress of mind of those days. If the Knights of Labour were not condemned by the Church, then the Church ran the risk of combining against herself every element of wealth and power. . . . But if the Church did not protect the working men she would have been false to her whole history; and this the Church can never be.[154]

Of all the many distinguished services which Cardinal Gibbons rendered to his Church and his country the championship of the Knights of Labor won for him the most enduring fame and the most grateful remembrance. As Bishop Wilhelm Emmanuel von Ketteler of Mainz had given both spirit and sustenance to the German Catholic social movement by his various activities and by his book, *Der Arbeiterfrage und das Christentum* (Mainz, 1864), and as Cardinal Manning by his written and spoken word and the leading role he played in the settlement of the London dock workers' strike of 1889 furnished an enlightened leadership to the Catholic Church in England, so did the work of Gibbons for the K. of L. give a new direction to American Catholics in their attitude toward the world of labor. In all the efforts he put forth in this cause from the time he first espoused the knights in the autumn of 1886 through the many pronouncements he made on

---

[153] *A Retrospect of Fifty Years,* I, X.

[154] "My Memories," *Dublin Review,* CLX (April, 1917), 171. At this point Gibbons paid tribute to the help he had received in the case of the knights from Cardinal Manning who, he said, "fought with me shoulder to shoulder for the rights of the Christian Plebs."

labor in the succeeding thirty-five years, Gibbons never approached it in any other light than as a problem with a deep moral significance in which, as a guide in the realm of morals, he felt he had a right to speak. While many of his utterances were of a general character, the prestige which he had gained with the American public gave to them a value and a significance which went far beyond their literal sense.

Cardinal Gibbons' reputation as a molder of Catholic thought on social questions was quickly insured once the full import of his memorial of 1887 had become known. It was only a few years after this time that the cardinal's distinguished fellow townsman, Richard T. Ely, professor of political economy in the Johns Hopkins University, published a volume in which he made a brief allusion to Catholic teaching on social problems. After paying tribute to Ketteler and Manning, he remarked that anyone who wished to familiarize himself with the attitudes of the Catholic Church on social questions should not overlook what he called Gibbons' "remarkable letter" on the Knights of Labor.[155] Two years before the cardinal's death Bishop Frederick W. Keating of Northampton told him that he had spent much time during the previous two months in the company of Gibbons' writings. He enjoyed them all, but he thought his plea for organized labor particularly fine and eminently reasonable in that period of renewed labor troubles.[156] More than half a century after Gibbons' defense of the Knights of Labor, Monsignor John A. Ryan, the distinguished moral theologian who had attained national fame for his work and writings on social questions, referred to this episode and said, "One of the first and also one of the most enduring contributions to my social education was provided by James Cardinal Gibbons." Ryan recalled that the last time he saw the cardinal was at Trinity College in Washington about a year before his death when the old churchman described at some length for Ryan and Dr. Kerby of the Catholic University of America his efforts in Rome to prevent the knights' condemnation. How dear to his heart these efforts had been was strikingly apparent to Ryan in the intensity of feeling which he displayed on that occasion which was over thirty

---

155 Richard T. Ely, *Socialism and Social Reform* (New York, 1894), p. 106.
156 120-H, Keating to Gibbons, Northampton, February 10, 1919.

years after the event. "He was a truly great man, was Cardinal
Gibbons," Ryan remarked, "and no small part of his greatness
was due to his social vision."[157]

The influence of the cardinal's action and writing lived, therefore, long beyond the time of the occasion that had called them
forth. They can be said to have offered the most striking contribution which came from the United States to the congeries of
events leading up to Leo XIII's encyclical, *Rerum novarum,* of
1891 and to the Catholic social movement of the twentieth century. At home the action of the cardinal in this instance helped
to shape the policy of the American Church toward labor unions
in the years ahead, and those who know something of the pattern
which developed will agree with the judgment of a leading American historian when he wrote, "The attitude of the Roman Catholic clergy toward the labor problem was greatly influenced by the
course of Cardinal Gibbons of Baltimore."[158]

---

[157] Ryan, *op. cit.,* pp. 18, 20–21.

[158] Arthur Meier Schlesinger, "A Critical Period in American Religion, 1875–
1900," *Proceedings of the Massachusetts Historical Society,* LXIV (1932), 542.

CHAPTER XIII

The Case of Henry George and Dr. McGlynn

THE second major social question in which Cardinal Gibbons was destined to play a prominent, if somewhat reluctant, role was the controversy which centered itself around the economic theories of Henry George and the advocacy of those theories by Dr. Edward McGlynn. In the turbulent years of the late nineteenth century when the evils of industrial society were making themselves felt with increasing rigor, it was natural enough that various panaceas should be offered to break the power of the monopolies and trusts and to mitigate the distress of the masses. Among these reform movements George's was closely related to the Knights of Labor, and like the knights it had for a time an important bearing on the Catholic Church of the United States. As with the knights, so in this case the immediate importance of the problem for the Church was of brief duration, but its implications were of more than passing significance and the final settlement of the question helped to shape the pattern which the American Church was to follow toward social problems in the years ahead.

It was in 1879 that there appeared from the pen of the self-made economist and reformer, Henry George, a volume entitled *Progress and Poverty*. Having experienced severe privation in his early years as a wandering journalist, George began a serious study of the ills of the industrial system with a view to finding a remedy. His observations in California and New York, and the things he read and heard on his many trips across the continent, convinced him of the evils of the capitalist order, and of the pressing need for reform lest the national wealth be diverted into even fewer hands and the poverty of the masses be rendered more acute. With this in mind George worked out an elaborate thesis in which land and its possession occupied a key position.

547

He contended that men were entitled to their fair share of land in the same manner that they were to water and air and any system which denied them access to the land was undemocratic. In order to eliminate the inequities of landholding, George proposed a land tax adjusted in such a way that the gain, or what was termed the "unearned increment" accruing by reason of advantageous location and the growth of a community, would be taken away. To the young reformer economic rent was a form of robbery and by virtue of having to pay such rent all elements of society received less return from their labors than was their due. George would, therefore, siphon off this economic rent in taxation and then abolish all other forms of contribution to the government. Land would not have to be distributed, so he said, but only its economic rent would be taken away. This system would eliminate monopolies since they would be grounded in appropriation of land values and thus, according to George, would there likewise disappear the periodic industrial depressions which afflicted American economy. In the end the single tax would, in his judgment, yield so much revenue to government that it could take over the railroads and telegraphs and inaugurate a vast program of other social services for the general populace.

While no one could honestly deny the abuses which the monopolies had created, the scheme put forth by Henry George contained a number of features which rendered it impracticable, and the very strong emphasis which he placed on land being the common property of all frightened many at a time when the growing menace of socialism appeared to be more than a distant cloud on the horizon. Although the American reformer had borrowed a number of his ideas from English forerunners like John Stuart Mill and Herbert Spencer, the publication of *Progress and Poverty* was the first opportunity for thousands of American readers to become acquainted with the promising theories of the single tax. The book enjoyed a tremendous vogue and the energetic crusade of its author in the United States, the British Isles, and elsewhere served to spread its message to an immense audience. When George sailed for Ireland in October, 1881, as a correspondent of the *Irish World* of New York, he was carrying his campaign to a country which was then in the midst of another of its recurrent tumults over the land question. George's affiliation with the Irish land leaguers not only brought him into contact with Michael Davitt and other Irish agitators of the period, but served to focus upon him the close scrutiny of Catholic bishops and priests both in the United States and Ireland who were deeply concerned over the settlement of the Irish land question.

Although there were doubtless many American Catholic readers of *Progress and Poverty,* it is safe to say that the author and his economic doctrines would never have become a problem to the Church had it not been for the stanch ally whom George found in Edward McGlynn, pastor of St. Stephen's Church in New York City.[1] Dr. McGlynn's first years in the priesthood were spent as an assistant to Father Thomas Farrell of St. Joseph's Church on Sixth Avenue. Farrell had been noted for his vigorous fight against slavery, and the interest of the older priest in social betterment no doubt had a good deal to do with attracting young McGlynn to a study of questions of this kind. In 1866 McGlynn was named pastor of St. Stephen's, then one of the most populous parishes in the entire country, and here he was daily brought face to face with the problem of unemployment and its attendant difficulties. It was the urge to get at the roots of the widespread unemployment he found among his parishioners that prompted him to a study of economic problems, and ultimately to an acceptance of the single tax doctrines of Henry George. McGlynn was a man of very strong convictions and he often held views which were quite unconventional for a Catholic clergyman. For example, as early as 1870 he had drawn the frowns of many of his colleagues by his open championing of public schools as against parochial schools in an interview which was published in the New York *Sun* on April 30 of that year.

In the intervening time McGlynn took up with the George movement and the arrival of Michael Davitt in the United States afforded the priest an occasion to give public expression to his

---

[1] There is no satisfactory biography of McGlynn. One of the most fully documented accounts of the controversy is to be found in Zwierlein, *The Life and Letters of Bishop McQuaid,* III, 1–83. Stephen Bell, *Rebel, Priest and Prophet. A Biography of Dr. Edward McGlynn* (New York, 1937) is not a definitive work and makes no use of the unpublished material in the archives of the Archdiocese of New York. These accounts can be supplemented by the brief sketch of McGlynn by John A. Ryan in the *Dictionary of American Biography,* XII, 53–54; for Henry George, cf. Broadus Mitchell's account, *ibid.,* VII, 211–215.

views on the single tax when he spoke at a meeting in August, 1882, in behalf of the Irish land leaguers. In this speech McGlynn espoused without reservation the teachings of George as a solution for the ills of the masses in the United States as well as in Ireland.[2] His views were reported to Rome and called forth a statement from Cardinal Simeoni to McGlynn's superior, Cardinal McCloskey, that the priest's utterances on the rights of property were socialistic in character and that he should, therefore, be reprimanded and if necessary suspended. McCloskey conferred with McGlynn and won a promise that he would make no further public addresses on the subject. There the matter was allowed to rest for the remainder of McCloskey's life, but when he died in October, 1885, he was succeeded in the See of New York by Michael A. Corrigan who took a much graver view of McGlynn's participation in the affairs of Henry George. The new archbishop's attitude became known when McGlynn, considering himself freed from the promise by the death of McCloskey, renewed his activities in the single tax crusade.

The occasion which brought a crisis in the relations of the archbishop and the pastor was the bid made by Henry George in the autumn of 1886 for the office of Mayor of New York. When it became known to Corrigan that McGlynn intended to address a rally of the Labor Party backing the George candidacy in Chickering Hall on October 1, the archbishop forbade him to do so. The priest refused to obey the command of his superior and as a consequence on the day following the meeting he was suspended from his priestly functions for a period of two weeks. While George was defeated in the election he made a surprisingly strong showing, and in the wave of enthusiasm that swept over his followers McGlynn enjoyed a major share of attention. Although the suspension of the priest did not become known immediately, the strained relations with his superior were ultimately found out with the result that the whole unpleasant story was widely aired in the press of New York and other cities during the ensuing months. Several weeks after the election Archbishop Corrigan, in pursuance of what he regarded as his duty to guide the faithful of his jurisdiction, issued a pastoral letter on November 19, 1886, at the close of the fifth synod of the Archdiocese of New York. The letter dealt with a number of subjects

---

[2] Bell, *op. cit.*, pp. 26–27.

but its principal emphasis was devoted to a defense of the right of private property. Corrigan vindicated the ownership of private property as a right founded on the natural law, and in support of his position he included a lengthy quotation from the encyclical of Pope Leo XIII, *Quod apostolici muneris,* of December, 1878, in which the Pontiff had stressed that right against the errors of socialism. Although he did not mention any names, it was obvious that the archbishop's pastoral was directed against what he regarded as the errors in the teaching of Henry George and his single tax advocates.[3]

In view of the amount of publicity given to the differences between Archbishop Corrigan and Father McGlynn — and their relations grew steadily worse with the priest's defiance of his superior — it would have been impossible for Cardinal Gibbons to remain unaware of the trouble that had arisen in New York. As was to be expected, however, the cardinal took no cognizance of the matter, since regardless of what views he may have held, it was entirely outside his jurisdiction. When the pastoral letter of the Archbishop of New York appeared its author had a copy sent immediately to Gibbons. The cardinal thanked Corrigan for his thoughtfulness and said that while he had not had time to read the pastoral thoroughly he had seen enough of it to appreciate its merits, and he felt that the remarks on land and private property were well timed and would go far to counteract the evil effects of loose utterances on the subject.[4] A few days later Gibbons relayed to Corrigan the favorable impression made by the pastoral on a number of clergymen to whom the cardinal had spoken, and he said that it had been applauded by the Baltimore press with the *Sun* publishing it *in extenso* and devoting a highly laudatory editorial to it.[5]

Meanwhile matters were going from bad to worse in New York. When McGlynn refused to cease his public addresses on the single tax he was suspended a second time and on December 6 there came a summons to Rome, a command which he likewise refused to obey. McGlynn maintained that there was nothing in George's teaching or his own that was contrary to the Church's

---

[3] Zwierlein, *op. cit.,* III, 7–11, reprints the leading passages of the pastoral pertaining to private property.
[4] AANY, Gibbons to Corrigan, Wilmington, Delaware, November 20, 1886.
[5] *Ibid.,* Gibbons to Corrigan, Baltimore, November 24, 1886.

doctrines. Until his suspension was lifted he would not comply with the orders of his archbishop or the Holy See, since to do so would be to give a tacit admission of the correctness of his superiors' action in penalizing him for views which he insisted were not in error. After discussing the matter with his consultors, Archbishop Corrigan on January 14, 1887, removed McGlynn from the pastorate of St. Stephen's Church and named Father Arthur J. Donnelly to succeed him.[6] On the day of the consultors' second meeting Corrigan explained for Gibbons the intransigeance of McGlynn in reaffirming his adherence to the doctrines of George and alleging futile reasons by way of excuse for not going to Rome, to which the archbishop added a request for a remembrance of the priest in the cardinal's prayers.[7]

All during the month of December there was tremendous excitement among the numerous friends and admirers of McGlynn, with the result that the press enjoyed a rare opportunity for lively reporting, even if much of it was founded on nothing more than rumor. For example, when the four eastern archbishops assembled at Philadelphia on December 16 for the hurriedly called meeting occasioned by the Abbelen petition of the Germans, some papers missed the point of the conference entirely and read into it the trouble over the Knights of Labor and McGlynn. The Cincinnati *Enquirer* of December 17 admitted that the archbishops' conference was a secret one, but that did not prevent them from hazarding the belief that Corrigan's suspension of McGlynn had formed "the leading subject" of the meeting. Archbishop Elder, who was aware of the real reason for the meeting in Philadelphia, denied that it had anything to do with the McGlynn case or the Knights of Labor and passed it off as a conference which dealt with certain questions that called for an exchange of views since the last plenary council of Baltimore.[8] The misleading news item in the Cincinnati *Enquirer* was

---

[6] AMSMC, There is a nineteen-page summary here on the meetings of the consultors of the Archdiocese of New York held on December 1 and 20, 1886, which was written by Patrick F. McSweeny, pastor of St. Bridget's Church, New York, and a consultor, to his brother, Edward F. X. McSweeny, a professor at Emmitsburg. McSweeny opposed the removal of McGlynn from his pastorate out of fear of the consequences that might ensue from McGlynn's numerous admirers among the masses.

[7] 82-H-8, Corrigan to Gibbons, New York, December 20, 1886.

[8] 82-I-7, Elder to Gibbons, Cincinnati, Christmas, 1886.

only a minor instance of how inaccurate and partisan reporting of the McGlynn case in the newspapers at this time made matters much more difficult. Those who were seeking a peaceful solution of the trouble had to contend with the fact that many of the priest's followers did not take the pains to verify the accuracy of what they read.

Up to the time of his departure for Rome in late January, 1887, to receive the red hat, Cardinal Gibbons had taken no part in the controversy over Henry George and Edward McGlynn. About a week before his departure he thanked Archbishop Corrigan for his invitation to be his guest while in New York. Although the acceptance of a previous invitation from Major Keiley of Brooklyn would prevent him from stopping with the archbishop, he assured Corrigan that the major share of his time on the Thursday before sailing would be given to him. Gibbons was likewise grateful for the copies of George's new publishing venture, the weekly *Standard,* which had begun publication on January 8 and which Corrigan's secretary had directed to Baltimore. In closing he told the archbishop, "I hope that God will give Your Grace strength to pass through the present trying ordeal."[9] A week later Gibbons was in New York where he received a visit at Keiley's home from the Reverend Richard L. Burtsell, pastor of the Church of the Epiphany and close friend and legal adviser of McGlynn. According to Burtsell's own account of the interview, he spent an hour with Gibbons going over all the details of the case and explaining that McGlynn refused to go to Rome since he believed he had been condemned without a hearing. Burtsell stated that the cardinal remarked he did not know McGlynn personally but that he had formed a high opinion of his character, that he had introduced a

9 AANY, Gibbons to Corrigan, Baltimore, January 20, 1887. A few days before he wrote Corrigan the cardinal had word from Bishop Moore who had recently been to New York. Moore felt blunders had been made on both sides. McGlynn had disobeyed and in that none attempted to defend him, but his suspension was not based on disobedience but on the supposed heterodoxy of George's land theories which he was ordered to retract and refused to do. The knowledge of the whole affair to the public came from Corrigan, not McGlynn, and, according to Moore, the archbishop telegraphed the New York *Tribune* that McGlynn had been ordered to Rome which, said Moore, was a grave error. If the case were brought to a formal trial in Rome, the Bishop of St. Augustine thought McGlynn would probably be reinstated. But so far he had remained passive, would not see his friends, and had declined to see Bishops O'Connor and Moore on the plea of illness (82-L-10, Moore to Gibbons, St. Augustine, January 15, 1887).

number of distinguished Baltimoreans to him, and that as far as the land theory was concerned, it was a very complicated and debatable subject. It was Gibbons' advice at this meeting that Burtsell should urge McGlynn to go to Rome and explain his views to the ecclesiastical authorities. The cardinal was quoted as saying he was glad to hear Burtsell's explanation, that he would use it at Rome where the question would be thoroughly investigated, and that he should tell McGlynn that Gibbons would see to it that if he consented to answer the summons of the Holy See as soon as he was again in good health he would go not on trial but to unfold a principle.[10]

Long before Gibbons reached the Eternal City, of course, the Roman officials had been made aware of the difficulties in the Archdiocese of New York. John Ireland, who had been in Rome for over two months, expressed his sympathy to Corrigan in the McGlynn case, as well as his astonishment that the man should have shown himself so disobedient and obstinate. As he said, "Had he come to Rome when called, how much scandal would have been avoided."[11] Three days after his arrival in Rome on February 13 the Cardinal of Baltimore had his first audience of Leo XIII during which the Pope raised the question of McGlynn. The Holy Father expressed his anxiety about the matter and mentioned McGlynn's refusal to come to Rome on the score of illness, adding that perhaps he was afraid to come, although the Pope made it clear that the case had not yet been judged by the Holy See. Leo XIII then instructed Gibbons to write to McGlynn and urge him to obey the summons. On the following evening Gibbons had an interview with Cardinal Simeoni in which the same wish was expressed to have McGlynn appear before the Roman authorities. All of this the Archbishop of Baltimore explained to Corrigan, and he added:

> In obedience to the H. Father's command, I will send a brief letter today detailing without note or comment the H. Father's conversation. As I do not know Dr. McGlynn's address, I will send the letter to the care of Dr. Burtsell.
>
> Whatever may be the upshot of his visit, I am sure you need have no fears of his being sent back to St. Stephen's. I told Canon

---

[10] AANY, Burtsell Letterbook, account of interview with Gibbons, January 28, 1887, pp. 332–338.

[11] *Ibid.*, Ireland to Corrigan, Rome, February 5, 1887.

Sparetti [*sic*] that this was out of the question, & said the same to the Cardinal [Simeoni], & if it were necessary I would say the same to the H. Father himself. His return to St. Stephen's would simply destroy your moral influence, & destroy Episcopal authority. Before I leave Rome, I will see to it that there is no fear on this score. But I have no apprehensions at all in the matter.[12]

True to his word, Gibbons on the same day sent the letter to Burtsell in which he refrained from adding any comment to the summary of his conversation with Leo XIII except to say in conclusion, "I may add that the Holy Father's and the Cardinal's words were expressed with paternal kindness."[13]

In the midst of the efforts which Gibbons and his colleagues, Ireland and Keane, were exerting that winter in Rome in behalf of the projected university and the Knights of Labor and to forestall the Abbelen petition concerning the German Catholics in the United States, the question of the teachings of Henry George took a turn that required their closer vigilance. After reaching Rome, Gibbons learned that there was a disposition in some circles of the curia to put the writings of George on the *Index of Prohibited Books*. The cardinal was decidedly opposed to such a move since he regarded it as being neither opportune nor useful. With that in mind he prepared a memorial on the question for Cardinal Simeoni in which he summarized his objections under four main headings. Gibbons contended that George was not the originator of his theories touching the right of property in land. Similar ideas had been expressed by Spencer and Mill and the world would judge it rather singular if the Holy See were to attack the work of one whom Gibbons called "a humble American artisan" instead of condemning the writings of his masters; however, if it was thought that the Holy See had a duty to condemn Spencer and Mill it would seem prudent to consult first with Cardinals Manning and Newman. Second, the cardinal pointed out that George's theories differed from those of communism and socialism, and in proof of his point he quoted the definition of com-

---

12 *Ibid.*, Gibbons to Corrigan, Rome, February 18, 1887, *Personal*.

13 *Ibid.*, Burtsell Letterbook, Gibbons to Burtsell, Rome, February 18, 1887, copy, pp. 2–3. One slight variation from Gibbons' summary to Corrigan was contained in his letter to Burtsell. In relating Leo XIII's remark that McGlynn may have been influenced against the trip to Rome by a fear of condemnation, Gibbons added to McGlynn's friend, "I replied that he may have had just grounds for apprehension as rumors were spread that his case was judged in Rome."

munism given by Valentino Steccanella in a work published by the Propaganda press five years before. In counterdistinction to communism's abolition of private property and the concentration of all goods in the hands of the state, Gibbons cited the doctrines of George in support of the absolute ownership of all the fruits of one's labors. Only in the matter of land, explained the cardinal, did George set a limitation on ownership by an extension of the *supremum dominium* of the state, and in this case he did not teach that the actual proprietors should be dispossessed but that a change in the system of taxation should be effected so that taxes should come from the land only and not from the fruits of industry.

At this point Gibbons stated that anyone who had studied the question of the relation of the state to the right of land ownership and its regulation by the laws of taxation, must recognize how complicated the subject was and how it would not admit of solution by a trenchant sentence from ecclesiastical authority. Moreover, the question was already before the American public in the political arena and there it would speedily find its end. George himself admitted his scheme could be put into operation only through legislation, and Gibbons maintained that it was certain no Congress would ever enact laws introducing such profound changes in social relations, nor would any President sign such a measure. In a country like the United States doctrinaires and visionaries, said the cardinal, did not get very far and, therefore, one could leave them alone with the certainty that their ideas would die of themselves. Under the third heading Gibbons alluded without mentioning names to the recent excitement in New York. He told Simeoni that he knew better than he did how necessary it was when there was a duty to speak the truth, that the times and circumstances be chosen for its expression in a way that would produce salutary results rather than fatal consequences. It would appear evident then, said Gibbons, that even if there was a certain need for a condemnation of the works of Henry George this would not be the time to do it. Finally he invoked the moral principle that a sentence should not be issued when the consequences would probably be contrary rather than favorable to the good end proposed. Gibbons held it as certain that if the writings of George were condemned it would give to them an importance that they would never otherwise enjoy and would excite the curiosity of readers so that thousands of additional copies would be sold, and thus the very influences which the condemnation sought to check and restrain would be immensely extended. Since this was a case that involved a practical people like the Americans in whose genius there was found little or no place for bizarre and impractical ideas, it seemed to the Cardinal of Balitmore, as he told Simeoni in conclusion, that prudence suggested that fallacies and absurdities be allowed to perish of themselves and that the tribunals of the Church not run the risk of giving to them an artificial life and importance.[14]

There was a good deal of similarity between the reasoning of Gibbons in the present case and that which he used in the memorial on the Knights of Labor which he had signed five days before. In both instances the cardinal revealed his distaste for measures of a harsh and negative character, and in both cases he correctly guessed that the phenomena which had called these social questions into existence were of a transitory nature and the Church's action against them would only serve to aggravate the situation and give to them an importance that they did not deserve. Likewise evident in both documents, was the keen awareness of the American mind which Gibbons so often displayed and which in the case of Henry George's doctrines, no less than with the knights, served to give the Roman officials pause about the wisdom of their policies and to afford them an enlightenment and direction in American affairs at a time when they were sorely needed.

While Cardinal Gibbons was exerting himself in Rome to prevent the Church's condemnation of the writings of George, the affairs of Archbishop Corrigan and Father McGlynn were growing progressively worse. The priest's removal from the pastorate of St. Stephen's had enraged his friends, both Catholic and non-Catholic, and the open demonstrations in his favor, fanned as they were by sensational and often inaccurate stories in the press, were creating a grave scandal and a serious threat to ecclesiastical discipline. Not only did the laity take sides, but the clergy themselves were divided with the great majority sup-

---

[14] AAB, Unclassified, Gibbons to Simeoni, Rome, February 25, 1887, printed copy in French entitled "La question des écrits de Henri George." The work cited by Gibbons in his memorial was that of Valentino Steccanella, S.J., *Del comunismo, esame critico filosofico e politico* (Roma, 1882).

porting the archbishop but a strong and articulate minority favoring McGlynn. McGlynn's own public statements became more and more intemperate as time went on with the result that many began to fear that he would leave the Church entirely.

Burtsell explained many of the recent details of the controversy for Gibbons in a letter which dealt harshly with Archbishop Corrigan, for what the writer stated was unfairness in his dealings with his unruly subject. The cardinal was probably a bit disconcerted in learning that his letter of February 18 which had summarized for Burtsell the audience with Leo XIII, was regarded by the canon lawyer as gratifying proof of what he termed "your earnest sympathy with Rev. Dr. McGlynn in his troubles. . . ." Gibbons was told that before the suspended priest would go to Rome he must first be reinstated at St. Stephen's and McGlynn's doctor was quoted as saying that his patient's heart condition would not then warrant a sea voyage.[15] Three days after writing this letter Burtsell cabled the cardinal asking what prospect there was of McGlynn's reinstatement, saying he would proceed to Rome if reinstated and remarking, "State of affairs here intolerable." The following day Gibbons cabled in return, "No prejudgment possible but immediate compliance with Holy See's call necessary."[16] It was apparent that the Archbishop of Baltimore had no intention of lending encouragement beyond what the instructions of the Holy See might warrant. Meanwhile he could only hope that McGlynn would obey the papal summons.

Toward the end of March, 1887, Gibbons took a brief holiday at Anzio whence he informed Corrigan of the success which had recently attended his efforts to win the Holy See's approval for the bishops' transfer of rectors of churches without a previous ecclesiastical trial. It was a subject about which Corrigan was naturally very much concerned just at this time, and Gibbons told him that they owed their success in good measure to Cardinal Howard, the English representative at the curia, whose

---

[15] 82-N-6, Burtsell to Gibbons, New York, March 8, 1887. Burtsell thanked Gibbons for his "frank and very able" statement on the Knights of Labor and expressed his delight that the American Church had, as he said, one so highly placed "who is so full as Your Eminence is of sympathy for our poor downtrodden and oppressed workingmen whose only safety and fortunately their lawful remedy is in organization for self defence."

[16] AANY, Burtsell Letterbook, Burtsell to Gibbons, New York, March 11, 1887, cablegram, copy, p. 9; Gibbons to Burtsell, Rome, March 12, 1887, cablegram, copy.

intervention in the matter Corrigan had solicited some time before. He remarked that he had heard nothing more in the McGlynn case and that he had very carefully abstained from any further action in that regard. Gibbons had hoped, he said, for the sake of the archbishop and McGlynn's own spiritual benefit that the latter would have obeyed his superiors, and he regretted to see that the question had now become mixed up with the labor problem. Revealing his sympathetic feeling for the Archbishop of New York, the cardinal said, "The strain upon you would try a stronger man."[17]

On the very day that Gibbons was at Anzio, Dr. McGlynn made one of his most famous speeches when he addressed an overflow audience in the Academy of Music on the subject of "The Cross of a New Crusade." While there was nothing particularly new in the speech, the speaker rose to great heights of eloquence and all the comments agreed that it was one of the most stirring orations heard in New York in a long time.[18] The circumstance of the occasion which especially irritated Corrigan was the presence on the platform of a number of New York priests. To the archbishop this was a source of scandal in their lending encouragement to one who was in his judgment contumacious toward the Holy See. The result was that the priests who attended were reprimanded and several of them were ultimately disciplined which, in turn, led to further recriminations in the press from both sides. Burtsell furnished Gibbons with information on these latest developments and included his own surmise that the attack on himself in the New York *Times* of April 5 had reached that paper through one of the Corrigan party, Father Thomas F. Lynch, pastor of the Church of the Transfiguration.[19]

While Gibbons was cautious about accepting the unsolicited versions of events supplied to him by Burtsell, he had confirmation from distant and independent sources of the harm which the McGlynn case was doing to the cause of religion in the United States. Bishop Fitzgerald of Little Rock warned that he feared for the worst and that McGlynn's latest utterances, to

---

[17] *Ibid.*, Gibbons to Corrigan, Anzio, March 29, 1887.
[18] Bell, *op. cit.*, pp. 79–87.
[19] AANY, Burtsell Letterbook, Burtsell to Gibbons, New York, April 1, 1887, copy, pp. 33–35; same to same, New York, April 5, 1887, copy.

his mind, showed an utterly un-Catholic spirit, and he gave as an instance of what he meant the priest's statement read at the memorial services on March 8 for the late Henry Ward Beecher.[20] Archbishop Elder was even more alarmed. He begged Gibbons to urge a decision at Rome, since he said good Catholics and even priests were growing perplexed and discouraged. To many, said Elder, it appeared that Rome was hesitating about supporting Corrigan's authority since four months after McGlynn had been called to the Holy See there was still no action. As Elder put it, "It almost looks like acknowledging that Rome had no right to call him & that he understood canon law better than the Propaganda does."

The Archbishop of Cincinnati remarked vaguely that others, taking advantage of the inaction, had begun to advocate the loosest doctrines about regard for authority, and what he termed, "even about the sufficiency of non-Catholic churches." In the circumstances Elder hoped that the Cardinal of Baltimore could avail himself of the opportunity to disabuse the Roman officials of their impression about the arbitrary disposition of bishops in the United States.[21] The same week the *Independent,* the New York Protestant weekly, editorialized under the title of "Dr. McGlynn and Cardinal Gibbons" on the controversies in Catholic ranks and instanced Gibbons' success with the Knights of Labor as showing how much better off McGlynn would have been had he obeyed the Church's authorities and carried his case to Rome. Had he done that, thought the writer, he would, like Gibbons, have been able to return in triumph but as things stood now McGlynn, advised by his own passion and Henry George, would sink out of sight. "Dr. McGlynn is nothing against the Church," said the *Independent,* "and St. Stephen's, big as it is, is nothing. They will be stamped out like a bubble."[22]

In the closing days of his Roman visit Cardinal Gibbons continued to receive and to give advice in the case. Corrigan

---

[20] 82-N-11, Fitzgerald to Gibbons, Little Rock, March 20, 1887. The tenor of McGlynn's remarks at the service for Beecher might easily have been taken as an effort to minimize the doctrinal differences between the various Christian churches as, for example, when he said Beecher taught better than others the essentials of religion in which all were agreed and, as McGlynn expressed it, none other so well understood how "to minimize the differences that seem to separate us." Cf. Sylvester L. Malone, *Dr. Edward McGlynn* (New York, 1918), p. 105.

[21] 82-P-7, Elder to Gibbons, Cincinnati, April 6, 1887.

[22] *Independent* (New York), April 7, 1887.

suggested to Elder that he cable the cardinal and urge him to seek "prompt and decided action" for the good of religious discipline, not only in New York but in the entire country.[23] Archbishop Ryan was also eager for a decision in McGlynn's regard, although he conceded that the principles behind George's theories would take more time for investigation.[24] Corrigan extended his gratitude directly to Gibbons for the manner in which he was handling the various interests of the American hierarchy at Rome, and he thought it proved the need of having a good representative at the Holy See for the American Church. He painted a dark picture for the cardinal of affairs in his archdiocese. He said:

> The McGlynn trouble now presents the phase of *organized* opposition to Episcopal authority on the part of some of his Sacerdotal supporters and admirers, e.g., Dr. Burtsell and Dr. Curran. It is no longer the case of a wound that may heal under the soothing influence of a poultice but it is an ulcer that needs the knife. Nothing less vigorous will be successful.[25]

By the time that the cablegram suggested by Corrigan to Elder had reached Rome, Gibbons had departed for Florence. When it was forwarded to him by Monsignor O'Connell the cardinal cabled Cincinnati in return, "Have advised holy see to renew efforts summoning McGlynn to Rome. Wire suggestion here."[26] On the following day he explained to Archbishop Elder, who had been acting as liaison man between Corrigan and Gibbons, that he had advised O'Connell to urge upon Jacobini, Secretary of the Propaganda, that the Holy See make another effort to get McGlynn to Rome. If he once more failed to obey, then, said

---

23 AAC, Corrigan to Elder, New York, April 8, 1887.

24 82-P-11, Ryan to Gibbons, Philadelphia, April 10, 1887, *confidential*. Ryan, too, was gratified at the settlement of the question about removal of pastors in the bishops' favor. Another prelate who found satisfaction in this decision was Cardinal Manning. He told Bishop Keane, "And I am rejoiced about the 'Remotio Rectorum.' I hope the wording is clear & safe. I should like to be fully informed as to Card. Simeoni's mind about the whole policy of Card. Gibbons' Paper. Mgr. Jacobini ought I think to go with it. Let me know this. And of any others. The state of the 'New World' is not the normal state of Christendom. But it is with the abnormal state that we have to do. We must deal with facts, not with memories, & lamentations. And to deal with facts we must go down into the midst of them. The Incarnation is our law & wisdom" (ADR, Manning to "My dear Lord" [Keane], Westminster, April 15, 1887).

25 82-P-12, Corrigan to Gibbons, New York, April 12, 1887. The second priest referred to by Corrigan was James T. Curran, assistant at St. Stephen's Church.

26 AAC, Gibbons to Elder, Florence, April 19, 1887, cablegram.

Gibbons, it would be the Holy See's business to determine whether and to what extent he should be punished for contumacy, and even whether he might already be regarded as contumacious.

Gibbons' personal chagrin at being characterized by the newspapers as a sympathizer with the refractory priest was made evident when he told Elder that to his regret "& even amazement" he learned from the papers that McGlynn's friends were speaking of him as the man's defender. Since the only possible ground for such an impression could be found in his letter to McGlynn through Burtsell, he had desisted entirely from writing further. He told the archbishop that he hardly knew McGlynn even by sight and had never corresponded with him, and that he had paid no attention to one or two communications which had reached him from McGlynn's friends. Since he had received no suggestion from Corrigan or any other American prelate, he said he had been at a loss to know what to do and, therefore, had hesitated to take any step on his own responsibility.[27] The next day the cardinal sent a second communication to Elder in which he advised that should the Holy See issue another summons, he thought it should be accompanied by a command for McGlynn to deliver no more speeches. Gibbons said he noted the inflammatory effect they were having on the audiences, and he regretted to see that in reporting these addresses disrespectful language was sometimes used of Archbishop Corrigan. The cardinal wondered if someone in the United States could not be found to prevail on McGlynn to stop making speeches. He concluded by saying that if no action was taken before he reached home, he would be very glad to unite with Elder and some of the other bishops in recommending a course of action to the Holy See. "You might communicate these views," said Gibbons, "to his Grace of N. York."[28]

There was no doubt at all that Cardinal Gibbons had been badly dealt with in this whole affair by the news items in the American press. He was persistently pictured by some newspapers as the defender of McGlynn against his archbishop, and in a number of instances statements of a nature to embitter the relations between him and Archbishop Corrigan were published on no better evidence than mere hearsay or rumor. For example,

---

[27] *Ibid.*, Gibbons to Elder, Florence, April 20, 1887.
[28] *Ibid.*, Gibbons to Elder, Florence, April 21, 1887.

on April 19 the New York *Morning Journal* carried a gossipy story to the effect that Monsignor Thomas S. Preston, Vicar-General of the Archdiocese of New York, and a certain Father Lynch, who was incorrectly called the archbishop's secretary, had tried to coerce the New York clergy into signing a statement endorsing Corrigan's handling of the McGlynn case so that the document could be used in Rome, as the *Journal* said, "against the efforts of Cardinal Gibbons and Bishop Keane." Moreover, the same paper went so far as to quote a supposed statement of Preston made at the dedication of St. Veronica's Church in the presence of ten or eleven priests, that Gibbons' part in the affair was easily accounted for since the cardinal, according to the quotation, "was a vain man seeking popularity. . . ."[29] It is not difficult to see how stories of this kind would contribute to bad feeling on both sides and lead to further misunderstanding and suspicion. The New York *Times* showed little sympathy for either Corrigan or Gibbons, since the policies of the one in the McGlynn case and the conduct of the other in defending the Knights of Labor led that paper to believe that the American Church was singularly ill served in its leadership. The *Times* of April 25 said:

> Both these prelates are obviously lacking in tact and understanding. Their errors will be viewed, not without unconcern perhaps, but certainly without sorrow, by the enemies of the Church. For the Church itself, if it really have an honest purpose to adapt itself to American institutions, it would seem to be a question worthy of serious thought whether the present policy of its agents in this country is either wise or safe.[30]

But regardless of the fact that the *Times* itself was obviously "without sorrow" over what it viewed as the bungling policies of the two archbishops, the latter continued their efforts to bring about a solution to the disturbance which for months had so greatly agitated ecclesiastical circles. In the hope that Rome

---

[29] This story in the *Morning Journal* furnished the occasion for a sharp exchange of correspondence between Corrigan and Keane on the subject of the latter's part in the McGlynn affair. Cf. AANY, Keane to Corrigan, Rome, May 1, 1887; Corrigan to Keane, New York, September 11, 1888, copy; Keane to Corrigan, Chicago, October 1, 1888; Corrigan to Keane, New York, October 14, 1888, copy; Keane to Corrigan, Baltimore, October 26, 1888.

[30] For a number of these newspaper items the writer is indebted to the unpublished master's thesis of Joseph F. Lekan, S.M., "James Cardinal Gibbons and the Press, 1868–1900," The Catholic University of America (1949).

would act if more evidence was placed in its hands, Corrigan forwarded to the Holy See a further set of documents covering various phases of the McGlynn trouble.[31] In anticipation of a decision by Rome and because the case was outside their jurisdiction, almost nothing was said publicly by any of the American bishops. Their general silence in reference to this and to other public questions puzzled Bishop Herbert Vaughan of Salford who told Corrigan that had the American bishops years ago spoken out on these matters, as the archbishop had done in his pastoral on private property, they probably would have molded, thought Vaughan, the greater part of the Catholic population of the United States on Catholic principles.[32]

The repeated efforts of the press to associate Gibbons with McGlynn's defense brought a timely rebuke from the leading Catholic newspaper of New York which would seem to have been partially inspired by the cardinal. The *Freeman's Journal* of April 30 carried an unsigned statement under a Roman dateline of April 8 in which astonishment was expressed at the "absurd rumors" about Gibbons' sympathy with the priest, and it was said that it could be authoritatively stated that the cardinal was amazed that any Catholic would believe he would countenance disobedience of this kind. The same issue published an editorial entitled "Cardinal Gibbons' Position" in which it took up the statement from Rome and gave a strong endorsement to the cardinal's integrity. The *Freeman's* announced they were happy to give the lie to the shameless use of the name of an absent prelate, "whose record," as the writer expressed it, "has been that of the purest obedience to and entire upholding of authority. . . ." A statement of this kind from a New York Catholic paper would be welcome reading to Gibbons who by this time had reached Paris on his return journey, for he had become genuinely apprehensive of the effect that all the garbled and distorted press reports might have on Corrigan and his attitude toward him. In an effort to put himself right with the Archbishop of New York the cardinal wrote him from Paris as follows:

> I have been sorely distressed by the continuation of your troubles, and deeply wounded by the insinuations thrown out in the papers that I was championing the cause of Dr. McGlynn. I most solemnly

---

[31] AAC, Corrigan to Elder, New York, April 25, 1887.
[32] AANY, Vaughan to Corrigan, Salford, April 28 [1887].

declare that my constant & prayerful desire has been to see an end to the trouble with honor to yourself & with the full maintenance of your Episcopal authority. I knew not what course to pursue in Rome except to urge his early departure for Rome, which would remove the cause of the trouble, & I know that Rome would investigate & decide the case in a manner satisfactory to yourself & the cause of justice.

I confess however to one error of judgment I innocently made, & that was in communicating my letter of Feb. 17 [sic] to Dr. McGlynn through Dr. Burtsell. The latter called on me on the evening that we dined with Mr. Keiley, & from the tenor of his conversation, I knew that he was friendly to Dr. McG. But it was later on that I discovered that he was such a partisan. The letter to which I refer, was the first & the last that I wrote, except a brief note of courteous reply addressed to a priest of another state in which I advocated obedience to authority. I never answered, or took any notice of any communication sent me on the subject.

In the Document on the Knights of Labor published in the "Moniteur" I took the precaution of excluding the paragraph referring to the suspended priest, not because it contained any argument against Your Grace, quite the contrary, but lest your opponents should try to distort it to their advantage. I was very sorry to learn that it was published in the Herald in the original French. Of course, they had the copy that was surreptitiously obtained. I hope the paragraph escaped observation.

I shall be most happy to aid you as far as I can in putting an end to the conflict. Abp. Williams will be here I hope tomorrow, & if he has any plan matured, I shall gladly cooperate with him.[33]

This lengthy explanation of his action reflected the anxiety that was uppermost at the time in the mind of Gibbons about the whole affair. And his misgivings were not without foundation, for despite his frank summary of what he had done and the honest avowal of his error in writing to Burtsell, the feeling of aggrievement at what he regarded as an interference in the business of his archdiocese by Gibbons and Keane continued to grow upon Archbishop Corrigan. The two metropolitans had entertained different views on such questions as the Catholic University of America and the Knights of Labor, but up to this point in their lives no problem had arisen which threatened so seriously to disrupt the general friendly relations of the Archbishops of Baltimore and New York as the case of Dr. McGlynn.

---

[33] *Ibid.*, Gibbons to Corrigan, Paris, April 30, 1887, *Personal.*

By May 12 Cardinal Gibbons had reached London where he had a meeting with Cardinal Manning and visited the headquarters of the Mill Hill Fathers to confer on matters pertaining to the Negro missions in his archdiocese. He refused to be interviewed and tried to keep his movements secret, although it was made known that his principal reason in coming to London was in the interests of the Negro missions and not to consult with Manning on the Knights of Labor.[34] The same issue of the New York *Herald* that published this item carried an interview with McGlynn given at Pittsburgh, in which Gibbons was pictured as the friendly medium through whom the original summons had reached him from Leo XIII. An unnamed member of St. Stephen's Parish was also quoted as saying that Bishop Chatard of Vincennes was guilty of securing a new order for McGlynn to proceed to Rome, and that through the efforts of Gibbons, Ireland, and Keane the Pope was led to declare that he saw nothing in the land theory contrary to the teachings of the Church and that he would like McGlynn to explain the question personally for the Roman officials. Leo XIII had declared nothing of the kind; in fact, within the same week McGlynn was handed a letter from Cardinal Simeoni in Jersey City where he had gone for a speech, in which he was told that if he did not appear at Rome within forty days after receipt of the letter he would be excommunicated.[35]

All of this information was, of course, transmitted through one channel or another to Gibbons during his stay in the British Isles, so that long before he landed in New York he was fully aware of the more critical turn which events had taken. Virtually every communication reaching him in these days suggested supreme caution on his part when he would arrive in the United States. In the opinion of Magnien, one of his closest advisers, McGlynn's behavior made his case "truly hopeless" and in the Sulpician's view he was fast losing the sympathy of many of his followers.[36] Bishop Keane who was still in Rome learned of the Propaganda's ultimatum of excommunication in forty days if the priest did not appear, and he gave the measure his hearty endorsement, provided only that the question be limited to the subject of McGlynn's discipline and not be permitted, as Keane

34 New York *Herald,* May 14, 1887.
35 Bell, *op. cit.,* p. 106.
36 82-Q-2, Magnien to Gibbons, Baltimore, May 14, 1887.

expressed it, "to drag us into a doctrinal & political discussion."[37] From Baltimore Father John Foley, too, warned Gibbons to watch his step in New York where any demonstration in his favor would be made use of by the followers of McGlynn.[38] Shortly before he sailed from Queenstown on the *Umbria* on May 29 he received a letter from Archbishop Corrigan who told of the distress he was experiencing at the hands of McGlynn's partisans who, he said, had stopped at nothing to misinterpret his every word and to attribute to him motives which never existed except, as the archbishop expressed it, "in their own perverse minds." He cited, moreover, some examples of how the press had distorted what he called Gibbons' own "innocent language" into different and bad meanings. Corrigan regretted deeply that the cardinal's kindness toward him in Rome had been so badly repaid, but he wished him to know that he was sincerely grateful for the efforts he had put forth in the interests of religion and legitimate authority.[39]

Although Gibbons had originally planned to go immediately to Major Keiley's home upon his arrival in New York, he apparently judged that the situation called for a change of plans since he cabled Corrigan from the high seas that he would come directly from the steamer to his residence.[40] Upon landing Gibbons first paid this public deference to the Archbishop of New York, after which he felt free to stop overnight with the Keileys before proceeding to Baltimore on June 7 for the reception which awaited him in his see city. While he was still in New York he received a somewhat detailed explanation in writing from Burtsell, who was at pains to clear his own name from the charge that he had been guilty of implicating Gibbons in a defense of McGlynn. In reply the cardinal very briefly thanked the canon lawyer for his words welcoming him home, said he had read his explanation with pleasure, and assured him that it was quite satisfactory.[41] But

---

[37] 82-Q-1, Keane to Gibbons, Rome, May 14, 1887.

[38] 82-Q-3, Foley to Gibbons, Baltimore, May 15, 1887.

[39] 82-Q-5, Corrigan to Gibbons, New York, May 16, 1887.

[40] AUND, Chatard Papers, Corrigan to Chatard, New York, June 1, 1887, microfilm. That Chatard was working in Corrigan's interests at this time is evident from the archbishop's thanks to him for what he called "the services which you have rendered this Diocese since your arrival in Rome. Thank God, your efforts have been very successful."

[41] AANY, Burtsell Letterbook, Burtsell to Gibbons, New York, June 5, 1887, copy, pp. 36–37; Gibbons to Burtsell, Brooklyn, June 6, 1887, copy.

beyond the demands of politeness Gibbons did not go, and his determination not to become further involved in the complicated and unpleasant business was revealed when Bishop Moore of St. Augustine, who was a strong defender of McGlynn and who had accompanied Gibbons from New York to Baltimore on June 7, informed Burtsell that the cardinal was not disposed to take any further steps in the case. Whether or not Moore got his information from Gibbons is not known, but at any rate, he told Burtsell that Corrigan was quite displeased with Gibbons, Keane, and Ireland for having, as he said, "interfered at all in the matter."[42]

Regardless of how anxious Gibbons might be to remain clear of the New York controversy, there were a number who continued to look to him in the hope that he might offer a way out of the impasse. One of Gibbons' most faithful admirers among the New York clergy was John M. Farley, the future cardinal. He told the Archbishop of Baltimore at this time of his fears that many souls would be lost because of what he termed "this unhappy trouble of ours," and he went on to say, "In the midst of it all Your Eminence is looked up to as the man of providence."[43] Of those who hoped that Gibbons might still be induced to act as an intermediary with the Holy See in McGlynn's behalf, the most persistent were Dr. Burtsell and Bishop Moore. In an exchange of correspondence during the midsummer of 1887 McGlynn's two friends discussed various angles of the case with Moore acting as spokesman with Gibbons.[44] When Burtsell learned that the cardinal had not handed in to the Propaganda the document he had sent him while he was in Rome, he at first thought Gibbons might be prevailed upon to commend him to the Propaganda so that his version of the case would get a favorable hearing. Moore did as it was suggested to him in

---

[42] *Ibid.*, Moore to Burtsell, Baltimore, June 8, 1887, copy.

[43] 82-U-3, Farley to Gibbons, New York, June 16, 1887.

[44] AANY, Burtsell Letterbook contains copies of this correspondence between June 20 and July 8, 1887, pp. 44–53. The cardinal was not home a week when another New York priest who had incurred the displeasure of Corrigan asked to come to Baltimore to see him about a number of important questions. Father Thomas J. Ducey, pastor of St. Leo's Church, thought his ideas might be helpful to Gibbons "whose power is so great and far-reaching for the good of souls and the true power of Holy Church in this 'Great Country' of ours" (82-T-6, Ducey to Gibbons, New York, June 12, 1887). There was no record of Gibbons' reply.

forwarding Burtsell's letter to Baltimore, adding a copy of a cablegram he had himself just sent to Simeoni, and hinting that a message to the Holy See from Gibbons approving Moore's steps would be helpful.[45]

But Gibbons was not to be easily drawn in again. His absence from home on a confirmation tour delayed his reply to Moore by almost a week. The timing was important, since Burtsell and Moore were working frantically to get action before the forty-day limit on McGlynn's compliance with Rome's command would run out and the ban of excommunication would be laid upon him. The cardinal explained to Moore the reason for his delayed reply, and he stated that in view of the character of Burtsell's letter sent to him at Rome in response to his own summary of the papal audience, he did not present the document to the Roman officials. Although the cardinal characterized the Burtsell letter as "most unsatisfactory & discouraging," nonetheless, he said he had communicated orally to Simeoni the excuses it contained for McGlynn's failure to make the trip, namely, his illness and his desire to have the suspension lifted before his departure. Gibbons reiterated to Moore his belief that McGlynn had shirked his duty in not going to Rome after his illness, and now that the forty days' grace had expired it was too late for him to comply with Moore's suggestion for intervention at the Holy See, even, he added, "if I deemed it expedient to do so."[46] It was evident from his policy during recent months that Gibbons did not regard it as expedient to chance further embroilment with the stormy New York priest. And when another McGlynn advocate, Father Sylvester L. Malone, pastor of SS. Peter and Paul Church in Brooklyn, attempted to gain his good offices he was asked by the cardinal's

---

[45] 82-W-5, Moore to Gibbons, St. Augustine, June 29, 1887. On June 23, 1887, for example, Burtsell wrote to Moore the following: "It seems to me that the very fact of Cardinal Gibbons not presenting my document might now be used by you or him as a means of getting both the Propaganda and the Doctor out of the difficulty. If the Propaganda was told that a document was sent by me intended for presentation of the Doctor's case to it through Cardinal Gibbons, which reached Rome by March 24th with the approval and co-operation of the Doctor, and as a beginning or opening of his defence the Propaganda would recognize that there was not the supposed flagrant contumacy and would probably suspend its action till I had a chance of being heard from. Propaganda would not heed me unless commended by you or the Cardinal" (AANY, Burtsell Letter-book, Burtsell to Moore, New York, June 23, 1887, copy, p. 46).

[46] 83-D-13, Gibbons to Moore, Baltimore, July, 1887, copy. The copy of this letter in Burtsell's Letterbook gives the exact date as July 8, p. 52.

secretary to excuse His Eminence from the intervention he had requested.[47]

Finally the forty days of grace expired without McGlynn making any move to comply with the Roman command, and on July 8, 1887, Archbishop Corrigan, following the instructions of the Holy See, issued a statement explaining that the priest had incurred excommunication. In pursuing this action the archbishop maintained that he was merely following the directive of Rome, and he explained to Archbishop Elder that the whole matter of the excommunication had originated and was accomplished in Rome without any suggestion from him.[48] Since this information was quickly relayed by Elder to Gibbons immediately after his return to Cincinnati from an interview with Corrigan, it raises the interesting question as to whether or not the cardinal had made a last-minute effort through the Archbishop of Cincinnati to head off the excommunication. Elder explained that the announcement of Corrigan's action had been sent to the newspapers before he met him which would seem to imply that any effort he might have made had come too late. Although there is no certainty that Gibbons had suggested this mission to Elder, it was fairly clear that the cardinal did not believe the extreme measure of excommunication would remedy matters. He forwarded a copy of the New York *Herald* to Denis O'Connell covering the announcement, and he said:

> I hope I am mistaken, but my impression is that it will lead to the loss of many souls, & to a weakening in some places of the reverence due to the Holy See. It was prudent not to require the reading of the excommunication in the churches; for, I dare say, there would have been a commotion, judging from the temper of the people as exhibited in the journals.[49]

But when three weeks later he furnished Corrigan with details about the preparation of an address of greeting to the Pope for the latter's jubilee he was careful to make no mention of his impressions. The Archbishop of New York was pleased with Gib-

[47] 82-V-8, P[atrick] J. Donahue to Malone, Baltimore, June 27, 1887, copy. Malone over thirty years later published a memorial volume on his friend entitled *Dr. Edward McGlynn* (New York, 1918), which was largely made up of appreciations of his life and work from friends and press clippings.

[48] 83-B-5, Elder to Gibbons, Cincinnati, July 11, 1887.

[49] ADR, Gibbons to O'Connell, Baltimore, July 15, 1887.

bons' efforts for the congratulations to Leo XIII and it prompted him to say, "One excellent result of the trial recently sent me by Divine Providence, is [a] very strongly increased devotion and attachment to the Holy See and its august occupant."[50]

Far from moderating the conduct of Father McGlynn, the promulgation of his excommunication seemed to goad him on to even greater excesses. He went forward with speaking tours for the Anti-Poverty Society which had been organized by the followers of Henry George in March, even though Corrigan had forbidden the faithful of his archdiocese to attend its meetings. On July 31 he delivered a scathing address in the Brooklyn Opera House on the subject, "The New Know-Nothingism and the Old," in which he used the most violent language in speaking of ecclesiastical authorities both in the United States and in Rome. Moreover, he employed the same subject and contents for an article in the *North American Review* the following month,[51] and so far had he now gone that even a faithful adherent like Bishop Moore began to doubt the possibility of solving the trouble, when he told Gibbons that on his visit with McGlynn the previous week he found him as obstinate as ever.[52] Moore, nevertheless, continued to act as the intermediary for several more letters from Burtsell who was endeavoring to solicit through Gibbons a more specific statement from Rome on the charges against McGlynn and to have the cardinal urge the Holy See to lift the excommunication, providing McGlynn would first promise to make the long-delayed journey.[53]

Whether the failure of Cardinal Gibbons to come forward as the champion of the excommunicated priest was directly responsible for the next act in the drama, it is not possible to say with certainty. At any rate, someone was apparently intent on forcing the cardinal's hand, for on September 9 the Brooklyn *Standard-Union* published an interview with an anonymous person who professed to know facts which made the many misleading and mendacious accounts up to this time seem pale, indeed. It was

---

[50] 83-F-4, Corrigan to Gibbons, New York, August 5, 1887.
[51] "The New Know-Nothingism and the Old," CXLV (August, 1887), 192–205.
[52] 83-G-12, Moore to Gibbons, Philadelphia, August 17, 1887.
[53] 83-K-2, Moore to Gibbons, Philadelphia, September 2, 1887, enclosing Burtsell's letter to Moore from Hotel Kaaterskill, Catskill Mountains, August 31, 1887 (83-J-8); 83-K-9, Moore to Gibbons, Philadelphia, September 5, 1887, enclosing Burtsell to Moore, New York, September 3, 1887 (83-K-4).

said that McGlynn had been excommunicated without a hearing, that Burtsell's defense of him sent to Gibbons had never been presented, but that despite all this he would be vindicated and ultimately reinstated at St. Stephen's. Archbishop Corrigan, it was hinted, would be removed from New York and made Rector of the Catholic University of America! As for Gibbons, he was said at first to have "sided more or less" with McGlynn, but when Corrigan's displeasure became known the cardinal deserted the cause at a critical moment because he wished to retain the archbishop's support for his own stand on the university and the Knights of Labor. The interview was shown to McGlynn the previous evening, said the *Standard-Union,* and he pronounced it true except for a few details. McGlynn then charged Gibbons with never presenting his defense at Rome, and when the Rector of the American College, in whose hands the document had been left, was recently pressed about the matter he was supposed to have replied that it was probably thrown into his wastebasket. In a final twist of the truth McGlynn was quoted as saying he felt it was Gibbons' duty to explain why he had not obeyed the orders of the Pope to notify him to appear at Rome.[54]

Naturally a story of this kind created a sensation and it was widely copied in other newspapers. So utterly false was it that Gibbons felt it could not be ignored, and for that reason he prepared an authorized statement which appeared in the Baltimore *Sun* of September 12. It read as follows:

> Shortly after his arrival in Rome in February last, Cardinal Gibbons, in an audience with the Holy Father, was requested by his Holiness to ask Dr. McGlynn to come to Rome. The next day the Cardinal complied with the instructions of the Holy Father; but as he did not know Dr. McGlynn's address, he wrote the letter to Dr. Burtsell, because he regarded him as a friend of Dr. McGlynn. Some weeks later Cardinal Gibbons received a reply from Dr. Burtsell, giving reasons and excuses why Dr. McGlynn did not go to Rome. As the answer from Dr. Burtsell was addressed not to Cardinal Simeoni, but to Cardinal Gibbons himself, the latter saw no reasons for handing the letter to the Propaganda.

---

[54] The Library of Congress file of the Brooklyn *Standard-Union* did not cover this issue so the New York *Herald* of September 10, 1887, which gave a full account of the story, was used instead. Among other fabrications in this interview was the tale that Mary Gwendoline Caldwell had withdrawn the $300,000 she had given for the new university.

Far, however, from suppressing its contents, he was very careful to communicate them to the cardinal prefect of the Propaganda. It may be added that Cardinal Gibbons was in no way authorized to act as an intermediary between Dr. McGlynn and his arch-bishop, and therefore scrupulously avoided interfering in a matter in which he had no direct concern, and his visit to Rome had quite a different purpose.

Knowing how reluctant the Cardinal of Baltimore was to enter in any way the field of public controversy, it was apparent that he viewed the fabrications of the *Standard-Union* with great gravity when he took the pains to issue a denial. Normally he ignored newspaper accounts of his conduct and policies, even when they were inaccurate, but the unfairness and mendacity of the author of this interview, along with the concurring com-ments of McGlynn, were too serious to be permitted to pass in silence. If Gibbons scored little success in convincing McGlynn and his friends of the correctness of his conduct, he had at least vindicated his good name before the general American public.

During the week following this episode Gibbons spent several days in Philadelphia at the centennial celebration of the United States Constitution. While there he met Bishop Moore, who again opened a discussion on ways of removing the scandal which was disrupting the peace of the Church in New York. Gibbons counseled the bishop not to go near McGlynn if he visited New York; but the following week after returning to Philadelphia Moore informed him that while in New York, as he confessed, "contrary to the advice you gave me, I saw McGlynn." The burden of the new approach was that McGlynn was now very calm and willing to listen to reason. If all censures were removed and the charges against him specified, he was perfectly willing to go to Rome and to stand trial. Because of what Moore regarded as his good disposition and the reasonable-ness of the condition McGlynn laid down, the bishop had written to Simeoni proposing that the priest's offer be accepted. Insofar as all this concerned Gibbons the Bishop of St. Augustine made his point in a brief concluding sentence, "If Your Eminence's good services could be still used in the case I would have the greatest confidence of a happy result."[55]

---

[55] 83-N-13, Moore to Gibbons, Philadelphia, September 24, 1887. In regard to the Brooklyn *Standard-Union* interview of two weeks before, Gibbons probably

But the day for the use of Gibbons' "good services" in regard to McGlynn had passed. He had, it is true, been sufficiently persuaded by the constant urging of Moore to bring up the subject of reopening the case to Archbishops Corrigan, Ryan, and Williams but, according to Corrigan's version of the matter, the Archbishops of Philadelphia and Boston had dissuaded the cardinal from entering into what Corrigan called "the trap cunningly devised by Dr. Burtsell." Corrigan told all of this to Archbishop Elder, along with the fact that Gibbons had given him Burtsell's and Moore's letters to read, and it was his view that after the McGlynn faction learned they could not employ the cardinal for their purposes, they then began the recriminations against him in the press. While Corrigan's resentment against Moore's part in the business was evident and while he had not been favorable to Gibbons' latest approach to him, the cardinal's conduct as described by the Archbishop of New York had been perfectly honorable, even if Corrigan did seem to imply that he thought Gibbons had been in danger of being taken in. Equally interesting in light of the events of the coming months was Corrigan's avowal to Elder that he felt Henry George's book should be placed on the *Index*. On this subject he wrote:

> The condemnation of H. George's book would, I think, be a great service to Religion; because several Priests unfortunately still uphold these doctrines, alleging that the H. See has not condemned them; consequently they may still be ventilated and sustained. I have already submitted this fact, recently, to the Holy See. If you think well of it, a letter to Propaganda in a similar sense would do good. As long as Priests freely absolve the Anti-Poverty rebels, what can I do? I cannot make it a reserved case, prudently, and so the evil festers and continues.[56]

In the midst of the excitement over McGlynn and his disobedience, the question of a judgment from the Church on the doctrinal aspects of George's writings had temporarily faded from view. But Rome had not been allowed to forget it, as

did not find it very consoling to be told by Moore, "The disclosure which appeared recently in a Brooklyn paper was made by Dr. [Edward] Malone, brother of Father [Sylvester L.] Malone, and contrary to the express agreement made with Dr. Burtsell in the matter when the information contained in the newspaper article was given. McGlynn and Burtsell admit that your Eminence has just cause to be indignant, and they are themselves sorely grieved over it."

56 AAC, Corrigan to Elder, New York, November 13, 1887.

Archbishop Corrigan indicated when he told his friend in Cincinnati that he had recently suggested a condemnation to the Holy See. It had been many months since Gibbons had submitted his memorial of February 25, 1887, to Simeoni on the subject, and the circumstance that brought the whole issue to life again in the United States was another of the mysterious leaks of the Church's private documents to the public press. On February 1, 1888, the New York *Herald* sprang a fresh surprise when it published Gibbons' statement against placing George's book on the *Index*. At once a whole chain of reactions was let loose accompanied by applause from the followers of McGlynn and George and expressions of incredulity and disapproval from their opponents. Father Patrick Hennessy, pastor of St. Patrick's Church, Jersey City, was delighted to learn, as he put it, "that the opinion which I have held on this George business from the beginning is identical with what Your Eminence has written to the Propaganda."[57]

The New York *Freeman's Journal* of February 4 showed only indignation and scorn in an editorial entitled "The 'Herald's' Enterprise." The *Freeman's* felt the whole document was either badly mistranslated or had even been invented by the *Herald*. It could not believe that Cardinal Gibbons would be guilty of what it saw as theological errors in the text where the cardinal had quoted from Steccanella's work on communism. Moreover, the fact that the document had Gibbons calling Henry George "an humble American workingman" also struck the *Freeman's* writer as proof of its lack of authenticity since George was neither humble nor a workingman. The editorial writer went on blissfully to declare that no request had yet been made to put the book on the *Index* — quite unaware, of course, of Corrigan's action — and it was his belief that whether or not the Holy See condemned the book it was certain that Rome regarded its ideas as "absurdly heretical." The *Freeman's* man felt that the outrage perpetrated by the *Herald* was all the more flagrant since, as he said, "Cardinal Gibbons' courtesy and scrupulous sense of respect due to others is so remarkable that, during his recent visit to Rome, he excited the enthusiastic admiration of all whom he met." The editorial in the *Freeman's Journal* was another interesting example of how thoroughly wrong the press could be

---

[57] 84-B-8, Hennessy to Gibbons, Jersey City, February 1, 1888.

in commenting on ecclesiastical matters, even when it was done from the highest motives and with the greatest respect shown to churchmen like Gibbons.

Cardinal Gibbons took the latest publication of his confidential correspondence with much more composure than he had shown a year before in the case of the Knights of Labor. It was not the *Herald's* revelation that now worried him, but rather something which he regarded as much more serious. The cardinal's anxiety was occasioned by word from Monsignor O'Connell that another attempt had been made to condemn the George book in Rome and the Roman rector advised that Gibbons solicit opinions from the hierarchy to be sent in to the Holy See against such action.[58] The cardinal was quick to respond to the new threat. He told O'Connell that the surreptitious publication of his memorial had produced one good result in that it had elicited the warm approval of that section of the American press that had commented on it. Time, said Gibbons, had confirmed the impression he formed in Rome and fulfilled the prediction he had ventured to make there, because the book was now almost forgotten and the doctrines it advocated had few adherents and they were outside the Church. He summarized once again his arguments against a condemnation of *Progress and Poverty* and maintained that the only people who would welcome it would be the Church's enemies. He alluded to the constant enmity of some toward the Church in the United States and said that Catholics had enough difficulties to contend with without provoking new ones. In conclusion he gave it as his judgment that if the American hierarchy were consulted in the matter he believed that with very few exceptions they would unite in deploring the condemnation of what he called a dying book.[59]

But regardless of how general he thought the sentiment against condemnation might be among the American bishops, Cardinal Gibbons was not prepared to leave matters to chance. He turned to his friend Archbishop Elder at once, outlined for him the danger of adverse action at Rome, and urged that if Elder agreed with him he should write the Holy See to say so. He cautiously followed O'Connell's instructions in telling Elder that his letter should reveal no knowledge of the threatened condemnation, but

---

[58] 84-D-4, O'Connell to Gibbons, Rome, February 25, 1888.
[59] 84-E-7, Gibbons to O'Connell, Baltimore, March 19, 1888, copy.

rather use the recent publication in the New York *Herald* as the basis for his representation.[60] Thus did Gibbons open his campaign with his colleagues of the hierarchy, and in the ensuing weeks he was busily engaged in soliciting letters from those whom he knew to be friendly to his point of view so that he might furnish Denis O'Connell with weapons to be used at the Holy See. The Archbishop of Cincinnati rapidly aligned himself with the cardinal, although he had written three months before to Simeoni against a condemnation so he now wondered if it was necessary to write again.[61] Gibbons definitely thought it was necessary. "We cannot too often & too strongly impress this thought on the H. See just now," replied the cardinal.[62]

The earnestness of Gibbons' intent was seen in his turning once more to Cardinal Manning. He outlined for the Archbishop of Westminster the substance of the new threat at Rome which he said was due to the Holy See's yielding to pressure from what he called "a certain quarter in this country"; and after a summary of his arguments against a condemnation of George's book, he begged Manning to assist in preventing such action, saying that he wrote especially because the Cardinal of Westminster was a member of the Congregation of the Index. Gibbons believed that not more than a half-dozen bishops in the United States would favor placing the book on the *Index,* and he concluded by saying that since Manning had given so much help to him the previous year in the Knights of Labor case he was prompted to call on him again.[63]

Knowledge of further support for the cause reached Baltimore soon thereafter when O'Connell gave the opinions of several American bishops then in Rome who were all against the condemnation of George. The Roman rector was apparently not very much concerned over the principles involved in the case since he remarked, "On account of the light in which it would place you, I oppose it."[64] Archbishop Ireland, as was to be expected, quickly rallied to Gibbons' call for a protest to Rome and he likewise asked Bishops Marty and Spalding to forward

---

[60] AAC, Gibbons to Elder, Baltimore, March 20, 1888.

[61] 84-F-1, Elder to Gibbons, Cincinnati, March 23, 1888.

[62] AAC, Gibbons to Elder, Baltimore, March 26, 1888.

[63] MP, Gibbons to Manning, Baltimore, March 23, 1888, *Private & Confidential.* This letter was published in Leslie, *Henry Edward Manning,* pp. 364–365.

[64] 84-F-7, O'Connell to Gibbons, Rome, March 25, 1888.

similar statements.[65] Ireland sensed the seriousness with which Gibbons viewed the matter, and several weeks later in expressing the hope that George would be kept clear of the *Index* he said, "If he is put on there will be a vacancy at Baltimore from a broken heart."[66] While Gibbons was receiving encouraging support from most quarters to which he had appealed, Archbishop Ryan would not oblige, saying that he preferred to remain neutral rather than to commit himself on the subject to Rome, although a year before he had told Gibbons it would be a great mistake to put the George book on the *Index* as it would give it an importance that would only tend to increase its circulation.[67] The cardinal accepted Ryan's refusal in good grace, and it was at this time that he first mentioned his preference for an encyclical from the Holy Father on the social questions of the day instead of a condemnation of George.[68]

Under the circumstances it was not surprising that three years before the publication of Leo XIII's *Rerum novarum,* Gibbons should suggest a papal encyclical to put a stop to the conflicting views on social questions that were then dividing American Catholics. Even McGlynn and George had come to a parting of the ways over support of President Cleveland's policy of tariff reduction with George intent on supporting Cleveland and McGlynn seeing such a policy as a serious diversion from the true program of the single tax movement and the Anti-Poverty Society of which he was president.[69] The confusion in Catholic ranks grew worse as time went on with McGlynn delivering a tirade on the Holy See on January 8, 1888, in an address called "The Pope in Politics," which was given in answer to one a short time before by Monsignor Preston, the vicar-general of New York, entitled "The Beneficence of the Pope's Influence in Politics." Bishop McQuaid, who continued to urge disciplinary

---

[65] 84-F-11, Ireland to Gibbons, St. Paul, March 26, 1888. Two years later McQuaid informed Gilmour in a letter of January 22, 1890, that twenty-three American bishops had written Rome against the condemnation of George's works. Quoted in Zwierlein, *op. cit.,* III, 66.

[66] ADR, Ireland to O'Connell, St. Paul, April 14, 1888.

[67] 84-G-4, Ryan to Gibbons, Philadelphia, March 28, 1888; 82-N-8, Ryan to Gibbons, Philadelphia, March 15, 1887.

[68] 84-H-2, Gibbons to Ryan, Baltimore, April 3, 1888, copy.

[69] Cf. Bell, *op. cit.,* pp. 165–169, 183–190. For the entangling relations of this whole question with the Knights of Labor case cf. Browne, *The Catholic Church and the Knights of Labor,* pp. 284–285, 292, 304, 333, 335–337, 344–345.

measures on Archbishop Corrigan for all concerned with the
rebel, felt that what he termed McGlynn's "crazy utterances" in
the speech of January 8 had finished him, and he believed that
those who were being led astray were now finding out that
Corrigan was right in the firm course he had followed toward one
whom he characterized as "this bad man."[70] The spirit of rebellion against ecclesiastical authority had, indeed, gone far, and
it was small wonder if those who had the best interests of
the Church at heart were alarmed when they witnessed the
repeated demonstrations and counterdemonstrations in New York.
This was to say nothing of the constant stream of literature that
poured forth from the secular dailies and such provocative items
in the Catholic newspapers as Burtsell's series of articles in the
New York *Tablet* under the general title of "The Canonical Status
of Priests in the United States."

With most of this turmoil Cardinal Gibbons was, to be sure,
acquainted and it was his firm conviction that a papal condemnation of the writings of Henry George would only add fuel to the
flames. For that reason he did not relax his efforts. Nor did the
latest intelligence from his Roman agent give reason for complacency. O'Connell cabled on April 14 for more letters from
the hierarchy, and in a letter of the same date he explained that
the issue was still uncertain and he was afraid that if they desisted
failure or reaction might set in. Abbot Bernard Smith, O.S.B., a
close friend of the American colony in Rome, concurred with
O'Connell in the belief that a personal message from Gibbons to
Leo XIII might serve a good purpose in the matter. The Roman
rector summarized the views of a number of the curial officials
for the cardinal, and he added, "No doubt there are some that
would glory in your humiliation, but I do not regard this last
battle as much, considering your vastly preponderating influence
here, if you stand firm."[71]

There was no lack of firmness in Baltimore and upon receipt of
the cablegram Gibbons again went into action to solicit the
desired letters from his friends in the hierarchy.[72] As a result of
his endeavor, the cardinal was able during the next few weeks

---

70 Quoted in Zwierlein, *op. cit.*, III, 58, with no date given for the letter.
71 84-I-5, O'Connell to Gibbons, Rome, April 14, 1888.
72 For example, AAC, Gibbons to Elder, Baltimore, April 15, 1888, *Personal;*
84-I-8, Gibbons to William H. Gross, Baltimore, April 16, 1888, copy.

to forward to O'Connell ten or more strong endorsements of his stand against condemnation of the George book which would, it was hoped, counteract the representations of Archbishop Corrigan and his followers in the opposite vein.[73] That the Corrigan party were not idle was clear from the fact that Simeoni told Monsignor O'Connell the books of Henry George had been sent to the Congregation of the Index not by himself but, as he expressed it, "by some of the American bishops"; and since the congregation had to pronounce on anything submitted to it some kind of a statement on the doctrinal aspects of George's writings was to be expected. With an eye on the coming presidential election campaign in the United States, O'Connell advised a direct approach to the Pope by Gibbons which would touch on the danger of a pronouncement before the election and how it might make George a hero of the Roman Inquisition and thus prove a handle to the Church's enemies.[74]

One of the methods used by the American hierarchy in these years to influence opinion in the Roman Curia was to insert articles in the *Moniteur de Rome* which was widely read in ecclesiastical circles. Archbishop Ireland was especially active in having published articles of this type and he was glad to call Gibbons' attention now to what he called "our American letter" in the *Moniteur* on the social question in the United States in which a condemnation of George's book was reprobated in the strongest language. The recent appointment of Cardinal Schiaffino as Prefect of the Congregation of the Index encouraged Ireland to believe that he might be of help since he referred to him as "our friend," and said that he had taken advantage of a letter of congratulations to emphasize his conviction that the good of religion demanded absolutely that George be left in

---

[73] Cf. 84-I-7, Gilmour to Gibbons, Cleveland, April 16, 1888; 84-I-9, Feehan to Gibbons, Chicago, April 17, 1888; 84-I-2, Elder to Gibbons, Cincinnati, April 18, 1888; 84-J-9, O'Connor to Gibbons, Omaha, April 23, 1888; 84-J-11, Heiss to Gibbons, Milwaukee, April 24, 1888; 84-I-12, Williams to O'Connell, Boston, March 26, 1888, copy. Cf. also ADR, O'Connor to O'Connell, Omaha, April 24, 1888; Northrop to Gibbons, Charleston, May 11, 1888; Haid to Gibbons, Belmont, North Carolina, April 30, 1888; Elder to O'Connell, Hot Springs, North Carolina, April 26, 1888; Janssens to O'Connell, Richmond, April 30, 1888; Kain to O'Connell, Wheeling, April 23, 1888; Heiss to Gibbons, Milwaukee, May 6, 1888.

[74] 84-I-12, O'Connell to Gibbons, Rome, April 17, 1888. O'Connell added a postscript on his failure to win a letter from Ryan of Philadelphia who declined to put himself on record against the congregation's taking any action.

oblivion.[75] Cardinal Manning, too, was still interesting himself in the case in behalf of Gibbons and his friends. The last he heard was that Rome had decided not to touch the George case and he hoped that the subject was now becoming clearer and quieter in the States,[76] for which Gibbons expressed pleasure in learning that in Manning's opinion there was no danger of George's book reaching the *Index*.[77]

But the shifting currents in Rome were apparently not always registered at Westminster, for Denis O'Connell let it be known in mid-May that the teachings of George were then under examination at the Holy Office. O'Connell acknowledged receipt of a letter from Cardinal Gibbons in which the latter had asked Leo XIII not to condemn George, and at the same time to treat the subject of private property in an encyclical. Since all the other bishops except Elder had urged absolute silence on the part of the Holy See and, too, since Gibbons had used the argument that it would be undignified for Rome to notice George with a condemnation, O'Connell now felt that the cardinal's latest letter to the Pope would only cause confusion in its present form. He had decided, therefore, not to submit it to the Holy Father.[78] As usual Gibbons accepted the advice of his Roman agent and a month later O'Connell was happy to learn that his view of the matter had been sustained by the cardinal.[79]

But for some unknown reason within the next six weeks the objection to a letter from Gibbons to the Pope touching both the George condemnation and the need for an encyclical was removed, for on July 30, 1888, the Cardinal of Baltimore wrote a detailed account of his position on Henry George to Leo XIII. All the familiar arguments were used again, such as George's dying popularity which would only be revived, the opportunity it would give to the Church's enemies, and the inopportuneness in view of

---

[75] 84-K-4, Ireland to Gibbons, St. Paul, May 7, 1888.
[76] 84-K-6, Manning to Gibbons, Westminster, May 8, 1888.
[77] Gibbons to Manning, n.p., May 23, 1888, quoted in Leslie, *op. cit.*, p. 365.
[78] 84-L-11, O'Connell to Gibbons, Rome, May 17, 1888.
[79] 84-P-7, O'Connell to Gibbons, Rome, June 17, 1888. Gibbons was told just at this time by Eduardo Soderini, the biographer of Leo XIII, that the work he was doing for the Church in the United States was given the greatest attention at the Vatican as well as all over Europe. Soderini wrote, "America is now much better known here & I hope it will be still more in the future. Your Eminence has the greatest merit in all that" (84-P-13, Soderini to Gibbons, Rome, June 20, 1888).

the coming presidential election, and the fact that only three or four of the American hierarchy would wish to see George's book put on the *Index.* He told the Pope that he did not pretend that the false theories of George should be tolerated by the Church, but if the Pontiff would permit him to say it, it was not by putting the book on the *Index* or condemning some propositions extracted from it that light would be shed on these problems. In his different encyclicals the Pope had defined and treated questions of the highest importance with a force, clarity, and wisdom that had convinced readers. These instructions which Leo XIII had given with the authority attaching to his apostolate and to his person were known and admired in the United States. A similar instruction in the same form, said Gibbons, on matters touching the right of property would bear the same authority. It would dissipate the shadows and have a salutary influence in solving the great questions which agitated and disturbed modern society.[80] Whatever may have been O'Connell's reason for his change of mind about what Gibbons should write to the Pope, he was now thoroughly satisfied. "Your letter on the George question," he said, "is masterly."[81]

While the Gibbons letter to Leo XIII doubtless carried great weight with the Holy Father, the minority of prelates who supported Archbishop Corrigan's side of the case had likewise made their position known to the Holy See, and in the fall of 1888 they enjoyed the advantage of having a very forceful advocate of their views when Bishop McQuaid made a trip to Rome. McQuaid was then in the midst of a heated controversy with one of his priests, Father Louis A. Lambert, pastor of St. Mary's Church at Waterloo, New York. Lambert had appealed to Dr. Burtsell to act as his canon lawyer in the dispute with McQuaid, and shortly before leaving Rochester the bishop heard a rumor that Lambert and Burtsell had gone to Baltimore where they had been told by the cardinal that he thought the Waterloo pastor had a good case against his superior. McQuaid informed Gibbons of the report, and he added, "The story is so absurd that I trouble you with it only to let you know how shamefully these parties are using your Eminence's name."[82]

---

[80] 84-T-9, Gibbons to Leo XIII, Baltimore, July 30, 1888, copy in French.
[81] 84-V-6, O'Connell to Gibbons, Rome, August 14, 1888.
[82] 85-H-5, McQuaid to Gibbons, New York, November 9, 1888.

Gibbons immediately sensed, of course, the serious implication this latest tale associating him with rebellious priests would have in the minds of Corrigan and his friends, and he, therefore, replied at once that Lambert had called on him some weeks before but that as soon as he mentioned his business he had promptly told him he would have nothing to do with his case, nor would he volunteer any opinion whatever in the matter. As for Burtsell, the cardinal said he had neither seen nor heard from him since he had left Rome.[83] It was well that Gibbons was able to give McQuaid so complete a denial, for the bishop was in a stormy mood and when he reached Rome he made the sparks fly in his denunciation of Lambert, McGlynn, and their kind. It was from the Eternal City that the Bishop of Rochester counseled Corrigan to forbid the Catholics of his archdiocese to attend meetings of the Anti-Poverty Society and to make infractions of his command a reserved case, that is, that ordinary confessors could not absolve penitents without special recourse to the archbishop. In closing his lengthy letter of December 20 he told his friend in New York, "Be clear, strong and bold, and not afraid."[84] Probably encouraged by McQuaid's forceful backing, Corrigan issued a statement on January 20, 1889, making attendance at meetings of the society a reserved case for the faithful on the grounds of the Pope having called McGlynn's opinions "false and pernicious" and the Congregation of the Inquisition having declared attendance at such meetings "an open and public sin."[85]

Periodically for two years now Cardinal Gibbons had been exerting himself to prevent the Holy See from condemning the works of Henry George. There can be little question but that the campaign he waged had its effects in Rome, but it must be remembered that Archbishop Corrigan was equally intent that the good of souls in the United States called for such a condemnation. Numerically the followers of Gibbons in the hierarchy were greater than the sympathizers with Corrigan but, nonetheless, the Roman officials were confronted with a flow of documentary evidence from both sides and once the question

---

[83] 85-H-6, Gibbons to McQuaid, Baltimore, November 10, 1888, copy. Lambert had come to Baltimore bearing a letter of introduction from Walter Elliott, C.S.P. (85-C-1, Elliott to Gibbons, Rochester, September 16, 1888).

[84] McQuaid to Corrigan, Rome, December 20, 1888, quoted in Zwierlein, *op. cit.*, III, 62–63.

[85] *Ibid.*, III, 63.

was laid before them by Corrigan they presumably felt they could not escape giving a judgment of some kind. As usual the Romans took their time but finally on February 6, 1889, the Congregation of the Inquisition gave a decision that the works of George had been found deserving of condemnation, and they transmitted their judgment to Cardinal Simeoni that he might forward it to Cardinal Gibbons. In doing so Simeoni stated that in view of the peculiar circumstances of the time and place, and by reason of the vigilance with which Rome credited the American hierarchy in guarding their people against doctrinal errors, the cardinals of the Inquisition had stated that the condemnation need not be published. It was forwarded, therefore, to Gibbons under the seal of the Holy Office with the added exhortation that the American bishops exercise their pastoral care and vigilance in quieting the controversy and in maintaining the integrity of sound doctrine.[86]

The decision would seem to have been a compromise between the Gibbons and Corrigan positions. Certainly the Cardinal of Baltimore would have been far more pleased had there been no decision of any kind, but he doubtless consoled himself that in its not being made public he had won at least a substantial victory. Corrigan could rightly afford to feel that the decision was a vindication of his view from the outset that the teaching of Henry George was not reconcilable with Catholic doctrine. But his disappointment in not being able to reveal his triumph was probably reflected in the remark of his friend McQuaid to Denis O'Connell when he said, "What's the use of it, if you can't

---

[86] 85-W-4, Simeoni to Gibbons, Rome, April 9, 1889. The pertinent passage of Simeoni's letter read as follows: "Libri in vulgus editi ab Henrico Georgio [sic] examini Supremae Congregationis S.R. et Universalis Inquisitionis fer. IV die 6 Februarii 1889 subiecti fuerunt, mihique demandatum, ut significarem Eminentiae Tuae eosdem damnatione dignos inventos fuisse. Attentis tamen peculiaribus temporum et locorum circumstantiis, et habita praesertim ratione zeli ac sollicitudinis, qua omnes sacrorum Antistites istius Reipublicae vigilant, ut fideles eorum curae concrediti, ab erroribus qui circumferuntur, serventur immunes; Emi. Patres Generales Inquisitores a condemnatione evulganda supersedendum censuerunt. Omnio enim confidunt, istarum regionum Episcopos una tecum industriam ac diligentiam esse adhibituros, ut quae Catholica Ecclesia de privatae proprietatis iure, vel si id terram respiciat, perpetuo docuit et pluries definivit, ac novissimis etiam temporibus per Summos Pontifices Pium IX, Litteris Encyclicis *Qui pluribus,* et SSmum. D. N. Leonem XIII, Litteris pariter Encyclicis *Quod Apostolici muneris,* inculcavit, fideles ac potissimum ecclesiastici viri, nulla eorum admixtione, retineant, atque a falsis theoriis, quas ea super re Henricus Georgius [sic] venditat, sibi caveant."

publish it?" To O'Connell himself the decision was a *"brutum fulmen,"* and he took from it at least the consolation that it had shown clearly how necessary the counterrepresentations of Gibbons and his friends had been.[87] There could be little question that the protests of the Gibbons party had slowed down the case and in the end accounted for the demand for secrecy. If there had been no such effort from that side the important reservation of silence would very likely not have been attached. At least the general American public would not be stirred up to new agitation over the case and the enemies of the Church were deprived of the opportunity of playing up the new Roman "aggression" against the liberties of American citizens. For that much — and it was a major point in his policy — Gibbons could breathe a sigh of relief.

But despite his oft-repeated reluctance to be drawn into the differences of Archbishop Corrigan with his clergy, Cardinal Gibbons was not yet free from the annoyance. When Corrigan early in 1890 removed Richard Burtsell from the pastorate of the Church of the Epiphany in New York City and appointed him pastor of St. Mary's Church at Rondout, New York, Burtsell was not ready to submit without a struggle. He took up his case with Rome and suggested to Cardinal Simeoni that the latter ask the opinion of Gibbons which, he believed, would be favorable to him. Although Burtsell had not previously asked permission of Gibbons to use his name, he did inform him of his action and he gave him an exact quotation of his words to the Prefect of Propaganda.[88] But Gibbons would not co-operate and he told Simeoni directly that he knew nothing of the case and would ask that he not request him to give any opinion.[89] Burtsell persisted and two months later called on Gibbons when he was in New York, only to be told that he would have nothing to do with the matter. Despite this admonition the canon lawyer sent a set of documents to Baltimore for the cardinal to read but Gibbons was quick to reply, "I send you back at once the documents which you forwarded to me and which have just arrived."[90] The Archbishop of Baltimore had already suffered deep embarrass-

[87] 86-C-12, O'Connell to Gibbons, Rome, June 14, 1889, *Private.*

[88] 87-H-11, Burtsell to Gibbons, New York, April 16, 1890.

[89] 87-M-7, Gibbons to Simeoni, Baltimore, May 17, 1890, copy in Latin.

[90] 87-P-5, Gibbons to Burtsell, Baltimore, June 10, 1890, copy.

ment over his well-intentioned efforts of three years before to have Burtsell act as an intermediary for the Pope's message to McGlynn, and now that he was in trouble himself with Archbishop Corrigan the cardinal had no intention of giving any possible grounds for further suspicion of his sympathies with the archbishop's troublesome subjects.

Gibbons was always a tactful man but the wounded feelings of the Archbishop of New York toward him caused the cardinal to exercise extraordinary means to avoid further offense and to heal, if he could, the breach between them. When he was asked by several prominent Catholic laymen in the spring of 1890 to lend his presence to the fair being planned for the benefit of Holy Rosary Mission at Castle Garden, New York, a home for friendless emigrant girls, Gibbons made known his sympathy for the cause and said he would have accepted gladly had Archbishop Corrigan been at home and expressed his pleasure in the matter. "But without some manifestation of his Grace's wishes," said Gibbons, "I feel a delicacy in accepting which I know you will appreciate."[91] The laymen then turned to Preston, the vicar-general, with their problem and the latter speedily assured Gibbons of a welcome and remarked that Corrigan would feel very much indebted to him for coming since, as the monsignor said, Holy Rosary Mission "is very dear to his heart."[92] The cardinal felt free to accept the invitation after receiving this assurance, but the presence of Burtsell on the day Gibbons opened the fair at Castle Garden did not improve matters in official circles in New York. Archbishop Ryan told Corrigan that he had lately preached in a colored church in Washington where he had met the cardinal who explained that he had declined to go to New York until invited by Preston; which prompted Ryan to make the rather snide comment, "Under the circumstances however, as I heard them from himself, the Mgr. could not have well avoided it."[93] Such a remark coming from one who was at the time posing as a peacemaker between New York and Baltimore was hardly helpful.

The absence of the Archbishop of New York on this occasion

---

[91] 87-K-1, Gibbons to Joseph J. Donahue and Eugene Kelly, Baltimore, April 26, 1890, copy.

[92] 87-K-3, Preston to Gibbons, New York, April 27, 1890.

[93] AANY, Ryan to Corrigan, Philadelphia, May 20, 1890.

was due to his having made a trip to Rome. Whether or not Corrigan being at the Holy See had given rise to fears in the United States that he might win a reversal of decision on the secrecy governing the judgment of Henry George, we have no way of knowing; but at any rate, Gibbons was happy to be told by Father John P. Farrelly, spiritual director of the American College, that he had spoken to Simeoni concerning American apprehensions lest the Holy Office should make a public pronouncement, only to be reassured that there was no question of such a thing happening. Archbishop Sallua had likewise told Farrelly that no step of that kind would be taken without first consulting Gibbons and the hierarchy.[94]

The thing that bothered the Cardinal of Baltimore most at this time, however, was the attitude of Archbishop Corrigan toward him. Regardless of the discretion employed by those most immediately concerned, the coolness between the two archbishops became known and afforded a subject for comment among both their friends and enemies. Among those who endeavored to bring about peace was Maurice Francis Egan, editor of the New York *Freeman's Journal,* following the death of McMaster. Egan was fearful that certain items appearing in his paper might have given offense to Gibbons. For that reason he made a trip to Baltimore with a view to making an explanation to the cardinal. In announcing his visit he said that the attitude of the *Freeman's Journal* toward Gibbons might be a small matter to the cardinal, but he wished him to know, as he put it, that "it is of grave importance to me, since it would give me intense pain should you misjudge me."[95] Egan used the visit to speak of the relations between the two archbishops and when he returned home he wrote Gibbons as follows:

> I took the liberty of telling Archbishop Corrigan that I had seen Your Eminence and that you had said the kindest and most affectionate things of him. He was genuinely pleased. I am heartily glad of it. It is a pity that he should ever have been led to misunderstand you.[96]

But it would take more than the diplomacy of Egan to bring about the desired effect. Another man who was trying his hand

---

[94] 87-M-8, Farrelly to Gibbons, Rome, May 19, 1890.
[95] AAB, unclassified, Egan to Gibbons, Brooklyn, June 20, 1890.
[96] *Ibid.,* Egan to Gibbons, Brooklyn, July 2, 1890.

at peace between Baltimore and New York in these days was Archbishop Ryan. He discussed with Gibbons the question of Burtsell's approach in his own case and learned that the cardinal had written to Simeoni asking that his opinion be not solicited about Burtsell and that his letter to this effect could be seen in Rome. If Burtsell's telling Rome to wait until Gibbons could be heard from before giving a judgment about his quarrel with Corrigan had delayed matters, that was no fault of the cardinal. In reporting all this to Corrigan the Archbishop of Philadelphia said, "He seemed most anxious that you should know this history of the facts if you were not already aware of it."[97] Corrigan admitted he knew of this particular letter, but he went on to say that if Gibbons was disposed to throw any light on other documents he had written to Rome, including his memorial against the condemnation of George's writings, he thought, as he expressed it, that "it would be more to the purpose."[98] At this point Ryan felt the time had come for direct communication between the two principals, so he sent the Corrigan reply on to Baltimore with that recommendation, to which he added, "I shall pray in the Holy Sacrifice, that a mutual understanding may result from patient explanation, & shall do whatever may be in my power to effect it. Of course both of you have but *one great motive*, but you are of totally different temperaments & schools."[99]

Following the advice of Ryan, the cardinal wrote a detailed explanation of all that had taken place from the time Burtsell first made his unsuccessful appeal to him for friendly intervention, including as well copies of the exchange of correspondence between him and the canon lawyer and his own letter to Simeoni. Then turning to Corrigan's reference to the previous documents which Gibbons had sent to the Holy See against the George condemnation, he made it clear that on this point his conduct had been dictated by his conscience and his opinion had not in the meantime changed. Gibbons frankly told the Archbishop of New York:

> I regarded & still regard that subject as neither local nor personal, but one affecting the general interests of the Church of the U. States. And while having no sympathy for George or his doctrines,

[97] AANY, Ryan to Corrigan, Philadelphia, October 23, 1890.
[98] 88-B-1, Corrigan to Ryan, New York, October 24, 1890.
[99] 88-B-2, Ryan to Gibbons, Philadelphia, October 26, 1890.

I deprecated a public condemnation as calculated in my judgment to do harm to religion.

I sincerely regret that my action in this matter did not accord with your judgment; but I assure you that it was prompted solely by a conscientious sense of duty & the interests of religion.[100]

There is no record of Corrigan's response to this explanation of the cardinal's action. Gibbons did not give up hope of a reconciliation and when word reached him a few days later that the archbishop's brother, Father James H. Corrigan, pastor of St. Mary's Church at Elizabeth, New Jersey, was gravely ill he sent a message of sympathy and promised to say Mass for him. In acknowledging his gratitude for the cardinal's sympathy, no mention was made by Corrigan of the explanation of the Burtsell affair.[101] The same week Gibbons was at pains to show the archbishop that he had instructed his lawyers to bring suit against the publisher of an unnamed book if they did not remove his name from it. Presumably the offending publication was critical of Corrigan since the cardinal told him, "It is a sore affliction to me that an unwarranted use of my name continues to be made in connection with the trials thro' which you have passed and which I hope are at an end."[102] This gesture brought regrets that Gibbons had been subject to such annoyance, a statement that his sick brother was now improved, but nothing more.[103] While the correspondence of the Archbishop of New York with Baltimore continued, therefore, in a polite but terse form, there was no acknowledgment that the cardinal's explanations had been found satisfactory.

Meanwhile the months passed and in May, 1891, there appeared the long-awaited encyclical on social questions when Leo XIII published *Rerum novarum*. Cardinal Gibbons, as we have seen, composed a letter of congratulations to the Pontiff and he took occasion to say that for a long time the Pope had been urged, and especially was this true in recent years, to condemn George's *Progress and Poverty*. But the desire of the cardinal, as he stated, had been that His Holiness should give Catholics a positive and explicit instruction on these matters

100 AANY, Gibbons to Corrigan, Baltimore, October, 31, 1890, *Private*.
101 88-C-3, Corrigan to Gibbons, New York, November 12, 1890.
102 88-C-4, Gibbons to Corrigan, Baltimore, November 14, 1890, copy.
103 88-D-1, Corrigan to Gibbons, New York, November 18, 1890.

rather than to reprove some of the false and dangerous propositions. Now with *Rerum novarum,* as he expressed it, "My desire has been realized, my hopes have been satisfied."[104] Monsignor O'Connell thought the cardinal's letter was well written but he told him that in view of the fact that the question of Henry George's teachings was now a thing of the past, he had not made Gibbons' letter public. "The excitement is no longer possible today," said O'Connell, "that was possible three years ago." Previous to the appearance of the encyclical the Roman rector had arranged for a series of articles in the *Moniteur de Rome* which were to be based on newspaper clippings forwarded to him by Gibbons, but now that the papal document had come out O'Connell had the articles suppressed.[105]

With the remaining phases of the controversy insofar as they related to Dr. McGlynn the Cardinal of Baltimore had little or nothing to do. The priest continued under the ban of excommunication until the coming of Archbishop Francesco Satolli to the United States in the capacity of papal ablegate to settle the school controversy of Archbishop Ireland. At that time an appeal was made to Satolli as the representative of the Holy See and McGlynn submitted a statement of his teaching on land which, in turn, Satolli gave over to the examination of four professors of the Catholic University of America where he was then in residence. The professors, Thomas Bouquillon, Thomas O'Gorman, Edward A. Pace, and Charles P. Grannan, examined the statement in the light of the recent encyclical and the Church's teachings generally and found nothing therein against faith and morals. Basing his judgment, therefore, on the professors' analysis, Satolli received McGlynn on December 23, 1892, at the university and late that evening issued a statement to the press that the priest had been freed from ecclesiastical censures and restored to the exercise of his priestly functions.[106]

---

[104] Vatican Archives, Gibbons to Leo XIII, Baltimore, June 22, 1891, photostat.

[105] 88-U-2, O'Connell to Gibbons, Rome, August 3, 1891, *Private.* Henry George was sufficiently exercised over the Pope's teaching on the right of private property to publish a challenge of *Rerum novarum* in *The Condition of Labor: An Open Letter to Pope Leo XIII* (New York, 1891).

[106] Bell, *op. cit.,* pp. 226–231, printed McGlynn's doctrinal statement. In an unpublished master's thesis done at the Catholic University of America in 1935 on the subject, "Rev. Dr. McGlynn's Statement on Private Land Ownership in the Light of the Teaching of Pope Leo XIII," Vincent A. McQuade, O.S.A., reached the conclusion, "Economically his proposals might be censured; theologically, they do not contain any false principles" (p. 45).

With the ban lifted, McGlynn after a few weeks proceeded to Florida where he spent considerable time preaching and giving lectures in the Diocese of St. Augustine under the friendly patronage of his loyal defender, Bishop Moore. The bishop was elated at the impression he made and the reception he was accorded on all sides, and when he received a letter from someone saying an apology was due from McGlynn, Moore thought, on the other hand, that an apology was due to the priest for five years of what he called "gross injustice," and Moore concluded his report to Cardinal Gibbons by saying that he would have no difficulty in putting his hand on the "culprit" from whom the apology was due.[107]

In the early summer of 1893 Dr. McGlynn finally made the long-delayed trip to Rome where he was received in a kindly manner by Pope Leo XIII and his Secretary of State, Cardinal Rampolla. He gave public expression to his gratification in responding to the invitation of the editor of the *Forum* for an article on the subject of "The Vatican and the United States." McGlynn had words of high praise for the establishment of a permanent apostolic delegation in this country with Satolli as delegate, and he took the occasion to say that the presence here of the Pope's representative would put a stop to the tyranny practiced by some bishops in governing their priests and people.[108] After his return from Europe there followed about a year and a half of uncertainty as far as his status in the Archdiocese of New York was concerned, but then in January, 1895, he was appointed by Archbishop Corrigan as pastor of St. Mary's Church at Newburgh, New York. In February, 1897, McGlynn contributed another article to the *Forum* in which he gave a glowing account of the success which had attended

---

[107] 91-H-9, Moore to Gibbons, St. Augustine, March 25, 1893. After McGlynn's reinstatement the press continued to print misleading accounts of the trouble. For example, the New York *Herald* of January 3, 1893, quoted an "ecclesiastic who occupies a high position in this archdiocese" to the effect that there would have been no excommunication for contumacy had not McGlynn's letter to Leo XIII been "burned by a high ecclesiastic into whose hands it was given to be transmitted to the Pope."

[108] XVI (September, 1893), 11–21. O'Connell told Gibbons shortly before that he had an opportunity of going to Norway and he took it. As he said, "It enabled me to avoid a meeting with Dr. McGlynn." He added, however, "Everything connected with Dr. McGlynn's audiences was most cordial" (91-R-1, O'Connell to Gibbons, Rome, August 1, 1893).

Satolli's mission as Apostolic Delegate to the United States.[109] The article appeared two months after Satolli had been made a cardinal and had returned to Rome. When copies of the article elicited letters of appreciation from Cardinals Satolli and Rampolla to the author, the Newburgh pastor transcribed the text of the messages from Rome in the belief that the Archbishop of Baltimore would be pleased to see them.[110]

In October of the year 1897 Father McGlynn pronounced the eulogy at the funeral of his old friend, Henry George. The two men had fallen out for a number of years but they were reconciled before George's death. But long before the author of the American single tax movement died the enthusiasm for his crusade had waned, and although certain of his followers continued their interest, the movement had for some time ceased to occupy national attention. There was no one who welcomed the breaking up of the single tax crusade and the Anti-Poverty Society with more glee than Bishop McQuaid, and in referring to the signs of disintegration he remarked to his friend Corrigan, "Protestants are now putting down Henry George's one tax theory, since Catholics, at the dictation of Card. Gibbons, declined to do so."[111] Gibbons had, indeed, exerted every effort to prevent the Church "putting down" the George theory in the sense of a formal doctrinal pronouncement, but he would have yielded not at all to the Bishop of Rochester in his satisfaction at the decline of the whole movement which he had predicted on more than one occasion.[112]

The case of Henry George and Dr. McGlynn proved to be one of the most unpleasant and painful episodes of Cardinal Gibbons' career. Insofar as George's teachings were concerned, the fight which the cardinal put up to prevent their condemnation by Rome sprang from the same strong conviction he had shown in the matter of the secret societies and the Knights of Labor, namely, that the way to handle such problems was not that of harsh decisions imposed by the Holy See. As with the

---

[109] "The Results of Cardinal Satolli's Mission," XXII (February, 1897), 695–705.

[110] AAB, unclassified, McGlynn to Gibbons, Newburgh, May 21, 1897.

[111] McQuaid to Corrigan, n.p., October 27, 1893, quoted in Zwierlein, *op. cit.*, III, 82.

[112] McGlynn outlived George by only a little over two years, dying at Newburgh on January 7, 1900.

knights, so in the case of George, Gibbons rightly guessed that the Church was here dealing with an ephemeral thing, and that if a certain amount of patience was exercised the difficulty posed by these cases would disappear of itself. The Archbishop of Baltimore was no more prepared to compromise doctrine than was a prelate like Archbishop Corrigan, but he knew and understood the American mentality much better than Corrigan and he was intent that the enemies of the Church in the United States should not find a new opportunity to charge a Roman aggression against American liberties if it could possibly be avoided. The final verdict of Rome on George's doctrines was not, of course, what the cardinal would have wished, but it is clear that the campaign which Gibbons and his friends waged against the condemnation had at least the salutary effect of preventing public fulminations against an economic theorist whose popularity was already in a state of serious decline when Rome handed down its secret judgment. The course of events ultimately sustained the cardinal's prediction about the temporary character of the single tax movement, for while it lived on among a few ardent followers for many years, its force was spent and it was deprived of the boon it would have experienced among many Americans had it been dignified by a public condemnation of the Holy See.

In regard to McGlynn the cardinal's intervention originally came in obedience to the command of the Holy Father that he should try to get the priest to Rome. In the fulfillment of that command Gibbons little dreamed that his letter of February 18, 1887, to Burtsell would be the occasion for picturing him as the defender of one who had set at defiance the commands of his own archbishop. Once the cardinal sensed the danger to which his well-intentioned efforts exposed him among McGlynn's friends and in the press, he strenuously fought against further involvement in the case. But the ire of Archbishop Corrigan had already been aroused and the damage was done. Repeatedly the cardinal endeavored to set his position right with the Archbishop of New York but for a period of some years he did not succeed. The detailed explanations of his actions by mail, the oral apologies for his conduct given to Archbishop Ryan to be relayed to New York, and the occasional friendly gestures

— all seemed to be received in a spirit of cold politeness that lacked entirely the suggestion of genuine forgiveness and a satisfaction of mind.

On the subject of his role in the cases of Corrigan's disobedient priests like McGlynn and Burtsell the cardinal's conscience was clear. He made his explanations in good faith and if they were not fully accepted he could only regret his failure to win back a prelate with whom for years he had been on close and friendly terms. But on one point even the demands of generosity toward an erstwhile friend and the need for harmony between New York and Baltimore could not move the cardinal. As he frankly told Corrigan on the question of a condemnation of George's book he still regarded that subject as neither local nor personal but as one affecting the general interests of the American Church. Gibbons sincerely regretted that his action in that matter did not accord with the archbishop's judgment, but since here he had responded solely to a conscientious sense of his duty there was no more that he could do about it. In all of this the Cardinal of Baltimore never questioned the sincerity of the Archbishop of New York, for Corrigan, too, obviously believed that he was in the right. Time alone would calm the ruffled feelings and bring fulfillment of the wish of Archbishop Ryan when he said that "there should be as perfect union as possible between Baltimore and New York. . . ."[113]

---

[113] 88-B-2, Ryan to Gibbons, Philadelphia, October 26, 1890.

CHAPTER XIV

The Apostolic Delegation

THERE was no event which served to emphasize more strikingly the mutually unsatisfactory relations existing in these years between the Holy See and the Catholic Church of the United States than the disciplining of Dr. Edward McGlynn. In the last quarter of the nineteenth century the number of appeals reaching the Holy See from American priests who were in trouble with their bishops grew steadily to the increasing annoyance of the Roman officials. In a considerable proportion of these cases Rome gave its judgment against the bishops which, in turn, caused irritation in the ranks of the American hierarchy who felt that Rome's leniency toward the priests was detrimental to episcopal authority. The answer of the Holy See to complaints of this kind from the prelates was frequently that the bishops did not keep Rome fully informed on these matters, and that in some instances decisions had to be made without benefit of a complete documentary coverage of the case from the bishop. Moreover, it was the opinion of some of the officials in the Roman Curia that the American bishops had on occasion shown an arbitrary disposition in dealing with their priests, and it was this conviction that in part lay behind the Propaganda urging so strongly at the time of the Third Plenary Council that either cathedral chapters be instituted in the United States, or that the diocesan consultors be given the right of "consent" rather than mere "counsel" to many matters wherein the bishops believed their personal decision was sufficient.

To the mind of the Holy See the remedy for this situation lay in the adoption for the American Church of what had long since become the normal practice in many of the countries of Europe and South America, namely, to have a resident representative of the Holy Father in this country. It was Rome's desire that this official should have preferably the rank of an apostolic nuncio who would enjoy diplomatic recognition from the American government, as well as possess full faculties from the Holy See to settle on the spot troublesome cases which might arise within the Church itself. In other words, the idea of Rome was a papal representative at Washington who would hold a dual status as was true at the time in such European capitals as Paris, Vienna, and Madrid. But to the overwhelming majority of the American hierarchy, as we shall see, this was not an acceptable answer to the difficulty of their relations with the center of the Catholic world, and from the earliest rumors of such an appointment it was vigorously resisted by many of the bishops. Many of the hierarchy, on the other hand, sought the accreditation of an American prelate residing in Rome who would, as in the case of Cardinal Howard for England, act as a liaison man for their business with the Holy See. With each side stoutly maintaining its own position, there was created something of an impasse until the closing years of the century when Rome imposed what was in the final analysis something of a compromise.

Long before the problem had become acute there had been some precedents for a representative of the Holy See in the United States, although in a few of these cases the result had not been happy. The earliest suggestion of a papal representative in Washington had come around 1819 from Father Robert Browne, O.S.A., a man who had given a great deal of trouble by his disobedience to the first three Archbishops of Baltimore.[1] In the following year, 1820, Joseph-Octave Plessis, Bishop of Quebec, acted on the request of Francesco Cardinal Fontana, Prefect of the Propaganda, to investigate the trustee troubles in the Church of New York.[2] On the occasion of the first two plenary councils of the American Church in 1852 and 1866 Archbishops Kenrick and Spalding respectively had been designated by Rome to act as apostolic delegates to preside over these councils. But when preparations were being made for the council of 1884 and the Holy See let it be known that it was

---

[1] Peter Guilday, *The Life and Times of John England, First Bishop of Charleston, 1786–1842* (New York, 1927), I, 288.

[2] Laval Laurent, O.F.M., *Québec et l'église aux Etats-Unis* (Washington, 1945), pp. 169–176.

going to appoint Bishop Luigi Sepiacci, O.S.A., as delegate to Baltimore, there was so firm a protest on the part of the American bishops, as we have already seen, that the idea of sending an Italian was withdrawn and Gibbons, in keeping with the precedents of 1852 and 1866, was named.

More than thirty years before the council of 1884 there occurred an incident which left a lasting memory in the minds of men of both Church and State. In June, 1853, there arrived in the United States the Apostolic Nuncio to Brazil, Archbishop Gaetano Bedini, who had been commissioned by Pius IX to come to this country to investigate the serious trustee troubles in Buffalo and other American sees. Bedini arrived just at a time when the nation was in a state of serious agitation over the Know-Nothing movement against Catholics and foreigners, and before the termination of his visit in February, 1854, he had been made the victim of numerous unfriendly demonstrations in various cities which in several cases almost reached the proportion of riots.

Acting in behalf of Bedini, Archbishop John Hughes of New York opened the question of the establishment of a nunciature at Washington with James Campbell, Postmaster-General in the cabinet of President Franklin Pierce, and a Catholic. Campbell made it known to Hughes that the President would be willing to receive a minister from the Papal States, providing it be understood that he would be only a political representative of the papal government, and he suggested that if a layman were named by Pius IX he believed there would be no difficulty.[3] This arrangement appeared acceptable to the American government since in 1848 the United States had named a fully accredited diplomatic representative to the Papal States with residence in Rome.[4] However, the Campbell suggestion of a layman to represent Pius IX at Washington solely in a political capacity apparently did not meet with the desire of Rome and nothing further came of the proposal at that time. All in all, therefore, the Bedini mission proved a failure from the viewpoint

---

[3] For the Bedini mission and the pertinent correspondence concerning the question of a nunciature at Washington cf. Peter Guilday, "Gaetano Bedini," *Historical Records and Studies*, XXIII (1933), 87–170.

[4] For the documents covering the diplomatic relations between the United States and the Papal States in these years cf. Leo F. Stock, Ed. *United States Ministers to the Papal States. Instructions and Despatches, 1848–1868* (Washington, 1933).

of both the Holy See and the American Church. Unfortunately, the American bishops had not been consulted in advance; if they had they might have spared the nuncio the painful experiences he endured by advising the Holy See of the inopportuneness of sending a representative to the United States when the Know-Nothing bigotry was at its height.

Nearly a quarter of a century later the Church of the United States received a visit from another papal envoy when George Conroy, Bishop of Ardagh and Apostolic Delegate to Canada, came to this country in 1878. Conroy met with no such vicious attacks as Bedini, and after an extensive tour of many of the American sees he paid a visit in mid-May to his former Roman schoolmate, Father Richard L. Burtsell, pastor of the Church of the Epiphany in New York. The delegate expressed his astonishment at the progress of the American Church and, according to Burtsell, he thought an apostolic delegate should be appointed to the United States. He would not recommend singling out the United States in this regard since it might prove odious, but if it should be the policy of the Holy See to appoint delegates elsewhere, then he felt it should be done here. It was Conroy's opinion that the delegate should not reside in Washington where he might be slighted by the President and the ambassadors of foreign powers but rather in New York where Cardinal McCloskey would maintain ecclesiastical precedence. Finally, he was represented as believing that the appointment should not be on a permanent basis but only for a time and according to the need.[5]

News of this kind was naturally calculated to increase the alertness of American Catholics about having a papal envoy in their midst, and the presence in this country from time to time of minor prelates from Rome who had no official standing but who, nonetheless, conducted themselves in an imprudent and officious manner did not improve matters. For example, the visits of Monsignori Filiberto M. Termos in 1882, Thomas J. Capel a year later, and Paolo Mori and Germano Straniero in

---

[5] AANY, Diary of Richard L. Burtsell, 1874–1878, May 14, 1878, p. 199. Some months later Bishop McQuaid was in Rome where he heard that Conroy had written "a most damaging report" on the American Church for the Holy See and he said he was going to try to secure a copy of it (74-E-2, McQuaid to Gibbons, Rome, December 10, 1878).

1886 all left an unhappy impression by these men touring the country, giving out newspaper interviews with observations on problems facing the Church here, and posing as representatives of the Holy See before the American public. Of these prelates only Straniero had anything approaching an official mission and his duty was simply to bring the red biretta to Baltimore for Cardinal Gibbons and no more.[6]

In the absence of a regularly established nunciature or apostolic delegation in the United States the conduct of the business of the Church with Rome had from the beginning of the hierarchy been channeled principally through the occupants of the See of Baltimore. In this respect the services of Cardinal Gibbons proved even more extensive than those of his predecessors. From the very outset of his tenure as Archbishop of Baltimore, Gibbons received a constant stream of inquiries from Rome for his judgment on such questions as the division of dioceses, the qualities of candidates for vacant sees, and the application of various aspects of canon law with respect to the American Church. Moreover, to Gibbons the Holy See entrusted special missions for the investigation and report of troubles which had arisen between a bishop and his clergy, as in the case of Bishop Rupert Seidenbush, O.S.B., Vicar Apostolic of Northern Minnesota, and his clergy in 1887, the dispute over property which arose between Bishop Gilmour of Cleveland and the Grey Nuns in Toledo in 1888, and the quarrel between Gilmour and one of his pastors which occurred the next year. This type of activity continued for almost the first twenty years of Gibbons' time in Baltimore and although he did not

---

[6] For Termos cf. AAC, Gibbons to Elder, St. Charles College, July 14, 1882; same to same, Baltimore, July 18, 1882; for Capel cf. 77-K-4, Capel to Gibbons, Philadelphia, September 8, 1883; 77-T-4, James O'Connor to Gibbons, Omaha, April 4, 1884; 78-I-3, Corrigan to Gibbons, New York, July 8, 1884; 79-A-2, Capel to Gibbons, Philadelphia, January 3, 1885; 79-I-1, Corrigan to Gibbons, New York, April 1, 1885; 82-I-3, Capel to Gibbons, Hicksville, California, Christmas Eve, 1886; for Straniero cf. 80-Y-3, Straniero to Gibbons, Rome, May 26, 1886; 81-B-5, D. J. O'Connell to Gibbons, Rome, June 2, 1886; AAC, Ella Edes to Elder, Rome, August 26, 1886; for Straniero and Mori cf. 81-U-7, O'Connell to Gibbons, Rome, September 8, 1886; ADR, Charles E. McDonnell to O'Connell, New York, September 15 and 26 and October 14, 1886; for Capel and Mori, 81-V-3, O'Connell to Gibbons, Rome, September 17, 1886; and Straniero, 82-F-11, Straniero to Gibbons, Barletta, Italy, November 30, 1886; 83-B-10, Gibbons to Straniero, Baltimore, July 12, 1887, copy; 88-L-4, Straniero to Gibbons, Rome, March 19, 1891.

hold the rank of apostolic delegate, except for the few weeks of the plenary council, actually there were many occasions when he performed the duties normally entrusted by Rome to one of that office. While he was not able, of course, to please all parties concerned in all these disputes, the cardinal's handling of the cases was generally successful and his services probably supplied in the minds of most of the bishops for any need they might have for an official representative of Rome in this country.

The first recorded opinion of James Gibbons on the subject of a permanent papal mission in the United States was occasioned by the visit which Bishop McQuaid of Rochester paid to Rome in the winter of 1878–1879. McQuaid was decidedly opposed to any such move, and while he had a number of reasons for his opposition, the fact that he had suffered a slight some years before from a visiting papal official probably had something to do with coloring his judgment. In 1875 Monsignor Cesare Roncetti had been sent to the United States with the red biretta for Cardinal McCloskey. McQuaid had invited the ablegate to visit Rochester and he had accepted, but then without any explanation Roncetti failed to stop in Rochester, although he spent three days in Buffalo. McQuaid felt justly aggrieved and he told his friend, Michael Corrigan, "When I take the trouble to invite a Roman Monsignor again, he will come to time according to promise."[7]

Incidents such as this, of course, only confirmed the strong-minded Bishop of Rochester in his views, and when a letter from the Archbishop of Baltimore reached him at Rome expressing opposition to an apostolic delegation for the American Church on political grounds McQuaid was fully prepared to agree. He told Gibbons that his repugnance to the plan arose chiefly from other reasons, although he conceded that the political one was a strong argument, and he assured him that he would use every judicious effort with all suitable persons from the Pope down "to put a stop," as he said, "to this *Delegate* arrangement." It was McQuaid's belief that had the recently deceased Prefect of Propaganda, Alessandro Cardinal

---

[7] McQuaid to Corrigan, n.p., July 12, 1875, quoted in Zwierlein, *op. cit.*, III, 3. The title "ablegate" is given by the Holy See to prelates whom it sends on temporary missions such as that of bearing the red biretta to a new cardinal who is absent from the residence of the Pope.

Franchi, lived he would have sent a nuncio to the United States. Franchi had put out feelers and he had his heart set on it, said McQuaid. As a remedy against what he called "such machinations," the bishop would have the American metropolitans speak up and make their minds known to Rome. He thought the disposition to listen to the American bishops in Rome was good and he felt convinced that the voice of the archbishops would be heeded.[8] After three weeks of further investigation and observation in the Eternal City McQuaid felt satisfied that the Roman authorities were determined on sending another delegate to Canada who would be commissioned at the same time to take a look at things in the United States. "This time," said McQuaid, "they will send an Italian," and he had heard that the office was being sought after by several prelates. To all of this McQuaid was, of course, opposed but he let Gibbons know that the chief blame for the condition lay with the American bishops, who did not keep the Holy See fully informed on trends in the Church of the United States. He fully believed that if there were two or three American prelates at Rome, "not afraid to speak," as he expressed it, they would be listened to. McQuaid himself had spoken out boldly but he was only one and, therefore, not of much consequence. But at least he was returning home content that he had done his best to bring about an arrangement that would be more satisfactory than the present one.[9]

A year and a half later Gibbons paid his first visit to Rome as Archbishop of Baltimore. His first impressions coincided with McQuaid's view regarding the source of trouble about Rome's legislation for the American Church. He told Archbishop Elder that from what he had seen he was now persuaded that if Rome at times departed from the letter of the conciliar legislation of Baltimore the fault was more at home than at the Holy See. Gibbons believed a remedy for these administrative snags could be found in the American Church having a strong and representative man resident in Rome, and he instanced England with a much smaller Catholic population as one branch of the

---

[8] 74-E-8, McQuaid to Gibbons, Rome, December 10, 1878; also published in Zwierlein, op. cit., II, 179–180.

[9] 74-G-2, McQuaid to Gibbons, Rome, January 1, 1879; also published in Zwierlein, op. cit., II, 180.

Universal Church that wielded more influence than the Americans by reason of powerful representation there.[10] He was alert on the subject of a delegate for the United States during his Roman visit, and in a later report of his activities to Elder he set forth a clear statement of the motives which governed his policy. He said:

> I spoke freely to one or more of the Cardinals & other officials on the inexpediency of sending us a Delegate. I would have mentioned the matter to the H. Father, if I were not assured that there is no danger of such a step being taken at least soon. I agree with you, & I believe that one of the certain results of such a step would be to create a school of service diplomacy, & another would be to retard the healthy progress of the Church & arouse complications with our government. If the danger is renewed, the Archbishops would do well to send a joint strong but temperate remonstrance. . . .[11]

Although the danger to which Gibbons alluded was not immediately renewed, the subject of American-Roman relations in ecclesiastical affairs continued a matter of concern to both sides. When the Fourth Provincial Council of Cincinnati was held in March, 1882, the need for the proper protection of American interests in Rome and the best means of communication were discussed, and although the bishops reached no positive recommendation, Gilmour of Cleveland informed Gibbons that a nuncio or delegate in the United States seemed unacceptable to everyone.[12] The Archbishop of Baltimore had already begun to canvass the views of a number of his fellow bishops on the advisability of having an American prelate established in Rome who would advise the Holy See on matters pertaining to this country. The response was sufficiently encouraging to warrant Gibbons sending a recommendation to Cardinal Simeoni in his own name and in the name of the other bishops urging that the plan be adopted.[13] But Rome took

---

[10] AAC, Gibbons to Elder, Rome, May 26, 1880.

[11] *Ibid.*, Gibbons to Elder, Rome, June 8, 1880.

[12] 76-P-11, Gilmour to Gibbons, Cleveland, April 21, 1882.

[13] Diary, October 20, 1882, p. 164. Archbishop Alemany was willing to conform to Gibbons' "wise proposition," although he found his affairs with Propaganda handled in a prompt and satisfactory manner (76-N-8, Alemany to Gibbons, San Francisco, February 10, 1882).

no action and when Gilmour paid a visit there some months later he was asked to write out his views on the subject of a Roman representative in the United States. The Bishop of Cleveland told Gibbons that he had responded as follows:

> To send a Legate from Rome to America would at present be injudicious, but to send an agent from America to Rome would not only be judicious but was necessary & would be acceptable, such Agent to be a bishop of experience & to be supported by a general levy pro rata on all the dioceses of America.

But Gilmour was not optimistic about the Holy See accepting his suggestion. Rome was determined, he said, to send here a representative, although it might be delayed until an American agent was tried in Rome if proper remonstrance was made; but if the American hierarchy neglected to make such remonstrance it was Gilmour's opinion that the "legate," as he called him, was sure to come.[14]

The recommendation of Bishop Gilmour for an American agent resident in Rome received a strong second when John J. Keane, Bishop of Richmond, visited the Holy See in the summer of 1883. Keane understood Gibbons' mind in the matter, and he fully agreed with the plan that the Archbishop of Baltimore had proposed to Simeoni some months before. During his stay in the Eternal City Keane had a number of conferences with Leo XIII, Cardinal Simeoni, and Archbishop Jacobini, the Secretary of Propaganda. From these conversations he had carried away two principal impressions. First, as he saw it there existed at the Holy See what he called a feeling that there was not a proper disposition of concord and union on the part of the American hierarchy toward the central government of the Church. The Romans had instanced the fact that some American bishops appeared to be lacking in politeness in not observing in their correspondence with the Holy See the proper style and methods of procedure, and to this Simeoni had added that it often happened that he wrote American bishops for information and did not even receive an answer. Keane agreed that this last, of course, was inexcusable, but the style in writing might be explained by ignorance of the proper

---

[14] 77-E-7, Gilmour to Gibbons, Cleveland, March 26, 1883.

forms and by a national brusqueness in the American character. However, such was certainly no indication of insubordination to the Holy See.

Keane's second impression dealt with the question of personal representation. Jacobini had confessed that he understood the American request for a representative at Rome to mean a sort of ambassador or plenipotentiary, something that no other hierarchy had. Simeoni, on the other hand, told Keane that when Leo XIII had spoken to a certain American bishop of his intention of sending a delegate to the United States the bishop had replied, "Oh we are independent, and would rather not have any one coming over to settle our business for us." Once more Keane conceded that either the bishop had expressed himself very poorly or the Pope had misunderstood him. He then explained that the American hierarchy shrank from the idea of a stranger coming to this country who would be immediately besieged by a crowd of malcontents and who would be unable to appreciate the circumstances or real nature of the cases laid before him. Simeoni's answer at this point was that the delegate would not be a tribunal for deciding cases at all, but only an envoy to investigate, gather information, and report to Rome.

The Prefect of Propaganda told Keane that Leo XIII had repeatedly urged him to send a delegate to the United States but that he had always replied he had no one suitable for the task. Simeoni thought an Irishman would be unacceptable to the French and Germans and a Frenchman would not please the Irish; consequently, only an Italian would be independent of all nationalities and he had no Italian with the necessary qualifications, and so there the matter rested. Keane again returned to the attack with a strong plea for an accredited American prelate in Rome who need not be an ambassador or a cardinal but who could, nonetheless, perform the functions for the American Church as Howard did for the English Church. To this Leo XIII had replied that he desired this himself, and he gave as an example the three German cardinals in the curia with whom he consulted on important negotiations he had to conduct relative to the Church in the German Empire. That, said Keane, was all the American bishops wished, and the report of the audience was concluded with the statement from the Holy Father that when the American metropolitans came to Rome in the autumn to prepare for the plenary council they could consult with him and all would be arranged to their satisfaction.[15]

Actually, however, no discussion of this question appears to have taken place in the fall of 1883 when the American archbishops were in Rome, and the minutes of the conferences at the Propaganda are completely silent on the point.[16] But the matter, nonetheless, did not die, for in the spring of 1885 before Gilmour started for the Holy See to help with the legislation of the Third Plenary Council Gibbons warned him that the talk of a delegate had been renewed.[17]

Gilmour arrived in Rome a month later and called to see Cardinal Manning who was then in the Eternal City. He reported Manning as "very clearly and openly opposed" to the idea of sending a delegate to the United States, and Bishop Dwenger of Fort Wayne, the man about whom the rumors of friendly relations with President Cleveland were circulating, as stating that he felt certain a nuncio or delegate was not contemplated by Rome.[18] But Gilmour's associate, Bishop Moore of St. Augustine, had picked up another variation which he relayed to Gibbons. On two or three occasions he had spoken to Jacobini about having an American bishop living in Rome, and the last time the Propaganda secretary had, according to Moore, "let the cat out of the bag," when he replied that the Americans wanted to tie Rome's hands. However, Jacobini had asked about the possibility of appointing one or two American bishops, either permanently or temporarily, to receive appeals in the United States and to treat matters there for Rome. Moore was agreeable to this proposal, providing there was also a prelate in Rome from the United States who could put matters into shape for the Propaganda and who could inform the officials

---

[15] 77-I-1, Keane to Gibbons, Florence, July 4, 1883.

[16] The only reference which the writer was able to find to a mention of this question during the Roman conferences of November–December, 1883, was a letter of Archbishop Ryan to Gibbons in which he wrote, "The Pope said (when we were in Rome) that he would select one recommended by the Archbishops who assembled in Rome in 1883 if he should determine on having a representative" (82-L-12, Ryan to Gibbons, Philadelphia, January 16, 1887).

[17] ADC, Gibbons to Gilmour, Cumberland, Maryland, May 9, 1885.

[18] 79-M-7, Gilmour to Gibbons, Rome, June 7, 1885.

of the value to be attached to testimony that came from this country. The Bishop of St. Augustine entertained the highest opinion of Jacobini's intelligence and ability, as well as of his good disposition toward the American Church.[19]

Just a week before Moore wrote his letter to the Archbishop of Baltimore there occurred an appointment which, to the mind of Gibbons, gave promise of solving the difficulty. On June 15, 1885, Denis J. O'Connell was named fourth Rector of the American College in Rome. This news rejoiced the heart of his patron in Baltimore, and Gibbons told Gilmour that he regarded the choice as not only a great blessing for the college but also a signal advantage for the American hierarchy who would find in O'Connell a wise and discreet intermediary between them and the Holy See. "He will discharge with zeal & ability," said Gibbons, "whatever commission may be entrusted to him."[20] O'Connell, who had been in Rome since the early spring to help with the legislation of the plenary council at the Propaganda, had already been active as an agent for Gibbons, and now that he was confirmed as rector he began a decade of service during which he served many of the American bishops as their Roman representative, although he never received any formal appointment as such nor any official recognition from the Holy See. The Roman rector had been from the outset fully cognizant, of course, of the question about a representative of the Holy See in the United States and six weeks after his appointment to the American College post he told Gibbons that Jacobini had said to him, "It is evident that we must appoint some one of the American Bishops our delegate in America."[21] Thus did the opinion at Rome swing back and forth at this time, but meanwhile no action was taken.

In the fall of 1885 matters took a new turn. In a confidential letter written in his own hand Cardinal Simeoni addressed an inquiry to Gibbons concerning his judgment on the propriety of Leo XIII sending a message of greeting and good will to President Cleveland. He gave as precedents for such a move the letters which the Pope had sent to the Emperors of China and Japan which had been very well received. If a communica-

---

tion could be sent to Washington with equal success it would be a source of consolation to the Holy Father who was then assailed by his enemies with such unfairness. The idea was Simeoni's own, and for that reason he wished it to be treated with the utmost confidence.[22]

The Archbishop of Baltimore replied after a few weeks to the inquiry of the Prefect of Propaganda, and while he expressed his thanks for the confidence reposed in him, he was at pains to lay before Simeoni a detailed explanation of why he thought such a letter would do more harm than good. The United States, he said, was largely a Protestant country with Protestant traditions. The article in the Constitution which provided that no religion should be favored had worked to the advantage of Catholics, for if any religion had been given a favored position it would have been the Protestant. True, the Catholic Church had made progress here, but Catholics were still a minority of eight out of fifty-five millions and the prejudices, however much buried they might seem at present, could easily be aroused again. American Catholics were in a position like that of the Catholics in England, and it was only by the exercise of prudence and moderation that they could hope to be and to remain strong. The American people were opposed to religious persecution but they were quick to resent favor to any particular religion and a letter from the Pope to the President would have the effect of uniting all the sects against the Church and making Catholics suspect of ambition, intrigue, and even of disloyalty.

Moreover, a letter from the Pope would embarrass President Cleveland. It was only in the last election that the Democratic Party had won after being excluded from power for twenty years. Most of the American Catholics were identified with that party and their opponents, the Republicans, would surely make the papal letter a weapon to be used against the Democrats. In these circumstances it was feared Cleveland might not make a reply that would be in keeping with the dignity of the Sovereign Pontiff and in accordance with the veneration with which Catholics surrounded his person. In the United States the real force was public opinion and public opinion would not be favorable to an exchange of letters such as suggested, even if Cleveland responded as fully and courteously as he should. At the moment both politi-

---

22 79-U-6, Simeoni to Gibbons, Rome, November 15, 1885.

cal parties were favorably disposed toward the Catholics and it would be unwise, said Gibbons, to do anything that might change these good dispositions.

He was happy to assure Simeoni, however, that personally the Holy Father was held in the highest esteem in this country, as was demonstrated by the universal admiration shown for his encyclicals like *Immortale Dei* by serious and intelligent Americans. Gibbons would have Simeoni know that he stood ready at all times to do whatever he could to foster cordial relations between the Holy See and the American government, but he did not believe that the sending of a letter from Leo XIII to Cleveland would accomplish that end.[23] The point of view outlined in this lengthy reply to the Prefect of Propaganda contained the sentiments which motivated Gibbons all through his life in opposition to the establishment of diplomatic relations between the two governments. While he was to be the intermediary a few years later of exchanges of letters between the Pope and the President, they occurred under the special circumstances of the centennial of the American Constitution and the golden jubilee of Leo XIII. In the present instance, however, he did not think the action suggested by Simeoni would be a wise one to follow up.

Just how real the threat of the appointment of a nuncio to Washington was it is difficult to determine. That there was a deep suspicion in the minds of a number of American bishops that Bishop Dwenger of Fort Wayne was engaged in some hidden action at Washington, there is no doubt. Denis O'Connell, who had returned to the United States for a visit, reported to Archbishop Corrigan that Dwenger had gone to Washington from Baltimore, and he added cryptically, "His companion says they are travelling for recreation."[24] Back in Rome a few months later O'Connell heard from an unnamed prelate that Monsignor Paolo Mori had attempted on his visit to the United States to open diplomatic relations and that Dwenger had made a trip to Washington with the same idea in mind.[25] News of this kind, of course,

---

[23] 79-Y-9, Gibbons to Simeoni, Baltimore, December 29, 1885, copy in French.

[24] AANY, O'Connell to Corrigan, Baltimore, February 24, 1886.

[25] 81-Q-3, O'Connell to Gibbons, Rome, August 1, 1886. There were others who had heard this version of Mori's visit and on better authority than O'Connell's unnamed prelate. John B. Stallo, who had become American minister to Italy in 1885 and who was friendly with Mori in Rome, informed Secretary of State Bayard in a private letter of April 2, 1887, that when criticism arose over Mori's

alarmed Cardinal Gibbons and others. Bishop Moore also had the story from O'Connell with added details. Moore quoted for Gibbons the pertinent passage from O'Connell's letter:

> Brisk correspondence between Card. Melcher [*sic*] and the West. There is reason for believing that Dwenger was called on to propose diplomatic relations with the Holy See and the U.S. and the attempt failed; report: "Impossible with present cabinet."

At this Moore was indignant and he poured out his feelings in a lengthy communication to the Cardinal of Baltimore, in which he vigorously protested against negotiations on so grave a subject being conducted behind the backs of the American episcopate. The Bishop of St. Augustine thought he knew the reason for secrecy, "probably because it is well known," he wrote, "that the Bishops of the U. S. are opposed to the project."[26] He followed this up with a similar letter to O'Connell in which he said he had described "Dwenger's escapade" for Bishop Gilmour, and he hoped O'Connell would keep Cardinal Gibbons fully informed of all he heard in Rome on the subject.[27] Gilmour was in complete sympathy with his Florida friend, and on a recent trip to Baltimore he had spoken fully with Gibbons on the subject of a nuncio and found, as he expressed it, that "He fully grasps the danger and impolicy of the move."[28]

Nor was the news at the end of the year 1886 more encouraging. Dr. O'Connell wrote that it appeared the United States was to have a nuncio after all and he heard that the main question then in the Pope's mind was the "dualism" of having a nuncio and a cardinal in the same country.[29] Apart entirely from the disturbing intelligence that the campaign was on again, Gibbons could hardly have taken seriously the remark about the question

---

activities in this country the latter showed him an autograph letter which he had from Cardinal Jacobini, papal Secretary of State, "from which," said Stallo, "to my astonishment, it appeared that the chief object of his mission had been to persuade the President, yourself, the Speaker of the House, etc., of the propriety of sending a diplomatic representative of the United States to the Holy See." Quoted in Charles Callan Tansill, *The Foreign Policy of Thomas F. Bayard, 1885-1897* (New York, 1940), p. xxxi.

[26] 81-S-2, Moore to Gibbons, St. Augustine, August 20, 1886.

[27] ADR, Moore to O'Connell, St. Augustine, August 31, 1886.

[28] ADC, Gilmour to Moore, November 5, 1886, copy.

[29] 82-G-9, O'Connell to Gibbons, Rome, December 10, 1886. Gibbons was also told by O'Connell that news of Simeoni's confidential letter to him of a year before had reached Rome through a leak from the United States.

of precedence since it was customary in capitals like Vienna and Paris to have a nuncio with the rank of an archbishop resident in the same city with the ordinary of the see who was normally a cardinal. He was far more concerned about the main business and, as he told Gilmour, he had received that week news from Rome that would put their worries over the German question "into the shade." He urged the Bishop of Cleveland to consult with Archbishop Elder as to what they should do. Gibbons suggested as one possibility that each province might prepare a protest to be sent to him which would set forth the dangerous consequences to be apprehended from such an appointment. The cardinal continued:

> What are to us the strongest reasons against the measure, would have little weight in Rome. The strongest arguments for us with the H. See are I think. 1. that the nuncio would have the official recognition from the government, & that this would be derogatory to the dignity of the H. See. 2. His presence here would serve to strengthen the statement of our enemies that ours is a foreign religion, paying homage to a foreign Power. It would arouse latent prejudices, & perhaps might occasion a repetition of the Bedini troubles.

While it is easy enough to appreciate Gibbons' reasoning on the second and third points advanced, it is difficult to see how he felt recognition of a nuncio by the government would be derogatory to the Holy See. There was no explicit statement of the reasons which seemed strongest to the American bishops in distinction to those which he felt would carry the most weight in Rome. In any case, the Cardinal of Baltimore was genuinely aroused. He told Gilmour in conclusion, "I am much exercised about it, but thus far have communicated the subject only to yourself. Our action must be calm, firm & respectful."[30]

But he soon extended his worries beyond the Bishop of Cleveland. Archbishops Elder and Corrigan were informed within a few days, and to the latter he said that before his departure for Rome to receive the red hat he would like to have the views of the metropolitans about a nuncio since the subject was likely to arise when he reached the Eternal City.[31] The cardinal was soon

---

[30] ADC, Gibbons to Gilmour, Baltimore, December 29, 1886, *Private*.

[31] AAC, Gibbons to Elder, Baltimore, January 3, 1887; AANY, Gibbons to Corrigan, Baltimore, January 7, 1887, *Personal*.

re-enforced with the opinions of his episcopal colleagues. Gilmour recalled his own memorial to the Propaganda at their request in 1882, and he now proposed that the American archbishops confer and come to a joint conclusion and then call their suffragans to get their support.[32] The Archbishop of New York regretted a nuncio as much as Gibbons, and he was particularly fearful that Dwenger might be chosen since he was believed at Rome to have *"immense political influence"* in this country.[33] Two days later Corrigan returned to the subject with the idea that if there must be a nuncio in the United States, it would be much better if Gibbons himself or Archbishop Williams would consent to fill the post.[34] Archbishop Ryan, too, was opposed to a nuncio, although he was inclined to think that an American prelate in the office of apostolic delegate might do good.[35]

After learning the opinions of a considerable number of the American bishops, Gibbons decided that there was not enough time left before he sailed to hold a formal meeting of the metropolitans. He had determined, however, as he told Gilmour, that unless subsequent developments caused him to change his mind when he reached Rome, he would advocate a delay in the matter until the archbishops could be heard from. If that counsel was not heeded then Gibbons would wish to know the choice of the American hierarchy for the office of nuncio, since he believed Gilmour was correct in his surmise that it would be an American. "The great, or principal objections," said Gibbons, "are removed

---

[32] 82-K-10, Gilmour to Gibbons, Cleveland, January 7, 1887. The "Canada muddles" referred to by Gilmour in this letter probably related to the quarrel between the bishops and the Society of Jesus over the legal title to the estates of the Jesuits which had been confiscated by the British government after the suppression of the Society in 1773. Prime Minister Honoré Mercier of the Province of Quebec undertook a settlement of the long-standing dispute in 1887. He secured the passage of a bill legally incorporating the Jesuits, and the apportionment of the sum appropriated as compensation was given over to Leo XIII to fix the ratio between the Jesuits, the Church, and Laval University. Cf. Robert Rumilly, *Histoire de la province de Québec* (Montreal, 1943), V, 281–289.

[33] 82-L-1, Corrigan to Gibbons, New York, January 8, 1887, *Private.*

[34] 82-L-6, Corrigan to Gibbons, New York, January 10, 1887, *Private.*

[35] 82-L-8, Ryan to Gibbons, Philadelphia, January 10, 1887. Ryan was more positive about the benefit to be derived from the appointment of a delegate when he wrote to Corrigan on the subject. He stated that an American in that office would help to silence the cry of "foreign allegiance" and decide matters of controversy among themselves more speedily (AABo, Ryan to Corrigan, Philadelphia, January 11, 1887, copy).

by having the appointee restricted to an American."[36] Following a suggestion of the Bishop of Cleveland, the cardinal urged upon Archbishop Elder that he call a meeting of his suffragans to get their views on the subject.[37] Moore in far-off Florida continued to fret at the prospect of Dwenger in Washington as nuncio, concerning whom he told Gibbons he could not think of "a more unfit selection. . . ."[38] To his friend, the Bishop of Cleveland, Moore urged that the American hierarchy strengthen Gibbons' hand by letters of protest since, as he said, "with him lies the remedy."[39]

The frequent mention of Dwenger as a possible candidate for the American nunciature presents a difficulty which is not easily solved. That the bishops took seriously the possibility that he might be appointed, there was no doubt; and yet there is little or no evidence — aside from periodic rumors and the bishop's own exaggerated notion of his power in Rome and Washington — to enable one to say whether or not he was really being considered for the office by the Holy See. In all likelihood the story owed its origin to the pompous manner in which he had conducted himself while he was in Rome with Gilmour and Moore in 1885 which annoyed his two colleagues so much, and to the fact that Dwenger seemed to fancy himself as a diplomat who enjoyed high prestige with some of the curial prelates as well as with certain government officials in Washington. Whatever the explanation be, a number of his fellow bishops were aroused over what they regarded as a real danger that he might convince Rome and Washington of his usefulness for the position, and they were determined at all costs to prevent him from succeeding in what they believed were his designs upon the office of nuncio.

This feverish activity among the American bishops on the eve of Gibbons' departure for Rome found an outlet to the public through the pages of the New York *Herald* of January 17, 1887. Rumors about the appointment of a nuncio had appeared previously in the press, and the *Herald's* Washington correspondent met up with a gentleman "well informed" on matters in the Church who gave him what was supposed to be an authentic

36 ADC, Gibbons to Gilmour, Baltimore, January 13, 1887, *Personal*.
37 AAC, Gibbons to Elder, Baltimore, January 13, 1887, *Private*.
38 82-L-10, Moore to Gibbons, St. Augustine, January 15, 1887.
39 ADC, Moore to Gilmour, St. Augustine, January 14, 1887.

story. Dwenger, it was true, had been in Washington some months before but on business of a purely private nature. The *Herald's* informant said that under the American form of government a nuncio could not possibly be accredited to Washington, nor would the Holy See try such an absurd move. Perhaps, there were one or two American bishops who would like to have "a papal inspector, so to speak," in the United States but it was certain not to happen. Cardinal Gibbons would be in Rome the following month and if the papal diplomats wished information of a reliable character about American political institutions he could furnish it.

Bishop Borgess of Detroit read this item in the *Herald,* and in connection with Elder's summons to a provincial meeting on the subject he wanted to know from Gilmour what they ought to do. Elder's suggestion of getting Rome to delay did not meet with Borgess' approval, since if the Holy See was determined on an appointment then the hierarchy of this country should speedily propose an American. Elder's hope for a delaying tactic was futile and Borgess feared, as he said, that it would only "insure us an Italian, when we least expect it."[40] Archbishop Williams was in Baltimore the week before Gibbons left and was reported by the cardinal as fully in accord with the other prelates on the need for blocking the appointment of Dwenger.[41] The day before Gibbons sailed for Rome the Bishop of Cleveland expressed to McQuaid of Rochester his belief that a nuncio was bound to come, and in that case he stated his preference for Corrigan, Williams, or McQuaid himself among the American bishops. With an eye to the political repercussions of such an appointment, Gilmour believed the next presidential campaign would be run on the issue of the nuncio and Catholicism. "Such a boon," said the bishop, "as it will be for the Republicans."[42]

---

[40] Archives of the Archdiocese of Detroit, Borgess to Gilmour, Detroit, January 19, 1887, copy.

[41] AABo, Gibbons to Corrigan, Baltimore, January 20, 1887, copy.

[42] *Ibid.,* Gilmour to McQuaid, Cleveland, January 28, 1887, copy. McQuaid's mounting unfriendliness to Gibbons at this time was reflected in his remarks to Archbishop Corrigan about the possibility of Dwenger being named nuncio. He wrote, "No one is so much to blame as Cardinal Gibbons himself. He gave prominence to Dwenger in the hope that the latter would favor his scarlet aspirations. Dwenger kept his part of the implied bargain. Why should not his Eminence favor D.? Dwenger, as Nuncio, would be the biggest thorn in the side of the Cardinal he ever could know. I would not pity him a bit" (McQuaid

Once he reached Rome the Cardinal of Baltimore exerted every effort to prevent the appointment of a nuncio to the United States. He was happy to report to Corrigan that Monsignor Straniero had been shelved, particularly since he had handed in to the Holy Father upon his return to the Holy See from this country, a report which strongly urged a nunciature despite his knowledge of the opposition of the hierarchy. Gibbons characterized the Straniero document as "insidious," adding his assurance to the Archbishop of New York that he would do all in his power to have the appointment definitely postponed.[43] The cardinal wrote in much the same vein to Archbishop Elder and said he intended to prepare documents on all the principal subjects affecting the American Church including the nunciature. After a week's residence in Rome Gibbons' conviction was strengthened that it was necessary to have a vigilant representative there from the United States in order to prevent what he termed "mischievous legislation."[44]

True to his word, the cardinal submitted to Leo XIII a formal request for the recognition of Dr. O'Connell as the representative of the American hierarchy. He outlined the need for someone to supply the Holy See with authentic information on American problems and who might act as liaison officer between Rome and the American bishops. He was convinced, said Gibbons, that of all the ecclesiastics in the United States no one knew both the civil and ecclesiastical conditions of this country more intimately than Denis O'Connell. He possessed the full confidence of all the bishops and he had the intelligence and discretion to

---

to Corrigan, n.p., January 26, 1887, quoted in Zwierlein, *op. cit.,* III, 151). With McQuaid's strong influence over the Archbishop of New York being brought constantly into play against Gibbons, it is small wonder that the archbishop's sensitive nature reacted to this prodding from Rochester in a way that was detrimental to good relations between New York and Baltimore.

[43] AANY, Gibbons to Corrigan, Rome, February 18, 1887, *Personal.* There was uneasiness in other quarters besides the American hierarchy. Baron Saverio Fava, Italian minister to Washington, was fearful of the restoration of diplomatic relations between the Holy See and the United States. On February 18, 1887, he inquired of Secretary of State Bayard if any application of this kind had been made. Bayard replied that it had not and he added, "that the indisposition of the Government of the United States to recognize any particular religion would probably prevent any such application being made; that it would be an anomalous condition of things. He said he was very glad to hear it." Quoted from Bayard's own account of the interview with Fava by Tansill, *op. cit.,* p. xxx.

[44] AAC, Gibbons to Elder, Rome, February 19, 1887.

handle the assignment. He asked the Pope, therefore, to accord the rank of counselor to the Propaganda to O'Connell and thus to confer on the American Church the good fortune and inestimable advantage of his official services.[45]

Following a practice which had begun some years before, Gibbons kept in close touch on all important questions with his friend Archbishop Elder of Cincinnati who shared the cardinal's views on most matters. Elder thought it would be an immense benefit if Gibbons could bring about the appointment of an American prelate to reside in Rome as their representative, and as a beginning he suggested that the Rector of the American College might be made a monsignor and receive an official post at the Propaganda.[46] Despite the support which O'Connell's appointment received from Gibbons and his friends, however, no official action was taken by the Pope, although the Roman rector continued to serve the American hierarchy in the capacity of their representative without official status. During this spring of 1887 the belief of Gibbons grew stronger that the plan for a nuncio had been blocked. He told Elder that he had hopes amounting almost to a certainty that the question would not be opened, or if it was, that the advice of the American prelates would be followed.[47] But three weeks later Gibbons reflected to his friend something less than certainty on the subject. Writing from Florence he hoped the nuncio was buried out of sight for some time and, he trusted, indefinitely, but his tone revealed that he did not feel entirely sure about the matter.[48]

In their anxiety over the question, a number of the American bishops urged Gibbons that he consent to fill the office himself. Bishop James O'Connor of Omaha fully appreciated the need of a competent person to act as the guardian of American interests with the Holy See, and he said he saw no reason why the cardinal could not render them this service. O'Connor suggested that the

---

[45] AABo, copy of a letter in French to Leo XIII, Rome, March 15, 1887. This document is not signed nor is it in Gibbons' handwriting, but from internal evidence it can almost certainly be said to have emanated from him.

[46] AAC, Elder to Gibbons, March 22, 1887, copy. It was at this time that Elder expressed his anxiety over the leaks of official Church business to the secular press. He thought it ought to be made the subject of a "grave complaint" to the Propaganda that the confidential papers of the American prelates were betrayed in this manner.

[47] *Ibid.*, Gibbons to Elder, Rome, March 31, 1887.

[48] *Ibid.*, Gibbons to Elder, Florence, April 20, 1887.

Archbishop of Baltimore might secure a coadjutor or an auxiliary bishop for the work of his see which would enable him to spend five or six months of the year in Rome. He instanced what he called "the attempted diplomatic *coup*" of Bishop Dwenger and the attempt to put Henry George's book on the *Index* as two examples of how necessary this representation was.[49] What reaction Gibbons showed to these suggestions we do not know, but there was one who would have more quickly put on his fighting armor had the suggestion taken on any indication of fulfillment. McQuaid was greatly annoyed that the second red hat for the United States had gone to Baltimore instead of to New York. Despite the fact that he opposed an Italian nuncio or delegate, he thought that anything would be preferable to Dwenger, and he was hopeful, too, that if the Italian delegation must come it would put a stop to what he called "the growing nonsense about Baltimore, *alias* the Sulpitians, being the head of the Catholic Church in the U. S."[50] Gibbons as nuncio or delegate would have been too much, indeed, for the Bishop of Rochester.

The departure of Cardinal Gibbons from Rome and his return to the United States did not set at rest the rumors that a nuncio would follow. The cardinal was anxious to quiet the press on the subject and, therefore, when Archbishop Corrigan sent a correspondent of the New York *Tribune* to Gibbons with a note of introduction, he decided that it was a good opportunity to give out a public statement. As he told Corrigan, he did not wish to be quoted directly so he authorized the correspondent to say that one who enjoyed the cardinal's utmost confidence had told him the following:

1. That the Holy See had made no overtures nor expressed any desire to send a nuncio to this country.

2. That as far as can be ascertained, the Holy See does not entertain such a desire.

3. That such an appointment would not be acceptable to our government.

4. Nor would it meet with the wishes of the American Episcopate.

While he had preserved his anonymity in the interview he realized, as he remarked to Corrigan, that people reading between

---

[49] 82-P-14, O'Connor to Gibbons, Omaha, April 20, 1887, copy.
[50] McQuaid to Gilmour, n.p., February 25, 1887, quoted in Zwierlein, *op. cit.*, III, 152.

the lines might conclude that the statement had been inspired by him, to which he added "perhaps all the better." He saw no danger of such an appointment, he said, if he could judge by the silence of the Holy See when he was there.[51] But the cardinal's attempt to put the nuncio question in the best light before the American public did not get by without a challenge. Dr. McGlynn, who had every reason to want a nuncio or delegate as a court to which he could appeal in his quarrel with Archbishop Corrigan, spoke on the subject in a speech in Buffalo in which he said the Holy See was trying to have an ambassador appointed to Washington, and in the face of Gibbons' denial McGlynn stuck to his story and implied that the cardinal, too, knew the true intentions of Rome.[52]

There would seem to be little doubt that the vigorous efforts made by Gibbons in his own name and in the name of his colleagues against a papal representative at the time of his Roman visit of 1887 had given at least a temporary pause to the Holy See. While not much more was heard of the subject for a year or two the Cardinal of Baltimore did not let down his guard. When Archbishop Elder appealed to him for a remedy against priests going over the head of the metropolitan's court to Rome, as was then the case with Father John B. Primeau, pastor of St. Louis Church, Toledo, in the Diocese of Cleveland who had appealed his dispute with Bishop Gilmour to the Holy See, Gibbons agreed that the numerous complaints of American priests to Rome with real or fancied grievances were deplorable. It prompted him to add, "I fear very much that the Holy See may use these appeals as a pretext for sending us a permanent legate or Delegate who would soon become the centre of intrigue, & the dignity & authority of the Ordinaries would be seriously impaired."[53] Here Gibbons touched on an aspect of the problem which was rarely mentioned in the correspondence of the American bishops with Rome on this subject but which, nevertheless, was of vital importance to them, namely, the fear of a derogation of their own episcopal powers if a nuncio or delegate should be established in this country.

---

[51] AANY, Gibbons to Corrigan, Baltimore, June 27, 1887, *Personal.*
[52] New York *Herald,* June 30, 1887.
[53] 85-T-14, Elder to Gibbons, Cincinnati, March 16, 1889; AAC, Gibbons to Elder, Baltimore, March 21, 1889.

The disquietude which the American hierarchy felt in the matter must have created a certain tenseness when, as we have seen, Archbishop Francesco Satolli was appointed to represent Leo XIII at the centennial of the hierarchy and the opening of the Catholic University of America in November, 1889. However, the visit passed off without incident and several weeks after the festivities in Baltimore and Washington Satolli returned to Rome. Not long after reaching the Eternal City he met Father Farrelly of the American College, to whom he confided that in the report of his American visit to Pope Leo and his Secretary of State he had expressed the opinion that more direct means of communication between the Holy See and the American Church were desirable. He requested Farrelly to inform Gibbons of this and to say that he suggested that the cardinal and two of the most prominent American archbishops should come to Rome during the year to treat of this subject with the Pope and the Secretary of State. Satolli revealed the differences that existed between the Vatican and the Propaganda on this question when he cautioned Farrelly to tell Gibbons that the subject must be kept strictly secret with no intimation whatever being allowed to reach the authorities at the Propaganda.[54] While it is exceedingly difficult to determine from the available evidence what the trouble was within the offices of the Holy See, it is certain that the Propaganda did not regard Satolli with favor, although he enjoyed a special place in the affections of Leo XIII. In any case, Satolli's suggestion about the visit of Gibbons and his two colleagues was not acted upon, but from this time on the Roman archbishop entered more and more into the picture.

At the time of Denis O'Connell's visit to the United States in the spring of 1890 he brought word that the talk of appointing one of the American archbishops as apostolic delegate was still going on in Rome. He mentioned to Archbishop Ryan the possibility that it might be Williams of Boston and Ryan, in turn, believed that if Cardinal Gibbons was not named it would surely be Williams or Corrigan.[55] That same summer the American

---

[54] 87-A-1, Farrelly to Gibbons, Rome, January 1, 1890, *Private*.

[55] AANY, Ryan to Corrigan, Philadelphia, May 20, 1890. Ryan told his New York friend that O'Connell was returning to Rome toward the end of the month and he added, "He has been evidently 'taking notes' around." Williams was in no way interested in the appointment as delegate. After O'Connell returned to Europe he informed Gibbons, "Abp. Williams wrote me saying 'if you hear

archbishops held the first of their annual conferences at Boston in accordance with the decision they had made at the Baltimore centennial. At Boston the archbishops voted to provide O'Connell with a secretary so that he might expedite the Roman business of the American Church. Moreover, it was the general opinion that he was deserving of higher honors and should be made a titular bishop. But the question of how these honors were to be secured brought about a divergence of opinion, with the result that the metropolitans finally agreed to leave the matter in the hands of Gibbons who would indicate their wish to Rome in a way that his prudence would suggest.[56] Although the American archbishops thus endeavored at Boston to enhance the prestige of their Roman agent, the record of their meeting revealed no mention of a nuncio or delegate in this country.

Meanwhile Monsignor O'Connell was doing all he could to keep the Cardinal of Baltimore fully abreast of Roman opinion on the subject of the representation of the Holy See in the United States. He held a detailed discussion with Domenico Jacobini, Secretary of the Propaganda, who told him he was deeply troubled by the irritation which the cardinals of his congregation had caused among the American archbishops by such acts as the appointment of Frederick Katzer to Milwaukee. Jacobini maintained that the Propaganda cardinals were of the opinion that the Americans were too independent and did not trust Rome. He was conscious of the fact that the Americans had an open and frank way of speaking and personally he preferred it, but some of the cardinals, said Jacobini, did not understand it and were determined to crush this spirit. He said that for himself he believed there were no better bishops in the world than the Americans, but he confessed that they seemed to him to be jealous of the Roman authorities, instancing their reluctance to have a delegate.

In reply O'Connell defended the prelates of the United States and said that if they did not seem to have trust in the Holy See, it might be because Rome had not treated them with sufficient confidence. As an example he cited the sending of Bedini in 1853

---

anything said about my name in connection with any new offices, you will place me under obligations by putting a stop to it.' Of course, if there were, that ends it" (87-V-4, O'Connell to Gibbons, Grottaferrata, September 6, 1890).

[56] 87-R-4, Minutes of the Meeting of the Archbishops, Boston, July 23-24, 1890.

without ever notifying the hierarchy, the plan to appoint Sepiacci in 1883 to preside over the Third Plenary Council, and the missions of Dwenger, Mori, and Straniero. "Was that," asked O'Connell, "a proof of confidence in the Episcopate?"

As a remedy Jacobini had suggested that O'Connell go directly to the Pope with the problem, but under no circumstances to let it be known that he had suggested it.[57] How soon the Roman rector carried out the suggestion we do not know, but some months later the duty of presenting the Peter's Pence from Gibbons' archdiocese gave an opportunity for discussion of the matter. His audience came at a time when there was great excitement over Cahensly's memorial on the German Catholics in the United States. Leo XIII assured O'Connell that he wished to calm and to reassure the American bishops on that question, and in the course of the audience the Pope turned to the subject of his representative. Gibbons' friend reported the conversation as follows:

"The whole evil is in this, that they do not want to have a representative of me there. If they had one of my representatives there now, that could speak to them the sentiments of the Pope, this trouble would never have happened. But for some reason of jealousy among themselves they don't want to have my representative there tho' I would only name some one acceptable to them all. Why don't they want the Pope there? If Christ were to return again to earth you would all rejoice to give him a welcome. Why not then receive his Vicar. No, if I had my *Nunzio* there all would go better and you would be rendered independent at once of the Propaganda and made depend immediately on the department of State." I said it was believed the presence of a *nunzio* w'd at once curtail the dignity of each individual Bp. "On the contrary," he said. "However" he said "I respect their sentiments in the matter, and I don't love them the less for it. Let us talk of something else." There was no tone of bitterness or of reproach in all this, it was the tone rather of sorrowful regret and of surprise.[58]

There was no doubt after this summary of the papal audience how the Pope felt about the matter, and the earnest desire he had to remedy the difficulties of Roman-American ecclesiastical relations through the medium of a personal representative here.

[57] 88-H-2, O'Connell to Gibbons, Rome, January 19, 1891.
[58] 88-S-1, O'Connell to Gibbons, Rome, July 1, 1891.

It was not long before Leo XIII was afforded a golden opportunity to accomplish his purpose. In 1892 there began serious preparations for the celebration of the 400th anniversary of the discovery of America which resulted ultimately in the opening at Chicago of the World's Columbian Exposition on May 1, 1893. During the course of the preparations it was made known that the managers of the fair were anxious to have an exhibit of old maps and charts which would illustrate the extent of geographical knowledge at the time that Columbus made his famous voyage. Many of the best maps of the late fifteenth century were preserved in the Vatican Library, and if the exhibit was to fulfill the hope of the planners a way would have to be found to secure a loan of the precious items from the Holy See.

It was Archbishop Ireland who conducted the preliminary negotiations with the board of commissioners of the fair. They unanimously consented to his suggestion that the Pope be invited to be an exhibitor and to send a representative. But at the last minute Thomas W. Palmer, president of the board, stepped in and said he feared there would be opposition to the fair from the anti-Catholic portion of the population if the Pontiff were sent such an invitation.[59] The refusal of Palmer to issue the invitation was reported to Cardinal Gibbons by Ireland and Richard C. Kerens, Republican national committeeman from Missouri who was a Catholic and high in the councils of the administration of President Harrison. Gibbons and Kerens agreed that the latter should see John W. Foster, Secretary of State, in an attempt to have him write the letter to Rome. Foster informed the cardinal of the desire of the fair officials to have on exhibit the Vatican maps, and he added,

it would afford me great pleasure to have the opportunity of a personal conference with you respecting the form of invitation which should be sent to His Holiness in furtherance of that object, in case you should approve of the suggestion.[60]

The result was a quite satisfactory handling of the matter through a personal conference of Gibbons, Foster, and Kerens. Foster agreed to make the request in the name of the United States government to Cardinal Rampolla, papal Secretary of State, the

[59] 90-F-4, Ireland to Gibbons, St. Paul, September 14, 1892.
[60] 90-F-3, Foster to Gibbons, Washington, September 14, 1892, *Personal*.

document to be transmitted to Rampolla by Gibbons. In describing the affair to John Ireland, the cardinal called the time he had spent in Washington arranging the details of the transaction, "one of the busiest, most anxious, and, I think, most successful days of my life."[61]

In pursuance of his promise, Secretary Foster wrote a letter to Rampolla in which he expressed the belief that a loan of the maps would be a manifestation on the part of the Pope of his regard for the United States which would be highly appreciated not only by the managers of the exposition but by the American people generally. Foster was at pains to have the Holy See know that the greatest care would be exercised to see that the documents were preserved without damage from the moment they were delivered into the hands of the agent of the American government, and he then presented an attractive alternative when he wrote:

> or, should his Holiness see fit to entrust them in the care of a personal representative who will bring them to the United States, I am authorized by the President to assure his Holiness that such representative shall receive all possible courtesy upon his arrival and during his sojourn in his country.[62]

The Holy See promptly granted the request for a loan of the maps and appointed a personal representative of the Pope to bring them to this country. Rampolla replied that Leo XIII had many reasons to entertain a special regard for the United States on account of the liberty which the Catholic Church enjoyed here, and for that reason he had decided to be represented personally at the ceremonies honoring Columbus' discovery by Francesco

---

[61] AASP, Gibbons to Ireland, Baltimore, September 16, 1892, copy. Ireland had been in Rome in the spring of 1892 fighting his battle over the schools. Alluding to this trouble, he told Gibbons that the Pope had taken the occasion of the American school controversy to revive the talk of a delegate (89-W-8, Ireland to Gibbons, Genoa, June 5, 1892). A month or more later he had reached Washington after visiting Gibbons in Baltimore. He recounted the visit for Denis O'Connell and it was evident that he had been working on the cardinal to get him to accept the Roman representative. He said, "At last I spoke of the delegate — telling that the delegate would be confided to him, that Leo was determined, that we must stand by Leo. He was delighted, & asked at once how we could get the delegate to Washington — away from New York. So all is settled, & all is right" (ADR, Ireland to O'Connell, Washington, July 11, 1892).

[62] 90-F-8, Foster to Rampolla, Washington, September 15, 1892, copy. This letter was sent from Baltimore in a covering letter of Gibbons to Rampolla of the same date (90-F-7).

Satolli, Archbishop of Lepanto, whose virtues and profound scholarship had won for him a high esteem. Rampolla then concluded, "His Holiness does not doubt that this decision of his will be received with pleasure by the Government, and feels sure that your Excellency will welcome the prelate with your accustomed courtesy."[63]

During the months preceding the arrival of Satolli for his second visit to the United States, a bitter controversy had been going on within the American Church over the issue of certain parish schools in the Archdiocese of St. Paul. We shall see more of this controversy later, but suffice it to mention here that the quarrel over the schools had widened the gulf between the Archbishop of New York on the one hand and the Archbishops of St. Paul and Baltimore on the other. It was a matter of importance, therefore, to Ireland and Gibbons that the arrival of Satolli at New York should be carefully handled. Weeks before Ireland had begun to lay his plans in a letter to Denis O'Connell in Rome. He wrote:

> If the Pope would do, as he said to me he would, remit Mgr. Satolli formally into Card. Gibbons' hands & mine, all is well. I would then do much which I cannot otherwise do. Meeting him in N. York & arranging there for his arrival, will give mortal offence. I think it is best to let [the] Cardinal do this, and yet he will not like to do it, unless special charge of Satolli is given to him. And yet it will never do to leave all to Corrigan. Write me at length on this matter. . . .
>
> By the way, I must consider also the Cardinal's susceptibilities, & unless I have some warrant for intermeddling, I will not be able to do much. If you can at all, obtain from the Vatican a few lines for me telling me to look after the "delegate", & aid him for [the] first few weeks.[64]

Gibbons was probably unaware of this particular aspect of Ireland's arrangements, but he did hold a conference with Kerens and instructed him to open correspondence at once with the Archbishop of St. Paul with a view to providing a revenue cutter to meet Satolli in the harbor of New York. The cardinal believed that by arranging matters with Charles Foster, Secretary of the

---

[63] Rampolla to Foster, Rome, September 28, 1892, quoted in Will, *op. cit.*, I, 465–466.
[64] ADR, Ireland to O'Connell, St. Paul, August, 20, 1892.

Treasury, no reasonable offense could be taken by the ecclesiastical authorities in New York. But as he told Ireland, "It would be very difficult for you to employ the services of private parties in N. Y. to provide a tug without exciting displeasure."[65] After giving these preliminary directions the cardinal left the reception of Satolli at New York for the most part in the management of Archbishop Ireland, although he appointed a party of Baltimore clergy to meet the ablegate when he landed and to escort him to Baltimore.

Archbishop Satolli, accompanied by Monsignor O'Connell from Rome and joined by Father Edward A. Pace of the Catholic University of America in Paris, arrived on the *Majestic* on October 12. They were met down the bay by the Baltimore delegation of clergy and a group of laymen aboard the revenue cutter *General Grant* which had been provided by the collector of the port of New York. After a brief stop in the city, during which they called on Archbishop Corrigan and took dinner with him, the ablegate and his party hurried on to Baltimore where they were the guests of Cardinal Gibbons.[66] Two days later Gibbons accompanied Satolli to Washington for a visit to Secretary of State Foster, and on October 18 the cardinal, the ablegate, Ireland, and O'Connell left for Chicago where Gibbons gave the invocation at the ceremonies dedicating the buildings for the Columbian Exposition and where they attended a reception and banquet honoring Vice-President Levi P. Morton.[67] From Chicago

---

[65] AASP, Gibbons to Ireland, Baltimore, September 21, 1892, copy.

[66] New York *Herald,* October 13, 1892. That the details of the reception had been carefully planned in a way that kept Archbishop Corrigan in the background was evident from a letter he received from Austin E. Ford, editor of the *Freeman's Journal.* Ford told Corrigan the day before the boat landed, "I have just seen Rev. Dr. O'Gorman, of Washington, who is here with a delegation from Cardinal Gibbons to receive Monsignor Satolli. He desires me to say to you, lest he should not be able to see you, that the Cardinal has arranged it so that an official character will be given to the reception. Mgr. Satolli is really the guest of the Government under the invitation of the Secretary of State, and will be received as such by the Collector of the Port, and his staff. The Collector will take Mgr. Satolli from the 'Majestic' in a U.S. Government vessel. The Baltimore Committee under Rev. Dr. Magnien will accompany the Delegate to your residence from the dock, and then take him on to Baltimore by special train which is in waiting" (90-J-7, Ford to Corrigan, New York, October 11, 1892, copy).

[67] Gibbons reported the friendly reception given to Satolli at Chicago by the officials of the American government and the directors of the fair when he transmitted a further letter of Secretary Foster to Cardinal Rampolla of November

Satolli traveled on to St. Paul with Ireland whose guest he was for nearly a month during the lapse of time before the annual conference of the archbishops, which was scheduled to open in New York at Corrigan's residence on November 16.

In one sense the visit of Archbishop Satolli was singularly ill-timed. Five and a half years before there had been organized in March, 1887, a society known as the American Protective Association with the avowed purpose of fighting the advance of the Catholic Church in the United States. The movement grew steadily and all through the 1890's the campaign of bigotry against the Church waxed strong and succeeded in arousing the fears and suspicions of thousands of Americans regarding the political designs of Catholicism. The appearance of the papal ablegate, of course, played directly into the hands of the A.P.A., and they made the most of it. From the outset of his visit Satolli was attacked in the A.P.A. press, and other papers, too, were soon carrying alarming rumors and false stories about his mission and the powers with which the Pope had invested him over the lives of American citizens.[68] So virulent was a section of the press in its assaults upon the papal envoy, that grave fears

---

1, 1892 (90-N-2, copy). He took occasion to tell the papal Secretary of State of the joy he felt at the cordial relations existing between Rampolla and Foster (90-N-3, Gibbons to Rampolla, Baltimore, November 2, 1892, copy).

[68] For the A.P.A. and Satolli's connection with the movement cf. Gustavus Myers, *History of Bigotry in the United States* (New York, 1943), pp. 223–245. Seven years after Satolli's coming the principal founder of the A.P.A., Henry F. Bowers, was asked if the delegate's visit had contributed to the growth of his organization. He replied that it had "very materially" done so. Bowers wrote, "We looked upon Satolli as a representative of the Propaganda at Rome to direct and influence legislation in this country, more especially his settling down in the city of Washington, and several moves which were made, which I cannot just now call to mind, which gave rise to an opinion at least that he was interfering with the public institutions of this country." Bowers to Humphrey J. Desmond, Clinton, Iowa, March 1, 1899, quoted in Desmond's *The A.P.A. Movement. A Sketch* (Washington, 1912), p. 15. Gibbons himself did not escape A.P.A. attacks. During the presidential campaign of 1892 his friendship with Grover Cleveland brought annoyance to the candidate when Cleveland was asked if it were true that there was a private wire from the White House to the cardinal's residence in Baltimore. Cleveland replied that he was almost ashamed to dignify the inquiry by an answer. He said, "I know Cardinal Gibbons and know him to be a good citizen and first-rate American, and that his kindness of heart and toleration are in striking contrast to the fierce intolerance and vicious malignity which disgrace some who claim to be Protestants." Quoted from a letter of Cleveland to William Black, Buzzard's Bay, Massachusetts, July 11, 1892, by Will, *op. cit.,* I, 537.

were entertained by some of the hierarchy that Satolli might encounter the same unfortunate experiences that had greeted Bedini forty years before. Although nothing so violent as the demonstrations against Bedini developed at this time, the early stages of the Satolli visit were conducted in an atmosphere sufficiently charged with tension to create in the minds of the American bishops the hope that he would not prolong his stay beyond the time necessary to transact his business.

When the archbishops of the United States assembled in New York in mid-November their main business was the controversy over the parochial schools. However, Satolli had another proposition to lay before the metropolitans besides Rome's decision on the school question. On November 17 the ablegate presented to the archbishops the great desire of the Holy Father to establish in the United States with their concurrence a permanent apostolic delegation. Cardinal Gibbons, who presided over all the sessions, then threw the subject open to discussion. All the archbishops, with the exception of Ireland, stated that they did not feel warranted in taking action on so important a matter until they had first consulted with their suffragans in view, as the minutes read, "of the serious difficulties connected with the subject." Satolli was informed of their decision and for the moment there the matter rested. Before the close of the conference Gibbons was instructed in a unanimous resolution to convey the thanks of the metropolitans to Satolli for the able manner in which he had discharged the duties of his "special mission" and their thanks were likewise to be extended to Leo XIII for sending to them so holy and learned a representative.[69]

The cardinal entrusted the task of composing the letter to the Pope to Archbishop Corrigan who furnished him some days later with a rough draft in which he alluded to the delegate question, but said that the country was not yet in a condition to profit from the establishment of a permanent delegation. Corrigan stated that if there were any changes which the cardinal wished to have made he would be happy to make them.[70] On the delegate question Gibbons suggested the insertion of a separate paragraph which would thank Leo XIII for sending so learned and excellent

[69] 90-Q-3, Minutes of the Meeting of the Archbishops, New York, November 16–19, 1892.
[70] 90-S-5, Corrigan to Gibbons, New York, November 30, 1892.

a representative to the United States on a temporary mission. A graceful compliment, he thought, would be gratifying to the ablegate and be sure to please the Pope. "It will also in some measure, I hope," said Gibbons, "offset the disappointment of his Holiness on finding that the Archbishops did not deem it advisable to ask for a permanent Delegate."[71]

Meanwhile Archbishop Satolli returned to Washington where he took up residence at the Catholic University of America. On December 3 he received certain faculties from the Propaganda for settling disputes between bishops and their priests. Bishop Keane, Rector of the University, was anxious that Cardinal Gibbons should understand clearly, however, that these were not the faculties of a delegate. Since Satolli was going to Baltimore to make this matter known to Gibbons, the rector wished to guard the cardinal against any possible misunderstanding and to have Gibbons impress upon the ablegate that he was to receive cases only as the Holy See did, that is, after they had passed through the court of the metropolitan. Keane added, "Were he *a court of first instance,* it is easy to imagine how much confusion & disorder would be occasioned."[72]

News of Satolli's increased faculties reached the public press, and Archbishop Elder was concerned when he read that the ablegate had increased powers and that Gibbons was alleged to have confirmed the truth of the report. The Cincinnati prelate was puzzled, but he was ready to accept whatever it might mean in a spirit of faith when he told the cardinal, "Well the Holy Ghost is always able to direct the course of events to the greater glory of God."[73] Whatever the new faculties given to Satolli by the Propaganda were, Gibbons must have thought them rather broad since he told Elder that he had asked Satolli to send copies to all the bishops, and by that time Elder had doubtless received Propaganda's document conferring, as he expressed it, "such ample powers" on the ablegate.[74] It was

---

[71] 90-U-1, Gibbons to Corrigan, Baltimore, December 7, 1892, copy. Gibbons had written on December 23 a letter to Leo XIII regarding the Satolli mission and the school question. Cf. Diary, p. 263.

[72] 90-T-4, Keane to Gibbons, Washington, December 4, 1892. A printed notification of Satolli's faculties for settling disputes between bishops and priests, approved by the Pope on October 30, was sent by Ledochowski to the American bishops (AABo, Ledochowski to Williams, Rome, November 8, 1892).

[73] 90-T-7, Elder to Gibbons, Cincinnati, December 6, 1892.

[74] AAC, Gibbons to Elder, Baltimore, December 10, 1892.

probably on the strength of these faculties that Satolli on December 23 absolved Dr. McGlynn from his ecclesiastical censures, an incident which, to be sure, did not endear the ablegate the more to Archbishop Corrigan.

The propositions which Satolli had submitted to the archbishops' conference in New York for settling the school question were not found acceptable to several of that body, and the proposal for the permanent delegation, with the exception of Archbishop Ireland, had met with their prompt refusal. When one reflects on how heated the controversy over the schools had been and how keenly many felt on the delegation, it is not to be wondered at that Satolli began to receive some unfriendly jibes from Catholic sources as well as from his enemies outside the Church. Cardinal Gibbons became aware of this public criticism of the papal envoy and he told Elder that he was deeply pained at the disrespect shown to Satolli in certain Catholic quarters. He believed it would grieve the Pope and hurt religion, and he explained to the Archbishop of Cincinnati that he referred to an alleged interview given out in Milwaukee against the ablegate, as well as an article which he saw quoted from the *Church Progress* of St. Louis, a Catholic weekly edited at the time by Conde B. Pallen.

There was, of course, grave discontent in New York with the Satolli mission due to his decision on Archbishop Ireland's schools, a discontent which was increased when the ablegate absolved McGlynn. Even before the decision in McGlynn's case, Corrigan informed his Roman friend, Salvatore M. Brandi, S.J., of his critical attitude toward Satolli. Brandi was in complete sympathy with the Archbishop of New York and felt that Satolli's action, which he characterized as a blunder and a fiasco, would cost him and John Ireland a severe reprimand. Brandi thought, too, that the proposal of the permanent delegation was a mistake and he said the *Osservatore Cattolico* of Milan had already carried the news and acquainted the Vatican with the refusal of the American archbishops. All of Corrigan's information had been communicated confidentially, said Brandi, to Cardinal Mazzella who agreed with them and suggested that the American archbishops send an official report of the whole business to Cardinal Rampolla.[75] It was apparent that Satolli's

---

[75] AANY, Brandi to Corrigan, Rome, December 12, 1892, *Private.*

enemies were not all concentrated in the United States. Once more someone betrayed the confidential business of the American hierarchy to the press. The propositions of Satolli concerning the schools, as well as his address to the archbishops in New York, were published in the papers after the metropolitans had agreed to keep these matters secret. Archbishop Elder received an English translation of the documents in pamphlet form a week after the meeting, with no indication of printer or place, and a little later the whole story appeared in the secular press with a dateline from St. Louis.[76] He was completely bewildered when still another pamphlet copy reached him with the name of the John Murphy Company of Baltimore. He told Gibbons, "I do not understand it all. There is mystery, & confusion naturally follows."[77] There was mystery and confusion, indeed, and some of it was in Baltimore. Gibbons informed his friend in Cincinnati that neither the minutes of their New York meeting nor the address of Satolli had been printed originally in his see city. He had been careful to keep these documents from the public eye and he had since learned that the Satolli speech was first published in a western city. To show Elder that he had not been remiss in his duty the cardinal explained:

> I was much worried for a while about the publication of the minutes of our meeting, especially as they were printed by Murphy & Co. & were dated "Baltimore." I made a searching investigation, & finally recd. a note from the Associated Press agent in Balto. stating with the authority of the principal manager that they did not emanate from Baltimore. But both the manager & the agent courteously refused to reveal the place or person from whom they came. . . . P.S. I enclose the notes recd. from the Press agents, declining to reveal

---

[76] On December 8, 1892, the New York *Herald* carried the text of the address of Satolli to the archbishops on the school question, saying it was here published in full for the first time. Four days later, in the issue of December 12, the same paper published the story from St. Louis of Satolli's failure to win them to his school propositions and to Leo XIII's wish for a delegate. The tenor of the account was that while Ireland was in Rome the previous summer he had gained the Pope and Rampolla over on these two subjects and now Satolli was learning how badly the Vatican had been misled about American opinion. Gibbons was supposed to have intervened to prevent the archbishops from rejecting the school propositions outright and to have suggested that they decline to sign them now and await further consideration.

[77] 90-W-2, Elder to Gibbons, Cincinnati, December 23, 1892.

the author of the publication of the minutes which I beg you to
return. "Mr. Morris" of the Balto. Sun was the gentleman I
employed to make the investigation.[78]

The Archbishop of Baltimore had already suffered much from
these leaks of private ecclesiastical business to the press, and
he was anxious now that his printing firm should be cleared
of any imputation of guilt in this latest episode.

But the trials of Gibbons and his colleagues at the hands of
the secular press were by no means at an end and they were,
in fact, at this time on the eve of one of the worst scandals
to date by reason of treachery in their own ranks and the lack
of ethical procedure on the part of certain newspapermen. On
January 3, 1893, the cardinal signed the letter to Leo XIII in
the name of the archbishops in which he outlined their reasons
for not wishing a delegate. The document was couched in the
most polite language but, nonetheless, Gibbons made it clear
that the Church of the United States was not ready for the
appointment. After congratulating the Pontiff on his approaching
golden jubilee, the cardinal alluded to the school question as it
was discussed in the recent meeting in New York, and referring
to that meeting, he said:

> It was discussed whether there could be had in this country
> what obtains almost everywhere else, a permanent Delegate of
> the Holy See. All, with one exception, agreed that it would not
> serve the best interests of the Church since the spirit of the people
> is not yet at a point where it would be favorably disposed to so
> great a benefit. It was their opinion that non-Catholics would be
> alienated from us to a greater degree, as though we wished to use
> the recent elections to attain some advantages, whatever they
> might be; this would certainly be a severe hardship both for us
> as well as for the State.
>
> Moreover the Delegate would now appear to be sent for no
> other reason than to include the Bishops of this country in his
> authority, which would injure the esteem which the people have
> for us.
>
> It might be added that there would not be lacking some who,
> due to calumny, would think that the Apostolic Delegate had been
> sent here precisely for the purpose of reporting to the Supreme

---

[78] AAC, Gibbons to Elder, Baltimore, December 26, 1892.

Pontiff about events over here, a calumny that evil men would use to blacken the good name of the Holy See.

Wherefore, after discussing the matter from all angles at our meeting, we judged it wise that nothing be done about this before we could obtain the advice of our suffragans.

The letter closed with high praise for Satolli's conduct of his mission and the assurance to the Holy Father that his ablegate had won the admiration of many who were, in turn, grateful to the Sovereign Pontiff for sending so representative a prelate to this country.[79]

The day following the mailing of this letter there appeared in the Chicago *Tribune* of January 5 and in other American papers a story from London that the Pope was "unusually irritated by the collapse of his project to appoint a nuncio to the United States." Within the next few days even more mendacious accounts of the Satolli mission were carried in the American papers as emanating from various European journals. For example, on January 6 the Chicago *Tribune,* on the authority of the *Corriere del Mattino* of Naples, stated that the ablegate's brusque manner had caused the Roman Curia to understand that the Americans would not tolerate the arrogance of its envoy and, therefore, Satolli had been recalled. In the face of these sensational stories a group of priests of the Archdiocese of New York were alleged to have signed a circular protesting against the attacks on Satolli, and stating that these attacks were instigated by certain bishops who opposed his presence here.[80] Gibbons, of course, read these accounts and when one version stated that the Catholic Club of New York had protested Satolli's mission, he made inquiry of Archbishop Corrigan concerning the report. Corrigan firmly denied any protest by the Catholic Club of his see city and as for himself, he said, "I never, for one instant, contemplated any disrespect to Mgr. Satolli; nor have I done aught to thwart his mission." Corrigan indignantly repudiated any personal connection with the attacks in the press, although he stated that two laymen had called on him on New Year's Day and revealed to him that they had written letters which appeared in the newspapers against the

---

[79] 91-A-3/1, Gibbons to Leo XIII, Baltimore, January 3, 1893, copy in Latin.
[80] Chicago *Tribune,* January 5, 1893.

ablegate. "The whole movement," said Corrigan a bit ambiguously, "was the spontaneous cry of a wounded Catholic conscience." But as for his own critics, he was disposed to silent forgiveness. "I pardon them from my heart, and try to imitate our B. Lord: 'Jesus autem tacebat.' "[81]

There was one critic of Corrigan in this instance who believed he had proof that the Archbishop of New York had inspired the press campaign against Satolli. John Ireland informed Gibbons that the discovery of what he termed a "conspiracy" was made by the Chicago *Post* and that before they went to press both he and Satolli were asked for an interview. Ireland said he had been shown autographed letters of Corrigan and Father Michael J. Lavelle of St. Patrick's Cathedral in New York, the first to a reporter in Chicago who used to do literary work for Corrigan when he lived in New York, the second to Maurice F. Egan. Egan, said Ireland, was ashamed that he was asked to be a party to the affair, but if need be he was willing to give over Lavelle's letter. Ireland was burning with indignation and a demand for action. He told the cardinal, "We have fallen upon sad times. Religion is suffering; Catholics are scandalized; Protestants laugh at us."[82] There was no doubt of the fact that scandal had been given and that the enemies of the Church, as Bishop Kain of Wheeling told Gibbons, "are chuckling over discord in our ranks."[83] Surely those who disliked Catholicism had rarely been given a better opportunity for rejoicing at the disunity within the hierarchy.

In the midst of the discord there suddenly came word from Rome that settled the main question, even if it did not fully quiet the storm. Gibbons received a cablegram from O'Connell which read, "American delegation established. Satolli first delegate."[84] The gordian knot had been cut by the personal action of the Pope and the American hierarchy were now faced by an accomplished fact. Gibbons immediately sent his congratulations to the new delegate in Washington who gratefully acknowledged what he styled this new and notable proof of the cardinal's charity toward him.[85] While the Archbishop of

---

[81] 91-A-5, Corrigan to Gibbons, New York, January 6, 1893.
[82] 91-A-7, Ireland to Gibbons, St. Paul, January 8, 1893.
[83] 91-A-8, Kain to Gibbons, Wheeling, January 9, 1893.
[84] 91-B-4, O'Connell to Gibbons, Rome, January 14, 1893, cablegram in Latin.
[85] 91-B-6, Satolli to Gibbons, Washington, January 15, 1893.

Baltimore yielded with his customary grace to an action of the Holy See which he had previously disapproved, he was now concerned about the fate of his letter to Leo XIII against the appointment which had been mailed ten days before the receipt of O'Connell's cablegram. When on January 18 there came a second cablegram from the Roman rector inquiring whether or not he should present the letter,[86] Gibbons hastily composed a communication to all the American archbishops asking them to advise him what they wished him to do. He told Elder that Bishop Chatard had just called and he had confided to him the problem which faced the metropolitans, and it was Chatard's advice that the letter to Leo XIII be withheld by O'Connell and sent back since the Pope's action was irrevocable and the presentation of their adverse views would only give pain to the Pontiff. To this Gibbons added, "I incline to the same view."[87] All the archbishops except two were in favor of withholding the document. Archbishops Riordan of San Francisco and Gross of Oregon City wired their opinion that it should be presented despite the Pope's action,[88] but the large majority made it safe for Gibbons to instruct his agent to return the document to him.

The American prelate who was most irreconcilable to the new delegation, however, was Bishop James Ryan of Alton. He lodged such vigorous protests with the Holy See in the form of cablegrams and letters that Gibbons was requested by both Cardinals Rampolla and Ledochowski to call him to time, and ask him to apologize to Rome for the improper and irreverent language he had used toward the supreme authority of the Holy See.[89] Gibbons did as he was requested and asked the

---

[86] 91-B-9, O'Connell to Gibbons, Rome, January 18, 1893, cablegram in Latin.

[87] AAC, Gibbons to Elder, Baltimore, January 19, 1893, *Personal;* AANY, Gibbons to Corrigan, Baltimore, January 19, 1893, *Private;* 91-C-1, Gibbons to the archbishops, Baltimore, January 19, 1893, copy.

[88] 91-C-2, Riordan to Gibbons, San Francisco, January 19, 1893, telegram; 91-D-11, Gross to Gibbons, Portland, January 31, 1893, telegram. Gross seemed to feel very strongly on the subject. He followed his wire with a letter two days later in which he said he believed that their views should be expressed "with all profound reverence" in spite of the Pope's action. Gross said there was no telling what the future would bring and their candid opinions would, he was sure, be received properly in Rome. However, he wished it known he would submit to Leo's decision if he had actually established the delegation, although, as he said, "there are so many wild and contradictory telegrams and stories now flooding our Pacific Slope, that it is no easy task to discern what in reality has been done" (91-E-1, Gross to Gibbons, Portland, February 2, 1893).

[89] 91-C-4, Rampolla to Gibbons, Rome, January 20, 1893; 91-D-4, Ledochowski

Bishop of Alton to come to Baltimore to see him;[90] but **Ryan wired** that the matter was now satisfactorily settled.[91] While the bishop had made amends to Rome his opinion was not changed, as he informed the cardinal two weeks later when he detailed all his objections to a permanent delegation in the United States. He blamed what he called the "clatter" of Archbishop Ireland and his followers for adding insult to injury which in the end, he thought, would undermine all authority, and he ended by suggesting that his letter be translated and sent on to the Holy See![92] Gibbons would have no part in forwarding so inflammatory a document to Rome, and he told Ryan he had better write another that would embody the sentiments of reverent obedience, although he ended with the assurance that he retained a personal regard and affection for the bishop and regretted the pain which the communications from the Holy See had caused him.[93]

Far from approving of Bishop Ryan's method of addressing the Holy See, the Cardinal of Baltimore's language in his communications with Rome was always highly respectful of its authority, and on at least this one occasion went beyond what was called for. Two weeks after the receipt of O'Connell's cablegram bearing the news of Satolli's appointment, Gibbons forwarded to Leo XIII his thanks for the establishment of a permanent apostolic delegation. He told the Pope that his personal sentiments even more than the circumstances urged him to express his gratitude and that the cablegram had brought him one of the great joys of his life, and he blessed from the bottom of his heart the Providence which had inspired this act of His Holiness and had induced him to execute it without delay. Nothing, said the cardinal, could have been more opportune since for some time there had been attacks upon Archbishop Satolli inspired and directed by men who were determined to hound him out of the country. Those who had at heart the true interests of the Church and the honor of the Holy See

---

to Gibbons, Rome, January 24, 1893. Ledochowski enclosed copies of three cablegrams from Ryan to the Propaganda.

[90] 91-E-3, Gibbons to Ryan, Baltimore, February 8, 1893, copy.
[91] 91-E-4, Ryan to Gibbons, Alton, February 11, 1893, telegram.
[92] 91-F-7/1, Ryan to Gibbons, Alton, February 24, 1893.
[93] 91-G-2, Gibbons to Ryan, Baltimore, March 1, 1893, copy.

reprobated these attacks but were without power to stop them. They had come in part from Catholics and even from some ecclesiastics who created and fomented them with every means in their power. Leo's action had put an end to this disorder, checked the intrigues, reduced to silence the most bitter of Satolli's opponents, and except, perhaps, in a few German journals one would not now find a single attack against the delegate in the Catholic press. Referring then to the reaction shown toward the appointment, Gibbons said:

> Satisfaction has been very' general in our ranks, and even those who have been surprised or even piqued by this exercise of your apostolic authority have already been led, or will soon be, by their personal reflection and by public sentiment to change their views and to accept with good grace the decision of Your Holiness, even to rejoice heartily in it.
>
> But, Most Holy Father, this is even more consoling, the entire nation, Protestants no less than Catholics, has manifested the highest appreciation for this establishment of a perpetual delegation and for the appointment of Mgr. Satolli, the great qualities of whom the press praises untiringly.
>
> Permit me to add, Most Holy Father, that this public sentiment of satisfaction and gratitude is everywhere proclaimed for Your Holiness. The Americans already had the highest esteem for your august person and the principles which inspire your conduct in the government of the Church. This recent act, the occasion which prompted you to do it, and the manner in which you carried it out increase their admiration and they rejoice quite openly to see the Catholic Church governed by a Pontiff with broad views, wise and firm, who knows the needs of their country and appreciates its institutions.

The Pope's present act, said the cardinal in conclusion, had enhanced this esteem, and he did not fear to say that what he had done would be an event that would have the happiest results for the Church of the United States and be an added glory for the pontificate of Leo XIII.[94]

Obviously the circumstances demanded a respectful acceptance of Leo XIII's action on the part of Gibbons and the American bishops as befitted those who owed allegiance to the supreme government of the Church. It was equally obvious that they

---

[94] 91-D-12, Gibbons to Leo XIII, Baltimore, January 30, 1893, copy in French in Magnien's handwriting but bearing the signature of the cardinal.

had been confronted with a *fait accompli* which they were power-less to reverse and, therefore, for reasons of prudence and common sense that they should have made their acceptance as graceful as possible. But allowing for all these various factors, the letter of Cardinal Gibbons, written less than four weeks after his declining in the name of himself and his fellow metro-politans to receive a permanent delegate, went beyond what was demanded in the case. There would not be the slightest reason to question the sincerity of the cardinal in deploring the attacks upon Satolli; this he had done from the time that they first began. But when he stated that the news of the permanent appointment had brought him "one of the great joys" of his life, that it had been well received by Protestants as well as Catholics, and that the news had silenced all opposition against Satolli, the Cardinal of Baltimore was, to say the least, taking a liberty with the truth to which he was not ordinarily accustomed. It was one thing to put the best possible face upon an inevitable fact; it was quite another thing to indulge in language which could not prevent a false impression arising in Rome concerning the general American reaction to the delega-tion. If Pope Leo XIII two years later on the occasion of a letter addressed to the American Church was to puzzle some by his reference to the general outpouring of joy at the establish-ment of the apostolic delegation, the Holy Father could readily be excused for reflecting the opinion expressed at this time to him by Cardinal Gibbons.

The cardinal was to suffer one more major embarrassment in connection with this case at the hands of the press. On February 5, 1893, the Baltimore *Sun* and other papers through-out the country carried under a Chicago dateline the text of Gibbons' letter of January 19 to the archbishops, in which he had notified them of the cablegram erecting the delegation and had asked their advice about presenting the joint letter of two weeks before in which they had declined to acquiesce in the Holy See's proposal. The reactions to this latest disclosure of confidential ecclesiastical business were immediate and far-flung. The New York *Daily Tribune* of February 6 called the leak "one of the most startling evidences of treachery in high places yet made public in the so-called Catholic controversy," and concluded that someone in the hierarchy was unworthy of his high station. Even the New York *Times* of the same date, ordinarily not friendly to Gibbons, showed sympathy with him in the present circumstances. The most bizarre twist came, however, from the Brooklyn *Eagle* of February 5 which, in addition to quoting Gibbons' letter, gave the text of an interview accorded a U.P. correspondent by one described as "a distinguished Catholic." This person stated that Cardinal Gibbons had deliberately withheld the opinion of the archbishops until the Pope had acted in creating the delegation, that Leo XIII would rebuke those who had misrepresented American opinion to him, and that he would censure the Cardinal of Baltimore. Various other versions of the affair were carried by the papers in the succeeding days with serious reflections upon the integrity not only of Gibbons but of Archbishop Corrigan and others.

In the emergency created by the dispatch from Chicago the close contacts of Archbishop Ireland with the American press once more were of service in ferreting out the culprit. He told the Archbishop of Baltimore:

> I have found out, beyond a doubt, that it is Conde Pallen of St. Louis who gave to the wires your letter to the archbishops and made upon it the malicious comments, which have shocked the country. This time the guilty party did not hail from New York. Pallen is the trusted agent of the St. Louis Jesuits. Your letter, he must have got through Father Brady. We live in fearful times; malice and fraud abound.[95]

---

[95] 91-E-5, Ireland to Gibbons, St. Paul, February 12, 1893. Ireland, who was still smarting under the attacks of the Jesuits and others in the school controversy, was grateful for Gibbons' recent words of encouragement and affectionate regard. He told him, "Without your sympathy and powerful help I should long ago have given up and gone under." The Brady mentioned by Ireland was Father Philip P. Brady, Vicar-General of the Archdiocese of St. Louis for the aged and enfeebled Archbishop Kenrick. Confirmation of Ireland's views regarding Pallen and Brady reached Gibbons two weeks later when Father James McCaffrey, pastor of St. Patrick's Church in St. Louis, described the exceedingly bad state of administration in that archdiocese due to Kenrick's enfeeblement. He said Brady and his group persisted in trying to make people believe that the archbishop was capable of fulfilling his functions. As for Pallen, he was openly an enemy of Gibbons and Satolli, said McCaffrey, and he was trying to throw cold water on all the delegate's actions. Regarding a coadjutor for Kenrick, he had overheard Father O. J. McDonald, manager of the *Church Progress* of which Pallen was editor, say, "If the Cardinal can have his way we will have a creature of his" (91-F-7, McCaffrey to Gibbons, St. Louis, February 24, 1893).

Corrigan had quickly repudiated any connection with the leak of the letter, for which he received the thanks of Gibbons and the assurance that he would make his denial public, since the cardinal said he owed it to the Archbishop of New York to put on record his warm appreciation of his words. Likewise he would see to it that the next issue of the Baltimore *Catholic Mirror* carried Corrigan's refutation of the calumny.[96] On February 25 the *Mirror* published an editorial to the effect that up to that time they had maintained silence in the matter of the Chicago dispatch, a policy which they would have continued had they not wished to thank Archbishop Corrigan for his statement, and to this the *Mirror* added that "in uttering these words we are voicing not only our own sentiments, but those of the cardinal himself." The New York *Times* picked up the *Mirror* item, gave to it their full assent, and in explanation of the role of Gibbons they said:

> Nothing could be further from his character than duplicity, or double-dealing of any sort. He would not make a public denial, however, especially of a thing of this sort, so unworthy of his notice, as he has steadily made it a rule to keep out of newspaper controversy. The author of the calumny may be safely left to his present obscurity and contempt, from which no one will attempt to drag him by an effort to administer public punishment.[97]

During the spring of 1893 the excitement over the press scandal of early February gradually died down, but the new delegate continued to be the subject of comment on both sides of the Atlantic. O'Connell expressed his delight at the form in which Gibbons had cast his letter to the Pope on the delegation, and with an eye to the cardinal's political fortunes in Rome, he added, "I think it was what was needed to put you right with the Pope." In an audience a few days before Leo XIII had

---

[96] AANY, Gibbons to Corrigan, Baltimore, February 18, 1893. The cardinal also added that he would have marked copies of the *Mirror's* editorial sent to some of the leading Catholic papers with the request that they reprint it.

[97] February 26, 1893. Ireland for one did not believe the public denial of Corrigan's part in the press scandal, and this on the strength of his talks with Michael Walsh, editor of the *Catholic Herald* of New York, who had gone back on Corrigan and had given over to Satolli some letters of the Archbishop of New York which plainly implicated him in the war against the delegation (ADR, Ireland to O'Connell, New York, April 29, 1893).

assured O'Connell that he would stand strongly behind Satolli, regardless of the opposition to him in the United States. The Vatican, said the Roman rector, was fully aware of the opposition and knew from what quarters it was coming and it had not improved the Holy See's esteem for certain persons. He confessed that as for himself he no longer counted for much with the Propaganda but he worked closely with the Pope and Rampolla and they were as firm as a rock. "My opinion is," said O'Connell, "that everything will be as you desire, in spite of an opposition that is rarely to be met with in the history of the Church."[98] A month later Gibbons informed Cardinal Rampolla of Bishop Ryan's repentance at his hasty cablegrams, and he went on to assure the Secretary of State that public sentiment in the United States was more and more in favor of the delegation. True, there was still criticism of Satolli, especially of his relations with McGlynn, but Gibbons believed that this would dissipate itself in time. He was doing all in his power to strengthen the delegate's position and he hoped the Pope would not hesitate to increase Satolli's moral authority still more by confirming his propositions on the school question.[99]

The press continued during this spring to make its contribution to confusion and misunderstanding on issues relating to the Church. On March 21, for example, the Wheeling *Register* carried a story that private word from Rome had been received in New York to the effect that Denis O'Connell had been named coadjutor to the Archbishop of Baltimore, who for some years had been thinking of seeking assistance, and it was supposed that he had asked for the monsignor as being one of his closest friends. Bishop Kain was taken in by the news item and commented to the rector of Gibbons' cathedral, "He stole a march on us!"[100] While this false story did no greater harm than to stimulate the curiosity of Gibbons' suffragans and priests, a more serious consequence was experienced two weeks later when the Detroit *Patriotic American*, an A.P.A. weekly, carried the text of a bogus encyclical of Leo XIII which by its threats against the lives and liberties of American citizens aroused a

[98] 91-E-6, O'Connell to Gibbons, Rome, February 13, 1893.
[99] 91-H-5, Gibbons to Rampolla, Baltimore, March 17, 1893, copy in French.
[100] AAB, unclassified, Kain to Cornelius F. Thomas, Wheeling, March 21, 1893.

widespread hatred of the Church and its representatives in this country.[101] Despite the patent falsehoods of the document it was reprinted up and down the land and many innocent Americans believed the fantastic tales with which it was filled.

In view of the uproar over the false encyclical and other propaganda of the same kind, it is little wonder that Cardinal Gibbons shied away from the suggestion made from Rome just at this time by J. E. Heywood, the representative of the United States Department of State for the Chicago exhibits from the Vatican. Heywood explained that all the governments, including even Turkey, were sending special envoys and gifts to Leo XIII on the occasion of the silver jubilee of his pontificate, and he felt embarrassed that this country had taken no action. He proposed that Gibbons take up the matter with President Cleveland, and probably knowing nothing of the cardinal's views on diplomatic relations between the two governments, Heywood hinted that a special envoy might prepare the way for what he termed "the establishment of some more important & more permanent diplomatic relations with the Holy See" at some future time.[102] In reply Gibbons offered the excuse that Cleveland's administration had begun a few days after the close of the Pope's jubilee. But Heywood was not to be put off and he returned a second attack with the plea of the mortification felt by the Americans in Rome that their government should be the only one that had not congratulated the Pope. "This fact," said the writer, "is noted here, & commented, as it could not fail to be."[103] But for the time being the cardinal had worries enough on his hands and he let the matter drop there, although several months later he was the medium through which a message and gift were sent to Pope Leo XIII from President Cleveland.[104]

Although he was not prepared just then to urge a presidential

---

[101] Desmond, *op. cit.*, p. 19. The false encyclical appeared in the issue of April 8, 1893.

[102] 91-J-3, Heywood to Gibbons, Rome, April 8, 1893, *Private & Confidential.*

[103] 91-L-3, Heywood to Gibbons, Rome, May 21, 1893.

[104] 91-R-1, O'Connell to Gibbons, Rome, August 1, 1893. O'Connell remarked, "I have the President's letter which is a gem." After he had presented the Cleveland letter to the Pontiff, O'Connell reported that Leo was "fairly delighted and smiled all over" (91-R-5, O'Connell to Gibbons, Rome, August 4, 1893). Cleveland likewise sent to the Pope a set of the *Messages and Papers of the Presidents* for the Vatican Library.

greeting for the Holy Father, the Cardinal of Baltimore was anxious to see that the apostolic delegate should be introduced to the new President. When an appointment was made for Satolli which he was not able to keep, Gibbons explained that the delegate would be unable for some weeks to call at the White House and, therefore, he was taking the liberty to suggest that Cleveland write Satolli a line of acknowledgment of the congratulations which the President had received from him.[105] In other ways, too, Gibbons was helpful in getting Satolli established in the United States. To a solicitation for his support for a home for the Apostolic Delegation which reached him from Father Patrick Cronin, chaplain of Blessed Sacrament Chapel in Buffalo, the cardinal promptly replied that the project met with his cordial approval.[106] When the board of trustees of the university met at Washington in April he submitted the matter to the five archbishops in attendance and they agreed that Gibbons should draft a letter to the hierarchy asking for financial aid of the measure.[107] However, the metropolitans were not able to show unanimity on the timing of the drive for funds as Archbishop Feehan wanted a delay until their annual conference scheduled for September in Chicago.[108] It was taken up again at that time and approval was won for the purchase of a house at Second and I Streets, N.W., in Washington, which had been erected in 1858 for Senator Stephen A. Douglas of Illinois, and had among its most recent occupants Associate Justice Joseph P. Bradley of the Supreme Court.[109] The delegate

---

[105] LC, Cleveland Papers, Gibbons to Cleveland, Baltimore, April 18, 1893. This letter is in the handwriting of Archbishop Ireland but signed by the cardinal. Gibbons was asked frequently by Satolli in his first years as delegate to give advice about disputes arising within the American Church, and in each case the cardinal supplied the delegate with all the information and guidance which he felt would help him. For example, when a conflict broke out regarding the naming of an administrator for the Diocese of Wheeling after the transfer of Bishop Kain to St. Louis, Gibbons was called on for his judgment (91-Q-9, Donato Sbarretti to Gibbons, Washington, July 29, 1893).

[106] 91-F-6, Gibbons to Cronin, Baltimore, February 22, 1893, copy.

[107] AAC, Gibbons to Elder, Baltimore, May 15, 1893.

[108] 91-L-1, Feehan to Gibbons, Chicago, May 20, 1893, *Private*.

[109] William J. Lallou, *The Fifty Years of the Apostolic Delegation, Washington, D. C., 1893–1943* (n.p., 1943), p. 37. The I Street house continued to be the residence of the delegation until September, 1907, when it was moved into the new building erected for that purpose at 1811 Biltmore Street, N.W. The present building at 3339 Massachusetts Avenue, N.W., was first occupied on March 27, 1939.

had been in residence at the Catholic University of America since his appointment, but on November 16, 1893, he moved into the I Street house. Meanwhile the collection continued among the bishops and by October, 1894, a sum of nearly $8,000 was on hand to be invested for the payment of taxes and insurance on the property.[110]

But there were more important negotiations awaiting Cardinal Gibbons in Satolli's behalf than the purchase of a house. Leo XIII and Cardinal Rampolla were fully aware of the resistance to the delegate, both at the Propaganda in Rome and on the part of Archbishop Corrigan in the United States, and if Monsignor O'Connell accurately reported their views they were determined to overcome the opposition. Corrigan, like most of the American bishops, had been opposed in principle to the establishment of the delegation, and when Satolli sided with Ireland in the school controversy and absolved McGlynn it naturally stiffened the archbishop's attitude. Added to these offenses in Corrigan's eyes was the sympathetic reception which Satolli gave to a committee from Epiphany Parish in New York who sought his intervention to have their former pastor, Dr. Burtsell, whom Corrigan had removed four years before, reinstated. The delegate intimated in a polite and tactful manner his thought that if Corrigan would condescend to honor the request it might, perhaps, render the petitioners more attached and deferential to the archbishop.[111] Regardless, however, of the politeness of Satolli's tone, Corrigan was certain to resent his favoritism toward those whom he considered as lacking in respect for his episcopal authority.

It was in circumstances such as these that Rampolla, at the request of Leo XIII, decided upon a positive move to heal the breach between the two prelates. He sent a confidential communication to Cardinal Gibbons in which he described the Pope's distress at the coolness between Corrigan and Satolli, and he requested Gibbons to intervene with his good offices to put a stop to the disagreement.[112] Two weeks after the receipt

---

[110] 93-L-4, Minutes of the Meeting of the Archbishops, Philadelphia, October 10, 1894. Even Bishop McQuaid, reluctant as he had been to see a delegate appointed, sent $600 as the initial contribution of the Diocese of Rochester. McQuaid to Gibbons, n.p., April 12, 1894, quoted in Zwierlein, *op. cit.*, III, 158.

[111] 91-L-8, Satolli to Corrigan, Washington, May 28, 1893, copy.

[112] 91-M-7, Rampolla to Gibbons, Rome, June 15, 1893, *Confidentielle*.

of Rampolla's letter the cardinal held a conference with Corrigan in which they discussed the trouble. In pursuance of their conversation the Archbishop of New York explained the circumstances which had prevented him from meeting the boat when Satolli landed in New York the previous October. Due to the fact, he said, that the Roman prelate had come in at 23rd Street whereas his steamer was scheduled to dock at 10th Street, it was impossible for him to know where he was going to land and to provide a carriage for his convenience. He was extremely pained when he later heard a report that he had failed in courtesy by not being at the dock to greet Satolli. "In one word," said Corrigan, "I was excluded from extending to him such courtesy."[113] All this the archbishop wished Gibbons to know so that it might prove useful to him in the discharge of his office as peacemaker. Gibbons thanked the archbishop for this explanation and, in turn, he told him that the only instruction he had given to the Baltimore clergy who had gone to New York to meet the ablegate was that they should pay their respects to Corrigan and then accompany Satolli to Baltimore. If Corrigan should have any new suggestion that might contribute to a cordial understanding he had only to command him. "You may rest assured," said the cardinal, "that I will do all in my power to effect the desired reconciliation, and it will be a happy day for me if I succeed."[114]

There was, indeed, necessity for a peacemaker, since apart entirely from the two principals, the words and actions of some of their followers contributed a good deal to keeping the feud alive. For example, when Archbishop Ireland met Satolli in Chicago in early June the cause of peace was probably not advanced by his reporting with evident satisfaction that the delegate hated Corrigan and regretted ever having put his foot inside the archbishop's house on Madison Avenue. Satolli, according to Ireland, was "far more advanced in all our ideas than we are ourselves."[115] Just what ideas he meant he did not say. But if peace was to come, others besides John Ireland needed to be calmed. Satolli had complained to Leo XIII of the opposition of the Jesuits to him, with the result that the

[113] 91-P-9, Corrigan to Gibbons, New York, July 17, 1893.
[114] 91-P-10, Gibbons to Corrigan, Baltimore, July 18, 1893, *Personal,* copy.
[115] 91-M-4, Ireland to Gibbons, St. Paul, June 13, 1893.

Pope was greatly displeased and ordered the General of the Society of Jesus to put a stop to these attacks. Father Brandi of the *Civiltà Cattolica* staff did not believe the charge was true since, as he told René Holaind, it was based on the false assumption that opposition to Ireland was opposition to the delegate. Nonetheless, when Brandi was ordered by Leo XIII to write an article in his journal favoring the American delegation he did so, as he said, "in fear and trembling," but he was glad to say it had pleased the Pontiff.[116] It was evident that the Pope was in earnest and that the critics of Satolli would have to step into line. Moreover, Leo XIII intended, as he told O'Connell, to urge upon Gibbons that he "display a little more authority" himself in the matter.[117]

Cardinal Gibbons waited until the return of Archbishop Satolli from his tour of the West before he broached directly the subject of the Archbishop of New York. He then wrote to the delegate and explained his commission from the Holy See and said he had learned with joy that Satolli intended to visit New York. When the visit was over Gibbons would meet the delegate either in Baltimore or Washington on a day convenient to him.[118] In the middle of August Satolli proceeded to New York where the way had been paved for him by Gibbons' earlier approach to Corrigan. The visit went off very well, with the archbishop preaching at Mass in the cathedral in the presence of the delegate, to whom he made several graceful allusions in the course of his sermon. In reporting the encounter to Baltimore both men seemed convinced of the happy results of their meeting and they were generous in their praise of each other.[119] Even

---

[116] AWC, Brandi to Holaind, Naples, July 26, 1893. The article in question appeared in the issue of August 5, 1893, of the *Civiltà Cattolica*.

[117] 91-R-5, O'Connell to Gibbons, Rome, August 4, 1893. O'Connell had a high opinion of his own standing with Leo XIII at this time. He told Gibbons, "I don't believe there is another man in Rome who speaks to the Pope as he permits me."

[118] 91-S-3, Gibbons to Satolli, Baltimore, August 9, 1893, copy in Latin in Bishop Keane's handwriting.

[119] 91-S-10, Satolli to Gibbons, New York, August 18, 1893; 91-T-7, Corrigan to Gibbons, Mount Saint Vincent's, August 30, 1893. In late November, 1892, as we have seen, Corrigan had composed the letter of the metropolitans to Leo XIII against the delegation at Gibbons' request. Several weeks after the reconciliation between Corrigan and Satolli in New York in August, 1893, Monsignor O'Connell informed Archbishop Ireland that this incident had been mentioned to him by Archbishop Augustino Ciasca, Secretary of the Propaganda, and

Ireland was glad that Gibbons had brought about the reconciliation for the sake of public edification, although he was sure many a poisoned shaft would be aimed at Satolli's ear, but he was still of the opinion at this time that the delegate would not waver in his friendship for them.[120] Bishop Keane quoted Satolli as saying that Corrigan had done all that could reasonably be asked, and the experience made the delegate hopeful that Gibbons could in like manner make peace between Corrigan and Ireland when the archbishops assembled in Chicago in September.[121]

The happy sequel to the New York visit was duly reported to Rampolla by the Cardinal of Baltimore who told him that the success that attended his efforts made him hope that a lasting peace would now reign among the American bishops. Apart from the public edification which had resulted, the visit of Satolli had an immediate effect, said the cardinal, in putting an end to the perfidious insinuations and anonymous attacks which until recently had been directed against the person and actions of the delegate.[122] Rampolla promptly acknowledged with thanks the work of Gibbons and told him that the Pope had highly praised the cardinal's able and efficient manner of carrying out the mission which they had entrusted to him.[123]

Since Gibbons' silver jubilee as a bishop was to be celebrated in October, he probably thought it a good opportunity to extend his peacemaking efforts by inviting Archbishop Corrigan to preach the sermon at the pontifical Mass in Baltimore. The Archbishop of New York agreed to fulfill the assignment, and while he stated at the outset of the sermon that Gibbons had

---

O'Connell had remarked that Corrigan had made his profession of faith in the delegate. Ciasca had replied, "There you are mistaken. Abp. C. was the first to give in his adhesion. We have his letters here, written long before the departure of Sat. asking the H. See to establish a delegation in America." If that were so, asked O'Connell, why had Corrigan opposed the delegation at the meeting of the metropolitans in New York in November, 1892? Ciasca answered that he had not opposed it but rather he had refrained from speaking in behalf of the delegation for fear of incurring odium before the other archbishops, to which Ciasca added, "We have his letter here. He wrote us that very evening and told us all" (AASP, O'Connell to Ireland, Rome, September 12, 1893, copy).

[120] 91-S-4/1, Ireland to Gibbons, St. Paul, August 11, 1893.
[121] 91-T-4, Keane to Gibbons, Washington, August 25, 1893.
[122] 91-T-10, Gibbons to Rampolla, Baltimore, August 30, 1893, copy in French.
[123] 91-W-2, Rampolla to Gibbons, Rome, September 13, 1893.

asked him not to make it a personal panegyric he felt justified in referring to the affection in which the cardinal was held by his priests and people, the very large number of prelates who had assembled to honor him, including "the venerated representative of the Holy Father," and the fact that Gibbons had been chosen by the Pope as a member of the senate of the Church as evidences of how deeply he had engraven himself on the hearts of those who knew him.[124] Corrigan's sermon of October 18, 1893, preached at Gibbons' invitation in the cathedral of Baltimore, made its contribution to setting at rest the talk about their differences and rivalry over public questions, even if it gave rise, in turn, in certain quarters where Corrigan was not liked to misgivings about Gibbons' loyalty and firmness.

By the close of the year 1893, therefore, the worst of the storm within the American Church over the apostolic delegate was over. True, matters did not run smoothly for Satolli during the remainder of his stay in the United States, but the hierarchy in general were by this time in the main reconciled to his presence. Ireland, who continued to watch closely over Satolli's fortunes, told O'Connell in the winter of 1894 that the delegate had grown discouraged of late at Propaganda's opposition to him, as well as at the plotting against him of certain prelates in this country. Even Gibbons had come in for some criticism from the man whose cause he had sought to champion. Satolli was quoted as saying that the cardinal was playing a double role and that the delegate was displeased with his visit to Father Henry A. Brann, pastor of St. Agnes Church in New York, after Satolli himself had refused to go there the previous year.[125]

Gibbons had further food for reflection on the difficult lot of a peacemaker when Bishop Keane visited Rome that summer. Leo XIII let the Rector of the University know his determination to give further public support to all Satolli's policies in the United States, again referred to the opposition in rather threatening terms, and said he would soon speak and act in a way that

---

124 Baltimore *Sun*, October 19, 1893. On August 30, 1893, Leo XIII sent his felicitations to Gibbons for his silver jubilee (91-T-8). In thanking him the cardinal described the celebration and told the Pontiff that he hoped his jubilee would confirm the peace and harmony in the American Church which Leo's letter had re-established among the bishops (92-Q-6, Gibbons to Leo XIII, Baltimore, November 3, 1893, copy in French).

125 ADR, Ireland to O'Connell, St. Paul, February 16, 1894.

would leave no doubt in the mind of anyone. It was from this source that Gibbons learned that his efforts to live on friendly terms with Archbishop Corrigan were meeting with criticism in Rome. One of Keane's professors, Thomas O'Gorman, had recently had an audience of the Pope during which Leo XIII had said complainingly, "But the Cardinal goes so much with *that Corrigan!*" Keane felt obliged to pass the remark on so the cardinal might know how matters were viewed at the Vatican. The Pope had complained, too, that it had been a long time since the Archbishop of Baltimore had been to Rome, which gave Keane a chance to urge the cardinal to make the trip as soon as he possibly could. After summarizing in great detail the state of opinion on various American questions as he found it at the Holy See and urging the visit from Gibbons, the bishop concluded, "Your Eminence can come with a brave and cheerful heart, will have no fighting to do, will only have to say *amen,* and put your seal on conclusions already ripe."[126] The implication seemed to be that if the cardinal was prepared to support the Pope in all the measures outlined by Keane and to temper his relations with Corrigan he could look forward to a very pleasant time on his next visit to Rome.

Six months before Cardinal Gibbons had an opportunity to discuss American affairs with the Pope in person, the Holy Father issued on January 6, 1895, his apostolic letter *Longinqua oceani* to the Church of the United States. The Pontiff had words of high praise for the progress which the Church had made under the freedom and liberty accorded to it by the government. He likewise spoke in strong support of the Catholic University of America and the American College in Rome, and the Third Plenary Council of Baltimore merited his commendation. But at this point he introduced the subject which Keane had said was uppermost in his mind, namely, the Apostolic Delegation. When the council of Baltimore had concluded its labors, said the Pope, the duty still remained of putting, so to speak, a proper and becoming crown upon the work. This he had done in establishing the delegation, and then Leo XIII went on to state the traditional and normal procedure of relations of the Holy See through a delegate, to give all the advantages that such an institution would have for American Catholics,

---

[126] 93-J-7, Keane to Gibbons, Pegli, July 31, 1894.

and to reassure those who might think that the presence of a delegate would be derogatory to episcopal power and dignity.[127] If there had been any lingering doubts about the Pope's forthright support of the delegation, those doubts were now laid once and for all by *Longinqua oceani.*

The Cardinal of Baltimore received the letter in the spirit in which it was written, and a few weeks later he wrote a message of thanks to the Holy Father in the name and by the request of the metropolitans of the United States.[128] In the spring the cardinal visited Rome and while later passing a few weeks in Germany he was glad to read in the Baltimore *Sun* what he called "a flat contradiction to a mischievous calumny" that he had been the bearer of a protest to the Holy See against Satolli and his mission. He wrote to Bishop Keane:

> I have never heard or thought of such a protest till I saw it in the paper, & I make it a rule to pay no attention to such lies. The truth is that I spoke warmly & most favorably to the Pope on the mission of the Delegate.[129]

The newspapers were still pursuing their fancies, but Gibbons had doubtless long since despaired of keeping straight the stories on the Church and its prelates in the public prints.

Gibbons had, indeed, remained loyal to the delegate even after there was unmistakable evidence that Satolli's sympathies were no longer with those to whom he had given his support during the first years of his residence in the United States. It is exceedingly difficult if not impossible to determine exactly for what reason and at what time the delegate's allegiance to men of the stamp of Ireland and Keane changed, but change it did. One of the clearest manifestations of this change appeared on April 21, 1895, when Archbishop Satolli spoke at the laying of the cornerstone of St. John the Baptist School at Pottsville, Pennsylvania. On that occasion the delegate was accompanied on his trip by Monsignor Joseph Schroeder of the Catholic University of America and Father August J. Schulte, former

---

[127] Wynne, *The Great Encyclical Letters of Pope Leo XIII,* pp. 320–335, prints the text of the document.

[128] Diary, February 26, 1895, p. 274.

[129] ACUA, Keane Papers, Gibbons to Keane, Wörshofen near Munich, July 12, 1895. According to the *Church News* of Washington for July 27, 1895, Gibbons had a denial of the false newspaper reports published in *Osservatore Romano.*

Vice-Rector of the American College in Rome, and it was evident from the way in which the German Catholic press featured the ceremony in this German parish that they regarded it as an event of more than ordinary importance.

In his speech Satolli expressed words of high praise for the warmth and sincerity of his reception at Pottsville, and he said that the work of the German Catholics in the United States could, in his mind, be characterized by three ideas illustrated in the Scriptures. First, they had the spirit of unity to live in harmony with each other in a way to make outsiders say, "See how they love one another!" Second, like the early Christians they had refuted the calumnies and false accusations brought against them by their exemplary lives and good works. "They rightly consider it to their honor," said Satolli, "to be called and recognized as Roman Catholic Christians and they evidence their feeling in an unequivocal way through their unfaltering devotion and attachment to the Holy See." Finally, citing St. Paul's advice to his converts to see that their conduct in public gave evidence of their private beliefs, the delegate defended the citizenship of the German Catholics, their language schools, their religious instruction, and their general contribution to American life. "The history of America in the past as well as in the present," he said, "testifies clearly that the German Catholics also stand second to none as good citizens of this great republic."[130]

From his speech at Pottsville it was apparent that Satolli was now with the German Catholics rather than with the so-called Americanizers in the Church, and it was probably true that his opinion on the German question colored his views on other matters which at the time were in dispute between the

---

[130] *Katholische Volkszeitung* (Baltimore), May 4, 1895. After the dismissal of Keane as Rector of the University in September, 1896, the Pottsville speech of Satolli was revived in the press. The Washington *Post* of October 28, 1896, spoke of the suppression of the speech in the second edition of Satolli's book, *Loyalty to Church and State* (Baltimore, 1895), and stated that it was rumored Frederick Z. Rooker, Secretary of the Apostolic Delegation, had caused the suppression. But the *Post* confessed there was much mystery about the whole affair and they stated, "In fact, it is one which would require the genius of a 'Sherlock Holmes' to unravel." All seemed to be agreed, however, that it was at Pottsville that Satolli's change of mind was first revealed publicly. As the *Post* put it, "It was in this speech that Cardinal Satolli gave the first intimation of his change of attitude on many questions."

liberal and conservative parties in the American Church. Yet despite his change of front, Gibbons did not alter his attitude toward the delegate and on January 5, 1896, he performed a final service for Satolli by conferring upon him the red biretta of his new rank as a cardinal in the cathedral of Baltimore, a ceremony at which there were present, among other prelates, Archbishops Corrigan and Ireland and among the priests Drs. McGlynn and Burtsell.[131]

Although Cardinal Gibbons was decidedly opposed from the very outset to an apostolic delegate in the United States, and even more so to a nuncio who would enjoy diplomatic recognition from the American government, throughout all the troublesome agitation which surrounded the question from the time it was first mentioned until the end of Satolli's mission in 1896 the cardinal remained entirely free from the acrimony that marked the controversy. He fought against the appointment in the conviction that it would increase anti-Catholic bigotry in the United States, and in this he was proven correct. Gibbons' keen appreciation of American public opinion and his fear that the powers of the bishops in their dioceses would be curtailed prompted him to state his views with force and clarity to his colleagues of the hierarchy and to give Rome a clear, if moderate and polite, indication of his disfavor. But through all the storm and stress he never lost a sense of his dignity and the charity which was owing to those who did not agree with him. When the appointment was finally made the cardinal accepted it in the spirit of obedience that should characterize any Catholic bishop in bowing to the will of the Supreme Pontiff. In only one instance could it be said that Gibbons was at fault, and that was in the exaggerated and fulsome language in which he thanked the Pope for the appointment. The circumstances being what they were his letter went quite beyond what the facts warranted and put too roseate a hue on the spirit in which the American Church had received the news.

In the nearly thirty years that elapsed from the appointment of Satolli to the death of Gibbons the latter had ample opportunity to see the usefulness of the Apostolic Delegation for the Church of the United States. Whatever misgiving the cardinal

---

[131] Cf. Reily, *op. cit.*, IV, 466–492, for a description of the ceremonies.

had entertained concerning the possible encroachment of the delegate upon the powers of the individual bishops had long since disappeared and the valuable services which the papal representative rendered to bishops and priests in settling disputes and acting as a liaison man for their business with Rome, convinced Gibbons of the worth of such an office. Not long after the departure of Satolli in 1896 the A.P.A. broke up and even among those outside the Church the voice of criticism was in large measure stilled, and the apostolic delegate came to be an accepted figure on the American Catholic scene with Gibbons and his coreligionists suffering little further pain or embarrassment from public attacks against the Pope's representative.

Through all the four administrations at the delegation in Washington which Cardinal Gibbons lived to see, his many acts of kindness and assistance to Satolli and his three successors earned for the cardinal the most generous expressions of gratitude from these men who served the Holy See in the United States. When, for example, Gibbons was in Rome in 1895 and informed Satolli that he had remembered him kindly to the Pope and Rampolla, it prompted the delegate to reply in his uncertain English, "With all this I do gladly and gratefully recall to my mind the many and many proofs of special benevolence of which Your Eminence made me the happy recipient ever since my arrival to this country."[132] When Satolli's successor, Sebastiano Martinelli, on whom Gibbons had likewise conferred the red biretta in the Baltimore cathedral on May 8, 1901, was ready to depart from the United States the following spring, he asked the cardinal to accept his sincerest thanks, as he expressed it, "for what you have done for me, & if you think that I may be, in some way, able to do something for Your Eminence be pleased to tell me."[133] Nine years later Diomede Falconio, the third delegate, was also made a cardinal and recalled to Rome, and in bidding farewell to Gibbons he wrote:

I beg to profit of this occasion to offer to your Eminence my sincerest best thanks for the great kindness which you have always shown to me, while I pray that God may prolong your days for the greater glory of the Church and of your beloved country.[134]

[132] 93-W-5, Satolli to Gibbons, Washington, July 25, 1895.
[133] 99-R-2, Martinelli to Gibbons, Washington, May 5, 1902.
[134] 107-R, Falconio to Gibbons, Washington, October 31, 1911.

The Cardinal of Baltimore had worked cordially and in close harmony with the delegates in the years after 1893. In this respect his attitude and conduct left nothing to be desired in Rome and reflected nothing of his previous opposition to the establishment of an apostolic delegation in the United States.

John Ireland, Archbishop of St. Paul.

CHAPTER XV

The School Controversy

AT THE time that Archbishop Satolli arrived in the United States in October, 1892, as the representative of Pope Leo XIII to the Columbian Exposition and as the bearer of a proposal for the establishment of a permanent apostolic delegation, the American Church was in the midst of one of the most acrimonious controversies in its history. The difficulty, which in one form or another had been with the Church for over a half century, related to the parochial schools. Ever since the trouble of Bishop John Hughes with the New York Public School Society in the 1840's, the problem had periodically caused tension and uneasiness between Catholics and many of their non-Catholic fellow citizens. The Church was intent upon the increase and spread of its parochial schools as a major safeguard for the religious faith of its children. On the other hand, the growing spirit of secularism in American society caused less and less emphasis to be placed upon religious instruction, and aroused resentment against any effort to provide means whereby the public schools of the nation might offer training in religion or whereby financial aid might be given to private religious schools. It would be untrue to say that by the later nineteenth century the majority of non-Catholic Americans had adopted the secularist point of view, but the fact was that an ever increasing number of them were of this opinion.

Fortunately, there were periods when the agitation over the issue of public vs. parochial schools slackened and during which sensible compromises were effected which worked to the advantage of both sides. For example, in May, 1870, Bishop Augustin Vérot, S.S., of Savannah made an arrangement with the school board of his see city, whereby the board took over the parochial schools of Savannah and was given power and responsibility for the repair of buildings, the hiring and testing of teachers, and the selection of textbooks, except in history, reading, and geography.[1] Three years later Father Patrick McSweeny, pastor of St. Peter's Church at Poughkeepsie, New York, worked out with the local school board a similar plan for the rental of his parish school for $1.00 a year with the board given jurisdiction in much the same manner as in Savannah. In Poughkeepsie, as in local communities of New Jersey, Connecticut, and Pennsylvania that had like arrangements, instruction in the Catholic religion was given after the regular school hours. These plans, which operated to the general satisfaction of those concerned, were brought about by mutual good will at a time when the issues were not clouded by ill-tempered attacks from unfriendly critics.

However, two years after the Poughkeepsie plan went into effect the question again entered the field of public controversy through the address of President Ulysses S. Grant delivered at Des Moines in September, 1875, in which he urged that not a dollar of funds allotted for public schools should ever be given to sectarian schools. The result was renewed excitement on all sides. Bishop McQuaid spoke in Boston the following February in defense of Catholic schools and their right to share in the taxes paid by Catholic citizens, for which he was sharply countered by Francis E. Abbot, founder of the Free Religious Association and editor of the weekly *Index* of Toledo, Ohio. On November 24, 1875, the Propaganda had issued an instruction to the American bishops warning against the danger to the faith and morals of Catholic children attending the public schools, and in June, 1876, the Republican Party at Cincinnati wrote a plank into its platform which echoed the views of Grant; and the Democrats, conscious of the Catholic vote, went only as far the same summer as to speak of preserving the public schools and the American doctrine of separation of Church and State. In the course of the public debate which followed harsh things were said by both Catholics and non-Catholics and the result naturally led to a deepening of prejudice all around.[2]

---

[1] For details of the Savannah plan cf. the Boston *Pilot*, February 15, 1873.

[2] For the background of the trouble on the school question cf. Daniel F. Reilly, O.P., *The School Controversy, 1891–1893* (Washington, 1943), pp. 1–38. Reilly's monograph is the most complete account of the subject, although it suffers some-

Although the unpleasantness aroused by the injection of this issue into the presidential campaign of 1876 gradually died out, the subject was revived in a more virulent form in the 1880's. The authorities of the Church in Rome, concerned for the faith of thousands of immigrant children reaching these shores, and yet wishing to hold themselves aloof from an American political question such as public funds for parochial schools, continued to urge the construction of more parish schools as the only remedy. On the eve of the Third Plenary Council in the fall of 1884 the Prefect of Propaganda, Cardinal Simeoni, exhorted Archbishop Gibbons to have the bishops build schools and not spend all their money on churches, as well as to have them see to the religious instruction of Catholic children attending the public schools.[3] The action which followed in the council on this subject was as advanced a one as the Church had yet taken in making it almost mandatory for pastors to erect parochial schools.[4] The accelerated pace in the spread of parish schools in the years after the council was noted, of course, by the A.P.A. which had been founded in 1887, and it was due in no small measure to the constant hammering away on the platform and in the press by A.P.A. orators and writers on the threat offered by the Catholic Church to the nation's public schools, that so much bitterness was engendered on the subject.

With the question very much in the public eye the officers of the National Education Association invited Cardinal Gibbons and Bishop Keane to address the annual convention of their organization on the topic of denominational schools at Nashville in July, 1889. The cardinal's brief paper, which was read by Keane at one of the sessions on July 17, was devoted to an explanation of why he regarded education as incomplete without religious instruction. Gibbons based his argument on man's spiritual nature and eternal destiny, and near the close of his remarks he instanced

---

what from a failure to consult the Corrigan side of the case in the Archives of the Archdiocese of New York. For an account of how this subject played a part in the political affairs of the Republicans cf. "The Attitude of the Republican Party toward Religious Schools, 1875–1880," by Sister Mary Angela Carlin, O.S.U., an unpublished master's thesis, The Catholic University of America (1948).

[3] 78-S-15, Simeoni to Gibbons, Rome, October 30, 1884.

[4] For a discussion of the council insofar as it related to parochial schools cf. Francis P. Cassidy, "Catholic Education in the Third Plenary Council of Baltimore," *Catholic Historical Review,* XXXIV (October, 1948), 257–305 (January, 1949), 414–436.

a way in which he thought the position of the public and parochial school systems could be made to work in harmony by
citing the example of Canada, although he did not enter into any
details about the financial help given to denominational schools
in the dominion. He recognized the difficulty of teaching religion
in the public schools where children of all faiths and of no
faith were in attendance, but aside from speaking of it as "a
grave problem beset with difficulties," he offered no practical
remedy.[5] It had been the cardinal's original intention to include
a brief statement near the end of his paper on the justice of a
division of public funds to benefit private schools, but some days
before the convention Keane warned him from Boston that he
should omit the reference. The bishop had spoken on the subject
to Archbishop Williams who was very much opposed to the
cardinal mentioning the point at all, since he thought it would
give rise to fierce resentment. Keane quoted Williams as saying,

> the suggestion, no matter how gently & hypothetically put by you,
> will inevitably be regarded, considering its source, as an authori-
> tative indication of Catholic policy, and will open up an issue here
> for which the Church is by no means prepared.[6]

Although the cardinal dropped all allusion to the matter except
for the oblique reference to Canada and phrased his entire paper
in the most conciliatory tone, he did not escape criticism, and
his paper and that of Bishop Keane were energetically challenged
by several opponents of private religious schools. Despite the
attacks Archbishop Ireland thought the Nashville convention had
been, to use his own words, "a grand thing for the Church."[7]

---

[5] *National Education Association. Journal of Proceedings and Addresses* (Topeka,
1889), p. 113. The papers of Gibbons and Keane, together with the rejoinders of
Edwin D. Mead and John Jay and five appendixes on the Catholic parochial
school, will be found here (pp. 111–179).

[6] 86-E-2, Keane to Gibbons, Boston, July 5, 1889.

[7] 86-G-10, Ireland to Gibbons, St. Paul, August 9, 1889. A year later the
Independent of New York ran a symposium in its issue of September 4, 1890,
on the subject, "The Catholics and the Public Schools." Among those who were
asked to contribute from the Catholic side were Gibbons, Ireland, and Father
James Nilan, pastor of St. Peter's Church, Poughkeepsie, New York. The cardinal's
remarks were headed "A Menace to Our Country," and while he said he did not
know any new idea he could add, he was glad that the subject was being
thoroughly discussed from various viewpoints. "Truth," said Gibbons, "will be
evolved from the clash of discussion." He then gave permission for the editor
to quote from his recent volume, *Our Christian Heritage* (pp. 489–495) wherein

John Ireland was accustomed to challenge and at times he rather enjoyed it, although it is doubtful if he did not sometimes grow weary during the prolonged struggle which lay immediately ahead of him and which made the opposition to Gibbons and Keane seem mild, indeed. The occasion which provoked the controversy was a speech of the Archbishop of St. Paul delivered before the same N.E.A. in his see city in July, 1890. The address was entitled "State Schools and Parish Schools," and at the very outset the speaker proclaimed in eloquent phrases his friendship and advocacy of the public schools, although, as he said, in the circumstances of the time he upheld the parochial school. He wished there was no need for the latter and if he had his way all American schools would be state schools. Nonetheless, the speaker made it plain that he saw no solution to the difficulty of the many varieties of the Christian religion in the United States in the teaching of a common Christianity in the schools. As he said, "In loyalty to their principles, Catholics cannot and will not accept a common Christianity."

This situation, therefore, called for a compromise in which the state could play a part. In Ireland's judgment the right of the state school to exist was beyond discussion, and since many parents would not fulfill their duty to their children in giving them an education, "the state," said the archbishop, "must come forward as an agent of instruction. . . ."[8] However, he maintained that the primary right to educate belonged to the parents, and if they performed their obligation by seeing to it that their children received in parochial schools an education that would properly fit them for citizenship, then they should be free of all interference. Ireland went on to point out the chief objection of Catholics to public schools, namely, their failure to teach religion, and to state his belief in the necessity of religious instruction for the complete education of the child. He admitted the differences between the public and parochial systems, and in an effort to offer a compromise he made the following proposal:

I would permeate the regular state school with the religion of the majority of the children of the land, be this religion as

---

there was reprinted his speech to the Nashville convention concerning the defect of public school education in barring the teaching of religion.

[8] John Ireland, *The Church and Modern Society*, I, 218. The text of the address is given here (pp. 217–232).

Protestant as Protestantism can be, and I would, as is done in England, pay for the secular instruction given in denominational schools according to results; that is, every pupil passing the examination before state officials, and in full accordance with the state program, would secure to his school the cost of the tuition of a pupil in the state school. This is not paying for religious instruction, but for the secular instruction demanded by the State, and given to the pupil as thoroughly as he could have received it in the state school.[9]

Aside from the emphasis on the state's right to educate, and his expansive remark about permeating the state school with the religion of the majority of the children, the suggestions made by Archbishop Ireland were not strikingly different from the arrangements already in operation in Poughkeepsie and other places. Why, then, one may ask, did his address give rise to such a storm of opposition? The principal reason probably lay in the personality and language of the speaker. Ireland had some time before this incurred the intense dislike of many German Catholics because of his forthright stand against the use of the German language in their numerous parish schools, and in the present instance they saw his proposals only in the light of a further attack upon their cherished institution. By his forceful views on such questions as the university, the secret societies, and the Knights of Labor, the archbishop had aroused the resistance of more conservative churchmen who believed that in Ireland's efforts to accommodate American Catholicism to the national spirit they detected the germ of European liberalism.

Moreover, the archbishop's manner of speech often gave an exaggerated notion of his ideas as, for example, when he exclaimed in a typically flamboyant passage of his address in St. Paul, "The free school in America! Withered be the hand raised in sign of its destruction!"[10] Read in their context the rhetorical flourishes of the archbishop sounded proper enough and were a true

---

[9] *Ibid.*, I, 229.

[10] *Ibid.*, I, 220. An interesting example of how Ireland caused comment by the expression of his ideas occurred two months before his St. Paul speech. Archbishop Ryan of Philadelphia told his friend, the Archbishop of New York, "Archbishop Ireland has created a sensation in Washington & through the country, by declaring that Catholics should admit the negroes to *social* as well as political and religious equality. His enthusiasm sometimes leads him too far, but his purity of intention is unquestionable" (AANY, Ryan to Corrigan, Philadelphia, May 20, 1890).

reflection of his personality, but when they were made to stand alone by those who disliked him they often furnished weapons to be used against him. Even the *Catholic Mirror* of Baltimore, which was ordinarily friendly to Ireland, felt it could not go along with what they called "The intense views of the prelate concerning the transcendent glories of our public school system."[11] And if the *Mirror* showed a lack of sympathy in the early stages of the controversy, other Catholic journals became savage in their attacks upon him.

A further factor contributing to the tumult over Archbishop Ireland's policies on the parochial school was, as we have mentioned, the A.P.A. The speech of July, 1890, deprived even this bigoted organization of suitable material for carping, but a year later the A.P.A. and others as well believed that they had found the secret behind Ireland's professed friendship for the American public school. Between August and October, 1891, two pastors of the Archdiocese of St. Paul, Fathers James J. Conry of Immaculate Conception Church at Faribault, Minnesota, and Charles Corcoran of St. Michael's Church, Stillwater, entered into agreements with their respective school boards to rent their parish schools for $1.00 a year with stipulations similar to those that had worked successfully in Poughkeepsie and other communities.[12] To these contracts Ireland gave his approval, with the result that when the details became known there was an immediate outcry that Ireland was trying to take over the public school system from within, and he now found himself advanced upon by extremists from the camps of both the Catholics and the A.P.A.

The close friendship and sympathy which Cardinal Gibbons felt for Archbishop Ireland were well known. Three years before the outbreak of the trouble over the schools the cardinal had given public testimony of his esteem for the Archbishop of St. Paul when he visited him on his way to Portland in September, 1887. At a reception held in his honor, Gibbons said he had watched Ireland's career for many years and in studying him he could not fail to love him. He regarded the archbishop, he told the St. Paul audience, "as a Providential messenger, sent to you by Almighty God to advance the interests of religion and

---

[11] July 19, 1890.
[12] Reilly, *op. cit.*, pp. 78–82.

the well being of society, because he has both objects in view."[13] While at times Gibbons grew fearful of the consequences of Ireland's blunt manner and speech in dealing with his opponents, during the more than thirty years they were destined to be associated together in the American Church the cardinal never retracted the tribute of 1887. Therefore, Gibbons was quick to sense danger to his friend when within six weeks of the time Ireland's address was delivered, the cardinal learned the disturbing news that someone had sent the text to Rome for examination.[14] Nor were his misgivings allayed two weeks later in hearing that while Monsignor O'Connell believed the archbishop would escape ecclesiastical censure this time, nonetheless, Simeoni was greatly troubled by the controverted speech.[15]

Uneasy as he was over the impression created in Rome about the Archbishop of St. Paul, the cardinal decided upon a personal defense of his friend. He emphasized to O'Connell the power of the archbishop in the United States who, he said, had more public influence than a half dozen of his neighbors among the bishops. Ireland's suggestions in regard to the schools had only been intended to secure for Catholic children attending public schools a Catholic education which was at present denied to them. Simeoni should know that there was not a bishop in the country who had done more to elevate and advance the Catholic religion than John Ireland, that he was honored and admired by the entire community, and that Protestants regarded him as a fearless and uncompromising champion of the Catholic faith, while Catholics venerated him as an eloquent exponent of their religion. Consequently, the circulation of even a rumor to the effect that he did not enjoy the entire confidence of the Propaganda or that he was under a cloud would do immense mischief to religion, discourage and dampen the zeal of Ireland, elate the Church's enemies, and sadden the hearts of Catholics. The representations against the archbishop at Rome were doubtless made, thought Gibbons, by men of narrow and contracted minds who did not understand the country in which they lived. "Had he been a dumb dog," said the cardinal, "no whelps would have barked at him here." Gibbons was saddened that such a man should suffer from malevolent

---

[13] *Northwestern Chronicle* (St. Paul), October 6, 1887.

[14] 87-U-1, O'Connell to Gibbons, Grottaferrata, August 22, 1890.

[15] 87-V-4, O'Connell to Gibbons, Grottaferrata, September 6, 1890.

tongues, and were the fact known he believed his sadness would be shared by the entire episcopate who were justly proud of their colleague.[16]

This letter of Cardinal Gibbons not only revealed the high value which he placed upon the qualities and services of Archbishop Ireland, but it showed as well the readiness which Gibbons so frequently displayed in coming to the support of those whom he believed to be the victims of unfair opposition, especially in the case of friends whom he loved as dearly as he did the Archbishop of St. Paul. An act of friendship such as Gibbons had performed in this instance would be likely to elicit the heartfelt gratitude of even a less generous spirit than that of Ireland, and when the cardinal informed him of what he had written to Rome there was immediate thanks forthcoming from St. Paul for what Ireland called "your promptness to extend over me, at the first sign of danger, the shield of your powerful influence." The archbishop was conscious of the harm which might result from a loss of his reputation at the Holy See. As he put it,

> Bishops are in fearful straits; their whole power is their influence; a word from Rome destroys this influence, and efforts will be made, whenever there is a chance to obtain that word. Our one hope is to be united, work together and hold by one another.[17]

There were, indeed, those who were prepared to use even an imaginary word from Rome to accomplish their purpose in thwarting Ireland. In fact, a few weeks later a rumor of Roman disfavor of the archbishop such as Gibbons had feared had already begun its mischievous work. A news item which appeared in the *Catholic Citizen* of Milwaukee and in other papers was widely circulated to the effect that the archbishop had been summoned to the Holy See to account for his conduct. Denis O'Connell regarded it as sufficiently serious to cable that he was authorized to contradict the report as absolutely false.[18] Thus in the school controversy, as in the public discussion of other major Catholic questions in this period, the press, both Catholic and secular and on both sides of the Atlantic, played a leading part in adding to the confusion and division of opinion by the

---

16 87-V-5, Gibbons to O'Connell, Baltimore, September 10, 1890, copy.
17 87-W-6, Ireland to Gibbons, St. Paul, September 23, 1890.
18 88-C-1, O'Connell to Gibbons, Rome, November 2, 1890, cablegram.

publication of constantly recurring rumors and false statements of this kind.

From the very outset of the trouble over the parochial schools, the question became deeply involved with the agitation over Cahensly and his German followers in the United States, with the result that until the storm subsided some years later there were no more persistent and voluble critics of Archbishop Ireland than the German Catholics. O'Connell informed Gibbons that they were lodging complaints at the Holy See against Ireland and they wrote, as the monsignor said, "as if there were no reliable Catholics in America but themselves." There was need, therefore, for counterrepresentations and Archbishop Jacobini had confidentially advised that the Cardinal of Baltimore should at once request the Pope to take no action on Ireland until he had heard from the American metropolitans. Not only did Rome show a strong dislike for Ireland's statement that he wished there was no necessity for parochial schools, but the *Corriera della Sera* of Naples had recently added to the uneasiness by giving a false version of the archbishop's address at the centennial of the American hierarchy at Baltimore in November, 1889.

For all these reasons it was important that Ireland should receive a prompt and strong defense of his school program from Gibbons. The cardinal was furnished with data on the systems governing Catholic education in a number of the European countries in order that he might use it in contrasting, to the advantage of the American situation, what obtained in Europe with what was being done in the United States.[19] Gibbons would need all the material he could gather, for on the same day that O'Connell wrote his letter Cardinal Rampolla addressed an inquiry to the Archbishop of Baltimore in which he said that the Holy Father desired to know exactly the opinion of Gibbons concerning the bearing of Ireland's school discourse on the educational principles of the Church.[20] It was important that the cardinal should put forth his best effort, since he was told by O'Connell that he believed the former's letter would decide the school question in much the same way that at the time he

---

[19] 88-D-6, O'Connell to Gibbons, Rome, November 24, 1890. The text of Ireland's address at the centennial of the hierarchy at Baltimore on November 10, 1889, can be read in his *The Church and Modern Society*, I, 71–101.

[20] 88-D-7, Rampolla to Gibbons, Rome, November 24, 1890.

thought the Holy See would follow Gibbons' direction in the case of the secret societies. At the Propaganda, said the cardinal's Roman agent, they still considered Gibbons as the guiding star of the American Church and, he added, "in all matters appertaining to that Church yr. opinion carries the greatest weight."[21]

With the counsel of his trusted adviser fresh in his mind, Gibbons prepared himself for another major statement of American policy for the guidance of the Holy See. He first outlined his intended approach to Archbishop Ireland, who promptly gave it his assent and supplied further facts about the parochial schools in his archdiocese. Ireland felt that apart from personal reasons a Roman rebuke for his address would be taken as a censure for his Americanism and as evidence of the hopeless foreignism of the Church. He detailed the attacks upon him of certain German Catholic papers like the *Amerika* of St. Louis and the *Columbia* of Milwaukee, both of which had said a condemnation of his speech was to come from Rome; and it was his belief that the German Jesuits in the United States were accountable for the opposition shown toward him by Cardinal Mazzella in the Eternal City. But the news of Gibbons' efforts in his behalf raised his spirits, and he told the cardinal, "I rather enjoy the predicament into which I have got."[22] When he received the draft of the cardinal's letter a week later he was, of course, deeply grateful. "I feel perfectly safe," he said, "so long as my case is in your hands."[23]

But beyond fair words and fragmentary impressions, the Archbishop of St. Paul forwarded to Cardinal Gibbons a lengthy and detailed analysis of his address of 1890 with comments on his intended meaning of certain passages and a summary of the

---

21 88-D-9, O'Connell to Gibbons, Rome, November 29, 1890. O'Connell told Gibbons that the Vatican and the Propaganda were deeply mortified at the leaks to the press of confidential documents of the Holy See. Recently the Propaganda had asked him to help them in tracing some of the betrayals to their authors. Archbishop Corrigan was then, said O'Connell, in possession of documents to which he had no right, and he thought this would be a favorable opportunity to follow it up since the copies of these unnamed documents had been carefully guarded at the American College and the monsignor concluded, therefore, they could have been secured only through theft or a violation of confidence in some quarter. "They know here," said O'Connell, "the Bps. are afraid to write to them on ac't. of these acts of treachery and I think they would be happy to hunt one act down."
22 88-E-4, Ireland to Gibbons, St. Paul, December 7, 1890.
23 88-E-5, Ireland to Gibbons, St. Paul, December 13, 1890.

criticisms which had been leveled against it in both the German and English language journals.[24] With all this material in his possession Gibbons then turned to Alphonse Magnien, S.S., for the composition of the document in French. The cardinal first emphasized the efforts which American Catholics had made and were continuing to make in behalf of parochial schools. But he informed Leo XIII that these efforts would never have other than a more or less limited success, since for various reasons circumstances would always make it necessary for a certain number of Catholic children to attend the public schools. That fact, therefore, had to be taken into consideration if the bishops were to accomplish their mission and provide proper education for their youth. But lest the Pope should form a false impression of the American public schools, Gibbons was at pains to explain in more detail their reason for omitting religious instruction. He said:

> It is true that in the public schools there is no religious education given, but, Most Holy Father, this is not, as in France, Italy and elsewhere, out of opposition to religion. Thank God, the public spirit in this country is fundamentally religious, and there is everywhere a great respect for liberty of conscience well understood and in the legitimate sense of the word. Consequently the religious question is set aside in the schools in order not to offend the sentiments of the children who attend them and the parents who send them there. The care of providing the religious education of the children is left to the Church and the Protestant sects.

Coming to Ireland's discourse, the cardinal stated that the archbishop knew better than anyone the feelings of the American public and the prejudices which existed in this country against the Church. Ireland had sought to use the occasion of his address to put an end to the divisions which occurred from time to time between Catholics and their fellow citizens, divisions which, as the cardinal expressed it:

> are caused above all by the opposition against the system of national education which is attributed to us, and which, more than any other thing, creates and maintains in the minds of the American people the conviction that the Catholic Church is opposed by principle to

---

[24] 88-F-8, Ireland to Gibbons, St. Paul, December, 1890. This document is printed as an appendix in Reilly, *op. cit.*, pp. 237–241.

the institutions of the country and that a sincere Catholic cannot be a loyal citizen of the United States.

If, said Gibbons, the first part of the speech in which Ireland paid his tribute to the public schools was read without preconceived ideas and with consideration for the principles which the archbishop set forth in the second section of his address, the cardinal found it impossible to see how anything reprehensible could be seen in it from the viewpoint of sound doctrine. When Ireland spoke of the state's right to educate he did not mean that right was unlimited, since he urged it only in the case of the parents' failure to exercise their primary right to educate their children. After quoting for the Pope a number of the most controverted passages of the speech, Gibbons then continued:

> It appears to me, Most Holy Father, that the various sentences in their context have no other meaning than this: The Catholics are not against state schools in principle; they recognize the great success of these schools; they desire neither their suppression nor diminution; what they ask is that the defects of the system be corrected, that religious teaching be given the place it is entitled to; in particular that Catholics be given the guarantees demanded by their conscience in the most important task of the education of their children, then these same Catholics will be glad to patronize these schools as their conscience will no longer oblige them, in order to have their parochial schools, to take upon themselves the heavy burdens which weigh upon them in the present circumstances.

In all of this, said Gibbons, there was nothing unreasonable, especially in a country of mixed religions like the United States.

But the opponents of the Archbishop of St. Paul had likewise suspected his faith because of his remarks concerning Protestantism. To the cardinal it was obvious that a religion, even an unorthodox one, that helped, as he said, "to maintain in the public mind belief in revelation and the supernatural order," was certainly preferable to atheism and unbelief. That, too, was the meaning of Ireland when he made his appeal for Protestantism. With these various factors in mind it would be, said Gibbons, a disastrous thing if the archbishop were condemned or even simply blamed. Protestants constantly proclaim that there can be no liberty of thought in the Catholic Church. To censure Ireland would give confirmation to this charge since he was a living challenge to such accusations. Furthermore, Ireland's zeal for religious education was proved by the fact that in his archdiocese there were 12,000 Catholic children attending parochial schools and there was hardly an important parish under his jurisdiction without one.

All these facts proved that the campaign against the Archbishop of St. Paul was not motivated by disinterested love of truth nor pure zeal for sound doctrine but found its roots in far less worthy motives. Ireland's soundness of doctrine was certainly established, although the ardor of his temperament and his enthusiastic character led him in the circumstances of the moment to use expressions which might defeat his thought by exaggerating it before his audience. Finally, if the Holy See deemed it proper to issue new instructions on education, it was the opinion of Cardinal Gibbons that these should not be made public before the American hierarchy had been given an opportunity to make its sentiments fully known, and if the Holy See wished him to do so the cardinal would be happy to lay the matter before the archbishops at their next meeting.[25] A copy of this elaborate defense of his views on the school question was forwarded in due time to Archbishop Ireland. Gibbons informed him that he had instructed Denis O'Connell to say at Rome, in case nothing objectionable was found in the address, that some expression of good will or approval of the archbishop's course of action by the Pontiff was desirable. The cardinal thought this would be a fitting rebuke to those who had questioned the soundness of Ireland's doctrine.[26]

During the course of the following week Archbishop Ireland was encouraged by the news dispatches from Europe — prematurely as it turned out — to believe that the case was settled in his favor. He attributed the outcome to Gibbons' generous friendship, and he added, "The word, grateful, would be but a poor expression of my heart's sentiments toward you." It was at this time that Ireland disclosed to the cardinal the fact that some months before an official of the Associated Press had sought from him a letter of introduction for one of their special agents to O'Connell with a view to securing a good local agent in Rome for Catholic news. The result was that Monsignor Eugène Boeglin

---

[25] 88-F-6, Gibbons to Leo XIII, Baltimore, December 30, 1890, copy in French, also printed in the translation of Pierre H. Conway, O.P., as an appendix in Reilly, *op. cit.*, pp. 242–247.

[26] AASP, Gibbons to Ireland, Baltimore, February 3, 1891, copy.

was chosen as the Roman A.P. agent for Catholic news and Boeglin was pleased and honored and would be, said Ireland, obedient to Denis O'Connell.[27] Ireland had thus provided what he thought would be a reliable channel for news coming out of Rome on the Church in the United States. But the first reports of action on the school question had not proved accurate, and a month later the archbishop was fretting at the delay in the Pope's decision. He hoped Leo XIII would say the right thing, not so much for himself as for the country. "If he is harsh towards our 'cherished institution,' " said Ireland, "harm will be done."[28]

In his letter to the Holy Father Cardinal Gibbons had stated that the views of Archbishop Ireland concerning the state's right to educate were held by various Catholic authorities whose orthodoxy had never been called in question, and in this connection he mentioned specifically Thomas Bouquillon, professor of moral theology in the Catholic University of America. Bouquillon had prepared some material on the school question which he had submitted to the judgment of the Abbé Magnien who thought that an article on the subject would do an immense amount of good and have the effect of putting an end to prejudice.[29] With this encouragement, the professor wrote an article and sent it to Father Ignatius F. Horstmann, editor of the *American Catholic Quarterly Review* in Philadelphia. But Horstmann declined to publish it unless Bouquillon would agree to tone down his views regarding the rights of the state in education, and in this opinion he stated that Archbishop Ryan agreed with him.[30] Unwilling to make the changes suggested by the Philadelphia editor, Bouquillon then turned to Gibbons for his advice as to what should be done. He outlined in a general way his ideas, but he remarked that he would not wish to publish anything that would give rise to trouble or reflect unfavorably on the university. For that reason he appealed to the cardinal as the head of the American hierarchy and the chancellor of the university for direction as to what course he should pursue.[31]

---

[27] 88-J-4, Ireland to Gibbons, St. Paul, February 11, 1891.
[28] ADR, Ireland to O'Connell, St. Paul, March 8, 1891.
[29] ACUA, Bouquillon Papers, Magnien to Bouquillon, Baltimore, January 9, 1891.
[30] *Ibid.*, Bouquillon Papers, Horstmann to Bouquillon, Philadelphia, May 11, 1891.
[31] *Ibid.*, Bouquillon Papers, Bouquillon to Gibbons, no date or place, copy.

Magnien was requested by Gibbons to reply in his name and to say that he regretted very much the view taken of the article in Philadelphia, and that he shared Bouquillon's sentiments both in regard to the teaching he set forth and the opportuneness of publication. The cardinal suggested, therefore, that the article be published in brochure form.[32] Gibbons had no realization, of course, of the furor that would ensue upon the appearance of Bouquillon's pamphlet later that year, but in the meantime he did not hesitate to give his approval to an authoritative Catholic statement of the case for the state in education from the professor. The refusal of the *Quarterly* to publish the Bouquillon article in no way surprised Ireland; it merely confirmed him in his low opinion of Archbishop Ryan and he exclaimed to Gibbons, "Oh, the servile timidity of some men!"[33] But what seemed timidity to John Ireland was with Ryan a conviction, since, as he explained to the cardinal, Bouquillon's efforts to prove the state's right to coerce in education might at once be applied to the circumstances of the Church's schools and be regarded as an invitation to compulsory education. The only power of compulsion which the Archbishop of Philadelphia would concede to the state was in the three R's since they seemed necessary to qualify a citizen to vote intelligently.[34]

From the early months of 1891 until the Bouquillon pamphlet came out in November the debate continued on the school question, although with nothing of the fury that characterized the exchange of views after that date. The news cabled from Rome through the Associated Press was highly favorable to Ireland on the matter of the schools, for which he thanked Boeglin and O'Connell. He believed the dispatches on the schools and the German question were creating a tremendous sensation and affecting Catholic opinion more than anything else could have done. While he was enthusiastic the archbishop, nonetheless, understood that the news dispatches would have little value unless the future pronouncements of the Pope or Propaganda sustained them on the schools.[35] He was strongly agitated that summer over these issues and he kept urging in vain for Gibbons to call a meeting of the archbishops.

---

[32] *Ibid.*, Bouquillon Papers, Magnien to Bouquillon, Baltimore, June 3, 1891.

[33] AAB, unclassified, Ireland to Gibbons, St. Paul, May 30, 1891.

[34] 88-Q-3, Ryan to Gibbons, Philadelphia, June 3, 1891.

[35] ADR, Ireland to O'Connell, St. Paul, May 21, 1891.

The news that the Vatican was seriously thinking of asking Archbishop Katzer and himself to go to Rome to present the two sides of the school question only annoyed Ireland. "Imagine," he said, "the insult to myself and to the Republic, to be brought to argue with Katzer, a man who knows as little of America as a Huron."[36] Calmer counsels tried their hand at this time when Bishop Spalding of Peoria published an article on "Religious Instruction in State Schools" in the *Educational Review,* the official organ of the National Education Association. Spalding took practically the same ground as Ireland had done a year before in the matter of the state's right to educate, and the only serious objection he raised to the public school was the same as the archbishop's, namely, its failure to provide for religious training.[37] Meanwhile Gibbons said nothing for publication, although he provided Archbishop Elder with Ireland's explanation of what had been done in the matter of the contracts for the parish schools in Faribault and Stillwater, Minnesota.[38]

In the last week of November, 1891, the American archbishops assembled in St. Louis for their annual conference and the celebration of Archbishop Kenrick's golden jubilee. At their meeting Cardinal Gibbons asked Archbishop Ireland to explain for the benefit of his fellow metropolitans the details governing the arrangements between the local school boards and the parish schools of Faribault and Stillwater which had been negotiated some weeks before. Ireland made his explanation, for which he received the explicit approval of several of the archbishops present, the open congratulations of Archbishop Williams, and no word of censure from his other colleagues.[39] As far as the meeting itself was concerned, therefore, the matter passed off without incident. However, the fact that the pamphlet of Dr. Bouquillon, *Education: To Whom Does It Belong?* appeared shortly before the archbishops convened was the circumstance that gave to their meeting an importance that it would not otherwise have had.

---

[36] 88-S-3, Ireland to Gibbons, St. Paul, July 2, 1891.

[37] II (July, 1891), 105–122.

[38] AAC, Gibbons to Elder, Oakland, Maryland, October 23, 1891.

[39] Will, *Life of Cardinal Gibbons,* I, 484–486. The minutes of the meeting at St. Louis on November 29 (89-D-5/1), which were drawn up by Ireland as secretary, make no mention whatever of the subject. The official report cited by Will (I, 485) was doubtless Gibbons' description of the Ireland school plan to Leo XIII, Baltimore, March 1, 1892, copy (89-Q-1).

On the day of the meeting the St. Louis *Globe-Democrat* gave a suggestion of the coming storm when it stated that the pamphlet, not yet in general circulation, was the subject of discussion among Catholics and others.[40] Even before the Bouquillon work became generally known news of it had reached the camp of the opposition, and some days before the meeting in St. Louis Bishop McQuaid expressed his pleasure to Archbishop Corrigan that Bouquillon was to be answered seriously. Reflecting his dislike of the university in Washington, McQuaid said, "Since the Professors of the U. have no students to teach, they take to the writing of pamphlets. They cannot let the U. die of inanition; they must bury it with contempt."[41] McQuaid was doubtless referring to the effort of Father René I. Holaind, S.J., of St. Francis Xavier College in New York, who wrote an answer to Bouquillon in a thirty-two page pamphlet called *The Parent First*.[42]

With the publication of the opposing pamphlets the controversy over the schools entered upon its bitterest phase, and during the following months the Catholic and secular press carried on about as angry a public debate as had yet divided the American Church. This is not the place to recount the story that enlivened the newspapers in those days. Suffice it to say that the question of how far the rights of the state extended in education and the relationship between the public and parochial schools ultimately involved most of the leading elements in the American Catholic body. Not only was the hierarchy divided on the subject, but the German Catholics and the Jesuits entered the fray against Archbishop Ireland while groups like the majority of the professors of the Catholic University of America and the archbishop's many

---

[40] November 29, 1891.

[41] AANY, McQuaid to Corrigan, Rochester, November 26, 1891.

[42] Holaind's pamphlet was published by Benziger Brothers in New York early in December. In his preface the author stated that he had received a copy of Bouquillon's work on November 19 and he referred to the fact that "the important meetings in which it must have great weight" would begin on November 28 (p. 4). From a letter of Holaind to Herman J. Heuser, editor of the *American Ecclesiastical Review,* it was obvious that his pamphlet was intended for the study of the archbishops at this meeting. He referred to Ireland's interview to the press against him, and he then remarked, "Now the pamphlet which caused the fuss did not reach St. Louis in time, although mailed carefully to St. Louis on the 24th of November" (ACHSP, Heuser Papers, Holaind to Heuser, Woodstock, December 16, 1891). The writer is indebted for the references in this chapter to the Heuser Papers to the kindness of Colman J. Barry, O.S.B.

admirers fought just as vigorously in his behalf. The fact that representatives of both sides supplied their European friends with letters and newspaper clippings accounted for the wide coverage which the debate received in the English and continental journals. By the early days of 1892 the question had become, probably to the surprise of all concerned, a matter of international interest and it was followed with more eagerness by European Catholics than they had shown over any American Catholic question since the Knights of Labor.

It was the New York *Herald,* which so often in this period was the first secular paper to print confidential Catholic news, that opened a particularly acute phase of the press war in its issue of December 13 with the supposed inside story of the archbishops' meeting at St. Louis, and the sensation which the Bouquillon and Holaind pamphlets were said to have produced on the Church's leaders. Ireland happened to be in New York at the time that the *Herald* story appeared, and he gave an interview which was published in that paper on the following day in which he referred scornfully to Holaind and his antiquated notions on modern education, lined up the Catholic papers who supported his position, and said it was not difficult to trace the story in the *Herald* of the day before to "the clique of foreign minded and shortsighted Catholics in St. Louis. . . ." The archbishop made it plain that he was thinking of the *Church Progress* of St. Louis, edited by Conde Pallen, and after an analysis of the work of Bouquillon and a statement of the Catholic complaint against the public schools for not teaching religion, he ended with a plea to the *Herald's* readers to regard Holaind's words as entirely his own and not those of the Catholic Church.

The Ireland interview was, to be sure, deeply resented by many of the German Catholics, the Jesuits in both the United States and Italy, and the followers of Archbishop Corrigan who were backing Holaind. But in less than ten days they had reason for further chagrin. On December 23 the Baltimore *Sun* and other papers published an unsigned cablegram from Berlin which summarized the attitude of the Church toward the state's rights in education in a number of European countries in a way that implied the Church's recognition of those rights, and it observed that the state schools wherein religious instruction was given seemed to be the practical ideal of Catholic parties on the continent. The cablegram obviously provided grist for Ireland's mill and he thanked Cardinal Gibbons for forwarding a copy of the *Sun* containing the item since the western papers had not yet published it. O'Connell and Boeglin had prepared the cablegram at much trouble to themselves, said Ireland, and forwarded it from Berlin, but this information was to be kept secret. "The facts given in it," said the archbishop, "should open the eyes of our Catholic extremists in America."[43]

Through all the noisy agitation in the press the Cardinal of Baltimore had thus far maintained silence, although he did not cease to work in private to insure the ultimate triumph of Archbishop Ireland. When one of his suffragans, Bishop Kain of Wheeling, responded to an inquiry from Simeoni with a lengthy vindication of Ireland's school policy in all its particulars,[44] Gibbons had a copy of Kain's letter sent on to St. Paul. The archbishop was delighted with Kain's response and he thought that if it did not enlighten Propaganda on the school question and set him right in Rome, then, as he expressed it, "the case is hopeless."[45] Yet the opposing faction, too, sought Gibbons' assistance in helping to banish the storm clouds which were gathering over the Church at this time. Archbishop Ryan reaffirmed his determination to keep the *American Catholic Quarterly Review* on the ground of principles and not allow it to touch the controversy as such, although Dr. George Wolff, editor of his archdiocesan weekly newspaper, the *Catholic Standard,* felt keenly the attack of Ireland's *Northwestern Chronicle* and was going to reply to it. "It is for moderate men who love the Church & truth more than party & victory," said Ryan, "to keep us from bitter division in face of a common enemy"; and then with a personal appeal to Gibbons he added, "it will require all the great tact with which God has blessed you, to aid in this important work."[46]

One of Ireland's chief enemies in Rome, Salvatore M. Brandi, S.J., who was a confidant of Archbishop Corrigan, did not allow his contacts with Gibbons to be interrupted by the controversy, and periodically the cardinal was supplied with long letters filled with Roman news on the American Church in Rome in which the

---

[43] 89-G-3, Ireland to Gibbons, St. Paul, December 28, 1891.
[44] 89-F-1, Kain to Simeoni, Wheeling, December 17, 1891, copy in French.
[45] 89-G-3, Ireland to Gibbons, St. Paul, December 28, 1891.
[46] 89-F-6, Ryan to Gibbons, Philadelphia, December 23, 1891.

Roman Jesuit, however, was careful not to show his hand too clearly. Gibbons was informed that Ireland's interview of December 14 in the *Herald* with its attack on Father Holaind, along with press clippings from the *Independent*, the *Church Progress*, and other papers had all been sent to the Holy See and the result was that the cardinals thought this noisy minority spoke for the majority. Brandi remarked that the Holy See's suspicion of liberalism in the Church of the United States was strengthened by those who at the other extreme wished, as he said, to appear more Roman than the Romans and who wrote and spoke of their opponents as liberals, revolutionary men, etc. He then stated:

> I am fully convinced and have not hesitated to assert it publicly and repeatedly that there is more genuine Catholicity in cities like Baltimore, Boston, Philadelphia, New York, etc., than in the eternal city of Rome and it is a disgrace to judge of the Catholic Church in the U.S., by the reports of a few unauthorized fanatics, who put together constitute but a very small minority. The true "liberal-Catholics" in the United States are few and well known.

The Jesuit editor then explained that he was the author of the recent article in the *Civiltà Cattolica* in defense of that journal against Bouquillon, but in it he had made no specific reference to the United States. Brandi may have hoped that his remarks concerning the horror of liberalism in the Roman curia would be a sufficient hint to Gibbons that he should now speak out.[47]

Cardinal Gibbons would have need of all the tact with which Archbishop Ryan credited him if he was to come through the present struggle with honor to himself and satisfaction to those who looked to him for leadership. That his moves were being watched by both friends and foes, there was no doubt. The death in early January, 1892, of Cardinal Simeoni prompted McQuaid to remark that the cardinals were going fast and that as the older ones died off Gibbons' chances for the Papacy were brightened. "The miracle of credulity," said the bishop to Denis

---

[47] 89-K-1, Brandi to Gibbons, Rome, January 18, 1892; a similar letter from Brandi was that of December 7, 1891, written at Rome (89-E-2). Another Jesuit who believed he had discovered the cardinal's real sentiments was Holaind. He told Heuser they were all very close to disaster and his [Holaind's] pamphlet was not one day too soon in the field, to which he added, "I thought always that his Eminence was merely coquetting with the movement, but I was mistaken" (ACHSP, Heuser Papers, Holaind to Heuser, Woodstock, January 25, 1892).

O'Connell, "is found in the fact that there are people, himself included, who believe that he has a ghost of a chance." McQuaid had just read in the newspapers that Ireland was going to Rome, and since it was not the time for his *ad limina* visit he was curious to know what took him there. Showing clearly what he thought of the archbishop and his friend in Baltimore, McQuaid told the monsignor:

> He is the head and front of the new liberalistic party in the American Church. If he would stay at home a little more, and mind his own diocese the latter would be the gainer. He is away from his diocese only a little more than Cardinal Gibbons.[48]

But if McQuaid was inclined to be harsh in his views of Gibbons and to expect little remedy from that quarter, there were those who believed that the Archbishop of Baltimore could do much to bring a solution to the current difficulties. Maurice Francis Egan was in entire sympathy with the cardinal's policy of silence on the school question. He felt that he knew the spirit of the American people too well to desire that the good which Gibbons had done by his insight and tact should be thrown away by the needless discussion of subjects best let alone. "Until we have a remedy," said Egan, "the school question ought to be let alone — I mean let alone as an object of 'resolutions.' "[49] And when Judge Edmund F. Dunne of Ohio, a Catholic lawyer, was quoted in the papers as attributing a false liberalism to the cardinal in the school controversy, a Protestant admirer who had read Gibbons' book, *Our Christian Heritage,* hastened to assure him of his support and to say that time and again he had pointed out to his acquaintances how effective an exponent he thought the book was to inspire everyone who had an unselfish desire to see the United States prosper in all that constituted true greatness.[50]

But regardless of how friendly or hostile might be the comments on Gibbons' part in the controversy, the burning issues involved in the trouble over the schools were not to be settled by that medium. True to his nature in facing opposition directly,

---

[48] ADR, McQuaid to O'Connell, Rochester, January 16, 1892.

[49] 89-L-1, Egan to Gibbons, Notre Dame, January 29, 1892. Egan set down here for the cardinal a lengthy description of how he thought Gibbons could make the *Catholic Mirror* of Baltimore a really influential newspaper.

[50] 89-N-4, John H. Keatley to Gibbons, Sioux City, February 17, 1892.

Archbishop Ireland sailed for Rome on January 16, 1892, armed with documentary weapons in defense of himself and of Dr. Bouquillon. His first report to Gibbons was encouraging. He found Leo XIII very cordial and a number of the other Roman prelates in an agreeable frame of mind, although the Italian journals controlled by the Jesuits were writing fierce articles against him and Bouquillon, and Miss Edes was ever watchful for issues of these journals, "steeped in gall" as Ireland said, so that she could hand them in to the Propaganda. He wanted to come out in the papers against the *Civiltà Cattolica* but his advisers would not allow it, and he had yielded to their view against his own judgment.[51] Meanwhile the cardinal was preparing a letter for the Pope which would embody the discussion of the Faribault-Stillwater plan of the archbishops at St. Louis. "I will make it as strong as possible, you may rest assured," he told the archbishop.[52] Within a few days the letter was finished and Gibbons' second lengthy apology for Ireland was forwarded to Rome. The cardinal covered much of the ground gone over in his letter of the previous December, but this time he detailed for Leo XIII the explanation which Ireland had made at his request before the metropolitans in St. Louis. Following that outline, Gibbons then told the Pope:

> After Mgr. Ireland's explanation and his answers, not one of the Archbishops offered a word of blame. Many were very explicit in their approval, and Mgr. Williams, Archbishop of Boston, whose authority is very great with us, did not hesitate to say that he congratulated his colleague on the result obtained, that his own

---

[51] 89-P-1, Ireland to Gibbons, Rome, February 21, 1892. On the Jesuits' biweekly journal cf. Antonio Messineo, S.J., "Civiltà Cattolica Centenary," *American Ecclesiastical Review,* CXXIV (June, 1951), 417–425; CXXV (July, 1951), 19–28. The first issue of this important periodical had appeared on April 6, 1850, at Naples but it was moved to Rome in September of that year. In 1891 Brandi joined the editorial staff of the *Civiltà Cattolica* after a residence of some years in the United States. In the period of the American controversies it was Brandi who contributed to the journal on questions affecting the American Church. Messineo says of him, "Brandi enjoyed the utmost confidence of Leo XIII and was considered his official interpreter" (p. 27).

[52] AASP, Gibbons to Ireland, Baltimore, February 25, 1892, copy. Ten days before Gibbons' letter to Ireland a further flare-up in the press prompted Holaind to write to Heuser and to say of Gibbons' vicar-general, " . . . Mgr. McColgan went to Murphy and told him that to sell my pamphlet was disloyalty to the Cardinal. Our liberals are as usual despotic in the extreme" (ACHSP, Heuser Papers, Holaind to Heuser, Woodstock, February 15, 1892).

wish would be to submit the schools of his diocese to a similar arrangement, and that he hoped to succeed, at least as to some.[53]

On the day he mailed this letter there came a cablegram from O'Connell to the effect that the tide had turned and that the Pope and Rampolla had espoused Ireland's cause. Naturally the news made Gibbons very happy and in his acknowledgment he not only showed his joy, but he revealed as well the depth of feeling which stirred him on the subject. He said:

> God bless the Pope. Yesterday I prayed at Mass that the Lord might inspire him & that right & justice should prevail. It is not the Faribault school that is on trial, but the question to be decided is whether the Church is to be governed here by men or by children, by justice & truth, or by diplomacy & intrigue, whether the Church is to be honored as a bulwark of liberty & order, or to be despised and suspected as an enemy of our Institutions.[54]

A week later the cardinal was still in a happy frame of mind when he reported to Ireland that the news dispatches about him from Rome were greedily devoured. "The rumor is sometimes whispered about you," he said, "that you will receive the red hat. The report, I fear, is too good to be true. Anyhow, God bless the Pope."[55] It was certainly true that Ireland and his Roman friends had the news dispatches well in hand. Week after week friendly American papers like the Boston *Pilot* reprinted news items from the *Moniteur de Rome* heavily freighted with laudatory references to the Archbishop of St. Paul. For example, on March 12 the *Pilot* carried a *Moniteur* story to the effect that Ireland had been received with marked favor by Leo XIII, and it did not hesitate to say that he was the most popular man in the United States, although his enemies would like to silence his voice and break his powerful influence. Reading news of this kind from the

---

[53] 89-Q-1, Gibbons to O'Connell, Baltimore, March 1, 1892, copy in French. This letter is also published in translation in Reilly, *op. cit.,* pp. 143–147.

[54] ADR, Gibbons to O'Connell, Baltimore, March 1, 1892.

[55] AASP, Gibbons to Ireland, Baltimore, March 8, 1892, copy. Needless to say, Ireland's enemies were likewise conscious of the impression created on American readers by the favorable news items taken in good part from the *Moniteur de Rome*. In an effort to discount their influence, Brandi told Heuser some months before, "The *Moniteur de Rome* is one of the poorest of all the Roman newspapers, and has no authority whatever. It is scarcely able to dispose of 500 copies" (ACHSP, Heuser Papers, Brandi to Heuser, Rome, November 16, 1891).

Eternal City, it was no wonder that the archbishop's friends beamed with pride and joy.

When the letter of Cardinal Gibbons reached Monsignor O'Connell he characterized it for Magnien as magnificent, remarked that Ireland was delighted, and said that about the only unsettled question now was the letter of vindication of the archbishop from the Pope. All Rome, said O'Connell, seemed to be going over to Ireland, and Cardinals Parocchi and Vannutelli had exclaimed, "Would to heaven we had such schools."[56] Bishop Keane joined in the chorus of rejoicing and felt that Gibbons' letter to Leo XIII, coming as it did when the tide was so favorably turned, must have a great effect in securing the complete victory for which they were all praying, and he added, "There must be a good deal of consternation in the ranks of the enemy."[57] If there was not consternation in the mind of one adversary of Ireland, there was at least some bewilderment about what were the real facts lying behind the exciting stories of Ireland's supposed triumphs in Rome. At the close of a letter on other business Archbishop Corrigan remarked to Denis O'Connell:

> You allude to Mgr. Ireland's case. If not indiscreet I would like to know what it is, and how it is progressing. The newspapers report matters so strangely, and with so much contradiction, that we are kept in the dark. For myself I am preoccupied with the new Seminary. . . .[58]

There was no doubt that the newspapers reported matters very strangely at times and the cautious reserve shown by Corrigan was fully justified, for the friends of John Ireland would have some anxious days before any real vindication of him was forthcoming from the Vatican.

For one blunder which occurred in the press at this state of the case the Archbishop of St. Paul was himself responsible. In his eagerness to score a point against his enemies, Ireland insisted that the editors of the *Civiltà Cattolica* publish a private letter of Cardinal Gibbons to O'Connell of three months before in which the cardinal had explained the circumstances, as he remembered them, of the St. Louis meeting in which Ireland had outlined the

---

56 ASMS, O'Connell to Magnien, Rome, March 15, 1892.
57 89-S-3, Keane to Gibbons, Washington, March 21, 1892.
58 ADR, Corrigan to O'Connell, New York, March 27, 1892.

Faribault-Stillwater school plan. The two sentences of the letter which gave rise to trouble were the following:

> The Archbishop expressed a willingness to discontinue this system, if his colleagues advised him. But he got no such advice, for the advantage is all on his side. The Archbishop answered several questions, put by his colleagues, and the result was a triumphant vindication of his course.[59]

Not only was the letter published without Gibbons' previous consent, but the editors of the Jesuit journal had at first protested against it and when they could not prevail they added, as Brandi explained to the cardinal, some editorial remarks which were not at all to the liking of Ireland.[60] As soon as the issue of the *Civiltà* for March 19 reached the United States it brought a prompt reaction from Archbishop Corrigan. He called Gibbons' attention to the item and remarked that on the principle of silence gives consent one might infer that all the archbishops had sanctioned the Faribault plan. He said he had no recollection of such sanction, the official minutes were silent on the subject, and another archbishop who was present confirmed him in the belief that no opinion of the Minnesota school plan's merits was asked at St. Louis.[61] It was now obviously up to the cardinal to offer an explanation.

Gibbons was prepared, despite Corrigan's doubts, to stand by the contents of his letter to O'Connell. The English text recently received from Brandi revealed, said the cardinal, that he had made three statements: (1) Ireland's willingness to discontinue the Faribault system; (2) that he got no such advice; and (3) that the archbishop answered several questions put to him by his colleagues. He then continued:

> These are facts. As none of the Prelates advised him to give up his plan, though this seemed to be the time & place to do so, if that plan had been considered to be truly objectionable, & as the archbishop's statements & answers to difficulties were such as to elicit an expression of dissent, I could not help believing & stating that his explanations were regarded as "a triumphant vindication of his course."[62]

---

[59] Reilly, *op. cit.*, pp. 140–141. The letter was dated December 18, 1891.

[60] 89-R-6, Brandi to Gibbons, Rome, March 11, 1892.

[61] 89-S-6, Corrigan to Gibbons, New York, March 28, 1892.

[62] 89-S-8, Gibbons to Corrigan, Baltimore, March 29, 1892, copy. The Gibbons

But Corrigan was not satisfied with this explanation, and it was almost certainly the Archbishop of New York to whom Ryan of Philadelphia referred when he told Gibbons that he had lately been asked by a certain prelate to give his recollections of the conference in St. Louis. Within the next few days there ensued an exchange of correspondence between Ryan and Gibbons in an effort to arrive at a clear understanding and agreement of exactly what had been said at the disputed meeting. Aside from certain differences over Ireland's remarks in explanation of the Faribault plan and what response he had received from his colleagues, the main objection of Ryan as stated to the cardinal arose from his impression that Ireland was trying to foist the school arrangement at Faribault and Stillwater on all the dioceses of the country as a general system. Ryan deplored the whole unfortunate affair and lamented its effect on the unity of the Church in the United States. "Much depends of [sic] Yr. Eminence," said the archbishop, "to effect the desired reunion. . . ."[63] Gibbons, too, regarded the Faribault scheme as a tentative one, and he fully shared the desire for peace and unity of his friend in Philadelphia. If these ends were to be attained the cardinal felt the bishops of the American Church must stand by one another, to which he added, "My custom has been to defend a brother Prelate whenever assailed." He said he was pained at the abuse heaped upon Archbishop Ireland, and he would suggest as one of the first means for restoring peace that the Catholic papers and periodicals stop their vituperation.[64]

Meanwhile Gibbons' letter to O'Connell published in the *Civiltà* continued to give trouble. Archbishop Ryan was plainly annoyed and he told the cardinal that O'Connell should never have let it out, "unless indeed," he added, "he had obtained your consent."

---

letter to O'Connell was reprinted from the *Civiltà Cattolica* in the Boston *Pilot* of April 9, 1892, and through this medium it quickly became known over the country. When Father Patrick Hennessy, pastor of St. Patrick's Church, Jersey City, read it in the *Pilot* he immediately sent congratulations to Gibbons and unburdened himself of a good deal of complaint against Corrigan. He said it was well known that Corrigan had urged Holaind to attack Bouquillon, that he had instigated Judge Dunne and the *Catholic Herald* of New York to decry Ireland, and that the views of Gibbons and his friends found the opposite of sympathy in New York. "The New York Prelate," said Hennessy, "rarely throws a *direct hand* — he works *behind others*" (89-T-6, Hennessy to Gibbons, Jersey City, April 9, 1892).

63 89-T-7, Ryan to Gibbons, Philadelphia, April 10, 1892.

64 89-T-9, Gibbons to Ryan, Baltimore, April 11, 1892, copy.

Ryan was embarrassed by a letter he had written some months before to Simeoni giving his views on the Minnesota school arrangement in which he had characterized it as a mere experiment. But Ireland's speech to the N.E.A. and his interviews in the New York *Herald* made it sound as though the system was intended for introduction universally in the country. It was probably unknown to Gibbons at the moment that Ryan was caught between his desire to remain friendly with the cardinal and his effort to appease Corrigan with his signature to a statement which would make it seem in Rome that Gibbons had given a false account of the affair in St. Louis. In his dilemma he told Gibbons:

> Of course Yr. Eminence only wrote about the plan *as presented to us by Abp. Ireland,* but it is said, that if we be silent now, Rome will place confidence in the assurance that we accept the plan in the same enthusiastic manner & light as the good Abp. of S. Paul. You may be satisfied that I will subscribe to no statement which will question your veracity. At the same time, I find myself, as I have said, embarrassed by my reply to Cardinal Simeoni's letter, which I presume is preserved in Rome.[65]

The cardinal hastened to disabuse Ryan of the notion that his private letter had been published with his consent. He said he would not have allowed it to be published had he been consulted and its appearance had given him much annoyance and pain. His first intimation of its publication was sent to him by Brandi and while he deeply regretted it Gibbons felt sure that Ireland had acted from pure motives.[66]

While these letters were passing back and forth between Baltimore and Philadelphia there was launched by Archbishop Corrigan, entirely unknown to Gibbons, an effort to get certain archbishops to go on record at Rome against the cardinal's interpretation of the events in St. Louis the previous November. It was this circumstance that made Ryan uneasy at the time in his correspondence with Gibbons. Corrigan drew up a document in which he expressed a contrary impression to that of the cardinal's letter published in the *Civiltà* regarding the assent of the archbishops to Ireland's school plan, and he sent it to the metropolitans with a request that it be signed. As he told Archbishop

---

65 89-U-2, Ryan to Gibbons, Philadelphia, April 16, 1892.
66 89-U-4, Gibbons to Ryan, Baltimore, April 18, 1892, copy.

Williams, "If you consent to sign it, or authorize me to affix your signature I will add it to several other names of Archbishops already obtained." But the Archbishop of Boston was not to be drawn in, and across the top of Corrigan's letter he wrote, "Ans. Ap. 11, 92. Prefer *not* to sign. Will see him in Washington. J. W."[67] However, the Archbishop of New York found six archbishops who were agreeable to his suggestion, and with these signatures obtained he forwarded the document to the Propaganda.[68]

Needless to say, the knowledge that seven of his colleagues had given their signatures to a contrary version of the facts he had written to the Holy See was the source of deep distress to Cardinal Gibbons. When several of the signatories learned through Magnien how hurt Gibbons was they hastened to give explanations of their intentions and the circumstances which accompanied their act, and in each case the archbishops protested their personal regard for the cardinal and their complete freedom from any thought of questioning his veracity before the Holy See.[69] But despite the apologies Gibbons continued for some weeks to be greatly upset. He told Ryan that at some future time he intended to make a statement to his colleagues in reference to the memorial of the archbishops. Revealing how keenly he felt he continued:

> It is a duty which I owe to myself and to the honored position which I fill, to vindicate my honor and my veracity. Conscious though I am of my integrity, I find it a grievous burden to live under a sinister imputation, and the last few days have been to me days of intolerable anguish.[70]

Although Magnien had known for some time about Corrigan's circular, Gibbons himself did not learn of it until he read the story in the *Church Progress* of May 14, and as Magnien told

---

[67] AABo, Corrigan to Williams, New York, April 9, 1892, *Private.*

[68] The St. Louis *Republic* of August 7, 1892, published the names of the seven archbishops as Corrigan, Feehan, Elder, Gross, Janssens, Katzer, and Ryan. Reilly, *op. cit.,* p. 153, n. 34.

[69] 89-U-6, Gross to Gibbons, Portland, April 19, 1892; 89-U-9, Riordan to Magnien, San Francisco, April 23, 1892; 89-V-13, Janssens to Magnien, Biloxi, May 10, 1892; 89-V-14, Elder to Gibbons, Cincinnati, May 19, 1892; unclassified, Ryan to Gibbons, Philadelphia, May 22, 1892; 89-W-7, Riordan to Gibbons, San Francisco, June 4, 1892.

[70] 89-W-1, Gibbons to Ryan, Baltimore, May 20, 1892, copy.

O'Connell, "I never saw him so deeply affected."[71] Only after the lapse of some weeks did the cardinal begin to be himself again and to see, as Magnien said, that he had made too much of the document of the seven archbishops. "There is something else he sees also," he added, "& I am glad of it, viz. that Abp. Corrigan cannot be conciliated, & he has made up his mind to act accordingly."[72] Gibbons was further consoled to learn from Ireland that Cardinal Ledochowski, the Prefect of Propaganda, was inclined to take the protest as the work of one man who had beguiled the other six into signing, and the Archbishop of St. Paul added, "He emphatically impressed on me the duty of assuring you of his utter confidence in the veracity of your report."[73]

Two months before this unpleasant episode occurred, the enthusiasm of several of Archbishop Ireland's lay admirers prompted them to set on foot a scheme to have him made a cardinal. Richard C. Kerens, Republican national committeeman from Missouri, and Austin Ford, editor of the New York *Freeman's Journal,* would seem to have been the prime movers. Kerens had an interview with President Harrison in which the chief executive was represented as cordially accepting the suggestion that he authorize a message to the authorities in Rome or Baltimore expressing his desire to see the archbishop honored.[74] Ford, who was in direct touch with Ireland in Rome, informed the archbishop that Kerens had seen Gibbons and that the cardinal had become, as he expressed it, "worked up over the thing." The only anxiety Gibbons had shown was over the means by which the President's message could be conveyed in a prompt and discreet way. Fearing a delay, Ford took it upon himself to cable Cardinal Rampolla that a message to the Pope from a high au-

---

[71] ADR, Magnien to O'Connell, Baltimore, May 14, 1892. Gibbons was becoming more and more worried about his confidential communications to the Holy See. Magnien told O'Connell that the cardinal's letter to the Pope on the school question had been given by the Pontiff to Propaganda and through that source it had reached Archbishop Corrigan. A month before Magnien expressed this same concern of Gibbons' to Ireland when he said the cardinal feared his letter to the Pope would be seen by Corrigan through the agency of Miss Edes or the *minutante* of the Propaganda (ADR, Magnien to "Your Grace," Baltimore, April 11, 1892).

[72] *Ibid.,* Magnien to O'Connell, Baltimore, May 31, 1892.

[73] 89-W-8, Ireland to Gibbons, Rome, June 5, 1892.

[74] ADR, Kerens to Ford, Fort Monroe, Virginia, March 24, 1892, telegram.

thority in Washington concerning a new American cardinal would be forthcoming in a few days.[75]

What exactly took place when Kerens called on Gibbons we do not know but, at any rate, the cardinal was thoroughly won over to the plan and about two weeks later he addressed a warm recommendation to Rampolla in behalf of Ireland's red hat. He said that he had heard apparently well-founded rumors that Leo XIII was thinking of giving the United States a second cardinal in the Archbishop of St. Paul, and he wished to say that of all the bishops in the country he did not know of one whose promotion under the present circumstances would be more opportune. Not only did Ireland's virtues and talents recommend him, but especially the force he exercised on American public opinion and the favor he enjoyed with the government. Gibbons had learned, he said, from an absolutely certain source that the President would be very gratified at the honor for Ireland, and Secretary of State James G. Blaine, who had the highest admiration for the archbishop, had entrusted to him a letter for Rampolla in which he, too, expressed the desire that Ireland should be raised to the cardinalate.[76] Gibbons' letter to Rampolla was forwarded to Monsignor O'Connell with the instruction that he should use his own judgment about presenting it, but O'Connell was warned in several communications from Magnien that the cardinal wished extraordinary precautions to be taken to prevent it from becoming known.[77] Thus did Gibbons make the first of several attempts to win a red hat for John Ireland, and although they failed of their objective, his efforts to secure for his friend the Church's

---

[75] *Ibid.*, Ford to Ireland, New York, March 29, 1892. *Confidential.* Ford said he feared to reply to Ireland's cablegram until he first got in touch with the cable manager and arranged for special precaution as to secrecy.

[76] 89-T-14, Gibbons to Rampolla, Baltimore, April 15, 1892, copy in French. In Blaine's letter to Rampolla he said Ireland was the most popular and widely influential prelate in the United States and highly respected by Protestants. He praised especially his work for temperance. In closing he emphasized that the honor would be pleasing to all classes and especially gratifying to himself. "The power of the Abp. of S. Paul wd. be enlarged if he could return home a prince of the Church" (AAB, unclassified, Blaine to Rampolla, Washington, April 15, 1892, copy).

[77] ADR, Magnien to O'Connell, Baltimore, April 17, 22, and May 14, 1892. Magnien was working hard for Ireland's red hat and urging O'Connell to do all he could to prevent the honor from going to New York.

highest honors made it evident how sincerely he espoused his cause and loved his person.

During the time the public debate over Ireland's school plan continued to rage in the press of the United States and Europe the cardinals of the Propaganda were quietly investigating all phases of the Faribault-Stillwater case and on April 21, 1892, they reached their decision which was confirmed by the Pope on the same day. The judgment of the cardinals was that, although they wished to derogate in no way from the legislation of the councils of Baltimore on parochial schools yet, taking into consideration all the circumstances, the arrangements at Faribault and Stillwater could be tolerated.[78] Although the official notification of the decision was not conveyed to Ireland until about ten days later, he learned of it and cabled the good news to Baltimore. Gibbons, of course, was elated and said he could hardly express the sense of relief and exultation which he felt on hearing of Ireland's victory. But in this moment of triumph the cardinal had fears that the archbishop's ardent nature might get the better of him and he, therefore, gave him a sage bit of advice. "Be sure," said Gibbons, "that no public expression will come from you which might be used by your enemies against you. Do nothing to wound or irritate. Your victory is a sufficient ground for the humiliation of others."[79] The advice showed Gibbons' horror of public recriminations as well as the knowledge he had of his friend's temperament and personality.

Within a week of the Propaganda's decision of April 21 the American papers became filled with dispatches from Rome concerning rumors of Ireland's vindication. But for the next two weeks they had nothing certain to go by. Then on May 5 the Ireland followers got a real jolt when Archbishop Corrigan arose at a dinner in Albany marking the consecration of Henry Gabriels as second Bishop of Ogdensburg, and read a cablegram which he said had come from someone high in authority at the Vatican. The words of the cablegram were, "Faribault system condemned. Special case tolerated."[80] Immediately the newspapers hummed with the sensational setback to Ireland and there was confusion

---

[78] Reilly, *op. cit.*, pp. 160–162, for Ledochowski's letter to Ireland transmitting the decision.

[79] AASP, Gibbons to Ireland, Baltimore, April 28, 1892, copy.

[80] Reilly, *op. cit.*, pp. 158–159.

on all sides. Abbé Magnien, who had attended the Albany cere-mony, immediately wired Gibbons, who had that very day received from Rome a rough draft of Propaganda's favorable decision in Ireland's case. The cardinal cabled at once to O'Con-nell to learn the true state of affairs and received in reply the following message, "Corrigan's cablegram absolutely false." Gib-bons quickly conveyed the news to Bishop Keane so that he might reassure anyone who inquired concerning the Corrigan announcement.[81] Amid the uncertainty which obtained for the next few days no one knew what to believe, but then on May 11 the New York *World* scooped all its rivals with the text of Ledochowski's letter to Ireland of April 30 which gave the deci-sion. Papers all over the country picked up the item from the *World,* and from this point on the debate shifted to the question of interpretation of the Roman decision. Here again the forces divided pretty much along the lines of their previous agreement or disagreement with Ireland, the enemies contending that the *tolerari potest* of the Holy See amounted to a condemnation of the Faribault plan, while the friends shouted loudly that it was a full blessing upon their hero.

In the midst of the public clamor Cardinal Gibbons held his peace and refused to be interviewed by the press on the subject of his interpretation of the decision. Privately, however, he told Archbishop Janssens of New Orleans that he had received an outline of Rome's judgment, and concerning it he said:

> It neither condemns nor approves, but tolerates the Faribault or Poughkeepsie plan. It enjoins a cessation of controversy, & urges that children not attending parochial schools, should be cared for. I have no reason to question the correctness of the information I received.[82]

The cardinal was more open about his reactions to the Rector of the University when he asked Keane, "Is not the news from Rome glorious? & is not the vindication so full as to leave no room for misrepresentation?"[83] But regardless of how clear the decision might seem to Gibbons, there were those who felt there was still ground for differences and, far from putting an end to the controversy, the Propaganda decision only gave rise to a

---

[81] ACUA, Keane Papers, Gibbons to Keane, Baltimore, May 6, 1892, *Personal.*
[82] AUND, New Orleans Papers, Gibbons to Janssens, Baltimore, May 7, 1892.
[83] ACUA, Keane Papers, Gibbons to Keane, Baltimore, May 11, 1892.

new, and in some ways an even more bitter, phase of the trouble. Try as he might to avoid being involved in the fight, the cardinal soon found himself compelled to take cognizance of what the press was saying about him in relation to the decision.

A reporter of the New York *Sun* called on him for an interview which Gibbons refused to give. However, this did not prevent the same paper in its issue of May 13 from stating that he had refused to comment on the decision concerning the Faribault case, to which they added, "other than to say that he differed with Archbishop Corrigan regarding the meaning of the decision." After printing this serious falsification the *Sun* sought to buttress its story by saying that Magnien, whom it characterized as "voicing Cardinal Gibbons' views," had declared that the Pope's decision conclusively sustained Archbishop Ireland. When the cardinal read this item he realized, of course, the impression that it would create on the Archbishop of New York, and for that reason he sent him the following explanation:

> The truth is that, while I candidly believe that the decision sustains Abp. Ireland, I refused to be interviewed at all, and I did not say a word on the subject to the reporter whom I chanced to meet in the passage as I was going upstairs. Whatever differences may exist I would not be so rude to your Grace as to express it for publication.
>
> I profit by the occasion to say that during my whole Episcopal career of 24 years, both in my writings and official utterances and conduct, I have been and am a consistent and unvarying advocate of Catholic education, and in sustaining Abp. Ireland in the Faribault Case, I do not think that I have departed from the principle underlying Catholic education.
>
> I have caused a brief editorial to be inserted in the *Mirror* contradicting the false statement sent to the *N.Y. Sun* and adding that I refused to be interviewed at all.[84]

True to his promise, Gibbons had published in the *Catholic Mirror* of May 21 an editorial note denying that he had given any opinion whatsoever to the *Sun* reporter, and saying, "While fully recognizing each one's right to have his opinion on the subject, he would be incapable of such discourtesy to a brother prelate whom he holds in so high esteem as to communicate any difference to the public press."

[84] 89-V-12, Gibbons to Corrigan, Baltimore, May 18, 1892, copy. This letter is printed in Reilly, *op. cit.*, pp. 168–169.

But if Gibbons felt incapable of communicating harsh views on a brother bishop to the press, there were those who did not. Archbishop Corrigan had given an interview on April 15 in which he stated that articles in the *Civiltà Cattolica* were submitted before publication to the Vatican for its approval, and since this Roman journal of the Jesuits had gone on publishing criticisms of Bouquillon's pamphlets and Ireland's school plan this could hardly happen if their contents were objected to by the Holy See. Whether designedly or not, this interview laid a background for the *Civiltà's* renewal of the campaign in its issue of May 18 in which it tried to explain away the *tolerari potest* decree of a month before as intended to be restricted solely to the two schools at Faribault and Stillwater while saying that the system itself was evil.[85] At this Ireland could not restrain himself, and in a Roman interview which was carried in the New York *Herald* on May 22 he let loose a blast at the *Civiltà's* interpretation which was followed a week later by the publication of a letter from Rampolla to Ireland in answer to the latter's inquiry concerning the official character of the *Civiltà* at the Vatican. Rampolla, much to the delight of the Ireland party, replied that it was in no way correct to say that the articles in this paper were submitted beforehand for revision and approval of the Holy See.[86]

With the publication of Rampolla's letter Archbishop Ireland concluded his Roman visit in high spirits and when he reached Genoa he wrote the story of his triumphs to Gibbons. He hoped the cardinal had admired the exchange of correspondence between himself and the papal Secretary of State; he had put in the names of Corrigan and the Jesuit provincial so there could be no mistake as to whom he desired the blow to strike. "The prestige of the Civilta," said Ireland, "is gone; the Jesuits never in the century received such a blow. This letter was my crowning victory." Rampolla and Ledochowski had thrown out strong hints about the red hat — they would see him soon again and only the great act the Pope was preparing would conclusively stop the opposition. "For myself," he added, "I am not much concerned." As for Archbishop Corrigan, he was ruined in Rome, and Miss Edes, his agent, was positively ordered out of the Propaganda by Archbishop Ignazio Persico, the secretary. Look-

---

[85] Reilly, *op. cit.,* p. 172.
[86] *Ibid.,* pp. 175–176.

ing forward to the meeting of the archbishops in New York in the fall, he said he would be prepared to silence Corrigan, to which he added a word to stiffen Gibbons' firmness for the coming meeting by saying, "Please, do not be afraid."[87]

Some weeks before Ireland quit Rome the Archbishop of New York put forth a further effort to head off a favorable decision in his adversary's case. On April 25 the bishops of the Province of New York were gathered for the consecration of Charles E. McDonnell as second Bishop of Brooklyn. They took the occasion to send Leo XIII a joint letter in which they asked him not to permit any decision which would endanger the parochial schools, and they added that he should not be influenced by any threat of impending persecution of the Church in the United States if he decided against the Faribault plan since no such danger existed.[88] The Pope replied on May 23. He made a plea for unity among the American bishops and counseled them to continue their efforts for parochial schools to which he gave his blessing. The Pontiff urged the prelates to work hard to induce the government in each of the states to acknowledge that nothing was better for the commonweal than religion; thus they should provide by wise legislation a teaching system supported by public expense, to which Catholics likewise would contribute, that would in no way hurt their conscience or offend their religion. On the point of a threatened persecution, the Holy Father said that since neither Ireland nor anyone else had made mention of this danger, it was clear that a mendacious public rumor had given rise to the wholly false notion which the New York bishops entertained.[89]

Since a month later Bishop McQuaid told a New York *World* reporter that the New York prelates had heard from one of their colleagues that both Ireland and Gibbons had communicated the threat of persecution to Rome, it is necessary to examine the facts.[90] In his first defense of Ireland in December, 1890, the

---

[87] 89-W-8, Ireland to Gibbons, Genoa, June 5, 1892.

[88] Zwierlein, *Life and Letters of Bishop McQuaid*, III, 171.

[89] The text of Leo XIII's letter is printed in Zwierlein, *op. cit.*, III, 171–174; Reilly, *op. cit.*, pp. 180–183.

[90] Zwierlein, *op. cit.*, III, 175. McQuaid expressed his indignation at the use of methods of this kind to bias the judgment of the Roman officials, and he instanced the threat of the loss of Peter's Pence five years before if the Pope did not declare in favor of the Knights of Labor.

Cardinal of Baltimore had twice stated that a condemnation of the archbishop would be disastrous for religion and the Church in the United States but he did not enter into particulars. However, near the close of his second letter to the Pope of March 1 Gibbons had said that silence on the part of the Holy See would be interpreted as a virtual condemnation of the conduct and views of Ireland. He then continued:

> If this opinion had been shared by the American public, as it assuredly would be in time, I fear that the national sentiment would be excited and that measures obnoxious to Catholics, would be proposed in school matters. There have been attempts in this direction; they have been checked for the present, but it is important not to renew them in creating or maintaining prejudice against ourselves.[91]

Therefore, apart from a general statement as to the disastrous results that would follow a condemnation and the expression of a fear that obnoxious measures concerning their schools would follow, Gibbons made no mention of persecution.

However, in the case of Ireland there was no such reserve. In his memorial to Propaganda in defense of Bouquillon's teaching on March 28 the archbishop linked the school question with the opposition his party was receiving from the foreign-born Catholics in the United States, and he clearly said that if Catholics generally joined in the attacks on American ideas and institutions with their foreign-born coreligionists there was a danger that the civil authorities would think the time ripe to oppress the Church as a hostile power. "It would be the hour," said Ireland, "of a formidable Kulturkampf."[92] A few weeks later in the elaborate statement of his case which he submitted to Cardinal Ledochowski he once again linked his foreign-born opposition in the United States to the school case in saying that public opinion regarded him as the representative of the party in the American Church which favored the government and his opponents as a danger to the Republic. As for himself personally, he cared very little what the consequences were, but for the country at large he had reasons for alarm. The Catholics were only one in eight in the United States and without wealth or influence, to which he added,

---

[91] 89-Q-1, Gibbons to Leo XIII, Baltimore, March 1, 1892, copy in French.
[92] Reilly, *op. cit.*, p. 268.

"a larger proportion than that of influence and population did not prevent a Kulturkampf in Germany."[93]

Served as he was by the skillful maneuvering of Ella Edes in getting confidential documents out of the Propaganda, Archbishop Corrigan knew what he was talking about. Ireland confessed to Cardinal Gibbons that in spite of all his effort to keep his memorial secret he had failed, and a copy had reached Corrigan. He knew Miss Edes was searching for it and his only conclusion was that she must have bought up the printer of the Propaganda.[94] In any case, the news soon became public and the New York *World* of June 26 published generous extracts from the memorial. It was obvious to all that Ireland had, indeed, used the threat of persecution as an argument to win his case, and that the statement of the New York bishops of the previous April had been based on fact. There followed another flutter in the press with Corrigan referring publicly to the Pope's "mistake" and Ireland for the time being reduced to comparative silence.[95] Amid all the excitement over the Propaganda document and its contents, the only hint of Gibbons' reactions came in a letter from Father Dyer of St. Mary's Seminary in Baltimore to Denis O'Connell in which he said the cardinal had commissioned him during the summer to send the monsignor newspaper clippings on the school controversy. Dyer told O'Connell:

> It is evident from the way the word "persecution" is used in the article of the New York World on the Pope's letter to the New York Bishops that they employed the word in their letter to the Holy Father. They have been very unskilful in not seeing that his Eminence & Archbishop Ireland speak of harassing measures, not persecution, & still more so not to recognize that they cannot make good their position without pleading guilty to the charge of having procured documents surreptitiously.[96]

The storm over the parochial schools had by no means ended, and Gibbons continued to feel its effects in various ways. Bishop Maes of Covington was irritated at the partisanship shown in

[93] *Ibid.*, p. 266.

[94] 89-W-8, Ireland to Gibbons, Genoa, June 5, 1892.

[95] The New York *Herald* of February 26, 1893, finally published the Ireland memorial in full which brought, in turn, a lengthy explanation from Ireland's archdiocesan paper, the *Northwestern Chronicle* of St. Paul, in its issue of March 4, 1893, about how the document had been obtained from the Propaganda. The explanation offered by Ireland's paper pointed clearly to Ella Edes as the culprit.

[96] ADR, Dyer to O'Connell, Baltimore, July 5, 1892.

Ireland's behalf by the professors of the Catholic University of America. Maes told Gibbons that he did not mean to enter into the merits of the controversy with the cardinal chancellor, but he did wish as a member of the board of trustees of the university to state emphatically that he thought the action of the professors was ruinous to the institution.[97] Gibbons fully agreed with Maes that everything should be done to avoid a weakening of confidence on the part of the bishops of the country in the university. He said he had written immediately to the rector when he received his letter, and he had asked two of the professors to come to Baltimore to discuss with him their part in the controversy. The cardinal was persuaded that if everyone accepted in good faith the decision of Rome there would be no need of interpretations from the doctors. "But so long as certain periodicals," said Gibbons, "will persist in minimising and distorting the decision of Rome, advocates on the other side will not be wanting in maintaining their side and in keeping up the unhappy controversy."[98]

But three weeks later the cardinal had more cheerful intelligence when John Ireland arrived in New York after his long stay in Rome and hurried on to Baltimore to see Gibbons. It was evident from the archbishop's report to O'Connell of this visit that he made every effort to reinforce his own point of view concerning persons and policies. He told the monsignor that Corrigan had just written Gibbons what he termed "a snubbing letter" and that Ryan of Philadelphia had been discovered supplying the *Katholische Volkszeitung* of Baltimore with articles against Gibbons. So the cardinal had agreed with him that they must never submit, but act and speak in such a way, as he expressed it, "to terrify his foes." Ireland had told him how strong they were and at every word the cardinal had seemed to grow erect and get into a position to fight. Moreover, O'Connell was informed of how pleased Gibbons was with him. "He is delighted with you, told me how much he is indebted to you, that he will forever stand by you."[99]

---

[97] 89-Y-1, Maes to Gibbons, Covington, June 11, 1892.

[98] 89-Y-4, Gibbons to Maes, Baltimore, June 16, 1892, *Personal,* copy. Gibbons told Maes, "I have given instructions to the managers of the 'Mirror' to express no views on the subject, except by publishing official or authoritative declarations regarding it, that may come from Rome."

[99] ADR, Ireland to O'Connell, Washington, July 11, 1892.

In much the same fashion Ireland continued through the summer in close touch with O'Connell and in most of his letters there was some reference to their colleague in Baltimore. Magnien paid the Archbishop of St. Paul a visit in August and they talked, said Ireland, for hours at a time. The archbishop found it amusing to hear Magnien describe how he had to maneuver to get Gibbons to write the letter in favor of his red hat. After it was written and signed the cardinal refused to mail it for a week, and when at last he consented Magnien rushed with it to the post office. When Gibbons began to doubt the wisdom of his action and drafted a cablegram to O'Connell ordering him not to present the document, Magnien had the message torn up. All of which led Ireland to make the rather ungenerous remark, "Gibbons is exactly the weak man we have imagined him but good at heart."[100] What was caution and prudence to the cardinal appeared as weakness to Ireland, but in the light of later events on the red hat it may be said that the archbishop would have been better served if he had had a little more of Gibbons' brand of weakness.

The summer of 1892 witnessed no abatement in the Catholic press of the harshness of debate over the parochial school question. In fact, it grew so bad that Archbishop Ryan hoped Cardinal Gibbons had escaped seeing the Catholic papers during his holiday, since in Ryan's judgment matters had reached the lowest ebb of personal abuse. He said he was thoroughly sick of the unnecessary fight and he had observed with pleasure that the cardinal had kept a prudent silence which, as he expressed it, was " 'masterly inactivity' just now."[101] The Rector of the University was in New York a few days later preparatory to sailing for Europe and he mentioned the scandal which the controversy was causing there.[102] When the press carried rumors of a rift between Gibbons and Ireland, the cardinal hastened to tell his friend that any effort at alienation would never succeed until he became so blind as not to see and admire honor, virtue, and

---

[100] *Ibid.*, Ireland to O'Connell, St. Paul, August 3, 1892. Ten days later Ireland confidently informed O'Connell that he and Gibbons would allow only one question to be considered at the autumn meeting of the archbishops, namely, how to provide religious instruction for children attending public schools. "We will balk Corr.," he said, "at every step" (*ibid.*, Ireland to O'Connell, St. Paul, August 13, 1892).

[101] 90-C-4, Ryan to Gibbons, Philadelphia, August 17, 1892.

[102] 90-D-2, Keane to Gibbons, New York, August 28, 1892.

heroism. "Fear not," said Gibbons, "be prudent and conservative in words and writings."[103]

By the time that Cardinal Gibbons in his capacity as chairman of the archbishops' annual conference began to lay plans for their autumn meeting, there had taken place a fundamental change in the situation governing the schools at Faribault and Stillwater, Minnesota. Hardly had Ireland arrived in St. Paul in mid-July before he was confronted with a serious revolt in the two communities on the part of both non-Catholic and Catholic opponents to his continuing the Dominican Sisters as teachers in the two schools. The Stillwater school board had terminated the contract of the sisters even before Ireland reached home, and the excitement at Faribault was only calmed sufficiently to permit a contract for one more year, but this, too, was later annulled as of October, 1893. The experiment, therefore, had proven a failure largely through the prejudices aroused over the arrangement, so that when the fall feeting of the archbishops was held the issue was no longer a practical one as far as the two schools were concerned. The meeting was originally scheduled for October 19 in New York, but due to the religious celebrations planned to mark the 400th anniversary of the discovery of America and the presidential election a week or so later, it was decided to postpone the date until November 16. In all the details preparatory to the conference Gibbons consulted in advance with Archbishop Corrigan. It was announced to the cardinal on September 12 that the Pope was sending Archbishop Satolli and in view of this fact proper arrangements had to be made by Corrigan for housing the ablegate as well as his other guests. In all this Gibbons co-operated fully with the Archbishop of New York who was grateful for his assistance in making certain the arrangements for their conference.[104]

Three months before the conference Gibbons received a request from Cardinal Ledochowski that the metropolitans first consult their suffragans on the question of the parochial schools before they met. This procedure would make the deliberations of the archbishops easier and give to their conclusions a greater

---

[103] AASP, Gibbons to Ireland, Baltimore, August 29, 1892, copy.

[104] AANY, Gibbons to Corrigan, Baltimore, August 29, 1892; 90-P-3, Corrigan to Gibbons, New York, November 8, 1892; AANY, Gibbons to Corrigan, Baltimore, November 9, 1892; 90-P-4, Gibbons to Corrigan, Baltimore, November 9, 1892, copy; 90-P-5, Corrigan to Gibbons, New York, November 10, 1892.

force, owing to the support they would have from the bishops.[105] McQuaid had long ago tried to insist on this point and he doubtless rejoiced to learn that the Prefect of Propaganda had given instructions that before all future conferences the suffragans should be consulted by their metropolitans. A further effort for unity and peace in the ranks of the archbishops was made in the early fall when Ryan made a trip to Baltimore to explain in person the circumstances surrounding another false newspaper story about his part in signing the Corrigan circular of some months before. He had been greatly shocked by Gibbons' reaction to the incident, and his visit, therefore, gave him an opportunity to disprove the falsehood and, as he added, "to restore, I trust, our former relations."[106]

As the time of the conference approached there were hopes in the minds of many that an authoritative decision from the metropolitans would put an end to the trouble. Father Walter H. Hill, S.J., of Sacred Heart Church in Chicago, told Gibbons that to him and many others the nub of the problem was to be found in this question: has the state any authority over the civil education of its citizens? Hill thought the answer was evidently and necessarily in the affirmative, but others differed and it was this fact that prompted him to look for a definite answer to stop the quarreling.[107] To this letter of the Chicago Jesuit, written in a kindly and moderate tone, the cardinal replied that he believed a decision would be issued. Whatever that decision might be, Gibbons thought they could not close their eyes to the fact that the great civilized governments of the world like Britain, France, and Germany exercised authority over the civil education of their citizens without a word of protest from the Church. "I heartily wish," said the cardinal, "that your views were shared by all those who are charged with the care of souls."[108]

The New York conference opened on November 16 and the ablegate of the Holy See was introduced to the metropolitans by Cardinal Gibbons.[109] Satolli read them an address in Latin and then laid before the archbishops for their consideration fourteen

---

[105] 90-B-3, Ledochowski to Gibbons, Rome, July 31, 1892.

[106] 90-E-9, Ryan to Gibbons, Philadelphia, September 12, 1892.

[107] 90-L-2, Hill to Gibbons, Chicago, October 26, 1892.

[108] 90-P-1, Gibbons to Hill, Baltimore, November 7, 1892, copy.

[109] 90-Q-3, Minutes of the Meeting of the Archbishops, New York, November 16–19, 1892.

propositions which were intended to compose the difficulties over parochial schools. At the outset the propositions espoused the further erection of parochial schools, but where there was no such school, attendance of Catholic children at the public schools was to be allowed with the permission of the bishops. Moreover, it was strictly forbidden for any bishop or priest either by act or threat to exclude from the sacraments parents who sent their children to the public schools. Another proposition stated that far from condemning the public schools, the Holy See would wish that the civil and ecclesiastical authorities should by joint action favor these schools, although it was added that the Church disapproved those features of the public schools which were opposed to the truths of Christianity and to morality. Thus the propositions definitely encouraged arrangements between the bishops and the local school boards in cases where due consideration was shown for the rights of both parties. For those Catholic children who attended the public schools it was urged that arrangements be made to see that they were taught religion, whether this be done by having the children assemble during free time to be taught their catechism or by some plan that would provide for catechism classes outside the public school building.[110] The general tenor, therefore, of the propositions was favorable to Archbishop Ireland's original stand on this question, and the fact that Satolli had spent most of the month preceding the conference in St. Paul was doubtless not lost on a number of the participants who probably suspected that the ablegate had been given careful guidance in his proposals.

Since the minutes of the meeting failed to furnish a complete account of what went on, it is necessary to depend on a letter of Archbishop Ryan to the Cardinal of Baltimore for these details. Ryan was with good reason worried that the English translation of Satolli's address and propositions would bring out in public the inside story of the New York conference which, as he said, would not prove very satisfactory reading to the public nor would it be very complimentary either to Rome or to the archbishops. The Archbishop of Philadelphia summarized for the cardinal how he thought the press stories would shape up:

First chapter. Rome directs us to call a meeting of our suffragans, that is, all the Bishops of the United States, & to confer with

---

110 The text of the propositions can be read in Reilly, *op. cit.*, pp. 271–276.

them on the Education Question & then with our & their opinions
& experiences to meet in NY & determine on something. Second
chapter. We meet in NY with our several reports, & before we
can interchange a thought, a pamphlet is sprung upon us, the
contents of which neither we nor our suffragans ever saw before & we
are asked (without consultation with the said suffragans & without
sufficient time to thoroughly examine this important document) to
sign it. This we declined to do without some changes & even then
we declare that we will only permit our approbation to be mentioned
without actually signing it. The Delegate consents, because there
would be little or no difference in the effect on the public. 3rd
chapter. He makes certain changes. We are silent & he takes this,
not unnaturally, for approbation. However we expect to see a last
version of the pamphlet with the proposed corrections. He arrives
next morning, makes an eloquent closing oration & then we bring
up additional objections. He leaves the Council chamber in anger
& declares that "he has been deceived" & refuses to return. 4
chapter. We depute the only prelate who voted for the pamphlet's
reception to declare to him we cannot permit our approbation to
be attached to it & we dissolve our meeting this being our *last
official act* after which the Archbishops of Boston & Chicago left.
During dinner our Delegate to Rome's Delegate arrives & says
blandly "that all is right." Mgr. Satolli will *simply* add to the
pamphlet the words "resolutis difficultatibus et actis emendationibus
requisitis," which before the public, will have the effect of the
originally required signatures. *To this we sent no reply* & the
Delegate acts & publishes not only the Latin but a popular English
version! No doubt the Delegate has sent the pamphlet to Rome &
I should not wonder if very soon we shall have the document
returned with Papal approbation & a permanent Papal Delegate
appointed! Abp. Ireland voted for this, & as the Holy Father told
me very positively that "he would never send a foreign Delegate
to us," it is quite possible Abp. Ireland will be the man appointed.[111]

With this explanation of what had transpired at the sessions in
New York it is easier to understand the confusion that followed.
On December 8 the New York *Herald* carried for the first time
the full text of Satolli's address to the metropolitans, which was
supplemented three days later by the somewhat sensational details that only one of the thirteen archbishops present voted to
accept the ablegate's propositions, namely, Ireland, and that consequently Denis O'Connell was hurrying to Rome the following

---

[111] AAB, unclassified, Ryan to Gibbons, Philadelphia, December 5, 1892.

week to try to save Satolli's school plan at the Holy See. On December 12 the *Herald* repeated some of these statements, adding that Gibbons had intervened to prevent the archbishops from rejecting the propositions outright with the suggestion that they decline to sign them just then and await further consideration. The *Church Progress* of St. Louis, previously mentioned as hostile to the Archbishop of St. Paul, promptly picked up the *Herald's* disclosures and in its issue of December 17 it carried two long articles purporting to give the views of Leo XIII and Archbishop Satolli on the subject, along with an editorial entitled, "The Pope and Mgr. Satolli," in which it was stated, "It will but require a reading of the two articles to see that Mgr. Satolli's opinion is not in the least the Holy Father's." In commenting on Satolli's address to the archbishops, the editor of *Church Progress* said there was no reason to doubt the authenticity of the document, but he added, "We do, however, question its authority." Satolli, according to Pallen, had no mission in the United States to settle the school controversy and his utterance had no more weight than that of a private opinion. "The reason of this opinion," said Pallen, "is not far to seek. Mgr. Satolli is a bosom friend of Archbishop Ireland."

Meanwhile Placide Chapelle, Coadjutor Archbishop of Santa Fe, who had acted as secretary of the conference, submitted his draft of the minutes to Gibbons and Corrigan who, with the exception of a few minor changes, gave their approval to his wording of the record.[112] But regardless of the silence of the official minutes on the subject of the opposition, certain archbishops were not so reticent. Gibbons was decidedly against a protest to the Holy See since he felt that the publication of Satolli's propositions made it certain that Leo XIII would sustain his representative and a protest now would be both unwise and useless. The cardinal assumed, as he told Ryan, that the legislation of the Third Plenary Council on parochial schools was beyond dispute and that not a single one of its decrees had been superseded or modified by Satolli's action.[113] Nonetheless, Archbishop Elder, who viewed the propositions as a serious undermining of the parochial school system, gathered his suffragans in Cincinnati

---

[112] 90-T-1, Chapelle to Gibbons, Brooklyn, December 1, 1892; 90-U-1, Gibbons to Corrigan, Baltimore, December 7, 1892, copy.

[113] 90-U-5, Gibbons to Ryan, Emmitsburg, December 9, 1892, copy.

on November 30 and forwarded a protest to the Holy See against the program outlined by the ablegate.[114]

Nor was the Archbishop of Cincinnati the only prelate who registered his objections to Satolli's proposals in Rome. Corrigan relayed his criticism of them to Father Brandi who, in turn, informed Cardinal Mazzella. The two Roman Jesuits were agreed that Satolli had made a serious blunder, and how he could ask the American hierarchy to accept his proposition, said Brandi, was a mystery to him. "I had thought," he said, "of publishing in January an article on the *Catholic* doctrine concerning education and have it ready for the press; but hesitate now for fear of giving personal offense to Mgr. Satolli."[115] Moreover, what appeared as a practical effect of Satolli's recommendations was made known to Gibbons when Bishop James A. Healy of Portland informed him that in one parochial school of 500 Canadian children in his diocese he had lost seventy-five who went off to the public school, confronting their pastor with the proposition that no bishop or priest should exclude parents from the sacraments who sent their children to a public school.[116] In spite of this the cardinal remained unshaken in his belief that the conciliar legislation of 1884 was still intact. He confessed to Healy that he regretted not having suggested in the meeting the insertion of a specific clause to this effect, but since Leo XIII had asked all the bishops to express their views to him on the propositions, he felt the Pope might issue an encyclical and, therefore, they had all better wait in peace until he had spoken.[117]

Although Cardinal Gibbons followed his customary policy of saying little for publication, in private he was busy urging the Holy See to confirm Satolli's proposals. Shortly before Christmas, in thanking the Pope for sending his representative, he alluded to the sensational accounts of the school question in some Catholic newspapers, and he said it was a matter of great moment to the Holy See that the ablegate's doctrine should not be changed or minimized.[118] A month later he followed this with a second letter to Leo XIII in thanks for the appointment of a permanent

---

[114] Reilly, *op. cit.*, pp. 211–213. Out of the ten suffragans of Cincinnati only one, Bishop John S. Foley of Detroit, refused to sign the protest.

[115] AANY, Brandi to Corrigan, Rome, December 12, 1892, *Private*.

[116] 91-B-2, Healy to Gibbons, Portland, January 12, 1893.

[117] 91-B-3, Gibbons to Healy, Baltimore, January 13, 1893, copy.

[118] 90-W-4, Gibbons to Leo XIII, Baltimore, December 23, 1892, copy in Latin.

delegate and here, too, Gibbons requested a formal papal blessing on Satolli's propositions in an encyclical on education.[119] The reports from O'Connell in the meantime encouraged Ireland to believe that all would turn out right in the end and that he would be sustained,[120] and about the same time the monsignor quoted Leo XIII as having said that while he might make a slight modification here and there he would in the main stand behind Satolli.[121] But while the news from the Eternal City continued to be bright, Gibbons took no chances, and when he informed Rampolla of the apology of Bishop Ryan of Alton for his indiscreet cablegrams on the Apostolic Delegation, he closed by saying that he hoped the Holy Father would not delay to augment still more the moral authority of Satolli by an official act confirming his propositions on the school question.[122]

Although he was willing to work privately for the Holy See's confirmation of the ablegate's document embodying the principles of the Minnesota school plan, the cardinal was not agreeable to having them publicly advocated for the Archdiocese of Baltimore. In early December the Baltimore *Sun* had printed a circular drawn up by a group of priests and laymen of the city which had urged an arrangement between the parochial and public school systems similar to that in Minnesota. On January 14, 1893, the *Freeman's Journal* of New York, which had stanchly supported Ireland through the whole fight, referred to the circular as coming from the cardinal. This Gibbons would not allow to pass, and the following week the *Catholic Mirror* of Baltimore corrected the mistake of its contemporary by saying:

> Without passing any judgment on the plan, it may be taken as certain that his Eminence is too deeply impressed with the necessity of Christian education to assent to any arrangement which would hamper or interfere in the slightest degree with the religious education which Catholic children should every day receive in the schools which they attend. We may add that this essential provision is expressed in the text of the circular itself.[123]

---

[119] 91-D-12, Gibbons to Leo XIII, Baltimore, January 30, 1893, copy in French.
[120] 91-E-5, Ireland to Gibbons, St. Paul, February 12, 1893.
[121] 91-E-6, O'Connell to Gibbons, Rome, February 13, 1893.
[122] 91-H-6, Gibbons to Rampolla, Baltimore, March 17, 1893, copy in French.
[123] January 21, 1893. The circular continued to give trouble to Gibbons throughout 1893. Late in the year H. K. Carroll of the staff of the *Independent* inquired if it was true that the cardinal and Satolli had signed such a document. He

That the cardinal supported parochial schools in his own arch-diocese was evident from the fact that in 1892 out of a total of 150 churches, of which ninety had resident pastors and sixty had not, there were ninety parishes to which a school was attached with a total enrollment of 19,000 pupils. These were figures that compared favorably with other American dioceses at the time.[124]

feared the effect it would have against the Church and he added, " . . . I believe that nothing would more quickly or thoroughly arouse public sentiment against your Church than the general belief that it is determined to secure a division of the public school fund" (AAB, unclassified, Carroll to Gibbons, New York, November 28, 1893). Gibbons denied his signature to the alleged circular and wrote across the letter of Carroll, "I am certain no such circular has any existence except in the imagination of people ever open to suspicion." Michael Walsh, editor of the *Catholic Herald* of New York, on the other hand, congratulated the cardinal on signing the document (AAB, unclassified, Walsh to Gibbons, New York, November 28, 1893). Gibbons' chancellor, Cornelius F. Thomas, answered Walsh and said, "In reply I would beg to say that the circular or petition to which you refer, is of several months standing, and is now revived. It emanated, not from his Eminence, [but] from a venerable priest of the Diocese. His Eminence is of the opinion that the moment is not opportune for the agitation of the question at least here in Maryland" (AAB, unclassified, Thomas to Walsh, Baltimore, November 29, 1893, copy).

[124] *Catholic Directory* . . . *1892* (New York, 1892), p. 72. The Archdiocese of New York, with almost four times the Catholic population of the Archdiocese of Baltimore, had 170 parochial schools with 40,631 children in attendance (p. 136). The Archdiocese of Milwaukee, with a very large German population and a total Catholic population of 30,000 less than Baltimore's 230,000, had 151 parochial schools with an attendance of c. 22,000 children (p. 111). When Father James R. Matthews of St. Mary Star of the Sea Church in Baltimore sought from the cardinal the previous summer permission to attempt a negotiation with the local public school authorities with a view to arriving at a plan along the lines of the Minnesota scheme, Gibbons replied as follows:

"You may try to effect an arrangement with the school commissioners on the following terms:

"1. You should have the selection & presentation of the teachers who must be good practical Catholics.

"2. The school commissioners will pay the salary of the teachers.

"3. The textbooks should contain nothing hostile to Catholic faith. (this point might not be urged at first, as it could be remedied afterwards & a judicious teacher could easily supply an antidote to the poison.)

"4. A certain time should be allowed each day of the school hours for catechetical instruction.

"5. The school house would be leased for one year, renewable at the end of the year.

"Of course the commissioners have the right to examine the teachers & to visit the schools.

"If you call on me we can discuss any details you may suggest" (90-A-3, Gibbons to Matthews, Baltimore, July 2, 1892, copy). The writer knows of no evidence that would indicate that the plan outlined above was ever carried into execution in Baltimore.

The widespread publicity given to the school question in the American Church by European journals naturally attracted attention and was responsible for some misunderstandings. When the text of the Satolli propositions reached England and was commented on by certain non-Catholic papers in a sense contrary to the manner in which the English Catholics had been furnishing elementary education to their children, the matter disturbed Herbert Cardinal Vaughan, Archbishop of Westminster, and he sought a clarification from Gibbons.[125] The Archbishop of Baltimore summarized for Vaughan the position of the two contending parties in the controversy. He said that one group was disposed to lease the Catholic schools to the public school authorities, with the provisions that the teachers be examined and the schools visited by the civil officials and with Christian doctrine taught at the beginning or end of the regular school hours. For these concessions, said Gibbons, the Catholic teachers would be paid by the school board and no objectionable textbook would be used. The second group, however, was unwilling to grant any concessions and they would receive state compensation without any condition attached. The cardinal then continued:

> What seems to me surprising is this that some prelates while opposing the first plan I indicated, sanctioned its adoption in particular cases in their own dioceses. There are to-day some fourteen dioceses in which certain schools are supported by the State on the conditions above named. The controversy in my judgment was more speculative than practical, for even if all Catholics were united in accepting the compromise of the first party, the State is not likely to make such concessions in the near future. Already the Protestant Ministers are protesting against granting any such favors, and the public at large outside the Church, look with jealous eyes on any interference with the present public school system.[126]

As the weeks wore on and there was still no official word from the Pope even so strong an optimist as Archbishop Ireland began to wonder. He told Gibbons he could scarcely believe that Leo XIII would go back on Satolli's propositions, but such pressure and unfair arguments had been brought to bear on Rome that he would be astonished at nothing. "Nor would I be much an-

---

125 91-G-3, Vaughan to Gibbons, Westminster, March 1, 1893.
126 91-J-6, Gibbons to Vaughan, Baltimore, April 17, 1893, copy.

noyed," said Ireland, "at anything that might occur; the war has hardened me.[127] But the Archbishop of St. Paul would not have long to wait, for on May 31 the Holy Father signed a letter to Gibbons in which he gave his judgment in favor of the acceptance of the disputed propositions of his delegate. The Pope was at pains to emphasize that the parochial school legislation of the council of 1884 was in no sense abrogated by Satolli's proposals, but he made it plain that the interpretations of the propositions which he had received from the opposition were totally alien to the mind of Satolli.[128]

Ireland and Satolli were, therefore, sustained and Gibbons was instructed by the Pope to communicate his letter to all the American bishops. The Cardinal of Baltimore expressed his thanks for the papal brief which had shown that there was no repugnance between the conciliar legislation and the delegate's propositions and he was grateful, too, that the Holy Father had put an end to the school controversy and brought a longed-for peace to the American Church.[129] Gibbons had the letter printed and distributed to the bishops in mid-June and even the strongest opponents in the hierarchy now subsided and insofar as the bishops were concerned the debate was over.[130] Archbishop Corrigan received the papal decision with a spirit of resignation, and in thanking Gibbons for his copy he said, "I trust the words of our Lord's Vicar will have the consoling effect of His own when He commanded the winds and the waves, and 'there came a great calm.' "[131]

There remained a few grumblings from minor figures in the controversy before complete peace settled over the field of battle. Brandi and his Jesuit colleagues, who had been scolded by the Pope at the instance of Satolli, wrote an article at the direction of Leo XIII in praise of the delegate for the *Civiltà Cattolica*. He told René Holaind, S.J., that it would appear in the issue of August 5 and deal with generalities, "and [it] confirms," he added, "the *true* meaning of the Pope's letter with regard to the school

[127] 91-M-4, Ireland to Gibbons, St. Paul, June 13, 1893.

[128] The text of the papal letter is given in Reilly, *op. cit.*, pp. 226–230.

[129] 91-Q-5, Gibbons to Rampolla, Baltimore, July 22, 1893, copy; published in translation in Reilly, *op. cit.*, p. 230.

[130] 91-N-1, Gibbons to Corrigan, Baltimore, June 17, 1893, copy; AAC, Gibbons to Elder, Baltimore, June 20, 1893.

[131] 91-N-5, Corrigan to Gibbons, New York, June 20, 1893.

question with an additional slap to the *Western Watchman*."[132]
Professor Bouquillon, a leader on the opposite side who had been
in friendly communication with Cardinal Rampolla since early
in 1892, went to Rome in the summer of 1893 where he was
received most cordially by the Pope, Rampolla, Serafino Cardinal
Vannutelli, and others. During his visit he wrote, at the suggestion of O'Connell and Boeglin, an article for the *Moniteur de
Rome* on the American delegation and three articles on the
Catholic University of America.[133] O'Connell confirmed the
friendly reception given to the professor at the Holy See, and
he remarked to Gibbons that Rampolla had told him to come
regularly to inform him fully on the situation.[134] The papal letter
of May 31 had, of course, vindicated Bouquillon as well as Ireland,
since serious charges had been brought against his teaching as
outlined in his several pamphlets on the state's right to educate.

As the time approached for the annual conference of the archbishops at Chicago in September, 1893, Ireland expressed the
hope to Gibbons that the meeting would be peaceful, and he
promised that he would certainly not open the war, "but if war
begins," he added, "I will wade in, despite your rappings." He was
thoroughly disgusted with Archbishops Corrigan and Ryan and
while he trusted that he would always know how to act toward
them as a gentleman and a Christian he would never forget their
cunning and deceit.[135] Actually the conference was comparatively
peaceful insofar as the school controversy was concerned. The
only untoward incident was Ryan's contention that a set of
resolutions which he had submitted at New York the year before
had been adopted, a point which Gibbons, Williams, and Corrigan
maintained was not true. After the Chicago conference Ireland
informed Monsignor O'Connell that Corrigan had gone out of
his way to show him attention and had even taken his part
against Ryan on the matter of the resolutions. It was Ireland's

---

132 AWC, Brandi to Holaind, Naples, July 26, 1893.

133 ACUA, Keane Papers, Bouquillon to "Monseigneur" [Keane], Rome, n.d.,
but he told the bishop he arrived in the Eternal City on July 29. For the papal
Secretary of State cf. *ibid.*, Bouquillon Papers, Rampolla to Bouquillon, Rome,
March 23 and September 16, 1892. Keane informed Gibbons of Bouquillon's
"splendid letter" from Rome where he said the professor had found the Pope,
Rampolla, and the two Vannutelli's "heartily with the University & against the
Jesuits" (91-T-4, Keane to Gibbons, Washington, August 25, 1893).

134 91-R-1, O'Connell to Gibbons, Rome, August 1, 1893.

135 91-S-4/1, Ireland to Gibbons, St. Paul, August 11, 1893.

belief that Corrigan for the time being felt that he was beaten.[136]

Cardinal Gibbons was, to be sure, happy that the storm was over. He told O'Connell that things had quieted down very much and he thought they were now in their ante-bellum normal condition. Michael Walsh, editor of the *Catholic Herald* of New York, who had been so violent an opponent of Ireland's school policy, was now advocating essentially the same thing, which prompted the cardinal to say, "We live in a strange world." Gibbons enclosed a copy of the minutes of the Chicago conference with instructions that O'Connell should not allow anyone to see it since they were pledged not to disclose the subjects of the meeting. He had sent a copy to Cardinal Ledochowski the day previous, and he added significantly, "Of course many things occurred at the meeting which are not recorded in the minutes." The cardinal transmitted at this time a further bit of news when he said the Sulpicians were going to lodge a formal complaint against the *Civiltà Cattolica* for its misrepresentation of their teaching on the school question and O'Connell would hear more of this soon.[137]

Magnien, the Sulpician superior in Baltimore, meant business on this matter and with the advice of Gibbons he sent a protest to the General of the Society of Jesus asking for an apology. Gibbons, he told O'Connell, wished that a copy of the protest should be shown to Rampolla and even to the Pope, but the monsignor was allowed to use his own judgment about this detail.[138] A few days later the Sulpician superior stated that Gibbons might himself write to Rampolla about the *Civiltà*, but he trusted that the Jesuits would do the right thing without waiting for last measures, "which," added Magnien, "I will certainly take, if necessary."[139] About three weeks later Magnien forwarded an article for insertion in the *Moniteur de Rome* if O'Connell thought it wise. He remarked that the slanders of the *Civiltà* had done St. Mary's Seminary no harm since their student

---

[136] ADR, Ireland to O'Connell, Chicago, October 4, 1893.

[137] *Ibid.*, Gibbons to O'Connell, Baltimore, October 6, 1893.

[138] *Ibid.*, Magnien to O'Connell, Baltimore, October 7, 1893. Magnien related that from all appearances Gibbons' jubilee celebration which was to be held on October 18 would be a grand affair. He was glad of it since it would confirm the cardinal's authority by the marks of universal respect he would receive. Bouquillon and Satolli thought Gibbons should go to Rome before the end of the year and O'Connell's own view of the matter would have weight with the cardinal, so Magnien urged him, "Give it very freely."

[139] *Ibid.*, Magnien to O'Connell, Baltimore, October 9, 1893.

body had increased even since his last letter, but he thought it might be a good thing if Father Brandi should read in print the view which was taken of what Magnien called "his mean little tricks."[140]

Meanwhile Cardinal Gibbons refused to be drawn into the public debate which marked the late days of 1893 over the issue of financial assistance from tax funds to the parochial schools. In thanking Pope Leo XIII for his letter of the previous spring on Satolli's propositions, he stated that he could now offer the Pontiff, following the Chicago meeting of the archbishops, the congratulations of all the metropolitans. All present had given their assent to the Pope's letter and all were equally persuaded, said Gibbons, that the letter would restore peace and harmony among them.[141] He made no allusion to the agitation which was just then filling the American press on the question of financial aid to the Catholic schools. The matter was rendered somewhat acute when it became known that Michael Walsh, editor of the *Catholic Herald* of New York, was leading a movement for this purpose with the idea of getting action in the state legislature. In the midst of the discussion the troublesome Baltimore circular of a year before was revived and the editor of the *Independent* of New York wrote to Gibbons to inquire if the suggestion of an arrangement between the public and parochial school systems of Baltimore had his blessing. The cardinal replied on December 7 and his letter was published in the *Independent's* issue of December 14. Gibbons said:

> Replying to your kind note, dated December 6th, I would beg to say that the circular which has appeared in some papers, alleging my action in presenting a claim for State aid for parochial schools, did not emanate from me and was not published with my authorization. Neither have I signed any petition to the Legislature for the purpose, and I am sure that Monsignor Satolli has not. Moreover, the paper in question is not something new. It appeared about a year ago without my sanction, and it has again appeared without my knowledge and consent.[142]

---

[140] *Ibid.*, Magnien to O'Connell, Baltimore, October 27, 1893.

[141] 92-Q-3, Gibbons to Leo XIII, Baltimore, November 1, 1893, copy in Latin.

[142] It is not unlikely that it was this circular to which Archbishop Ryan was referring when he told Gibbons, "Monsignor McColgan has done the right thing — at the wrong time. The present wave of bigotry must pass over before anything can be effected" (92-U-7, Ryan to Gibbons, Philadelphia, December 7, 1893).

One who said that for a long time he had been pained by the agitation of the school fund question by indiscreet Catholics, congratulated the cardinal on this letter as being timely, wise, and conservative. He thought there was nothing to be gained from trying to divide the school fund among the denominations, and that all non-Catholics would unite against the Catholics if that were done.[143]

The last unpleasant episode connected with the school controversy which Gibbons was called upon to arbitrate involved the continuing fiery attacks by Father David S. Phelan, editor of the *Western Watchman* of St. Louis, on the Jesuits. Phelan had been striking hard at the society for some time, accusing Cardinal Mazzella and Father Brandi of engaging in a Roman conspiracy against the American Church and its interests. Cardinal Rampolla asked Gibbons to use his name and influence to put a stop to Phelan's offensive conduct.[144] The cardinal brought the matter to the attention of John J. Kain, Coadjutor Archbishop of St. Louis, who deplored the priest's action as much as Gibbons, but who said Phelan was so stormy a character that Kain was at first a bit fearful of what he might do if he were ordered to stop.[145] However, within a few days the editor called on Kain and promised to behave himself and to write a letter of apology to Gibbons.[146] The cardinal informed Rampolla of Phelan's good dispositions and told him that he had disavowed his attacks on the Jesuits which were provoked, said Gibbons, by the imputations against his personal and priestly character which had appeared in the *Civiltà Cattolica*.[147]

---

[143] 92-V-8, Felix A. Reeve to Gibbons, Washington, December 19, 1893.

[144] 93-B-7, Rampolla to Gibbons, Rome, January 25, 1894. It was just at this time that Ireland was trying to rouse Gibbons and Keane to give a substantial sum for the support of Monsignor Boeglin as the agent for A.P. dispatches on the Church from Europe. Gibbons at first objected to being obliged, as Keane told O'Connell, "to resort to such measures in work like ours." But he finally agreed to give $1,000 (ADR, Keane to O'Connell, Washington, January 5, 1894). Ireland gave O'Connell credit for doing what he could not have done, namely, of waking up Gibbons and Keane in the interest of Boeglin (*ibid.*, Ireland to O'Connell, St. Paul, January 11, 1894).

[145] 93-C-3, Kain to Gibbons, St. Louis, February 10, 1894.

[146] 93-C-5, Kain to Gibbons, St. Louis, February 13, 1894.

[147] 93-D-1, Gibbons to Rampolla, Baltimore, March 2, 1894, copy in French. Two months later Gibbons reported again to Rampolla to say that the difficulties in St. Louis were all settled. Phelan had made an act of submission to Kain and expressed his sorrow for his attacks on the bishops and their administration,

Regardless of the clamor which the A.P.A., some ill-advised Catholics, and others continued to make on the issue of the relations between the public and parochial schools the controversy was, to all intents and purposes, over by the last months of 1893. From the very beginning, as we have seen, Cardinal Gibbons took a firm position in defense of Archbishop Ireland and held to it throughout. Although he gave no sanction for his own Archdiocese of Baltimore to any plan similar to that of Faribault and Stillwater, he felt that in the Minnesota arrangement Ireland was fully justified and worthy of support. He was convinced as well of the commanding position which the archbishop held with the American public and he was determined that his prestige should not be damaged by a Roman rebuke. To that end he exerted every effort to prevent a condemnation in the conviction that it would prove damaging to the Church and, too, because he believed that a good deal of the opposition to Ireland was based on mean and unworthy motives.

Yet in all this Gibbons as usual confined his action as much as possible to private channels, and there was no one who was more deeply pained than the cardinal at the bitter and hateful tones which the debate took among the American Catholics themselves, to say nothing of what was hurled at the Church and its representatives from the platform and press of those outside its fold. Throughout the controversy Gibbons was compelled from time to time to suffer the embarrassment and pain of misrepresentation of his views and action in the press, and one of the last recorded references made by him to this trouble related to a dispatch from Europe which he read in the Baltimore *Sun* while he was visiting in Germany in July, 1895. He had recently come from Rome where he had had an audience of the Holy Father who was represented as thinking less favorably of Ireland's school plan as a result of his talk with the cardinal. "As a matter of fact," said Gibbons to Bishop Keane, "the school question was not once mentioned in my conversations with his Holiness."[148]

---

and Kain, on his side, had published and read in all the churches of the archdiocese a circular accepting Phelan's apology and the archbishop's congratulations to him on his submission which had honored him as a man and as a priest (93-G-6, Gibbons to Rampolla, Baltimore, May 11, 1894, copy in French).

[148] ACUA, Keane Papers, Gibbons to Keane, Wörshofen near Munich, July 12, 1895.

Errata

545, l. 9	'assured,' not 'insured'
551, l. 8	Insert 'should' before 'be allowed'
558, l. 10	'to learn' in place of 'in learning'
565, l. 3 from bottom	'problem' in place of 'probelm'
584, Note 86, l. 10	'omnino' in place of 'omnio'
585, l. 8 from bottom	after 'he' insert 'be not requested,' in place of 'not request him'
593, l. 18–19	Insert 'ephemeral' in place of 'temporal'
617, l. 17	Insert 'check' in place of 'pause'
617, l. 21	'priests' ' instead of 'priests', apostrophe after the last 's'
640, l. 12	Insert 'golden' for 'silver' and 'episcopacy' instead of 'pontificate' in next line
648, Note 129, l. 1	'Wörishofen' instead of 'Wörshofen'
693, l. 17	Insert 'meeting' in place of 'feeting'